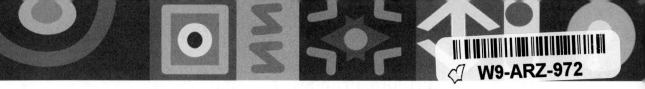

Understanding Human Differences

MULTICULTURAL EDUCATION FOR A DIVERSE AMERICA

Kent L. Koppelman
University of Wisconsin—La Crosse

with

R. Lee Goodhart
Faculty Emeritus
University of Wisconsin—La Crosse

PEARSON

Boston   New York   San Francisco
Mexico City   Montreal   Toronto   London   Madrid   Munich   Paris
Hong Kong   Singapore   Tokyo   Cape Town   Sydney

Dedicated To

Burt Altman and Dick Rasmussen

Who showed us the meaning of the word "good"
to precede the nouns: colleague, mentor, friend,
and human being.

Series Editor: Traci Mueller
Series Editorial Assistant: Janice Hackenberg
Senior Editorial-Production Administrator: Beth Houston
Editorial-Production Service: Kathy Smith
Executive Marketing Manager: Amy Cronin Jordan
Composition and Prepress Buyer: Linda Cox
Manufacturing Buyer: Andrew Turso
Cover Administrator: Linda Knowles
Electronic Composition: Publishers' Design and Production Services, Inc.

For related titles and support materials, visit our online catalog at www.ablongman.com.

Copyright © 2005 Pearson Education, Inc.

All rights reserved. No part of the material protected by this copyright notice may be reproduced or utilized in any form or by any means, electronic or mechanical, including photocopying, recording, or by any information storage and retrieval system, without written permission from the copyright owner.

To obtain permission(s) to use material from this work, please submit a written request to Allyn and Bacon, Permissions Department, 75 Arlington Street, Boston, MA 02116 or fax your request to 617-848-7320.

Between the time Website information is gathered and then published, it is not unusual for some sites to have closed. Also, the transcription of URLs can result in typographical errors. The publisher would appreciate notification where these errors occur so that they may be corrected in subsequent editions.

Library of Congress Cataloging-in-Publication Data

Koppelman, Kent L.
    Understanding human differences : multicultural education for a diverse
  America / by Kent L. Koppelman with R. Lee Goodhart.
      p. cm.
  Includes bibliographical references and index.
  ISBN 0-205-40842-7
    1. Multicultural education—United States. 2. Discrimination—United States.
  I. Goodhart, R. Lee. II. Title.

LC1099.3.K66 2005
370.117'0973—dc22

2004044424

Printed in the United States of America

10 9 8 7 6 5 4 3 2 1   08 07 06 05 04

Contents

CHAPTER 10   Sexism: Where the Personal Becomes Political 195

SECTION 4

The Challenge of Diversity to American Institutions 290

Preface

Why Do We Need to Understand Diversity?

Americans live in the most racially, ethnically, and socially diverse country on earth. Yet too often we live, work, and play as if our own social, gender, or religious group is the only one about which we need be concerned. To enjoy the advantages of our national diversity, we believe that every reader must seek as many facts and consider as many issues as possible to enhance effective interaction with individuals from diverse groups. This book is not a collection of essays providing multiple perspectives on diversity—there are many books that already do that; this book uses research to examine problems, misperceptions, and the potential of the diversity that exists in the United States. We believe that understanding diversity is the prerequisite to valuing the diversity in our society.

If we are to value and respect diversity, then we must not only value and respect different groups, but also respect and value opinions that differ from our own. We need not agree with everything others might say, but our expressions of disagreement should follow a consideration of all available information that has been communicated within a context of mutual respect.

The issues this book addresses are not new; human beings have struggled with them in one form or another for centuries, as is illustrated by the quotations from individuals of different eras that appear in each chapter. Chapters in this book are presented in an inquiry format. After a brief introduction, each chapter consists of related questions with responses based on research from a variety of disciplines as well as author expertise. As the references illustrate, information for this book has been collected from studies in a broad array of behavioral sciences, including education, psychology, sociology, anthropology, history, science, and literature.

The focus of Section 1 is upon individuals and interpersonal relationships. Chapter 1 defines terms essential for discussing diversity issues: Being able to make clear distinctions between terms such as *bias, prejudice,* and *bigotry* is critical for a conversation about problems related to individual and group differences. Chapter 1 also introduces the concept of values. The values promoted by a particular culture will shape the values, beliefs, and actions of individuals living within that culture. Our cultural values define who we are and what we think is important; they shape the ideals that we embrace.

Section 1 also examines issues affecting all individuals, especially those living in a diverse society: communication, conflict, and conflict resolution; the causes of prejudice and the impact of prejudice in society; and the ways that prejudices are learned.

Section 2 provides a historical context to illustrate how cultural biases were reflected in our evolving society. This context must be understood prior to examining the issues in Section 3, which describes intergroup relations in our diverse society. Section 2 describes the foundations of oppression as observed in early interactions between European settlers intent on conquering and colonizing America and indigenous people who initially assisted, and later opposed, the unceasing flood of immigrants to America. The attitudes of descendants of immigrants toward each successive wave of new immigrants reveal the difficulty of sustaining the ideal of America as a land of opportunity and freedom. Anti-immigrant sentiment was even directed against new arrivals from the same or similar racial or religious backgrounds, and eventually came to include blatantly racist and anti-Semitic attitudes.

The final chapter in Section 2 reviews the development of alternative perspectives as expressed by Americans on immigrants and the diversity produced by immigration, including the idea (or ideal) of pluralism, also called *cultural pluralism.* The rationale for promoting pluralism in a diverse society is examined as well as the strategies that we can use to promote pluralism.

Section 3 describes various ways in which different minority groups have been oppressed in our society. Our description of relations between dominant and subordinate groups includes an analysis of current cultural, individual, and institutional behaviors. Examples illustrate cultural biases against certain groups; individual prejudices, myths, and stereotypes believed by members of the dominant group about members of subordinate groups; and institutional policies and practices that benefit dominant group members but disadvantage subordinate group members.

Section 4 discusses changes that have already occurred in various institutions in the United States, reflecting a shift toward pluralism. This final section describes opposition to efforts that will move individual attitudes and institutional practices toward an acceptance of pluralism as the most appropriate response of a diverse society. The final chapter includes implications for future changes as the United States struggles with the challenges inherent in its status as the most diverse society in the world.

The Conceptual Framework for this Book

Understanding human differences is an ongoing challenge. Initially, scholars focused on *individual attitudes and behaviors;* later, they described the influence of *cultural expectations* in shaping individual attitudes. Finally, scholars addressed *institutional policies and practices* in which either discrimination was intentional against minority groups or it was an unintentional outcome. Vega (1978) describes a conceptual framework incorporating these three elements to understand human differences and the oppression of minority groups by dominant groups. This conceptual framework provides the basis for the organization of our book as we examine individual attitudes and actions, the evolution of cultural biases, and the establishment of discriminatory institutional practices (see Figure F.1).

To understand human differences, Vega's conceptual framework allows us to analyze American cultural, individual, and institutional behaviors. In exploring culture, the objective is to describe *cultural norms and standards.* What images are associated with the ideal? Any culture will associate particular images with the ideal woman, the ideal man, and the ideal family. For many Americans, those images are primarily white, middle-class people living in a nuclear family. Norms and standards are powerful determinants of individual expectations and behaviors, represented by the arrow pointing from culture to individual. Once we understand norms and standards, we can begin to understand what is meant by *cultural biases.* In a multicultural society, cultural biases can be detrimental to minority groups whose norms or standards do not conform to those of the dominant culture.

Once we understand the influence of culture on individuals, we can analyze *individual beliefs, attitudes, values, opinions, actions, and inactions;* sometimes what a person chooses *not* to do reveals as much as his or her actions. Although individuals are influenced by their cultural norms and standards, the Vega conceptual framework portrays that arrow as double headed, meaning that when significant numbers of individuals accept cultural norms, express their agreement, and behave in accordance with them, the cultural norms and standards are reinforced. With regard to human differences, an analysis of individual behavior must identify the influence of *prejudice* on individual comments, actions, and inaction.

Finally, we analyze *institutional practices, policies, and standard operating procedures* that are influenced by cultural norms and standards as well as by individual attitudes and behavior. To the extent that they reflect cultural norms and standards as well as individual attitudes and behaviors, institutions also reinforce them. To relate institutions to human differences, the analysis must focus on discrimination, identifying both ways in which the institution intentionally discriminates against certain groups and ways in which the institution unintentionally advantages certain groups and disadvantages others.

Although the Vega conceptual framework describes the intricate relationship between the three areas—cultural, individual, and institutional—chapter narratives of necessity deal with each discretely. Readers are asked to keep in mind the double-headed arrows signifying that all three areas are interlocked with each other to create the following relationships:

FIGURE F.1

A Conceptual Framework for the Study of Intergroup Relations

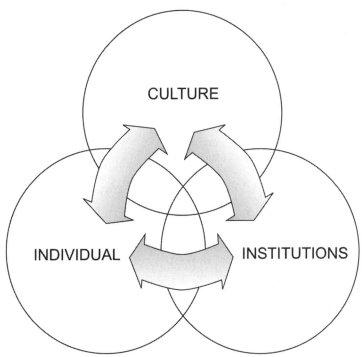

1. Cultural norms and standards influence and are reinforced by individual attitudes and behaviors and institutional policies and procedures.
2. Individual attitudes and behaviors influence and are reinforced by cultural norms and standards and by institutional policies and procedures.
3. Institutional policies and procedures influence and are reinforced by cultural norms and standards and individual attitudes and beliefs.

Before concluding our discussion of Vega's conceptual framework, consider this example to illustrate how interreliant culture is with individual and institutional behaviors. Although many forms of family exist in the United States, our cultural bias is for the nuclear family (the norm). Influenced by this cultural bias, Americans tend to form nuclear families. Even when people with a cultural tradition of extended families immigrate to the United States, they tend to form nuclear families within a few generations, sometimes reversing convention

with elderly parents receiving care in nursing homes rather than at home.

American institutions have encouraged the formation of nuclear families because they are more able to relocate in an age in which mobility of workers is highly desirable for employers across the nation. In an analysis of discrimination, problems may emerge for minority subcultures that value extended families if they maintain that value rather than adjust to the cultural norm. As this example illustrates, Vega's conceptual framework helps to clarify the complexity of intergroup relations by describing the related factors involved in the oppression of minority groups by a dominant group.

Discussion Exercises

To assist in the examination of serious ethical questions, exercises for group discussion are provided at the end of each chapter. Based on particular issues addressed in each chapter, suggested activities encourage readers to reflect on and discuss issues or aspects of issues that involve ethical or moral dilemmas. The exercises are not designed to manipulate readers into making a "politically correct" solution, but to hear the variety of responses from others and to appreciate the complexity of individual, institutional, and cultural issues in America today.

The Intent of this Book

The information provided in this book is intended to challenge readers to think and talk about issues that each of us must consider as citizens in a multicultural society; we do not necessarily intend to change reader values, although we do intend to challenge attitudes based on incomplete or erroneous information (see Chapter 1 for a description of the difference between *values* and *attitudes*). When students have finished reading this textbook, we hope their attitudes reflect a sound grasp of the issues presented (Appendix A contains an attitude inventory to assess any change). Diversity brings benefit as well as challenge, but the surest way to gain the benefit is to meet the challenges with a firm foundation of knowledge and insight that is based upon research from all behavioral sciences. While our narratives address a variety of questions, our answers included within those narratives may raise other questions, especially ethical questions, which readers must answer for themselves.

The intent of this book is to clarify our understanding of human differences and the role they play in interpersonal and intergroup relations. The Vega conceptual framework allows us to recognize how the interlocking circles of cultural biases, individual attitudes and actions, and institutional policies and practices have produced inequities that continue to polarize many Americans and that all too often prevent Americans from achieving ideals first expressed over two centuries ago when dreamers imagined a radical new concept, a nation where each person was given the freedom to be whoever he or she wanted to be.

Student Reaction

The following are comments that came from students who field-tested an early draft of *Understanding Human Differences* as part of Professors Koppelman and Goodhart's class at the University of Wisconsin—La Crosse:

"If you had asked me whether I needed to know more (about diversity) at the beginning of the semester, I probably would have said no . . . Now my views have changed . . . I have been challenged to think about many issues and differences in society. I have learned a lot about myself and I have come to a better understanding of prejudice and white privilege."

"I have come to realize that many comments I used to make and the language I used was stereotypical and racist. I have gained such an understanding of the diversity in our society."

"I was confronted with many things I never thought about before. I never thought about how Indian mascots were offensive. My eyes have been really opened as to how others are treated and discriminated against."

"I did not fully understand that (as a white person) I had the odds in my favor when looking for housing, employment, or even shopping in a store. It is a strange feeling to know that I have an advantage over someone else because of what I was when I was born."

Supplements

Instructor's Manual/Test Bank

Written by the authors, this resource was designed to acquaint instructors with the text, its structure, format, and individual sections, including formal and informal assessment of student attitudes with regard to human differences. It also includes:

- Answer keys to objective activities that appear in the review and discussion sections at the end of each chapter.
- Chapter-by-chapter explanation of review and discussion activities that are subjective in nature.
- A Human Relations Attitude Inventory (also included in the student text), as well as an in-depth, research-based analysis of the validity of the instrument as a means of assessing change in student attitudes toward diversity.
- Recommended readings by chapter.
- A glossary of terms and definitions.
- 350–400 questions from the computerized test bank.

TestGen Computerized Test Bank

The printed Test Bank is also available electronically through our computerized testing system: TestGen. Instructors can use TestGen to create exams in just minutes by selecting from the existing database of questions, editing questions, or writing original questions.

MyLabSchool

Free when packaged with a student access code. Contact your local representative for more details!

Discover where the classroom comes to life! From video clips of teachers and students interacting to sample lessons, portfolio templates, and standards integration, Allyn & Bacon brings your students the tools they'll need to succeed in the classroom—with content easily integrated into your existing course.

Delivered with Course Compass, Allyn & Bacon's course management system, this program gives our students powerful insights into how real classrooms work and a rich array of tools that will support them on their journey from their first class to their first classroom.

VideoWorkshop for Multicultural Education CD-ROM

Available free when packaged with the textbook, the CD-ROM contains five modules of three- to ten-minute digitized video clips featuring snapshots of teachers and students in real classroom settings. The VideoWorkshop CD comes with a Student Study Guide, containing all the materials needed to help students get the most out of this exciting media product. With questions for reflection before, during, and after viewing, this guide extends classroom discussion and allows for more in-class time spent on analysis of material. An Instructor's Teaching Guide is also available to provide ideas and exercises to assist faculty in incorporating this convenient supplement into course assignments and assessments. (Visit www.ablongman.com/video workshop for more details.)

Acknowledgments

This book, like so many others, has been a collaborative project. Although an author must always take full responsibility for any flaws, the assistance of the various colleagues who contributed to the completion of this book is deeply appreciated.

The first to be thanked are those faculty members serving on the University of Wisconsin–La Crosse Faculty Development Committee who reviewed this project and approved a leave to complete the book. Thanks also to Traci Mueller at Allyn & Bacon for her encouragement and support throughout this lengthy process. Several people read and responded to specific chapters, including: Richard Morehouse, Laura Nelson, Matthew Taylor, Al Gedicks, Joe Feagin, Greg Wegner, Jim Parker, Sandi Krajewski, John Magerus, Craig Fiedler, Charlotte Erickson, and Mark Sweet. And a special thanks to Kathy Smith, whose conscientious and careful editing made the final editing process a relatively painless and even positive experience, which resulted in a better book.

The director and staff of Murphy Library at the University of Wisconsin–La Crosse were especially helpful in locating references and securing books from other libraries, as was Shana Joseph who served as the initial research assistant for this project. Another special thanks goes to Susan Beauchamp for her assistance, advice, and diligence in identifying numerous valuable resources, and for the many long hours she spent locating appropriate images and obtaining permissions for the book's illustrations.

We would also like to thank the following individuals who reviewed drafts of the manuscript: Funsho Akingbala, University of Texas–Austin; Kay Benjamin, Cleveland State University; Norvella Carter, Texas A&M University; George Meadows, Mary Washington College; Fred Ramirez, California State Univeristy—Fullerton; Anne Sirota, University of California—Los Angeles; and Sharon Thomas, Miami-Dade College.

Finally, we thank our wives, Jan and Karla, who not only supported our efforts to complete this project but who discussed issues and questions as the book evolved into its final form.

There are so many more people who have contributed directly and indirectly to this book that it is not possible to name them all: authors whose work was influential even though they may not be included in the references; students who discussed issues in class and unfailingly came up with insights that provided a fresh perspective; and colleagues who have shared ideas in presentations and conversations, all of whom created a rich context that benefited the writing of this book.

Kent L. Koppelman
R. Lee Goodhart

Individual Attitudes and Interpersonal Relations

Section 1 examines individual human differences. From the beginning, we human beings have been social animals; interpersonal relationships are the bedrock of our social nature. How we perceive and react to others is a complex combination of values, attitudes, beliefs, assumptions, and behaviors.

Chapter 1 explores individual values in terms of our cultural context. We can be expected to share certain dominant cultural values, but we

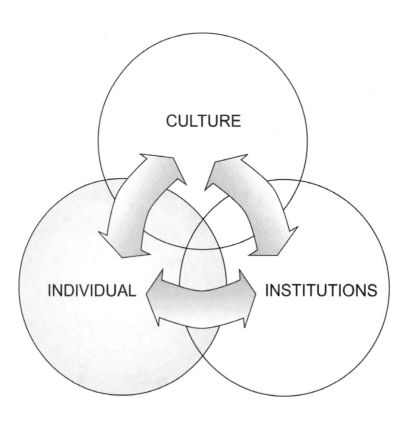

need to understand how individuals learn values in families and communities, and also how those values affect our individual behavior. The chapter also provides definitions for a number of important terms and concepts such as race, ethnicity, nationality, and minority. It is essential to have shared meanings of such terms and concepts in order to understand how individual human differences stem from the influence of groups.

Perceptions of, or reactions to, human differences may result in conflict; however, conflict does not have to become a destructive force. Chapter 2 investigates interpersonal communication beginning with an analysis of misperceptions about communication. With the help of a communication model, the chapter explains elements of communication, the origins of interpersonal conflict, and certain attitudes that promote conflict resolution.

Chapter 3 explains how negative behaviors can result from prejudice, creating conflicts harmful to individuals and communities. Since the word prejudice is often confused with other terms, distinctions are made between important and related terms: bias, stereotype, prejudice, bigotry, and discrimination. The chapter also describes factors that promote prejudice in our society and the rationalizations that Americans employ to avoid identifying and confronting their prejudices.

Prejudice is not innate, but is learned, and Chapter 4 illustrates how prejudices are learned in the United States, emphasizing the role of culture as reflected in everyday conversational words and phrases. Pejorative terms that are frequently employed in name-calling, from the playground to the corporate boardroom, demean people just as do the use of informal and formal labels that define and demean various groups. Prejudice can indeed lead to discrimination, yet theories also explain certain kinds of discrimination that do not evolve from prejudice.

Understanding Ourselves and Others: Clarifying Values and Language

"I have striven not to laugh at human actions, not to weep at them, nor to hate them, but to understand them."

BARUCH SPINOZA (1632–1677)

"May you live in interesting times" is a Chinese curse. It implies that life is easier and more enjoyable when nothing out of the ordinary or controversial happens. As Americans living in a complex, multicultural society, we certainly live in interesting times. Is it the best of times or the worst of times? Like the question about whether the glass is half empty or half full, the answer is the same: It's a personal decision. We can choose to be engaged in the challenges and opportunities of diversity issues, or we can retreat and resign ourselves to an attitude of indifference or even despair. Because America is not only a diverse society but also a democratic one, we have the freedom to choose our perceptions, assumptions, and behaviors.

If we take Spinoza's quote seriously, we need to understand all kinds of diversity—including opinions, appearances, values, and beliefs—as well as the categories of race, ethnicity, social class, gender, sexual orientation, and disability. The study of human diversity obviously requires an examination of social groups that encounter discrimination. However, in addition to focusing on the sociocultural differences between groups, we must also acknowledge the importance of *individual* differences. Each of us wants to be recognized as an individual. Our experiences are affected by multiple factors, including whether we are white or a person of color, female or male, from a low-, middle-, or upper-income family, or from a rural, suburban, or urban home. Each person's opinion offers a unique perspective that only the individual expressing it can fully understand. The task for us as listeners is to understand as best as we can the ideas, values, and beliefs articulated by the individuals we encounter.

What is the difference between beliefs and values?

Kniker (1979) suggests that beliefs are inferences about reality that take one of three forms: descriptive, evaluative, or prescriptive. A *descriptive belief* is exemplified by those who argued that the world was not flat but round because they observed boats sailing off to the horizon and recognized that the hulls disappear while sails are still visible. An *evaluative belief* is illustrated by Winston Churchill's conclusion about democracy based on his reading of history: He understood why some called democracy the worst form of government, but found it to be better than all other forms of government that had been attempted thus far. An example of a *prescriptive belief* would be the recommendation that students take a role in creating classroom rules because research showed that students who help create rules are more likely to be cooperative and abide by them. All beliefs are predispositions to types of action. Rokeach asserts that a cluster of related beliefs creates an **attitude;** he defines **values** as "combinations of attitudes which generate action or deliberate choice to avoid action" (Kniker, 1979, p. 33).

THE ROLE OF VALUES IN HUMAN DIFFERENCES

Rokeach is saying that values determine our choices: Values are the foundation for actions we choose to take—or to avoid (see Figure 1.1). What value do Americans place on wealth? For some, money and possessions are the primary measures of success. They admire others who are rich and successful, and they define their own worth by their income and wealth. For others, money is not a priority. Their main concern is to make enough money to support a comfortable lifestyle, however they choose to define it. There are also people who believe the Biblical caution that love of money is "the root of all evil," and refuse to let wealth play an important role in their choices. Their behavior is a reflection of their values. While serving as vice president to John Adams, Thomas Jefferson was once turned away from a prominent hotel because his clothes were soiled and he had no servants with him. After the proprietor was told whom he had refused, he sent word to Jefferson, offering him any room in the hotel. Having been accepted into another hotel, Jefferson sent a reply politely refusing the offer of a room, noting that if the hotel

FIGURE 1.1   The Relationship of Values, Beliefs, Attitudes, and Choices

Source: Kniker, C. *You and values education.* Copyright © 1979. Reprinted by permission of Pearson Education, Inc., Upper Saddle River, NJ.

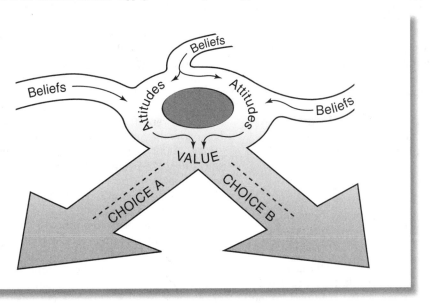

proprietor did not have a room for a "dirty farmer," then he must not have a room for the vice president either (Botkin, 1957).

What is the relationship between a person's values and behaviors?

America has a history of social commentary on the role of values in people's lives, and scholars engage in research examining the relationship between expressed values and behavior. Searching for consistent patterns in values research is challenging. However, one theme from social critics has been repeatedly supported by research and case study: There is a *consistent inconsistency* between what we say we value and our actual behavior (Terry, Hogg, and Duck, 1999; Aronson, 1999; Lefkowitz, 1997; Myrdal, 1944).

The tendency for Americans to say we believe in a certain value and then engage in contradictory behavior is a curious and yet consistent pattern. Contradictory behavior by human beings has been criticized and even ridiculed by essayists, novelists, and observers of American society. In 1938, the Carnegie Foundation invited Swedish social economist Gunnar Myrdal to the United States to conduct a study on the "American Negro Problem." Myrdal (1944) went far beyond a study of racial relations: He attempted to identify and understand the core values of American society.

In his analysis of Myrdal's research, Risberg (1978) identified nine values that Americans perceived as the defining values of the culture:

1. Worth and dignity of the individual
2. Equality
3. Inalienable rights to life, liberty, property, and the pursuit of happiness
4. Rights to freedom of speech, press, religion, assembly, and private association
5. Consent of the governed
6. Majority rule
7. Rule of law
8. Due process of law
9. Community and national welfare (pp. 5–6).

Despite the consensus about them, Myrdal observed that all of the values were regularly contradicted by American behavior. He provided examples from his observations, primarily based on race relations, to illustrate his conclusion.

What inconsistencies exist between American values and American behaviors?

Although Americans have always tended to emphasize individuality, American society quite consistently has demanded conformity. We Americans always seem to be uncomfortable with differences, often minimizing or ignoring them. In the turbulent era of the 1960s, many young people protested the Vietnam War, challenging authorities on college campuses and elsewhere in American society. Young men and women defied traditional

> The primal principle of democracy is the worth and dignity of the individual
>
> **EDWARD BELLAMY (1850–1898)**

gender roles in their choice of lifestyles and music, but most Americans did not celebrate this youth counterculture as an expression of individuality; instead, many denounced their behavior. Families were sundered and social critics predicted the downfall of American values. The protests passed, and expectations that Americans should conform have continued.

The influence of peers on individual behavior illustrates the seductive power of conformity. Social psychologists studying the influence of peer pressure have reported that people in groups engage in behaviors they would not undertake as individuals (Haag, 2000; Terry, Hogg, and Duck, 1999; Aronson, 1999). According to LeBon (1968), when individuals congregate, the group "presents new characteristics very different from those of the individuals composing it" (p. 27). In a study of young men who had assaulted homosexuals, Franklin (2000) found that many of the men she interviewed expressed tolerant attitudes toward homosexuality even though they admitted that when they were with friends, they participated in verbal or physical assaults on people perceived to be gay.

When questioned, 35% said they were motivated by a desire to prove their "toughness" and to become closer to the friends who engaged in anti-gay behavior.

Contradictory behavior also is illustrated in the belief that Americans value equality. The Declaration of Independence proclaims that the United States is founded on the belief that "all men are created equal," and yet the man who wrote that statement owned slaves. During World War II, boxing champions Joe Louis and Sugar Ray Robinson signed up for military service. At a bus stop in Alabama, a military policeman insisted that the two "colored soldiers" move to the rear of the station. When they refused, they were arrested. After an officer had reprimanded them, Louis responded, "Sir, I'm a soldier like any other American soldier. I don't want to be pushed to the back because I'm a Negro" (Mead, 1985, p. 231). Although racial inequality has diminished to some degree in the United States, the gap between the wealthy and poor has become greater than ever. A Chairman of the Board for the First National Bank of Chicago admitted that it was difficult to defend an economic system that permitted such a wide disparity of income as existed in the United States (Terkel, 1980, p. 23).

The United States also was founded on the rule of law and the belief in a justice system that would be fair to everyone, yet people with wealth and status are routinely able to circumvent our ideal. The view that our courts favor those who can afford the best lawyers is widely recognized and is often portrayed

> The law, in its majestic equality, forbids the rich as well as the poor to sleep under bridges, to beg in the streets, and to steal bread.
>
> **ANATOLE FRANCE (1844-1924)**

in films and on television. Despite the contradiction, Americans continue to believe that justice can prevail in a courtroom and they are resentful of cases where they believe it has not. Many people were upset by the verdict at the O.J. Simpson trial, believing his acquittal was the result of his wealth, status, and the skill of costly attorneys. Since the reaction

tended to split along racial lines, it may be more useful to look at the case of Claus von Bulow, who was tried and convicted for attempting to murder his wife. He subsequently hired the famous defense attorney Alan Dershowitz, who identified a legal technicality that necessitated a new trial for his client. At the retrial, the jury acquitted von Bulow of attempted murder (Wright, 1983). No one except von Bulow knows if he is guilty or innocent; however, there are poor people in prison today because they could not afford to hire a lawyer as skilled as Alan Dershowitz.

What Myrdal observed and reported in the 1940s continues to be true today: Americans behave inconsistently and engage in actions that contradict their expressed values. Myrdal's observations reinforced what American social critics had been saying for many years and what research and case studies have documented since the 1940s. These observations require some explanation, and it seems logical to begin by examining how people choose their values.

Are values individually chosen or are we taught to accept certain values?

The way American values are taught plays a major role in the values we hold. Individuals, subcultures, and institutions are involved in teaching values; parents, teachers, peers, clergy, relatives, and youth counselors are just a few examples. By studying how individuals and organizations in America teach values to children and youth, Raths, Harmin, and Simon (1966) identified seven traditional approaches (pp. 39–40).

A first way to teach values is to (1) *set an example.* Parents and teachers are supposed to be role models for children and youth. Young people are also told to emulate various individuals—from historical leaders to contemporary athletes whose achievements are attributed to practicing certain values. In similar fashion, schools and other organizations use (2) *rules and regulations* to promote certain behaviors in children and youth (and adults) that represent important values. Learning punctuality is considered important enough that teachers send children to the principal's office for a tardy pass if they are late for class. This example is especially interesting since the child securing the tardy pass from the principal cannot be in the classroom while the other children engage in some kind of learning activity, which is supposedly the primary purpose for requiring students to attend school.

Another approach is to (3) *persuade or convince* others to accept certain values. Respectful discussions with reasonable arguments can be an effective means of convincing someone that the values being espoused are appropriate for living a good life. Related to this is an (4) *appeal to conscience* in which a parent or teacher may challenge a child or youth who seems to advocate an inappropriate value or belief. This approach is illustrated when a teacher responds to a student making an inappropriate comment by saying, "You don't really believe that, do you?" The point of such questions is not to give the student a chance to explain or defend what he or she said, but to bring a subtle and insistent form of moral pressure intended to coerce the student into rejecting an unacceptable point of view.

Parents often teach values by offering (5) *limited choices.* By limiting choices, parents intend to manipulate children into making acceptable decisions. If a mother values cooperation and tells her children that family members should share in household duties, what can she do if one of her children refuses? She asks one child to wash dishes twice a week, but the child hates to wash dishes and refuses. The mother might say: "Either you agree to wash dishes twice a week or you will not be allowed to play with your friends after school." The child is restricted to two options in the hope that he or she will choose to do the dishes, reinforcing the mother's original objective of wanting her children to learn the value of sharing domestic responsibilities.

Organizations have employed the approach of (6) *inspiring* people to embrace certain values, often by sponsoring a "retreat" with inspirational or motivational speakers or a social function where the combination of speakers, films, and activities is designed to have emotional or spiritual impact. Although religious groups employ this approach, corporations sponsor events to inspire employees to work harder to achieve personal or group goals, and in doing so, contribute to the achievement of organizational goals.

Some religious groups and secular organizations emphasize (7) *religious or cultural dogma* to teach val-

ues. To accept beliefs without questioning them is to be **dogmatic.** If a Christian with dogmatic beliefs were questioned, he or she might say "That's what the Bible says," or, similarly, a dogmatic Muslim might say "This is what it says in the Qu'ran," even though people have interpreted the teachings of Jesus and Muhammad in different ways. Even early Christians held widely divergent views on the meanings of the life and words of Jesus (Pagels, 1979). Dogmatic beliefs stifle debate by emphasizing tradition: "This is what we have always believed."

Dogmatic beliefs also can be found in a secular context. When someone questions a value based on cultural beliefs, a dogmatic response might be

> When people are free to do as they please, they usually imitate each other.
>
> ERIC HOFFER (1902–1983)

"We've always done it this way." The appeal to tradition in opposing change has been employed in such controversies as using Native Americans as school mascots and including the Confederate flag in the official flags of some southern states. Only in 2003 did Georgia change its state flag to remove the confederate symbol.

Understanding how values are taught provides some insight in answering the question about why people consistently behave in ways that contradict their expressed values. Each of the seven traditional approaches to teaching values seems to be based on a common assumption, and that assumption might explain the inconsistencies.

How does the way values are taught explain the inconsistency between values and behavior?

What do the seven traditional approaches to teaching values have in common? They are all based on an assumption that certain prescribed values are to be taught, and that the individuals being instructed should accept them. The person teaching values—the teacher, parent, scout leader, minister, priest, rabbi, imam, or employer—knows what values are appropriate. The goal is to persuade the student, child, parishioner, or worker to accept those values. In actuality, each approach is a form of **indoctrination,** where the intent is to dictate cultural values that must be accepted rather than assist people in deciding what are right and wrong values.

This assumption shared by all seven traditional approaches to teaching values in America caused Raths et al. to question whether all approaches were primarily successful in convincing people to say the right thing, yet not do the right thing. If this is true, there are important implications for how values should be taught. It is neither ethical nor prudent to teach values that are advocated but not practiced in our everyday lives. This does not teach values, but, rather, hypocrisy. If the goal of teaching is to help learners to understand what they genuinely believe and what values they choose to incorporate into their behavior, those who teach must recognize the limitations of coercing children and youth to feign acceptance of prescribed values. For Americans to behave consistently with our expressed values, we must demonstrate authentic commitment to them.

Why should anyone be concerned about inconsistencies between values and behavior?

If we understand our values and consistently act upon them, it is more likely that our choices will reflect our highest ideals. We are constantly confronted with moral dilemmas that challenge our values and require us to make difficult choices. Scholars still try to explain how citizens as well educated and intelligent as those of Germany could betray their moral values and participate in, or deliberately ignore, the execution of gypsies, homosexuals, people with mental disabilities, and more than six million Jews. Being clear about one's values and acting consistently upon them leads to the kind of moral reasoning and behavior that result in satisfactory resolutions to conflict situations. During the 1930s, when Fiorello La Guardia was mayor of New York, a Nazi government official was scheduled to visit the city. Mayor La Guardia did not want to receive the German visitor, but had no choice. The German Consulate requested police protection, fearing that Jewish militants might attack their representative in retaliation for Nazi atrocities. La

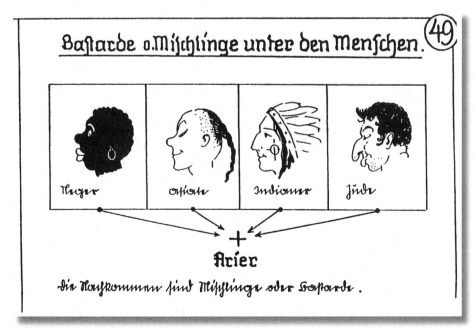

FIGURE 1.2 Nazi Educational Materials In Nazi Germany, educators were expected to teach values and beliefs in support of Aryan superiority and anti-Semitism, as reflected in this illustration of different races.

From: Burgstaller, "Bastards and Mixed Bloods under the People," *Erbelhre,* 1941, p. 49.

Guardia agreed to provide police protection, and he made sure that every police officer selected to guard the Nazi diplomat was Jewish (Mann, 1965).

Should parents rather than schools teach values to their children?

The question of who should teach values is a rhetorical one. Both parents and schools in America are expected to contribute to the development of children's value systems. We constantly encounter people who reveal their values in everyday words and actions. Teachers model their values whether or not they consciously choose to do so. The question is not whether values should be taught, but how they should be taught.

Of the many approaches Kniker (1977) identified for teaching values, the most effective approaches allow children and youth opportunity for discussion and debate, employing activities that stimulate them to think about their beliefs, hear other perspectives, and consider what effect different decisions could have for others as well as themselves. Discussing values, related behaviors, and possible consequences exposes young people to perspectives of others; evaluating arguments about values from their peers can help them decide which ones seem more attractive, compelling, and meaningful. In the process, we learn not only what values are important to us, but also to accept people with values different from our own.

As adults, we do not tend to make decisions about values at a particular point in time and then never change our minds. Our values are based on beliefs and attitudes that change frequently, resulting in an ongoing process where decisions are made and re-evaluated throughout our lives. Culture, geographical location, parents, and life experiences influence each person's decisions. Each individual must determine what he or she believes is best, and the cumulative decisions individuals make influence the evolution of our society (Bellah, et al., 1991;

> Consciously we teach what we know; unconsciously we teach who we are.
>
> **Don Hamachek (Contemporary)**

Zinn, 1990; Lappe, 1989). School classrooms are part of this journey. Teachers must present students with moral dilemmas and trust that when our children and youth are given the freedom to choose, they will be capable of making ethical decisions.

What problems can interfere with making ethical decisions?

One of the main problems in making ethical decisions about human differences is confusion concerning the language employed to address those differences. Many essential words or phrases are either common terms with a history of misuse or unfamiliar terms. Confused language often reflects the discomfort people feel toward sensitive issues.

> How often misused words generate misleading thoughts.
>
> **Herbert Spencer (1820–1903)**

For example, the word *racism* did not appear in most English dictionaries until the 1960s. As the civil rights movement gained momentum and attracted considerable attention from the media and people across America, we could no longer avoid using the term. Similarly, the word *sexism* did not appear in dictionaries until the early 1970s, as the women's movement became increasingly successful at bringing issues concerning the treatment of women to public attention (Miller and Swift, 1977).

Using inaccurate or ambiguous language creates problems when we are addressing sensitive, uncomfortable issues. To be coherent and meaningful in our discussion of human differences, we must clarify our vocabulary and agree to specific appropriate meanings for significant words and concepts.

DEFINING TERMS RELATED TO HUMAN DIFFERENCES

One would expect that consultation with any scholarly authority would provide definitions for a term such as *prejudice,* but the scholarly world is not free from confusion. Some textbooks have defined *prejudice* as a prejudgment that could be either positive or negative; this definition confuses prejudice with *bias,* a feeling in favor of—or opposed to—anything or anyone. *Stereotypes* always refer to people, and also can be positive or negative. As with stereotypes, prejudice always refers to people, but prejudice is always negative.

This chapter includes a series of definitions intended to clarify terms referring to human differences. Definitions throughout the text are based on the work of scholars from various fields in the behavioral sciences, including racial and ethnic studies, women's studies, education, sociology, and anthropology. Unless cited, definitions reflect a distillation of common themes identified in several scholarly sources (Schaefer, 2004; Herdt, 1997; Andrzejewski, 1996; Feagin and Feagin, 1996; Simpson and Yinger, 1985; Levin and Levin, 1982). The following series of definitions makes distinctions and indicates relationships between the terms.

Bias A preference or inclination, favorable or unfavorable, which inhibits impartial judgment.

Stereotype A positive or negative trait or traits ascribed to a certain group and to most members of that group.

Prejudice A negative attitude toward a group and persons perceived to be members of that group; being predisposed to behave negatively toward members of a group.

Bigotry Extreme negative attitudes leading to hatred of a group and persons regarded as members of the group.

Discrimination Actions or practices carried out by a member or members of dominant groups, or their representatives, that have a differential and negative impact on a member or members of subordinate groups.

Notice that each of the first four terms above represents attitudes of greater intensity than the previous one. Regarding bias and stereotypes, attitudes can be either positive or negative and can influence a person's perceptions of a person or group. Having a *bias* related to a group creates an inclination to favor or dislike an individual from that group. *Stereotyping* a group indicates an expectation that most members of the group will behave in certain positive or negative ways. No positive option exists for prejudice or bigotry because of the greater intensity of these attitudes. *Prejudices* are negative attitudes based on a prejudgment of a group; *bigotry* involves hatred and represents a harsher form of prejudgment against a person or group. Note that whereas bias, stereotype, prejudice, and bigotry relate to attitudes, discrimination refers to actions taken that demonstrate negative attitudes. A person can have a bias, a stereotype, a prejudice, or even be a bigot and still not engage in any kind of negative or positive behavior. Unless an individual's attitudes are publicly expressed, others may not be aware of them. Discrimination can be seen and documented, and it can cause physical and emotional harm.

How do negative attitudes develop?

We learn various biases, stereotypes, and prejudices as we grow up. We can be biased in favor of or against certain kinds of foods, types of books, styles of clothing, or types of personalities. Bias can affect decisions about what we eat, read, or wear; it can influence our choice of friends. A stereotype assumes that individuals possess certain human traits simply because they are members of a particular group. Although some traits are regarded as positive—such as blacks have rhythm, Asians are good in math—other traits are viewed as negative—certain groups are lazy, shiftless, dishonest, or violent. Although negative stereotypes are regarded as unacceptable, many people accept positive stereotypes. The problem with positive stereotypes is that they cause us to have specific expectations for individuals and groups even though we have little or no evidence for these assumptions. A positive stereotype may sabotage the process of forming a realistic and accurate perception of an individual.

At a Midwestern university, three Asian American women employed by a student services office reminisced during a coffee break about their undergraduate days. They complained about how difficult math classes had been and laughed as they recalled some of their coping strategies. The student services director, an African American, walked into the room, overheard what they were saying, and interrupted their discussion to chastise them for "putting yourselves down." He said they should stop. He also said he was disappointed in them and departed.

After the director left, the three women initially were too surprised to speak. Once they started talking, they realized they were angry because his comments suggested that he assumed they all had good math skills and were not being honest when discussing their lack of math ability. The women thought the director viewed them as individuals; they were angry and hurt when they realized that he had allowed a stereotype to distort his perception of them. They were especially upset because they had not expected a person of color to believe in a stereotype—even a positive one about the math abilities of Asians—but apparently he did.

If negative stereotypes reinforce negative biases, prejudices can develop, and prejudices are always negative. Although prejudice is only an attitude, negative attitudes often lead to negative actions against an individual or a group. Taking negative action might strengthen the prejudices of a person until they become the intense hatred of bigotry, which is the basis for white supremacist groups such as the Ku Klux Klan, neo-Nazis, and the Aryan nation. Because hatred is such a strong emotion, bigots are more likely to express their hatred with *actions*, including violence. Negative behaviors are often directed against individuals from social groups based on such differences as race, ethnicity, or nationality.

What is the difference between race, ethnicity, and nationality?

Race is not a scientific concept, but a social reality dictated by the color of one's skin, even though skin color as a basis for human categorization is absurd. African Americans are identified as black, yet the skin color for many African Americans is more accurately described as brown. Contrary to the racist term "redskin," the skin color for Native Americans is not red. Yellow is an inaccurate description of skin color for those of Asian heritage. At an elementary school in Minneapolis, young children created a poster with the title "The Human Rainbow." The first band of their rainbow was colored with a light brown crayon, making a very pale brown band, and each band above it was a slightly darker shade of brown until the outer band, which was colored in such a dark brown color that it almost looked black. The children had created a realistic way of representing and understanding the effect of melanin on the color of human skin.

The concept of race is both easy and difficult to discuss. Most Americans believe they know the meaning of the term, yet we have no specific set of racial categories acceptable to the scientific community. Racial schemes have been devised with dozens of categories or only three—Caucasoid, Negroid, and Mongoloid. In the 1930s, scientists such as anthropologist Franz Boas challenged theories describing a hierarchy of races (Gosset, 1963). In 1937, American historian Jacques Barzun bluntly denounced the spuriousness of race as a legitimate scientific concept:

[Racial classifications] come and go and return, for the urge to divide mankind into fixed types and races is evidently endless. Each attempt only illustrates anew how race-groupings have been shaped not by nature but by the mode of thought or the stage of mechanical efficiency that mankind valued at the moment. The history of these attempts confirms . . . that race-theories occur in the minds of men for an ulterior purpose. (1965, p. 196)

The series of paintings on "Caste" from the Spanish Colonial era (see Figure 1.3) supports Barzun's point about the historical effort to find ways to divide and label human beings. Most anthropologists today assert that there is only one race, the human race, and that different groups within it simply represent variations whose differences often can be understood as accommodations to environmental influences (Olson, 2002; Marks, 1995).

Although race is based upon perceptions of physical differences, **ethnicity** is based upon cultural differences (Jones, 1997). Ethnicity refers to the historic origins of an individual's family. For immigrants to the United States, ethnicity identifies their country of origin or that from which their ancestors came: Poland, Mexico, China, Italy, Cuba, Ethiopia, Russia, or Iran. For those whose ancestors emigrated from different countries of origin, eth-

> In claiming the unity of the human race we resist the unsavory assumption of higher and lower races.
>
> ALEXANDER VON HUMBOLDT (1769–1859)

FIGURE 1.3 Eighteenth Century Paintings of "Castas" A series of South American paintings from the eighteenth century identifies categories of people (such as Indian, Spanish, or Chinese) and names the children of mixed marriages. For example, the child of a Spanish and African couple is a Mulatto, and the child of a Spanish and Mulatto couple is a Morisco. In the three paintings below, the artist illustrates how descendants of a Spanish and Indian couple can regain status as a white person. The child of the Spanish and Indian couple is a Mestizo, the child of a Spanish and Mestizo couple is a Castiza, and the child of a Spanish and Castiza couple is considered Spanish.

Source: De Espanol, y India, na ce Mestiza (190.1996.1), De Espanol, y Mestiza, Castiza (190.1996.3), and De Espanol, y Castiza, Espanol (190.1996.2). c. 1775, Francisco Clapera, Jan and Frederick Mayer Collection, Denver Art Museum.

nicity can represent a choice about personal identity based on culture. As Dalton (2002) explains it:

> [Ethnicity] describes that aspect of our heritage that provides us with a mother tongue and that shapes our values, our worldview, our family structure, our rituals, the foods we eat, our mating behavior, our music—in short, much of our daily lives. (p. 16)

Most Americans identify more than one ethnic group as part of their heritage, and for that reason ethnicity may have little meaning because of a lack of strong cultural identification with one of those groups. Some of us with multiple ethnic heritages may claim a stronger cultural affinity with one of the groups. A person may be a mixture of Irish, German, and Swedish ancestry and yet, perhaps because her surname is Irish or because Irish traditions were more strongly promoted in her family, she identifies most strongly with being Irish (Banks, 1994).

For Native Americans, ethnicity generally refers to tribal affiliation: Apache, Kwakiutl, Cherokee, Seminole, Mohawk, Hopi, or Lakota. For most African Americans, ethnic identity was obliterated by the experience of slavery, making it practically impossible to trace one's heritage to a specific tribal group such as Hausa, Ibo, Tsutsi. The introduction of the term "African American" in the 1980s was intended to provide an "ethnic" label for black people as distinct from race (Dalton, 2002). Because of the unique preservation of his oral family history, Alex Haley (1976) was able to reconnect with his ethnic group as described in the book, *Roots*.

Nationality refers to the nation in which one has citizenship. To ask people about their nationality is to ask where they reside or what nation is identified on their passport. People curious about someone's ethnic heritage have often asked, "What is your nationality?" instead of "What is your ethnic background?" Being asked about one's nationality may be considered quite insulting because it implies that the questioner does not perceive the other person as American but as belonging to another country. What do the terms *race, ethnicity,* and *nationality* have in common? They each refer to people considered to represent minority groups in the United States.

What are minority groups and why are they called minority groups?

The term **minority group** does not necessarily imply anything about the number of people in the group; however, it does imply something about their power. Minority group members possess limited power compared to members of a dominant group. It is possible for a minority group to be larger than a dominant group because it is the group's lack of power that defines it. When the white minority held power in South Africa, black South Africans were the majority in terms of numbers, but they were considered a minority group because they lacked power under the racist system of Apartheid. Women in the United States are included as a minority in affirmative action plans and equity proposals even though they are numerically the majority because historically they have not held as much power as have men.

A person in a minority group must overcome obstacles—handicapping conditions—related to their group identification based on such factors as race, ethnicity, gender, sexual orientation, socioeconomic status, religion, or disability. Some people refer to minority groups and diversity as if the two terms are synonymous, but **diversity** refers to the presence of human beings with perceived or actual differences based on a variety of human characteristics. Diversity exists both in classrooms having no minorities and in classrooms where all students are African American; too often, these differences can result in some children being stigmatized and marginalized by other children. The concept of diversity includes minority groups as well as groups identified according to differences based upon age, marital status, parental status, educational status, geographic location, physical characteristics, and other factors that influence individual personality and behavior. As Banks (2001) has noted, it is imperative to recog-

nize the interactions of all these variables in order to understand individual behavior.

How do minority groups function in our society?

In any society, you can find a group hierarchy where preferred groups occupying superior positions disregard groups that are devalued by that society. Preferred people constitute the dominant group and usually control major political, social, and cultural institutions of that society. Terry (1993) described the relationship of dominant and subordinate (or minority) groups by using an "up/down" metaphor. To determine who is *up* or *down* in a society, one must discover which groups have the most wealth, status, and power, and which have the least. In the United States, a person becomes an *up* by belonging to these groups: Caucasian, male, middle or upper class, Christian, heterosexual, or nondisabled. A *down* belongs to one or more of these groups: nonwhite, female, lower class, non-Christian, homosexual, bisexual, transgender, or disabled. Most individuals will represent a mixture of memberships in these up or down groups.

With reference to his metaphor, Terry suggests that ups don't know much about downs, and think they don't need to know about them because downs are not regarded as socially important. Ups do not compete with downs; they move in different circles. The only time ups become concerned about downs is when downs start getting "uppity" by challenging the power structure or the status quo by engaging in marches, demonstrations, or some other kind of protest about an issue. The response of ups is likely to be "What do these people want?" because they genuinely do not know. They are "dumb ups" when it comes to understanding issues affecting downs. By contrast, downs know a great deal about ups because they must; it is essential for their survival and for their success. To achieve whatever goals they have set for themselves, downs have to understand ups so that, as Terry says, they know what the ups are up to (pp. 194–196).

It is tempting to assume that if someone is a down in one category, that person will be more sensitive to downs in a category where he or she functions as an up. Unfortunately it doesn't seem to work that way. When people are behaving as part of

FIGURE 1.4
Nationalities of Ethnic Immigrants to America

Source: Schaefer, R.T. *Racial and ethnic groups,* 9/e. Copyright © 2004. Reprinted by permission of Pearson Education, Inc., Upper Saddle River, NJ.

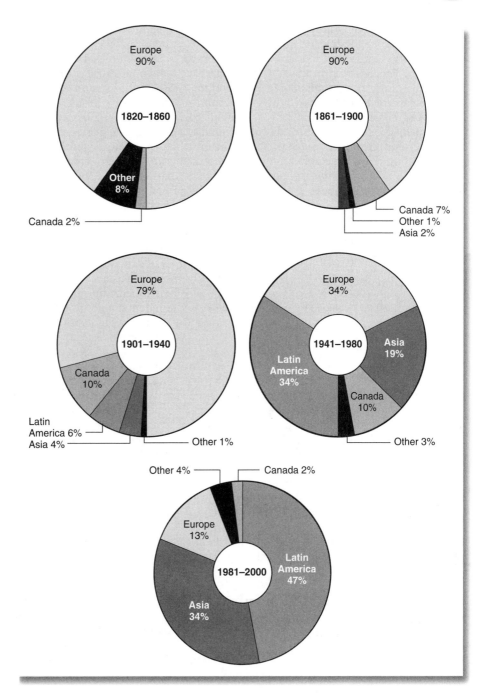

an up group, they tend to be "dumb ups." It's as if there are separate file folders; their experiences in one category stay in that file and don't influence other files. People living in poverty can be racist; people of color can be homophobic; gays and lesbians can be prejudiced against immigrants; immigrants can be sexist; women can be prejudiced against people with disabilities; and people with disabilities can be prejudiced against welfare recipients.

Terry's "up/down" metaphor provides a useful way of thinking about the complexity associated with a society that includes a variety of minority

> It is well to remember that the entire universe, with one trifling exception, is composed of others.
>
> JOHN ANDREW HOLMES (1789–1876)

groups. Subordinate groups must function within structures and cope with attitudes created and promoted by the dominant group. Schools can be used to illustrate this point. As Delpit (1995) noted, children from low-income families don't tend to do as well in school because "the culture of the school is based on the culture of the upper and middle classes—of those in power" (p. 25). Sometimes subordinate group status is only temporary and serves a useful function (such as children and youth), but as Miller (2001) noted, temporary membership in subordinate groups must not be confused with persistent social problems of those whose subordinate status is ongoing (such as racial and ethnic groups).

How has our society responded to social problems experienced by minority groups?

Ryan (1976) described two radically different approaches involved in addressing social problems. The **exceptionalistic perspective** focuses on individuals; it perceives all problems as local, unique, and unpredictable. Since problems are seen as a consequence of *individual* defect, accident, or unfortunate circumstance, proposed remedies must be

tailored to fit each individual case that is an "exception" to the general situation. A criticism of this approach is that it treats only *symptoms* of problems and not causes; exceptionalistic remedies have been derided as "Band-Aid solutions" that alleviate but do not solve problems.

Ryan describes an alternative approach, a **universalistic perspective** that views social problems as systemic, beginning in fundamental social structures within a community or a society. Since social structures are inevitably imperfect and inequitable, the problems that emerge are predictable and preventable because they do not stem from a situation unique to one individual but rather from conditions common to many. The universalistic perspective emphasizes engaging in research to collect and analyze data and to identify patterns that predict certain outcomes. Once patterns and root causes are identified, appropriate solutions can be created and implemented through public action, institutional policy, or legislation. Because research takes time, the universalistic approach has been criticized since it does not address the immediate consequences of problems or assist people who are currently suffering from particular problems.

To illustrate the difference between exceptionalistic and universalistic perspectives, Ryan describes two responses to the problem of smallpox. An exceptionalistic approach would be to provide smallpox victims with medical care to help them recover; a universalistic approach would first demand legislation to fund inoculation of the population to prevent the disease from spreading. The contrast is similar to a metaphor from Kilbourne (1999) about bodies floating down a river and ambulances being called to rescue the drowning people. Although rescuing people from the river is important, it is also important to send someone upstream to investigate how people are falling in (p. 30).

The metaphors illustrate a need for both approaches. While people are engaged in studying problems, help must be provided to those who suffering right now. If everyone goes upstream to discover how people are falling into the river, no one is left to save people who are drowning; if everyone stays downstream to rescue drowning people, the cause of the problem will never be found. Neither perspective can be neglected whatever efforts are employed to solve social problems.

AFTERWORD

The chapter began by discussing diversity and individuality. Holding differing values is part of both diversity and individuality. The values we choose are influenced by our membership in groups defined by such factors as race, ethnicity, gender, and social class; however, the ultimate decision to embrace certain values is up to the individual. Almost everyone holds some values similar to those of their parents, and almost everyone holds some values different from those of their parents. We share values with friends; yet we hold some values that are different from theirs. Values are part of the landscape of human differences, a part of what we need to understand in order to appreciate diversity.

Language is the primary tool we use to pursue understanding. We can observe and evaluate the behaviors of others, but we will never understand them without interacting with them or reading what they have written. Confusing or ambiguous language is like a smudge on the lens of a microscope; it prevents us from having a clear understanding of our subject. This chapter has tried to clarify some confusing terms so that our view is not distorted as we begin our study of human differences.

When Jewish author Isaac Baashevis Singer was asked if he believed people had free will, he replied, "Of course we have free will, we have no choice." As citizens of a democracy, we have many choices. As human beings living in a diverse society surrounded by diverse global cultures, trying to understand human differences would seem to be a necessary choice. For every reader who has already made that choice, this book offers insights and information to enhance your understanding. For readers who have not made that choice, this book may help to create an understanding of why the choice is necessary. But it is still each person's choice to make; as Singer said, we have no choice about that.

TERMS AND DEFINITIONS

Attitude A cluster of particular related beliefs, values, and opinions

Beliefs Inferences a person makes about reality that take one of three forms: descriptive, evaluative, or prescriptive

Bias A preference or inclination, favorable or unfavorable, that inhibits impartial judgment

Bigotry Hatred of a group and members of that group

Discrimination Actions or practices by members or representatives of dominant groups that have a differential and negative impact on members of subordinate groups

Diversity The presence of human beings with perceived or actual differences based on a variety of human characteristics

Dogmatic To accept beliefs one has been taught without questioning them

Ethnicity Identification of an individual according to his or her national origin and/or distinctive cultural patterns

Exceptionalistic perspective Views social problems as private, local, unique, exclusive, and unpredictable, a consequence of individual defect, accident, or unfortunate circumstance, which requires that all proposed remedies be tailored to fit each individual case

Indoctrination Instruction whose purpose is to force the learner to accept a set of values or beliefs, to adopt a particular ideology or perspective

Minority group A subordinate group whose members have significantly less power to control their own lives than do members of a dominant, or majority group

Nationality The nation in which an individual has citizenship status

Prejudice A negative attitude toward a group and anyone perceived to be a member of that group; a predisposition to negative behavior toward members of a group

> Freedom is the right to choose: the right to create for yourself the alternatives of choice. Without the possibility of choice and the exercise of choice, human beings are not human but instruments, things.
>
> ARCHIBALD MacLEISH (1892–1982)

Race A social concept with no scientific basis that categorizes people according to obvious physical differences such as skin color

Stereotype A positive or negative trait or traits associated with a certain group and any member of that group

Universalistic perspective Views social problems as public, national, general, inclusive, and predictable; a consequence of imperfect and inequitable social arrangements which require research to identify their patterns and causes so that remedial institutional action can be taken to eliminate these problems and prevent them from reoccurring

Values Combinations of attitudes that generate action or the deliberate choice to avoid action

REFERENCES

Andrzejewski, J. (Ed.). (1996). Definitions for understanding oppression and social justice. *Oppression and social justice: Critical frameworks*. Needham, MA: Simon & Schuster.

Provides definitions for a variety of terms essential for discussing intergroup relations.

Aronson, E. (1999). *The social animal* (8th ed.). New York: W.H. Freeman.

Presents an overview of research in social psychology and describes people behaving inconsistently with their expressed attitudes in Chapter 2 on Conformity.

Banks, J.A. (2001). Multicultural education: Characteristics and goals. In J.A. Banks & C.A. McGee Banks (Eds.), *Multicultural education: Issues and perspectives*. New York: Wiley.

Describes the evolution of multicultural education, the importance of group identification, and how implementation of multicultural education meets the needs of diverse students.

Banks, J.A. (1994). The complex nature of ethnic groups in modern society. In *Multiethnic education: Theory and practice* (3rd ed.). Boston: Allyn & Bacon.

Describes ethnic diversity in the United States, assimilation issues that have historically confronted ethnic groups, and how ethnicity influences individual identity in contemporary society.

Barzun, J. (1965). *Race: A study in superstition* (Rev. ed.). New York: Harper & Row.

Explains why race is a pseudoscientific concept with an Appendix of racial (mostly racist) quotes from authors, scientists, and mystics.

Bellah, R., Madsen, R., Sullivan, W., Swidler, A., & Tipton, S. (1991). *The good society*. New York: Vintage.

Presents quantitative and qualitative data from interviews with Americans talking about what values and behavior are necessary for creating a good society.

Botkin, B.A. (1957). *A treasury of American anecdotes*. New York: Bonanza Books.

Includes over 300 anecdotes about famous, infamous, and ordinary Americans; the Jefferson anecdote originally appeared in a German Almanac published in Pennsylvania.

Dalton, H. (2002). Failing to see. In P. Rothenberg (Ed.), *White privilege: Essential readings on the other side of racism*. New York: Worth.

Discusses race and ethnicity and how white has been defined as the norm in the U.S. making white people oblivious to the role of race in the formation of their identity.

Delpit, L. (1995). *Other people's children: Cultural conflict in the classroom*. New York: The New Press.

Examines issues in teaching children of color, including inequalities and the imbalance of power that create obstacles to learning.

Feagin, J., & Feagin, C. (1996). Basic concepts in the study of racial and ethnic relations. In *Racial and ethnic relations* (5th ed., pp. 6–26). Upper Saddle River, NJ: Prentice Hall.

Explains major terms and concepts in intergroup relations and includes a glossary for all terms used in the book.

Franklin, K. (2000). Anti-gay behaviors among young adults. *Journal of Interpersonal Violence 15*, 339–363.

A survey of 484 young adults concerning their participation in name-calling, physical violence, or threats against homosexuals.

Gosset, T.F. (1963). *Race: The history of an idea in America*. Dallas: Southern Methodist University Press.

Describes attitudes about race in colonial America, the evolution of this concept into a pseudo-scientific theory in the nineteenth century, and its debunking by scholars in the 1930s.

Gould, S.J. (1981). *The mismeasure of man*. New York: W. W. Norton.

Describes the misguided attempts by scientists to categorize human beings by race.

Haag, P. (2000). *Voices of a generation: Teenage girls report about their lives today*. New York: Marlow.

Examines responses of more than 2,000 females, ages 11 to 17, to six questions revealing a variety of explicit and implicit issues related to their public and privates lives.

Haley, A. (1976). *Roots.* Garden City, NY: Doubleday.

Describes the author's use of family stories to establish his ethnic background in Africa.

Herdt, G. (1997). *Same sex, different cultures: Exploring gay and lesbian lives.* Boulder, CO: Westview.

Reviews anthropological and cross-cultural evidence on attitudes toward sexual orientation and provides a glossary of essential terms.

Jones, J. (1997). *Prejudice and racism* (3rd ed.). New York: McGraw-Hill.

Integrates data from psychology, sociology, and history to explain the relationship between prejudice and racism in their appropriate sociocultural historical context.

Kilbourne, J. (1999). *Deadly persuasion: Why women and girls must fight the addictive power of advertising.* New York: The Free Press.

Argues that advertising is a pervasive cultural phenomenon that encourages people to objectify each other in a way that diminishes the quality of human relationships.

Kniker, C.R. (1977). *You and values education.* Columbus, OH: Charles E. Merrill.

Summarizes theory and research concerning values and describes alternative approaches to teaching values in schools.

Lappe, F.M. (1989). *Rediscovering America's values.* New York: Ballantine.

Presents a dialogue with one perspective emphasizing individualism and the other perspective emphasizing communitarianism and egalitarianism.

LeBon, G. (1968). The mind of crowds. In R. Evans (Ed.), *Readings in collective behavior.* Chicago: Rand McNally.

Examines the general characteristics of crowds and crowd behavior, especially the influence of emotional and moral factors on the behavior of crowds.

Lefkowitz, B. (1997). *Our guys: The Glen Ridge rape and the secret life of the perfect suburb.* Berkeley: University of California Press.

Explains the contradictions reflected in the upbringing and behavior of "All American" boys from the suburbs who gang rape a mentally retarded girl.

Levin, J., & Levin, W. (1982). *The functions of discrimination and prejudice* (2nd ed.). New York: Harper & Row.

Describes the functions of prejudice for both the majority and minority groups; describes causes and effects of prejudice; and provides definitions of critical terms.

Mann, A. (1965). *La Guardia comes to power: 1933.* Philadelphia: J.B. Lippincott.

Describes how Fiorello La Guardia became mayor of New York City. (This is the second installment of a two-part biography, with volume one covering La Guardia's life from 1882–1933.)

Marks, J. (1995). *Human biodiversity: Genes, race, and history.* New York: Aldine de Gruyter.

Provides evidence for the consensus in the scientific community that there is no scientific basis for the concept of race.

Mead, C. (1985). *Champion: Joe Louis—Black hero in white America.* New York: Charles Scribner.

Describes the life and boxing career of Joe Louis and his struggles with racism.

Miller, C., & Swift, K. (1977). *Words and women.* Garden City, NY: Anchor Press/Doubleday.

Analyzes sexism in the English language and provides many examples; discusses the inclusion of racism and sexism in dictionaries on page 141.

Miller, J.B. (2001). Domination and subordination. In P. Rothenberg (Ed.), *Race, class and gender in the United States: An integrated study* (pp. 86–93). New York: Worth.

Describes complex perceptions and interactions between dominant and subordinate groups.

Myrdal, G. (1944). *An American dilemma: The Negro problem and modern democracy.* New York: Harper & Row.

Describes values and contradictions in American culture and how they relate to the pervasive prejudice in American society.

Olson, S. (2002). *Mapping human history: Discovering the past through our genes.* Boston: Houghton Mifflin.

Describes human history as revealed by recent research on DNA that has concluded that human beings share a common African ancestor and do not consist of separate races.

Pagels, E. (1979). *The Gnostic gospels.* New York: Vintage.

Examines Gnostic beliefs as related to debates among early Christians regarding beliefs about Christ's resurrection and divinity, monotheism, and gender roles in the church.

Raths, L., Harmin, M., & Simon, S. (1966). *Values and teaching: Working with values in the classroom.* Columbus, OH: Charles E. Merrill.

Addresses the issue of traditional approaches to teaching values as forms of indoctrination and describes these approaches.

Risberg, D.F. (1978, June 18). *Framework and foundations: Setting the stage and establishing norms.* Paper presented at the first annual National Conference on Human Relations, Minneapolis, MN.

Describes the development of Human Relations as an academic discipline incorporating knowledge from other disciplines but creating its own structure, paradigms, and language.

Ryan, W. (1976). *Blaming the Victim* (2nd ed.). New York: Vintage.

Explains exceptionalistic and universalistic perspectives on pages 17–20.

Schaefer, R.T. (2004). *Racial and ethnic groups* (9th ed.). Upper Saddle River, NJ: Pearson.

Provides information on racial and ethnic minorities but also includes chapters on women, religious diversity, immigrants, and cross-cultural comparisons.

Simpson, G.E., & Yinger, J.M. (1985). *Racial and cultural minorities: An analysis of prejudice and discrimination.* New York: Plenum.

Examines causes and consequences of prejudice and discrimination in the U.S. and includes definitions of important terms and concepts.

Terkel, S. (1980). *American dreams: Lost and found.* New York: Ballantine.

Interviews diverse people about their perceptions of America, including First National Bank board member Gaylord Freeman.

Terry, D., Hogg, M., & Duck, J. (1999). Group membership, social identity, and attitudes. In D. Abrams & M. Hogg (Eds.), *Social identity and social cognition* (pp. 280–314). Malden, MA: Blackwell.

Examines how attitude–behavior consistency is influenced by both congruence of individual attitudes with group norms and the significance to the individual of group membership.

Terry, R.W. (1993). *Authentic leadership: Courage in action.* San Francisco: Jossey Bass.

Examines six leadership styles by defining leadership as the ability to frame issues correctly and to respond to issues by using power legitimately and ethically.

Wright, W. (1983). *The Von Bulow affair.* New York: Delacorte.

Provides a detailed review of the case; also of interest is the film "Reversal of Fortune" (based on Alan Dershowitz' book) available on videotape (Warner Brothers, 1990).

Zinn, H. (1990). *Declarations of independence: Cross-examining American ideology.* New York: HarperCollins.

Examines American beliefs and inconsistencies between behavior and ideals.

Summary Exercises

Summarizing exercises are provided in which groups of three to five students can delve deeper into the content presented in the chapter. Two types of summary exercises presented are:

1. Focus review
2. Term and concept review

Summary Exercise #1 In your triad or group, create at least five summarizing statements that restate what was presented in the chapter.

Recommended steps:

A. Paraphrase and condense rather than debate the merits of the concepts presented.
B. Write the statements in your personal note-taking journal.
C. Be certain that all members agree on the wording of each statement.
D. Following the creation of five statements, select two to read to another triad or group.
E. Discuss the chapter with that triad or group based upon your paraphrased concepts

Summary Exercise #2 In your triad or group, refer to the terms and definitions presented at the end of this chapter. Explain how each relates to your better understanding the concept of how values are transmitted through our language.

Caution: This will take time, but these terms are vital to know as you learn how we perceive human differences.

Recommended steps:

A. Place a star (*) next to any terms that are unclear to you.
B. Place a hash mark (#) next to those terms that you feel you comprehend.
C. Canvass your group for all terms that are unclear; share your understanding so that each term is discussed (1–3 minutes); record page numbers from the text for reference to each term.
D. As discussion occurs, add remarks in your personal note-taking journal about each term and its definition.

E. As a group, review the remaining terms and their definitions to be certain of your comprehension.
F. Enter explanations into your note-taking journal or beside the terms in your text.

Personal Clarification Exercises

Personal clarification exercises, such as team or dyad discussions, provide opportunity to confirm for oneself the existence of concepts presented in the chapter text. In Chapter 1, the following two exercises are intended to provide an honest basis for discussion of personal values.

1. A Survey of Current Issues
2. What Are Your Ethics? Questionnaire

Clarification Exercise #1 A Survey of Current Issues

Directions: This exercise asks you to consider each policy to the extent that you have an opinion about the issue it exposes.

Part One: Read each of the statements below. As you proceed, discuss each item and then agree upon a number that most accurately reflects the sentiments of your *entire* discussion group.

A Survey of Current Issues

For the statements on page 20, circle a 5 if you agree strongly, a 4 if you agree, a 3 if you are undecided, a 2 if you disagree, and a 1 if you disagree strongly.

Part Two: After everyone in the group has responded to all 10 statements, discuss your responses. If there are areas of strong disagreement, take time to have each person explain why he or she feels strongly about this issue. The purpose is not to change anyone's mind or reach a consensus, but to understand and respect differences of opinion.

Clarification Exercise #2 What Are Your Ethics?

Directions: In the same groups of five, consider each of the situations below. Your natural inclination toward a solution will reveal your own personal ethics profile. Analyzing your ethics and those of others will afford you an opportunity to understand

	SA	A	U	D	SD
1. Health care costs are too high.	5	4	3	2	1
2. Immigration policies are too loose and need to further restrict the number of people allowed to enter the United States.	5	4	3	2	1
3. Bilingual education should exist in all states.	5	4	3	2	1
4. A time for voluntary, silent prayer should be part of every school day.	5	4	3	2	1
5. We should hold parents legally responsible for the actions of their children.	5	4	3	2	1
6. The U.S. government has the responsibility to help countries in need of aid throughout the world.	5	4	3	2	1
7. Environmental laws are too strict, costing workers their jobs.	5	4	3	2	1
8. The right to carry a gun should be restricted by law.	5	4	3	2	1
9. Military spending must be continued to keep the United States strong.	5	4	3	2	1
10. Information on human sexuality should be taught in schools.	5	4	3	2	1

your own values and how they may have been learned.

Part One: Read aloud the questions below. Privately select the solution that you believe to be most appropriate.

What Are Your Ethics?

1. X tells you, in strict confidence, that she is having an affair. Her partner, Y, asks you straight out: "Is X having an affair?" Do you:
   A. Lie and say you don't know.
   B. Tell the truth.
   C. Say: "Ask X."
   D. Ask Y if he wants to talk about his relationship problems with X.
2. You work for a large company that is investing a lot in finding a treatment for AIDS. You discover that a colleague is leaking research information to your company's competitors. Do you:
   A. Take no action.
   B. Report your colleague.
   C. Think: "Good, the drug will be more widely and cheaply available if it's made by more than one company."
   D. Raise the issue with your colleague.
3. Your home is burglarized and your TV stolen. Actually, it had just broken down, irreparably, and was worthless. You have insurance, but do you:
   A. Claim it and look forward to getting a new one.
   B. Tell the insurance company the truth.
   C. Assert that it was better than it was, and enjoy ripping off the insurance company.
   D. Claim it in full and appease your conscience by donating to charity.
4. Someone approaches you on the street and hassles you for money for "a cup of coffee." It's obvious that he really wants the money for alcohol. Do you:
   A. Apologize for not giving.
   B. Tell him you don't believe him.
   C. Do as your mood dictates—whether it means giving or not.
   D. Give something—because you generally do.
5. Your small child is starting school. In your area, children have to attend the nearest school, which in your case has low academic standards. Do you:
   A. Move where schools are better.
   B. Write a letter of complaint to your political representative or local newspaper explaining why you object to the local school.

C. Look for private alternatives.

D. Send your child to the local school and get involved to try to raise academic standards.

6. You don't own a car—and you're proud of it—but you're neglecting your aging parents because there's no public transportation to their home. Do you:

A. Look into a car-share scheme.

B. Hold on to your green ethics and keep giving car drivers a hard time.

C. Get a car, putting your human relationships first.

D. Campaign for better public transportation and rent or borrow a car when you really have to.

7. You have it on the best authority that your political representative has a secret lesbian relationship. The politician is married with children and, like most in her profession, exploits her family credentials to promote her career. She also abstains from voting on gay-rights issues. Do you:

A. Decide that her sex life is private—but ask for regular gossip updates.

B. "Out" her to the press—or write to inform her that this is what you intend to do if she does not make a statement herself.

C. Write to her, telling her that it's being a politician that she should be ashamed of.

D. Reason that homophobia is a powerful destructive force, so it's acceptable to remain closeted.

FROM: *NEW INTERNATIONALIST*, ISSUE NO. 289, "HOW ARE WE TO LIVE?" P. 11. REPRINTED WITH PERMISSION.

Part Two: When all items have been read aloud and you have selected a personal response for each item, talk with each other in order to that all group members agree on three or four items for general group comparison.

Part Three: Explain to the group the values you hold that led you to select your responses. Make notes in your journal about how many different values are represented in discussion of the best solutions to these issues. The Instructor's Manual has a description of your ethics based on your responses to the seven questions. Your instructor may choose to have you discuss this.

Intergroup Exercises

Intergroup Exercise #1 A Mutual Support Dilemma

Directions: In groups of five, read the case situation explained below. Prepare to discuss it with those in your assigned group. Regardless of your gender, in your group, respond to each of the questions listed at the end of the story. Plan to explain your group position to the entire class.

Part One: Read the case study below. You may read independently or aloud within your group.

The Story of Mary and Luke: A Mutual Support Dilemma

Mary and Luke were married during their senior year in college. After their graduation, Mary took a secretarial job in the registrar's office of the university where Luke was attending graduate school. Mary worked for five years while Luke completed his doctoral degree. Their first and only child was born the second of the five years and Mary missed only two months of work at that time.

Luke has now been offered an assistant professorship at a prominent eastern school and is eager to accept it. Mary has applied and been accepted into graduate school at the University of Chicago. She is eager to accept the assistantship that she has been offered.

Mary argues that Luke should give her the chance for an education now that he has completed his. She also reminds him that he has been offered a job at the Chicago Junior College. Luke says that he intends to take the job in the east and that Mary can find someplace out there to go to school.

If Mary refuses to follow him, Luke promises to file for a divorce and seek custody of their three-year-old daughter.

Part Two: Questions for discussion:

1. What would you do if you were Mary?
2. What advice do you have for Luke?
3. How could this situation be handled so that neither Mary nor Luke loses?
4. Does your group agree that either Mary or Luke lose?

Part Three: Explain to your reconvened class those responses at which you mutually arrived. Record in your note-taking journals the three principal outcomes for Mary and Luke. Take a poll or a majority vote of the group regarding what they wish to be the outcome.

Intergroup Exercise #2 Expert Advisor Selection Activity

Directions: A group of fifteen experts, considered miracle workers by those who have used their services, has agreed to provide these services for the members of this group. Their extraordinary skills are guaranteed to be 100 percent effective. It is up to you to decide which three of these people can best provide you with what you want. The experts and their qualifications are listed below.

Part One: In groups of three or five, review the qualifications of each expert advisor

Expert Advisor Selection Activity

1. *Dr. Dorian Grey* A noted plastic surgeon, he can make you look exactly as you want to look by means of a new painless technique. (He also uses hormones to alter body structure and size.) Your ideal physical appearance can be a reality.
2. *Susan Surenuff* A job placement expert. The job of your choice, in the location of your choice, will be yours.
3. *Jedediah Methuselah* Guarantees you long life (to the age of 200) with your aging process slowed down proportionately. For example, at the age of 60 you will look and feel like 20.
4. *Dr. Masters Johnson* Expert in the area of sexual attraction and compatibility, she guarantees that you will be the perfect male or female who will contribute to a successful marriage.
5. *Dr. Yin Yang* An organic expert, she will provide you with perfect health and protection from physical injury throughout your life.
6. *Dr. Knot Not Ginott* An expert in dealing with peers, he guarantees that you will never have any problems with your peers again. They will accept your values and your behavior.

7. *Fay Cultipower* An expert on authority, she will make sure that you are never again bothered by authorities. Her services will make you immune from all control which you consider unfair by the administration, the police, and the government.
8. *"Pop" Larity* He guarantees that you will have the friends you want now and in the future. You will find it easy to approach those you like and they will find you easily approachable.
9. *Dr. Sandy Smart* She will develop your common sense and intelligence to a level in excess of 150 I.Q. It will remain at this level through your entire lifetime.
10. *Rocky Fellah* Wealth will be yours, with guaranteed schemes for earning millions within weeks.
11. *Dwight D. Degawl* This world famed leader will train you quickly. You will be listened to, looked up to, and respected by those around you.
12. *Dr. Otto Carengy* You will be well liked by all and will never be lonely. A life filled with love will be yours.
13. *Dr. Claire Voyant* All of your questions about the future will be answered, continually, through the training of this soothsayer.
14. *Dr. Hinnah Self* Guarantees that you will have self-knowledge, self-liking, self-respect, and self-confidence. True self-assurance will be yours.
15. *Prof. Val U. Clear* With her help, you will always know what you want, and you will be completely clear on all the muddy issues of these confused days.

Part Two: Discuss with group members each of the fifteen experts. As needed, ask clarifying questions, such as "Could this person . . . ?" or "Do you believe that she could also . . . ?"

Part Three: Select those you think could be of value to you personally. Narrow your selection to the three who are most likely to help you achieve your goals.

Part Four: Explain to your group why you selected the three expert advisors that you did. You need not apologize for your selections, since the needs upon which you based your selection will not be the same as the needs of others in your group. Ask any questions you have about the rationale others used to select their expert advisors.

CHAPTER 2

Communication, Conflict, and Conflict Resolution

"If I were to summarize the single most important principle I have learned in the field of interpersonal relations it would be this: Seek first to understand, then to be understood."

STEPHEN COVEY (1932–)

Communication seems simple. One person talks, and other people listen to understand what the speaker is saying; when the first person stops talking, another person responds, perhaps to agree or disagree with the first speaker. Nothing seems complicated here, so why is there so much misunderstanding that often leads to conflict between individuals, groups, organizations, and nations? One answer was suggested in the 1960s film "Cool Hand Luke," in which Paul Newman as Luke, an inmate, keeps breaking the warden's rules. As he prepares to punish Luke once again, the warden says, "What we have here is a failure to communicate." Actually it's not that Luke doesn't understand the rules; the problem is he doesn't *respect* the rules, so he violates them. By *communication*, the warden means that Luke has not demonstrated his understanding that he must conform to the rules.

COMMUNICATION AND CONFLICT

In communication, there is more going on than speaking, listening, and comprehending one another's words. Understanding communication requires some knowledge of the purpose served by that communication and what attitudes support it.

Spitzberg (1990) reported that we interact with other people 70% of the time we are awake. Communicating effectively is an asset in one's personal and professional life, especially when conflicts occur. And conflicts are likely to be resolved only if those people involved communicate effectively.

What is an appropriate definition of communication?

Most people assume that the term *communicate* refers to interpersonal communication, but mass media represent another form of communication. Kougl (1997) offers a practical definition of **interpersonal communication:** "A dynamic process of interaction between people in which they assign meaning to each other's verbal and nonverbal behavior" (p. 7). Two features of this definition provide clues about how communication can lead to conflict: *assign meaning* and *nonverbal behavior.*

How does assigning meaning lead to conflict?

We not only listen to words; we also make assumptions about what the other person means. If our assumptions are accurate, there is no problem, but if they are not, the result is likely to be a misinterpretation of the message. Sometimes we deliberately make inaccurate assumptions because we don't agree with another person, so an assumption is made to prove the other person wrong. This was illustrated on an Oprah Winfrey program featuring parents who opposed their children's interracial dating. One white father had made several prejudicial comments by the time Jane Elliott, a human relations consultant, came on the program to give her perspective. As Elliott explained her perceptions of racism in America, the white father interrupted her.

Father: Other countries don't have racism?

Jane: Other countries *do* have racism. Absolutely other countries do have racism.

Father: So why . . . you're saying America this, America that. We're born in a racist society. Fine and dandy, but what I'm getting from you is that we're the only ones that are racist.

Jane: Did I say that?

Father: But that's the impression I'm getting from you.

Jane: No, you *choose* to get that impression from me. Not everyone is getting that impression from me. You do because you want to. That's a choice you're making.

Father: So I'm making an assumption on your part.

Jane: You're making an assumption that will defend your position. It's an indefensible position.

Father: You're not the person that says because white people like chocolate and chocolate milk they want to be black, are you?

Jane: I think you said that; you didn't hear that from me. (To the audience) Did you hear me say that? (Audience: "No")

Father: No, at, I mean, no, at some other time, on some other program.

Jane: Do you really think I'd say that?

Father: (shrugs) I don't know.

Jane: You see, what we're dealing with here is mental illness. Racism is mental illness.

Elliott exposed the father's deliberate misinterpretation by identifying his erroneous assumptions (notice the emphasis on *choice* in her comments). He assumed she was engaging in "America bash-

> The meanings of words are not in the words; they are in us.
>
> **S. I. HAYAKAWA (1906–1992)**

ing" so he asked about racism in other countries to detract from the problem of racism in the United States, and he assumed that she was out of touch with reality and might believe the absurd notion about liking chocolate. After Elliott identified the two distortions of her comments and beliefs, she addressed the cause of the problem—his racial prejudice. Using his comments as her example, she then made the point to the audience that racism makes people do and say "crazy" things.

On another talk show, Phil Donahue played devil's advocate to civil rights activist Charles King, Jr. In explaining racism, King said it was painful when black people described their experiences with racism to white people who refused to believe that what the black people said was true. The dialogue continued:

Donahue: What you say isn't true all the time.

King: The majority—Look there are—

Donahue: Just because you're black doesn't mean what you say is true. That's very Messianic and you know better than to say that. (Audience applauds)

King: Now what you just witnessed there was a defense that white people use to black people all the time. (Audience: "No, no") It is. Listen to this, listen to this. He said something there that was true. Just because you are black doesn't make what you say always right, which gives other white people the argument that a lot of what I am saying is wrong.

Donahue: No, it doesn't. It just—no it doesn't. (Audience: "No, no")

King: Why did you bring it up then?

Donahue: You did. You brought it up!

King: No. What white people do is exaggerate what black people are saying. What he said was—I never said I am black so everything I say is true. I never—

Donahue: Yes, you did. You just said that.

King: I never said that!

Donahue: What did you say?

King: You exaggerated what I said to put it on an extreme so that you could be right. I never said just because I'm black, I'm always right! I never have said that. This audience should certify that I didn't say that. You said that.

Like Elliott, King is able to identify the cause of the miscommunication—that he was talking about black people telling the truth about racism and Donahue exaggerated the statement to make it sound as if King had claimed that he always spoke the truth. This transforms what King said into an extreme statement that can be rejected. King also argued that the tactic is a common rhetorical device employed when white people discuss racism: By exaggerating legitimate claims of racism, they can deny their legitimacy and, therefore, deny the problem. Both examples deal with verbal behavior, but of course misunderstanding and conflict can also stem from nonverbal messages.

How does nonverbal communication lead to conflict?

Hecht and DeVito (1990) define **nonverbal communication** as "all the messages other than words that people exchange" (p. 4). Estimates of how much meaning is taken from interpretations of nonverbal communication have been as high as 93%, although Burgoon (1985) estimated that 60–65% is more realistic. Children don't tend to find as much meaning from nonverbal behavior as do adults; still, parents and teachers must be conscious of their nonverbal cues, especially when they express disapproval or take disciplinary action. For a child to understand what adults mean, messages must not be contradicted or confused by nonverbal messages (Kougl, 1997).

Disciplinary action may be required in response to a child's unacceptable behavior—perhaps the child is teasing or taunting other children. The adult says: "Teasing is bad. It hurts people's feelings. It may make them angry and it certainly makes me angry. You must stop doing this or no one will like you and no one will want to play with you." The message is clear and provides good reasons, includ-

ing self-interest, for the child to change his or her behavior. However, if this message is accompanied by angry looks, a loud voice, and gestures such as the adult pointing or jabbing a finger at the child, the good advice may get lost. The message the child gets is not that the behavior is bad but that "I'm bad" or "She hates me."

Children receiving this message are not likely to change their behavior, but to persist in it, either as a way of rebelling against the adult who has made this negative comment about them, or as a self-fulfilling prophecy: "She says I'm bad so I might as well be bad." Being told that certain *behavior* is unacceptable implicitly offers a child the power to choose. Children may not think they can change who they are, but they know they can change their behavior. If they hear an adult make a negative judgment about who they are, they can do nothing about that. Conflicts arising from such misinterpretations of nonverbal messages also occur among adults.

The need to assign meaning and the influence of nonverbal messages address two misconceptions about communication: (1) that communication simply means telling people something and (2) that communication is a verbal process to transmit messages using only words. Teachers who are committed to being good communicators understand the need to seek constant feedback from students to ensure that the knowledge they impart is being understood. Postman and Weingartner (1969) criticized educators for taking an "inoculation approach" in which teachers communicate information to students as if inoculating them against ignorance. When student grades on tests reveal that students didn't retain much information, the teachers' reaction is similar to that of a physician who doesn't understand why a vaccine had no effect when she knows she injected it. In discussing classroom communication, Kougl (1997) emphasized that teaching is not just talking; it involves more than words, as is true of all communication.

> Communication is something so simple and so difficult that we can never put it into simple words.
>
> **T.S. MATTHEWS (1901–1991)**

FIGURE 2.1   According to Ekman (2003), expressions of contempt and disgust are often used to indicate hatred of another. Prior studies have indicated that expressions of hatred and anger are often confused. In these two photographs from Ekman's research, one expression represents contempt and the other is anger. Try to identify the emotion represented in each facial expression. (For the answer, see the Ekman annotation in the References at the end of the chapter.)

Source: Used by permission of Paul Ekman.

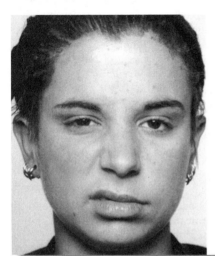 

What are other misconceptions about communication?

Of the many misconceptions about communication identified by Stone, Singletary, and Richmond (1999), the following five examples are especially important to recognize:

Communication is a natural human ability.
Communication is a good thing and should be encouraged.
Communication will solve all our problems.
Communications can break down.
Communication competence is equal to communication effectiveness. (pp. 56–61)

Communication is a natural human ability.
In a longitudinal study of three communities in the Piedmont Plateau region of the Carolinas, Heath (1983) described the way children learned communication skills and how skills varied depending on how the children had been taught. Heath found

that low-income white parents taught language to children by reading storybooks with a moral for each tale. Parental communication style was didactic and authoritarian; their children memorized Bible verses, learned strict rules for right and wrong, and were severely punished for lying. When the children went to school, they did well initially because learning activities and communication styles of teachers were similar to what they had experienced at home. The children obeyed teachers, looked for a single meaning—the moral—of a story, and memorized material as required.

As the children from low-income white families progressed through elementary school, however, they encountered activities requiring critical thinking and creativity. They had trouble making up stories because it seemed like lying. They struggled to make sense of stories with multiple meanings and to identify and analyze different perspectives for strengths and weaknesses. Their life experiences had not prepared them for reading, thinking, and communicating at any level of complexity. As they approached middle school their grades declined, as did their confidence. The majority never achieved academic competence in school, and some dropped out before finishing high school.

Heath described the language learning of Black children from low-income homes as a more creative process where children listened to adults tell stories that often had no particular moral point; these stories related what happened at work or in the neighborhood or gossip about "crooked politicians . . . or wayward choir leaders" (p. 168). Adults often told stories with a basis in fact, but with embellishment. When the stories got too far removed from reality, the teller was accused of "talkin' junk." In addition to hearing stories, boys developed language skills to respond to teasing based on "feigned hostility, disrespect and aggressive behavior" while girls became proficient in language by making up songs when skipping rope (p. 85). Both boys and girls practiced telling stories and, like adults, learned to embellish their stories with fictional details.

Black children from low-income homes came to school with highly creative communication skills, but they did not do well in the early elementary classes because they were not as adept at memorization or sticking to the facts. They saw many meanings to a story other than the simple moral the teacher wanted. As the students struggled with their assignments and growing feelings of inadequacy, they lost confidence in themselves as learners. When they finally encountered the more creative and complex learning activities later in elementary school, they were not successful because they had given up the possibility of success.

Heath noted that the children who succeeded in school at all levels were from middle-class homes, black as well as white, where their parents had read to them and had asked for didactic meanings of stories but also encouraged engagement in creative and analytical activity. A parent might read a story and then ask, "Would you have liked to go fishing with Little Bear? What do you think you would have caught?" (p. 250). Middle-class children came to school with a range of communication and language skills: They were successful at memorization and didactic activities during early elementary years; they were also able to adjust to activities emphasizing creativity or critical thinking in later years. Heath's research demonstrated that learning to communicate is not a natural human ability but a product of the cultural and social context one experiences as a child.

Communication is a good thing and should be encouraged.   Communication is a tool, and tools can be employed for good or bad purposes. Hitler used oratorical skills to arouse feelings of Aryan superiority and to deepen the anti-Semitic prejudices of Germans into a hatred that condoned persecution and execution. Martin Luther King, Jr. employed his oratorical skills to urge nonviolent resistance to oppression, warning his followers not to hate oppressors but to focus on the cause of justice. With any communication it is essential to ascertain the speaker's purpose and then determine whether that purpose is a good one.

It is also important to recognize when additional communication is not necessary, when the time has come to take action. Martin Luther King, Jr. deplored the "paralysis of analysis" as when people continue to talk about problems without ever doing anything. Of course it is essential to be thoughtful before acting, taking time to consider alternatives and consequences before deciding on a course of action, but there comes a time when one must stop analyzing every possible outcome and take action. After taking action, it is important to consider the consequences to determine whether to continue or choose another tactic. It is what Freire (1970) meant by the term **praxis**—taking action to address injustice and then reflecting upon the effectiveness of the actions taken as the person or group continues their activities.

> Think like an active person; act like a thoughtful person.
>
> **HENRI BERGSON (1859–1941)**

Communication will solve all our problems. Communication has the potential to solve problems, but it also has the potential to create them. In a speech to college students, poet Maya Angelou noted that whenever anyone asks, "Can I be brutally honest?" she always says "No" because she does not want to encourage anyone to do anything brutally. Whether information is accurate or inaccurate, truthful or distorted, if communication is delivered brutally it will be hurtful, and hurting people will create problems rather than solve them. We can communicate honestly without being brutal; we can show respect and sensitivity to the feelings of any person or group we encounter.

Ironically, some communication addresses problems with no *intent* of solving them. Berne (1996) described such interaction as playing "games." In the "Ain't it Awful" game, two people talk about a problem, not to solve it but to affirm each other's perceptions, sometimes at the expense of another. Imagine two teachers discussing a student. One describes Danny's misbehavior; the other responds with a similar story about something Danny did in her class, and they continue to exchange stories. The teachers are not trying to understand the boy's behavior to help him; instead, each is telling the other: "You and I are all right. Danny is the problem." When their conversation ends, both teachers walk away believing they are not to blame or obligated to do anything. Their communication has not solved Danny's problem, but it has made them feel better.

Another game Berne has described is "Yes, but . . ." where one person comes to another asking for advice, but actually wanting something else. For example, Luis is a teenager who is having problems with his parents. He goes to his best friend for advice. His friend suggests several strategies, and each time Luis says either (a) he tried that (or something similar) and it didn't work, or (b) he thought about doing that but explains why the suggestion wouldn't work. After the friend has exhausted all possible strategies he can think of, he may say something like, "Well I don't know what else to tell you. I don't know what else you can do." At this point, Luis walks away saying, "That's okay." The friend may be frustrated that he could not help solve the problem, but for Luis, the point of the conversation was to hear that he had done everything he could and there was nothing more for him to do. Now he can say the problem is not his responsibility; it is up to his parents. Both "Ain't it Awful" and "Yes, but . . ." involve a "solution" only in the sense that someone gets what he or she wants from the interaction, but the communication is not intended to solve the problem.

Communications can break down.   Most of us have used this particular misconception about com-

munication to justify ongoing conflicts. Rebellious teenagers say their parents don't understand them; husbands and wives complain that their partners don't appreciate them; workers may go on strike claiming that management isn't bargaining in good faith. In such cases, we may rationalize that our conflict cannot be resolved because communication has broken down. When machines break, they stop; however, communication cannot break down because it never stops, even if people stop talking to each other. Their communication could be hearsay or it could be nonverbal; it could consist of interpretations by one person about perceived decisions and actions of another.

Communication occurs because one person wants or needs to know what the other is thinking

> Information voids will be filled by rumors and speculation unless they are preempted by open, credible, and trustworthy communication.
>
> **JEAN KEFFELER (CONTEMPORARY)**

about or doing; a person may make decisions to do (or not to do) something based on assumptions about someone else. One person may decide not to attend a Christmas party so that a co-worker will know he is still angry with her, or he may decide to attend the party but not speak to the co-worker or make eye contact. In an extreme example, Dylan Klebold and Eric Harris had stopped responding to the taunts of some classmates and endured the verbal abuse at Columbine High School in silence, but when they went home, they left written and videotaped records of their repressed rage and their plans for revenge (Brown and Merritt, 2002). Communication can be ineffective or effective, but communication does not stop. If *verbal* exchange ceases, communication in some other form—whether words or actions—will replace it.

Communication competence is equal to communication effectiveness.   This is a misconception few college students should believe since almost every college student is familiar with professors who are knowledgeable about their subject matter but ineffective at communicating that knowledge. We are competent to communicate on a topic if we have sufficient knowledge of it; however, possessing knowledge does not mean that we can communicate in a way that is easily comprehended.

A major function of teacher education programs consists of preparing people to be effective at organizing and communicating information. Whether they are lecturing or using alternative means of delivering information, teachers must understand what studies have concluded about effective ways of helping people learn. To assess how effectively they deliver information, teachers must also evaluate how well students learn. Tests and other forms of assessment may measure student learning; more importantly, they reveal how effectively the teacher communicated.

Except for those in teacher education, most college professors learn how to communicate from mentors or self-study. Many professors have acquired the skills to become good teachers, yet the misconception that communication competence equals communication effectiveness is often the basis for student complaints that they aren't learning because a professor is incompetent. Professors may have **communication competence** because they have the knowledge needed for communication and may even have published articles and books on their specialty, yet they may not display **communication effectiveness** because they lack the appropriate skills to communicate effectively in a classroom.

How does effective communication occur?

Numerous excellent models have been developed that examine the communication process and analyze communication to ascertain why misunderstandings occur (Stone, Singletary, and Richmond, 1999; Schramm, 1973). The following model describes four factors involved in interpersonal communication. Each instance of a person interacting with another is influenced by these four cumulative factors (see Figure 2.2).

A Circular Model of Communication

1. Attitudes toward people or groups
2. Observations and assumptions
3. Conclusions and judgments
4. Verbal and nonverbal action

FIGURE 2.2 The Circular Model of Communication

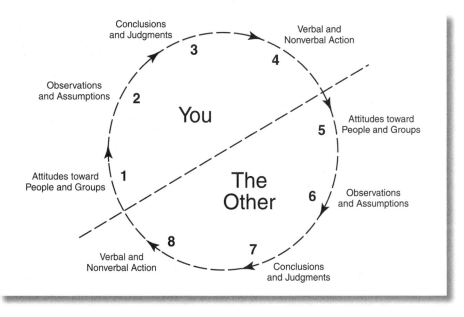

First, the communication process is grounded in an individual's *attitudes toward people or groups.* All people develop a general attitude about their interactions with others. Some of us are trusting, others are suspicious; some are willing to share ideas, others are reserved; some are motivated by dominance and control, others function with an egalitarian view. Our attitudes may change because of those involved in our interactions. Our interactions with family are different than they are with strangers. We communicate differently within same-gender groups than in mixed groups or with people of the opposite gender. Our behavior is different with others of our own race or ethnic group as opposed to being in mixed groups or with individuals from another race or ethnic group. Having prejudices or stereotypes about a particular minority group will certainly influence our interactions with a member of that group.

Second, our *observations and assumptions* about another person shape the communication between us before anything is said. Our initial reaction may be friendly and accepting, aloof and suspicious, or even hostile and rejecting, depending upon the appearance of the other person and sometimes upon which behaviors we choose to observe—a phenomenon known as **selective perception.** If an individual believes a stereotype about someone from a certain group, that stereotype is likely to be reinforced by selective perceptions.

How do our observations influence our assumptions? What if a person were introduced to a long-haired young white male who was dressed in torn overalls and wore a red bandana around his head? Based on observation, one might assume that the young man has rejected our materialistic society by imitating college students from the 1960s who questioned authority figures and rebelled against middle-class values, conformity, and the Vietnam War. These observations and assumptions are now taken to the next level.

The third step, *conclusions and judgments,* refers to the values and beliefs we employ to draw conclusions or to judge others. In the example of the young man with long hair, various people observing him and making reasonable assumptions could come to different conclusions. One person may have been in college in the 1960s and remember it as an exciting time that had a profound influence on his life. His initial reaction may be a positive conclusion: "That young man reminds me of myself

when I was his age." Conversely, someone who was taught to respect authority and appreciate the material comforts of our society and whose goal is to acquire material comforts may make a negative judgment, perhaps making additional assumptions about the young man smoking marijuana or using other illegal drugs. Prejudice and negative stereotypes lead to negative assumptions, which result in a negative judgment of another person.

The fourth and final step in the process is *verbal and nonverbal action.* When individuals meet, one person will say or do something to initiate interaction. Doing something might be as simple as smiling or frowning, making eye contact with the other or looking away. Nonverbal behavior employing such body language can initiate communication as much as words, often just as powerfully.

What does this communication model suggest about conflict resolution?

If conflict occurs during interaction, how can we resolve it? Our most common response is to focus on the action taken, on the words or behavior that initiated the conflict. For example, elementary teachers often witness conflict during recess where one child insults or hurts another. Some teachers respond by making the perpetrator apologize: The problem was the child's action, so the teacher forces the child to take another action to offset the first. This response focuses on the symptoms of the conflict and not the cause, so it is not likely to result in a resolution. Since the child may not feel genuinely sorry, what is learned from such an apology is a lesson in hypocrisy—being forced to say something that is not true.

Effective conflict resolution rejects superficial attention to actions and analyzes other factors to identify probable causes of the conflict. As Schramm (1973) stated, "The full significance of acts of communication is seldom on the surface" (p. 23). For this reason, most strategies for resolving conflicts are intended to get past surface meanings: Expressing "I" messages (Gordon, 2000); engaging in transactional analysis (Harris, 1993); using empathy to promote understanding (Rogers, 1980); and negotiating "Win/Win" strategies (Jandt, 1985). Still, even a proven approach may be ineffective if the people involved do not accept the value of the techniques employed. The following analysis employs the four factors of communication that preceded the conflict to understand the cause of the conflict.

The situation concerns a father and Abby, his daughter. Abby is talking on the telephone and making plans to meet with some friends whom her father doesn't like.

If Abby and her father were to resolve their conflict by focusing on what each one said and did, resolution would be unlikely but resumption of the quarrel would be quite likely. Instead, they could analyze factors involved prior to their argument to determine common ground upon which to create a resolution. The cause of their quarrel stems from the father exercising his authority as a parent in

	FATHER	ABBY
Interpersonal and Intergroup Attitudes:	Loves his daughter and wants her to be happy.	Loves her father, but resents the authority he has over her.
Observations and Assumptions:	Remembers Abby as an obedient child, but she has been rebellious since becoming a teenager; she has been challenging his authority and questioning his decisions rather than giving him the respect he deserves.	Perceives her father as using his authority to control her and not being fair to her; expects him to interfere with decisions that she believes she has the right to make by herself.
Conclusions and Judgments:	Believes that Abby's behavior is a personal rejection of him; he has also concluded that Abby's friends have encouraged her to reject him by disobeying him.	Values independence and wants more freedom; regards her father as hypocritical for denying her what he values; ready to rebel against attempts to control her.
Nonverbal and Verbal Action:		Hangs up the phone and says "I'm bored so I'm going out to meet my friends."
	Questions her choice of friends—"Why are you always hanging out with that bunch? Can't you find any other friends?"	
		"You are always criticizing my friends! You have no right to tell me who to be friends with!"
Conflict:	Becomes angry at her disrespectful tone of voice (which he expected to hear); tells her she cannot leave the house and orders her to her room.	Becomes angry about his attempt to control her (which she expected), shouts "Just leave me alone!" and runs off, slamming the door behind her.

FIGURE 2.3 United States: Past and Future   As ethnic diversity increases in the United States, being aware of cultural differences will become increasingly important.

Source: Schaefer, R.T. *Racial and ethnic groups,* 9/e. Copyright © 2004. Reprinted by permission of Pearson Education, Inc., Upper Saddle River, NJ.

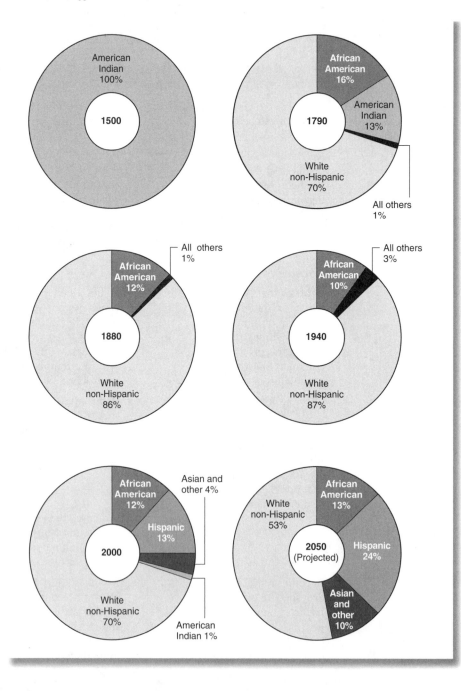

conflict with Abby's desire for greater independence. They will need to discuss their conflicting assumptions and desires. The father must understand that adolescents typically resent parental authority and not take her rebelliousness personally. Abby must recognize her father's authority as legitimate. A resolution is likely to come from agreements about the father supporting Abby's desire to be more independent and Abby recognizing his concern to protect her from the consequences of what he perceives as bad decisions. The causes of an interpersonal conflict will rarely be found in an analysis or discussion of individual behaviors; they are more likely found in observations, assumptions, conclusions, or judgments made about each other, and sometimes in contrasting attitudes toward people and groups.

How can attitudes toward people or groups create conflict?

When people involved in interpersonal communication identify themselves—or are identified by others—as part of a specific group (such as by race or ethnicity), individual attitudes can be significantly influenced. In a multicultural society such as the United States, it is probable that people, especially in urban areas, will interact with others who are different by race, ethnicity, nationality, or religion. How much the cultures of different nationalities or people of different racial or ethnic groups affect communication will depend upon how much each person knows about the culture of the others.

Cultural awareness

Kimmel (2000) identified levels of cultural awareness:

Cultural chauvinism Belief that one's culture is the best, superior to all other cultures; feeling no need to learn about other cultures.
Tolerance Awareness of cultural differences, recognition that differences stem from the country of origin for that person (or his/her ancestors); no judgment of cultural differences as inferior, simply as different ways of thinking or behaving.
Minimalization Minimizing cultural differences by emphasizing a universality of human needs

and behaviors as a means of creating a stronger sense of relationship or connectedness with culturally different people.
Understanding Recognizing that reality is shaped by culture and that each person's reality is different from that of a person from a different culture; having no judgment of different cultural realities; accepting and respecting cultural differences (cultural relativism).

Communication conflicts occur readily between people at the cultural chauvinism level, and they also may occur at the tolerance and minimalization levels. Only when people understand cultural differences and practice cultural relativism is it likely that conflicts between people from different cultures can be avoided or resolved.

CULTURE, COMMUNICATION STYLE, AND CONFLICT

Differences in cultural norms can cause misunderstanding and conflict. In the United States, business executives usually engage in minimal personal conversation before discussing a proposal at a group meeting. In some other cultures, communication is commonly expected to focus first on personal matters—questions about the person's health, family, or interests—before business is discussed. Ismail (2001) stressed how the global marketplace requires business executives to be knowledgeable about and employ appropriate communication strategies concerning use of direct speech, acceptable levels of informality, attitudes about time, and expressions of emotion in order to negotiate successfully with people from other cultures.

What are some communication style differences that are based on culture?

In the United States, it has become acceptable to take a direct approach to conflict resolution, with each party openly expressing their concerns. In other cultures, people are expected to show sensitivity to the feelings of others by taking an indirect approach to resolving conflicts. In some cultures, people tend to speak in a linear progression, going

> The test of a first rate intelligence is the ability to hold two opposed ideas in the mind at the same time, and still retain the ability to function.
>
> F. SCOTT FITZGERALD (1896–1940)

from one idea to the next, but in other cultures, people digress, often telling stories or anecdotes to illustrate their point. Cultures also reflect differences in nonverbal behavior. In Arab cultures, people tend to stand much closer in conversation than do Americans. In the United States, men greet one another with a firm handshake; in France, anything other than a quick handshake is considered rude; in Ecuador, greeting a person without offering one's hand is a sign of special respect. In the United States, the forefinger to thumb gesture means "okay"; in France, it signifies that something is worthless; and in Brazil, the gesture is considered obscene (Jandt, 1998).

Differences in communication styles have also been identified in subcultures in the United States. Kochman (1981) described how black and white children learn to express aggression. For most middle-class white people, aggressive language is viewed as a harbinger of aggressive behavior. "Fighting words" are words that may provoke a physical confrontation. Most white children learn to repress aggressive feelings and maintain a calm demeanor even though they may be furious. If they begin using language aggressively, it is likely that a fight is imminent. For some black males, however, words can be used aggressively without a conflict. Foster (1986) described how urban black male children may taunt one another in a playground game known by different names including "sounding" or "playing the dozens." Situations may become intense and emotional; however, a fight will only occur if a child gives an obvious signal such as making a fist to indicate that he is angry.

The contrast between the reactions of black and white people to aggressive language can lead to misunderstanding. Imagine two black children still playing the insult game as they come back to their classroom after recess. The teacher tries to intervene, but the boys continue to insult each other. A

black teacher may recognize the childhood game and firmly tell them to stop, but a white teacher may perceive the boys as engaged in a hostile quarrel, and order them to the principal's office. If the principal asks them why they were sent, they are likely to say they don't know. When the principal says their teacher saw them fighting, they will vigorously deny it, insisting that they were just teasing each other. Because the teacher has made this "false accusation," they might think she doesn't like them and become hostile to her in return.

Kochman (1981) describes another difference in communication styles concerning the conduct of arguments. White people are encouraged to present unbiased, objective arguments, but black people tend to accept the existence of bias and are skeptical of claims of objectivity. Although white people have been taught to argue in a calm, dispassionate manner, people in many black communities defend their beliefs passionately. In debates, black people do not expect impersonal or dispassionate arguments and may distrust people who are not passionate. Expressing ideas passionately during an argument is regarded as a measure of sincerity. In white society, the norm in debating issues is to repress emotions because they are believed to interfere with keeping an open mind. For many white Americans, arguing passionately seems confrontational; they think it exacerbates conflict and makes consensus less likely.

> Misunderstandings and inertia cause perhaps more to go wrong in this world than slyness and evil intent.
>
> JOHANN WOLFGANG VON GOETHE (1749–1832)

The potential for misunderstanding about how arguments are conducted was revealed in a televised program showing academics discussing racial issues in which a white professor misperceived a black professor based on his communication style. The black professor was making an eloquent and passionate argument. The white professor sitting beside him appeared uncomfortable, yet displayed no emotion. As the black professor paused before concluding, the white professor remarked in a defensive tone of voice but without facial expression, "Well you don't have to be so angry." Startled by the interruption, the black professor looked over at his white colleague and said, "Excuse me, you are mistaking anger for intensity."

In describing communication style differences, the intent is not to find fault with any group or person, nor is it to say that one communication style is better than the other. What is important is to understand that communication styles are influenced by cultural heritage; we should not make assumptions about others based on their communication style. If a conflict occurs in a group whose members are different races or cultures, individuals in the group must articulate their perceptions about the cause of the conflict to see if everyone has a similar perception. Understanding our perceptions of others provides a basis for resolving culturalmisunderstandings and conflicts. Meanwhile, research suggests that differences in communication styles create misunderstandings between men and women as well.

How does gender influence communication styles?

Communication differences based on gender are said to originate in differences in the way boys and girls are socialized. Traditionally, Americans have encouraged boys to be aggressive and girls to be nice; this has been documented in studies of children's play activities. American boys tend to play outdoors, typically in competitive games that require groups and involve aggressive behavior; they resolve disputes by engaging in debates in which everyone participates. In contrast, girls tend to play indoor types of games in small groups or with a friend; these games involve conversation and collaboration, and a quarrel will usually disrupt the game (Honig, 1998; Pearson, 1985).

Gender differences persist even as children leave childhood behind. Some scholars believe that male aggressiveness in conversation is revealed in studies where men interrupt women more than women interrupt men (Pearson, 1985), but Tannen (1994) argued that it is simplistic to say such behavior is always a dominance issue. Reviewing communication research on gender differences, Burgoon (1985) reported that women are more competent than men at giving and understanding nonverbal

messages. Grumet (1990) found that women tend to have more eye contact than men and to pay more attention to their conversational partner.

Differences in degree of eye contact and face-to-face interaction often reflect differences in how women and men express intimacy. Tannen (1990) described differences in male and female communication styles originating in childhood and continuing into adult years. In one study with subjects ranging from children to young adults, two people of the same age and gender were taken to a room, seated in chairs placed side by side, and asked to talk about a serious topic. The younger boys had trouble with the task; they didn't move the chairs, did not make eye contact, and spent much of their time shifting restlessly and talking about not wanting to talk. Males of all ages would sit in the chairs in their original position with minimal face-to-face interaction. At all age levels, female partners either moved the chairs or positioned themselves to face each other; they began talking immediately on a serious topic as requested.

High school boys express intimacy through aggressive behavior. Pushing, shoving, even punching each other is an indication of a close friendship. As adults, men transform aggressive physical behavior into aggressive verbal behavior. For example, American men will be careful expressing disagreement with someone they don't know very well, but they will bluntly disagree with and even use sarcasm with a close friend. It is a sign of intimacy and trust when men don't have to "pull their punches" with each other.

From childhood through adulthood, American women tend to express intimacy by engaging in face-to-face interactions and expressing concern for the other person's feelings. For most, outright disagreement is regarded as a threat to intimacy, a lack of sensitivity or respect. When a woman disagrees with another woman, she will often begin by saying something positive or something they agree upon, and then address the issue about which they disagree. The difference in male and female communication styles creates opportunities for misunderstanding. If a man and a woman have an intimate relationship and discuss an issue on which they disagree, he may make direct, honest comments because he feels so close to her, but she may interpret his harsh comments as insensitive, disrespectful, and even contemptuous of her opinions.

With such an emphasis on competition and aggression, boys become men who directly express wants, needs, or demands. With such an emphasis on cooperation, being nice, and caring about how others might feel, girls become women who are concerned about not imposing their wants or demands, preferring consensus. A man might attempt to convince someone to do what he wants, but a woman is more likely to ascertain whether the other person is interested in doing what she wants to do. Tannen (1990) argues that this difference may be a basis for historic gender stereotypes which have contributed to misunderstandings and conflict: men perceiving women as devious and cunning, and women perceiving men as arrogant and intimidating.

How do gender differences in communication styles lead to misunderstanding and conflict?

Imagine a woman coming home from work, greeting her husband, and then remembering, "Oh John, I meant to stop at the store and pick up a few things, but I am so tired I forgot to do it. This has been such a rotten day." She is indirectly asking him to go to the store for her, yet he may not get the message. Even if he tries to be sympathetic—"I'm sorry to hear that"—she will be upset if he doesn't offer to go to the store. If he wanted her to go to the store he would ask her directly; he needs to understand that her socialization and her communication style does not allow her to make demands as he would.

In a similar example, after leaving early for a long trip, a couple has been driving all morning on the interstate and it's almost noon. She sees a sign advertising a restaurant she likes at the next exit, points it out to him, and says, "Would you like to stop there and get something to eat?" He hears her comment not as an indirect request, but as a genuine question. He wants to drive for another hour before stopping to eat, so he says "No" and drives on. When he realizes that she is upset, they discuss the reason, and he criticizes her for not explicitly stating what she wanted. She thinks he should be able to understand that she did tell him in a manner that took account of his feelings. She believes that she has been sensitive and he has not. He believes

she was being dishonest while he was being straightforward with her.

The reason for identifying gender differences is not to blame men or women, nor to say that one communication style is better than another. What is important is to recognize the diverse ways people communicate so that differences in communication styles do not result in conflict. Knowing the influence on communication style of such factors as gender or culture provides a basis to prevent misunderstandings. If people recognize problems as possibly stemming from a difference in communication styles, they can modify their interaction to communicate more effectively (Ismail, 2001; Jandt, 1998).

CONFLICT RESOLUTION

Sometimes resolving conflicts seems hopeless. Groups have been in conflict for centuries; individuals take unresolved conflicts to their graves. Obviously, conflict resolution is not easy, and most people approach conflict with apprehension. In a study by McCorkle and Mills (1992), every metaphor chosen by participants to describe conflict was negative, often involving feelings of helplessness and of being an innocent victim.

With potential for so much misunderstanding, how are conflicts resolved?

Conflict offers opportunity for constructive change, if all parties are prepared to make concessions and to establish a context conducive to resolution. Deutsch (2000) identified values that participants must share if they want to resolve conflict: fallibility, equality, reciprocity, and nonviolence (pp. 34–35).

Fallibility refers to accepting the possibility of being wrong. In conflict, people are customarily presented with evidence and arguments. However, presenting evidence will not help resolve a conflict if participants refuse to acknowledge that their position could be wrong. During deliberations in a jury room, the foreman of a jury said he believed the defendant was guilty and that he would not change his mind. Another jury member pointed out that such an attitude violated the jury process that requires discussing and debating evidence, listening to arguments with an open mind, and changing one's mind if justified by the weight of evidence or arguments. Although still believing the defendant guilty, the foreman admitted the jury member was right, and agreed to listen with an open mind. Ultimately he changed his mind.

Equality refers to the belief that every human being, regardless of status, occupation, or wealth, deserves to be treated respectfully, with consideration for his or her values, beliefs, and behavior. It is an acknowledgment that every human life has value and that no one should be treated unjustly. In another jury trial, some members of the jury began to criticize testimony of two overweight and casually dressed female witnesses, based on their appearance rather than on what they said. Another juror chastised them for their negative attitudes and argued that if the jury was to render a just verdict, they should focus on the evidence the women presented, not on how they looked. Other jurors agreed.

Reciprocity means that participants in a conflict must behave toward others with the same sense of fairness and attentiveness that they would want for themselves—a restatement of the golden rule that appears as an ethical principle in practically all cultures, or as modified by Confucius: "Do not do to others what you would not like yourself" (Waley, 1938, p. 162). Apparently Confucius believed one did not have to be good to others as long as no harm was done to them. Either way, the feeling of reciprocity is essential for participants in a conflict if they hope to negotiate a resolution to it.

To value *nonviolence* is to believe that the only genuine solutions are peaceful ones. As Deutsch explained in his fourth shared value, coercing others into accepting an imposed solution winds a long and tragic path through human history marked by brutality and blood, civil and global wars, leaving little evidence that solutions imposed by the strong on the weak are effective—or lasting—solutions.

In the context of the four shared values proposed by Deutsch, conflict need not be a destructive event; it can be a constructive opportunity. Appleton (1983) quotes educational philosopher John Dewey: "Conflict is the gadfly of thought. It steers us to observation and memory. It instigates to invention. It shocks us out of sheep-like passivity" (p. 185). If participants use effective negotiation

> The man who strikes first admits that his ideas have given out.
>
> **CHINESE PROVERB**

strategies, they may be able to identify sources of conflict and determine appropriate solutions leading to improved relations between people.

Johnson, Johnson, and Tjosvold (2000) identified effective negotiation strategies to engage in what they termed **skilled disagreement.** Their first strategy for engaging in skilled disagreement is similar to what the jury member described in the fallibility anecdote: that all parties (1) agree to emphasize rationality, seek the best possible answer based on the available evidence and arguments, and be willing to change their position when justified by the evidence. Another strategy is that participants (2) agree that criticizing an idea is not criticizing those who propose the idea—that their worth as human beings is separate from their ideas.

It is also important that participants (3) make a conscious commitment to encourage others to contribute to discussion and to listen thoughtfully to the contributions they make. To ensure the process is effective, it is helpful when participants (4) restate ideas if they're not clear on what was said so that everyone understands the issue from all perspectives being presented. Finally, it is essential that participants (5) remember that the problem and any recommended solution will affect everyone; they must not be focused upon winning a debate but upon arriving at a collaborative solution everyone can support (pp. 70–71).

AFTERWORD

Even if we say exactly what we want to say, we can never assume that the meaning is heard and understood in the way we intend. Miscommunication happens when people do not check with others to ensure that they were understood. When misunderstandings are not clarified at the time they occur, they can cause people to become antagonistic toward others, thereby laying the foundation for an eventual conflict.

Conflict resolution is not easy, yet it's better than coping with unresolved conflict. It is in everyone's interest to embrace the values that make conflict resolution possible and to practice communication strategies necessary for engaging in skilled disagreement. Conflict—from intimate disagreements between husbands and wives to global disputes among nations—is inevitable. The resolution of conflicts, however, is not inevitable. We must choose to engage in and be committed to the process of conflict resolution. The quality of individual lives, and the quality of life for communities and for countries depends on the willingness of people to choose to resolve conflicts rather than hopelessly perpetuate them.

> All wars are civil wars, because all men are brothers . . . Each one owes infinitely more to the human race than to the particular country in which he was born.
>
> FRANCOIS FÉNÉLON (1651–1715)

TERMS AND DEFINITIONS

Communication competence Having sufficient knowledge of a subject to communicate accurate information about that subject

Communication effectiveness Having the skills to communicate information in order to be easily understood

Cultural chauvinism An attitude that one's culture is the best, superior to other cultures

Interpersonal communication A dynamic process of interaction between people in which they assign meaning to each other's verbal and nonverbal behavior

Minimalization An attitude about other cultures that reduces importance of cultural differences and emphasizes the universality of human needs and behaviors in order to create a stronger sense of relationship with all people

Nonverbal communication Those messages other than words that people exchange, also called "nonverbal behavior" or "nonverbal messaging"

Praxis Taking action to address injustice and then reflecting upon the effectiveness of the actions taken as the person or group continues their activities

Selective perception Paying attention to behaviors of another person that reinforce our expectations for that person

Skilled disagreement Strategies that have been proven effective in achieving a successful resolution to conflicts

REFERENCES

Appleton, N. (1983). *Cultural pluralism in education: Theoretical foundations.* New York: Longman.

Examines how the United States has become pluralistic, how American education has responded to pluralism, and what our pluralistic society might look like in the future.

Berne, E. (1996). *Games people play: The psychology of human relationships.* New York: Ballantine.

Examines the purposes behind conversational "games" and analyzes a number of them, then provides suggestions to promote more honest interactions.

Brown, B., & Merritt, R. (2002). *No easy answers: The truth behind death at Columbine.* New York: Lantern Books.

Describes the bullying and taunting of Dylan Klebold and Eric Harris by other students that resulted in their murder spree and suicides at Columbine High School.

Burgoon, J.K. (1985). Nonverbal signals. In M. Knapp & G. Miller (Eds.), *Handbook of interpersonal communication* (pp. 344–390). Beverly Hills, CA: Sage.

Reviews research to describe the nature, structure, and social functions of nonverbal communication including the impact of cultural norms, gender, and social status.

Deutsch, M. (2000). Cooperation and competition. In M. Deutsch & P. Coleman (Eds.), *The handbook of conflict resolution* (pp. 21–40). San Francisco: Jossey-Bass.

Describes constructive and destructive forms of competition and the implications of a cooperative orientation for more effectively resolving conflicts.

Ekman, P. (2003). *Emotions revealed: Recognizing faces and feelings to improve communication and emotional life.* New York: Times Books.

This cross-cultural study of nonverbal communication reveals the effectiveness of facial expressions in communicating meaning. [The picture on the left was anger; on the right, contempt.]

Foster, H.L. (1986). *Ribbin', jivin', and playin' the dozens* (2nd ed.). Cambridge, MA: Ballinger.

Describes verbal and nonverbal communication of urban black youth to prevent misunderstandings and to provide teachers with effective interaction strategies.

Freire, P. (1970). *Pedagogy of the oppressed*. New York: Seabury.

Analyzes the dynamics of oppression including the role of the oppressor, the responses of the oppressed, and the consequences of oppression for both.

Gordon, T. (2000). *Parent effectiveness training: The proven program for raising responsible children*. New York: Crown.

Describes a variety of strategies for parents to use not only to resolve conflicts with their children but also to teach children how to make responsible choices.

Grumet, G.W. (1990). Eye contact: The core of interpersonal relatedness. In J. DeVito & M. Hecht (Eds.), *The noverval communication reader* (pp. 126–139). Prospect Heights, IL: Waveland.

Presents an overview of research related to the significance of eye contact on relationships and the function of eye contact in interpersonal communication.

Harris, T. (1993). *I'm OK—You're OK*. New York: Morrow/Avon.

Uses Berne's theory of Transactional Analysis (TA) to explain how TA can become an analytical tool to understand interactions with others and resolve conflicts.

Heath, S.B. (1983). *Ways with words*. Cambridge, UK: Cambridge University Press.

Describes how children learn language in three distinct communities and the consequences of the way they have learned language with regard to their ability to be successful in school.

Hecht, M.L., & DeVito, J.A. (Eds.). (1990). Perspectives on nonverbal communication: The how, what and why of nonverbal communication. *The nonverbal communication reader* (pp. 3–17). Prospect Heights, IL: Waveland.

Reviews research to describe the characteristics of nonverbal communication and to explain the relationship between verbal and nonverbal communication.

Honig, A.S. (1998). Socio-cultural influences on gender-role behaviors in children's play. In D.P. Fromberg & D. Bergen (Eds.), *Play from birth to twelve and beyond: Contexts, perspectives, and meanings* (pp. 328–347). New York: Garland.

Describes gender differences in play activities, stereotyping in toy preference, and the influence of parents, peers, and television on children's play.

Ismail, N. (2001, September). Communicating across cultures. *Victoria, BC: Pertinent Information*. Available *http://pertinent.com/pertinfo/business/yaticom.html*

Examines factors that affect communication between people from different cultures and offers suggestions for improving such cross-cultural interactions.

Jandt, F.E. (1998). *Intercultural communication: An introduction* (2nd ed.). Thousand Oaks, CA: Sage.

Describes how cultural norms and values create a context for communication and how understanding different cultures is necessary for successful intercultural communication.

Jandt, F.E. (1985). *Win-win negotiating: Turning conflict into agreement*. New York: Wiley.

Provides examples of conflicts that failed to reach a satisfying conclusion and describes alternative strategies that have proven to be more successful in resolving conflicts.

Johnson, D.W., Johnson, R.T., & Tjosvold, D. (2000). Constructive controversy: The value of intellectual opposition. In M. Deutsch & P. Coleman (Eds.), *The handbook of conflict resolution* (pp. 65–85). San Francisco: Jossey-Bass.

Explains how conflict can be constructive and reports on the positive results of research involving people who were taught to use the strategies for "skilled disagreement."

Kimmel, P.R. (2000). Culture and conflict. In M. Deutsch & P. Coleman (Eds.), *The handbook of conflict resolution* (pp. 453–474). San Francisco: Jossey-Bass.

Describes the influence of culture on individual communication and the need to practice cultural relativism to avoid conflict in intercultural communication.

Kochman, T. (1981). *Black and white: Styles in conflict*. Chicago: University of Chicago Press.

Explains differences in communication styles commonly used by black and white people in urban America and how those differences can lead to conflict.

Kougl, K. (1997). *Communicating in the classroom*. Prospect Heights, IL: Waveland.

Analyzes the dynamics of communicating in a classroom, including communication problems that often occur, and describes optional strategies for responding to those problems.

McCorkle, S., & Mills, J.L. (1992, Summer). Rowboat in a hurricane: Metaphors of interpersonal conflict management. *Communication Reports* 5(2), pp. 57–67.

Examines the relationship between the metaphor selected by an individual to describe conflict and how that individual addressed conflict situations.

Pearson, J.C. (1985). *Gender and communication.* Dubuque, IA: William C. Brown.

Reviews gender research on a range of issues such as perceptions, self-image, sex roles, language, and media images; analyzes each issue's influence on men and women.

Postman, N., & Weingartner, C. (1969). *Teaching as a subversive activity.* New York: Delta.

Advocates that teachers use the inquiry method in their teaching and provide a relevant curriculum so that students become critical thinkers who are interested in their learning.

Rogers, C. (1980). *A way of being.* Boston: Houghton Mifflin.

Describes the philosophical basis for his professional practice and provides examples from his person-centered approach to therapy; Chapter 7 focuses on the value of empathy.

Schramm, W. (1973). *Men, messages, and media: A look at human communication.* New York: Harper Row.

Provides a historical overview of communication and uses research to analyze the functions of contemporary communication; communication models are explained in the appendix.

Spitzberg, B.H. (1990). Perspectives on nonverbal communication skills. In J. DeVito & M. Hecht (Eds.), *The nonverbal communication reader* (pp. 18–22). Prospect Heights, IL: Waveland.

Describes how nonverbal communication contributes to communicating effectively and provides a rating scale to measure nonverbal communication skills.

Stone, G., Singletary, M., & Richmond, V.P. (1999). *Clarifying communication theories: A hands-on approach.* Ames: Iowa State University Press.

Explains the theoretical foundations for communication, examines aspects of interpersonal communication and mass communication and describes communication research methods.

Tannen, D. (1990). *You just don't understand: Women and men in conversation.* New York: William Morrow.

Discusses how gender influences communication styles and explains how conflicts between men and women can result from these communication style differences.

Tannen, D. (1994). *Gender and discourse.* New York: Oxford University Press.

Six essays on language and gender including such topics as conversational strategies, issues of power, and the impact of culture and status on linguistic strategies.

Tavris, C., & Wade, C. (1984). *The longest war: Sex differences in perspective* (2nd ed.). New York: Harcourt Brace Jovanovich.

Examines a wide range of gender issues by reviewing research in anthropology, biology, human sexuality, education, psychology, and sociology.

Waley, A. (Ed.). (1938). *The analects of Confucius.* New York: Vintage.

Provides the social and political background for the philosophy of Kongfuzi (Confucius) and an annotated translation with explanations of references to events and individuals.

Summary Exercises

See page 19 for exercises to help you summarize the main points and define key terms in this chapter.

Personal Clarification Exercises

In Chapter 2, one exercise with four related parts provides an honest basis for discussion of interpersonal communication conflicts.

The Listening Test:

1-A   What Is Listening?

1-B   Are You Listening?

1-C   I Know You Think You Heard What I Said . . .

1-D   How Did It Feel? Summary Discussion Activity

Explanation of clarification exercises: Three activities outlined below provide illustration and practice with listening skills. Each activity is designed with a time limit, and your group leader or convener will have the responsibility of coordinating the times, role selection, and follow-up for each experience. None of the activities is meant to embarrass you or force you to reveal values that you prefer not to share.

The Listening Test

Clarification Exercise #1-A What Is Listening?

[Groups of 4] [Time: 5 minutes]

Directions: As a test of the listening skills of your group, each group member is asked to be able to summarize accurately what a speaker just said—at any point in your conversation. As the basis for this activity, discuss the following two questions:
  • What is the importance of listening?
  • Is it a skill that needs to be developed like any other skill?

Clarification Exercise #1-B Are You Listening?

[Teams of 2] [Round One: 5 minutes] [Round Two: 5 minutes]

Directions: In pairs and facing each other, one team member acts as the listener and the other takes the role of speaker. A time will be indicated when team members reverse roles for this activity.

  • *Listener role:* To use good nonverbal body language while listening; to not speak during this exercise; to let your partner do all the talking.
  • *Speaker role:* To explain to your partner how you value the first concept provided below. (Speaker B is asked to explain the second concept below.) As the basis for this activity, focus on the concepts that: (A) Listening is the best way to save time and effort and (B) Most of my friends seem more intent on telling me something than upon listening to what I have to say.

Directions for Follow-up to Exercise #1B: Join with another partnership team to assess the success of your experiences.
  • *Listener A:* At the end of Round One, tell your Speaker partner what you heard him or her tell you about why listening is the best way to save time and effort.
  • *Listener B:* At the end of Round Two, tell your Speaker partner what you heard him or her tell you about why most of his or her friends seem more intent on telling something about themselves than upon listening to what others have to say.

Clarification Exercise #1-C I Know you Think you Know What I Said, But . . . [Teams of 2]

Directions: [Round One: 8 minutes]
  • *Partner A (Speaker):* Your task is to deliver a two-minute description of a film, television show, or story that positively portrays a person who is different from you in some way (race, culture, social class, ethnicity, disability, sexual orientation, etc.). When your group leader says "Begin," you may begin. When your group leader says, "Stop," stop immediately even if you are in the middle of a sentence.
  • *Partner B (Listener):* If your leader has said "Stop," tell your partner the last five words he or she just spoke.
  • *Partner A (Speaker):* When instructed, continue your description from the point where you were interrupted. At the second "Stop" command, complete your current thought and conclude.

- *Partner B (Listener):* After your partner has stopped for the second time, summarize all of what the other person has said to you. Do not attempt to repeat the entire conversation.
- *Partner A (Speaker):* After listening to the summary, tell your listener whether or not the summary accurately reflects what you said. Explain how it could have been more complete, or what was omitted.

Directions: [Round Two: 8 minutes]

- Reverse roles. Partner A becomes the Listener, Partner B becomes the Speaker. Repeat each step so that the listening and speaking skills of each partner are exercised.

Clarification Exercise #1-D How Did It Feel?

Summary Discussion Activity [Whole group] [10 minutes]

Directions: Following your participation in one, two, or all three of the activities above, please place your chairs into a discussion group circle to respond to the questions below:

How Did It Feel? Summary Follow-Up Activity

1. In Exercise 1-A: How well did you summarize what your group members said? What good advice did you receive about how to improve?
2. In Exercise 1-B: How well do you think you listened to the explanations of your partners? Can you repeat—at this time—what was the best point in his or her explanation?
3. In Exercise 1-C: How many of you remembered the previous five words of your speaker when you heard "Stop"? Was that difficult or easy? Why?
4. Overall: What was the most difficult part of the activities that you completed? What made each challenging?
5. Listeners: Could you have sustained your concentration for 10 minutes? For 40 minutes? Why or why not? How long do you think the activity could have been for you to have continued to listen well?

6. What is different about how you listened in these exercises and how you normally listen to others? Would it be better if you listened as intently all the time? Why? When would it not be better?

ADAPTED FROM *BUILDING CULTURAL BRIDGES*

Intergroup Exercises

For Chapter 2, a role-play exercise promotes discussion about communication conflicts that we often experience.

Intergroup Exercise #1 Difficult Dialogues: Resolving Communication Conflicts

Directions: Read the following four scenarios; select one to use as the basis for a scene that your group will act out for the class. With others in your group, develop a story of what might occur in the scenario selected. Create a cast of characters so that each person in your group is significantly involved; each person in your group must have a part to play.

Part One: Discuss possible ways that you could improvise your selection into a 4–5 minute story that carries out the situation described. Assign roles, add characters to include everyone in your group, and imagine possible conversation that could occur. Take approximately 10 minutes to establish your characters, create a rough script, and set your scene.

Part Two: Explain your scene and introduce the cast of characters. Then present your scenario to the class. Be prepared to remain in character following your scene in order to answer questions from the audience. [Audience: follow the interpersonal communication between characters as well as the story.]

Difficult Dialogues: Resolving Cultural Conflicts—What Would You Do?

1. Eric, an African American student, is new to Metro State University. During the first week of classes, he is put in a discussion group where he becomes friends with Bob, who is white. As the semester goes on, he meets many black students

at the Multicultural Resource Center and becomes friends with several of them. One day, two of his black friends see Eric eating lunch with Bob and they don't come over to their table. Eric begins to worry that his black friends might see him as a "sell out" for having a white friend, but he and Bob have had a lot of fun together and he doesn't want to end their friendship. What does Eric do?

2. Maria, a Hispanic student, is upset by the behavior of three white girls in her Art Appreciation class. They seem to be friends because they are always together and they always sit in the back of the room and talk until class begins. Maria notices that they stop talking whenever she comes near them. If she starts to walk by them, they will suddenly become quiet and stare at her, and the expression on their faces is not friendly. What could Maria do?

3. Ben, a Native American student, hears one of his Native American friends talk about African Americans in a very demeaning way. Ben does not like to hear such prejudicial comments, but

he notices that his other friends smile and seem to agree with these comments. What could Ben do?

4. Kim, a white student, tells Amy, an Asian student, that she is very lucky. When Amy asks why Kim thinks she is lucky, Kim says Amy must be getting a lot of money to go to college since she is a minority. This comment upsets Amy even though she has heard it before. In the past, she has tried to ignore such comments, but she doesn't feel like ignoring it today. What could Amy say or do?

Part Three: All cast members face the audience. Characters should respond to audience questions about what they were thinking and feeling in the roles they portrayed. [Audience: Questions are important.]

Part Four: Cast of characters: Please make final remarks about yourselves to bring out any feeling or attitude that you think is important but has not been questioned.

CHAPTER 3

Understanding Prejudice and Its Causes

"It is so much easier to assume than to prove; it is so much less painful to believe than to doubt; there is such a charm in the repose of prejudice, when no discordant voice jars upon the harmony of belief."

W.E.H. LECKY (1838-1903)

Prejudice is an attitude; it is not an action. Whether you are looking at definitions in a dictionary or reading scholarly writing, you will inevitably encounter puzzling uses of the term *prejudice*. Some sources suggest that prejudice involves a hatred of others, but hatred is bigotry. Based on their study of world cultures, anthropologists have argued that people everywhere in the world have prejudices, yet they do not claim that hatred—or bigotry—is widespread.

Confusion in our language is caused by a definition that suggests prejudice is synonymous with bigotry. That is why many of us deny we are prejudiced: A bigot hates, and we are certain we don't hate anyone. In addition, we deny the pervasiveness of prejudice because we don't observe widespread hatred in the world; thus, confusing prejudice with bigotry creates misunderstanding about the nature and extent of prejudice.

CONCEPTIONS AND MISCONCEPTIONS OF PREJUDICE

What are examples of misconceptions about prejudice?

We confuse prejudice with bias, stereotypes, and bigotry. As defined in Chapter 1, bias is a mildly positive or negative feeling about someone or something; and to stereotype is to associate positive or negative traits with a group of people. **Prejudice** is a stronger feeling, but it is always negative, and it always refers to a group of people. Prejudice predisposes us to behave negatively toward certain others because of a group to which they belong. And when prejudice reaches the intensity of hatred, it becomes bigotry.

Some dictionaries define *prejudice* as the process of forming opinions without looking at relevant facts, yet people with prejudices may examine relevant facts and simply interpret them to confirm their prejudices. Other definitions describe prejudice as being irrational, implying that those we acknowledge as rational could not possibly be prejudiced. The problem here is that rational people also hold prejudices; we know this from reading what they wrote. Aristotle claimed that a woman was an inferior man. Abraham Lincoln believed black people were intellectually inferior to white people. Carroll (2001) quoted Martin Luther warning German Christians, "do not doubt that next to the devil you have no enemy more cruel, more venomous and virulent, than a true Jew" (p. 368). However, their prejudices did not deter any of these men from achieving significant improvements in human rights.

It is easy to smile at ancient racist or sexist attitudes and to denounce past prejudices as absurd, yet often we do not recognize current widespread prejudices that future generations may find just as absurd. In fifty or one hundred years, what will people think about the programs for the poor in the United States today? Or how people with disabilities were so often isolated or ignored? Or how gay men and lesbians were condemned by so many people?

> There are, in every age, new errors to be rectified, and new prejudices to be opposed.
>
> SAMUEL JOHNSON (1709–1784)

How widespread is prejudice?

Although this book focuses on attitudes in the United States, prejudices are not limited to one country or one race. People living in nations around the world possess negative attitudes toward others within their own borders or close to them. Prejudices have been ignored, promoted, or tolerated, but rarely challenged. When prejudice has been challenged, the case often has become a *cause célèbre,* as when Emile Zola published "J'accuse," an essay denouncing anti-Semitism in France's prosecution of Alfred Dreyfus for treason (Bredin, 1986). Persistence of prejudice was illustrated by Jean Paul Sartre's 1945 description of French anti-Semitic attitudes as Jews returned to France following World War II, even though French people were aware of Nazi concentration camps and of the genocide against the Jews (1976).

Today, nations around the world are being forced to confront historic prejudices because of economic globalization and population migrations that have created major demographic changes. Some responses to immigration have revealed the persistence of historic prejudices. In the opening paragraph of their book on prejudice and discrimination, Simpson and Yinger (1985) describe this phenomenon:

> Western European nations discovered that "guest workers," whom they have employed by the millions, are something more than cogs in an economic machine.

And, for example,

> England, with a steady migration of people from India, Pakistan, Bangladesh, Africa, and the West Indies, found herself faced with problems of a color bar and passed an unprecedented law limiting immigration. Pressures against persons of Indian descent in the new nations of East Africa not only reshaped intergroup relations in those lands but influenced Britain's restrictive immigration policy. . . . (Russia) not only struggles with questions of equity and control of her own racial and cultural minorities but finds that her ancient fear of

45

the "Mongol hordes," now the Chinese, intrudes into international relations. (p. 3)

As long as people lived in relative isolation from others, prejudice against those who were far away was not necessarily harmful. In a global economy requiring functional and respectful relationships between nations, prejudice can be a destructive force both in the world and in individual societies, especially diverse societies (Gioseffi, 1993). Despite its pervasiveness, prejudice may or may not be acted upon. It is not inevitable that we must be controlled by our prejudices; those who can identify their stereotypes and prejudices may choose to control them. Education can confront such negative attitudes both in the media and in our language to help students unlearn prejudices they have been taught, and also understand why it is in everyone's best interest not to act on prejudices. The basis of our hope for a better America and a more peaceful world is for teachers to make such a commitment and to fulfill it in their classrooms.

How are prejudices reflected in American media and language?

To understand how prejudices are transmitted in our culture, we need only observe some of the prevalent images of racial or cultural groups in society. As Giroux (1998) said:

> My concern with such representations . . . lies not in deciding whether they are "good" or "bad" but in analyzing them in relation to the pedagogical work they are doing. That is, what knowledge, values, and pleasures do such representations invite or exclude? (p. 27)

Look for magazine advertisements that depict Native Americans, Asian Americans, or Hispanic Americans. Why is it that most advertisements seem to use African American models to reflect diversity? If people of color are included in advertisements, why are they often featured in ways that reflect historic stereotypes? Native Americans are almost never portrayed as contemporary people but

FIGURE 3.1

Source: John Branch, *San Antonio Express-News.*

as nineteenth century warriors; Asian Americans are often shown working at computers or in math-related professions; Mexican Americans are presented as gardeners or servants. Problems of omission and stereotyping affect other groups as well: People with disabilities are invisible, blue-collar workers are usually stereotyped, if they appear at all, and women appear frequently in advertisements as sex objects to sell products. Still, we typically don't recognize these advertisements as stereotypes because these images are so familiar that they seem not to be stereotypes at all, but rather to portray reality. This is one reason so many white Americans do not understand why Native Americans find offensive the use of Indian mascots for sports teams.

Negative perceptions are also embedded in everyday language. When people negotiate the price of a product they might say they "Jewed him down" on the price. Parents and teachers have been overheard telling children to stop behaving "like a bunch of wild Indians." Boys are regularly ridiculed by comments such as "he throws like a girl" or "he's a sissy." And then there are jokes, many of which are based on racial, ethnic, gender, or other prejudices. When we complain that some jokes aren't funny, we are likely to be told we don't have a sense of humor: "It was a joke!" Just a joke.

> I am, in plainer words, a bundle of prejudices—made up of likings and dislikings.
>
> **CHARLES LAMB (1775-1834)**

Chapter 4 will focus on the issue of how prejudices are learned, but in this chapter we are trying to understand what prejudice is and how it influences behavior. The influence is always negative because prejudice is always negative.

Why can't prejudice be positive?

Some people misuse the term *prejudice* by saying they are prejudiced *for* something, but a prejudice is a negative attitude. A milder attitude of liking or disliking anything or anyone is a bias; however, the concept of prejudice involves learning to fear, mistrust, and strengthen stereotypes we have been taught about other groups of people. Once we learn to be prejudiced against a certain group, we tend to *behave* in negative ways toward others who appear to be members of that group. Negative behavior is discrimination: We no longer merely hold a negative attitude—we have acted upon that attitude.

CONSEQUENCES AND CAUSES OF PREJUDICE

With regard to discriminatory actions, Allport (1979) identified five negative behaviors caused by prejudice: (1) *verbal abuse* against others occurring among friends or resulting in name-calling directed at others from a particular group. Name-calling can escalate into (2) *physical assaults*. The victim doesn't even have to be a member of the despised group to be assaulted; anyone could be a victim by being perceived as one of "them." When a large group of ethnic Hmong from Southeast Asia settled in a Wisconsin community of 50,000 people, some local citizens did not accept them. A Japanese foreign exchange student who attended a college in that community was severely beaten by a white male in the mistaken belief that his victim was Hmong. Another common example of violence based on misperceptions is that heterosexual men have been physically assaulted because they were perceived to be gay.

When prejudice reaches its most extreme form, bigotry, behavior promoted by hatred can include (3) *an urge to kill* certain "others." Acting on one's hatred can lead to behavior that today we call a "hate crime." In 1982, two Detroit men lost their jobs at an automobile factory and believed it was due to the popularity of imported Japanese cars. When they encountered Vincent Chin, a Chinese American, they mistakenly thought he was Japanese. Motivated by hatred and rage, they brutally murdered him. If homicidal rage spreads, it might lead to **genocide**—the systematic and deliberate extermination of a nationality or a racial or ethnic group (Feagin and Feagin, 1996).

Bigotry is required for people in power to attempt the extreme act of genocide, but prejudice

FIGURE 3.2 **Neighborhood Preference of White Respondents**

In a study cited by Farley (2000), subjects were shown diagrams of neighborhoods consisting of 15 homes with an X on the home in the center of the neighborhood indicating the subject's home. Each shaded home represented an African American family. White respondents were asked: How comfortable would they feel in each neighborhood? If they were uncomfortable, would they leave? Would they move into such a neighborhood? The percent not willing to live in those neighborhoods where only one-fifth or one-third of homeowners were African Americans illustrates attitudes that produced white flight.

Neighborhood Diagram

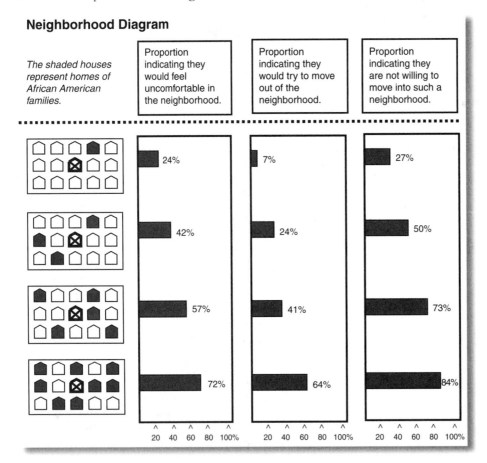

may give bystanders a reason to ignore such actions. Anti-Semitic prejudice in Germany was a major factor contributing to the Nazi extermination of six million Jews during the Holocaust. Before and during World War II, most Germans (also Poles, Austrians, and others) did nothing to protest or interfere with the death camps. After the war, they claimed they didn't know what was going on; persuasive evidence has been gathered to refute their claim (Goldhagen, 1996).

In contrast to confrontational negative behavior stemming from prejudice and bigotry, a more passive negative response to prejudice is to avoid members of other groups. We do this by (4) *limiting our interactions* with people from racial or ethnic groups other than our own. Measuring attitudes about avoiding others was the focus of research by Bogardus; this study used a Social Distance Scale in which people encounter a list of racial, ethnic, and religious groups and are asked to rank them in order of preference (Schaefer, 2004). People consistently reveal a preference for those groups most like themselves, and they have less regard for people from groups they perceive as least like themselves.

Another way to avoid certain groups is (5) to *engage in or condone discrimination* in such areas as education, employment, and housing. To illustrate this behavior, consider how people choose what sort of neighborhood they want to live in. In the 1960s, when courts ordered urban school districts to desegregate, many school administrators responded by busing students to different schools, a controversial solution that caused massive movement of white families from urban neighborhoods to racially segregated suburbs, the **white flight** phenomenon. Despite the passage of the 1968 National Fair Housing Act, studies have documented the preference of most white Americans to live in racially segregated neighborhoods (Massey, 2001; Farley, 2000). As Massey noted, the Fair Housing Act "theoretically put an end to housing discrimination; however, residential segregation proved to be remarkably persistent" (p. 424).

What factors promote the development of prejudice?

Considerable research has been conducted addressing the question of how individuals become prejudiced. Some studies suggest that elitist attitudes foster prejudice. **Elitism** is the belief that the most able people succeed in society and form a natural aristocracy while the least able enjoy the least success because they are flawed in some way or lack the necessary qualities to be successful. This condescending attitude promotes the belief that those in the lower levels of society deserve to be where they are and that successful people have earned their place in society. Unsuccessful people are often held responsible for their failure. Elitist attitudes are a major factor in studies based on social dominance theory (Howard, 1999; Stephan, 1999).

The eugenics movement beginning in the late 1800s argued that an individual's genetic inheritance determined his or her fate and that environment played little or no role in human development (Selden, 1999). Based on this argument, proponents of the eugenics movement in the United States were promoting elitist attitudes. Selden quoted American biologist George W. Hunter, author of several biology textbooks widely used in schools between 1914–1941, who expressed this elitist attitude clearly:

> Those of low grade intelligence would do little better under the most favorable conditions possible, while those of superior intelligence will make good no matter what handicaps they are given. (p. 75)

Other studies suggest a link between prejudice and attitudes about power. Some people express a **zero-sum** attitude, a highly competitive orientation toward power based on the assumption that the personal gains of one individual mean a loss for someone else; therefore, to share power is regarded as having less power. According to Levin and Levin (1982), an individual with a zero-sum orientation toward power tends to be a person with strong prejudices. Thurow (1980) has described the adverse consequences for society when a zero-sum orientation is prevalent. Studies also suggest that people with authoritarian personalities tend to be more prejudiced, although other studies refute the idea (Farley, 2000). Some have even proposed that prejudice is innate, but there are no scientific studies to support that claim.

To be as pervasive and persistent as it has been, prejudice must serve some purpose and offer some benefit to individuals or to society. Having reviewed

> Everyone is a prisoner of his own experiences. No one can eliminate prejudices—just recognize them.
>
> EDWARD R. MURROW (1908-1965)

research concerning causes of prejudice, Levin and Levin (1982) identified four primary causes, and within these causes, functions of prejudice that sustain it. The four causes include (1) personal frustration, (2) uncertainty about a person based on lack of knowledge or experience about the group to which they belong, (3) threat to one's self-esteem, and (4) competition among individuals in our society to achieve their goals in relation to status, wealth, and power.

How does frustration cause prejudice?

The frustration-aggression hypothesis maintains that as frustration builds, it leads to aggressive action. Frustration causes tension to increase until a person chooses to act upon the frustration to alleviate the tension. Jones (1997) and others have called this the "scapegoat phenomenon." The word **scapegoat** derives from an ancient Hebrew custom described in Leviticus 16: 20–22, where each year the Hebrew people reflected on their sins during days of atonement. At the end of that time, a spiritual leader would stand before them with a goat, lay his hands on the goat's head, and recite a list of the people's sins, transferring the sins of the people to the goat—which was then set free. In modern America, the term generally refers to blaming a person or group for problems they did not cause.

When we take aggressive action—from verbal abuse to physical violence—we inevitably cause harm to others. Since most individuals define themselves as "good" according to some criteria, they will usually find a way to rationalize their actions as being good or at least justified. When Southerners lynched black people in the late nineteenth and early twentieth centuries, they justified their actions by insisting that all blacks were lazy, lustful, or liars. Using the Kafkaesque reasoning that all blacks were guilty and therefore it didn't matter what crime a black person was accused of committing, they executed victims with no regard for whether that specific black person was guilty of a crime.

Ironically, data from some studies have shown that aggressive action may not alleviate frustration, but instead may exacerbate it. In one study, two groups of subjects were asked to allow medical technicians to take physical measurements of their bodies. After taking the measurements, the technicians made derogatory comments intended to make the subjects angry. One group was taken to the technician's "supervisor" if they wanted to complain; the other group was not. The researchers thought that members of the group being allowed to "vent" their anger would feel less hostile toward the technician afterwards, yet those who complained reported stronger feelings of hostility than the subjects who were not allowed to complain (Aronson, 1999). The findings suggest that identifying a scapegoat upon which to vent one's frustration does not solve a person's problems, and it may make matters worse.

The implication that finding a scapegoat does not solve problems is illustrated in domestic abuse cases. When a man takes out his frustrations by abusing his partner, he has to justify his actions. It is common for men arrested for domestic abuse to explain their behavior by saying, "She made me do it," or "She kept nagging and wouldn't shut up." This not only depicts the man as a victim (the suffering husband), but also it reinforces the stereotype of nagging wives, providing the husband with an excuse for assaulting the woman he once claimed to love. Because violence escalates with each domestic abuse complaint from the same home, it is obvious that blaming one's spouse or partner doesn't solve the problem; it may possibly cause the abuser to become more violent toward those interfering with his actions.

Because of the high rates of injury and death to police officers responding to domestic abuse cases, many American cities, counties, and states require officers to file abuse charges directly, even over the objections of the one abused. Courts often mandate counseling for abusers to address and understand how gender prejudices and stereotypes created negative attitudes leading to abuse, and to teach abusive men effective, nonviolent strategies for managing anger. The role of gender stereotypes in contributing to domestic abuse illustrates another major cause of prejudice—uncertainty.

What do stereotypes have to do with uncertainty and how do they cause prejudice?

Most of us only have knowledge of the groups to which we belong; often we do not know much about other groups. In the United States, schools

FIGURE 3.3 This drawing has been used for research and in classrooms. One person is shown this picture and whispers a description of the entire scene to another person, who then whispers the description to another person until each person in the room has heard it. The last person is asked to describe the scene to everyone. Typically, the person describes a poorly dressed black man with a weapon preparing to attack a well-dressed white man, thus illustrating the power of racial stereotypes.

have historically implemented curricula reflecting perspectives, contributions, and experiences of the dominant (white) group; many of our neighborhoods still tend to be segregated by race or social class. The result is that people from different racial and ethnic groups have few opportunities to learn about one another. Because of our lack of accurate information, we may believe in stereotypes as a way to convince ourselves that we know about certain groups. Our stereotypes can be reinforced by images or information contained in such media as advertisements, textbooks, and films.

When a person actually encounters individuals of a different race, ethnicity, or social class, selective perception of the behaviors of those individuals often reinforces his or her stereotypes. Stephan (1999) reported on one study where subjects were presented with equal amounts of positive and negative information about a group to which they belonged (in-group) and a group to which they did not belong (out-group). Subjects tended to recall more positive information about the in-group and more negative information about the out-group. According to Stephan, negative attitudes in our memory tend to increase over time.

Selective perception was illustrated in another study where two groups of subjects viewed consecutive videotapes: The first videotape was of a fourth-grade girl playing with friends, and the second videotape was of the same girl taking an oral test in school where she answered some difficult questions correctly, but missed some easy questions. Although the second videotape was the same for both groups, the first videotape shown to one group was the girl playing in a low-income neighborhood and first videotape shown to the other group was the girl playing in a high-income neighborhood. After watching both videotapes, subjects were asked to judge the girl's academic abilities. Those who saw her playing in the low-income neighborhood rated her academic ability lower than those who saw her playing in the more affluent neighborhood. Whether the subjects focused more on the girl's correct or incorrect answers appeared to have been influenced by the neighborhood where they believed she lived and stereotypes associated with affluence and poverty (Aronson, 1999).

Researchers have also shown that becoming more knowledgeable about others helps people to overcome stereotypical perceptions. In a psychiatric hospital with an all-white staff, patients acting violently were either taken to a "time out room" or subjected to the harsher penalty of being put in a straightjacket and sedated. In the first month of a research study, both black and white patients were admitted. Although the black patients admitted were diagnosed as being less violent than the whites, they were four times more likely to be put in a straightjacket and sedated by the staff if they became violent. The discrepancy in the white staff's use of restraints suggests that they believed in the stereotype that black people were more prone to violence. As the staff became better acquainted with the patients, the staff responded to violent incidents with more equal use of restraints for both black and white patients (Aronson, 1999). Stereotypes that portray a group as being prone to violence, lazy, or less intelligent can influence a person's behavior; stereotypes can also play a part in a person's self-esteem being threatened, which is another major cause of prejudice identified in research.

How does threat to self-esteem cause prejudice?

In the United States, people are encouraged to develop self-esteem by comparing themselves with others. We do so by grades in school, music contests, debates in speech, and athletic competitions. But what happens when positive self-esteem is achieved by developing feelings of superiority to someone else? Or when we achieve our sense of superiority by projecting our feelings of inferiority onto another person or group? If we believe in the innate superiority of our group compared to other groups, then we believe we are better than anyone who is a member of the inferior group. If members of an inferior group become successful, their achievements threaten those whose self-esteem was based on feelings of group superiority and unconsciously transforms a condescending attitude into prejudice.

People of color confront the issue of self-esteem based on race as a cause of prejudice when they encounter white people whose self-esteem is threatened by their achievements or success. The first African American to teach at Harvard University Law School commented:

> You have to simultaneously function on a high level and try not to upset those whose racial equilibrium is thrown off when they recognize that you are not incompetent, not mediocre, and don't fit the long accepted notions about persons of color that serve as unrecognized but important components of their self-esteem. (Bell, 2002, pp. 66–67)

When we possess this kind of self-esteem, we are insecure and easily threatened. Coleman (1997) argued that people perceiving others as inferior "are more likely to identify and maintain negative stereotypes about members of stigmatized groups" (p. 222).

> If we believe absurdities we shall commit atrocities.
>
> **VOLTAIRE (1694–1778)**

Studies suggest that part of the self-esteem for many men derives just from being male. In Michigan, over a thousand children wrote essays about what their lives would be like if they were the opposite gender. Although almost half the girls found many positive things to say about being male, 95% of the boys could find nothing positive to say about being female (Sadker and Sadker, 1994). Similar attitudes appear among adults. In their research on self-esteem, Martinez and Dukes (1991) reported that males displayed higher self-esteem than did females, and that white males had the highest self-esteem of all groups.

When male self-esteem derives from perceiving one's gender as superior, it is easily threatened by women's achievements. American men often rationalize female achievements by attributing women's success to reasons other than competence. Their rationalizations may be characterized by resentment or anger, which intensifies the prejudice that created the initial illusion of superiority. If a woman receives the promotion a man wanted, he might complain that she is "sleeping her way to the top." Since self-esteem based on a belief in gender superiority is an illusion, it is ultimately inadequate because the individual has done nothing to earn it. Fearing that an "inferior" person might receive rewards the "superior" individual desires is related to the fourth primary cause of prejudice: competition for status, wealth, and power.

How does competition for status, wealth, and power cause prejudice?

There is evidence that competition fosters prejudicial attitudes. Jones (1997) described a study at a summer camp where Boy Scouts were given time to become acquainted and to develop friendships before being divided into two groups and housed in separate bunkhouses. The groups were divided so that approximately two-thirds of each boy's friends were in the other bunkhouse. The two groups were encouraged to play a series of competitive games such as tug-of-war, football, and baseball. Boys who had liked each other began to intensely dislike each other and to engage in name-calling. Although

there was solidarity within groups, friendships that had been established with boys from the other group no longer existed. After competitive games were concluded, researchers brought the boys together, but animosity remained until the boys were given tasks that required them to cooperate with each other. Working together to achieve a common goal reduced the hostility and resulted in the boys again making friendships with individuals from the other group.

THE PERPETUATION OF PREJUDICE

People want to be successful and will try to promote their own self-interests. When members of one group believe that individuals from another group are becoming more successful than they are, they may become angry at those individuals—even hostile toward the entire group—by rationalizing an advantage other than talent or skill that is responsible for their success. White American males sometimes resent affirmative action because they believe it provides women and racial or ethnic minorities an advantage in being hired and promoted. Resentment from economic competition for good jobs with high salaries and status fosters prejudice. Since humans are intelligent enough to identify these various causes of prejudice, it seems logical to assume that people should be able to recognize that they have prejudices and attempt to eliminate them.

How are prejudices perpetuated?

A major factor in the perpetuation of prejudice is the tendency to rationalize prejudices and the negative behaviors prejudices promote. As Gioseffi (1993) has noted, "Just as individuals will rationalize their hostile behaviors . . . so nations do also" (p. xvii). Vega (1978) described rationalizations taking three forms: denial, victim-blaming, and avoidance. To unlearn our prejudices and develop effective ways of confronting prejudices expressed by others, we need to recognize these rationalizations so we can make an appropriate response when they are expressed.

Denial rationalizations

In making **denial rationalizations,** we refuse to recognize that there are problems in our society resulting from prejudices and discrimination. Such claims are astonishing in their ignorance, yet they continue to be made. In response to assertions of racism, the most common denial rationalization is the reverse discrimination argument that claims that women and minorities receive the best jobs because of affirmative action programs. Is there any truth to this claim?

According to population demographics, women now comprise almost half of the workforce; another 10% consists of males of color, which means that white males constitute about 40% of the work force (Daft, 2003). A job paying an annual salary of $50,000 or more is a criterion to identify which jobs involve some degree of authority, status, and decision-making power. How many of these jobs are in the hands of white males? It would be consistent with their proportion of the workforce if white males had slightly less than half of these jobs, yet according to the Bureau of Labor Statistics (2001), white males hold over three-fourths of these positions, about twice as many as the percent of white males in the workforce. Claims that white males are unfairly discriminated against as a result of affirmative action policies would appear to be dubious (see Table 3.1).

The most common denial rationalization related to sexism is the "natural" argument, which denies gender discrimination, claiming that it is natural for women to do some things better than men, and for men to do some things better than women. This denial rationalization is offered as an explanation for why men and women have historically held certain types of jobs. The argument does not explain the difference between the skills of a tailor (predominantly men) compared to a seamstress (predominantly women) to justify the differences in their compensations. Nor does it explain why construction workers (mostly males) should be compensated at a greater rate than college educated social workers (mostly females). Historically, women have been paid less than men for doing the same work, and occupations dominated by women still receive lower wages than occupations dominated by men (Bureau of Labor Statistics, 2001). This is the reality, but denial rationalizations have little to do with reality.

The most subtle denial rationalization is personal denial illustrated by the man who says, "How can I be sexist? I love women! I married a woman. I have daughters." This seems a reasonable statement: Someone denying he has gender prejudices does not appear to deny the existence of widespread prejudice against women—but the statement actually does imply a more sweeping denial. Psychologically, most people feel they are normal, average

> People prefer to believe what they prefer to be true.
>
> FRANCIS BACON (1561-1626)

TABLE 3.1

Annual Incomes of Full-Time Workers in the United States

RACE/GENDER	MEDIAN WEEKLY EARNINGS			
	1990		2000	
White males	$494	(100%)	$669	(100%)
Black males	$361	(73.1%)	$503	(75.2%)
Hispanic males	$318	(64.4%)	$414	(61.9%)
White females	$353	(71.5%)	$500	(74.7%)
Black females	$308	(62.4%)	$429	(64.1%)
Hispanic females	$278	(56.3%)	$364	(54.5%)

Source: U.S. Census Bureau (2001)
Statistical Abstract of the United States.

people. If a person denies being prejudiced, he or she is actually denying that most other normal, average people are prejudiced as well. The real meaning of such a statement is that the speaker does not believe prejudice and discrimination are serious problems in society. If someone argues this point, the person making this denial rationalization might resort to victim-blaming responses because the two are closely related.

Victim-blaming rationalizations

People employing **victim-blaming rationalizations** reject the notion that prejudice and discrimination are problems in society, even though they admit that problems exist. The problems they identify, however, are typically deficiencies or flaws in members of minority groups (Ryan, 1976). Victim-blamers focus on the group being harmed by societal prejudices and insist that society doesn't need to change: The group needs to change. Victim-blamers urge individuals to stop being so sensitive or so pushy, to work harder, and to quit complaining. Group members are told they are responsible for whatever problems they must overcome.

Victim-blaming often occurs among people who want to believe in a just world. In one study, subjects observed two people working equally hard at a task. By a random decision, researchers gave one of the workers a significant reward when the task was completed; the other worker received nothing. When asked to rate how hard the two people had worked, the subjects tended to describe the person who received nothing as not working as hard as the person receiving the reward. Aronson (1999) concluded his analysis of this study by suggesting that "we find it frightening to live in a world where people, through no fault of their own, can be deprived of what they deserve or need" (p. 299).

People who engage in victim-blaming rationalizations often go beyond blame to propose solutions. By defining the problem as a deficiency existing in the victimized group, every solution proposed by a victim-blamer involves what *they* need to do because *they* are the problem. The rest of us need do nothing. Rape is increasing on college campuses? That's a woman's problem, so what they need to do is to wear less provocative clothing, avoid going out late at night, and learn to defend themselves by taking martial arts classes or carrying pepper spray. What to do

about the men who rape isn't addressed. Because victim-blamers offer solutions, it is easy to confuse victim blaming with some avoidance rationalizations.

Avoidance rationalizations

Unlike denial and victim-blaming, **avoidance rationalizations** recognize the problems in society stemming from prejudice and discrimination. This is a significant difference from the previous rationalizations. Even though a person making avoidance rationalizations admits there are problems, he or she will not address them and will rationalize a reason to avoid them. Ways to avoid confronting issues include offering a solution that addresses only part of a problem, or suggesting a false solution that does not address the problem at all.

If college administrators decide to confront prejudice by requiring students to take an ethnic studies course, that requirement will address a small part of the problems caused by racial prejudice and discrimination. Learning more about ethnic groups is a good idea, but if colleges are serious about actively opposing racism and improving race relations, administration and faculty must recruit diverse students, hire diverse faculty, and promote cultural diversity through workshops and seminars both on campus and in the community.

A false solution that does not address the problems of sexism whatsoever is the proposal that "sexism would just disappear if we didn't pay so much attention to it." Problems created by sexism did not suddenly appear and they won't disappear unless people engage in actions to confront, challenge, and change sexist attitudes, policies, and laws. The only way any society can solve problems and improve conditions is to analyze a problem, create appropriate solutions, implement the solutions that seem most likely to be effective, and, after time passes, assess the impact of these solutions.

Another form of avoidance rationalization involves making an argument that distracts from the issue or question being discussed. Imagine a group of people discussing efforts that could be made to increase social justice in our society. Suddenly someone says, "You're being too idealistic. We are never going to solve this problem because we're never going to have a utopia." The speaker was not arguing for the creation of a utopia, a perfect society, but for ways to improve society. By making the reasonable statement that utopias are not possible, the speaker has shifted the focus of the conversation to a different topic that avoids the issue. It is not realistic to believe that it is possible to create a perfect society, but it is possible—in fact, essential—to believe that any society can be improved.

In a discussion about the need for child-care centers at worksites, someone might say "I support the idea, but it takes time; it's not going to happen

> [There is a] strangely irrational notion that there is something in the very flow of time that will inevitably cure all ills. Actually time is neutral. It can be used either destructively or constructively.
>
> **MARTIN LUTHER KING, JR. (1929–1968)**

overnight." A reasonable response, except if the discussion ends with that comment, what has been achieved? To implement any solution successfully, it is necessary to clarify what is entailed: What needs to be done? Who will do what? Which actions should be done next month? What can we expect in the next six months? Who will determine whether the solution is working and how will that be determined? Saying a solution takes time may be true, but it is still necessary to discuss what must be done to implement it. To avoid that discussion is to avoid the problem. Problems are not solved by talk or the passage of time, but by taking some kind of action.

Is prejudice part of human nature?

There is no study concluding that prejudice is an innate part of human nature. The most fundamental truth about prejudice is that it is learned. Rationalizations like the ones just described illustrate how people can resist changing their negative attitudes and perpetuate the prejudices they have learned. Some people despair of ever solving problems that result from prejudice, yet the fact that

prejudice is learned offers hope: Anything that can be learned can be unlearned.

AFTERWORD

If prejudice were part of human nature, people would be justified in feeling despair because the implication would be that human beings eventually will destroy each other. But there is no evidence to support the idea that prejudice is innate. Instead, studies have consistently concluded that prejudice is learned. Prejudice can be reduced by the provision of accurate information, by affective educational experiences, by formal and informal learning, and by establishing equitable workplace policies and practices. Prejudices can be unlearned by by good teaching and by friends challenging one another's negative attitudes. And even though some people may not be able to give up their prejudices, they can learn how to manage them. When we can identify our prejudices and understand how we learned to be prejudiced, we can choose not to act on these prejudices.

When we make positive choices, we offer humanity the best reason to have hope for the future. It was the positive choices human beings have made throughout history that resulted in genuine human progress. If our society is to benefit from its diversity, it will be because enough Americans have chosen to regard diversity as an asset and to confront their prejudices. Those who make such positive choices today will shape the nature of the society in which our children and their children must live.

> Prejudices, it is well known, are most difficult to eradicate from the heart whose soil has never been loosened or fertilized by education; they grow there, firm as weeds among stones.
>
> **CHARLOTTE BRONTË (1816–1855)**

TERMS AND DEFINITIONS

Avoidance rationalization A response to a social problem—such as injustice toward a minority group—that acknowledges the existence of a problem but avoids confronting the problem by offering partial or false solutions or by using arguments that do not address the situation as in "Yes, but you should have seen how bad it was last year."

Denial rationalization A response to a social problem—such as injustice toward a minority group—that does not acknowledge the existence of a problem but insists instead that no injustice has occurred as in "That's not discrimination, men have always been the boss; it's just the way things are meant to be."

Elitism The belief that the best people ascend to a place of superiority in society and represent a natural aristocracy, while those who are not successful are viewed as lacking the necessary qualities to be successful within society

Genocide The deliberate and systematic extermination of a particular nationality, or racial, ethnic, or minority group

Prejudice A negative attitude toward a group and anyone perceived to be a member of that group; a predisposition to negative behavior toward members of a group

Scapegoat An individual or a group of people blamed for another person's problems or difficulties; identifying a scapegoat is often employed to justify one's taking a negative action against that individual or group

Victim-blame rationalization A response to a social problem—such as injustice toward a minority group—that identifies the problem as a deficiency in the minority group and not a societal problem, as in "If poor people want to escape poverty they just have to be willing to work harder."

White flight The migration of white families from an urban to a suburban location because of court rulings to desegregate urban schools

Zero sum An orientation toward power and resources based on assumptions of scarcity, as when struggling to achieve goals, one person gains at the expense of another. The belief that sharing power means a reduction of power

REFERENCES

Allport, G. (1979). *The Nature of Prejudice.* Reading, MA: Addison-Wesley.

Examines prejudice and its consequences for individuals who act on prejudice as well as those victimized by prejudice.

Aronson, E. (1999). *The social animal* (8th ed.). New York: W.H. Freeman.

Presents an overview of research in social psychology and describes patterns and motives revealed in these studies concerning human behavior.

Bell, D. (2002). *Ethical ambition: Living a life of meaning and worth.* New York: Bloomsbury.

Discusses six factors that are critical in determining the quality and meaningfulness of one's life: passion, courage, faith, relationships, role models, and humility.

Bredin, J. (1986). *The affair: The case of Alfred Dreyfus.* New York: George Braziller.

Describes the historical background and the ensuing controversy surrounding this notorious example of anti-Semitism.

Bureau of Labor Statistics. (2001). Chapter 1: Counting Minorities: A brief history and a look at the future. *Report on the American Workforce.* Washington DC: U.S. Department of Labor. Retrieved April 12, 2003, from *http://ww.bls.gov/opub*

Analyzes statistics pertaining to the American workforce and the role and nature of the participation in that workforce by women and minorities.

Carroll, J. (2001). *Constantine's sword: The church and the Jews, a history.* Boston: Houghton Mifflin.

Examines the history of relations between the Catholic Church and the Jews and explains the basis for the historic pattern of anti-Semitism that still exists in the church.

Coleman, L.M. (1997). Stigma. In L. Davis (Ed.), *The disability studies reader* (pp. 216–233). New York: Routledge.

Discusses the origin of the concept of stigma and analyzes the reasons why some differences in human beings are valued and others are stigmatized.

Daft, R.L. (2003). Managing diverse employees. *Management* (6th ed., pp. 436–468). Versailles, KY: Thompson Southwestern.

Discusses diversity in the workforce and how corporate culture is accommodating diversity.

Farley, J. (2000). *Majority-minority relations* (4th ed.). Upper Saddle River, NJ: Prentice Hall.

Discusses the research on authoritarian personalities in Chapter 2 (pp. 23–29) and racial segregation in U.S. neighborhoods in Chapter 10 (pp. 290–306).

Feagin, J., & Feagin, C.B. (1996). Glossary. *Racial and ethnic relations* (5th ed., pp. 501–504). Upper Saddle River, NJ: Prentice Hall.

Provides definitions of major terms and concepts in intergroup relations.

Gioseffi, D. (Ed.). (1993). *On prejudice: A global perspective.* New York: Anchor.

Contains excerpts from historic and contemporary authors from around the world describing the existence and consequences of human prejudice.

Giroux, H. (1998). *Channel surfing: Racism, the media, and the destruction of today's youth.* New York: St. Martin's.

Analyzes media images, especially films, and their impact on children and youth.

Goldhagen, D.J. (1996). *Hitler's willing executioners: Ordinary Germans and the Holocaust.* New York: Knopf.

Presents evidence for the controversial thesis that Germans readily collaborated in the Nazi Holocaust.

Howard, G.R. (1999). *We can't teach what we don't know: White teachers, multiracial schools.* New York: Teachers College Press.

Integrates theory, research, and personal experiences to describe problems created by racism and white privilege and discusses actions to bring about positive changes.

Jones, J. (1997). *Prejudice and racism* (2nd ed.). New York: McGraw Hill.

Integrates data from psychology, sociology, anthropology, biology, political science, and history to explain prejudice and racism and the relationship between them.

Levin, J., & Levin, W. (1982). *The functions of discrimination and prejudice* (2nd ed., p. 202). New York: Harper & Row.

Examines the causes and effects of prejudice summarized on two flow charts.

Martinez, R., & Dukes, R.L. (1991, March). Ethnic and gender differences in self-esteem. *Youth & Society* 22(3), pp. 318–339.

Presents findings from a study of self-esteem in a multiracial population of students in grades 7–12 who attended the largest school district in Colorado Springs, Colorado.

Massey, D.S. (2001, January). Residential segregation and neighborhood conditions in U.S. metropolitan areas. In N. Smelser, W. Wilson, & F. Mitchell (Eds.), *America becoming: Racial trends and their consequences.* (ERIC Document Reproduction Service No. ED449286.)

Describes how segregation has increased in recent years, especially for blacks, as well as the nature of segregation for Hispanics and Asian Americans.

Ryan, W. (1976). *Blaming the victim* (2nd ed.). New York: Vintage Books.

Describes and analyzes victim-blaming attitudes toward blacks in the inner cities.

Sadker, D., & Sadker, M. (1994). *Failing at fairness: How America's schools cheat girls.* New York: Charles Scribner.

Discusses how boys are favored and girls are discriminated against in schools; describes the Michigan study in Chapter 3, "The Self-Esteem Slide" on pp. 83–85.

Sartre, J.P. (1976). *Anti-Semite and Jew.* New York: Schocken.

Describes French anti-Semitism expressed after World War II despite French people's awareness of the Nazi Holocaust.

Schaefer, R.T. (2004). *Racial and ethnic groups* (9th ed.). Upper Saddle River, NJ: Pearson.

Reviews changes in the composition of U.S. immigrants and anti-immigrant sentiments in Chapter 4: Immigration and the United States (pp. 102–131); discusses findings of research using the Social Distance Scale in Chapter 2: Prejudice (pp. 36–71).

Selden, S. (1999). *Inheriting shame: The story of eugenics and racism in America.* New York: Teachers College Press.

Examines the development of the eugenics movement in the United States and what lessons should be learned from it.

Simpson, G.E., & Yinger, J.M. (1985). *Racial and cultural minorities: An analysis of prejudice and discrimination.* New York: Plenum.

Provides an in-depth examination of prejudice and discrimination, including studies that used the Social Distance Scale (pp. 94–97).

Stephan, W. (1999). *Reducing prejudice and stereotyping in schools.* New York: Teachers College Press.

Reviews theories of prejudice and stereotyping, examines conditions to promote changes in negative attitudes, and describes techniques for improving race relations in schools.

Thurow, L. (1980). *The zero-sum society.* New York: Penguin.

Describes economic implications when a society accepts and acts on zero-sum thinking.

United States Bureau of the Census. (2001). *Statistical abstract of the United States.* Retrieved, March 19, 2003, from *http://www.census.gov*

Provides historic and current statistical data on the demographics of the U.S. workforce (at the web site, look for Statistical Abstract under "Special Topics").

United States Department of Labor. (2000). Earnings differences between women and men. Available from the Women's Bureau under *Facts on Working Women*. Retrieved, June 22, 2003, from *http://www.dol.gov/dol/wb*

Examines the history of the wage gap between men and women and analyzes the impact of such issues as age, occupation, and education.

Vega, F. (1978). *The effect of human and intergroup relations education on the race/sex attitudes of education majors*. Unpublished doctoral dissertation, University of Minnesota, Minneapolis.

Discusses the development of individual racist and sexist attitudes from cultural and institutional influences and measures the impact of a course on those attitudes.

Summary Exercises

See page 19 for exercises to help you summarize the main points and define key terms in this chapter.

Personal Clarification Exercises

In Chapter 3, two exercises are intended to provide an honest basis for discussion of personal prejudice.

Clarification Exercise #1 Rationalization Issues in Race and Gender: Illustrations and Explanations

Directions: In teams of two and with the aid of your text, analyze each set of rationalizations in order to learn to recognize why each illustration exemplifies the kind of rationalization with which it is placed.

Part One: In teams of two, review the examples provided for victim-blame, denial, and avoidance rationalizations. Agree with your partner about how each statement fits its placement.

Rationalizations on the Issues of Racism and Sexism: Illustrations and Examples

Denial: The denial rationalization rejects the existence of the problem. The speaker truly doesn't recognize that there is a problem! Or the speaker may recognize that there is a problem, but denies that anything can ever be done about it by using or implying "That's just the way things are."

1. "When I see minorities on television, most of them are happy; they're always singing and having a good time. I don't think racism is a problem any more . . ."
2. "I'm fed up with all these people accusing me of being racist and sexist and all the other things and blaming me for all their problems. I've heard it all before and I'm tired of it. Besides, my ancestors never owned slaves. I had nothing to do with it then and I have nothing to do with it now."
3. "We'd all be better off training these people for some useful trade, something they can more easily adapt to, instead of lowering our academic standards at our colleges and universities

or hiring them for jobs without the proper qualifications."
4. "Women are just naturally emotional and soft-hearted. They are not equipped to make the hard decisions required of people in positions of authority."

Victim-Blame: The victim-blame rationale makes reference to a *specific* person or group and either directly or by implication blames that person or group for having created their own misfortune. The speaker refuses to accept responsibility for the plight, even though that person or an allied group may have been highly responsible.

1. "The problem with radical minority organizations is that they are often led by minorities who are extremists."
2. "The problem today is that minorities and women think that everyone owes them a living."
3. "The solution to the Indian problem is in the hands of the Indians. If they forget about the old ways and join in our modern technological society, they'll do just fine."
4. "What's all this stuff about police brutality? If people break the law, they deserve whatever treatment they get."
5. "The problem with the women's lib movement is that it is led by a bunch of sexually frustrated, female sexists."

Avoidance: The avoidance orientation accepts the existence of the problem but attempts to avoid it. Avoidance rationale may propose a false or inadequate solution, or make a statement that attempts to sidetrack the listener away from the real issue. The effect of this orientation is the misplacement of the problem leading to faulty or incomplete solutions focusing on victims, such as the need for more research, more law enforcement, more remedial programs.

1. Don't you think these people have gone too far with all this sitting in, protecting law breaking, and demanding? After all, there are established procedures for people to air their grievances in our society.

2. Yes, we have a lot of problems in our society, but if we were all just good Christians, we could learn to love one another.

3. Yes, but isn't this all part of human nature? Aren't we all prejudiced in one way or another? And, isn't everybody discriminated against in some way, shape, or form?

4. I have the right to like or dislike anybody I want and the First Amendment of the Constitution guarantees me the right to say so.

5. I know America has problems, but I'm proud to be American; I think you should love it or leave it.

Clarification Exercise #2 Rationalizations: Victim-Blame, Denial, and Avoidance

Directions: This exercise provides everyday statements we might hear; each one is a specific kind of rationalization. Based upon the text, the activity above, and upon your group discussion, identify the statements below according to one of the three types of rationalizations.

Part One: In teams of two, select which passages would most likely represent an **avoidance** of a problem. Then select those in which the speaker employs a **denial** rationalization—that the problem either does not exist or that the speaker is suggesting "That's just the way things are." Finally, locate **victim-blame** statements where there is a specific person or group being charged with its own downfall or problem.

Rationalizations for Our Prejudices

Directions: Decide whether the following statements represent a **denial** of the problem (D), a **victim-blame** that it is the speaker's problem (D/VB), or an **avoidance** of the problem (A).

____ 1. Women and minorities are getting everything their way. They are taking away our jobs and pretty soon they are going to take over everything.

____ 2. What we have here, basically, is a failure to communicate. We must develop better programs in interpersonal communications to address this issue.

____ 3. This is the way these people want to live. You can't change poor people; they can't help the way they are.

____ 4. We must move with deliberation on these issues. Real change takes time. We have to educate people.

____ 5. All those women on welfare have it made. All they do is stay home and make babies while the rest of us have to work and pay taxes to support them.

____ 6. I can't figure out what to call all these people. Why can't we all just be human instead of black, Chicano, Latino, Native American, or Asian American?

____ 7. Indians are their own worst enemy. They should stop fighting amongst themselves and get together on whatever it is they really want.

____ 8. If blacks want to make it in our society, they are going to have to get rid of those dreadlocks and other weird hair styles, the baggy clothes, funny handshakes, and they better start speaking better English.

____ 9. Yes, but in the old days, race and sex discrimination were much worse. And even today, women and minorities are much better off in this country than anywhere else in the world.

____ 10. Women are just too sensitive about sexism. They need to look at these things less emotionally and much more rationally.

____ 11. We need more programs in African American studies, Latino studies, Native American studies, and Asian American studies to learn about all the contributions these groups have made to our society.

____ 12. Feminists are pushing too hard for the changes that they demand. They are hurting themselves more than they are helping.

____ 13. I understand that some people face more difficulties than others, but this is a free country and I believe that anybody who is willing to work hard enough can be successful.

Part Two: When you have completed this exercise and you are instructed to move ahead, compare your responses separately with those of two other teams. Explain your reasoning for each and develop extensions of the definitions provided in order to better recognize denial, victim-blame, and avoidance rationalizations.

Part Three: Select any two from each of the three categories—D, VB, and A—and rewrite them to be the fourth kind of statements—those *without* rationalization.

Part Four: At the appropriate time, share your revised statements with those of others within the total group. Explain why you chose to rewrite them as you did.

Intergroup Exercises

In Chapter 3, two exercises promote discussion about values and ethical behavior in modern American society.

Intergroup Exercise #1 The Liver Transplant Problem

Background: Today, the only medical procedure available to save the lives of persons suffering from diseases of the liver is an organ transplant. Unfortunately, there are not enough livers to take care of all cases now, and there will not be enough in the near future to save the lives of all those who need such an operation to survive.

Your role: The decision about which people can be saved must be made on criteria other than medical criteria. Your hospital has decided that the best way to select persons for a transplant is by setting up a volunteer citizens panel to make the decisions. You are on the panel and you receive a Profile Sheet of applicants for transplants (see below). Doctors have screened all patients already, and all have equal prognosis for medical success.

Problem: There is now *one* liver available for one of the persons on the list. A decision must be made quickly. All those not served are expected to die soon. The availability of other livers cannot be anticipated, although if other livers become available, additional persons on the list could receive transplants.

Directions: In a group of four to five people, identify one person from the list to receive the liver currently available. Your panel is asked to deliver a *unanimous* decision regarding the person to be the liver recipient. As you deliberate, discuss your values and consider those of others related to the process being utilized and the criteria that you propose.

Liver Transplant Recipient Profile Sheet

Code	Age	Race	Sex	Marital Status	Religious Affiliation	Children	Occupation
A	24	Black	M	Married	Moslem	None	Postal worker
B	45	White	M	Married	Atheist	2	Executive
C	39	Asian American	F	Divorced	Buddhist	None	Medical Doctor
D	40	White	F	Married	Jew	3	Housewife
E	23	White	M	Unmarried	Episcopal	None	PhD student
F	40	White	F	Unmarried	Pentecostal	9	Welfare Mother
G	28	Native American	M	Unmarried	Native	3	Seasonal Worker
H	30	Latina	F	Married	Catholic	7	Housewife
I	19	White	M	Unmarried	Baptist	None	Special Student

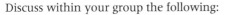

Discuss within your group the following:

1. The criteria you develop for choosing the recipient.
2. Why you believe that the person you chose best fits your criteria.
3. How your panel comes to a single selection of a recipient.

Notes about recipients:

A. Devotes time to volunteer work for black organizations
B. Possible candidate for U.S. Senate
C. College physician and women's liberation speaker
D. Active in local synagogue and charitable activities
E. Middle states chair of a gay rights task force
F. Advocate and organizer of welfare mothers
G. State chair, Indian Treaty Rights Organization
H. Blind and physically disabled
I. Cognitively disabled

Individual Exercise #1 I'm Not Prejudiced, But . . .

Directions: Read privately each of the following statements and respond as honestly as you can about whether or not you have felt, expressed, or heard within your family similar thoughts in the past. Enter your responses next the each number below. Your responses should be one of the following: S = Sometimes, O = Often, N = Never. Share those responses that you wish to discuss.

I'm Not Prejudiced, But . . .

1. If I'm in a social setting and a joke with racial overtones is told, I laugh.
2. When I'm walking on campus and I see a group of people of another race coming toward me, I feel uneasy.
3. I don't see the point in separate ethnic courses such as Native American History, or African American Literature.
4. People who are United States citizens should not identify themselves with hyphenated names such as Asian American or Irish American. We should just be Americans.
5. Racism is not a high priority topic for me.
6. Since Asian Americans have been able to pull themselves up from hardship and discrimination, other minorities should be able to do the same.
7. I believe that minorities are responsible for their own poverty.
8. Placing too much emphasis on the ethnic and racial identity of minority students just makes race relations worse.
9. Flying a Confederate flag or having one in your dorm room should not be seen as a racist act.
10. I can see having multicultural education in urban schools, but I don't see why they should have multicultural education in rural or suburban schools.

Learning the Language of Prejudice

"No one has ever been born a Negro hater, a Jew hater, or any other kind of hater. Nature refuses to be involved in such suicidal practices."

HARRY BRIDGES (1900–1990)

What Harry Bridges said about bigotry is also true of prejudice. No one is born prejudiced, yet all human beings learn prejudice along with everything else as they pass from infancy to adulthood. Prejudices will vary depending upon family, friends, location, and racial or ethnic group; some are simply embedded in culture, specifically in language. One way to understand the history of prejudice in the United States is to examine how immigrants were perceived by those already established as American citizens. To be accepted, immigrants were expected to adopt American cultural traits and integrate themselves into society. Insistence that immigrants reject their cultural heritage and adopt dominant cultural norms is a historical pattern that persists in American society.

How has language reflected negative attitudes toward immigrants?

As immigrants became assimilated, they often shared existing American attitudes of suspicion, and even hostility, toward newer immigrants, the "foreigners" in their midst. Changes in immigration laws document a tug-of-war between those who advocated inviting others to America and those who wanted newcomers to return to their homeland. If immigrants came to America, they were usually expected to assimilate quickly. **Assimilation** placed enormous pressure on new arrivals; to assimilate meant to abandon their roots, their native cultures and traditions, and even their native language, and to replace them with the traditions, customs, and language of standard American culture. Language especially has been a significant issue in the assimilation process. Immigrant school children were punished if they were caught speaking their native language.

Assimilation expectations endure: To be different often arouses suspicions, stereotypes, and prejudices. The Hmong, American allies during the Vietnam War, were persecuted when Laotian communists took control. In the 1980s, Hmong refugees entering the United States became a significant presence in communities and public schools across the nation. A large number of Hmong families settled in a small, midwestern community. In the local high schools, white students resented those students talking to one another in the Hmong language in the hallways. The white students were uncomfortable and seemed to believe that by talking in their native language, Hmong students were demonstrating a reluctance to "become American" by maintaining their culture and their differences.

In the past, many ethnic immigrants have tried to preserve their culture. While striving for economic success, Chinese Americans established Chinese schools and German Americans built German schools to maintain their cultural heritage. Americans have been slow to understand that the loss of native language also results in a loss of cultural identity (Macedo and Bartolome, 2001). The process of Americanization has usually been effective with the children of immigrants; second and third generations of immigrant families tend to adopt American norms, unfortunately losing more of their cultural heritage with each generation. Despite this success at homogenizing different groups coming to America, our dominant American society has sent out curiously mixed messages about language.

Carlos Cortes (2002) tells the story best. When he started school he was fluent in Spanish, but teachers told his parents not to speak Spanish so that Carlos could focus on learning English. He was so successful in school that he ultimately earned a college scholarship. When Carlos enrolled in a liberal arts program, he discovered that there was a requirement to learn a foreign language. Suddenly it was desirable to be competent in another language, like Spanish. Carlos wondered why he had not been allowed to remain proficient in Spanish as a child. He enrolled in Spanish to relearn the language he had lost, and many years later wrote two versions of his dissertation, one in Spanish and one in English, to emphasize the value of being bilingual.

CULTURAL BIASES IN LANGUAGE

The U.S. Bilingual Education Act passed in 1968 was intended to help students maintain fluency in their native language while learning English, but resistance to bilingual education in the United States has been strong. Opponents believe bilingual/bicultural education allows (and even encourages) immigrants to maintain and perpetuate cultural differences, illustrating the ongoing suspicion of immigrants as foreign, different, and some-

how not "American." These opponents were successful in 2002 when the Bilingual Education Act expired after thirty-four years and was not renewed (Crawford, 2002). Distrusting people because they seem different is a major factor in how people learn to be prejudiced, but people also learn prejudices from negative attitudes embedded in the language itself.

How are negative attitudes embedded in language?

Language is an important source for understanding the values and norms of any culture. Analyzing language reveals not only assumptions, beliefs, values, and priorities of a culture, but also prejudices. Scrutiny is not limited to words alone, but also how words are used. For example, in Germany there are two words meaning *to drink: trinken* and *saufen. Trinken* is used to refer to humans drinking and *saufen* refers to animals drinking. When someone drinks alcohol to excess and becomes publicly inebriated, Germans may use the word *saufen* to refer to that person's drinking behavior. The criticism concerning public intoxication is obvious.

An eighteen-year-old German student stayed with a college professor during a high school cultural exchange program. A few days before his final weekend in America, Franz related a recent conversation he had with with his new American friends. As they planned a farewell party for their German visitors, several high school seniors joked about "getting hammered." Franz wasn't certain, but he assumed they were talking about getting drunk at this party and asked his host if that was what they meant. After being told his assumption was correct, Franz expressed surprise. In his culture, such talk would be equivalent to saying, "Let's plan to behave stupidly, to embarrass ourselves in front of people." Influenced by his cultural beliefs, Franz was astonished that anyone would actually plan to do something so ridiculous. Language is a cultural mirror, but words also reflect on the individual choosing to use them.

What difference does our choice of words make?

Some people argue that the influence of language is overrated, that it's not the words we use but what we mean by them—our intent. If someone didn't intend to cause harm by the words he or she used, then no harm was caused. But studies show that word choice *does* makes a difference in people's reactions to situations. In one study, subjects were shown a videotape of a multiple-car accident. One group was asked to estimate the speed of the cars when they "smashed" into each other; the other group was asked to estimate the speed when the cars "hit" each other. Subjects in the group with the word "smashed" in their instructions had consistently higher estimates for car speed than the subjects who heard the word "hit" (Aronson, 1999).

Language is a powerful tool, a reflection of culture and an influential teacher. Language teaches us cultural norms, standards, and values, transmitting them from one generation to the next. Prejudices are transmitted as well. Prejudice is not something we are born with, it is learned. An important question to answer is: How is prejudice learned? By examining English words and phrases, we can identify some blatant and some subtle lessons in prejudice that are being taught to American children as they learn the language of their culture.

What examples of racial prejudice exist in our language?

One pattern observed in the English language has been called the **Black/White syndrome.** Scholars report that this language pattern emerged in English long before the British knew that people described as *black* were living in Africa (Moore, 2000). Although the pattern likely originated in Biblical language referring to Satan, evil, and hell as black or dark, it has been argued that a consistently negative pattern for references to *black* affected British perceptions of Africans and that negative connotations for blackness were readily applied to all dark-skinned people they encountered. A negative pattern for black has persisted in the English language as can be seen in familiar phrases: black deed, black day, black hearted, black mass, black magic, the Black Death, black thoughts, black looks, and blacklist.

> One may no more live in the world without picking up the moral prejudices of the world than one will be able to go to Hell without perspiring.
>
> **H.L. MENCKEN (1880–1956)**

In contrast, references to *white* in the English language follow a consistently positive pattern: telling little white lies, having a white wedding, cheering White Knights (in Shining Armor), indicating approval by saying "that's really white of you," and even engaging in white-collar crime (perceived as less harmful than other crimes). Some authors have exploited the pervasive black/white pattern by deliberately using *white* as a negative term, invoking images of sterility, death, or evil to shock readers with unexpected associations. Robert Frost employed this reversal in some of his poems, and it was no accident that Herman Melville chose to make Moby Dick, the symbol of evil in Ahab's obsession, a white whale.

Although other colors relating to nonwhite racial groups are used negatively, the pattern is not as persistent as in the black/white syndrome (Watson and Johnson, 1972). Red is used to describe being in debt ("in the red"), possibly involving a lot of red tape, especially if the person is caught red-handed. Yellow is associated with cowardice (yellow streak down his back) and is used to designate cheap, sensational, tabloid-style journalism. Children are surrounded by messages pertaining to color, even with something as simple as using crayons and finding one called "flesh" that is closer to the color of the flesh of white people than other groups. Although some changes have occurred, many negative messages remain about human differences.

What examples of gender prejudice exist in our language?

Unlike many other languages, English does not have a neutral pronoun that includes men and women, so the word *he* is used to refer to someone of indeterminate gender and *man* has traditionally been used in words or phrases where the referent could be female (even though there are neutral nouns such as *human* and *people*). A principle in English common law was that when a man and woman married, they became one, but that "one" was the man; if a woman owned property prior to marriage, legal rights to dispose of that property passed to her husband.

Some linguists continue to insist that *man* is generic when used in words such as *businessman, chairman, congressman, fireman, layman, mailman, policeman, salesman, spokesman,* and *statesman,* but studies do not support the claim. Arliss (1991) described studies using subjects ranging from elementary children to adults; all concluded that generic language invoked mental images of males.

In a study reported by Miller and Swift (1977) involving 500 junior high students, one group of students received instructions to draw pictures of "early man" engaged in various activities and to

> Sometimes [prejudice] is like a hair across your cheek. You can't see it, you can't find it with your fingers, but you keep brushing at it because the feel of it is irritating.
>
> **MARIAN ANDERSON (1897–1993)**

give each person drawn a name (so researchers could be certain that a man or woman was the subject of the drawing). The majority of students of both sexes tended to draw only males for every activity identified except the one representing infant care, and even for that activity, 49% of boys drew a male image. A second group of students was instructed to draw pictures of "early people" engaged in the same activities and to give each human figure drawn a name; once again, the majority of the humans drawn by both sexes were male. It is possible that the phrase *early people* sounded strange and that many students translated it as "cave men" and drew male pictures. The third group of students was asked to draw pictures of "early men and early women," once again giving names to human figures. Only in this group did the figures drawn by students include a *significant* number of female images, but even with these instructions, some students of both sexes drew only male figures.

Because of their commitment to gender equality, feminists have lobbied various professional groups to replace sexist language with **inclusive language.** The goal is to change our culture by replacing sexist terms with terms that are not only more inclusive (including both men and women) but also more accurate. Feminists have succeeded in persuading several organizations to change *guidelines* in their writing manuals to promote nonsexist language as the preferred form for their professional publications. The fifth edition of the style manual of the American Psychological Association includes writing conventions employing language free of racist and sexist implications (see Table 4.1). Despite such progress, scholars still describe considerable sexist language in common words and phrases. Do we have a man-made product if it is manufactured in a factory employing only women? Can an organization "man the desk" with women? Does brotherly love include sisters? Does the opinion of the common man include women or are women "uncommon"?

Alternatives for sexist terms exist: a product is handmade, women can staff the desk, and the average person can give his or her opinion. But is inclusive language also more accurate? To use the common expression "founding fathers" denies the importance of women's historical role. The presence of immigrant families distinguished the settlements in what became the United States from New World settlements of the French (primarily men—trappers and hunters) and Spanish (primarily soldiers—*conquistadors*). Evans (1989) insists that compared to New World settlements of other nations, the presence of women and children in the English colonies had an impact on how American society evolved, and that the truth of our historical development is distorted by language denying women's presence. Such prejudicial messages occur not only in individual words but also in common cultural expressions.

What are some common expressions reflecting prejudicial attitudes?

In addition to words and phrases, negative connotations in traditional cultural expressions teach lessons about race, gender, and other human differences. Responding to a request for help by saying

GENDER	
PROBLEMATIC	**PREFERRED**
man a project	staff a project, hire personnel, employ staff
man–machine interface	user–system interface, person–system interface, human–computer interface
manpower	workforce, personnel, workers, human resources
man's search for knowledge	the search for knowledge
mothering	parenting, nurturing [or specify exact behavior]
The authors acknowledge the assistance of Mrs. John Smith.	The authors acknowledge the assistance of Jane Smith.
cautious men and timid women	cautious women and men, cautious people, timid men and women, timid people
RACIAL AND ETHNIC IDENTITY	
PROBLEMATIC	**PREFERRED**
The 50 American Indians represented . . .	The 40 American Indians (25 Choctaw, 15 Hopi, and 10 Seminole) represented . . .
We studied Eskimos	We studied Inuit from Canada and Aleuts
The articulate Mexican American professor	the Mexican American professor

TABLE 4.1

Language Recommended by the American Psychological Association

Source: Publication Manual of the American Psychological Association (5th ed.) pp. 71–72, 74–75.

"Who was your nigger last year?" reveals contempt for historic roles forced upon black people, first as slaves and later as domestic servants. Although we no longer use names like Sambo and Aunt Jemima or the caricatures associated with them (see Figure 4.1), we still have "Indians" representing sports teams.

We can find people who believe that "Behind every good man there's a good woman," or "The hand that rocks the cradle rules the world," or "A woman's place is in the home." People who endorse attitudes implied in such comments are likely to argue that the expressions are a tribute to women's power and to the important role they have played and continue to play rather than seeing them as putting women in "their place."

We also find social class prejudice in common expressions such as "Where there's a will there's a

> Nobody talks more of free enterprise and competition and of the best man winning than the man who inherited his father's store or farm.
>
> **C. WRIGHT MILLS (1916–1962)**

FIGURE 4.1 Despite the commercial advantage of maintaining a familiar face on one's product, Quaker Oats felt that the old image (B) of Aunt Jemima was too much of a stereotype and updated her image in the 1960s (A).

(A)

(B)

way," a seemingly harmless attempt to encourage children and youth to try hard and do their best. But it has a more critical meaning embedded in it: If all it takes to be successful is to have the will to succeed, then those people who are not successful are at fault for their failure. Such a simplistic view rejects issues of prejudice and discrimination in favor of a belief that those who fail just didn't "try" hard enough. This belief leads to blaming the victim

and provides an ethical escape for middle-class people. A person can attribute his or her success to having worked hard and ascribe other people's poverty to their not working as hard, which reinforces the stereotype of poor people as either lazy or incompetent. Believing this is the reason for poverty relieves any responsibility for a middle-class person to feel obligated to help the poor. One need only say, "They should work hard like I did," and turn away.

THE LANGUAGE OF LABELS

The majority group has created derogatory names for members of minority groups. When a dominant group has the power to label a subordinate group, others will consistently associate that label with individuals from the subordinate group. The power to label results in the power to define the people in a group, not only for the dominant group, but sometimes for the members of the labeled group as well. In recognition of the power of such labels, many groups have engaged in efforts to label themselves in a positive way. In the 1960s, many in the group that the majority had labeled "colored people" or "Negroes" rejected the majority group's names and chose to call themselves "Blacks." This was accompanied by calls for "Black Power" and claims that "Black is Beautiful." Many black people continue to prefer that designation because they believe it makes a positive contribution to an individual's sense of identity. Since the 1960s, "African American" has also become a popular choice among black people and others as a positive label for this group.

When a majority group has the power to label and define those belonging to a minority group, they also can control subordinate group members, obviously by limiting their opportunities, but sometimes in more subtle ways as well. Macedo and Bartoleme (2001) compare the term *migrant,* which most often labels Latinos seeking economic opportunity in the United States with the term *settlers,* which is used to designate English and other Europeans immigrating to America to improve their economic opportunities. Reactions to the two terms are significantly different even though both terms describe people engaged in a similar quest.

How have labels been used to define and control groups of people?

The idea that the power to label equals the power to define, which equals the power to control is illustrated by an example contrasting two people who love to watch college football. One is a married college professor, the other a young man labeled mentally retarded and living in a group home. On Saturday morning, the professor and the young man are watching college football games on ESPN. As noon approaches, both decide to have hot dogs for lunch. Both put hot dogs in pans of water, turn on the stove, and return to their respective living rooms. Both resume watching football and forget about the boiling hot dogs until the water boils out and the smell of burnt hot dogs causes both to run into their kitchens to turn off the stove.

The professor's wife might say he forgot about the hot dogs because of his obsession with football and others might joke about absent-minded professors. With regard to the other man, people are most likely to say, "Well, he's retarded, you know." For a person labeled "mentally retarded," behaviors, especially negative behavior, are often explained by that single factor. Rules, guidelines, and policies are created to prevent people labeled mentally retarded from engaging in certain activities or from being hired for certain jobs. A label has defined them as people not to be trusted; thus, their opportunity is limited and those limiting them feel justified that it's "for their own good." The young man will be labeled mentally retarded for his entire life: The quality of his life will be controlled and determined primarily by that label.

Labels such as "cognitively disabled" are official, formal, bureaucratic terms; others are informal and societal—terms used or heard by people in everyday life. The existence of **derisive labels**—terms reflecting a sense of contempt or ridicule based on factors such as race, class, disability, sexual orientation, and gender—and their variety suggest the extent to which prejudices exist. Words such as *nigger, spic, chink, buck,* and *squaw* represent only a few of the racist terms in English. Wessler (2001) described the observations of elementary educators who have heard children using such labels, especially during recess where children may feel they have more freedom to express themselves. Stephan (1999) insists that reducing prejudice requires that teachers help children become aware of the tendency to attach negative labels to others. Not only are such words heard on the streets and playgrounds of America, but some even show up in instructional materials such as maps, textbooks, or activities.

One theory of the origin of the word *squaw* is that it derives from a French word meaning vagina and was used by early French trappers to indicate that they wanted sex, usually followed by an offer to pay or barter something (Chavers, 1997). Other linguists claim that *squaw* has a more neutral origin, merely referring to a woman, but as Green (1975) demonstrated, its use has been consistently negative. The word *squaw* can still be found in elementary school materials and in names for lakes and other geographic sites around the United States.

Because they objected to the term, high school students in Minnesota successfully lobbied the state legislature to change the names of state geographical sites containing *squaw,* yet at least one white community in Minnesota, Squaw Lake, refused to change. Chavers (1977) reports that students have lobbied other state legislatures to delete *squaw* in geographic sites or town names because the word is offensive and insulting to Native American women.

What is the impact of labels on individuals who are labeled?

Wright (1998) wrote that very young children are only minimally aware of skin color and often unaware of race. Asked about her skin color, a three-year-old black girl wearing a pink and blue dress responded, "I'm pink and blue. What color are you?" At about the age of four children begin to understand that skin color is permanent, yet they do not regard it as negative. At five years of age, children are likely to become more interested in differences of skin color and may ask teachers many questions; they also begin to be aware of race and societal attitudes about racial differences. However, true racial awareness does not tend to become a significant issue until children are eight or nine years old. Because of children's growing awareness of skin color and racial attitudes, teachers must consciously confront name-calling and other forms of prejudice in their classrooms and on the playground.

Racist name-calling usually involves blatant, ugly words that carry harshly negative connotations: *coon, jungle bunny, gook, greaser, wetback, timber nigger.* What impact does it have on a child to hear such words? Sometimes members of a subordinate group believe and internalize myths, stereotypes, and prejudices expressed about their group by the dominant group; the result is termed **internalized oppression.** Even for those who do not internalize the negative messages, being called derisive names, especially by other children, has an impact on children and youth. Anthropologist Jamake Highwater, who was orphaned, Native American, and gay, commented upon the many derisive terms he heard as a child:

> At first, the words had no meaning to me. Even when I was told their meaning, I couldn't easily grasp why they were supposed to be shameful. . . . [They] were whispered in the classroom and remorselessly shouted when adults were not around. On the playground. In the locker room. In the darkness of the balcony at Saturday movie matinees. Those were the words that filled my childhood.
>
> They were words that aroused a sense of power and self-aggrandizement for those who shouted them; they brought shame and humiliation in those at whom they were shouted. Words were weapons, fired in rapid succession in order to hold back an intrusion of outsiders—the "them"—aliens, deviants, perverts, and barbarians. Words were a psychological Great Wall of China, staunchly guarding the frontiers of conformity and an unrelenting notion of the superiority of insiders. (1997, p. 24–25)

Highwater believes that *derisives,* derogatory terms, damage individuals in the dominant group as well as those in subordinate or minority groups because derisive language creates boundaries. Derisive terms define the oppressor as superior and the oppressed as inferior. Herbst (1977) agrees that such terms create suspicion, fear, and contempt in members of dominant groups and arouse frustration and anger in individuals from subordinate groups. In his struggle for social justice, Martin Luther King (1963) insisted that his followers not hate oppressors, but instead hate oppression. Some groups have tried to take over certain words, to "own" them and reshape them in order to make them less

> Race prejudice is not only a shadow over [racial minorities], it is a shadow over all of us, and the shadow is darkest over those who feel it least and allow its evil effects to go on.
>
> **PEARL BUCK (1892–1973)**

hurtful. African Americans, especially urban blacks, have taken the word *nigger* for their own purposes, as can be heard in their rap music. Gay men and lesbians, especially young people, are using the word *queer* as a generic term for the gay community, and courses in queer studies have sprung up on college campuses in an attempt to change formal, bureaucratic language.

How can negative bureaucratic language be as harmful as social derisive terms?

When we think of derisive terms, we usually think of informal, social labels. Derisive terms for social class such as *hillbilly* or *redneck,* often have a regional origin, but may become widespread as in *white trash,* a term that evolved into a variety of forms including *trailer park trash.* Yet some argue that the most harmful derisive terms for low-income people come from formal sources such as government reports and scholarly studies; these terms include *culturally deprived, culturally disadvantaged, welfare households, inner city residents.* What images do such terms conjure? Derisive bureaucratic terms are powerful purveyors of negative images primarily because they have the sanction of authority behind them.

In addition to negative images, derisive bureaucratic terms send a negative message. Being labeled *culturally deprived* represents a form of blaming the victim. What group are we talking about? What do they lack? The term *cultural deprivation* suggests that poor people lack an ability to appreciate arts and humanities; it does not acknowledge the reality that they are economically deprived and need financial assistance for such things as job training, employment, and better health care. Labeling poor people *culturally deprived* implies that a deficiency in cultural qualities, perhaps certain values, is the cause of their problems.

People with disabilities are labeled with derisive social and bureaucratic terms. Around the world people have heard and told "moron jokes" as children, and Linton (1998) argues that when children insult others by calling them *retard*, *dummy*, *cripple*, or *gimp*, they are asserting a claim to normalcy and rejecting those who are deviant and unacceptable because of disability. In a bureaucratic setting, the term *handicapped* labels people as deviant. For more than fifty years, people with disabilities have objected to the term *handicapped* and have lobbied with some success to have it removed from common bureaucratic usage. Derisive bureaucratic terms are also represented by such phrases as *the retarded* and *the disabled*. These terms isolate one adjective for a disabled person and make it a noun to label the group. According to Charlton (1998),

> Prejudice blinds, ignorance retards, indifference deafens, hate amputates. In this way do some people disable their souls.
>
> **MARY ROBINSON (1944–)**

people with disabilities persistently object to the practice of labeling them with such adjectives because "their humanity is stripped away and the person is obliterated, only to be left with the condition—disability" (p. 54).

To understand what Charlton means, imagine a person who is either active or acquiescent, bold or bashful, cynical or compassionate, devilish or devout, and now add *disabled* to the description. If the last adjective is singled out and made a noun, that word defines the person being imagined. Using a term like *the disabled* defines and diminishes people with a disability because it focuses on only one aspect of their existence. Historically, non-disabled people in America all too often have viewed disabled people as unable to take care of themselves. "The retarded" and "the disabled" have been institutionalized and the action was justified by claims that it was "for their own good." The history of institutionalized people with disabilities illustrates the power of everyday language labels to define and ultimately control the quality of life for those who have been labeled.

How are derisive labels integrated into everyday language?

In informal settings, many Americans continue to employ derisive terms to label groups of people, even when such language is no longer as acceptable in formal settings. On a playground, children may not be punished for expressing derisive terms that a teacher will not tolerate in a classroom. Despite some improvement, there are still "acceptable" derisive terms expressed even in formal settings. Perhaps the most common ones heard today in malls and school hallways are those related to the issue of sexual orientation.

FIGURE 4.2   Advertisement for Halloween Costumes

In this advertisement from a costume shop, the images are clearly based on stereotypes for low-income people, but in case the reader might miss the point, the derisive labels are included.

Children used to be limited to the term *sissy*, and as they got older, the language escalated to *fairy* or *fruit*. Today, even elementary children can be heard calling one another a *faggot*. Although they may not know for certain what the word means, they know it is a negative term (Wessler, 2001). In the 1960s, male homosexuals began using the term *gay* to label and define themselves in a positive way. Unfortunately, American adolescents have co-opted the term and changed the meaning, so that saying "That's so gay!" is a negative comment. Women athletes have to be careful not to look too *butch* or they might be called a *dyke*. The language of prejudice is everywhere.

Is it so difficult to believe that we have learned to be prejudiced? How could we not learn at least some prejudice when we have been surrounded by so many derisive terms? The pervasiveness of derisive terms causes victims of prejudice to react strongly—even to ambiguous language. When a speaker refers to a minority group as *these people* or when someone in conversation makes a comment about *you people*, referring to the group to which the listener belongs, the listener may become suspicious. The person making the ambiguous reference may not be influenced by prejudices or stereotypes, but when listeners have heard derisive terms all their lives, is it fair to say they are being "oversensitive" or "paranoid"? Yet American men often make such comments about women's reactions to derisive terms.

What derisive terms have promoted negative attitudes toward women?

American men in all socioeconomic levels tend to express names for women, such as *doll* or *peach* or *honey*, that may have been intended as compliments, but describe women as other than human. Comparing women to something pretty or sweet to eat objectifies them, reducing women from persons to pleasurable "things" in a man's life.

Throughout America, women experience the insincerity of objectifying compliments. Imagine two women friends having a conversation in a bar, when they are interrupted by a man who flirts with one of them. He may be full of *sweeties* and *babes*, but if the woman firmly and unequivocally rejects

him, she is likely to hear *bitch* or *dyke* or another hostile term. The compliments last as long as women are pleasant, responding to men by giving them the attention they want.

A plethora of derisive terms exist for women, often with obvious sexual overtones such as *slut*, *whore*, and *tramp*. In contrast to the clear deprecation of such terms, derisive language directed at men often sends a mixed message. It may be intended as an insult to call a man a *prick* or a *bastard*, but it can also be interpreted as the speaker being envious of the man's power or position. Men may feel that they have to be tough, ruthless, and relentless if they are going to be successful in the "dog eat dog world," and such language could be regarded as a compliment to a man's prowess, his masculinity.

What terms for men are considered derisive?

In the English language, unambiguously derisive terms for men often accuse a man of being feminine. No little boy wants to be called a *sissy*; no man wants to be called a *wimp* or a *pussy*. Baker (1981) argued that although a man may resent being called a name that implies he acts like a woman, it is even more insulting to be called a name suggesting that a woman controls him, that he's *pussy whipped*. Men often use such language in a joking manner, but the message is serious.

That it is an insult for a man to be compared to a woman was delivered loud and clear at a summer festival where my wife and I were standing in line with our daughter to get her face painted. A dunking booth nearby was not open yet, but a man and his son were getting it ready. Three young men came up to the booth and volunteered to be dunked. The man thanked them but said he had all the volunteers he needed. Animated by the alcohol they had consumed, the three of them badgered the man for several minutes before they finally left. As they walked away, the man at the booth said, "Goodbye girls!" One of the young men turned around immediately and shouted, "What the fuck did you call me?" Whereas the older man's comment illustrated ordinary sexist attitudes, the violence of the young man's response was both surprising and disturbing as he came storming back, seemingly determined to start a fight. It didn't matter that this was a father with his young son nearby; the young man had been insulted and he was ready to resort to violence to defend his manhood.

Having observed this confrontation, my wife shouted sarcastically to the young man, "Oh, what a terrible thing to be called!" He looked over at us. I had visions of this young man coming to ask belligerently if this was my wife and threatening both of us, but other women standing in line also shouted similar comments. As the young man looked at the line of people, his face betrayed his confusion. His body had swelled up with anger, but now it seemed to deflate. His shoulders drooped and his expression became almost sheepish. As he approached the man at the dunking booth, he was still angry but not to the point of engaging in violence. After a brief conversation, a security officer appeared to escort the young man away. Considering the hostility aroused by such a flippant remark, one has to wonder about the attitudes males are being taught concerning women. Is it possible for a man to hate the idea of being called a female and not subconsciously hate women as well?

Perhaps the place where the most demeaning comments about women can be heard are the locker rooms where men readily refer to a woman as a *piece of ass* or a *cunt*. Outside of locker rooms, when men are talking in a group, such terms of contempt not just for women perceived as promiscuous, but for all women are also used. Referring to a woman with words related to a part of her body transforms her from a person to a thing; using words related to her sexuality reduces her significance to her ability to give a man pleasure. Her sexuality is being defined as impersonal, purely physical, and is reflected in locker room comments such as: "Put a bag over their head and they're all alike" or "They're all the same from the waist down," statements that demean and dehumanize women and demonstrate male sexist attitudes. A woman's primary value is being defined as the sexual pleasure resulting from an impersonal act. Is it any wonder that date rape has become so pervasive in a culture where young men are surrounded by sexist language—and other forms of sexism—every day of their lives?

What are other sources of sexist messages in our society?

Prejudice is also learned from our culture as reflected in television programs and films, in newspapers and magazines, in media and print advertising, in popular music, and on the Internet. Aronson (1999) described a study in which two groups of subjects watched television. One group viewed commercials where women were portrayed as sex

> You can tell the ideals of a nation by its advertisements.
>
> **NORMAN DOUGLAS (1868–1952)**

objects or as housewives subservient to their husbands. Another group watched nonsexist commercials containing scenes such as a husband cooking dinner for his wife. A third group watched no television at all. Afterward, subjects in all three groups answered questions about their futures. All males in all three groups expressed high expectations. Females who had watched nonsexist commercials expressed goals similar to the male subjects. Females who had watched sexist commercials or no commercials did not tend to anticipate promising careers or notable achievements. Perhaps female subjects viewing no commercials for the study had already accepted cultural messages about gender roles.

What negative cultural messages about other groups have been identified in media?

Many scholars have analyzed negative messages in media based on race, ethnicity, gender, social class, sexual orientation, and other factors (Coltrane and Messineo, 2001; Entman and Rojecki, 2000; Kilbourne, 1999; Giroux, 1998; Kamalipour and Carilli, 1998; Kuhn, 1996; Spring, 1992; Faludi, 1991; Wolf, 1991; and Wu, 1972). From what we have learned from these analyses of images in American culture promoting prejudice, the question we must now ask is: How can Americans identify their own prejudices and unlearn them?

PREJUDICE, PRIVILEGE, AND DISCRIMINATION

The difficulty in acknowledging and confronting our prejudices is that we make rationalizations to justify our attitudes. Being unaware of our prejudices seems attractive to those who are privileged by the way things are. An American who is white, male, middle-class, nondisabled, and heterosexual is privileged in our culture (Rothenberg, 2002; McIntosh, 2001). The person who fits all categories except for one (such as being female) loses some benefits, but is still rewarded. People who appear to benefit from the way society is structured prefer to keep their advantage, even if it means that others may experience discrimination.

What causes discrimination to occur in our society?

For years we believed that discrimination was caused by prejudice; therefore, the way to reduce discrimination was to reduce prejudice. Efforts were made in schools and in popular culture to address and reduce prejudice, and they produced positive results. In recent years, research has shown a *significant decrease in prejudice;* however, studies have reported *little decrease in discrimination* (Astor, 1997). Based on efforts by scholars seeking alternative explanations, Feagin and Feagin (1986) described three theories of discrimination: the interest theory, the internal colonialism theory, and the institutionalized discrimination theory, all of which identify historic and contemporary forces responsible for inequities being perpetuated without the involvement of prejudice.

How does the interest theory explain discrimination?

The **interest theory** describes discrimination resulting from people protecting their power and privilege. Instead of being motivated by prejudice, people discriminate against individuals from subordinate groups because of self-interest. For example, white males may object to affirmative action programs not because of their prejudice, but from fear of policies that might reduce their opportunities to be hired, retained, or promoted. Homeowners might persuade neighbors not to sell their home to a family of color because they are worried about what will happen to property values. Discrimination is a function of protecting one's interests; this is similar to the internal colonialism theory.

How is self-interest involved in the internal colonialism theory?

The **internal colonialism theory** of discrimination is an analysis of how privilege was created in the United States when the dominant group—white male Europeans—exploited subordinate groups to assume control of America's resources: land from American Indians, unpaid labor by African slaves, and wages and property of wives. Furthermore, by gaining control over resources and exploiting them to their advantage, certain white male Europeans achieved positions that provided them access to technological developments and control of industrial developments in the United States, including military technology. Once they are in a position of power, people will do what they can to maintain their advantage and stay in power.

Although initially established by force, unequal distribution and control of economic and political resources eventually became institutionalized. The theory of internal colonialism asserts that continued domination of nonwhites and women by white males is maintained by the way that institutions function in the United States. Internal colonialism theory creates the foundation on which the theory of institutionalized discrimination was built.

How is discrimination explained by the institutionalized discrimination theory?

Those who developed the theory of institutionalized discrimination accept the historical analysis of the internal colonialism theory, but they focus on how discrimination occurs in contemporary settings. **Institutionalized discrimination theory** describes institutional policies and practices that have a different and negative effect on a subordinate group in a given society. This theory examines how privilege and advantage are embedded in an organization's *norms,* its regulations, informal rules, and roles—social positions with their attendant duties and rights. The goal of an analysis based on this theory is to understand the mechanisms and methods that lead to discrimination in institutional policies and practices. Similar to the internal colonialism and self-interest theories, institutionalized discrimination theory is not concerned with prejudice (what U.S. courts have termed "evil intent"), but upon the assumption that much discrimination today is unintentional.

When a number of women in city government in an urban area were interviewed for a research project, one department head explained how a group of female department heads had solved a problem. At the end of a workday, the women tended to leave immediately because of family responsibilities such as picking up children and preparing meals. Male department heads tended to meet for a drink after work once or twice a week, and to play golf together on weekends while women department heads spent that time with their families. At meetings where they had to make decisions about funding for programs, female department heads were frustrated by their inability to be as effective as their male counterparts in supporting each other.

The women understood why the men had an advantage. Because of their social activities, male department heads knew more about each other's departments, so they could make informed arguments in support of each other's programs. To create a similar advantage for themselves, the women started meeting together one evening every month (child care provided) to talk about their programs and needs, and to prepare for debates on funding priorities. As a result of their efforts, a greater amount of funding was distributed to departments headed by women.

The institutionalized discrimination theory provides a realistic basis for understanding discrimination: The actions of the male department heads were not based on a prejudice against women; rather, they were doing their job in accordance with historic practices that benefited their departments. The women understood that the solution was not to berate the men, but to devise a strategy to offset advantages already established for male department heads. Although informal institutional procedures favored the men, the women found a way to "play the game" more effectively. Although discriminatory actions can still be a direct result of prejudice

on the part of people making decisions, it is more likely that causes for discrimination stem from reasons far more subtle and complex.

AFTERWORD

The future of young people in school today will be dramatically different from experiences of their grandparents and even their parents. Social change is occurring at an incredibly rapid pace, so much so that many people struggle to understand what is going on and others simply resist change altogether. At times it is difficult to determine if we are going backward or forward. The U.S. Supreme Court accepted racial segregation in the 1896 *Plessy* v. *Ferguson* decision, but in 1954 it called for racial desegregation of schools in *Brown* v. *Board of Education.* Although decades have passed, this country has yet to achieve the goal of bringing children of all races together in schools, and there is even evidence that this goal is being abandoned.

In a poll of 1001 Americans aged eighteen to twenty-nine conducted by the Arthur Levitt Public Affairs Center (2000), 50.3% said that segregation was acceptable as long as everyone had equal opportunity, clearly echoing a return to the *Plessy* v. *Ferguson* principle. Discouraged by ongoing white resistance to integration, some minority leaders now advocate a neoseparatist strategy that accepts the current status quo of racially segregated schools, but demands that resources be provided to ensure that schools attended primarily by students of color are funded as well as and have facilities equal to those attended primarily by white students.

Anything that we have learned, we can *unlearn.* Because prejudice remains so extensive and pervasive, there is much to unlearn. Some say we must teach children and youth to be tolerant of differences, but that should not be the final goal. Ultimately all people, especially those living in a diverse society, should strive to go beyond tolerance to acceptance—even excitement—about differences. The ultimate goal for a diverse society is to teach people to recognize how human differences enhance individual development and contribute to the richness of the experiences available in that society. In the coming years, citizens of our diverse society will have some critical choices to make, and the consequences will vary depending on what those decisions are. Each person must determine whether he or she will be committed to identifying and unlearning personal prejudices. To make such a profound and idealistic commitment is to take the first step toward working for social justice.

> This country will not be a good place for any of us to live in unless we make it a good place for all of us to live in.
>
> THEODORE ROOSEVELT (1858–1919)

TERMS AND DEFINITIONS

Assimilation The process whereby immigrants adopt cultural traits of the host country in order to be identified with that country and integrated into the immediate society

Black/White syndrome A pattern in the English language consisting of negative meanings for phrases by employing the term *black* and positive meanings for phrases using the term *white*

Derisive labels Names that reflect attitudes of contempt or ridicule for individuals in the group being named

Inclusive language Language that is not gender-specific, but inclusive of both genders

Institutionalized discrimination theory The treatment of others based on institutional policies and practices that have differential and negative effects upon subordinate groups in a society

Interest theory The suggestion that people may engage or acquiesce in discriminatory actions based on a desire to protect their power or privilege

Internal colonialism theory The concept of control and exploitation of subordinate groups by an older, more established and dominant group within a given society

Internalized oppression Occurs when members of a minority group believe myths, stereotypes, and prejudices held and expressed by members of a dominant group to define that group as inferior to the dominant group

REFERENCES

Arliss, L.P. (1991). *Gender communication*. Englewood Cliffs, NJ: Prentice Hall.

Analyzes sexist language in Chapter 3, "Debates about Language and Sexism."

Aronson, E. (1999). *The social animal* (8th ed.). New York: W.H. Freeman.

Presents an overview of research in social psychology. The multiple-car accident study is in Chapter 3, "Social Cognition," and the television commercial study is in Chapter 7, "Prejudice."

Arthur Levitt Public Affairs Center. (2000). *Race*. Retrieved April 21, 2003, from *http://www.hamilton.edu/levitt/survey_past*

Co-sponsored by the NAACP, the poll was conducted by Zogby International of Utica, New York, under the supervision of Dr. Philip Klinkner from Hamilton College.

Astor, C. (1997, August). Gallup poll: Progress in black/white relations, but race is still an issue. USIA electronic journal, *U.S. Society & Values 2*(3), 19–212.

Highlights information from a Gallup Poll Special Report on "Black/White Relations in the United States;" access the complete poll at *http://www.gallup.com*

Baker, R. (1981). "Pricks" and "chicks": A plea for persons. In M. Vetterling-Braggin (Ed.), *Sexist language: A modern philosophical analysis* (pp. 161–182). Lanham, MD: Littlefield, Adams.

Explores sexist attitudes in our society as expressed in sexual slang.

Charlton, J.I. (1998). *Nothing about us without us*. Berkeley: University of California Press.

Examines the status of people with a disability in various cultures.

Chavers, D. (1997, March 17). Doing away with the "S" word. *Indian Country Today 16*(37), 5.

Describes efforts of high school students to force Minnesota to change the names of state geographic features that include the word "squaw."

Coltrane, S., & Messineo, M. (2001, March). The perpetuation of subtle prejudice: Race and gender imagery in 1990s television advertising. *Sex Roles: A Journal of Research* (pp. 363–390).

Describes how television commercials reinforced racial and gender stereotypes.

Cortes, C. (2002). *The making—and remaking—of a multiculturalist*. New York: Teachers College Press.

Describes the author's life and includes anecdotes about his childhood in Chapter One.

Crawford, J. (2002, Summer). Obituary: The bilingual education act, 1968–2002. *Rethinking Schools 16*(4), 5.

Provides an overview of the history of bilingual education, the opposition to it, and the contradictory research on its effectiveness with students.

Entman, R.M., & Rojecki, A. (2000). *The black image in the white mind: Media and race in America.* Chicago: The University of Chicago Press.

Assesses white attitudes toward blacks and analyzes the contributions of media (network news, advertising, television programs, and movies) in shaping those attitudes.

Evans, S. (1989). *Born for liberty: A history of women in America.* New York: The Free Press.

Provides evidence of the influence of women on the colonies and the nation that emerged.

Faludi, S. (1991). *Backlash: The undeclared war against American women.* New York: Crown.

Examines sexist messages from the media in Part 2, "The Backlash in Popular Culture."

Feagin, J., & Feagin, C. (1986). *Discrimination American style* (2nd ed.). Malabar, FL: Krieger.

Describes the three alternative theories of discrimination on pages 7–12.

Giroux, H.A. (1998). *Channel surfing: Racism, the media, and the destruction of today's youth.* New York: St. Martin's.

Analyzes media images and their impact on children and youth.

Green, R. (1975). The Pocahontas perplex: The image of Indian women in American culture. *Massachusetts Review 16*, 698–714.

Discusses the historic use of the term *squaw* by the dominant culture.

Herbst, P. (1997). Ethnic epithets in society. In *The color of words: An encyclopedic dictionary of ethnic bias in the United States* (pp. 255–259). Yarmouth, ME: Intercultural Press.

This essay, an appendix to the dictionary, describes the purpose of ethnic slurs and their effect on those who use them.

Highwater, J. (1997). *The mythology of transgression: Homosexuality as metaphor.* New York: Oxford University Press.

Describes the impact of derisive language directed against a child perceived by others as "different" is found in Chapter 2, "Inside the Walls" (p. 23–30).

Kamalipour, Y.R., & Carilli, T. (Eds.). (1998). *Cultural diversity and the U.S. media.* Albany: State University of New York Press.

Examines problems concerning the representation of diverse groups (racial, ethnic, or religious) in the media (network news, television programs, movies, and textbooks).

Kilbourne, J. (1999). *Deadly persuasion: Why women and girls must fight the addictive power of advertising.* New York: The Free Press.

Argues that advertising is a pervasive cultural phenomenon that encourages people to objectify each other, which diminishes the quality of human relationships.

King, Jr., M.L. (1963). *Strength to love,* Philadelphia: Fortress.

Contains many sermons addressing the idea of not hating oppressors, including "Loving Your Enemies."

Kuhn, L. (1996). Exposing a woman-hating culture. In J. Andrzejewski (Ed.), *Oppression and social justice: critical frameworks* (5th ed., pp. 335–346). Needham Heights, MA: Simon & Schuster.

Explains similarities of mainstream media images of women with pornographic images and discusses what influence these images have on violence against women.

Linton, S. (1998). Reassigning meaning. In *Claiming disability: Knowledge and identity* (pp. 8–33). New York: New York University Press.

Discusses "nice words" and "nasty words" for disabled people, and explains why some people with disabilities have begun to use the word *crip* in a positive way.

Macedo, D., & Bartolome, L.I. (2001). *Dancing with bigotry: Beyond the politics of tolerance.* New York: Palgrave.

Examines issues concerning language, race, ethnicity, and limitations of teaching tolerance; the discussion of *migrant* vs. *settlers* is in Chapter 1, and Chapter 2 discusses bilingual education.

McIntosh, P. (2001). White privilege: Unpacking the invisible knapsack. In P. Rothenberg (Ed.), *Race, class, and gender in the United States: An integrated study* (5th ed., pp. 163–176). New York: Worth.

Explains the nature and extent of white privilege and provides a specific list of examples illustrating white privilege.

Miller, C., & Swift, K. (1977). *Words and women.* Garden City, NY: Anchor Press Doubleday.

Explains the study of junior high students' drawings of "early man" along with other studies concerning the sexism of generic terms in Chapter 2, "Who Is Man?"

Moore, R.B. (2000). Racism in the English language. In K. Rosenblum & T. Travis (Eds.), *The meaning of difference: American constructions of race, sex and gender, social class, and sexual orientation* (2nd ed., pp. 451–459). Boston: McGraw Hill.

Examines the origins and implications of many racist words and phrases.

Nilsen, A.P. (1977). Sexism as shown through the English vocabulary. In A.P. Nilsen, H. Bosmajian, H.L. Gershuny, & J.P. Stanley (Eds.), *Sexism and language* (pp. 27–41). Urbana, IL: National Council for Teachers of English.

Explains the nature and extent of sexism in language with numerous examples.

Rothenberg, P. (Ed.). (2002). *White privilege: Essential readings on the other side of racism.* New York: Worth.

Fourteen essays that examine such issues as white images and self-image, white conformity, white privilege, and how white people can combat racism.

Spring, J. (1992). *Images of American life: A history of ideological management in schools, movies, radio, and television.* Albany: State University of New York Press.

Analyzes how political and economic factors influence the ideas and values disseminated not only by the media but by teachers in classrooms.

Stephan, W. (1999). *Reducing prejudice and stereotyping in schools.* New York: Teachers College Press.

Reviews theories of prejudice and stereotyping, examines conditions to promote changes in negative attitudes, and describes techniques for improving race relations in schools.

Watson, G., & Johnson, D. (1972). Race and ethnic barriers in psychological relationships. In *Social psychology: Issues and insights* (pp. 304–341). Philadelphia: J.B. Lippincott.

Discusses racial differences, the perceptions related to skin color, the consequences of racial prejudice, and actions that can be taken to reduce prejudice.

Wessler, S.L. (2001, January). Sticks and stones. *Educational Leadership 58*(4), 28–33.

Describes the degrading and even violent language children use in schools and the impact of this language on its victims.

Wolf, N. (1991). *The beauty myth: How images of beauty are used against women.* New York: Doubleday.

Analyzes the ways in which the "consumer culture" manipulates women's images for profit but to the detriment of both women and relationships between women and men.

Wright, M.A. (1998). *I'm chocolate, you're vanilla: Raising healthy black and biracial children in a race-conscious world.* San Francisco: Jossey-Bass.

Describes the changing awareness of skin color and social attitudes about race during child development and recommends strategies to preserve children's resilience and optimism.

Wu, C. (Ed.). (1972). *"Chink!" A documentary history of anti-Chinese prejudice in America.* New York: World Publishing.

Reprints speeches, newspaper articles, and political cartoons documenting anti-Chinese prejudice; includes excerpts from movies, textbooks, and magazines in Chapter 2, "Overt Agitation."

Summary Exercises

See page 19 for exercises to help you summarize the main points and define key terms in this chapter.

Personal Clarification Exercises

In Chapter 4, two exercises promote reflection concerning personal prejudices.

Clarification Exercise #1 My Experiences with Culture, Race, and Ethnicity

Directions: Reflect on what age(s) over your life span you have had personal, direct contact with someone of a different culture, race, and ethnicity.

Part One: Using the chart below, begin with the earliest recollection and move forward to the present.

1. What was the setting: home, school, family? What was the nature of the contact: dinner guest, classmate, and playmate? Follow the sections below to complete your own recollection of experiences with culture, race, and ethnicity.

MY AGE	PERSON OF DIFFERENCE	SETTING	NATURE OF CONTACT

2. Identify your earliest exposures to different others through movies or television shows, including newscasts. What was the story about?

My Age	Person of Difference	Media	Nature of Story

3. Identify your earliest exposure to different others through newspapers, storybooks, novels, or magazines. What was the story about?

My Age	Person of Difference	Media	Nature of Story

Part Two: Prepare to explain to others the impressions these experiences made on you at the time and your reactions to them then and now. Have your reactions changed over time?

Clarification Exercise #2 The Liberated I.Q. Activity

Directions: Read each item carefully. Note any implications that are made and any inferences that you are making. Also check for any assumptions that are contained in the work before writing your response. Please write your response rationale for each entry before comparing responses with your class. Plan to share your responses with two others to discuss the issues of culture, bias, stereotype, and prejudice that might arise.

1. Should a husband help his wife most of the time with homemaking and child care?

   Yes _____ No_____ Comment:

2. Should a husband usually ask his wife's opinion before making decisions about major purchases or investments?

   Yes _____ No_____ Comment:

3. Should a husband approve of his wife's working outside of the home, although it interferes with her homemaking and child-care duties?

   Yes _____ No_____ Comment:

4. Should a husband be willing to let his wife take the initiative sexually?

   Yes _____ No_____ Comment:

5. Should a husband be pleased when his wife expresses informal opinions about political or intellectual matters, even if her views differ from his?

   Yes _____ No_____ Comment:

6. Should a husband ever have reason to agree to watch his children or to baby-sit when his wife is unable to do so?

   Yes _____ No_____ Comment:

7. After reviewing your responses to the questions above, would you rate yourself relatively liberated?

   Yes _____ No_____ Comment:

Intergroup Exercises

Intergroup Exercise #1 Words and Phrases That Hurt: Implications of Language

Directions: Look at each of the following ten statements and determine the implications of the language that could hurt people. Conclude with your assigned team member what explanation of each statement you could provide to your discussion group.

1. A white person to a person of color: "We must have law and order."
2. In a discussion of inequitable school funding, a white person to a black person: "You can make your schools as good as ours."
3. A white person to a black acquaintance: "You're different from most blacks."
4. A white employer announcing the intention of integrating the workplace: "Of course, we will make sure we only hire a *qualified* minority applicant."
5. In response to court-ordered desegregation, a white parent to a black parent: "Why do you want to send your children to our schools?"
6. A white person to a Chicano: "I don't understand what you people want."
7. A white person to a person of color: "Our old neighborhood used to be good when I lived there as a kid, but look at it now!"
8. A white person to a black person: "The death of Martin Luther King, Jr. was a terrible loss to your race."
9. A Gentile to a Jew: "Oh, you're Jewish? I didn't realize you were Jewish—you sure don't act like one."
10. A white person to a Native American: "I think your people have made great progress."

Intergroup Exercise #2 Cultural Images: An American Stereotype Discussion

Directions Part One: Read the item below that appeared in *Time* magazine March 3, 1923, regarding discussion and objection to a statue proposed to honor black women of the Old South. Study the implication of the impact of cultural imprinting on those cited in the story.

"Black Mammy" Debate in Washington, D.C.

In dignified and quiet language, two thousand Negro women of the Phyllis Wheatley Y.W.C.A. protested against a proposal to erect at the Capitol a statue to "The Black Mammy of the South." A spokesman carried the resolution to Vice President Coolidge and Speaker Gillette and begged them to use their influence against "the reminder that we come from a race of slaves."

This, of course, will rebuke forever the sentimentalists who thought they were doing honor to a character whom they loved. They desired to immortalize a person famous in song and legend. But that person's educated granddaughters snuffed out the impulse by showing that they are ashamed of her.

Part Two: Whole group participation in "Black Mammy." Questions for discussion:

1. What appears to be the attitude of the writer toward "Negro women" in the first paragraph? In the second paragraph? Why do you think the attitude of the author changes?

2. The proposal for a statue came from Southern legislators, many of whom were raised by black nannies. Were they sincere in wanting to honor this cultural image that had personal meaning for them? If Congress had erected a statue of "The Black Mammy of the South," how do you think white and black people would view that statue today?

3. Is there a comparable situation today involving white people insisting on maintaining a cultural image for another (nonwhite) group of people? Explain.

Cultural Foundations of Oppression in the United States

Beginning with Native Americans, Section 2 examines historical information about how cultural values and norms of European colonists in America encouraged oppressive attitudes and actions toward those who were different. Oppressive colonial attitudes and actions were reinforced in response to ethnic and religious diversity contributed by subsequent waves of immigration. Understanding how early American culture fostered oppression aids in our understanding how anti-oppressive attitudes and actions are promoted in response to the diversity existing in America today.

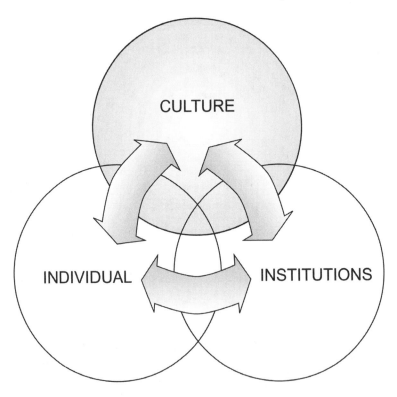

Chapter 5 describes the negative attitudes of Europeans toward native peoples of America and how people with negative attitudes were able to justify the conquest of Native Americans and dispossession of their lands. Although native cultures had much to teach the incoming settlers who were unfamiliar with the biodiversity in America, until recently, we largely ignored this information. Oppressive behaviors toward American Indians has continued through the subsequent centuries, and even today native peoples struggle to maintain their cultures and their status.

Chapter 6 describes how ethnic diversity of immigrants historically has been perceived as threatening to white supremacist attitudes of the majority group. Historic attempts have been made to curb immigration to America, especially of immigrants perceived as not being satisfactorily white enough, and to justify anti-immigration efforts through the early twentieth century quasi-science of eugenics. Because of the reform of immigration laws in 1965, ethnic diversity of immigrants has dramatically increased, and the chapter concludes with a description of anti-immigrant activities that underscores the persistence of these attitudes on the part of a significant percentage of the American population.

Chapter 7 focuses on the religious diversity of immigrants and the challenge that diversity has always represented to the creation of a free society. The religious diversity of people who settled in America eventually led to a shared concern that religious differences not be used to justify persecution, and the concept of religious freedom was included in the first amendment to the Constitution. The principle was established, but reality did not conform to it. Although members of different Protestant faiths began to accept one another as equals, Catholic, Jewish, and atheist immigrants were discriminated against and denied certain civil rights. Although Catholics and Jews finally achieved a status as equals, the 1965 immigration reform resulted in an unprecedented increase in Muslims and persons of other religions—such as Buddhists, Hindus, and Sikhs—with no relation to the dominant American faiths that embraced the Judeo-Christian tradition. Once again the United States is being challenged to live up to its principle of providing religious freedom that acknowledges and accepts people from diverse faiths as equal partners in our religiously diverse nation.

In response to the cultural history described in the preceding chapters, Chapter 8 identifies four perspectives that describe individual reactions to racial, ethnic, and religious diversity in America. The most recent perspective, pluralism, emerged in the 1920s and today is challenging this history of oppression by calling for Americans to recognize the value of diversity and the contributions diverse groups have made, and continue to make, to American society. Since the problems related to this diversity are ongoing and will be discussed in the next section, this chapter emphasizes pluralism as a force for change, for a new direction in our society in response to the diversity that not only exists but is increasing.

CHAPTER 5

The Roots of Oppression: The Subjugation of Native Americans

"Everyone likes to give as well as to receive. No one wishes only to receive all the time. We have taken much from your culture . . . I wish you had taken something from our culture for there were some good and beautiful things in it."

CHIEF DAN GEORGE (1899–1991)

C hief Dan George identified a persistent problem in relationships between **indigenous people,** those who were established in the New World, and European colonists. Although we can attribute many colonial living practices and governance policies to Native American influence, early colonists never seemed to value the culture, history, and knowledge of American Indians. Beginning with Columbus and perpetuated by those who came after, colonists barely acknowledged Indians as human, recognizing them only as "savages" who were tolerated but considered extremely dangerous. From the time of Columbus, it was clear that indigenous people in America would be viewed as obstacles to be overcome or eliminated.

COLONIZERS AND COLONIZED IN THE NEW WORLD

One of the requirements for those who came to the New World was to be on good terms, at least initially, with the people who already inhabited the land. When Columbus stepped ashore on the

Caribbean island he called Hispaniola to greet the Arawaks, it is estimated that at least 500 nations of indigenous people were scattered throughout the Americas. Columbus established the pattern carried out by the colonists who followed. After a brief period of peaceful relations, the Columbus party began to engage in oppressive and hostile actions against the Arawaks in order to control and then exploit native resources for profit. When Arawaks resisted, Columbus and his men drove them away and claimed their land (Loewen, 1995).

Although Columbus was initially impressed with the gentle, peaceful nature and physical beauty of the Arawaks, that didn't stop him from taking a number of them back to Spain to auction as slaves. When many of them died, he relinquished this scheme and looked for other ways to profit. He noticed Arawaks wearing gold jewelry and asked them to bring him gold. They insisted that there was only a little gold on their island, but Columbus did not believe them. He demanded that they bring him gold and warned them not to return without it. If any Arawaks came back empty-handed, Columbus ordered his men to cut off their hands to intimidate the rest into complying (Zinn, 1999). The beautiful people were now "savages" who were cheating Columbus of a deserved reward; he had to demonstrate to them that he would not be deceived.

Although he never found gold, in a short time Columbus and his followers managed to almost exterminate the Arawaks. Almost. Josephy (1994) explains that the European conquerors of America and their descendants eventually exterminated nearly half of the 500 nations of indigenous people and almost eradicated the cultures of nations that survived. Almost.

What motivated Europeans to come to the New World?

The first colonists who came to America gambled on having better lives—the origin of the American Dream. For generations they had survived difficult conditions in England and across Europe. It had not been easy; just staying alive had been an achievement. Disease was rampant and early death could be anticipated. Walls surrounded most European cities to protect them from outside attack; clouds of war either hovered overhead or thundered on the horizon (Tuchman, 1978). As Barzun (2000) wrote:

> Violent events were to be typical of European life till the middle of the 17th century. Riots, combat, sieges and sacks of towns, burnings at the stake, and escape by self-exile repeat without letup. (p. 15)

When Europeans came to colonize the New World, they had been well prepared by their life in the Old World to do what was needed to survive.

At first, food was their primary need for survival, especially in the dark days of that first dreadful winter at Plymouth. Jennings (1976) described starving colonists digging up the graves of recently buried natives to get the corn that they knew had been buried with the bodies. By observing native practices, colonists eventually learned useful information: They saw natives eating certain plants or preparing food a certain way, such as making succotash, and they imitated them. Colonists preferred

the food they had eaten back home, but they did what was necessary to survive. Once settlements were established, colonists wanted more than survival: They wanted land to build more communities to create a "New England," and only the Indians stood in their way.

WHAT'S IN A NAME

Although the term "Native American" has become widely used, there is still not a consensus among native peoples about the generic term they prefer. Popular author Sherman Alexei is adamantly against the term, preferring to be called an American Indian. Some prefer to be called "indigenous people" while others are content with the traditional label of "Indian." In this chapter, all of the terms are used to reflect this diversity of preferences. The only consensus among all of the indigenous people is their preference to be identified by their tribal affiliation such as Hopi, Apache, Sioux, Mohican, Kwakiutl, or Inuit. In conversations with individual American Indians, one would do well to follow Beverley Tatum's advice—ask the individual what his or her preference is, then use that term.

What did Europeans learn from Native Americans?

As Chief Dan George lamented, most colonists seemed unwilling to listen or to learn from indigenous Americans; when they did, they rarely gave the natives credit. English settlers in America tended to build on existing Indian settlements and they walked on paths well worn by Indians, many of which eventually became the roads of the new nation. Benjamin Franklin was impressed by the governance structure developed by representatives of several Indian nations to create their Iroquois League, and he borrowed heavily from the Iroquois to formulate his "Albany Plan," the basis for the Articles of Confederation that was the first form of government implemented in the United States (Weatherford, 1988). Although he borrowed ideas from the Iroquois League, Franklin did not acknowledge Indian influence on his work, and he remained prejudiced against them until late in his life. An example of Franklin's prejudice is revealed in a letter to James Parker about the need for the colonies to establish a union:

> It would be a very strange Thing, if six Nations of ignorant Savages should be capable of forming a Scheme for such an Union and be able to execute it in such a Manner, as that it has subsisted for Ages, and appears indissoluble; and yet that a like Union should be impracticable for ten or a Dozen English Colonies, to whom it is more necessary. (Le May, 1987, p. 444)

Unlike Franklin, most colonists did not care to learn from or imitate Indian culture, knowledge, or intertribal customs. They learned what was necessary for basic survival, but their goal was to import to America the culture and traditions of their European heritage. This goal reflects an ethnocentrism behind their unwillingness to value and learn from the indigenous peoples. **Ethnocentrism** is the belief that one's own race, nation, or culture is superior to all others. Ethnocentrism was illustrated by colonial choices for settlement names. Dutch settlers called their community *New* Amsterdam; the city was later taken by the English and its

> God teaches the birds to make nests, yet the nests of all birds are not alike.
>
> **DUWAMISH PROVERB**

name was changed to *New* York. Many settlements were named in this way or without even adding the term "new," a fact easily confirmed by comparing city names on current maps of New England states with city names on maps of England. Williams (1954) described another example of colonial ethnocentrism when English colonists noticed a bird that reminded them of an English robin. We still call this bird a robin today, even though it is not an English robin, nor is it even related to the English robin.

What could the European settlers have learned from Native Americans?

If Europeans had listened and observed more carefully, they could have learned much from Native Americans. The following four areas provide a few examples.

Foods and Medicines European settlers did not want to eat food initially unfamiliar to them such as potatoes, peanuts, corn, squash, tomatoes, peppers, and pumpkins. These foods were later exported around the world and had a major influence on various nations. Many Asian and Southeast Asian cultures incorporated American peanuts and chili peppers into their cuisines. And in Europe, many American foods became associated with certain nations. As Weatherford (1988) wrote, "It is difficult to imagine what Ireland would be today without the potato" (p. 64). Similarly, it is difficult to imagine what Italian food was like before the American tomato became part of that cuisine. According to Weatherford, the introduction of American foods in Europe ended the "episodic famines" that had been a major factor limiting population growth.

The land produced more than food; it offered an array of herbal medicines to those who understood the medicinal value of certain plants. Native American shamans had such knowledge and could have taught Europeans the cure for many diseases. Scurvy is a disease caused by vitamin C deficiency resulting in bleeding gums and fatigue; it often afflicted people sailing on ships because fruit didn't last long on a voyage. Native Americans knew how to cure scurvy centuries before Europeans stumbled upon the cure when German sailors on boats stocked with sauerkraut found that they did not tend to get the illness (Weatherford, 1988).

Suzuki and Knudtson (1992) estimate at least 75 percent of prescription drugs derived from plants were discovered based on clues stemming from the healing practices of the indigenous peoples of the world. Scientists now work openly with Native American shamans to conduct experiments based on their knowledge of the healing qualities of certain plants. According to Harvard botanist Richard Schultes, every time a shaman dies, "it is as if a library had burned down" (Gell-Mann, 1994, p. 339). Scientists are anxious to discover if specific chemical elements in plants that may be responsible for healing effects can be reproduced in labs and made publicly available. Indian activists express resistance to such projects because pharmaceutical companies rarely credit or compensate Native

Americans for the knowledge and assistance they provide. The same corporations that vigorously demand "intellectual property rights" for their discoveries seem to deny the same rights to Native Americans.

Hygiene Spring (2001) reports that Europeans referred to Indians as "filthy savages" not because Indians were dirty but because of their "seemingly unrepressed sexuality" (p. 10). In fact, Europeans had a lot to learn about good hygiene from natives who believed in frequent bathing. Although Roman ruins across Europe and the Middle East document the fondness Romans had for baths, the decline of their empire prompted the decline of bathing. A major factor in this decline stemmed from disapproval of public bathing by the early Christian church because its leaders feared that nude people mingling together in a public bath might inspire lust. Europeans also mistakenly believed that too much bathing was unhealthy; they thought that using water to wash one's face and hands was acceptable, but bathing exposed one's entire body to the air, leading to colds and other more serious health problems.

Instead of bathing, Europeans would dry-rub themselves with alternative cleansers such as sand, ashes, or pumice stone. For royalty and aristocracy, strong perfumes disguised offensive body odors. According to Smith (2001), Queen Elizabeth I of England took a bath once a month, "whether she needed it or not" (p. 348). Spain's Queen Isabella, even more modest than Elizabeth, proudly stated that she had taken only two baths in her life: when she was born and when she was married. It is no wonder that perfume was so expensive and so highly valued.

Governance and Gender Equality Europeans could have learned to view women differently and to share power with women by including them in decision making. Because of conflicts with Indians, Virginia colonists in 1642 arranged a meeting with a Cherokee delegation led by Outacite, who had been instructed to negotiate for a peaceful resolution. As he approached the colonial delegation, Outacite wondered aloud why he saw no women. Upon hearing that the colonists had brought no women, Outacite returned to his people saying he did not believe he should negotiate because the

FIGURE 5.1

The use of Indian images on medicine bottles in the 1800s suggests that Americans were aware that Indians understood the medicinal value of plants. Instead of acquiring that knowledge, entrepreneurs created concoctions (usually including alcohol), put an image of an Indian on the bottle, and sold the bogus medicine to naïve customers.

Source: Pictures of Record, Inc.

colonists were missing half the people needed for the negotiation. Perdue (1998) also described a 1757 meeting of the South Carolina Governor's Council to which Distinguished Cherokee leader Attakullakulla had been invited. He began his remarks by asking why there were no women on the Council. The Cherokee even had women on their war councils, earning them the colonists' contempt (Woodward, 1988).

Wagner (1996), a feminist scholar, has described possible influences that Native American views of women might have had on the ideals of the nineteenth century women who demanded property rights and voting rights which women in many indigenous societies already enjoyed. If an unmarried colonial woman owned property, it was legally transferred to her husband when she married; in the event of a separation or divorce, the husband kept the property (Evans, 1989). By contrast, if Indian women owned property, it remained in their control regardless of their marital status (White, 1993; Woodward, 1988). In terms of political power, Indian women belonging to the Iroquois League did not serve on the governing tribal council, but they selected the men who served.

Ecology   Native Americans have long expressed environmental concerns, offering an ecological perspective to honor the land and its treasures. Many Indian cultures viewed nature not as a mechanical world of cause and effect, but one where spirits animated plants, animals, and even rocks. Human beings shared a spiritual kinship with the natural world and were obligated to live in harmony with it. For years, indigenous people in the Americas have protested the exploitation of nature practiced by our dominant culture. Suzuki and Knudtson (1992) cite a declaration from one of the most ancient consistently functioning governments, known today as the Iroquois Confederacy, which deplores the destruction of forests by industrial entrepreneurs, the depletion of wildlife by sports hunters and pesticides, the pollution of the air by factories, the pollution of water and poisoning of fish by industry and agribusiness, and the toxic wastes deposited in chemical dumps across the country (pp. 238–239).

In recent years, Americans have begun to embrace the environmentalism always expressed by indigenous people. We now have an Environ-

> Take only what you need and leave the land as you found it.
>
> ARAPAHO PROVERB

mental Protection Agency to preserve the quality of our air, water, and land. Many old, deteriorating dams built on rivers across America are not being repaired, but torn down because of the damage they have caused to the environment. There is a growing recognition of the importance of preserving the natural world. Although the Iroquois declaration laments the fact that so many people in the dominant society "display no love for the life of this planet," it calls on others to participate in preserving the life that is left, to "carry out our function as caretakers of the land" (Suzuki and Knudtson, 1992, pp. 240–241).

What relationships did colonists have with native people?

Instead of learning new lessons from Native Americans, colonists practiced lessons already learned about conflict and survival, conquest and subjugation—and to the victor belonged the spoils. An example of how the game was played occurred at an early European settlement near the mouth of the Connecticut River. As with other European immigrants, the Connecticut settlers at first were friendly in their interactions with the Pequot and Narragansett Indians; indeed, they were dependent on them. Jennings (1976) described this dependence:

> Colonists of Jamestown, Quebec, and Plymouth immediately allied themselves to nearby natives to guarantee security . . . The necessity for native alliance was not merely a matter of armed manpower; it was desirable and indeed indispensable because of massive European ignorance. To the European who lacked woodcraft, knew not the native trails, and imagined gothic horrors in every copse, the familiar hunting parks of the Indians were lethal wilderness. The European "settlers," who knew nothing of tillage methods in America and were often revolted at the labor of farming, depended on Indian gardens for subsistence between the deliveries of cargoes from overseas. (p. 33)

As more settlers came to the Connecticut settlement, Fort Saybrook was built and stocked with guns and ammunition. The Pequots and Narragansetts were aware of this, but were not certain what it meant. After all, they were friends with the settlers; they had offered help and signed treaties. Then Narragansetts killed a colonist, John Oldham, in revenge for an unnamed outrage, probably the outbreak of smallpox that took the lives of 700 Narragansett people.

With military might sufficient to ensure victory and Oldham's death as an excuse, General John Endecott was sent to Fort Saybrook to lead an attack on the Narragansetts and on innocent Pequots as well. After some early skirmishes, the Pequots requested a conference and met with Lieutenant Lion Gardiner to determine if they could stop fighting and resume their peaceful relations. Gardiner's reply demonstrated that he wasn't prepared to lay down his arms. Because of Dutch brutality during their Indian wars, the Pequots asked Gardiner if it was true that the Europeans did not just kill the men they fought, but also their women and children. They were sure Lieutenant Gardiner would deny such a vicious accusation; he only said, "they should see that hereafter" (Jennings, 1976, p. 212).

The representatives understood Gardiner's meaning, and returned to tell their people of this disturbing threat from their (formerly) friendly neighbors.

In response, the Pequot tried to recruit Indian allies, including their old enemy the Narragansett, to join forces against the English, but were unsuccessful.

CONTESTED LAND AND NEGOTIATED TREATIES

Land was the source of contention between immigrants and natives. In today's American elementary schools, children are often taught that Columbus planted the flag of Spain in the soil of the New World to claim the land for Spain, implying that Spain and indigenous Americans would resolve their competing claims to the land either by fighting or by negotiating some kind of treaty agreement. Although war is generally not regarded as an admirable way to resolve conflicts, the practice of engaging in war to gain land was not unusual in the history of European nations who always seemed to be involved in some struggle to conquer others. Conquered lands were taken by the victor and inhabitants subjected to foreign rule. Kings received tribute or paid tribute to other kings who had conquered them.

The problem with assumptions we make about land claims in the New World is that they are not accurate. According to Berkhofer (1978), the only

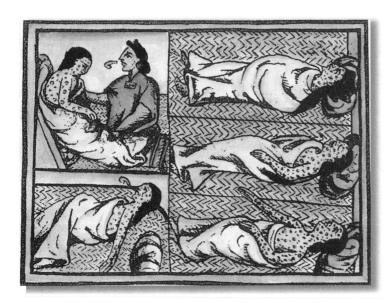

FIGURE 5.2

This drawing shows Mexican Indians dying of smallpox; like many other diseases brought by Europeans, there was nothing in Indian immune systems to counter it. During Pontiac's Rebellion in 1764, the U.S. Army gave smallpox-infested blankets to Shawnee and Delaware Indians who came to Fort Pitt to negotiate peace. The rebellion ended within a year because so many Indian villages were devastated by smallpox.

Source: The Granger Collection, New York.

land that could be claimed by a foreign country was uninhabited land, a legal principle known as "vacuum domicilium," whereas inhabited land was another matter. Even in 1492, international law recognized property rights of indigenous people. Those who lived and farmed and hunted on the land were acknowledged as rightful owners of that land. Grants and charters given to explorers allowed them to claim land they might discover under the principle of "terra nullius":

> Terra nullius was an ambiguous term, however, for it could mean lands totally vacant of people or merely not inhabited by peoples possessing those religions and customs that Europeans recognized as equal to their own under the international law. (p. 120)

Why were colonists and native peoples unable to establish a peaceful relationship?

When Columbus planted the Spanish flag, he was claiming the legal right for Spain to own the uninhabited lands or to purchase the land if it was determined that indigenous people had a legitimate claim to it. Most of the legal claims for land inhabited by Native Americans were not made under the

principle of "vacuum domicilium" because the natives made it clear through words and deeds that the land on which they lived belonged to them, just as they belonged to the land. To resolve the ambiguity of making a "terra nullius" claim, European nations wanting to take possession of Indian land created a new concept called "occupatio bellica," which referred to a peaceful seizure of land that was being underutilized by the indigenous people.

What was viewed as "underutilized" to Europeans might have been regarded as fully utilized by indigenous people; still, the principle provided the opportunity to take possession of land by peaceful means. An example of "peaceful means" was to erect crosses marked with the royal seal throughout the land desired, and then sign agreements with indigenous people who may have been bribed or forced to concede the land and then depart.

Nomads were the only exception to the principle of property rights for indigenous people. Defined as a "pastoral people" wandering over vast expanses of land and never staying in one place, nomadic groups were not granted a legal claim to the land over which they traveled. Often colonists described the indigenous people they encountered as nomadic to justify their claims to land they had not purchased. Were these indigenous inhabitants nomadic? A group might occupy one site for many

FIGURE 5.3

Indian housing is typically represented in movies and educational textbooks by the tipis or wigwams of Plains Indians. This drawing portrays an Indian village in New England with structures later copied by the U.S. Army for its "Quonset huts."

Source: Stock Montage, Inc.

years and then, usually as a consequence of decreasing crop productivity due to soil depletion, they would pack their belongings and move. After many years at another site, they would move again. It was not uncommon for a group to return to a site abandoned decades before where soil was now replenished and could once again provide bountiful crops. Needless to say, this does not fit the standard definition of *nomadic.*

Some historians still insist that the designation of indigenous people as "nomadic" was legitimate. Although many Plains Indians such as the Sioux or Cheyenne were nomadic and followed historic migratory patterns, most of the indigenous Americans lived in villages and grew crops. Maize (corn) was one of many agricultural products unknown in Europe prior to the colonization of the New World. Indian farmers domesticated maize and developed several different varieties, including the kind we now call "Indian corn" (Weatherford, 1988). If indigenous people living in such villages protested or used force to remove those encroaching upon their land, the result was usually armed conflict eventually leading to the Indians' defeat and removal. This was a common procedure for resolving conflicting claims for land.

Why did Native Americans agree to negotiate and sign treaties?

Early treaties almost always involved cession of Indian lands to colonists. From the earliest days, fur traders purchased furs by trading guns and ammunition, metal traps, kettles, and other items that simplified Indian life; each of these items also made Indians dependent on the European traders. As trade continued, Indian demand for goods exceeded their ability to provide enough animal pelts and natives became indebted to fur traders. Often treaties were signed in which Indians gave up a portion of their land to pay their debts (Satz, 1991).

Treaties were sometimes negotiated under threat of war to force Indians to surrender land so colonists could establish settlements; they were also negotiated in the aftermath of armed conflict between the two groups. Most American Indian nations were not warrior cultures and were usually unable to overcome European, and later American, military superiority.

After being defeated, groups of Indians were often forced to move elsewhere, which sometimes resulted in conflicts between the exiled Indians and the Indian nations whose land they had entered. Following armed conflict between indigenous peoples, victors would often integrate into their society the surviving members of the defeated group, usually consisting primarily of women and children (Josephy, 1994). When Americans began to move westward, the land made available to Indians diminished until eventually the Indians were relegated to small parcels of land to which they were restricted by treaties.

Treaties were negotiated so long ago; why are they still being enforced?

A **treaty** is a legal document negotiated between two sovereign nations to resolve claims of land ownership and other issues such as hunting or fishing privileges. Each nation of indigenous people was legally regarded as a sovereign state; treaties were not to be made between sovereign states and individual state governments but with another sovereign state: the United States. Treaties were written stating that they would be maintained in perpetuity, meaning forever, or in the language of some treaties: "as long as the grass grows and the sun shines."

The problem was that one of the sovereign states signing treaties, the United States, never seemed to keep its promises. Despite the inclusion of language to indicate clearly that all parties agreed that provisions of the treaty were meant to be permanent and enforced in perpetuity, in reality the U.S. government failed to honor its guarantees of "perpetuity." Frequently, terms of treaties were violated during the lifetimes of those who had been the negotiators. Josephy (1994) and Wilson (1998) report that the United States has violated virtually every treaty made with the indigenous people.

> They made many promises, so many I can't remember, but they only kept one. They promised to take our land, and they took it.
>
> **RED CLOUD (1822–1909)**

During the 1970s, critics of negotiations with the Soviet Union to reduce the numbers of nuclear weapons said the United States could not trust the Russians to keep their promises because they would find a way to violate treaty provisions. Native Americans were especially amused by the critics' concerns about the possibility of Russian treaty violations. A century earlier, Red Cloud, one of the most powerful and influential leaders among the Lakota (Sioux) tribes, had denounced the U.S. government for its treaty violations. Native American elders remembered the words of Red Cloud and many other leaders who gave similar warnings about the danger of making treaties with the United States government.

Why were Native American treaties consistently violated?

When U.S.–Indian treaties were signed, the land designated for indigenous people was often deemed expendable to the United States. When that land became desirable, Indians were usually forced to surrender it to American interests. When enough settlers migrated to Wisconsin, the Winnebagos— originally Ho Chunk—were removed to Nebraska and Kansas. Many refused to leave and hid from authorities; others left but eventually returned (Bieder, 1995). As settlers demanded more land, treaties with Indian nations were broken or renegotiated. Land indigenous people still possessed was often unwanted and couldn't easily be farmed. Eventually, land that was undesirable for settlement became targeted for confiscation when discoveries of coal, oil, or uranium deposits made it valuable.

The Cherokee were forcibly removed to the territory of Oklahoma despite the fact that they had legal deeds to land in Georgia where they had built homes and businesses. The U.S. Supreme Court respected the legality of Cherokee claims and ruled in their favor when they protested the removal order. Despite his sworn duty to uphold the Constitution of the United States and to carry out the decisions of the Supreme Court, President Andrew Jackson chose to ignore the Supreme Court justices and refused to enforce their ruling upholding Cherokee land claims. Federal troops brutally marched the Cherokee to Oklahoma, resulting in many deaths during the journey that is now called the *Trail of Tears* (Wallace, 1993).

Treaties initially designated the entire Oklahoma territory as Indian country, and several Indian nations occupied the land. But the relentless thirst for cheap land resulted in the United States renegotiating that treaty. The Indian tribes in Oklahoma were relocated to the least desirable land in the territory, and settlers were invited to claim the rest. No one cared about Indian land in Oklahoma until oil was discovered there. Time to renegotiate the treaty. Similarly, an 1868 Treaty of Fort Laramie declared that the Sioux would permanently retain lands sacred to them in the Black Hills—until gold was discovered there. Time to renegotiate the treaty. Although it may not be possible to repair the damage done to indigenous people who were stripped of their lands, it is important that contemporary historians report accurately the devious means by which Native American subjugation was accomplished (Wilson, 1998; Josephy, 1994).

Indian land was confiscated not only for settlement but also for its resources, and a dominant white society benefited from its continual assault upon Native American land and resources. Historian David Wrone has calculated that 19.5 million acres of land taken from one indigenous group alone, the Chippewa, resulted in enormous wealth gained by the United States. Besides taking possession of the land, the resources from the land included "100 billion board feet of timber; 150 billion tons of iron ore; 13.5 billion pounds of copper" (Gedicks, 1993, p. 51). In addition, other resources taken from Indian land included water, ports, fish, fowl, and game, all of which contributed to a profitable tourism industry that has yielded considerable wealth to members of the dominant society who gained access as a result of renegotiated treaties.

Unfortunately, a similar pattern exists today. Although land was lost, many treaties signed near the turn of the century affirmed rights of indigenous people to hunt and fish on traditional tribal lands outside the boundaries of Indian reservations. For native people, being able to hunt and fish on former tribal land was a critical concession; to others, it may have seemed an innocuous benefit when the treaty was signed, especially given the amount of land Indians were being forced to relinquish. As hunting and fishing have become profitable tourism activities, there have been increasing numbers of complaints that the treaties are old and should be abrogated. White people in areas promoting outdoor recreational activities have protested Indian hunting and fishing privileges guaranteed "in perpetuity" by the treaties. It is easy to imagine some form of the following dialogue taking place:

"The treaty was signed a hundred years ago. How long are we supposed to abide by it?"

"The treaty says it is to be enforced in perpetuity."

"In perpetuity? You mean forever? You've got to be kidding!"

"That's what it says. That's what the U.S. government agreed to."

"I'm sure they didn't really mean forever!"

"You may be right, but Indians did mean it."

The pattern remains the same. A treaty giving indigenous people land or rights that seemed of little value at the time is taken from them when it becomes valuable. Ironically, we call people "Indian givers" who want something back that they have given to someone. Will this pattern finally be broken, or will the tourism industry continue to be the latest villain to violate and force a renegotiation of Indian treaties?

Indigenous people have responded to this issue by an insistence on maintaining **Indian Sovereignty,** which Deloria (1993) explains as the legal right of Indian nations to "define themselves and to

> A people without faith in themselves cannot survive.
>
> **Hopi Proverb**

act as unique entities" (p. 388). But while Native Americans are defending the legal status of treaties and insisting that treaty rights are essential to their survival, not enough white people are listening, which reinforces what Chief Dan George expressed at the beginning of this chapter: Members of the dominant society in the United States have a history of not listening to, or learning from, subordinate groups, especially indigenous people.

CURRENT CONCERNS OF INDIGENOUS PEOPLE

Anthropologists have identified Native Americans as the first immigrants to America, crossing a land bridge along the Bering Straits 15,000 years ago. Native Americans insist that they have always been here. Increasing archaeological evidence, reluctantly accepted by some, makes it difficult to ignore the conclusion that indigenous people appear to have been living in both North and South America for more than 30,000 years, long before the land bridge came and went (Chatters, 2001; Parfit and Garrett, 2000). Disputes over Native Americans' origins—whether or not they came from somewhere else—is only one example of ongoing disagreements between the dominant society and indigenous people.

Berkhofer (1978) described one of the major issues for indigenous people: the images of "Indians" projected to themselves and to others. According to Berkhofer, white people tend to hold one of the following two images of Indians: the noble savage who lived long ago and was exterminated or the contemporary Indian who has lost his culture and been degraded by white men's ways. Most school textbooks of American history and American literature reinforce the former image by presenting information and images about Native Americans through the end of the nineteenth century; twentieth century Indians don't appear, implying to children and youth that Native Americans were a people who lived long ago and then ceased to exist, except perhaps for a few living on reservations. What should Native American children and youth make of this? How do they explain to their peers that the books are wrong? Would their peers listen?

Many American schools continue to present inappropriate and even negative perspectives on Native Americans in textbooks and educational materials. As long as history textbooks continue to present Indians as a nineteenth century phenomenon, the only images children will have of Indian people will be based on stereotypes of the Plains Indians wearing moccasins and headdresses. Ask a child what kind of home Indians live in and you're likely to hear "tepee."

Children are not taught the historic diversity of Native American cultures. Diversity was reflected

> (White people) are trapped in a history which they do not understand; and until they understand it, they cannot be released from it.
>
> JAMES BALDWIN (1924–1987)

in the variety of housing—the long houses of such Northeastern woodland Indians as the Wampanoag; Pawnee earth homes later copied by Midwest pioneers for their sod houses; grass houses of the Wichita; adobe houses of the Navajo; log houses of Northwestern Indians including the Kwakiutl. Textbooks also suffer from an absence of information on contemporary Native Americans. Children are not taught about Indians living in urban areas or

FIGURE 5.4

about current issues such as the resistance by reservation Indians to the use of their land as sites for dumping toxic wastes or other forms of environmental exploitation (Hendry, 2003).

Some of the ways schools teach or reinforce Indian stereotypes go beyond the textbook. Freire (1970) wrote, "The more the oppressors control the oppressed, the more they change them into apparently inanimate things" (p. 45). An Indian mascot is such a "thing." Connolly (2000) documents that many Native American individuals and tribal councils across the nation have clearly stated that Indian logos and mascots for sports teams are racist and offensive. They have asked schools and colleges displaying such images to discontinue this practice. Most sports fans say they don't see what is so offensive, insisting that these mascots are meant to honor and show respect for Native Americans. Apparently we only honor Indians when Indians don't ask us to do something we don't want to do, such as eliminating Indian mascots. We argue that Indian mascots honor a proud, fighting spirit; meanwhile we criticize or ignore Indians who proudly fight to eliminate the use of Indian mascots.

What is the current status of relations between Native Americans and the dominant society?

One of the few facts about contemporary Indians that is widely known by white people—and often resented—is that Indians operate casinos. If any U.S. state sanctions gambling activity, then by federal law it is legal for Native Americans living on reservations in that state to operate gambling casinos. Although Indian Sovereignty allows Indian people the right to have casinos, less than 1 percent of the total Native American population makes substantial revenue from gambling. American Indians have been criticized for operating casinos, even though profits often have been employed to purchase land, build or improve schools, offer academic scholarships, support job-training programs, create jobs, and fund an array of projects intended to improve opportunities for Indian people and perpetuate their culture. Casinos do not exist on all Indian reservations, nor do all Indians approve of them. Especially among tribal elders, casinos on reservations have raised ethical and spiritual questions. In time, it may become more apparent whether casinos have been a blessing or a curse.

Indigenous people struggle with a variety of issues. Despite the financial gains from casinos on a few reservations, many living on reservations still confront consequences of their forced assimilation into the dominant society such as extremely high unemployment rates, low school completion rates, widespread domestic abuse, and considerable alcoholism. Tribal elders have witnessed the deterioration of cultural traditions and ancient beliefs and fear that the survival of their people is in jeopardy. Some American Indians are opposing mining companies and other corporate enterprises that have identified resources on reservation land and are engaged in activities to secure mineral or water rights (Gedicks, 1993; Matthiessen, 1984). It is an ongoing struggle for indigenous people, a struggle for survival.

AFTERWORD

Human evolution is a story of survival, but once physical survival as a group is assured, human beings create cultures. The struggle for survival of the many indigenous cultures in America began when the first European colonists stepped on American shores. The roots of oppression grew in the cultural and physical conflict that followed; this oppression eventually encompassed African slaves, Chinese laborers, Latino migrant workers, and other immigrants of color. The subjugation of Native Americans illustrates an oppression that has been directed not only against racial and ethnic groups in the United States, but against other subordinate groups as well. Oppression of Indians and others by the dominant American society can be understood by using the following definition from Andrzejewski (1996):

> **Oppression** exists when any entity (society, organization, group, or individual) intentionally or unintentionally distributes resources inequitably, refuses to share power, imposes ethnocentric culture, and/or maintains unresponsive and inflexible institutions toward another entity for its supposed benefit and rationalizes its action by blaming or ignoring the victim. (p. 56)

Four areas for observing oppressive behavior are identified in this definition: culture, resources, power, and institutions. When colonists settled in the New World they did not recognize existing cultures of indigenous peoples, but instead attempted to impose European culture. American colonists did not coexist peacefully with Native Americans by sharing land and resources; instead colonists, and later most Americans, employed their power to take the land and its resources away from indigenous people, forcing them from their homes, relocating them, and relegating them to less and less land, leaving them with minimal reservation lands.

Institutionally, colonists and representatives of state and federal governments have managed laws and agencies charged with interpreting or enforcing laws to legitimize their acquisition of Indian land, whether by force, deceit, or threat. When Indians in the past or present have protested, they have often been ignored or told that what was being done was for their benefit. Even when the stakes are not as high, as in the protest against Indian mascots, members of the dominant society continue to ignore Indians or to insist that such mascots are a good thing because they honor and preserve "Indian heritage." The roots of a particularly vicious form of oppression have flourished in this paradise to which the colonists came in pursuit of the same freedom and opportunities that have been denied to indigenous people.

These roots of oppression have expanded over the years and have affected other individuals of color who also came to the United States seeking the same vision of freedom and opportunity that brought the first colonists. We are now a nation of nations, a people who have come from all over the world in pursuit of the happiness promised by a free society. If the United States is to be a pluralistic society embracing diverse groups, it must make sure not only that the first Americans are not excluded, but also that they are given a special place in our diverse national family. There is still much to learn from Native Americans. The time has come to listen.

> It is in remembering that our power lies, and our future comes. This is the Indian way.
>
> ANNA L. WALTERS (1946–)

TERMS AND DEFINITIONS

Ethnocentrism The belief that one's race, nation, or culture is superior to all others; also individual actions or institutional practices based on that belief

Indian sovereignty The legal right of Indian nations, confirmed by their treaties with the U.S. government, to define themselves and to act as unique entities

Indigenous people A racial or ethnic group that is well established in an area before the arrival of a new group; a group that may be but does not need be native to the area in which it is established

Nomads A group of persons with no single fixed abode who move from place to place in search of food and water

Oppression Actions of one entity, such as a society, organization, group, or individual, that intentionally or unintentionally for its supposed benefit: distributes resources inequitably, refuses to share power, imposes on others its ethnocentric culture, and/or maintains unresponsive and inflexible institutions toward another entity, and ultimately rationalizes its actions by blaming or ignoring the victim entity

Treaty A formal, legal agreement between two (or more) nations involving terms of peace, trade, and other matters as agreed to by the negotiating parties

REFERENCES

American Rivers. (2000). *River issues: Dam removal.* Retrieved June 28, 2002, from *http://www.amrivers.org*
Describes the rationale and evidence for not rebuilding deteriorating dams across the United States because of ecological damage they have caused.

Andrzejewski, J. (1996). Definitions for understanding oppression and social justice. In J. Andrzejewski (Ed.), *Oppression and social justice: Critical frameworks* (5th ed., pp. 52–59). Needham, MA: Simon & Schuster.
Provides definitions for a variety of terms essential for discussing intergroup relations.

Barzun, J. (2000). *From dawn to decadence: 500 years of Western cultural life (1500 to the present).* New York: HarperCollins.
Discusses significant historical events as well as the intellectual contributions of those individuals who have had a lasting impact on the culture of the western world.

Berkhofer, Jr., R. (1978). *The white man's Indian: Images of the American Indian from Columbus to the present.* New York: Vintage Books.
Examines legal manipulations by Europeans with regard to land claims in the new world. See especially "The Colonial Foundations of White Indian Policy" (pp. 115–134).

Bieder, R.E. (1995). *Native American communities in Wisconsin, 1600–1960: A study of tradition and change.* Madison: The University of Wisconsin Press.
Describes the history of Indian tribes in Wisconsin and examines the impact of efforts at the state and federal level to promote their assimilation.

Chatters, J.C. (2001). Routes of passage. In *Ancient encounters: Kennewick Man and the first Americans* (pp. 239–264). New York: Simon & Schuster.
Addresses archeological discoveries that place human beings in North and South America much earlier than can be accounted for by the Bering Strait theory of migration.

Connolly, M.R. (2000, September/October). What's in a name?: A historical look at Native American-related nicknames and symbols at three U.S. universities. *The Journal of Higher Education 17*(5), 515–548.
Examines the Indian mascot issue by focusing specifically on efforts to change the mascots at the University of Illinois, Miami of Ohio, and Eastern Michigan University.

Deloria, P. (1993). Sovereignty. In B. Ballantine & I. Ballantine (Eds.), *The Native Americans: An illustrated history* (pp. 384–462). Atlanta: Turner.
Defines and describes Indian sovereignty as a historical concept and explains why it continues to be an important concern for Native Americans.

Evans, S. (1989). *Born for liberty: A history of women in America.* New York: The Free Press.
Describes the experiences of women in America beginning with indigenous women and including women of color as well as the European women immigrants.

Freire, P. (1970). *Pedagogy of the oppressed.* New York: Seabury Press.
Analyzes the dynamics of oppression including the role of the oppressor, the responses of the oppressed, and the consequences of oppression for both.

Gedicks, A. (1993). *The new resource wars: Native and environmental struggles against multinational corporations.* Boston: South End Press.

Examines Indian resistance to corporate exploitation globally and efforts in Wisconsin to protect the environment by opposing mining plans of two multinational corporations.

Gell-Mann, M. (1994). *The quark and the jaguar: Adventures in the simple and the complex.* New York: W.H. Freeman.

Integrates knowledge from research in the sciences, primarily physics, to explore various issues such as the need to preserve cultural and biological diversity (Chapter 21).

Hendry, J. (2003). Mining the sacred mountain: The clash between the Western dualistic framework and native American religions. *Multicultural Perspectives* 5(1), 3–10.

Contrasts patterns of western thought with the perspective of Native Americans especially with regard to their views of nature and the protection of the environment.

Jennings, F. (1976). *The invasion of America: Indians, colonialism, and the cant of conquest.* New York: W.W. Norton.

Describes the conflict between the Pequot and Narragansett Indians in Chapter 13.

Josephy, Jr., A. (1994). *500 nations: An illustrated history of North American Indians.* New York: Knopf.

Provides information on conflicts between Indians and the dominant society, the treaties made and broken (served as the basis for the PBS documentary "500 Nations").

Le May, J.L. (Ed.). (1987). *Benjamin Franklin: Writings* (pp. 442–446). New York: Library of America.

Franklin's comment can be found in "Securing the Friendship of the Indians: A letter to James Parker."

Loewen, J. (1995). *Lies my teacher told me: Everything your American history textbook got wrong.* New York: The New Press.

Describes distortions and omissions in high school history textbooks, including the lack of accurate information on the treatment of the Arawaks by Columbus.

Matthiessen, P. (1984). *Indian country.* London: Flamingo.

Analyzes conflicts between Indians and the dominant society, where land continues to be the source of the dispute.

Parfit, M., & Garrett, K. (2000, December). Hunt for the first Americans. *National Geographic* 198(40), 40–64.

Explains how recent archaeological discoveries have changed the way anthropologists think about prehistoric Native Americans.

Perdue, T. (1998). *Cherokee women: Gender and culture change, 1700–1835.* Lincoln: University of Nebraska Press.

Examines the role of women in traditional Cherokee society and how that role was changed by contact with European colonists and ongoing relations with the dominant society.

Satz, R.N. (1991). Chippewa treaty rights: The reserved rights of Wisconsin's Chippewa Indians in historical perspective. *Transactions* 79(1). Eau Claire: Wisconsin Academy of Sciences, Arts and Letters.

Describes the relationship between the Chippewa Indians and the U.S. government, the treaties they signed, and the subsequent curtailment and violation of treaty rights.

Smith, V. (2001). Cleanliness. In P. Sterns (Ed.), *Encyclopedia of European social history: From 1350 to 2000* (Vol. 4, pp. 343–353). New York: Scribner.

Describes how attitudes and practices with regard to cleanliness have evolved since the Middle Ages (from a six-volume encyclopedia).

Spring, J. (2001). *Deculturalization and the struggle for equality: A brief history of the education of dominated cultures in the United States* (3rd ed.). Boston: McGraw Hill.

Presents a concise history of racism in the United States with special attention given to the impact of school policies on members of subordinate groups.

Suzuki, D., & Knudtson, P. (1992). *Wisdom of the elders: Honoring sacred native visions of nature.* New York: Bantam Books.

Provides information on Native American knowledge of herbal medicine, their perceptions of nature, and their efforts to interact harmoniously with nature.

Tuchman, B. (1978). *A distant mirror: The calamitous 14th Century.* New York: Ballantine.

Includes graphic descriptions of the difficulties for the average European prior to the discovery of the new world.

Wagner, S.R. (1996). *The untold story of the Iroquois influence on early feminists.* Aberdeen, SD: Sky Carrier Press.

Presents evidence to support the argument that nineteenth century feminists were influenced by their awareness of women's rights in Native American societies.

Wallace, A. (1993). *The long, bitter trail: Andrew Jackson and the Indians.* New York: Hill & Wang.

Describes the forced removal of the Cherokee to Oklahoma known as the "Trail of Tears."

Weatherford, J. (1988). *Indian givers: How the Indians of the Americas transformed the world.* New York: Fawcett.

Identifies specific examples of Indian knowledge or products borrowed by Europeans and, that in some instances have been associated with Europe (the Irish potato, German chocolate).

White, R. (1993). Expansion and exodus. In B. Ballantine & I. Ballantine (Eds.), *The native Americans: An illustrated history* (pp. 211–299). Atlanta: Turner Publishing.

Describes the failed efforts of Native Americans to reconstruct the world destroyed by contact with whites, and the institutions and values created to replace what was lost.

Williams, W.C. (1954). The American background. *Selected essays of William Carlos Williams* (pp. 134–161). New York: Random House.

Examines colonial ethnocentrism and provides several examples such as the misnaming of the robin.

Wilson, J. (1998). *The earth shall weep: A history of native America*. New York: Atlantic Monthly Press.

Describes the history of Native American nations and relations with the dominant society.

Woodward, G.S. (1988). *The Cherokees*. Norman: University of Oklahoma Press.

Presents the history of the Cherokee nation and their struggle to maintain their culture and sovereignty despite the "trail of tears" and treaty violations.

Zinn, H. (1999). *A people's history of the United States*. New York: HarperCollins.

Provides a detailed account concerning Columbus and the Arawaks in the first chapter, "Columbus, the Indians and Human Progress."

Summary Exercises

See page 19 for exercises to help you summarize the main points and define key terms in this chapter.

Personal Clarification Exercises

In Chapter 5, two exercises promote discussion about our sensitivity to issues of oppression.

Clarification Exercise #1 Finding Bias in Instructional Materials

Directions: In teams of two, identify all biased information contained in the statements below that were originally developed as an elementary punctuation exercise. Passages can be identified as Cultural Imposition, Exotic Creatures, Ethnocentric Attribution, or Stereotype (Overgeneralization). Based upon these categories, when you find that biased items exist, explain to your teammate in what way that word, phrase or sentence is biased and which category that item best represents. Underline the word or words that you judge need replacement. When you have completed discussing and revising all items, prepare to share with other teams your identification and revisions of the words and phrases, and the reasoning that prompted your modifications. Before moving to another item for discussion, be satisfied with your own understanding of bias in that passage.

Bias in Instructional Materials

1. Indians lived in our country many years before the white man.
2. Have you ever seen an Indian?
3. Indians belong to the red race.
4. Their skin is of a copper color.
5. Most of the men are called warriors.
6. The women are called squaws.
7. Do they live in wigwams and tepees?
8. The red man's name for corn was maize.
9. Were bows and arrows used for hunting by the Indians?
10. A group of Indians living together is called a "tribe."
11. Do little Indian girls and boys play games?
12. The squaws carried their babies on their backs.
13. What does each Indian tribe call its "leader."
14. The leader of each tribe is called a "chief."
15. A few Indian tribes still live in the western part of our country.

Clarification Exercise #2 The Mascot and Place Name Game

Directions: In groups of four to five:
A. List as many American Indian mascot names or publicly recognized place names as you can. Recall names from public or parochial elementary, middle, or secondary schools, from professional sports teams, from structures or natural sites, and from terms that are said or assumed to honor Native Americans. You may include such mascot names as Atlanta Braves, place names such as Squaw Peak, and terms such as "Wild as Indians." Consider carefully historic site names before including them on your list.
B. Merge your lists with those of others in the class as a public display for all to see. Discuss and clarify any terms that are unclear.
C. Agree upon a system to categorize your Native American names into at least three different subgroups. Revise your lists under those headings.
D. Develop an all-group explanation of how some names are disrespectful to Native Americans.
   • To your knowledge, are any terms or names acceptable to Native Americans?
   • How might a Native American explain that place names and mascots are not acceptable?

Intergroup Exercises

In Chapter 5, two exercises promote discussion about our sensitivity to issues of oppression.

Intergroup Exercise #1 Cultural Condescension Activity: The New Kid Comes to School

Directions: In groups of five,
A. Read the situation described below.
B. Then, select a person to be the non-Indian, another to be the teacher, and three to be classmates.
C. Discuss the situation presented. *New student:* Prepare to act the way that character must think and feel; get ideas from others in your group. *Teacher:* Understand the role that the teacher is playing in

this classroom; discuss with others his or her character and how the teacher is being positive, but understand what perspective he or she presents. *Children:* Discern how you are cooperative but limited in your understanding of the American white culture.

D. Next, in your groups, read your parts aloud as a reader's theater rehearsal; add as much interpretative inflection as possible. Continue the scenario into at least one additional episode before stopping this exercise.

E. When you stop, each character should write in his or her personal note-taking journals at least one paragraph explaining how he or she felt.

F. Join together with those same characters from other groups. Explain to the entire class what thoughts went through your minds as you portrayed those characters and what you wrote in your journals. Begin with the Teachers, then the Children, and last those who were the "non-Indian" new classmates.

The New Kid Comes to School

Imagine that you are *not* a Native American, a "non-Indian" elementary student walking into a classroom where everyone else—teacher and students—is American Indian. When you walk in, all of the students are at the front of the room chatting with the teacher. She looks up:

"Ah, the new student. Welcome! Have a seat. You're a non-Indian aren't you? We were just talking about your people."

The children look at you; some giggle and whisper to each other. None of the people in the room looks or sounds like the people in your family. You look around the room. There are dolls in a bed and pictures on the wall and faces on book covers, but none of them has eyes or hair or skin color like you and your family. Then you notice one poster on a bulletin board with people who look like you—the poster says, "Thanksgiving: A Non-Indian Holiday." The poster has a grotesque picture of a non-Indian woman in Reeboks and a Pilgrim hat, holding a dead turkey in one hand and a machine gun in the other. Your classmates giggle when they look at the poster.

"Look at those funny shoes," you hear someone whisper. You look down at your favorite pair of Reeboks and sit quickly at a desk, shoving your feet out of sight. The teacher begins to speak.

"Now class, it's very important to remember that our non-Indian friends are not responsible for what their forefathers did. They stole our land and ruined our forests, but that was a long time ago. We're not going to talk about that today. Now, who can tell me what kind of houses the non-Indians live in?" Several students raise their hands; the teacher calls on a student.

"Their houses are square with red tile roofs."

"That's right, and who are the people living in them?" Most students don't know, but one or two raise their hands enthusiastically. The teacher nods at one of them.

"The mother and father and the children."

"Very good." One student seems puzzled and raises his hand. "Yes, do you have a question?"

"What about the grandmother and grandfather?"

"Oh no, they don't have their grandmother or grandfather live with them like we do; they send them away to special places called retirement homes." The children seem surprised, even shocked, and call out "Why?"

"I don't know why, children. Perhaps later on we can ask our new student about this. Now, next week during Thanksgiving we'll have a unit on Non-Indians. We'll make a Non-Indian town out of clay. It's called a 'suburb.' Can you say 'suburb'? Non-Indians sleep in separate rooms in their homes and they have little houses near or attached to their homes where they keep their cars. Here is a Non-Indian hat." The teacher pulls out a Pilgrim's hat and keeps talking . . . .

MODIFIED FROM: CLARK, DEWOLF, & CLARK "TEACHING TEACHERS TO AVOID HAVING CULTURALLY ASSAULTIVE CLASSROOMS," *YOUNG CHILDREN*, JULY, 1992

Intergroup Exercise #2: Athabaskan Teaching Lesson Activity

Directions: In discussion groups:

1. Read the "Note" below. Next read the story: "Athabaskan Teaching Lesson." Then,

2. In your discussion groups:
   - List at least five possible outcomes where the lesson being taught in the story below could

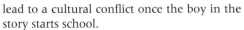

lead to a cultural conflict once the boy in the story starts school.

- Discuss what teachers need to do in order to make the most of any culture they encounter.

3. Be prepared to present your group list of items to the other discussion groups for a final discussion of cultural differences in the education of children.

Note: In Cultural Conflict in the Classroom, Lisa Delpit wrote that in Alaska, native Eskimo children of the Athabaskan society often perceive white teachers as "unbelievable tyrants" who tell them when to go to the bathroom, when to go to lunch, and when to put your work away whether you are finished or not. To Alaskan communities like those of the Athabaskans, Delpit reports that these are "foreign and dangerous" concepts.

In contrast to the rhetoric coming from American educators about teaching thinking skills, the reality may be that we are not teaching children to be independent thinkers, but to be dependent on external authority "for direction, for truth, for meaning." Too often, Delpit writes, American teachers have insisted upon finding meaning solely from books and tend to teach children to believe things are true even when truths conflict with their own common sense.

An Athabaskan Teaching Lesson

A little boy went out with his grandfather and other men to hunt bear. After capturing a bear and placing it in a pit for skinning, the grandfather sent the boy for water to assist in the process. As the boy moved away from the group, his grandfather called after him, "Run, run, the bear is after you!" The boy tensed, started to run, then stopped and calmly continued walking. His grandfather called again, louder, "Run, run I say! This bear is going to catch and eat you!" But the boy continued to walk. When the boy returned with the water, his grandfather was very happy. He had passed the test. The purpose of this test was to teach the boy to disregard the words of another, even a wise and trusted person like his grandfather, if the advice did not make sense according to his own perceptions. To the Athabaskan Alaskan Indian people, it is essential that each person learn to rely on his or her own observations.

FROM: **OTHER PEOPLE'S CHILDREN: CULTURAL CONFLICT IN THE CLASSROOM LISA DELPIT (1995, PP. 101–102)**

CHAPTER 6

Nativism: The Paradox of Xenophobia in a Nation of Immigrants

"We are all citizens of one world; we are all of one blood. To hate someone because he was born in another country, because he speaks a different language or because he takes a different view on a subject, is a great folly."

JOHN COMENIUS (1592–1670)

A s British colonists settled in America, they struggled with the issue of ethnic diversity because the need for more people to settle this new land conflicted with their **xenophobia**—the fear of or prejudice against people from other nations. There was no such struggle with racial diversity. As Kammen (1972) noted, European colonists came to America with racist notions of primitive Africans and savage Indians that justified enslaving them; seeds of white supremacy were sustained—and nurtured—on American soil. Ethnic diversity, however, was different. As the dominant ethnic group, British immigrants witnessed people from other European nations coming to the colonies, creating the difficult task of coexistence in a diverse community of immigrants. The challenge of devising an appropriate response to diversity has never been fully resolved. Instead, America has been enmeshed in an ongoing paradox of established immigrants fearing each wave of newcomers.

As the dominant ethnic group, how did British colonists react to diversity?

Part of the dilemma of ethnic diversity was the determination of British colonists to retain their identity. The French who settled to the north in Canada had readily adapted to Indian ways, especially with regard to economic practices such as trapping and through intermarriage with Native American women. The Spanish came as conquerors, but after their conquest, they still required Indian labor to sustain their control of conquered territory. Like the French, the Spanish borrowed cultural elements from conquered peoples, and intermarriages produced what would eventually be termed a new race: "La Raza."

Those who settled the English-speaking colonies tended to emigrate in family groups. Although some immigrants came to seek their fortune and return home, most came to establish permanent settlements. The British came as subjects of the English king, prepared to create an English colony as an extension of Britain. Although settlers occasionally used information gained from Indians about such things as edible plants and food preparation, their goal was to recreate as much of the Old World as was possible in the New World.

The problem with recreating the Old World was that it was not possible to make the colonies into a *New England.* In addition to British colonists (English, Scottish, and Irish), significant numbers of Dutch, German, and French colonists arrived, as well as small groups from other European countries and adventurers from parts of the world other than Europe. Germans in particular were as adamant as the English about maintaining their cultural heritage. They lived together in communities, spoke to each other in German, posted signs in German, imported books from Germany, and founded schools where their children were taught in German.

By the beginning of the eighteenth century, British colonial leaders became so alarmed by German behavior that some called for restricting or excluding Germans from further immigration. Benjamin Franklin believed it was necessary to Anglicize the Germans because of the size of their population. As their numbers continued to grow, he feared that the Germans would "shortly be so numerous as to Germanize us instead of us Anglifying them" (Feagin, 1997, p. 18). Although Franklin obviously shared the desire of British colonists to Anglicize the colonies, he also recognized positive attributes of German immigrants and the contributions they were making to colonial development: "All that seems necessary is to distribute them more equally, mix them with the English, and establish

> Law is a reflection and source of prejudice. It both enforces and suggests forms of bias.
>
> DIANE SCHULDER (1937–)

English schools where they are now too thick settled" (Brands, 2000, p. 219).

Franklin was concerned with Anglicizing Germans and all immigrants who were not from Britain and, therefore, unfamiliar with British customs and language. In 1749, he sponsored the establishment of a school that included no foreign language instruction. His desire to Anglicize foreign colonists was also reflected in the views of President George Washington: "The more homogeneous our citizens can be made . . . the greater will be our prospect of permanent union" (Kammen, 1972, p. 74). Perhaps the desire for a more homogeneous citizenry was the reason the New American Congress passed a law in 1790 that limited citizenship in the United States to immigrants who were "white" persons. This early expression of xenophobia would lead to the growth of nativism in the United States.

CAUSES OF XENOPHOBIA AND NATIVISM IN THE UNITED STATES

Assimilation refers to a process in which immigrants adopt cultural traits from their host country and are absorbed into society. British colonists preferred a homogeneous population of immigrants who could be assimilated into a dominant Anglo culture, but immigrants from other countries often demonstrated a persistent wish to maintain their own ethnic heritages. Their desires contributed to the development of xenophobia in response to the constant infusion of ethnicities among immigrants to America. When established immigrants, who considered themselves "natives," felt threatened by the many non-British immigrants in their midst, organizations based on nativist concerns would appear. Feagin and Feagin (1996) define **nativism** as "an anti-immigrant ideology that advocates the protection of native inhabitants of a country from [new or potential] immigrants who are seen as threatening or dangerous" (p. 503).

DID AFRICANS IMMIGRATE TO AMERICA?

According to Smedley (1999), some Africans came to Jamestown as laborers in 1619. A slow but steady stream continued to immigrate to the colonies, especially after tobacco became an important colonial export. Like many European immigrants, most Africans came as indentured servants. After completing the designated years of service, Africans were free to look for work, move to another town, and even vote. Some purchased land or businesses and some even purchased slaves. The existence of slaves has made it difficult for historians to determine how many Africans freely immigrated to the colonies in the early years. By the eighteenth century, the colonies passed legislation separating the group identified as "Negroes" from other servants, leading eventually to the designated status of "permanent, hereditary slavery" (p. 94). Although small numbers of free Blacks continued to exist in the colonies and in the new nation, the enslavement of the vast majority of Africans made the experiences of all African Americans considerably different from those of most other immigrants.

Franklin's desire to Anglicize non-British immigrants and Washington's desire for a homogeneous population can be described as a benign form of nativism based on nationalistic concerns. Although nationalism represents one of the primary themes of nativist activities in the United States, two additional themes have characterized many nativist attitudes and actions: anti-Catholicism and anti-radicalism.

Nativism as anti-Catholicism

Although the religious beliefs of Benjamin Franklin, Thomas Jefferson, and other founders of the American republic were quite different from those of most Christians today, at its birth the United States was a nation strongly influenced by Protestant Christianity. The presence of Catholics had been tolerated throughout the colonial period, but by 1820, the 200,000 Catholics in the United States stimulated anti-Catholic sentiment, especially in urban areas. By 1850, there were almost two million Catholics in the United States; the Irish alone constituted 42% of that foreign-born population (Fuchs, 1990).

Under President John Adams, eligibility for citizenship was established as a minimum of fourteen years residency; this was reduced to five years during Thomas Jefferson's presidency. A political party calling itself "Native Americans" began forming in some of the larger cities; the party lobbied vigorously against immigrants becoming eligible for citizenship after five years. The Native American party insisted on a residency of twenty-one years before an immigrant was eligible for citizenship. Their main concern was voting, arguing that immigrants coming from nations governed by monarchs were not prepared to be self-governing. Since an immigrant came with:

> all his foreign habits, prejudices and predilections . . . can it be believed that he can disburden himself so completely of these, and have so learned to fulfill the duties of a citizen of the United States, in the very short term of five years?" (Myers, 1960, p. 111)

At first, the Native American party encouraged people to welcome immigrants and only opposed their eligibility for citizenship after five years; however, by 1843, the movement had become hostile to continued immigration of both Irish and Catholics. In Philadelphia, the Native American party held a meeting in an Irish district of the city, initiating a confrontation between Protestants and Catholics; the violence that followed culminated in an angry mob setting fire to many buildings, and was reported in newspapers around the country. Federal troops were called in to restore order, which was no easy task, and peace prevailed for a little more than a month before mobs attacked a Catholic church and troops fired at the crowd to force them to disperse. Two more days of violence resulted in two soldiers being killed and twenty-six soldiers wounded.

Nativism as anti-radicalism

Both anti-Catholicism and prejudice against the Irish fueled the nativism movement that flourished briefly in the 1850s, but the other negative sentiment contributing to the success of nativism was anti-radicalism. Most immigrants admitted to the United States in the first decades of the nineteenth century were overwhelmingly impoverished European laborers with minimal skills and little education. Some were sponsored by American capitalists to be contract laborers paid less than the wage native workers would accept. As new immigrant workers adapted to life in the United States, they came to realize how they were being exploited; many joined or helped create unions to demand better wages and benefits by engaging in strikes, marches, and protests. Nativists saw union actions as un-American, especially when the "foreigners" expressed socialist, anarchist, or other radical ideas. The antagonism toward what was regarded as radical activities by recent immigrants was clearly and frequently expressed on the editorial pages of urban newspapers (Higham, 1955):

> "Our National existence and . . . our National and social institutions are at stake."
> "These people are not Americans, but the very scum and offal of Europe."
> "There is no such thing as an American anarchist."
> "Europe's human and inhuman rubbish." (p. 55)

The first quotation illustrates the nationalism often expressed in nativist sentiments; the other quotations reveal hostility and a dehumanized view of the perceived "radicals." The un-American implication in each statement is central to the nativist perspective. Nativist concerns at that time also had to do with the decreasing amount of land available for immigrants in the midwest and west; as a result, immigrants increasingly settled in urban areas. Because many immigrants were moving from southern and eastern Europe, land reformer Henry George commented "What, in a few years more, are we to do for a dumping ground? Will it make our difficulty the less that our human garbage can vote?" (Higham, 1955, p. 42). The issue of immigrants becoming eligible for citizenship and voting continued to fuel individual xenophobia, and nativist political actions document a fear of the potential political power of incoming immigrants.

NATIVISM, POLITICS, AND SOCIAL CHANGE

The Native American party never gained political dominance, yet by the 1850s it had prepared the way for the rise of the "Know-Nothings," a somewhat secret movement whose members were told to respond to any question about the organization by saying that they knew nothing about it. Staunchly anti-immigrant and anti-Catholic, Know-Nothings

FIGURE 6.1

This Know-Nothing flag reveals the group's relationship to the Native American Party. The American Eagle is surrounded by flags and is perched behind a ballot box labeled "Twenty-One Years," the length of residency the Native American Party demanded for immigrants prior to being granted citizenship and voting rights.

Source: Photo courtesy of the Milwaukee Co. Historical Society.

were concerned with what they perceived as the growing political influence of Catholics; these fears were confirmed by President Franklin Pierce's appointment of a Catholic, James Campbell, to be the nation's Attorney General.

How successful were the nativists in their political activities?

The Know-Nothings fielded candidates for the American Party, and in 1854 elected nine governors, eight (of 62) senators, and 104 (of 234) members of the House of Representatives (Myers, 1960). In the 1856 elections, Know-Nothing members used force and threats to keep immigrants from voting and encouraged election-day riots in Louisville, Kentucky, and in St. Louis, Missouri. When the Whig Party refused to nominate Millard Fillmore for a second term as President, the American Party nominated him as their candidate. Despite the success of other American Party candidates, Fillmore received only eight electoral votes.

Reaction to the political success of the Know-Nothings was swift. In Congress a resolution was submitted, then voted down, condemning secret organizations and citing the Know-Nothings as a specific example. Political and religious leaders across the nation denounced the activities of the Know-Nothings, including the young political aspirant Abraham Lincoln, who wrote in a letter to a friend:

> As a nation we began by declaring that "all men are created equal." We now practically read it, "all men are created equal except Negroes." When the Know-Nothings obtain control, it will read: "All men are created equal except Negroes, foreigners, and Catholics." (Myers, 1960, p. 146)

Why did nativism fail to become a dominant movement in the United States?

The political success of nativism in the 1850s was brief because the issue of slavery began to take precedence over anti-Catholic prejudice and fears, and it divided the Know-Nothings. By the end of the Civil War, the Know-Nothings and the American party were no longer a political force, although the nativist fears that fueled their activity persisted as a major influence in the United States. As the

American people debated the issue of slavery, American capitalists continued to sponsor importation of labor from overseas to keep wages low and profits high.

Throughout U.S. history, a significant percentage of Americans consisted of recent immigrants or children of immigrants who appreciated the opportunities in America and vigorously opposed attempts by nativists to restrict immigration. Meanwhile, there was constant pressure from society to promote the **Americanization** of immigrants, and public schools carried out societal expectations by encouraging immigrants to abandon their heritage and conform to American ways (Pai and Adler, 1997). Nativist attitudes in the United States continued to wax and wane, our xenophobia historically balanced by those who believed in America as a place for oppressed people to achieve freedom and fortune.

The demand for Americanization of immigrants intensified in the late 1800s as the majority of immigrants were not Northern Europeans—Greeks, Italians, Slavs, and Jews—people who did not conform to the Anglo ideal. Due to an economic downturn in the 1890s, nativism experienced a renewed popularity with American people; then in the ebb and flow of xenophobia, nativist fears succumbed to a confidence inspired by the United States triumph in the Spanish American War and by heroes such as Teddy Roosevelt. Although nativists never again succeeded in sponsoring an independent political party, events in the early twentieth century would establish the foundation for their greatest political triumphs.

What influenced twentieth-century nativist attitudes in America?

It seemed certain to most Americans that if the United States was going to become a dominant political and economic power in the world, immigrants were needed in the labor market of its dynamic economy. But when World War I began, attitudes changed. Nativism surged again, driven by feelings of nationalism and anti-radicalism. German-Americans were singled out for especially opprobrious treatment and their loyalty to the United States was questioned. Rumors abounded that German-Americans were spying for Germany.

Because German-Americans insisted on maintaining their dual identity as Americans of German

> There is no room in this country for hyphenated Americans.
>
> **THEODORE ROOSEVELT (1858–1919)**

FIGURE 6.2

Hull House in Chicago, one of the first settlement houses, has been preserved and is open to visitors.

Source: Courtesy of the Chicago Landmarks Commission

descent, people of influence such as Teddy Roosevelt admonished them by denouncing all immigrants who claimed a dual identity. German-Americans were surprised by such criticisms. From colonial times they had maintained their culture, language, and traditions through separate schools, organizations, and newspapers. Because of their industriousness, efforts to preserve their German heritage had been tolerated by American society until World War I, when nativist individuals and organizations attacked German-Americans for keeping themselves separate and not assimilating to an Anglo ideal.

During World War I, surging patriotism intensified the demand that immigrants be Americanized quickly. Although this nationalism was a less abrasive form of nativism, it became more virulent when reinforced by anti-radical attitudes. Radical organizations were attacked as un-American, especially radical unions like the International Workers of the World, the "Wobblies." Nativists accused certain immigrants of espousing ideas that were disloyal to the country and demanded their deportation.

German-Americans were not the only targets of anti-American accusations. **Anti-Semitism**—having prejudices, stereotypes, or engaging in discrimination against Jews—increased with the success of the Russian Revolution in 1917. Jews were associated not only with communism, but also with international financiers who profited from the war. After World War I, nativists continued to complain that the Anglo ideal for America would disappear if diverse European ethnic groups continued to emigrate; however most Americans seemed to believe that those who came eventually would assimilate into the dominant culture.

By the 1920s, a revised perspective was being expressed. In settlement houses such as Hull House in Chicago, people providing social services began to appreciate the diversity of the immigrants. Social activist Jane Addams, co-founder of Hull House, and University of Chicago philosopher John Dewey described the advantages of diverse cultures and the value of people maintaining their heritages while still learning, as Benjamin Franklin had recommended, the language and customs of American culture. Although resentment toward Germans slowly dissipated after the war, anti-Semitism persisted as part of a new development in xenophobic attitudes in the United States.

What new development affected xenophobic attitudes in the United States?

In 1899, William Z. Ripley, an economist from the Massachusetts Institute of Technology, published a "scientific" study identifying and describing three European races: Teutonic, Alpine, and Mediterranean (Higham, 1955). Based on emerging theories about race, Nativists argued that for U.S. citizenry to achieve unity, immigrants of the blue-eyed, blonde-haired Teutonic type (also called

FIGURE 6.3
This advertisement from a 1923 *Time* magazine warns its readers that the days of white supremacy may be numbered and urges white people who want to do something about it to read Stoddard's book, *The Rising Tide of Color.*

Three books by LOTHROP STODDARD

The Revolt Against Civilization

"The reason why this book has attracted such an extraordinary amount of attention is not far to seek. It is, so far as we know, the first successful attempt to present a scientific explanation of the world-wide epidemic of unrest that broke out during the Great War and still rages in both hemispheres."—*Saturday Evening Post.* $2.50

The New World of Islam

This book is *true*—current events are bearing it out in startling fashion. "He has presented, in compact and readable form, what did not exist before in any language: a short, concise account of the modern Mohammedan world and its reaction to the invasion of the West."—*Atlantic Monthly.*   With maps. $3.00

The Rising Tide of Color

White world supremacy is in danger. The world-wide ascendancy of the white race, apparently so unshakable, is in reality threatened by the colored races. This is a startling book, one for the reader who is able to stand up against the impact of new ideas. It is a clear, sharp warning to the whites, and an appeal for white solidarity.   With maps. $3.00

© Bachrach   LOTHROP STODDARD
From early manhood he has prepared himself, by wide travel and extensive study, to qualify as a true expert on world affairs. His is the mind of a trained observer who has received the soundest scientific training.

"Nordic" or "Anglo Saxon") should be given preference. Senator Henry Cabot Lodge of Massachusetts called for an end to all further immigration to the United States, and Teddy Roosevelt chastised Anglo Saxon women in America for contributing to the possibility of "race suicide" by not producing as many children as immigrant women (Brodkin, 2002). In the aftermath of World War I, pessimism about diverse groups being able to assimilate into an Anglo Saxon American culture fueled racist sentiments expressed in widely read books such as Lathrop Stoddard's *The Rising Tide of Color.*

Madison Grant (1916/1970) provided the most influential expression of this pessimism in *The Passing of the Great Race, Or the Racial Bias of European History.* Grant rejected the idea that immigrants from other than Nordic heritage could achieve the Anglo Saxon ideal; thus the "Great Race" of Anglo Saxons was doomed to disappear in America. Claiming that his ideas were grounded in the emerging science of genetics, Grant concluded that intermarriage between races produced degraded offspring who would revert to lower qualities contained in their parents' genes. Referring to Ripley's three European races, Grant stated, "The cross between any of the European races and a Jew is a Jew" (p. 16). Although many of his contemporaries rejected Grant's anti-Semitism and did not share his concern for the decline of Anglo Saxon superiority, many Americans, including well-known automaker Henry Ford, expressed similar beliefs. Anti-Semitism and racism were incorporated into traditional xenophobic attitudes.

NATIVISM AND RACISM

Nativists used the new racist concern for preserving the nation's Anglo Saxon heritage to sound the alarm about the numbers of immigrants from southern and eastern Europe—80% of all U.S. immigrants from 1900–1910. Stanford University's

> [America can have] a unity created by drawing out and composing into a harmonious whole the best, the most characteristic, which each contributing race and people has to offer.
>
> JOHN DEWEY (1859-1952)

Ellwood P. Cubberley echoed their concerns in his history of education textbook (1919):

> These Southern and Eastern Europeans were of a very different type from the North and West Europeans who preceded them. Largely illiterate, docile, lacking in initiative, and almost wholly without the Anglo-Saxon conceptions of righteousness, liberty, law, order, public decency, and government, their coming has served to dilute tremendously our national stock . . . our national life, for the past quarter of a century, has been afflicted with a serious case of racial indigestion." (p. 338)

Nativists triumphed in 1924 with the passage of an immigration law establishing quotas for immigrants based on country of origin. The quotas ensured that immigrants from northern Europe (the so-called "Nordic" type) would constitute the majority of U.S. immigrants, guidelines that remained largely unchanged for the next four decades.

What groups were affected by the addition of racism to xenophobia?

This new racist form of nativism was directed not only against people of color, but also against white people perceived as not being white enough, which often meant not sharing the common prejudices of the white majority. This was especially observed in southern states. In 1898, debates at Louisiana's state constitutional convention focused on who would be denied the right to vote. Although blacks were the main targets, Italians were considered "as black as the blackest negro in existence" (Barrett and Roediger, 2002, p. 32). Because of such perceptions, some Italians were victims of southern violence in the nineteenth century. In Tallulah, Louisiana, five Sicilian immigrants owned businesses that served primarily black customers. Local whites resented the immigrant storekeepers because they treated black people as equals. Before long, the locals fabricated a quarrel over a goat and lynched the five Sicilians (Higham, 1955).

The idea of perceiving Italians, Irish, or others as separate races based on their national origins seems strange today; yet most Americans, including members of identified "races," accepted this designation. In the 1930s, an Irish campaign manager representing an Irish politician made the following speech at an Italian neighborhood meeting to ask the Italian men to vote for his candidate in the upcoming election:

> Maybe I'm the only Irishman here, but this is not a racial contest. You don't select your man because of his race. There are too many who cry him down because of that. But these people that sit behind closed doors and discriminate against a man because of his race have no place in American life . . .
>
> This district don't house men and women that vote only because of their racial strain. For the immigrants of your race and my race, I have no apology. In the time of need, we answered the call of our country. One of the largest quotas of men was sent out from this district. At that time there was no discrimination because of a man's race, there was no turning men back for that reason. We sent out boys by the thousands in order that we might enjoy the blessings of free government. Here we never turn down a man because of his race or creed. (Whyte, 1955, p. 227)

The idea of national origin defining separate races declined as skin color became the primary determinant of racial identity. As revealing as it is to read the xenophobic comments directed against immigrants of European origin at the beginning of the twentieth century, it is even more enlightening to study the comments directed against immigrants of color. By the 1920s, racist attitudes had become clearly established as a factor influencing xenophobia in response to Spanish-speaking immigrants, principally Mexicans, and especially Asian immigrants including the Japanese and Chinese.

How did nativist attitudes create problems for Asian immigrants?

The first Chinese immigrants in the early 1850s tended to be men lured to California by the promise of finding gold. Like the Chinese who came later, the men planned to return to China after they made their fortune on the "Gold Mountain." By 1870, 63,000 Chinese had come to America, with more than 75% living in California. Although well received at first, the Chinese were soon targeted by the surge of nativist sentiment of the 1850s, as demonstrated by slogans such as "California for Americans" and by the levying of a tax on all those mining for gold who were not U.S. citizens (Takaki, 1993). The Chinese, of course, couldn't become citizens, since the 1790 law restricted citizenship to whites only.

Chinese who were discouraged from mining for gold found work as laborers building the western portion of the transcontinental railroad. Owners of the railroad paid the Chinese less than they paid native workers. When Chinese workers went on strike for higher wages, they were denounced by local newspapers and literally starved into submission when railroad owners cut off food supplies (Takaki, 1993). Some Chinese laborers eventually returned to China, but many stayed, especially in San Francisco.

Wherever they settled, Chinese men continued to be paid low wages, many of them in agricultural jobs. White laborers resented them, and they did not receive much sympathy from the predominantly white public who perceived the Chinese as maintaining a separate identity and as unwilling to become Americanized. White workers would occasionally target Chinese men who maintained traditions such as the "queue," a long single braid of hair worn down their back. Chinese laborers complained of white men grabbing or even cutting off their queue.

In 1871, mob violence resulted in the deaths of twenty-one Chinese immigrants in Los Angeles; in 1885, twenty-eight Chinese railroad workers were killed in Rock Springs, Wyoming (Fong, 2000; Wu, 1972). The violence continued. During an economic recession in the 1890s, unemployed white workers rioted, beating and shooting Chinese workers. Confronted with such hostility and violence, some Chinese avoided competing for jobs with white workers; instead, they pooled their resources to start their own businesses such as general stores, restaurants, or laundries. Although Chinese immigrants constituted less than 1% of the U.S. population in 1882, Congress passed the **Chinese Exclusion Act** prohibiting Chinese immigration for the next ten years; it was renewed for another ten years in 1892, and renewed indefinitely in 1902. The door to the "Gold Mountain" was closed.

Were Chinese immigrants the only targets of anti-Asian xenophobia?

A similar pattern occurred for the Japanese. Having been recruited to Hawaii by plantation owners as cheap labor, 150,000 Japanese men and women immigrated to the United States between 1880 and 1908 (Takaki, 1993). The Japanese government hoped to avoid problems Chinese men had encountered by encouraging Japanese women to immigrate, but it seemed to make no difference to California nativists, who still complained about the number of Japanese in the state. In 1905, California newspapers initiated a campaign against the "**Yellow Peril**" based on the belief that Japanese immigrants, like the Chinese, could not or would not assimilate into American culture.

Nativists insisted on excluding the Japanese from further immigration. After the California legislature passed a resolution calling for the prohibition of Japanese immigration, President Theodore Roosevelt negotiated a **Gentleman's Agreement** in 1908. The Japanese government agreed to issue no more passports to Japanese workers beyond those already in the United States and their close relatives. Unlike the Chinese, Japanese could use this loophole to bring wives—"picture brides"—and families to the United States until 1920, when exclusion became complete.

How did Americans respond to the immigration of Spanish-speaking people?

The combination of nativism and racism was also found in the experiences of Latinos in the United States; especially egregious was the plight of Latinos who were not immigrants. In the aftermath of the Mexican-American War, 100,000 Mexicans suddenly found themselves living in territory belonging to the United States, and Mexican landowners were forced to defend their land claims in U.S. courts. Despite assurances that legitimate claims would be honored, most Mexican landowners lost their land. Since legal arguments were conducted exclusively in English, landowners had to hire white lawyers with whom they had no pre-existing relationship or influence. Those who lost their court cases also lost their land; other Mexican landowners sold part of

Immigrants of color never have . . . (been) fully assimilated into U.S. society. They instead join a racially stratified society with deep inequalities (that) will forever deny them the opportunity available to their white counterparts to be fully integrated into the national community.

KEVIN JOHNSON (1958–)

their land to pay legal fees. Some landowners won their cases, only to return home to find white squatters on their land refusing to leave. With no support from local law enforcement, many were forced to sell their land. Only a few Mexican landowners held onto the land they owned before the war (Feagin and Feagin, 1996).

The decision by Mexican laborers to migrate to the United States for work has been a pattern for over a century. In the late 1880s, Mexican workers in the Southwest built or restored old Anasazi irrigation ditches, cleared land for planting, and picked cotton. They worked in mines and for the railroads; yet like Chinese, Japanese, and other minority workers, they were paid less than whites even when they did the same work. In 1903, Mexican and Japanese farm workers formed a union, went on strike for better wages, and won, but they knew the union could not survive unless it affiliated with the American Federation of Labor (AFL). AFL President Samuel Gompers agreed to the affiliation if the union would expel its Asian members; Mexican workers refused, and the union was not able to maintain its existence without AFL support.

Latinos from Central and South America also immigrated to "El Norte" in search of jobs and opportunities. Sometimes they were escaping from oppressive governments or death threats, yet they still encountered xenophobia similar to that of other immigrants of color. Today, this reaction is related to changes in U.S. immigration laws that overturned the most significant nativist achievement—the 1924 immigration law.

IMMIGRATION REFORM AND THE RESURGENCE OF NATIVISM

As the civil rights movement gained momentum, allegations of racism were made in many areas. President John Kennedy admitted to inequities in immigration policies based on the 1924 law.

FIGURE 6.4 The cartoonist is satirizing the contrast between the noble ideas expressed in the Emma Lazarus poem on the Statue of Liberty with the reality of immigration policy.

Source: ©1981 by John Trevor, *Albuquerque Journal.* Reprinted by permission.

Attorney General Robert Kennedy characteristically stated the issue more bluntly, "As we are working to remove the vestiges of racism from our public life, we cannot maintain racism as the cornerstone of our immigration laws" (Eck, 2001, p. 7). In 1965, Congress amended immigration laws to eliminate the racially biased National Origins Quotas. From 1968–1993, 80% of the people immigrating to the United States came from Central or South America, the Caribbean, and Asia (Roberts, 1997). The influx of Latino immigrants spawned a renewed xenophobia, especially in California.

How have changes in U.S. immigration laws affected nativist attitudes and actions?

The most obvious example of nativist attitudes and actions in recent years occurred in 1994 with the passage in California of **Proposition 187,** which mandated the denial of many basic services to anyone suspected of being an illegal alien. Proposition 187 was opposed by associations whose members would have to enforce its racist provisions: the California School Board Association, California Parent-Teacher Association, California State Employee Association, and California Organization of Police and Sheriffs; the law was approved despite their opposition. Majorities of voters from all ethnic groups opposed Proposition 187; 78% of Latino votes represented the largest majority, but the small percent of minorities who voted for the law in combination with the 54% of white voters who approved the measure resulted in its passage by a substantial majority (Tatalovich, 1997).

Teachers, doctors, nurses, case-workers, and other social service providers were required by Proposition 187 to engage in racist actions: They were compelled to deny services to people based on such factors as "physical appearance," including complexion, height, and hair color; the way the person was dressed; and their speech, speaking with a foreign accent, in "broken" English, or in a foreign language. Professionals in the human services were relieved when the courts declared this law unconstitutional. The xenophobic attitudes responsible for the success of Proposition 187 have also been reflected in another recent and ongoing example of nativist activity—the English Only movement.

How is the English Only movement an example of xenophobic behavior?

The **English Only** movement calls for making English the "official language" of the United States, working toward that goal on a state-by-state basis. The movement is not a recent phenomenon; its resurgence represents a renewal of an older form of nativism disguised as a concern for literacy. The origins of the movement can be found in legislation first proposed by nativists in 1887 requiring immigrants to pass a literacy test; nativists would promote this requirement for the next thirty years. Although the test only required immigrants to be literate in their native language, it was still rejected by the majority in Congress. When nativists finally convinced enough legislators to pass the bill, both Democratic and Republican presidents vetoed it until it was passed over President Wilson's veto in 1917 (Delgado, 1997).

Nativists were supported in their crusade to require literacy tests by scholars and scientists within the growing ranks of the eugenics movement. *Eugenics* was the term describing responses to recent discoveries concerning the role of heredity in human development. British scientist Francis Galton defined **eugenics** as "the study of agencies under social control that may improve or repair the racial qualities of future generations, either physically or mentally" (Lynn, 2001, p. 4). Before the Nazis tainted eugenics with their emphasis on race purification and genocidal activities, some American scholars endorsed the eugenics movement. They were concerned about what they perceived to be a degeneration of the mental abilities of Americans, believing there was a racial component to the problem represented by immigrants whom they regarded as a primary cause of this decline of intelligence in America.

Although the eugenics movement never attracted a majority of academics, some in the eugenics camp were influential scholars: Robert Yerkes of Harvard (President of the American Psychological Association), Lewis Terman of Stanford, and Edward Thorndike from Teachers College, Columbia University (Selden, 1999). Because of their academic interests, Yerkes, Terman, and Thorndike were responsible for developing early intelligence tests (see Table 6.1). When Henry God-

TABLE 6.1 Sample Questions from the World War I Army Mental Tests

Alpha and Beta Tests developed by Psychologists Robert Yerkes, Louis Terman, and Henry Goddard assisted by Carl Campbell Brigham, Founder of Educational Testing Service (ETS)

These sample questions reveal how culturally biased and inappropriate the early tests of "intelligence" could be; yet such tests were used with immigrants to determine which ones were of acceptable intelligence and which were "feeble minded."

FROM ALPHA TEST 8:

2. Five hundred is played with: rackets   pins   cards   dice
3. The Percheron is a kind of: goat   horse   cow   sheep
7. Christy Mathewson is famous as a: writer   artist   baseball player   comedian
10. "There's a reason" is an "ad" for a: drink   revolver   flour   cleanser
19. Crisco is a: patent medicine   disinfectant   tooth-paste   food
29. The Brooklyn Nationals are called the: Giants   Orioles   Superbas   Indians
32. The number of a Kaffir's legs is: two   four   six   eight
35. The forward pass is used in: tennis   hockey   football   golf
38. The Pierce Arrow car is made in: Buffalo   Detroit   Toledo   Flint

Source: Owen, David. *None of the above: The truth behind the SATs,* 1999, p. 176.

dard implemented intelligence tests with the immigrants at Ellis Island, he reported that 80 percent were "feeble minded" (Brodkin, 2002).

Because some respected scholars supported it, the eugenics movement flourished from 1910 to 1940, shaping the content of biology textbooks, reinforcing popular views concerning white supremacy, and contributing to the growth of anti-immigrant attitudes. One legacy of the eugenics movement is the standardized testing used to measure academic achievement that students still take today—but testing is not the only legacy of the eugenics movement.

Established in 1937 to promote eugenics policies, the Pioneer Fund advocated the forcible removal of "American Negroes" to Africa. The first Pioneer Fund President, Harry Laughlin, wrote the Model Eugenical Sterilization Law adopted by thirty states in the United States and Nazi Germany. Laughlin proposed that Adolf Hitler be given honorary membership in the American Eugenics Society. The Pioneer Fund continues to support scholars working on race-based IQ theories, including work employed in support of the controversial comments about race made in *The Bell Curve* (Herrnstein and Murray, 1994). The Pioneer Fund also supported a recent book by Lynn (2001) arguing in favor of eugenic principles, and has continued to be a major funding source for the English Only movement (Tatalovich, 1997).

What appropriate actions can the United States take to encourage immigrants to learn English?

Immigrants have always tended to learn English out of necessity for economic and social well-being. Today, fewer than 14% of Americans speak a language other than English: less than 6 percent of Americans speak no English (Wiley, 1997). Despite these facts, the English Only movement has been successful in promoting state legislation to establish English as the official language. Almost half the states have existing laws declaring English as the official language. Some laws are largely symbolic, and no penalties are enforced and there is no prohibition against teaching foreign languages or implementing and supporting bilingual programs. However, some state laws prohibit their governments from printing materials in other languages.

> We must get rid of fear; we cannot act at all till then. A man's acts are slavish, not true but specious; his very thoughts are false, he thinks as a slave and coward, till he have got fear under his feet.
>
> THOMAS CARLYLE (1795–1881)

Since Spanish is the first language of a significant percentage of immigrants, English Only laws prevent recent immigrants who are trying to learn English from having access to useful information. Such laws may also prevent legally eligible people from voting (Tatalovich, 1997). Whether symbolic or harmful, English Only laws reflect the xenophobic reaction of a great many people in the United States against many of our recent immigrants, primarily people of color whose first language is not English and who may not yet be literate in English. English Only laws justify the antagonism some individuals feel toward people speaking a different language; at times this antagonism even results in violence.

Why do xenophobic attitudes promote violent behavior?

Today, immigrants or people who appear to be immigrants can still be victims of violence. Recent Cambodian, Vietnamese, and Hmong immigrants can attest to this. White shrimp fishermen in Texas threatened Vietnamese fishermen when shrimp became scarce. In Wisconsin, a young white male attacked a Japanese exchange student whom he mistakenly believed was a Hmong immigrant. Xenophobia encourages individuals to see recent immigrants as "foreign"; instead of applauding their hard work and success, xenophobia causes people to criticize immigrants for taking "our" jobs. This kind of prejudice against foreigners can intensify into hatred, and hatred often leads to violent behavior.

A dramatic example reported by the national media occurred in 1982 when a Chinese American named Vincent Chin was murdered. Two automo-

bile workers attributed the recent loss of their jobs to the success of imported Japanese cars. When they encountered Vincent Chin, they mistakenly thought he was Japanese and beat him to death with a baseball bat. As often happens with national news stories, the crime and the arrest of the perpetrators were widely reported, but not the resolution of the case. Chin's killers were allowed to plead guilty to manslaughter and their punishment for taking the life of a human being was to be placed on probation for three years and to pay a fine of $3,780 (Chang, 1997, p. 250).

What American nativist attitudes exist today?

Anti-immigrant sentiments are widely expressed in America, and immigrants, including children, hear what is being said about them. As part of a longitudinal study, immigrant youth in high schools were asked what most Americans think about "people from my country"; 65% of their responses were negative—being stupid, lazy, thieves, and gangsters (Suarez-Orozco and Suarez-Orozco, 2001). Negative perceptions are fueled by myths widely believed by Americans concerning "foreigners" legally or illegally entering the United States. Some myths refer specifically to immigrants with refugee status. According to the United Nations, a *refugee* is a person "unable or unwilling to return to his or her country because of a well-founded fear of persecution . . . based on race, religion, nationality, or membership in a particular social group or political party" (Pipher, 2002, p. 18). The following myths reveal current nativist attitudes about immigrants and refugees.

> MYTH #1: Immigrants arrive ignorant, penniless, with very little formal education and immediately have to go on welfare.

Macedo and Bartolome (2001) record an example of this myth being expressed by a former president of Boston University complaining about the number of Cambodians in Massachusetts: "There has to be a welfare magnet going on here. . . . Why should Lowell be the Cambodian capital of America?" (p. 11). In fact, immigrants often have been professionals in their country of origin—doctors, professors, and engineers. Although the figure varies each year, 20% to 25% of U.S. immigrants have earned college degrees (Sorenson and Enchautegui, 1994). Still, even those arriving with college educations may take minimum-wage jobs because institutions or professional organizations in the United States may not recognize their practices, skills, or degrees, forcing them to return to school to be certified in their profession or retrained in related fields. Despite obstacles of language and culture, the percentage of immigrants, including refugees, receiving welfare is approximately the same as native residents (Center for Immigration Studies, 2002; Limon, 1996). The statistics about modern immigrants to the United States document that they rarely become permanent recipients of public assistance.

Immigrants are consumers who pay rent and buy groceries and other products that help to strengthen the economy. Most studies of the economic impact of immigrants report that they ultimately benefit local economies, even taking into account the services that may be required to assist them during their first few years in the country. For example, one Urban Institute study reported that immigrants pay more in taxes than the cost of providing services to them (Cole, 1996). Despite such contributions, some Americans persist in viewing

> All the people like us are We,
> And every one else is They.
>
> **RUDYARD KIPLING (1865–1936)**

non-white immigrants as a problem, such as the Massachusetts man quoted in Macedo and Bartolome (2001) who called a local talk radio program to complain about the recent wave of immigrants: "Why should we be supporting these bilinguals? . . . The problem with Brockton is the Haitians, the Hispanics, the Cape Verdeans that are ruining our neighborhood" (p. 12). The man's hostility is illustrated by his transforming what could be regarded as an asset—the ability to speak more than one language—into a derogatory slur: "bilinguals."

MYTH #2: Immigrants cling to their culture, language, and traditions, and refuse to assimilate into the American "melting pot."

New immigrants have always maintained their cultural heritage, in part because their identity has been profoundly shaped by the native culture. When immigrant children become adults, they typically integrate their cultural heritage with American culture, producing a hybrid of traditions and values taken from both. As for learning English, it is not unusual to find that immigrants are multilingual when they arrive; often English is one of the languages they know. Those not fluent in English will learn it eventually to survive. Recall the earlier figure: Less than 6% of immigrants in the United States have not learned English.

Immigrants pay taxes, send children to schools, serve in the military, and are affected by local political decisions. Recent immigrants have demonstrated their desire to be actively engaged in our democratic society by participating in voter registration efforts and transporting voters to the polls for elections. Since the Constitution leaves the issue of voting qualifications up to the local government, some cities have responded by giving voting rights to immigrants who are not yet citizens. As populations shift globally, 100 nations now allow an individual to have dual citizenship, but the United States has traditionally resisted this idea. The assimilation of immigrants is further complicated by a backlog of those pursuing naturalization, a process that can take years if not decades before they are granted legal permanent resident status, and the process has been delayed even further since the 9/11 tragedy (Wucker, 2003).

MYTH #3: The United States is taking more than its fair share of immigrants; other countries need to take more.

The main difference between U.S. immigration and that of other countries is that more diverse groups are admitted to the United States than are accepted by other countries. Between 70% and

80% of immigrants around the world are refugees. The United States accepts less than 1% of the refugees, while several other countries admit a higher percent. According to the 2000 Census, immigrants constituted 10 percent of the U.S. population, whereas in 1900, they constituted 15% (Pipher, 2002; Passel and Edmonston, 1994).

People who express concerns about excessive admission of immigrants to the United States often refer specifically to Mexicans, who constituted 25% of all legal immigrants in the 1990s, and an undetermined number of illegal immigrants. Current xenophobic attitudes have demanded restrictions on Mexican immigration and more money for border patrols to keep out illegal immigrants. Mexican immigration has not diminished, but increased border scrutiny has caused legal Mexican immigrants to stay in the United States rather than return home for fear they might not be allowed re-entry: The number of those returning to Mexico plummeted in the 1990s. Although stricter border enforcement has not kept illegal immigrants from coming, it has resulted in three times as many deaths of those attempting to enter the United States (Massey, 2003).

> MYTH #4: The main problem with U.S. immigration is the large number of illegal immigrants getting into the country.

Illegal immigrants make up 13% of the immigrant population and about 1% of the U.S. population. According to the Census Bureau, the number of illegal aliens in the United States is not increasing; it has remained stable (Fix and Zimmerman, 1994). The popular image of illegal aliens is that of Mexicans illegally crossing the border into the United States. In fact, most Mexicans in the United States arrive legally, often recruited by employers, and only become illegal by remaining after their work visas expire.

The United States has a visa waiver program for residents of 22 selected countries, mostly in Western Europe, whose citizens can come to America for up to 90 days simply by purchasing a round-trip travel ticket. The Immigration and Naturalization Service (INS) reports that many people who come with such visas stay well beyond the 90-day limit, also becoming illegal aliens. According to the INS

data, major abusers of the privilege come from France, Sweden, and Italy (Hernandez-Truyol, 1997). So why is it that only Mexicans are viewed as "illegals"? The stereotype of Mexicans sneaking across the United States border illustrates not only xenophobia, but racism.

> MYTH #5: Immigrants are taking jobs away from Americans.

The fear of losing jobs to immigrants persists despite the fact that immigrants customarily have been hired for minimum-wage jobs that are difficult to fill. According to a Cato Institute study, immigrants do not increase joblessness, even in lowest-paid worker categories. For as long as there has been immigration, business owners have insisted, and continue to insist, that immigration is necessary to sustain U.S. economic growth. Studies have found that an influx of immigrant labor may create new jobs: One Los Angeles County study of a decade of immigration reported that Mexican immigrants created 78,000 new jobs (Cole, 1996).

As in the past, it is employers who are demanding immigrant labor for available jobs. In 1986, the U.S. government made it a crime for an employer to hire undocumented workers; now, many employers hire subcontractors to supply them with workers, thus placing the risk of arrest on the subcontractors for hiring undocumented workers. Unions have begun to accept the reality of immigrant labor and have been attempting to organize workers—especially laundry workers, janitors, hotel housekeepers, and waiters. These unions have become the main voice representing immigrant concerns (Massey, 2003).

A new and possibly growing problem may be the fault of businesses that urge opening immigration to more workers: the use of H1(b) visas and professional visas for entry into the United States. During the labor shortage of the 1990s, American companies increased their use of H1(b) visas to recruit qualified workers for vacant jobs, and there have been allegations of abuse concerning the use of these visas. Recent trade pacts signed by the Bush administration relax H1(b) rules to allow into the United States additional thousands of workers from countries with whom the United States has free trade agreements. If this problem continues, immigration laws in the United States will likely be revised once again. Maintaining fairness in addressing the diversity and complexity of immigration issues in the American economy is an ongoing challenge, but the goal should be to provide opportunity to immigrants, no matter when they came to the United States, as they try to achieve their American Dreams.

AFTERWORD

This history of immigration demonstrates that there have been and still are diverse but clearly defined attitudes toward immigration on the part of American citizens, political leaders, and representatives of business and industry. Although entrenched workers sometimes resent the economic competition, our society has always benefited from the willing labor of immigrant workers. We have also benefited from the cultural diversity represented by immigrants from so many different nations. Although some have complained that immigrants do not assimilate and have repeatedly insisted that immigrants should rid themselves of their old culture, history teaches us that there is no royal road for immigrants trying to adjust or adapt to a new culture; in reality, there are diverse pathways. Each immigrant may take a different route, but each will end at the same destination—becoming an American.

> America, it would seem, is miraculously both singular and plural, organized and scattered, united and diffused.
>
> HENRY KARIEL (1924–)

TERMS AND DEFINITIONS

Americanization The demand that immigrants to the United States reject their ethnic or cultural heritage and conform to American ways as defined by the dominant group

Anti-Semitism Having anti-Jewish prejudices or stereotypes, or engaging in discrimination against Jews

Assimilation A process whereby immigrants adopt cultural traits of the host country in order to be identified with that country and integrated into the immediate society

Chinese Exclusion Act A law prohibiting Chinese immigration to the United States

English Only A movement in various states demanding that legislatures make English the official language of the state, with the eventual goal of having the federal government make English the official language of the United States

Eugenics The study of agencies under social control that may improve or repair the racial qualities of future generations, either physically or mentally

Gentleman's Agreement The Japanese government guaranteed the U.S. government that it would issue no more passports (as of 1908) to Japanese workers except those already in the United States or their close relatives

Nativism An anti-immigrant ideology advocating the protection of "native" inhabitants of a country from new or potential immigrants who are viewed as threatening or dangerous

Proposition 187 A California proposal approved by voters to deny certain social services (such as medical services) and public benefits (such as a public education) to anyone suspected of being an undocumented immigrant

Xenophobia Fear of or prejudice against people from nations other than one's own

"Yellow peril" The term for the belief that Chinese and Japanese immigrants could never assimilate into American culture, and therefore threatened the unity of American society

REFERENCES

Barrett, J.R., & Roediger, D. (2002). How white people became white. In P. Rothenberg (Ed.), *White privilege: Essential readings on the other side of racism* (pp. 29–34). New York: Worth.

Discusses the process of Americanization of immigrants to the United States with attention to the use of white privilege as an inducement for immigrants to conform to the majority.

Brands, H.W. (2000). *The first American: The life and times of Benjamin Franklin.* New York: Doubleday.

Describes Franklin's development as a scholar, entrepreneur, political leader, and the influence he had on the emerging nation.

Brodkin, K. (2002). How Jews became white folks. In P. Rothenberg (Ed.), *White privilege: Essential readings on the other side of racism* (pp. 35–48). New York: Worth.

Discusses the racism and anti-Semitism that has characterized anti-immigrant sentiment and the factors that resulted in the ultimate acceptance of white ethnic immigrants.

Center for Immigration Studies. (2002). *Immigrants in the United States—2002: A snapshot of America's foreign-born population* (p. 13). A panel discussion sponsored for the National Press Club in Washington, D.C. Retrieved July 12, 2003, from *http://www.cis.org/articles/2002/snapshotpanel2002.html*

Analysis by panel members of a variety of immigration issues; comments on welfare by Robert Suro, Director of the Pew Hispanic Center.

Chang, R.S. (1997). A meditation on borders. In J.F. Perea (Ed.), *Immigrants out!: The new nativism and the anti-immigrant impulse in the United States* (pp. 244–253). New York: New York University Press.

Explains how the concept of borders heightens the perception of foreign for anyone outside of those borders.

Cole, D. (1996). The new Know-Nothingism: Five myths about immigration. In J. Andrzejewski (Ed.), *Oppression and social justice: Critical frameworks* (5th ed., pp. 152–154). Needham, MA: Simon & Schuster.

Describes some popular myths about immigration and provides information disproving each of these myths.

Cubberley, E.P. (1919). *Public education in the United States.* Boston: Houghton Mifflin.

Describes how schools were established in the United States and the influences that shaped the development of American public schools.

Delgado, R. (1997). Citizenship. In J.F. Perea (Ed.), *Immigrants Out!: The new nativism and the anti-immigrant impulse in the United States* (pp. 318–323). New York: New York University Press.

Discusses recent proposals directed toward making U.S. citizenship more difficult to obtain.

Eck, D.L. (2001). *A new religious America: How a "Christian Country" has become the world's most religiously diverse nation.* New York: HarperCollins.

Examines the growth of diverse religions in the United States, especially with regard to immigration patterns since 1965, and describes its impact and potential.

Feagin, J. (1997). Old poison in new bottles: The deep roots of modern nativism. In J.F. Perea (Ed.), *Immigrants out!: The new nativism and the anti-immigrant impulse in the United States* (pp. 13–43). New York: New York University Press.

Presents an overview of the development of nativist sentiment in the United States from the early 1800s to the present.

Feagin, J., & Feagin, C. (1996). Basic concepts in the study of racial and ethnic relations. In *Racial and ethnic relations* (5th ed., pp. 6–26). Upper Saddle River, NJ: Prentice Hall.

Provides definitions of essential terms and concepts for intergroup relations.

Fix, M., & Zimmermann, W. (1994). After arrival: An overview of federal immigrant policy in the United States. In B. Edmonston & J. Passel (Eds.), *Immigration and ethnicity: The integration of America's newest arrivals* (pp. 251–285). Washington DC: The Urban Institute Press.

Analyzes trends in immigration and public policy in the United States and provides a description of both express and de facto immigrant policies of the federal government.

Fong, T.P. (2000). The history of Asians in America. In T.P. Fong (Ed.), *Asian Americans: Experiences and perspectives* (pp. 13–30). Upper Saddle River, NJ: Prentice Hall.

Describes the historical experience of Asian immigrants to the United States.

Fuchs, L.H. (1990). *The American kaleidoscope: Race, ethnicity and the civic culture.* Hanover, NH: University Press of New England.

Argues that immigrant groups have been successful in embracing and practicing basic social and political principles of U.S. society.

Grant, M. (1970). *The passing of the great race, Or the racial basis of European history* (Rev. ed.). New York: Arno Press. (Original work published 1916)

Expresses fears that the white race may be losing its position of supremacy in the world.

Hernandez-Truyol, B.E. (1997). Reconciling rights in collision: An international human rights strategy. In J.F. Perea (Ed.), *Immigrants out!: The new nativism and the anti-immigrant impulse in the United States* (pp. 254–276). New York: New York University Press.

Discusses the basis for advocacy of human rights globally and in the United States and argues that Proposition 187 is a violation of those human rights principles.

Herrnstein, R.J., & Murray, C. (1994). *The bell curve: Intelligence and class structure in American life.* New York: Free Press.

Analyzes research to argue that differences in intelligence stem from race/ethnicity and are genetically determined and that economic success or failure is determined by intelligence.

Higham, J. (1955). *Strangers in the land: Patterns of American nativism, 1865–1925.* New Brunswick, NJ: Rutgers University Press.

Describes the growth of anti-immigrant sentiment in the United States, culminating in significant anti-immigrant policies and legislation of the 1920s.

Kammen, M. (1972). *People of paradox: An inquiry concerning the origins of American civilization.* New York: Vintage.

Analyzes and attempts to reconcile contradictory aspects of American culture as revealed in the history of the colonial experience and in the emerging nation.

Limon, L. (1996). Testimony on use of welfare by immigrants. Retrieved, April 12, 2003, from *http:// www.hhs.gov/asl/testimony.html*

Presents data from surveys conducted to determine immigrant use of welfare services. (At the Web site, go to 1996 file and scroll to February 6 [1996] testimony.)

Lynn, R. (2001). *Eugenics: A reassessment.* Westport, CT: Prager.

Provides background on the historical formulations of eugenics, gives examples of how eugenics has been implemented, and discusses the role that eugenics could play in the future.

Macedo, D., & Bartolome, L.I. (2001). *Dancing with bigotry: Beyond the politics of tolerance.* New York: Palgrave.

Examines issues of language and limitations in multicultural education; the first quote is from John Silber, who was Chair of the Massachusetts State Board of Education at the time.

Massey, D.S. (2003). Closed-door policy. *American Prospect 14*(7), 26–28.

Analyzes recent trends in Mexican immigration to the United States and the impact of U.S. government reactions taken in response to these trends.

Myers, G. (1960). *History of bigotry in the United States.* New York: Capricorn.

Describes the historic targets of bigotry since colonial days, with emphasis on Catholics, Jews, and immigrants, and the actions taken against these minorities by the majority.

Pai, Y., & Adler, S. (1997). Schooling as Americanization: 1600s–1970s. In *Cultural foundations of education* (2nd ed., pp. 55–91). Upper Saddle River, NJ: Merrill Prentice Hall.

Describes the evolution of the Americanization concept and its implementation in schools.

Passel, J., & Edmonston, B. (1994). Immigration and race: Recent trends in immigration to the U.S. In B. Edmonston & J. Passel (Eds.), *Immigration and ethnicity: The integration of America's newest arrivals* (pp. 31–71). Washington DC: Urban Institute Press.

Examines 1980s immigration and compares to immigration trends from 1880 to 1920.

Pipher, M. (2002). *The middle of everywhere: The world's refugees come to our town.* New York: Harcourt.

Presents stories about a variety of recent immigrants, including the conditions that forced them to immigrate and the difficulties they encounter trying to adjust to American culture.

Roberts, D. (1997). Who may give birth to citizens: Reproduction, eugenics, and immigration. In J.F. Perea (Ed.), *Immigrants out! The new nativism and the anti-immigrant impulse in the United States* (pp. 205–219). New York: New York University Press.

Discusses proposals to deny citizenship to children of undocumented immigrants, relating this to the eugenics movement and other historical examples of racism.

Selden, S. (1999). *Inheriting shame: The story of eugenics and racism in America.* New York: Teachers College Press.

Analyzes the development of the eugenics movement in the United States in the early twentieth century and what lessons should be learned from this development.

Smedley, A. (1999). The arrival of Africans and descent into slavery. *Race in North America: Origin and evolution of a world view.* Boulder, CO: Westview.

Describes the arrival of Africans to America and how they lost their equal status with other immigrants.

Sorenson, E., & Enchautegui, M.E. (1994). Immigrant male earnings in the 1980s: Divergent patterns by race and ethnicity. In B. Edmonston & J. Passel (Eds.), *Immigration and ethnicity: The integration of America's newest arrivals* (pp. 139–161). Washington DC: Urban Institute Press.

Examines how the earnings of immigrants are affected by trends in skill composition and the length of time immigrants have lived in the United States.

Suarez-Orozco, C., & Suarez-Orozco, M. (2001). *Children of immigration.* Cambridge, MA: Harvard University Press.

Describes the lives of recent immigrants based on the authors' longitudinal study and other studies, and examines the difficulties they face as they try to assimilate.

Takaki, R. (1993). *A different mirror: A history of multicultural America.* Boston: Little Brown.

Describes the experience of diverse racial and ethnic groups in the United States.

Tatalovich, R. (1997). Official English as nativist backlash. In J.F. Perea (Ed.), *Immigrants out!: The new nativism and the anti-immigrant impulse in the United States* (pp. 78–102). New York: New York University Press.

Examines the English Only movement as an example of the new nativism.

Whyte, W.F. (1955). *Street corner society: The social structure of an Italian slum.* Chicago: The University of Chicago Press.

Presents an ethnographic study of an urban Italian neighborhood in the 1930s.

Wiley, T.G. (1997). Literacy and language diversity in the United States. Available from AskERIC, *http:// eri-cir.syr.edu/* (ERIC Document Reproduction Service No. ED440557).

Provides statistics and commentary concerning language diversity in the United States.

Wu, C. (Ed.). (1972). *"Chink!" A documentary history of anti-Chinese prejudice in America.* New York: World Publishing.

Reprints speeches, newspaper articles, and political cartoons documenting anti-Chinese prejudice; examples related to mob violence against Chinese in California are provided in Chapter 3, "Chinaman's Chance."

Wucker, M. (2003). Civics lessons from immigrants. *American Prospect 14*(7), 45–46.

Examines efforts of recent immigrants to express political concerns and play an active role in addressing local issues.

Summary Exercises

See page 19 for exercises to help you summarize the main points and define key terms in this chapter.

Personal Clarification Exercises

In Chapter 6, two exercises promote discussion about our sensitivity to issues of oppression.

Clarification Exercise #1 It Is Uncomfortable When . . . Exercise

Directions: Identify a friend, relative, neighbor, or other acquaintance that you know has been uncomfortable or in some way resentful because of a situation similar to one or more of the situations described below. Explain to your group members how that person has explained his or her discomfort. What do you think creates that discomfort? Why should (or shouldn't) your friend or acquaintance be justified in harboring those feelings? If you can recall a time when you held similar feelings, explain how and why you felt the way that you did in that situation.

It Is Uncomfortable When . . . The Situations

Situation A—School Three Mexican American high school students are conversing in Spanish on the way to their third period classes; they look at you as you walk by and seem to begin talking on a new topic as you, a white person, make eye contact with them. Perhaps they are talking about you.

Situation B—Work A work group of Pakistani day laborers are talking in Hindi, their native language, near where you are sitting alone on a break from the same job. While working, they seem friendly and almost deferential to you, a person of approximately the same age; in their group, however, they seem to be talking about the white laborers, such as yourself; from the inflection and body language of their conversation, you have a notion that they are resentful of what they might see as a white privilege.

Situation C—Travel Somali airport luggage handlers are working feverishly to check in baggage from a long line of people in preparation for your flight; although they ask their questions in English to those in line, as they interact among themselves in their first language, you can't help suspecting that they are frustrated with the impatience of those in line and especially, when your turn comes, with you.

Situation D—Dining Out You have planned for a long while to eat out at a trendy French restaurant with three friends; you are seated immediately, but in passing, the Maître'd makes a comment to your waiter that everyone at your table felt was a discourteous remark. Although no one could adequately translate the comment, and even though it was not delivered with telegraphing body language, it seems to have placed you and your friends in some discomfort, as if you were not welcome.

Clarification Exercise #2 What I Know Is . . . What Do We Know about Hyphenated Americans?

Directions: In a society as diverse as that in many parts of the United States today, immigrant cultures are sometimes strongly demonstrated, as in those described below. After reading each item, explain to a teammate what you know and how you tend to feel about the subcultural diversity illustrated within each category. If possible, explain what knowledge you have and/or the feelings you hold about those differences. Be careful not to trade stereotypes! Finally, if you dare, attempt to explain any animosity or frustration in tolerating those cultural differences.

1. Differences in social interaction:
   A. How loudly some racial or ethnic groups seem to talk in conversation.
   B. Direct eye contact between conversants is prohibited in some cultures.
   C. Some family sizes are large and seem to be happy living together, even in smaller spaces than actually needed.
   D. Physical contact in public between men and women is forbidden, and neither is walking together allowed.
2. Differences in dress:
   A. Women from a number of countries wear a traditional sari, many of them of exquisitely beautiful fabrics.
   B. The Sikh male turban is part of culture and religion.

C. The burqua for Muslim women may be required by cultural and religious policy.
D. Male Hasidic Jews wear black suits, hats, and pius/payess.

3. Differences in cultural traditions:
A. Preparing foods from many countries involves ingredients that are not familiar to many of us whose parents and grandparents have more thoroughly integrated customs and foods into a standard American fare.
B. National celebrations such as Cinco de Mayo and Syttende Mai are often unknown to a majority of Americans, even though American citizens with heritages from different countries work to keep their homeland traditions alive.
C. The significant events of a culture can be observed through seasonal rituals, religious occasions, wedding ceremonies, and family activities and vary according to ethnicity, religion, and country, such as gathering for H'mong New Year and for funeral rites.

Intergroup or Individual Exercises

In Chapter 6, two exercises promote discussion about our sensitivity to issues of oppression.

Intergroup Exercise #1 The Four Corners Exercise—Taking a Stand: How Can I Support These Statements?

Directions: Have each participant count off with numbers from 1 to 4.
A. In corners clearly marked,
Those identified as 1s move to the corner of the room marked "Strongly Agree."
The 2s move to the corner marked "Agree."
The 3s move to the corner marked "Disagree."
The 4s move to the corner marked "Strongly Disagree."
B. Once in corners, have the groups take 3–5 minutes to adopt and discuss the merits of the position of their assigned corner as related to the statements below.

C. Have group members read the first statement and, after brief discussion, list at least three plausible arguments to support the position represented. In turn, groups will present their arguments (position) to the class.
D. Next have groups read, discuss, and present the second statement.
E. Continue with group presentations and explanations of all five statements.
F. When all positions are presented and explained for each of the items below, move the class to regular seating to discuss together:
   • How did you feel about developing and articulating your group arguments?
   • Did some arguments seem strange, illogical, or embarrassing?
   • Have you heard these arguments from others?

Comment: Results of the statements developed in this exercise will illustrate both positive and negative attitudes that exist in our society—the point of the activity. Discussion is expected not only to present valid arguments for each position, but also to discuss the cognitive and affective quality of argument.

Taking a Stand: How Can I Support These Statements?

1. The United States is a Christian nation, and we are at risk of losing that distinction by letting all these Buddhist, Muslim, and Hindu immigrants settle here.
2. The problem is not immigration but illegal aliens coming into the United States when they have no right to enjoy our country.
3. Immigrants have always brought new ideas and energy to our country; we have benefited in the past and we are still benefiting today.
4. The United States accepting so many refugees has become a problem because so many of them don't speak English and have no job skills for our society.
5. The United States should accept any H'mong immigrant who wants to come here given everything they did for us during the Vietnam War.

Intergroup Exercise #2 Difficult Dialogues Experience

Directions: In groups of three, develop a dialogue based upon the scenario below. Use the situation as the basis for your 5-minute role-play of the situation. Remain in character at the conclusion of your skit and respond to class questions about motivation, purpose, or intent behind your comments during the scene. Each team of three is asked to complete their 5-minute role-play, regardless of similarity to others performed.

Difficult Dialogues: A Mathematical Question

Characters:
- Hispanic advanced placement female high school junior
- Muslim female high school senior—and highest achiever
- White male high school senior student in upper 2% of his class [See below]

A student makes the following statement in a mathematics class: "I'm glad to be in a class where issues of race and culture and diversity aren't important. Everyone knows that most of the great mathematicians were from Europe. Anyway, it doesn't matter here."

CHAPTER 7

Religious Diversity: The Struggle for Religious Freedom

"I wish you had a religion, Peter . . . Oh, I don't mean you have to be Orthodox, or believe in heaven and hell and purgatory and things. I just mean some religion. It doesn't matter what. Just to believe in something!"

(ANNE FRANK)

The character of Anne Frank makes her comment about religion in "The Diary of Anne Frank," a play based on the journal she kept during World War II until the Nazis found her. Her story has frequently been used to introduce students to the horrors of the Holocaust. At the play's end, Anne's father reads her diary and the audience hears Anne say, "In spite of everything, I still believe that people are really good at heart" (Goodrich and Hackett, 1956). Both comments affirm the goodness of humanity, regardless of differences between people. Neither comment seems to be controversial, yet some Christians have demanded that children not read the play because the remark about religion suggests that all religions are equally valid. Usually those who complain believe that one religion, their religion, is the only true faith.

RELIGIOUS DIVERSITY IN COLONIAL AMERICA

Americans have confronted religious controversy since early colonial times when immigrant groups arrived with an array of diverse beliefs and minor-

ity faiths contended with the power of a dominant faith to survive. Honoring the principle of **religious freedom**—the right to worship according to one's individual beliefs—has been an ongoing struggle in America, and the history of our efforts to achieve it is the focus of this chapter.

Although religious freedom does not deny an individual's right to disagree with the beliefs and practice of another religion, it does require acceptance of divergent beliefs, as long as they don't infringe on the rights of others. The constitutional separation of church and state principle was established to resolve the problem of diverse faiths in America, and although the principle is appropriate, efforts to achieve religious liberty and the freedom to worship have been a source of dramatic conflict throughout American history.

How did the first colonists deal with religious diversity?

Puritans came to the New World to practice their religion freely, yet they had no intention of allowing others the same freedom. When Anne Hutchinson expressed religious sentiments contrary to Puritan teaching, she was excommunicated and then exiled in 1637. Roger Williams was exiled as well because he advocated respect for all religious faiths and for separation of church from state, a principle not inherent in either Puritan cultural heritage or that of other European immigrants. To re-establish Old World practices, dominant religious groups such as the Anglicans in Massachusetts expected their faith to be designated the **established church** of their colony and to be supported by an allotment of local tax dollars. Miller (1976) described this perspective, "The established religion with its educated ministers and stately rituals was an important element in creating or re-creating the world they left behind" (p. 26).

English colonists discovered that it was difficult to create an established church in the New World. Parishioners wishing to take care of their families could not afford to give their churches much financial support; therefore, the need for support from colonial governments was greater than had been required in England, which placed a significant fiscal burden on scarce colonial revenues. Furthermore, immigrants represented diverse faiths—Presbyterians, Quakers, Baptists—who were resentful when colonial tax revenues were expended to support a church to which they did not belong.

Religious resentment was mutual. Northern colony Puritans particularly disliked Quakers because of their ecstatic worship and their practice of allowing women to be church leaders. In Massachusetts, blasphemy laws were enacted to force Quakers out, threatening them with death if they returned. When they did return, authorities promptly arrested them; four Quakers were executed between 1659 and 1661. The executions stopped only because authorities in Britain were embarrassed, insisting that Quakers be sent to London for proper trials (Miller, 1976).

Most American colonies enacted blasphemy laws directed at those who did not belong to the colony's majority faith. Blasphemy was defined as an individual denying the truth and authority of the Bible. If anyone denied the divinity of Christ he could be executed or at least lose his property. Although violating blasphemy laws usually did not result in death, punishments could be quite severe, especially for freethinkers and atheists. According to a 1699 Maryland law, blasphemers, typically people who were using language that degraded Christ, the Apostles, or the Holy Trinity, were to be branded with a "B" for a first offense, have a hole burned through their tongue with a red-hot iron for a second offense, and have their property confiscated for a third offense. In a humanitarian gesture, some colonies allowed blasphemers to avoid punishment by publicly asking to be forgiven (Myers, 1960).

As colonies designated "established churches," blasphemy laws also required ministers from other churches to register as "dissenters" and agree to practice only after receiving colonial approval. Dissenting ministers sometimes refused to register and preached whenever they wished; however, they were often arrested, sometimes with an effect opposite of what was intended. At one point when Baptist ministers were being aggressively pursued, arrested, and jailed for unauthorized preaching, the number of Baptist converts increased dramatically (Miller, 1976). Conversion efforts were customarily focused on those colonists who attended but were not members of a church, or upon those not attending a church, a majority in the colonies.

By 1775, more than 150 years since the first colonists arrived, approximately 10% of Americans were church members (Lippy, 1994). Although groups such as Puritans and Quakers came to the colonies to plant the seeds of faith in fertile ground, most immigrants came instead to escape physical destitution and moral despair. They hoped to achieve material success: to own their own land and to provide for their families. They wanted a better life on earth, not in heaven. Preachers from minority faiths focused on those who attended church with little enthusiasm or those who may have found a better material life but longed for satisfaction of spiritual needs. The competition for converts intensified the desire for religious freedom.

How did the colonies promote the concept of religious freedom?

Because of the influence of Roger Williams, William Penn, and Lord Baltimore, the colonies of Rhode Island, Pennsylvania, and Maryland declared religious freedom for those of any faith. Puritans regarded their faith as a "light to the world," so they often forced people to accept it. Williams argued that people could not develop true faith through coercion, and expressed the need for a "wall of separation between the garden of the church and the wilderness of the world" (Nord, 1995, p. 135). With a Baptist majority in Rhode Island, the arrival of Quakers tested the colony's commitment to religious freedom. Williams personally disliked Quakers and attacked them in his writings, but general tolerance prevailed as religious freedom was maintained, attracting some intolerant Puritans and a small group of Jews settling in Newport. Quakers eventually became the dominant religion in Rhode Island (Miller, 1976).

William Penn believed that God spoke directly to individuals through the conscience and that this was the basis for a commitment to religious freedom. Penn undertook deliberate efforts to bring to Pennsylvania people from diverse faiths: Anabaptists, Presbyterians, Puritans, Roman Catholics, and others who had no religious conviction. Pennsylvania was the first colony to experiment with the idea of denominational churches instead of an established church; no church received state assistance, nor did the state interfere in church affairs. Members of a denomination were not expected to withdraw from the world, but to participate in it.

As might be expected, Pennsylvania's "holy experiment" was not without problems. Because

> (If) Papists and Protestants, Jews and Turks, may be embarked in one ship . . . none of the Papists, Protestants, Jews or Turks (should) be forced to come to the ship's prayer or worship nor compelled from their own particular prayer or worship, if they practice any.
>
> **ROGER WILLIAMS (1603–1683)**

Penn was a Quaker, Quakers had more government influence than other denominations, and for a time they functioned as an informal established church. Although Quaker dominance caused friction, compared to other colonies, Pennsylvania and Rhode Island provided the clearest alternative to the Old World tradition of state support for an established church.

Founded by Lord Baltimore, Maryland was originally intended as a refuge for English Catholics. The principle of religious freedom was self-serving since Catholics constituted a minority even among the first contingent settling Maryland, and Catholicism remained a minority faith throughout the colonial period. Still, Baltimore's commitment to religious tolerance attracted immigrants from diverse faiths. But Maryland's experiment was not successful: The Church of England became its established church in 1702. Since three other faiths—Anabaptists, Presbyterians, and Quakers—had more members, the Church of England was established on condition that religious tolerance would be maintained. Such tolerance was reserved for the currently residing religious groups; incoming Jews and Unitarians were not allowed to settle in Maryland at that time (Hudson, 1973).

How was the principle of religious freedom established in all the colonies?

As the mid-seventeenth century approached, a significant event (later termed the "Great Awakening") promoted the principle of religious freedom, beginning with ideas in the widely read writings of Jonathan Edwards and other New England ministers. Concerned about the "extraordinary dullness" of people's faith, Edwards challenged individuals to demonstrate personal commitment to their faith in their everyday lives. In 1740, English preacher George Whitefield presented his similar challenge to colonial people, with dramatic results.

Although Protestant ministers throughout the colonies invited him, Whitefield avoided churches, preferring to speak in open fields. His sermons stimulated people's emotions as much as their intellect, and audiences responded enthusiastically. Whitefield insisted that being a Christian was not about belonging to a particular church, but being committed to faith and demonstrating that commitment in

FIGURE 7.1

Whitefield's impact on colonial America is commemorated in this statue on the University of Pennsylvania campus..

Source: Photo courtesy of the University of Pennsylvania.

everyday life. Ironically, his sermons resulted in a huge increase in church attendance and church members. Nord (1995) describes a sermon in Philadelphia where Whitefield looked up to the sky and shouted:

> Father Abraham, whom have you in heaven? Any Episcopalians? No! Any Presbyterians? No! Any Independents or Methodists? No, no, no! Who have you there? . . . We don't know those names here. All who are here are Christians . . . Then God help us to forget party names and become Christians in deed and truth. (p. 103)

The impact of the Great Awakening on religious freedom was that it denied the significance of differences between Protestant sects. Prior to the Great Awakening, Protestants belonged to one sect or another, each defining itself as the "true faith." This **sectarian** view of Christianity gave way to a consensus about what it meant to be Christian: accepting others, doing good deeds, and ignoring theological controversy. The Great Awakening replaced a sectarian approach to Christianity with a **denominational** view based on the perception of a singular Protestant church that is called—denominated—by many different names such as Anglican, Lutheran, or Baptist. Although the denominational view united Protestants, Catholics were not included.

THE EMERGING CONCEPT OF RELIGIOUS FREEDOM

In the mid-eighteenth century, Europeans were making significant discoveries based on scientific inquiry. Isaac Newton alone was responsible for discovering the principles of gravitation and light; he also developed differential calculus and even had time to invent the reflecting telescope. The dissemination of ideas and inventions during this era, eventually called "the Enlightenment," created an increased respect for science and a diminished belief in miracles and the supernatural. Some argued that religious truths, like scientific truths, would be discovered by human reason, not through divine revelation. This thinking led to the birth of **Deism,** a religious philosophy based on rationality that was devoid of mysticism. Deists acknowledged that God created the universe, but insisted that human beings must use their intellects to understand the rational principles by which the universe functioned. In response to the increased emphasis on rationality and the scientific method as the

> I do not believe in the creed professed by the Jewish church, by the Roman church, by the Greek Church, by the Turkish church, by the Protestant church nor by any church that I know of. My own mind is my own church.
>
> **THOMAS PAINE (1737–1809)**

preferred means of ascertaining truth, many intellectuals rejected all religious faiths. Although some American colonists declared themselves **atheists,** denying the existence of God, the religious philosophy of Deism was more appealing than atheism to Christian intellectuals in the colonies.

What was the relationship between Deism and Christianity?

Deism dismissed much of what constituted traditional Christian beliefs. Deists believed God created the world and a system of natural laws that governed it. Although they believed that God would reward or punish the soul after death, they did not believe that God was an active force in the everyday world. Thomas Jefferson and Benjamin Franklin were among many who were attracted to Deism as a religious philosophy. Although Deists denied the divinity of Christ, they tended to admire his moral teachings; therefore, many Deists attended churches of various denominations while others never went to church. Although Deist views were not popular among the general public, the principles of Deism influenced several people who would write the documents that transformed the thirteen colonies into the United States of America. Curiously, these "enlightened" founders did not include religious freedom in the Constitution, but incorporated the principle in the first of ten amendments that became known as the Bill of Rights.

Why was religious freedom guaranteed in the Bill of Rights but not in the Constitution?

By the time of the Revolutionary War in 1776, four colonies had guaranteed the right of people to worship as they chose: Rhode Island, Pennsylvania, Delaware, and New Jersey. The Church of England remained the established church in other colonies; however, during the war one colony after another ceased providing church support. By the war's end, only Massachusetts, New Hampshire, Connecticut, and Virginia continued to have established churches. In 1786, the new nation was still struggling to function under its first constitution, entitled the Articles of Confederation, when Virginia approved its statute guaranteeing religious freedom that would eventually become the model for the nation.

When the delegates met to write the Constitution of the United States, most of them did not question the issue of religious freedom, but accepted the principle that each citizen had the right to worship as he or she chose. The delegates did debate other issues, however, such as what civil rights should be granted those who were not Protestant. New Jersey's Constitution stated that every office holder had to be Protestant, a provision not revised until 1844. Some states required all those seeking public office to recite an oath that they had no allegiance to any foreign power— "ecclesiastic as well as civil" (Myers, 1960, p. 46). Of course, a devout Catholic could not take such an oath, which was the reason it was required. Some states merely demanded that an office holder be a Christian; Maryland, which eventually permitted Jews to settle, stood alone as the only state that allowed Jews to vote and hold public office. Obviously, Jefferson's wall between church and state had yet to be built.

As they wrote the Constitution, the authors affirmed the principle of religious freedom by stating "No religious Test shall ever be required as a Qualification to any Office or public Trust under the United States" (Article VI). When completed, this was the only reference to religion in a Constitution that made no reference to God. To secure consensus

> The government of the United States of America is not in any sense founded on the Christian Religion.
>
>   **JOHN ADAMS (1735–1826)**

for the Constitution, the question of having an established church was left to each state. Since religious freedom was a well-established principle in most states, the authors may have thought there was no need to include such a statement until it became obvious that several amendments would be necessary before enough states would ratify the Constitution. Eck (2001) describes how Jefferson used the "Statute for Religious Freedom" he had written for Virginia's legislature in 1786 when he drafted the First Amendment's explicit guarantee of religious freedom.

Nord (1995) argued that much of the impetus for religious freedom stemmed from the Enlightenment belief that "natural reason, operating in a free culture, was the way to the truth" (p. 108). Yet most church leaders supported the First Amendment for similar reasons. They did not advocate state-sponsored churches because they believed it was appropriate that only those churches that attracted enough members should survive. Ministers such as Ezra Stiles believed that through competition, truth would prevail: "Here Deism will have its full chance; nor need libertines . . . complain of being overcome by any weapons but the gentle, powerful ones of argument and truth" (Hudson, 1973, p. 110). Connecticut and Massachusetts supported a state church until Connecticut declined to subsidize the Congregational Church in 1817, and Massachusetts disestablished the Congregational Church in 1833 (Myers, 1960).

Did the First Amendment establish religious freedom in the new nation?

Although the freedom to worship according to one's personal religious beliefs was guaranteed in the Bill of Rights, it was guaranteed in principle more than in practice. Having a minority faith could affect one's political rights. As the Constitution was being ratified by the thirteen states, only three of them—Pennsylvania, Maryland, and Delaware—permitted Catholics to vote. Within five years of the Constitution's ratification, three more states—South Carolina, Georgia, and New York—granted the vote to its Catholic citizens, and eventually the remaining states did the same (Myers, 1960).

Because of their numbers, Jews exercised limited political influence, encountering intolerance early in the colonial period when Jewish immigrants were forced to depart from Boston as soon as they arrived. More than three decades after the Constitution was approved, Maryland was the only state where Jews could vote or hold public office. During the Civil War, General Ulysses S. Grant expelled Jews from areas he had reclaimed by military conquest for the United States; however, President Lincoln rescinded Grant's order (Miller, 1976). North Carolina granted civil rights to Jews in 1868; New Hampshire granted Jews the right to vote in 1876.

Was any group actively persecuted for their religious beliefs?

Religious freedom was violently denied to the followers of Mormonism, the Church of Latter-day Saints, which was founded on the revelations of Joseph Smith in the early 1800s. After his *Book of Mormon* was published in 1830, Smith found followers captivated by his new vision of the past and his responses to major religious controversies of the day. He aroused animosity among traditional Christian denominations by his promotion of polygamy and other ideas deemed unconventional and unacceptable in American society. Smith's first church in Ohio was not welcomed, and when the members moved to Missouri, they were attacked and forced to leave, eventually settling in Nauvoo, Illinois. They lived there for only a few years before Smith was arrested and incarcerated at nearby Carthage, where a masked mob broke into his cell, shot and killed him. Miller (1976) declared, "The rise of Mormonism tested the American dedication to religious liberty, and the nation ultimately failed the test" (p. 111).

When Brigham Young replaced Smith as leader for the Church of the Latter-day Saints, he realized that Mormons would not be guaranteed religious freedom if they remained in the United States. In 1847, Young persuaded his Mormon followers to undertake an ambitious journey of a thousand miles, finally stopping to settle on land that belonged to Mexico. One year later, as the Mexican-American War ended, the Great Salt Lake Valley where the Mormons had settled became part of the United States. Since there was no one close enough to persecute the Mormons, they successfully populated the territory of Utah and applied for statehood. Their application was denied six times until 1897, when they changed their state Constitution to renounce polygamy (Kosmin and Lachmin, 1993).

Religious freedom was also not extended to those who rejected religious beliefs. Atheists in Virginia could be arrested for publicly professing that God did not exist. In 1833, Abner Kneeland was arrested and incarcerated in Massachusetts for questioning the divinity of Jesus, his miracles, and his resurrection. Kneeland was convicted under the state's blasphemy law and sentenced to sixty days in jail; however, his conviction resulted in

F IGURE 7.2

The Mormon Trail

To escape persecution, the Mormons headed west and did not stop until they had left the United States and reached the safety of Mexican territory.

Source: © by Intellectual Reserve, Inc.

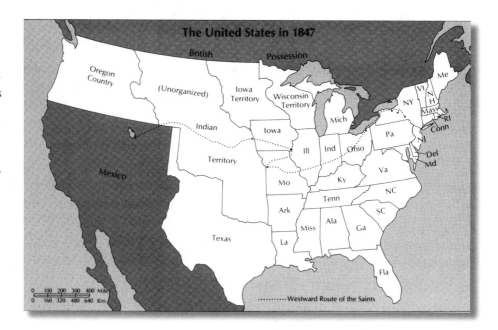

vigorous protests. Kneeland was the last person convicted of blasphemy in Massachusetts, although the law was not repealed for many years (Miller, 1976).

How religiously active were Americans in the nineteenth century?

Rigorous requirements for membership in Protestant churches endured from early colonial times into the nineteenth century. By 1800, approximately one of fifteen adults were members of an established church, increasing to one in eight by 1835, but these numbers do not accurately reflect American involvement in religion. According to Hudson (1973), "The number of people attending Sunday morning worship in the 1830s was usually three times the membership of the church" (p. 130). The rising number of religious periodicals also illustrates the general interest in religion: Ten were available in 1800, but the number of such periodicals increased to approximately 850 over the next four decades (Lippy, 1994).

THE RISE AND FALL OF ANTI-CATHOLICISM

In contrast to the slow but steady growth of members in Protestant churches, membership in the Catholic Church increased dramatically. By 1850, the number of Catholics in the United States had expanded from several hundred thousand to nearly two million. Between 1820 and 1865, of approximately two million Irish immigrants to the United States, over one million were Catholic (Kosmin and Lachmin, 1993). Because of its assistance to Irish immigrants, the New York City political and labor organization known as Tammany Hall became a powerful force influencing the city and state of New York, which intensified anti-Catholic sentiments.

What was the impact of large numbers of Catholic immigrants?

Immigrants have almost always provoked hostility in some Americans, but the arrival of so many

Catholics fueled Protestant fears and created an atmosphere of suspicion and distrust. Because the Catholic Church had persecuted, tortured, and even killed those who defied its authority in the past, Protestants believed that Catholics would not hesitate to employ any tactic that would convert Protestants to the Catholic faith. Several popular novels such as *The Awful Disclosures of Maria Monk* described Protestant women being kidnapped and confined in underground cells in convents and subjected to unspeakable tortures.

Following a fistfight between laborers at a Charlestown, Massachusetts, convent and brickyard workmen, the workmen spread rumors that the convent had imprisoned a woman just as the novels suggested. Although published results of an investigation said there was no truth to the rumor, a mob gathered and set fire to the convent. No police or militia appeared. Ten fire engines responded to the call, but the fire brigades insisted they could not act without orders from a magistrate, so they watched as the convent was destroyed. A meeting of Protestants called by the mayor of Boston produced a formal statement denouncing the mob's actions, but the Catholic Church never received compensation for its losses (Myers, 1960).

> We have just enough religion to make us hate,
> But not enough to make us love one another.
>
> **JONATHAN SWIFT (1667–1745)**

Why was hostility directed against Catholics?

The 1830s and 1840s was the era of Native American and Know-Nothing parties promoting **anti-Catholicism** and anti-immigrant sentiments. The Know-Nothings dedicated themselves to reducing a perceived growth of Catholic power and influence. Anti-Catholic prejudices were also reflected in public school textbooks where priests were depicted as living in luxury, oblivious to the poor and hungry, and the Catholic Church was described as the enemy of freedom and knowledge because of its history of religious persecution and its suppression

of the Bible (Miller, 1976). It is not surprising that at this time the Catholic Church felt compelled to create an alternative school system, increasing Protestant animosity toward Catholics.

Protestants were not opposed to separate schools for Catholics, but in 1840, Bishop Hughes of New York created controversy when he petitioned the New York Public Schools Society for funds to support Catholic schools. Hughes argued that separate schools for Catholic children had become necessary because of anti-Catholic materials in public schools. Protestants objected to using tax dollars to teach "Catholic dogma," and accused the Bishop of trying to undermine public schools. Hughes provided excerpts from textbooks that ridiculed Catholicism, including one book in which the Catholic Church was accused of encouraging drunkenness in order to maintain its hold on church members who would reject the "Romish religion" if they could only think rationally (Myers, 1960). Although the New York Public Schools Society denied Hughes' petition for funds, they agreed to remove anti-Catholic content from textbooks and to exclude from school libraries books that clearly promoted anti-Catholic prejudice. Although this seemed to solve the problem in New York, growing anti-Catholic sentiment would lead to the shocking events of the Philadelphia Bible Riots.

What were the Philadelphia Bible Riots?

In 1844, the Philadelphia School Board approved the substitution of the Douay (Catholic) Bible for Catholic students when Bible reading was required. The Native American party called for a meeting in Kensington, an Irish Catholic district in Philadelphia, to protest the use of the Catholic Bible in public schools. The meeting provoked area residents, who attacked participants and forced the meeting to end. Native American party leaders insisted on a second meeting in Kensington, which resulted in violence that left one person dead and 50 wounded.

The following day, a large crowd gathered to approve a resolution in support of teaching the Protestant version of the Bible in public schools. The meeting soon became uncontrollable, and when the mob heard shots fired from a nearby building, they set fire to that building and went on a rampage. Troops were called in, but before they could restore order, several homes had burned, eight men were dead, and sixteen were wounded. The night was quiet, and there was no further violence the next morning. Most of the soldiers withdrew.

By mid-afternoon, a Protestant mob gathered once again, setting fire to a Catholic Church and a nearby row of houses whose tenants were Irish. Troops were re-called, but before they arrived, the mob attacked another church. This time the police surrounded the church, but the mob drove them off with bricks and stones and set fire to that church and a Catholic school, and the fire spread to frame houses nearby. The troop commander summoned to Philadelphia declared martial law. Property losses from the riots included forty-five homes, two churches, and a school. Violence flared again a month later, and by the time the Philadelphia Bible Riots were finally over, 58 people had been killed and 140 wounded. The Native American party blamed the Irish for the deaths and injuries and even for the destruction of churches and homes in Irish neighborhoods (Ravitch, 1999; Myers, 1960). Although anti-Catholic sentiment would remain strong for another decade, other issues and events would command the nation's attention.

What caused anti-Catholic sentiments in the United States to subside?

Nord (1995) concluded, "The politics of race and the Civil War put the politics of anti-Catholicism to rest" (pp. 73–74). Although the Great Awakening unified Protestant churches, they were split over the slavery issue. During the Civil War, Catholic soldiers fought and died as bravely as the Protestant soldiers beside them, and anti-Catholic sentiments declined. After the war, anti-Catholic prejudice still existed and flared up on occasion, yet it never reached the level that fostered the rise of the Native American and Know-Nothing parties. Another factor in the decline of anti-Catholic prejudice after the Civil War was that the Catholic Church was no longer the only serious opponent for Protestant churches. Religious diversity in the United States was about to increase dramatically.

How did religious diversity increase following the Civil War?

After the Civil War, immigration to the United States surpassed pre-War levels. By 1900, there were 75 million Americans, 25 million of whom were foreign-born adults and their children. The number of Roman Catholics in the United States increased from two million in 1850 to four million in 1870 to twelve million by 1900. Although Protestants continued to be the dominant group, one-third of Americans who claimed church membership in 1920 were members of the Catholic Church (Hudson, 1973).

Catholic immigrants came from Germany, Ireland, Poland, Italy, and Czechoslovakia, their ethnic diversity creating tension in the Church. Not only did they speak different languages, but also they had different traditions and customs related to their worship. The Church's inability to resolve ethnic differences led to the creation of the Polish National Catholic Church in the 1890s and the Lithuanian National Catholic Church in 1914. Protestant churches faced similar challenges. The majority of Protestant immigrants were Lutherans whose diversity resulted in Finnish, Icelandic, Swedish, Danish, German, and Norwegian Lutheran churches. By 1900, Hudson (1973) suggests there were at least twenty-four different kinds of Lutheran churches.

Diversity also resulted from missionaries proselytizing Native Americans and former slaves. Minimal efforts to reach either group had been made prior to the Civil War because both groups had been perceived as heathen. Early European colonists were convinced that Native Americans engaged in witchcraft and worshiped the devil. In 1670, Samuel Clark said of Indians, "Their chief God is the Devil whom they call Oke, and [they] serve him more from fear than love" (Lippy, 1994, p. 38). The Great Awakening had generated some enthusiasm for conversion efforts, but Native Americans who accepted Christianity usually blended the new beliefs with their old ones. Even when Protestant missionaries went to frontier territories, their primary focus was upon white settlers, the majority of whom did not belong to a church, because of concerns that Catholic missionaries would convert these pioneers first.

Following the Civil War, missionaries visited reservations to create schools for Indian children, with the federal government supporting missionary efforts by banning many tribal religions (Hendry, 2003). By the 1870s, government funds supported Protestant and Catholic schools for Indian children even though Catholics could not obtain federal tax money to educate their own children. Protestants typically established off-reservation boarding schools, whereas Catholics tended to establish boarding schools and day schools on reservations (Fraser, 1999).

Slave owners had been reluctant to convert their captives, and as late as the 1850s, conversions were minimal. Slaves persisted in spiritual beliefs they brought from Africa, and as with the Indians, white colonists perceived them as practicing "black magic," or being in league with the devil. When slave owners did convert slaves, it was a Christianity emphasizing submission to divine and earthly authorities with the promise of eternal life in heaven as their reward for enduring slavery in this life (Lippy, 1994).

Following the Civil War, Protestant missionaries made it their goal to reach the 3.5 million newly freed slaves. Former slaves who had converted to Christianity no longer wanted to attend the churches their owners had forced them to attend, especially when the church still expected them to sit in the back seats and to have no voice in church affairs. Separate churches for freedmen were established, the majority being Baptist, with Methodists a distant second. By 1916, 43% of blacks were members of a church, a higher percentage than for the white population (Hudson, 1973).

As racial and ethnic groups added to the diversity, so did the creation of new faiths. Madame Blavatsky borrowed from eastern religions to create the Theosophical Society, declaring that profound truths were the basis for all religions. William Miller was abandoned by "Millerites" in 1844 when his prediction about Jesus returning did not come true. Many of his former followers turned to Ellen Harmon White, whose spiritual revelations included hygienic practices and dietary restrictions for the faithful to ensure the return of Jesus; White's followers became Seventh Day Adventists. Mary Baker Eddy responded to the growing importance of scientific research by founding Church of Christ, Scientist. Eddy spoke of an Eternal Mind as the source of life, and that disease was a consequence of mental error. Christian Scientists sought to overcome the illusions that have been the source of all

human troubles (Lippy, 1994). Adding to the complexity of diverse faiths in the late nineteenth century, all immigrants were not simply Christian.

What non-Christian religions were included among immigrants?

Immigrants to the United States included members of non-Christian religious groups. On the west coast, Buddhists among Chinese and Japanese immigrants established a Young Men's Buddhist Association in 1898. On the east coast, 1.5 million Jews came to America between 1880 and 1905 to escape anti-Semitism in Russia, Poland, Rumania, and Austro-Hungary. Hudson (1973) cites an advisor to the Czar predicting the consequences of new Russian policies: "One-third of the Jews will emigrate, one-third will be baptized, and one-third will starve" (p. 332).

Diversity increased within the Jewish community as well. In 1880, most of the 250,000 Jews in the United States were descendants of German-speaking Jews from central Europe affiliated with Reform Judaism; Jews emigrating later from Eastern Europe were more likely to be Orthodox than Reform. According to Hudson, more than three million Jews had immigrated by 1920, with Orthodox Jews outnumbering Reform Jews. The largest Jewish group, larger than the number of all religious Jews combined, were those not affiliated with any synagogue; many of them were Zionists whose activity was more likely to be political than religious.

America also experienced an increase in people professing no religion. Darwin's theory of evolution and other scientific advances caused many people to question the validity of religious faith. English scientist Thomas Huxley declared himself an **agnostic,** believing that one could neither prove nor disprove the existence of God. Lawyer and orator Robert

> A believer is a bird in a cage; a freethinker is an eagle parting the clouds with tireless wing.
>
> **ROBERT INGERSOLL (1833–1899)**

Ingersoll published *Why I Am an Agnostic* in 1896 and traveled across America questioning many aspects of Christianity. Still, some scholars reconciled Darwin's ideas with religion by believing in God, just not in specific denominational doctrines. The Christian majority reacted by punishing those who strayed from conventional beliefs as well as nonbelievers. In 1878, Alexander Winchell publicly rejected the Genesis version of creation, and Vanderbilt University trustees asked him to resign. When Winchell refused, they abolished his position. In 1886, James Woodrow was removed from his faculty position at Columbia Theological Seminary for advocating the possibility of reconciling Darwin's ideas with those of the Bible (Hudson, 1973).

Did increasing numbers of non-Christians cause anti-Catholic prejudice to diminish?

Although racial prejudice became more dominant than religious prejudice after the Civil War, a large Catholic immigration fueled anti-Catholic attitudes. Protestant leaders called for tolerance, yet others said tolerance meant a lack of religious commitment, an indifference to the true faith, and urged Protestants not to give equal status to any other religion. Psychologist William James questioned whether human beings could live with the ambiguity of tolerance for conflicting religious ideas because it would challenge individuals "to think in two contradictory ways at once" (Marty, 1987, p. 67).

Forced to disband by federal troops during Reconstruction, the Ku Klux Klan was revived in 1915. In their efforts to promote and maintain white supremacy in the United States, the Klan employed tactics of intimidation including threats and violence. Although their primary targets were blacks and foreigners, as a Christian group, its members were also hostile to Catholics and Jews. Membership in the Klan increased every year for ten years, peaking at two million in 1925; it fell to 100,000 by 1928. At a 1941 rally in Charleston, the Grand Dragon of North Carolina was heckled and booed by many of the 3,000 who attended (Myers, 1960). The last time the Klan's anti-Catholicism would be seen on the national stage was in the presidential election of 1928.

How did the 1928 election demonstrate anti-Catholic prejudice?

The Democratic Party nominated Alfred E. Smith, the first Catholic to run for president. Some political and religious leaders hailed the nomination as evidence of growing religious tolerance; others saw it as a threat to the social order. The Klan and other anti-Catholic organizations insisted that the Vatican was directing Smith's campaign with a Jesuit committee assigned to persuade Protestants to ignore Smith's religion as an issue. Presbyterians were urged to vote for the Republican candidate. Methodists were urged to vote for the man who prayed the same way they did. Myers (1960) quoted an excerpt from an anti-Catholic magazine claiming that Smith would get not only the Catholic vote, but also "the Jew and Negro vote . . . gamblers, the red-light and dope-ring vote . . . the Jew-Jesuit movie gang (vote) who want sex films and Sunday shows to coin millions through the corruption of youth" (p. 268).

Although anti-Catholic prejudice contributed to Smith's defeat, it is not clear how large a role it played. Democrats were the minority party, the economy was doing well, and Republican candidate Herbert Hoover was widely respected. Despite the anti-Catholic assault, Smith received 40% of the vote, more than the Protestant Democratic candidates had received in the two previous elections (34% in 1920, 28% in 1924). Smith had a higher percentage of votes than a majority of Democrats running for Congress in that election (Hudson, 1973).

After Franklin Roosevelt was elected President in 1932, Catholic participation in national politics became common, and the question of whether a Catholic could be elected President was answered in 1960 when Americans chose John F. Kennedy. It is possible that Kennedy's election was not so much a measure of increased religious tolerance as it was an indication of what has been called the "Americanization of Religion." Since World War II, attitudes of American Catholics gradually diverged from a strict recognition of Roman Catholic Church doctrine and more closely allied with attitudes of the Protestant majority. By the 1990s, polls documented Catholic attitudes as similar to Protestant attitudes on such issues as abortion, birth control, ordination of

FIGURE 7.3

The Ku Klux Klan had its highest membership when the group sponsored this 1925 march in front of the nation's capitol.

Source: Photo courtesy of Brown Brothers.

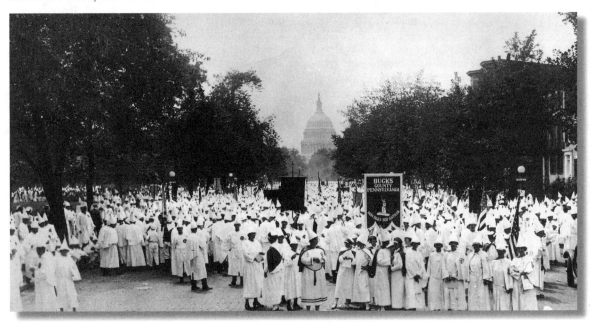

women, and marriage of priests (Kosmin and Lachman, 1993).

How were Jews affected by the "Americanization of Religion"?

In the late 1880s, Jews contended that they should be regarded as another denomination and accepted in the same spirit as Methodists, Baptists, or Lutherans. They were unsuccessful partly because at that time Jews were defined as a race more than a religion, a transformation that began in 1451 when the King of Castile endorsed a blood purity statute (*limpieza de sangre*), declaring that Jews who converted to Christianity could not hold office in the Catholic Church. Carroll (2001) explained that the concern for blood purity was "a shift from a religious definition of Jewishness to a racial one" (p. 347). By the nineteenth century, the transformation in Europe of societal perceptions of Jews from religious to racial was complete. Nazi Germany could justify arresting Jews who had converted to

Christianity because "once born a Jew, always a Jew" (Wegner, 2002, p. 152).

ANTI-SEMITISM IN AMERICA

By 1870, American public school textbooks referred to Jews as "a race" with traditional stereotypes of Jews as greedy, selfish, and manipulating. Jews were described as unethical entrepreneurs who tried to monopolize certain professions and as the devious power behind the throne in many European countries (Miller, 1976). In 1879 the term **anti-Semitism** was employed for the first time by a German journalist to express his opposition to the Jewish "race." In his essay, Wilhelm Marr made the paradoxical argument that although Jews were inferior to Aryans, they were a threat to Aryan world dominance (Carroll, 2001). Reacting against such pervasive stereotypes, one Jewish writer complained, "In

> Anti-Semitism is a noxious weed that should be cut out. It has no place in America.
>
> **WILLIAM HOWARD TAFT (1857–1930)**

the popular mind, the Jew is never judged as an individual, but as a specimen of a whole race whose members are identically of the same kind" (Eck, 2001, p. 303). This judgment would continue in the "popular mind" for many more decades.

From 1890 to 1914, Jews accounted for 10% of all immigrants. With increased numbers of Jews in America, anti-Semitism was at least as strong as earlier anti-Catholicism. Ironically, despite their experience of oppression, Catholics joined Protestants in vilifying Jews. In the popular press, Eck (2001) found Jews presented as undesirable aliens who could not assimilate because they were "incapable of grasping American ideals" (p. 50), although many Jews refuted the view by achieving extraordinary success, especially in higher education. As the number of Jews at Harvard escalated from 6% in 1908 to 22% in 1922, the president of Harvard proposed establishing a quota for the number of Jews Harvard would accept. Faculty rejected his plan, but Harvard still limited the number of Jews for many decades. Other colleges established quotas for Jewish enrollment anywhere from 3% to 16% (Dinnerstein, 1994).

In what ways was anti-Semitism promoted?

Anti-Semitism had several popular advocates. In the 1920s, one was Henry Ford. In his role as publisher of a weekly newspaper, *The Dearborn Independent*, Ford printed the text of "The Protocols of the Elders of Zion," which documented the activities of a Jewish conspiracy plotting a revolution to undermine Christian civilization and establish Jewish supremacy throughout the world. Ford's popularity made it likely that his readers would take his warning seriously. In a poll taken in 1923, *Collier's* magazine reported that 260,000 people—over one-third of those polled—endorsed Ford to run for President (Ribuffo, 1997).

Shortly after Ford published "Protocols," the document was exposed as a forgery concocted in the late 1890s by Russian loyalists supporting the Czar. In response to this revelation and to a legal action for slander brought by a Jewish businessman, Ford wrote a letter of apology, promising not to publish anti-Semitic articles again, but the damage had been done. Ford ceased publishing his newspaper, yet he continued to maintain and express anti-Semitic attitudes. In 1938, Ford traveled to Germany to receive a medal from Adolph Hitler in honor of his anti-Semitic actions, and two years later in England during an interview with the *Manchester Guardian*, Ford insisted that "international Jewish bankers" caused World War II (Ribuffo, 1997).

In the 1930s, President Franklin Roosevelt invited many Jews into his cabinet, and over vigorous objections, he appointed a Jew to the Supreme Court, Felix Frankfurter. However, anti-Semitism found a spokesman in a priest named Charles Edward Coughlin. In his popular radio show, Father Coughlin attacked President Roosevelt, communists, and Jews. Although reprimanded for his attacks on the president, Church superiors did not criticize Coughlin's anti-Semitism because he disguised it in anti-communist rhetoric (Myers, 1960).

In 1938, Coughlin revealed his anti-Semitic attitudes by reprinting "The Protocols of the Elders of Zion" despite the evidence of its forgery. Nineteen thousand people attended a gathering in Madison Square Garden where Coughlin gave a speech, while surrounded by banners declaring "Smash Jewish Communism!" and "Stop Jewish Domination of Christian America!" Coughlin's use of rumor and distortions of fact to castigate Jews was challenged by Jewish groups, denounced by Protestants, and contradicted by his embarrassed superiors in the Church. He was forced to abandon his radio program in 1940, but for the next three years, young men belonging to his "Christian Frontier" organization roamed the streets in several large cities, affixing obscene materials to Jewish businesses or synagogues and even assaulting Jews they chanced to encounter (Myers, 1960).

During World War II, anti-Semitism intensified. Dinnerstein (1994) quotes an Irish soldier who was disturbed by the anti-Semitism of soldiers who told him that:

All the Jews stay out of the army, or if they get in, they are given commissions—the President is a Jew—you can't get a defense contract unless you are a Jew—Jews own 80% of the nation's wealth—Jews got us into the war. (p. 137)

According to a poll conducted during the war, over half of Jewish soldiers in the armed forces had changed their names to generic American surnames to avoid anti-Semitic remarks from other soldiers. Even Jews in Roosevelt's cabinet were excluded from private clubs catering to people in power. By the end of the war, 58% of Americans agreed with the statement, "Jews have too much power in the United States" (Dinnerstein, 1994, p. 146).

> (The Jew) always talks about the equality of all men, without regard of race or color. Those who are stupid begin to believe that.
>
> ADOLPH HITLER (1889–1945)

What influence did the Holocaust have on American attitudes?

Learning about the horrors of the Holocaust changed American attitudes toward Jews after World War II. Many returning veterans deplored anti-Semitism and other prejudices they had witnessed. Hollywood produced films exposing the prejudice and bigotry of anti-Semitism in America, and one of them, "Gentleman's Agreement," won the Oscar for Best Picture in 1947. Editorials in many newspapers and magazine articles reinforced the idea that anti-Semitism was no longer acceptable in the United States. Although it was in the 1950s that "under God" was added to the Pledge of Allegiance and "In God We Trust" to U.S. currency to emphasize U.S. opposition to "godless communism," being a Catholic, Protestant, or Jew was less important than being someone who believed in the Judeo-Christian God (Fraser, 1999).

In his 1955 analysis of religion in America, *Protestant-Catholic-Jew*, sociologist Will Herberg wrote that Catholics and Jews reflected American attitudes as much as Protestants did. An "Americanization" of religion meant that each faith "regards itself as merely an alternative and variant form of being religious in the American way" (p. 278). Herberg admitted that the majority of Americans were still anti-Semitic, but they knew it was inappropriate to act on their feelings. *Look* magazine reported that Hitler had made anti-Semitism unequivocally disreputable. A series of polls in the 1950s reported Americans expressing increasingly positive attitudes toward Jews. Discrimination against Jews still occurred, especially in such prestigious professions as law and medicine, yet doors had opened, especially to colleges and universities. By 1965, *Time* magazine reported that "anti-Semitism is at an all time low," and that overt expressions of anti-Semitism were "out of fashion" (Dinnerstein, 1994, p. 171). However, a national immigration law was passed in 1965 that would challenge Americans with a new religious dilemma.

THE IMPACT OF IMMIGRATION REFORM ON RELIGIOUS DIVERSITY

The 1924 U.S. immigration law had prohibited Asian immigration, and strict quotas ensured that the majority of American immigrants would be white and Christian. When President Lyndon Johnson signed the Immigration and Nationality Act of 1965, not only did the racial makeup of incoming immigrants change dramatically, so did their religious affiliation. From 1960 to 1990, Asians constituted more than 5 million of 15 million immigrants to the United States. From 1990 to 1999, the Asian population in the United States grew 43% to total almost 11 million people, among them 4 million Buddhists. Approximately 170,000 Hindus live in New York City alone. Nationwide, America can claim over 6 million Muslims, more than the number of Presbyterians and equal to the number of Jews (Eck, 2001). There are increasing numbers of children from diverse faiths: About 20% of students attending public school in the United States identify as "religious minorities" (Clark, Vargas, Schlosser, and Allmo, 2002).

Although proportions of those representing different religions have changed, what has not changed is the importance of religion. According to Elshtain (2001), data from the 2000 census report that 90% of Americans believed in God and 70% were members of a church, synagogue, or mosque. To appreciate this variety of faiths, Americans must confront stereotypes. We often make assumptions about an individual's religion based on their ethnicity, although there is religious diversity within any religion. An old stereotype is that Irish Americans are Catholic, even though the majority of Irish Americans are not. Most Asian Americans are not Buddhist or Hindu but Christian, as are most Arab Americans, and most American Muslims are not Arabs (Kosmin and Lachman, 1993).

What were the consequences of the reform of American immigration laws?

Unfortunately, recent immigrants continue to encounter prejudice as Americans persist in their past religious animosities and revert to learned stereotypes. After the 1995 bombing of the Murrah Federal Building in Oklahoma City, television broadcasts suggested that it was a terrorist attack and that authorities were pursuing "Middle Eastern-looking" men; the backlash was immediate. Islamic centers across the nation were sites for drive-by shootings and bomb threats. Muslim students on college campuses were assaulted. Muslim parents kept their children home for fear they would be taunted or even assaulted in school.

What the media did not report was the presence of Muslim firefighters rescuing victims of the bombing, Muslim physicians working to save victims' lives, and individual Muslims and Muslim organizations donating money to help the families of the victims. Despite their efforts, Muslims were denied an opportunity to participate in the nationally televised memorial service featuring words of consolation from President Clinton and representatives of Catholic, Jewish, and Protestant faiths.

Often when Americans act on their religious prejudices, it does not occur at a national level. Eck (2001) described a number of incidents that occurred across the nation. During the 1990s, an Islamic Center in Quincy, Massachusetts, was a site

of arson, as was a Minneapolis mosque. In Memphis, a man fired a shotgun at Muslims going to their mosque. Since September 11, 2001, religious violence has escalated, especially toward Muslims. A Virginia mosque was defaced with graffiti such as "Muslims Burn Forever." A man drove his car through the plate glass doors of a Cleveland mosque, bullet holes were found in the stained glass of an Ohio mosque, and a Texas mosque was firebombed. And violence hasn't been restricted to Muslims. In Boston, a Buddhist temple was vandalized, and Hindu temples were vandalized in Houston and Detroit, and in Illinois and New Jersey. An Egyptian businessman who had resided in the United States for twenty years was shot and killed in his California store. He was a Christian.

It is heartening that most Americans reject the violent discriminatory acts of bigots. Neighbors and community advocates for victims of violence directed at religious groups have responded with kindness, sympathy, and offers of support. Positive responses have consistently countered negative actions against recent immigrants of diverse religious faiths. Since 1991, Muslim chaplains have joined Protestant, Catholic, and Jewish chaplains to open each session of the House of Representatives and the Senate with invocations (Kosmin and Lachman, 1993). A Hindu priest was asked to serve as chaplain to open a September 2000, session of the U.S. House of Representatives.

The largest enclosed shopping facility in the United States is the Mall of America in Minneapolis, Minnesota. In recognition of the religious diversity in America's suburbs, mall administrators created an interfaith group called the Mall Area Religious Council to promote interfaith dialogue and conversations between people of different religions and cultures. Is American interfaith support a harbinger of the future as business and community leaders come to terms with the implications of religious diversity? At a Whirlpool manufacturing plant in Nashville, Tennessee, a Muslim employee quit when he was refused permission to perform his midday prayers; those Muslim employees who remained prayed secretly. After a Muslim support group intervened, Whirlpool managers agreed to schedule afternoon coffee breaks to accommodate the Islamic prayer schedule (Eck, 2001).

Universities and colleges have increasingly promoted interfaith dialogue. Wellesley College developed a Multi-Faith Council, Chapman (CA) University created an All-Faiths Chapel, and Johns Hopkins University instituted an Interfaith and Community Service Center; in each, faiths as diverse as Baha'i, Buddhist, Christian, Jewish, Muslim, and Hindu may come to worship or to talk with members of other faiths. Interfaith discussions not only address commonalities between faiths, but encourage honest dialogue concerning differences in beliefs (Eck, 2001). It is essential that students at colleges and universities engage in religious discussions, because religious freedom requires understanding of different faiths. Public and private educational institutions from elementary grades through high school must also play a critical role in fostering that understanding.

How have schools taught students about the concept of religious freedom?

The history of American education reveals a gradual secularization of public schools. Public schools in the United States originally did not teach about religious freedom; they reinforced Protestant beliefs, causing Catholics and Jews to establish schools for their children in addition to or instead of public schools. History credits Horace Mann with shaping public schools in the United States, yet he was denounced as the "archenemy of the Christian church" for advocating that the Bible should be read—but not interpreted—in school because Biblical interpretation should be a parental prerogative (McMillan, 1984, p. 85). When Bible reading was eliminated, *McGuffey's Reader* became the most popular public school textbook. It referred to God and used Protestant perspectives to deliver its moral lessons. Later revisions of McGuffey eliminated overt religious language but maintained a sermonizing tone. By 1870, most Protestants agreed that a sectarian religious perspective should not be pre-

sented in public schools, but that a nonsectarian Christian perspective was essential (Nord, 1995).

Starting in the 1940s, U.S. federal courts wrote several decisions related to the constitutional guarantee of religious freedom being enforced or contradicted in schools (see Table 7.1). The next sixty years of court rulings would challenge schools to eliminate their Christian bias and to become more **secular,** reflecting the civic culture and not promoting any religious perspective. United States courts have ruled that schools are forbidden to force students to say the Pledge of Allegiance, compel students to pray, begin the day with devotional reading from the Bible, have a minister, priest, or rabbi give a prayer at graduation, post the Ten Commandments in classrooms or hallways, or teach religion disguised as science—"creationism"—as a scientific alternative to evolutionary theory (Fraser, 1999; Allen, 1996; McMillan, 1984).

In 2002, the Ninth Circuit court created a controversy in *Newdow* v. *United States Congress* by ruling that the inclusion of the phrase "under God" meant the Pledge of Allegiance served a religious, not a secular purpose. The court concluded that schools could not have students recite the Pledge even if they are allowed to choose not to participate because the school setting is a coercive context that puts pressure on students to conform to the majority (Pauken, 2003).

How can public schools teach about religion in a way that respects all religions?

As federal and district courts ruled on what schools could not allow, they also provided guidelines for constitutional activities. Schools were encouraged to teach objectively about all religions, and even about the Bible. As Justice Clark wrote:

> It might well be said that one's education is not complete without a study of comparative religion or the history of religion and its relationship to the advancement of civilization. It certainly may be said that the Bible is worthy of study for its literary and historic qualities. (McMillan, 1984, p. 163)

Although schools cannot force students to pray, schools cannot prevent a student from praying, as long as the prayer does not create a disruption. If

> The First Amendment has erected a wall between church and state. That wall must be kept high and impregnable.
>
> **JUSTICE HUGO BLACK (1886-1971)**

1943	*West Virginia* v. *Barnette* (brought by a Jehovah's Witness family): No child could be forced to stand and recite the Pledge of Allegiance.
1947	*Everson* v. *Board of Education*: Students attending parochial schools could be transported to their schools on buses provided for public school students.
1962	*Engel* v. *Vitale*: Students attending public schools could not be forced to recite state written prayers.
1963	*Abington Township* v. *Schempp*: Public schools could not insist that students recite the Lord's prayer or any prayer nor require "devotional Bible reading."
1968	*Epperson* v. *Arkansas*: An Arkansas law forbidding the teaching of Darwin's theory of evolution in school was ruled unconstitutional.
1971	*Lemon* v. *Kurtzman*: Established a three-part test for subsequent cases. The principle of separation of church and state was not violated if the statute, policy, or practice under consideration: (1) had a secular legislative purpose; (2) did not foster excessive government entanglement with religion; (3) neither advances nor inhibits religion as its primary purpose.
1980	*Stone* v. *Graham*: A Kentucky law requiring a copy of the Ten Commandments posted in every public school classroom was declared unconstitutional.
1985	*Wallace* v. *Jaffree*: Since the intent of an Alabama law requiring a moment of silence was "to return prayer to the public schools," it was unconstitutional.
1987	*Edwards* v. *Aguilar*: Schools could not teach creationism as an alternative to evolutionary theory because creationism was based on religious beliefs and did not satisfy the criteria to constitute a scientific theory.
1990	*Westside Community Schools* v. *Mergens*: If a public school allows community groups to use its facilities, religious groups must have equal access.
1992	*Lee* v. *Weisman*: Schools could not include prayers offered by religious leaders (of any faith) at graduation ceremonies; if a school policy or practice has a coercive effect, it is unconstitutional.

TABLE 7.1

Court Rulings on Religion in Public Schools (a selection of significant cases)

Source: Between Church and State: Religion and Public Education in a Multicultural America by James Fraser, 1999.

students representing a religious group want to use school facilities, they have the same right of access as any community group.

In 1999, the U.S. Department of Education sent comprehensive guidelines on issues related to religion in public schools to every public school in the nation. A committee of diverse religious and educational leaders had developed the guidelines that include legal assurances for recommended practices (al-Hibri, 2001). Teaching *about* religions has now been incorporated into national and state standards for teachers (Douglass, 2002); following the guidelines will ensure that schools address those standards by providing accurate information about fundamental beliefs of the world's major religions.

AFTERWORD

Although historically, the Protestant majority in the United States resisted accepting other faiths vigorously, at times even violently, Protestants of all denominations accepted each other on equal terms and eventually accepted Catholics and Jews. Will the faiths of new immigrants—Hinduism, Buddhism, Islam, and other non-Christian religions—become acceptable to the dominant Judeo-Christian groups in America? Although U.S. courts have consistently upheld the principle of religious freedom, schools will also have an important role to play.

In the past, public schools were part of the problem, promoting Protestantism and reinforcing anti-Catholic and anti-Semitic attitudes. As schools became more secular in response to the religious diversity of immigrants, they engaged less in proselytizing and contributed to the resolution of conflicts among Protestants, Catholics, and Jews. Because current immigration has increased non-Christian religious diversity in the United States, it is important that public schools continue to affirm court decisions and use the guidelines offered by the Department of Education. Students need to learn more about other religions and to discuss issues such as Elshtain's comment: "My freedom is not in opposition to yours, but each of us together is free insofar as we sustain respect and recognition for others" (2001, p. 48).

If the United States is to be successful as a religiously diverse society, it is essential that "the principal religious groups not only claim freedom for themselves, but affirm equal freedom for others, whatever their beliefs may be" (Katz and Southerland, 1968, p. 269). As students learn about diverse religions they may also come to appreciate why religious freedom was guaranteed in the Bill of Rights, and why it has been so difficult to achieve that ideal.

> We cannot live in a world in which our economies and markets are global, our political awareness is global, our business relationships take us to every continent, and the Internet connects us with (the world) . . . imagining that somehow the one we call God has been primarily concerned with us and our tribe.
>
> DIANE ECK (1945–)

TERMS AND DEFINITIONS

Agnostic A belief that human beings cannot prove or disprove the existence of God

Anti-Catholicism Expressing stereotypes about or prejudices against Catholics or discriminating against Catholics

Anti-Semitism Having anti-Jewish prejudices or stereotypes, or engaging in discrimination against Jews

Atheism Believing that God does not exist

Deism A belief that God created the world and the system of natural laws that governed the world, but was not a presence (and did not play a role) in everyday life

Denominations A perspective on diverse Protestant faiths that views all of them as a singular Protestant church with different names (denominations)

Established church When one church is declared the official faith of a political unit (a colony or state) and tax revenues are used to fund this church

Religious freedom/religious liberty The right to worship in any church of one's choice consistent with that church's beliefs and practices

Sectarian A perspective on diverse Christian churches or sects in which an individual regards his or her own sect as the "true faith"

Secular The civic culture of a society not reflective of religious perspective

References

al-Hibri, A.Y. (2001). Standing at the precipice: Faith in the age of science and technology. In A. al-Hibri, J.B. Elshtain, and C.C. Haynes (Eds.), *Religion in American public life: Living with our deepest differences.* New York: W.W. Norton.

Explains how the Industrial Revolution produced a mechanistic model and how it has affected the United States, including how the country approaches issues such as the separation of church and state.

Allen, R.S. (1996). *Without a prayer: Religious expression in public schools.* Amherst, NY: Prometheus.

Provides the human story behind the Supreme Court cases on religion in public schools, including the consequences for those individuals who brought those cases forward.

Carroll, J. (2001). *Constantine's Sword: The church and the Jews, a history.* Boston: Houghton Mifflin.

Examines the history of relations between the Catholic Church and the Jews and explains the basis for the historic pattern of anti-Semitism that still exists in the church.

Clark, C., Vargas, M.B., Schlosser, L., & Allmo, C. (2002). It's Not Just "Secret Santa" in December: Addressing educational and workplace climate issues linked to Christian privilege. *Multicultural Education,* Winter, 53–58.

Describes the ways Christianity is affirmed or promoted in subtle and blatant ways at work and in schools, and provides a religious dilemma at a worksite for group discussion.

Dinnerstein, L. (1994). *Anti-Semitism in America.* New York: Oxford.

Summarizes the experience of Jews in America and the various forms of anti-Semitism they have encountered from the colonial period to the present.

Douglass, S. (2002). Teaching about religion. *Educational Leadership,* 60(2) 32–36.

Reports findings from a study of the inclusion of religion in national and state teaching standards and discusses resources and strategies for implementing these standards.

Eck, D.L. (2001). *A new religious America: How a "Christian Country" has become the world's most religiously diverse nation.* New York: HarperCollins.

Examines the growth of diverse religions in the United States, especially with regard to immigration patterns since 1965, and describes both its impact and its potential.

Elshtain, J.B. (2001). Faith of our fathers and mothers: Religious belief and American democracy. In A. al-Hibri, J.B. Elshtain, and C.C. Haynes (Eds.), *Religion in American public life: Living with our deepest differences* (pp. 39–61). New York: W.W. Norton.

Defines the concept of the civil society in America while examining how responsibility for religious rights has become increasingly relegated to the courts in the United States.

Fraser, J.W. (1999). *Between church and state: Religion and public education in a multicultural America.* New York: St. Martin's.

Describes the history of religious diversity in the United States from the colonial beginnings to the present, and examines the critical court cases on religious freedom.

Goodrich, F., & Hackett, A. (1956). *The diary of Anne Frank.* New York: Random House.

Presents ideas and events recorded in Anne Frank's diary; this Pulitzer Prize-winning play was first performed on Broadway in the fall of 1955.

Hendry, J. (2003). Mining the sacred mountain: The clash between the Western dualistic framework and Native American religions. *Multicultural Perspectives* 5(1), 3–10.

Contrasts patterns of western thought with the perspective of Native Americans especially with regard to their views of nature and the protection of the environment.

Herberg, W. (1955). *Protestant-Catholic-Jew: An essay in American religious sociology.* Garden City, NY: Doubleday.

Examines the status of religion in the United States in the early 1950s and explains how the three major religions have achieved equal status in American society.

Hudson, W.S. (1973). *Religion in America: An historical account of the development of American religious life* (2nd ed.). New York: Charles Scribner.

Describes the religious life of Americans from separate faiths moving toward common principles and eventually toward the pluralistic attitudes necessary for religious liberty.

Katz, W., & Southerland, H. (1968). Religious pluralism and the Supreme Court. In W. McLoughlin & R. Bellah (Eds.), *Religion in America* (pp. 269–281). Boston: Beacon Press.

Examines the role played by the Supreme Court in moving the United States from a nation tolerating religious diversity toward the goal of promoting religious pluralism.

Kosmin, B.A., & Lachman, S.P. (1993). *One nation under God: Religion in contemporary American society.* New York: Crown.

Analyzes results from the 1990 National Survey of Religious Identification with data from 113,000 Americans; this was one of the most extensive religious surveys ever conducted.

Lippy, C.H. (1994). *Being religious, American style: A history of popular religiosity in the United States.* Westport, CT: Praeger.

Describes religious beliefs and practices of Americans from colonial times to the present that supplement or replace beliefs and practices from traditional religions.

Marty, M. (1987). *Religion and republic: The American circumstance.* Boston: Beacon.

Examines contemporary religion in the United States and the role of environment in the development of American spirituality and the concept of civil religion in relation to pluralism.

McMillan, R.C. (1984). *Religion in the public schools: An introduction.* Macon, GA: Mercer University Press.

Examines the historical background of the separation of church and state principle and provides the written Supreme Court decisions on major cases with minimal editing.

Miller, G.T. (1976). *Religious liberty in America: History and prospects.* Philadelphia: Westminster.

Provides a history of conflicts related to religious diversity in the United States and progress made toward religious liberty with an emphasis on the period prior to the twentieth century.

Myers, G. (1960). *History of bigotry in the United States* (Rev. ed.), G. Christman (Ed.). New York: Capricorn.

Describes the historic targets of bigotry since colonial days, with emphasis on Catholics, Jews, and immigrants, and the actions taken against these minorities by the majority.

Nord, W.A. (1995). *Religion and American education: Rethinking a national dilemma.* Chapel Hill: The University of North Carolina Press.

Addresses current dilemmas involving religion in public schools and establishes a middle ground to accommodate religion while maintaining the principle of religious liberty.

Pauken, P. (2003, January). *I Pledge Allegiance to the Curriculum: The establishment clause and the legal balance between educational authority and individual rights.* Presented at the Hawai'i International Conference on Education, Honolulu.

Reviews court cases concerning the First Amendment's guarantee of religious liberty and the legal principles that have evolved, especially with regard to religion in the schools.

Ravitch, F.S. (1999). *School prayer and discrimination: The civil rights of religious minorities and dissenters.* Boston: Northeastern University Press.

Provides an overview of the history of religious intolerance and currently legal religious practices in public schools and provides a model statute to promote religious freedom.

Ribuffo, L.P. (1997). Henry Ford and the international Jew. In J. Sarna (Ed.), *The American Jewish experience* (2nd ed., pp. 201–218). New York: Holmes & Meier.

Traces Henry Ford's involvement in anti-Semitism through a series of articles in his newspaper and describes Ford's impact on anti-Semitic attitudes around the world.

Wegner, G.P. (2002). *Anti-Semitism and schooling under the Third Reich.* New York: Routledge Falmer.

Describes the Nazi educational philosophy and the anti-Semitic curriculum and pedagogy developed by German educators to promote Nazi ideas about race and racial purity.

Summary Exercises

See page 19 for exercises to help you summarize the main points and define key terms in this chapter.

Personal Clarification Exercises

In Chapter 7, two exercises promote discussion about our sensitivity to issues of oppression.

Clarification Exercise #1 Separation of Church and State Activity

Directions: Read the December 5th situation below. Then decide which requests for changing school policy from the following list will be implemented (Agree) and which requests for change will be rejected (Disagree). If your team members do not know a term, ask your instructor to define it for you. Upon completion of your group's consideration of the twelve proposed rule changes, compare your team recommendations with those of another team; explain your rationale for agreement and disagreement; be prepared to present your larger group rationale for each rule change and for each rule that your group feels should not be changed.

Separation of Church and State in Schools Activity

The Situation: It is December 5th. As a citizen and parent, you have been publicly assigned to a select committee to examine a list of new school district policies that has been proposed by a group of Jewish parents. Twenty-five percent of the students in the district are Jewish, 15% have no religious affiliation, and 60% declare some sort of Christian affiliation.

Proposed District Policies:

Breaks and Absences

1. Vacation breaks during the school year will be established without regard to religious holidays.
2. Jewish children will be excused when they are absent on Jewish holidays.
3. Jewish teachers will not be charged with personal leave when they are absent during Yom Kippur and Rosh Hashana.

Religious Holidays

4. No celebration of Christmas as part of the school curriculum.
5. No celebration of Hanukkah as part of the school curriculum.
6. No creche shall be displayed in school.
7. No Christmas trees shall be displayed in school.
8. No gift exchanges or Christmas parties in class.

Curricular and Extracurricular Activity

9. Impact of religious values on historic or current events and issues will be examined and discussed in the classroom.
10. The Holocaust will be studied as part of the World War II unit and as part of the history of Western civilization.
11. No extracurricular activity will be scheduled on Friday evening.
12. No songs that refer to Jesus Christ will be sung in the winter music program.

Clarification Exercise #2 Religious Freedom in the United States: What Is Your Judgment?

Directions: Many people have come to America because of the guarantee of religious freedom, although there have always been issues about how far that freedom can go. In a 1999 study of 675 workers from six different faiths, 20% reported that they had experienced or witnessed religious discrimination in their workplace. The following list contains incidents that have actually occurred. Ask your instructor for clarification of terms as needed. Your task is to determine which items you believe violate the rights of people to behave in accordance with their chosen faith.

Religious Freedom in the United States

1. Should a Sikh be allowed to wear his turban on a hard-hat job even though it appears to be a violation of safety regulations?
2. Can a soldier who is a member of Wicca practice his or her religion on an army base?
3. Should Muslims be forced to build their temple with a "Spanish" architectural style that will

match the other buildings in a southern California community instead of building it based on their traditional temple architecture?

4. Because a Jainist student attends the high school, must the cafeteria staff clearly mark the contents of the meals prepared so that the student can be assured of eating only vegetables?

5. Can an Arabic woman teaching in a public school wear her traditional head covering in her classroom?

6. Should members of the Native American Church be allowed to ingest peyote because this drug has historically been part of their religious rituals?

7. Should a Florida city council allow members of the Santeria faith to engage in animal sacrifice because it is traditionally part of their religious practice?

8. Should a Sikh student come to school with the symbolic knife (kirpan) he is required to wear following his initiation?

9. Should Muslim employees be given time to perform obligatory prayers during the workday?

10. Do Seventh Day Adventist or Jewish employees have the right to be excused from work on Saturday because it is their Sabbath?

11. Can Buddhist practitioners who work as clerks be required to participate in company prayers prior to the beginning of their work shift?

Intergroup Exercises

In Chapter 7, two legal case study exercises promote discussion about our sensitivity to issues of oppression.

Intergroup Exercise #1 The Case of Zachary Hood

Directions: Read "The Case of Zachary Hood." Then, based on previous court rulings provided in this chapter and especially the "Lemon test," determine what you believe the courts should decide.

The Case of Zachary Hood

The setting is a first grade classroom in a public school. The teacher tells the students that they may read a story of their choice to the entire class as a reward for doing well in reading. Zachary Hood tells the teacher that he wants to read a story from *The Beginners' Bible* where Jacob and his brother Esau are reunited. The story does not mention God.

The teacher is concerned. If she allows Zachary to read this story will she violate court rulings about appropriate or inappropriate inclusion of religion in public schools? Will this make it appear that she is endorsing the Bible, and therefore Christianity, as a religion? The teacher decides not to allow Zachary to read the story to the class, but she asks him to read it to her privately.

Zachary is hurt by the teacher's decision and doesn't understand why he couldn't read his story. He goes home and tells his parents, and they call the school and meet with the teacher and the principal several times to discuss the issue, but they can come to no resolution. Zachary's parents file a lawsuit against the school.

ADAPTED FROM: *FROM BATTLEGROUND TO COMMON GROUND: RELIGION IN THE PUBLIC SQUARE OF 21ST CENTURY AMERICA* BY CHARLES C. HAYNES IN *RELIGION IN AMERICAN PUBLIC LIFE: LIVING WITH OUR DEEPEST DIFFERENCES* (MARTIN MARTY, ED.) NEW YORK: W. W. NORTON & COMPANY, 2001, PP. 111–112

Intergroup Exercise #2 Difficult Dialogues: Converting Heathens—Are Our Religions Safe?

Directions: In groups of three, develop a dialogue based upon the scenario below. Use the situation described as the basis for your 5-minute role play of what conversations might occur. Do not revise the race and/or ethnicity of your characters. Remain in character at the conclusion of your skit in order to respond to class questions about motivation, purpose, or intent behind your comments during the scene.

Are Our Religions Safe?

Characters:
- Second-year college student majoring in mathematics and computer software design with a strong Missouri Synod Lutheran background
- Returning adult naturalized American student of Kuwaiti descent who schedules classes carefully in order not to miss Muslim prayers
- College instructor in comparative religions to the students above; born of Jewish mother and formerly Hasidic father [See page 148]

In the comparative religions class, the topic of proselytizing arises. After some discussion, the second-year student indicates to the returning adult that she will "Pray for him" because of an explanation that Islamic rule allows people to accept the religions of others and not to convert others to the faith. (A Buddhist exchange student indicates that he feels there are admirable qualities in all faiths, and chooses not to debate merits of Lutheran superiority.) The mathematics major insists even more that those of other faiths must accept her definition of Christianity in order to be accepted into heaven and that it is their duty to do so by seeking out others in their homelands.

Intergroup Exercise #3 Create a Memorial: Religion, Friendship, and the Neighborhood

Directions: Sometimes we are asked to carry out requests on behalf of others. In this case, your team is asked to create a neighborhood memorial service. As a highly responsible team of three, obtain as much information as possible before putting your plan into action. First, read and discuss the situation that is presented below. Then, develop four to six questions regarding information that you need before creating the event that is your responsibility; prepare to ask your questions to others in order that you can complete your task.

Create a Memorial: Religion, Friendship, and the Neighborhood

The Situation: Four long-time neighborhood friends have perished in a dreadful automobile accident. You and two other neighbors of the group have been asked to create an ecumenical memorial service that represents the faiths of those who died. Interestingly, each of the four represents a different faith: Muslim, Christian, Atheist, and Jew.

Part One: Ask your questions to the assembled group, all of whom are interested in your task. Help to answer the questions of others who have been charged with developing similar proposals for the closure to the incident.

Part Two: Discuss (1) What could be appropriate as a fitting memorial service for your friends and (2) What guidelines you will provide to the six speakers who have been invited to conduct the occasion.

Part Three: Present your plan to the group. Explain the rationale for your program to the class, and specify the guidelines that you will give to the speakers.

Part Four: Following the completion of each team's proposal and guidelines, create a single event using the combined wisdom of your whole group: What will the service look like? When will it be held? Not held? What kinds of appeals to spirituality and to conscience would be appropriate? Not appropriate? On behalf of your four friends, how can their disparate contemporary religious perspectives be reconciled? Why is—or isn't—this task difficult? In what ways is the idea of a memorial service appropriate for your neighborhood?

CHAPTER 8

Rejecting Oppressive Relationships: The Logic of Cultural Pluralism for a Diverse Society

"In the United States, we have the richest mix of ethnic groups, of racial groups, of global experience that the world has ever known and it is this richness of this mix that yields our incredible creativity and innovation. We have not even begun to experience the real potential of our fantastic human resource mix—our competitive edge in the global economy."

JAMES NAISBITT (1929–)

James Naisbitt, author and respected consultant, provides corporate clients with analyses of data and trends to facilitate corporate decision making related to many pertinent social issues. In his remarks above, Naisbitt confronts a reality that is becoming unavoidable: the diversity of human beings in the United States that is steadily increasing. America has become more diverse than any other nation in the world.

DIVERSITY IN THE UNITED STATES

In 2050, non-Hispanic whites will constitute 53% of the U.S. population; white males will represent about 26% of the population and many of them will be retired, resulting in about half of the workforce consisting of people of color (Schaefer, 2004). For the social security system to continue to provide its promised benefits, people of color will need jobs that pay living wages. All Americans must care about diversity because in our complex, technological society we are already highly dependent upon each other.

The most dramatic demographic changes in the immediate future will occur in bellwether states such as California, Texas, and Florida. According to Smith and Edmonston (1998), over half of the workforce in Texas will be black or Hispanic by 2035, a demographic prediction that does not include other workers of color who are currently part of the Texas workforce: Native Americans, Asian Americans, and Pacific Island Americans. Since predicted demographic changes have not yet occurred in many areas of the United States, it is possible for some of us to ignore population diversity. Still, even if we focus on the present, it is difficult to be oblivious to population changes occurring through immigration and internal migration in America.

Based on data from the 2000 census, Pipher (2002) reported that one in ten people in the United States was born in another country and that one in five children in school is a child of recent immigrants. Historically, immigrants tended to settle in urban areas of a few states, primarily New York, California, and Florida, but immigrants now live in smaller cities of all states. Pipher illustrates this point by observing that in a Lincoln, Nebraska, newspaper "Our obituary column . . . is filled with Hrdvys, Andersens, Walenshenskys, and Muellers. But the births column . . . has many Ali, Nguyen, and Martinez babies" (p. 6).

Demographers track movement of people in society, yet none can predict accurately what the mix of people will be in the future. Demographers tend to be conservative in their speculations, yet the harbingers of change to come surround us. Pipher (2002) provides this example: Police in Nashville, Tennessee, have computers that explain laws and basic words for simple requests or demands in twenty languages. Rather than debate demographic predictions, it is more pertinent to consider how the current white majority responds to population changes.

How have members of the majority responded to diversity?

The history of the United States reveals that the dominant white majority has never been consistently respectful of the rights of subordinate groups. The American majority has maintained a suspicion, even distrust, for people regarded as "other" whether by race, ethnicity, national origin, religion, or by some other aspect that makes them different. Distrust and suspicion continue, and are being met with increasingly militant attitudes by subordinate groups, causing many in the majority to define diversity as a problem in today's society.

The threat of ethnic divisiveness has become a popular topic among media pundits and some scholars. Columnist George Will criticizes higher education's efforts to advocate for diversity, chastising institutions for engaging in "political correctness." Skeptical of the recent emphasis on diversity, Arthur Schlesinger, Jr. (1991) argued that promoting multiculturalism would lead to the "balkanization" of the United States. Others refer to ethnic conflict in the former Yugoslavia as an example of the dangers of promoting ethnic affiliations. In the wake of the destruction of New York's World Trade Center, Americans assaulted and killed Arab Americans and vandalized mosques in several U.S. cities. The violent responses occurred despite appeals from religious and political leaders, including President Bush, emphasizing that Islamic faith is not responsible for terrorist actions. Misguided responses do not bode well for our future as the nation with the most diverse population on earth.

It is imperative that Americans understand how we benefit from diversity and that we learn more about about previous and current contributions of diverse groups in our society because the real threat to our nation is not diversity but ignorance. Some Americans are choosing to focus on opportunities in a diverse society rather than upon problems in areas such as business, community, and education. This issue does not simply affect the United States; rather, it is global. Naisbitt and Aburdene (1990) were among the first to describe global societies becoming culturally homogenized in the 1980s. Looking ahead to the twenty-first century, they predicted a "backlash against uniformity" as people struggled to "assert the uniqueness" of their culture in the global village: "As our outer worlds grow more similar, we will increasingly treasure the traditions that spring from within" (p. 120).

> We are now at the point where we must decide whether we are to honor the concept of a plural society which gains strength through diversity or whether we are to have bitter fragmentation that will result in perpetual tension and strife.
>
> **JUSTICE EARL WARREN (1891–1974)**

ATTITUDES ABOUT DIVERSITY

Historians have long maintained that to understand the present, we must understand the past. In terms of diversity, the best way to understand historic attitudes toward societal diversity is to examine how Americans have responded to immigration, the primary source of our diversity. Although some Americans have been (and still are) guilty of anti-immigrant sentiments, many have expressed positive beliefs about immigrants assimilating into society. By reviewing past and present attitudes concerning immigration, Gordon (1964) described consistent ideological perspectives with regard to ethnic diversity: Anglo conformity, melting pot, and pluralism. Brooks (1996) and others have described a fourth perspective: separatism. Taken together, the four perspectives represent historic and contemporary American views on ethnic diversity. Curiously, despite the persistence of these ideological points of view, Anglo conformity has been and continues to be the dominant perspective on racial and ethnic diversity in the United States.

What does it mean to have an Anglo conformity perspective?

Cole and Cole (1954) first identified **Anglo conformity** as the efforts of English colonists to institute American values, norms, and standards perpetuated ever since. Anglo conformity is an extension of English culture and European civilization. It rejects diversity in favor of homogeneity, maintaining that everyone should conform to values, norms, and standards determined by the Anglo founders of the country and modified by a continuing white majority.

Anglo conformity requires that immigrants stop speaking native languages and use only English as soon as possible. Anglo conformity requires immigrants to abandon their ethnic heritages—the customs, ceremonies, clothing, and traditions of their former culture. Even if their native lands are European, immigrants have been expected to adopt American ways and to become similar to everyone else. Barrett and Roediger (2002) explained that people of color have found Anglo conformity to be a problem because it "took place in a nation obsessed by race. For new immigrant workers the processes of 'becoming white' and 'becoming American' were connected at every turn" (p. 30). Since immigrants of color could never become white, they could never completely achieve the goal of Anglo conformity: to look and act just like the members of the white majority.

When referring to individuals assimilating into society, social scientists often use the term *Americanization*, yet it still refers to Anglo conformity.

Early in our nation's history, Americanization was a process of assimilation applied even to children of indigenous people. In the late 1800s, as public schools were expected to be responsible for the Americanization of immigrant children, schools created by the Bureau of Indian Affairs (BIA) were expected to "Americanize" Native American children. Indians had long been viewed as an obstacle to U.S. expansion and occupation of new territories; Adams (1995) quoted a liberal reformer who argued that "We must either butcher them or civilize them, and what we do we must do quickly" (p. 2). The insistence on Americanizing Indian children led to the creation of BIA boarding schools. As illustrated in the photographs of Navajo student Tom Torlino (Figure 8.1), BIA boarding schools were a dramatic example of the Anglo conformity ideal.

How did the BIA boarding schools promote Anglo conformity with Indian children?

At first, Indian schools were established on reservations, but being close to parents meant Indian children would return home and go "back to the blanket"—back to Indian values and behaviors. Parental influence defeated one of the major purposes of BIA schools, which was, as Adams (1995) explained, to teach values: "to respect private property . . . to realize that the accumulation of personal wealth is a moral obligation" (p. 22). In order for the BIA to be more confident of success in its Americanization efforts, Indian children were taken to boarding schools away from reservations, where

> Two deer, two owls will behave differently from each other. I have studied many plants. The leaves of one plant, on the same stem, none is exactly alike. . . . If the Great Spirit likes the plants, the animals, even little mice and bugs to do this, how much more will he abhor people being alike, doing the same thing.
>
> **JOHN LAME DEER (1903–1976)**

FIGURE 8.1

Anglo conformity is vividly illustrated in these two pictures of a Navajo student, Tom Torlino, before and after being enrolled in a BIA boarding school.

Source: Princeton Collections of Western Americana, Princeton University Library

they were not allowed to return home even on weekends. Although years passed before anyone recognized the absurdity of trying to Americanize Native Americans, the boarding school experiment ultimately failed. Their emphasis on conformity, uniformity, and individual achievement were too contrary to intrinsic Indian values.

Which immigrant groups benefited from Anglo conformity?

Northern European ethnic immigrants to the United States could more easily achieve Anglo conformity. To insist that people Americanize—dress, talk, think, behave, and conform fully to the white majority—is an advantage for those with white skin. However, white advantage created frustration and anger for people of color, who rejected their heritage and native language and who imitated white behavior but could not overcome the disadvantage of skin color; they could not be as successful as their white peers. As Americans of color were denied rewards given to white ethnic groups, some with lighter skin opted to claim white skin—"passing for white"—although some who succeeded paid a psychological price. Their success illustrated the

power of Anglo conformity and contradicted the concept of America as a melting pot.

What does it mean to describe America as a melting pot?

The **melting pot** perspective is that immigrants to America need not relinquish their entire racial or ethnic heritage. Instead, the idea was that ethnic differences would blend into the dominant culture to create a new identity, an American identity, made up of cultures and customs carried to America by all immigrants. This perspective was first articulated by eighteenth century French immigrant Hector St. John de Crevecouer, who said of the United States: "Here individuals of all nations are melted into a new race of men" (Schlesinger, 1991, p. 12). Others such as Ralph Waldo Emerson also alluded to a melting pot concept, but Americans scarcely responded.

It was in 1908 when Israel Zangwill established this engaging and popular metaphor in the American imagination as his successful play, *The Melting Pot,* opened in Washington, D.C. during a tidal wave of immigration. The melting pot has been especially attractive in intellectual, artistic, and political circles with its compelling image of Americans as a blend

The energy of the Irish, Germans, Swedes, Poles, and Cossacks, and all the European tribes—and of the Africans, and of the Polynesians—will construct a new race, a new religion, a new state, a new literature.

RALPH WALDO EMERSON (1803–1882)

FIGURE 8.2

A political cartoon illustrating the idealistic image of the melting pot. Even though Japanese and Blacks are included in the pot, anti-Irish prejudice is revealed in the caricature of an Irishman with a knife in one hand, the Irish flag in the other, and the caption which reads: "The Mortar of Assimilation — and the One Element That Won't Mix."

Source: Courtesy of Michigan State University Museum.

THE MORTAR OF ASSIMILATION — AND THE ONE ELEMENT THAT WON'T MIX.

of cultures. In the following excerpt, David, a Russian Jew, describes the metaphor but also defines the limits of the melting pot:

> America is God's Crucible, the great Melting Pot where all the races of Europe are melting and re-forming! Here you stand, good folk, think I, when I see them at Ellis Island, here you stand in your fifty groups, with your fifty languages and histories, and your fifty blood hatreds and rivalries. But you won't be long like that, brothers, for these are the fires of God you've come to—these are the fires of God. A fig for your feuds and vendettas! Germans and Frenchmen, Irishmen and Englishmen, Jews and Russians—into the Crucible with you all! God is making the American! (1915, p. 33)

Despite rhapsodic oratory, notice the absence of references to people of color. Blacks, Latinos, Asians, and Native Americans are excluded. Only northern Europeans are invited to this highly selective melting pot; even members of certain white ethnic groups such as Greeks or Italians need not apply! As Laosa (1974) noted, the melting pot favored "the white Anglo-Saxon Protestant (WASP) group and . . . [neglected] certain 'culturally different' groups" (p. 136). Anglo conformity was actually reflected in government policy and educational programs, but the idea of America as a melting pot remained an idea; a belief about America embraced by some, rejected by others.

People of color first questioned the melting pot concept, criticizing it as a myth that had nothing to do with the reality of America's diversity. People of color were not only excluded from the melting pot, they weren't sure they wanted to be included. To them, melting meant giving up their ethnic identification, its history, and its traditions, to be accepted in America. Although the melting pot was supposed to be the combination of all subcultures into a new and superior culture, Laosa (1974) described the process as a "melting away of subcultures [and] the preponderance of the dominant group over the others" (p. 136). People could talk about a melting pot, but Anglo conformity was the reality.

The melting pot perspective de-emphasized differences and emphasized instead the need to disregard diversity and accept immigrants as Americans as long as they learned to speak English and became citizens. The most common expression of the melting pot perspective today is the argument that people should be **color-blind,** that people should ignore a person's skin color. Americans will often say: "When I look at you I don't see color, I just see an American (or a student or a neighbor)."

People of color often are offended by the color-blind approach, arguing that it implies a negative attitude about race. When white people say they don't notice the color of anyone's skin, people of color find it difficult to believe: White Americans seem to advocate being color-blind only when it relates to skin color. People of color question why someone should be oblivious to skin color but not to other colors in the world—flowers, sunsets, animals, rainbows? Seldon (1996) believes the answer indicates a discomfort with those whose skin color is not white. To be color-blind is to pretend that a person is white in order to be able to associate with them, work with them, or view them in a positive way. Color-blindness indicates an attitude about skin color differences that is as negative as anything advocated by the separatist perspective.

How is the separatist perspective negative?

Separatism is the most pessimistic of the four perspectives, yet it may also be the easiest to recognize. Separatists believe that different racial and ethnic groups ought to be apart; they should have their own places and "be with their own kind." The goal of separatism is for diverse groups to tolerate each other. Separatism is based on the premise that ineradicable differences exist between groups of people and that differences inevitably cause hostility. The logical outcome is to believe that different groups must have their own places separate from others and should interact only when necessary. The best a person can hope for is peaceful co-existence.

At different times, both majority and minority group members have advocated for the separatist perspective. Before the Civil War, white separatists advocated for African Americans being relocated to Africa, and some Americans assisted a number of former slaves in creating a new African nation called Liberia. Even President Lincoln considered the idea, but abandoned the project after hearing a vehement rejection of the proposal at a White House meeting with a group of prominent African

Americans including Frederick Douglass (Martin, Jr., 1984). In the 1920s, Marcus Garvey promoted the goal of supporting black entrepreneurs to create a self-reliant black society (Cronon, 1955). For a contemporary example, Appleton (1983) described Switzerland as a "segregated pluralism where the country is divided into four distinct cultures" with four languages (p. 26). Although German speakers in the northern and eastern cantons constitute 70% of the population, 21% live in western cantons and speak French, 8% live in south-central cantons and speak Italian, and 1% living in the Alps speak Romansh.

Although there are separatist groups in the United States today, they attract few followers and most are perceived as hate groups such as the Aryan Nation or Black Muslims. Although not all separatists advocate hatred, they tend to subscribe to the pessimistic separatist premise. Some call for a separate state for African Americans; others reject the concept of integrated schools in favor of returning to the *Plessy* v. *Ferguson* principle of separate but equal education for white children and children of color. Contrasting views will continue to be part of the mix of voices reacting to diversity; however, pluralism is now challenging the dominance of Anglo conformity.

> We are not fighting for integration . . . We are fighting for recognition as human beings.
>
> **Malcolm X (1925–1963)**

What attitudes about diversity does pluralism promote?

Pluralism (also known as **cultural pluralism**) refers to the equal coexistence of diverse cultures in a mutually supportive relationship within the boundaries of one nation (Pai and Adler, 1997). As first articulated by philosophers Horace Kallen and Alain Locke in the 1920s, pluralists believe that people in a diverse society such as the United States should have the right to preserve their cultural heritage and not be forced to abandon it to conform to a dominant culture (Menand, 2001). Pluralism is based on the belief in "equality of opportunity for all people, respect for human dignity and the conviction that no single pattern of living is good for everyone" (Pai and Adler, 1997, p. 102). Beginning in the 1960s, the National Association for the Advancement of Colored People and professional organizations such as the National Education Association have actively promoted pluralism.

Advocates for pluralism believe that diversity is not a difficulty to be overcome, but a positive attribute of a society. American pluralists do not refer to being tolerant of others; to pluralists, tolerance is an inadequate response in a nation as diverse as the United States. As Eck (2001) writes, "Tolerance can create a climate of restraint but not one of understanding. . . . It is far too fragile a foundation for a society . . . [as] complex as ours" (p. 72). In a society guided by pluralistic beliefs, people appreciate differences because everyone is enriched by a diverse society. To pluralists, individuals have the right to maintain and be proud of their racial, cultural, ethnic, or religious heritage.

Separatists say that human differences will never disappear and will always cause conflict. Melting pot advocates ignore differences to avoid problems arising from them. Anglo conformity advocates demand the elimination of differences based upon the assumption that a homogeneous society will be a more harmonious one. By contrast, pluralism encourages individuals to identify themselves in terms of their heritage in addition to identifying themselves as American. Individuals who embrace pluralism tend to identify themselves as Italian American or Polish American, as African American or Arab American, as Mexican American or Cuban American, as Chinese American or Hmong American. The identification means they perceive their identity as being shaped by their racial or ethnic heritages as well as by a more homogenous American culture. A recent adaptation in response to persistent criticisms of "hyphenated Americans" has been to refer to "Americans of Japanese (or other) descent." With regard to preserving one's cultural heritage, some have asked how Italian must an Italian American be? From a pluralist perspective, it is up to each individual to decide how much of the customs, traditions, and language of an ethnic heritage he or she wants to maintain.

Because pluralism promotes bilingual education and maintenance of one's native language, those in the English Only movement seem to misunder-stand the pluralist position as a rejection of the need for English as a common language for all Americans. English Only groups in various states have organized to lobby for legislation establishing English as the official language of that state, with the ultimate goal of eliminating the use of all other languages. Of course, a society including diverse language groups needs a common language, and English has been and continues to be the common language for the United States. Can people become fluent in English without losing the language spoken in their home? Students the world over are taught to be fluent in more than one language. Should children and youth in America who are fluent in a language learned at home be taught English at school while maintaining their first language fluency? Pluralists argue that speaking different languages is a fundamental part of a diversity that enriches our society: People proud of their heritage should not be forced to give up the language associated with it. The concept of pluralism is consistent with American values about individuality and freedom, and as the diversity in our nation increases, it becomes increasingly necessary for Americans to reject Anglo conformity in favor of pluralism.

Why should American society become pluralistic?

Anglo conformity remains the dominant perspective among Americans, even though numerous individuals and organizations advocate pluralism and question the appropriateness of Anglo conformity in a society as diverse as the United States. Although these advocates encounter resistance, they have articulated persuasive arguments in support of the practice and promotion of pluralism in America. Here are five of their compelling reasons:

(1) *The failure of Anglo conformity* has been described by many social critics. Although a majority of Americans has historically endorsed Anglo conformity, it has been ineffective because its demand for conformity contradicts the historic identity of the United States. Eck (2001) observed "America is a nation formed not by a race or a single people, but by the ideals articulated in the succession of founding documents, beginning with the Declaration of Independence" (p. 74). American immigrants have succeeded because they have accepted and embraced the civic culture of the

United States as described by those founding documents; to require conformity based on race, religion, or other human differences in a society with such diversity is by nature unrealistic and illogical (Fuchs, 1990).

Sociologists who note that Anglo conformity has failed in America argue that it is inherently unjust to those who cannot conform adequately because they are not white or Protestant (or at least Christian). People unable to conform have endured oppression, and many are still being oppressed today. Racial and ethnic minority groups are still disproportionately represented in the data on human suffering such as infant mortality rates, unemployment statistics, welfare rolls, inadequately funded schools, and unsafe neighborhoods. The availability of goods and services and accessibility to education and opportunity have been inequitably distributed in the United States based on factors of race, gender, social class, sexual orientation, and disability. Respect and self-respect have also been inequitably gained, an issue that goes beyond equity to raise an ethical question about a lack of human compassion.

(2) *The impact on self-consciousness and self-determination* refers to the impact of being perceived as different on one's efforts to develop the kind of positive self-consciousness that is essential for individuals to be confident in their ability to determine goals and to achieve them. If people consciously feel proud of who they are, it is easier to set goals and to believe they can be reached. Appleton (1983) argued that a primary purpose of democracy is to "provide an opportunity for individuals to choose who and what they will become" (p. 57). It is difficult for people to develop a sense of personal pride and to believe they can achieve their goals when they feel their abilities are constantly being doubted. As people struggle against negative attitudes based on group identification, they are more likely to feel alienated from society.

Sometimes when a majority demands conformity, even being successful can cause problems for minority groups. Other people from an individual's group may be suspicious of his or her achievement and wonder if success means the person has "sold out." In a society that does not value diversity but demands conformity, it is difficult for people from minority groups to define who they are and to be proud of what they have achieved. If prejudicial attitudes are perpetuated in a diverse society, some will be denied their fundamental right to be respected. Being respected by other people is important for developing a positive consciousness of self and a belief in self-determination that ought to be an American's birthright.

(3) *The necessity for human interdependence* concerns the extent to which people depend upon others. Individuals interact in any society; as a society becomes more complex, people inevitably become more dependent upon each other. A complex society relies on technology, cooperation, and division of labor. Some people grow food, some build homes and furniture, some sell and service cars, and so on. People rely upon others to provide the goods and services needed in their daily lives. It is also essential that those in the workforce are paid well enough to support the social security system for retired workers. In any society, but especially in a democratic society, people rely upon each other. According to Pai and Adler (1997) "a democratic society is necessarily pluralistic . . . because it is founded on a belief in the intrinsic worth of individuals and their unique capacities to become intelligent human beings" (p. 109); therefore, becoming a pluralistic society promotes positive relations between individuals in all areas and from all groups within that society.

The lack of a pluralistic perspective concerning racial and ethnic interdependence in the United States contributed to problems in the past. When drug use began to increase in urban ghettos and barrios in the 1950s and 1960s, the larger society ignored it. No one seemed to care what "those people" did to themselves because we did not understand that interdependence means social problems cannot be confined. By the 1970s, drug use by urban and suburban white people increased significantly, and today the entire society is confronted with an enormous health and economic problem because of the availability and use of illicit drugs. Drug use became a significant problem in the United States because the majority did not appreci-

> Pluralism is the greatest philosophical ideal of our time.
>
> **John Dewey (1859–1952)**

ate the interdependence of diverse groups in American society.

White people are not alone in misunderstanding social interdependence. When AIDS first appeared, most people, including people of color, ignored the disease because it seemed to affect only the gay community. Some people said—and some still say—that AIDS was a punishment from God upon homosexuals. It was only when the virus spread to heterosexuals in highly publicized cases that the U.S. government began providing funds for research to find a cure. In the meantime, thousands of human beings died.

Human interdependence exists everywhere, but in a diverse, democratic society such as the United States, citizens must advocate and practice pluralistic attitudes to ensure that our society functions as effectively as possible to be a good place for all (Locke, 1989). The Boy Scout study described in Chapter 3 illustrates this point. When boys competed with each other, hostility developed between groups, but hostility was eliminated when they cooperated to achieve a mutual goal. As Aronson (1999) concluded, "The key factor seems to be mutual interdependence—a situation wherein individuals need one another and are needed by one another in order to accomplish their goal" (p. 332). This is not a new insight. More than three centuries ago, poet John Donne wrote "Any man's death diminishes me . . . therefore never send to know for whom the bell tolls; it tolls for thee" (Simpson, 1967, p. 101).

(4) *The recognition of diversity as an ideal* implies that people must promote the idea that our diversity constitutes the best possible situation. One need only consider what has already occurred as a result of the diversity in the United States: Some of the best art, music, and literature ever created in America was a consequence of borrowing from different cultural traditions. Our modern English language has evolved by adopting words from languages of other cultures as diverse as those of Spain, Germany, France, Italy, Mexico, as well as from African and from Native American dialects (Claiborne, 1983). A major argument for promoting English as a world language is its ability to accommodate infusion of words from other cultures—proving its flexibility and accessibility.

Diversity is regarded as positive when people engage in solving problems. If we all examined problems the same way, we would generate similar solutions. Williams (2003) described a problem-solving conference where a chemical company invited 50 employee women and people of color together with the company's top 125 predominantly white male managers. When divided into problem-solving teams, half of the groups consisted of white males only and half included diverse members by both gender and race. Afterward, the company CEO said, "It was so obvious that the diverse teams had the broader solutions. They had ideas I hadn't even thought of. . . . We realized that diversity is a strength as it relates to problem-solving" (pp. 442–443).

Diversity is also valued in the natural world: The more diversity there is in nature, the more likely it is that human life will adapt as new conditions arise. We have become concerned about endangered species and the destruction of rainforests: If diversity in nature is diminished, whatever potential usefulness we find in a species of plant or animal will be lost permanently. If diversity in nature can be appreciated and valued, should it be so difficult to appreciate diversity in human beings?

(5) *The current existence of diversity* is perhaps the most compelling argument for promoting pluralism. If some quality is characteristic of a society, it makes sense that we value it rather than deny it or try to pretend that it didn't exist. If most of the players on a basketball team are tall, a coach will take advantage of their height to create offensive and defensive strategies. If the tall players graduate and next year's team is short and fast, the coach will take advantage of speed and quickness by creating new offensive and defensive strategies. As the most multicultural society in the world today, we must realize the advantages of diversity and embrace pluralism to capitalize upon our advantages.

Other arguments for pluralism challenge us to think about how our society is changing and what sort of society it could become. To perpetuate Anglo

> Commandment Number One of any truly civilized society is this: Let people be different.
>
> **DAVID GRAYSON (1870–1946)**

conformity is to perpetuate the current fear and hostility of certain groups for each other and the conflicts between them. However, changing societal attitudes to a pluralistic perspective offers hope. Human beings have always encountered problems and conflicts, but in a diverse society, conflicts and problems are more likely to be resolved if everyone were to demonstrate pluralistic attitudes.

VALUING INDIVIDUAL DIFFERENCES

The evidence that Americans already value diversity becomes most apparent when people are asked: "Would you want to live in a society where everyone was the same?" Americans often reply that they would not want to live in such a society. It is an American belief that each person is unique, and most of us are proud of those factors that establish our individuality. The United States has always consisted of people from different races, cultures, and religions. If we value our own uniqueness, it is logical and consistent to value what is unique in others. Pluralists value human differences. Sooner or later, all Americans should embrace pluralism because no other perspective regards differences as an asset for a society. Still, to be a pluralist requires more than claiming to value diversity; pluralism

must be practiced. As Ecks (2001) noted, "diversity alone is not pluralism. Pluralism is not a given but must be created. Pluralism requires participation and attunement to the life and energies of one another" (p. 70). Individuals and organizations committed to pluralism are actively working to bring about social change in the United States and to transform social attitudes from our traditional acceptance of Anglo conformity to acceptance and promotion of pluralism.

Must one be actively involved in change to be a pluralist?

Terry (1975) has developed a matrix (see Figure 8.3) based on the idea that people can be either prejudiced against one or more groups (racist, sexist, homophobic) or they can demonstrate pluralistic attitudes toward diversity. According to Terry, people also can be active or passive in their prejudices or their acceptance of diversity. The matrix identifies four different positions: (1) people may actively assert and promote their prejudices; those with such strong prejudices are typically perceived as extremists (such as a bigot or a male chauvinist). (2) People may be prejudiced without expressing those ideas or behaving in ways that obviously reflect prejudice; they do not disagree with bigots or chauvinists, but do not tend to articulate their ideas on behalf of causes. People in this group passively accept the status quo that has been shaped by past prejudice and thereby perpetuate injustice in our society. They are conformists. They like things as they are and they would like to see them stay that way.

In another position (3) people may reject prejudiced ideas and sympathize with victims of social injustice, but not express their views. Although opposed to prejudice and discrimination, they don't want to risk causing trouble or upsetting anyone, so they say nothing—and do nothing. Similar to those who are passive in their prejudice, people in this group conform to the status quo. By their conformity they help to perpetuate problems that are known to be part of the status quo. There is little difference between prejudiced people and people opposed to prejudicial ideas and actions if they are both passive in their behavior. It is not possible to claim to have pluralistic attitudes and be passive because passivity perpetuates social injustice.

FIGURE 8.3 Matrix for Oppressive and Anti-Oppressive Behaviors

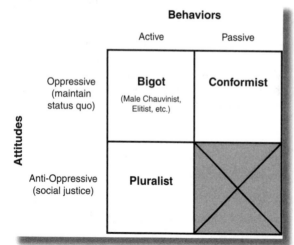

Tatum (1997) describes the existence of prejudice and its benefits for the dominant group as similar to a moving walkway at an airport. People who actively engage in prejudice not only step on the walkway, yet they keep walking as well. People who are passive, whether their attitudes are prejudiced or opposed to prejudice, merely step on the walkway and let it carry them along. To be actively opposed to prejudice and the benefits it brings to the dominant group, people must step off the walkway as soon as they recognize its function. Using Tatum's metaphor, to escape the moving walkway means to be actively involved in promoting social justice.

To promote social justice, (4) people must reject prejudiced ideas, articulate pluralistic attitudes, and act on a new consciousness of human differences. To be a pluralist requires not only positive attitudes, but also a commitment to engage in activities to change social injustices in our society. Contrary to those who promote being "color blind," pluralists argue that it is not consciousness of color that is the problem, but that people's consciousness of color and other differences has tended to be negative. Whites may feel uneasy around someone who is not white. Middle- or upper-class people may have contempt for welfare recipients. Nondisabled people feel pity for people with disabilities. Men may be condescending to women. What is needed is not to ignore differences but to consciously develop a positive attitude toward human differences. Put simply, unless we are part of the solution, we are part of the problem.

What kinds of activities can create social change?

If one has power to address a problem, one need only decide how to use that power to solve the problem. If individuals or groups do not have power to make a desired change, they may employ tactics to persuade those with power to implement the solutions they advocate. The tactics—deliberate and conscious strategies—employed to achieve social change in the United States are as old as the birth of our country as illustrated in the Declaration of Independence and in the writing of John Adams, Thomas Jefferson, Thomas Paine, and others responsible for revolution against England and for eventual American independence. Terry (1975) identified six tactics historically employed to promote social change.

The most basic tactic is to engage in (1) a *dialogue* with those in power to convince them to implement a proposed change. If dialogue fails, people might organize (2) a *confrontation* of some kind: a march, a sit-down strike, or a rally. Confrontation dramatizes the need for change by public demonstration to show that people are concerned about an issue. The goal of confrontation is either to revive a dialogue that had been terminated or to pressure those in control to develop a greater sense of urgency about finding a solution.

If both dialogue and confrontation fail, those advocating change might (3) apply *economic pressure* to those individuals or organizations unwilling to change. Pressure usually takes the form of a **boycott** of products or services related to the issue in dispute. The best-known example of this tactic was the Montgomery bus boycott that lasted more than a year and ended only when the courts ruled in favor of desegregation of public transportation. The bus boycott launched the career of Martin Luther King, Jr., and brought national attention to the civil rights movement (Williams, 1987; Wright, 1991). More recently, Néstlè Corporation was the target of a boycott based on concerns about the marketing strategies Néstlè had employed to sell infant formula in third world countries (Infact, 2003).

In addition to boycotts, economic pressure can be applied through discrimination litigation calling for major economic penalties. In the 1990s, 1,300 African American employees at Coca-Cola brought a class-action lawsuit charging the corporation with discrimination in performance reviews, pay, and promotions. They won the case and were awarded $192 million. To improve the corporate image in the aftermath of the lawsuit, Coca-Cola committed additional resources to diversity issues including "increasing its use of minority suppliers, instituting a formal [diversity] mentoring program, and instituting days to celebrate diversity with its workforce" (Jones and George, 2003, p. 130).

People demanding change often initiate or support (4) *research* designed to examine data relevant to the issue being confronted. Research of a specific issue or problem might define the nature of the problem and perhaps identify its causes. Researchers may or may not recommend specific solutions to address problems, but the purpose of research is to provide information in support of a persuasive argument about changes being proposed to those in control.

Another tactic is to establish (5) an *inside-outside alliance* where a member of a decision-making body (such as a board of directors, city council, or school board) collaborates with a group demanding change. This tactic may involve persuading someone who is already in the decision-making group of the benefits of the changes advocated, or it may mean working to elect a candidate or influence an appointment to the decision-making group of someone who is sympathetic to the need for change. Once elected or appointed, the person selected can represent and articulate arguments for change advocated by outside groups. Jones and George (2003) provide the example of an insurance and annuity company committed to diversity that owned almost a million shares of Nucor Corporation; they exerted pressure on Nucor to add more women and people of color to its board of directors.

When all else fails, people resort to (6) *violence* to demonstrate their frustration and to dramatize the need for change. This tactic might involve destruction of property or an assault on people or both. The use of violence is typically an unplanned and spontaneous reaction such as the Los Angeles riots of 1992 in response to the acquittal of the police officers who had been videotaped beating a black man, Rodney King. When violence is planned, most often it is meant primarily to be a symbolic gesture, such as the Boston Tea Party of 1773.

In the past, violence erupted when frustration over an issue reached a point where people most affected could no longer control their rage, usually responding destructively to a specific incident. During the Civil War, if wealthy young men were drafted, they avoided military service by paying poor and often unemployed men to take their place. The poor knew that these young men were being exploited and that most of them would probably be killed in the war, and their anger resulted in the 1863 Draft Riot in New York City. More recently, riots occurred in several cities in 1968 following the assassination of Martin Luther King, Jr.

> A nation without the means of reform is without the means of survival.
>
> EDMUND BURKE (1729–1797)

Violence rarely resolves problems primarily because incidents igniting riots are typically only symptoms of larger problems. Even if symptoms are addressed following a riot, the causes of those symptoms will eventually create new problems.

In the last half of the twentieth century, people of color participated in riots, especially in urban areas. This has caused many Americans to associate violent tactics for change with people of color, but many groups have resorted to violence at one time or another. In fact, the history of riots in the United States reveals that white people have most often been the group causing riots (see Table 8.1). Jones (1997) reported on the historical record: "With few exceptions . . . previous racial riots had consisted of interracial fighting or the destruction of black communities by white mobs" (p. 46).

In identifying tactics, Terry noted that the first five not only represented nonviolent approaches but also illustrated *the critical role education must play* if individuals and groups are to engage in nonviolent change. The skills and means necessary to engage in nonviolent tactics are related to what we teach in our schools. To be persuasive in dialogue requires the kinds of communication and problem-solving skills students are taught in school. To engage successfully in confrontation, it is essential to understand how to work effectively in groups; from elementary school through college, students are provided opportunities to participate in collaborative activities and projects. In addition, students are taught how to deliver an effective public speech in school, and skillful confrontation requires one or more individuals with an ability to articulate the group's concerns to the public.

Although economic pressure may not seem to relate to schools but simply to the economic resources one controls, studies show that people earn higher salaries based upon the level of education they have completed (Bonilla-Silva, 2001; Department of Labor, 2000). Organizing a successful boycott requires sufficient numbers of people in a community with economic resources to create pressure on those resisting change, and that largely depends upon how much education the people have completed. The level of education an individual has completed is also a major factor in employing the tactic of an inside-outside alliance. The perception of an individual's credibility as a legitimate candidate for election or appointment to a

TABLE 8.1

Riots in America: A Selected List of Riots in the United States Since the Nation Began

Year	Name/Location	Cause
1788	Doctors' Riot/New York City	Medical students digging up bodies
1834	Election Riots/Several cities	Allowing recent immigrants to vote
1835	Abolition Riots/Several cities	Opposing abolitionist efforts
1844	Bible Riots/Philadelphia	Use of Catholic Bible in public schools
1863	Draft Riots/New York City	Corruption and injustice in draft laws
1877	Railroad Riots/Baltimore, Pittsburgh, Chicago, others	Workers striking for fair pay riot in response to militia being called in
1885	Anti-Chinese Riots/Rock Springs, Wyoming	Opposing the railroad's use of Chinese labor
1908	Race Riot/Springfield (IL)	(False) allegation by a white woman of being raped by a black man
1917	Race Riot/East St. Louis	Blacks hired to replace white workers on strike
1921	Race Riot/Tulsa (OK)	(False) allegation by a white woman of an attempted rape by a black man
1942	Zoot Suit Riot/Los Angeles	Allegation that sailors were assaulted by "pachucas" in Zoot Suits leads to sailors attacking Mexican Americans
1965	Watts Riot/Los Angeles	"Routine" traffic stop sparks protest against unjust treatment by police and legal system
1967 1968	Race Riots/Detroit, Newark and other cities	Protesting police brutality against black suspects, other local racial injustices, and the assassination of Martin Luther King, Jr.
1992	Race Riot/Los Angeles	Protesting white jury acquitting white police officers caught on videotape beating a black man (Rodney King)

decision-making body is typically influenced by his or her educational achievements.

Finally, education also plays a pivotal role in research. Although studies can be conducted by anyone with a basic knowledge of principles of effective research, those results that are widely disseminated and that influence public and corporate policies tend to come from studies conducted by people with college experience. Violence is the only tactic that does not require education; as Jefferson wrote in the Declaration of Independence, it is the approach people will choose when they believe no other options exist. It is essential that schools provide people with the skills and means for engaging in nonviolent tactics to address issues of social injustice.

AFTERWORD

The United States today is a society struggling with its internal diversity at the same time that it attempts to understand and adjust to the external diversity of the global village. Americans have much to learn from other nations' experiences with diversity. Historically, societies dominated by Western Europeans have

> Be the change you want to see in the world.
>
> MOHANDIS K. GANDHI (1869–1948)

been intolerant of differences, persecuting those who did not think or act in accordance with what religious or political authorities deemed acceptable, causing conflicts between religions, ethnic groups, and countries. Even when tolerance was practiced, Zeldin (1994) argued that it was for the wrong reasons: "Not out of respect for other people's views, not out of deep knowledge of what they believe, but in despair of finding certainty. It meant closing one's eyes to what other people believed" (p. 272).

Being more diverse than all of Europe, the United States is engaged in a debate between maintaining Anglo conformity or promoting pluralism in response to diversity. Zeldin (1994) explained why advocating tolerance is inadequate: "The tolerated are increasingly demanding to be appreciated, not ignored, and becoming more sensitive to [the] contempt lurking behind the condescension. They do not want to be told that differences do not matter" (p. 272). Pluralism goes beyond tolerance, requiring understanding and acceptance of differences. Many American institutions are responding positively to diversity and taking public positions on the issue. Eck (2001) praised the following statement from the Girl Scouts:

> Pluralism means being inclusive and respectful of people or groups with different backgrounds, experiences, and cultures . . . although you can have diversity without pluralism, you cannot have pluralism without valuing diversity. (pp. 76–77)

If Americans are to demonstrate pluralistic attitudes, educators must teach all students about diversity, and how individuals from diverse groups have contributed to our society. If the changes needed to improve and sustain this society are to come as a consequence of nonviolent tactics for change—from discussion and debate in the context of mutual respect—teachers must help students develop the abilities to use nonviolent tactics effectively. How schools can fulfill this role and what pluralistic policies and practices illustrate the changes happening in the United States will be the focus of the final section of this book, but first it is necessary to understand the problems experienced by diverse groups in our society.

> We are all Americans who, because of our cultural heritage, contribute something unique to the fabric of American life. We are like the notes in a chord of music—if all the notes were the same, there would be no harmony, no real beauty, because harmony is based on differences, not similarities.
>
> ROSA GUERRERO (1934–)

TERMS AND DEFINITIONS

Anglo conformity Views the values, norms, and standards of the United States as an extension of English culture because the English were the dominant group during the colonial era and when the new nation was emerging

Boycott To abstain from using, buying, or associating with a group, organization, or nation to protest an injustice and to force the other to address this injustice

Color-blind A response to race based on the belief that a person should not notice or consider the skin color of another

Melting pot The conceptual belief that when immigrants from diverse racial/ethnic backgrounds come to the United States they blend into the culture and, mixed together with those who have come before, develop into a new, distinctly American identity

Pluralism (Cultural Pluralism) The equal coexistence of diverse cultures in a mutually supportive relationship within the boundaries of one nation

Separatism The conceptual belief in the notion of establishing entirely separate societies for each distinct racial, ethnic, or other groups that exist within a society

REFERENCES

Adams, D.W. (1995). *Education for extinction: American Indians and the boarding school experience, 1875–1928.* Lawrence: University Press of Kansas.
Describes the establishment of the Bureau of Indian Affairs boarding schools and examines their impact on the Indian students who attended them.

Appleton, N. (1983). *Cultural pluralism in education: Theoretical foundations.* New York: Longman.
Examines how the United States has become pluralistic, how American education has responded to pluralism, and what our pluralistic society might look like in the future.

Aronson, E. (1999). *The social animal* (8th ed.). New York: W. H. Freeman.
Presents an overview of research in social psychology and describes patterns and motives revealed in these studies concerning human behavior.

Barrett, J.R., & Roediger, D. (2002). How white people became white. In P. Rothenberg (Ed.), *White privilege: Essential readings on the other side of racism* (pp. 29–34). New York: Worth.
Discusses the process of Americanization of immigrants to the United States with attention to the use of white privilege as an inducement for immigrants to conform to the majority.

Bonilla-Silva, E. (2001). *White supremacy and racism in the post-civil rights era.* Boulder, CO: Lynne Rienner.
Examines why blacks and other racial minorities remain behind whites financially, and in terms of occupation, health, educational attainment, and other social indicators.

Brooks, R.L. (1996). *Integration or separation?: A strategy for racial equality.* Cambridge, MA: Harvard University Press.
Explains why racial integration and separatist movements have not been successful in the United States, and discusses how a "limited separation" approach could be a successful alternative.

Claiborne, R. (1983). *Our marvelous native tongue: The life and times of the English language.* New York: Times Books.
Describes the evolution of English as a language and the influences and contributions from cultures around the world that shaped it.

Cole, S.G., & Cole, M.W. (1954). *Minorities and American promise.* New York: Harper Brothers.
Provides a framework for discussing diversity; critiques Anglo conformity and melting pot models; and describes how interactions between groups can produce cultural unity.

Cronon, E.D. (1955). *The story of Marcus Garvey and the universal Negro Improvement Association.* Madison: University of Wisconsin Press.
Describes the ideals and aspirations—the rise and fall—of Marcus Garvey.

Eck, D.L. (2001). *A new religious America: How a "Christian Country" has become the world's most religiously diverse nation.* New York: HarperCollins.
Examines the growth of diverse religions in the United States, especially with regard to immigration patterns since 1965, and describes its impact and its potential.

Fuchs, L.H. (1990). *The American kaleidoscope: Race, ethnicity and the civic culture.* Hanover, NH: University Press of New England.
Argues that immigrant groups have been successful in embracing and practicing basic social and political principles of U.S. society.

Gordon, M. (1964). *Assimilation in America: The role of race, religion, and national origins.* New York: Oxford University Press.
Reviews research on immigration and assimilation, and discusses the emerging perspectives on ethnic diversity: Anglo conformity, melting pot, and cultural pluralism.

Infact (2003). About Infact. Retrieved May 20, 2003, from *http://www.infact.org/aboutinf.html*
Provides information about the organization including their participation in the Néstle boycott.

Jones, G.R., & George, J.M. (2003). Managing diverse employees in a diverse environment. In *Contemporary management* (3rd ed., pp. 112–149). New York: McGraw Hill.
Describes increasing diversity among consumers and in the workforce.

Jones, J. (1997). *Prejudice and racism* (2nd ed.). New York: McGraw Hill.
Integrates data from psychology, sociology, and history to explain the relationship between prejudice and racism in their appropriate sociocultural historical context.

Laosa, L. (1974). Toward a research model of multi-cultural competency-based education. In W. A. Hunter (Ed.), *Multicultural education through competency-based education* (pp. 135–145). Washington, DC: American Association of Colleges for Teacher Education.

Discusses the value of cultural diversity and the need for competency-based programs to prepare teachers to work with culturally diverse students.

Locke, A. (1989). *The philosophy of Alain Locke: Harlem renaissance and beyond,* L. Harris (Ed.), Philadelphia: Temple University Press.

Discusses the relevance of pluralism for democracy in several essays including "Pluralism and Intellectual Democracy" and "Pluralism and Ideological Peace."

Martin Jr., W. (1984). *The mind of Frederick Douglass.* Chapel Hill: The University of North Carolina Press.

Describes influences on Frederick Douglass's intellectual development.

Menand, L. (2001). *The metaphysical club.* New York: Farrar, Straus, Giroux.

Discusses the evolution of ideas that led to the philosophy of pragmatism and explains how this influenced Horace Kallen and Alain Locke's concept of cultural pluralism.

Naisbitt, J., & Aburdene, P. (1990). Global lifestyles and cultural nationalism. In *Megatrends 2000* (pp. 118–153). New York: William Morrow.

Discusses the assertion of cultural uniqueness in response to homogenization caused by globalization.

Pai, Y., & Adler, S. (1997). *Cultural foundations of education* (2nd ed.). Upper Saddle River, NJ: Merrill Prentice Hall.

Discusses the relationship between pluralism and democracy in Chapter 4, "Cultural Pluralism, Democracy, and Multicultural Education: 1970s–1990s" (pp. 93–136).

Pipher, M. (2002). *The middle of everywhere: The world's refugees come to our town.* New York: Harcourt.

Describes the nature of recent immigration to America using some statistical data; the book is primarily based on interviews with immigrants.

Schaefer, R.T. (2004). *Racial and ethnic groups* (9th ed.). Upper Saddle River, NJ: Pearson.

Provides information on racial and ethnic minorities but also includes chapters on women, religious diversity, immigrants, and cross-cultural comparisons.

Schlesinger, Jr., A. (1991). *The disuniting of America: Reflections on a multicultural society.* Knoxville, TN: Whittle Books.

Provides an overview of the various historical perspectives on ethnic diversity.

Seldon, H. (1996). On being color-blind. In J. Andrzejewski (Ed.), *Oppression and social justice: Critical frameworks* (5th ed., pp. 297–298). Needham, MA: Simon and Schuster.

Analyzes the implications of asserting a "color-blind" perspective.

Simpson, E. (Ed.). (1967). Meditation 17. *John Donne: Selected prose* (pp. 100–101). London: Oxford University Press.

Considered one of the most profound statements about the connectedness of human beings.

Smith, J.P., & Edmonston, B. (1998). *The immigrant debate: Studies on the economic, demographic, and fiscal effects of immigration.* Washington, DC: National Academy Press.

Analyzes data on external immigration and internal migration of U.S. racial minorities.

Tatum, B.D. (1997). *"Why are all the black kids sitting together in the cafeteria?" and other conversations about race.* New York: Basic Books.

Explains the development of racial identity in adolescents and the subtle and overt racial barriers that inhibit the cross-racial dialogues Americans need to initiate and sustain.

Terry, R.W. (1975). *For whites only* (2nd ed.). Grand Rapids, MI: William B. Eerdmans.

Discusses the need for white people to embrace pluralism and describes the tactics to be used to promote social change.

United States Department of Labor (2000). *Earnings differences between women and men.* Available from the Women's Bureau under *Facts on Working Women.* Retrieved April 12, 2003, from *http://www.dol.gov/dol/wb*

Provides information on the history of the wage gap between men and women.

Williams, C. (1968). *Manifesto.* Ann Arbor: Michigan Education Association.

Presents a rationale for advocating for cultural pluralism in our schools.

Williams, C. (2003). Managing individuals and a diverse work force. In *Management* (2nd ed., pp. 343–371). Versailles, KY: Thomson Southwestern.

Explains why diversity is being promoted in the corporate world, discusses the benefits of diversity, and discusses principles for being an effective manager of diverse employees.

Williams, J. (1987). *Eyes on the prize: America's civil rights years, 1954–1965.* New York: Viking Penguin.

Describes the Montgomery bus boycott in Chapter 3 (pp. 59–89); also of interest is Episode 1, "Awakenings: 1954–1956," of the PBS documentary "Eyes on the Prize: America's Civil Rights Years" (Blackside, Inc., 1986).

Wright, R.H. (1991). *The birth of the Montgomery bus boycott.* Southfield, MI: Charro Press.

Provides a first-person account of the crucial first four days of the boycott.

Zangwill, I. (1915). *The melting pot.* New York: Macmillan.

Presents the melting pot perspective. [Also of interest, "Moscow on the Hudson," a contemporary melting pot perspective available on video (Columbia Pictures, 1984).]

Zeldin, T. (1994). *An intimate history of humanity.* New York: HarperCollins.

Examines private lives and relationships, but expands to explore a universal human history through a variety of perspectives, employing a wide range of knowledge.

REVIEW AND DISCUSSION ACTIVITIES

Summary Exercises

See page 19 for exercises to help you summarize the main points and define key terms in this chapter.

Personal Clarification Exercises

In Chapter 8, two exercises promote discussion about our sensitivity to issues of oppression.

Clarification Exercise #1 Differing Views: America's Ethnic Composition Activity

Directions: Do you hear or participate in conversations that reflect your perspectives about American racial and ethnic relationships? In this activity, identify each statement by its perspective on ethnic diversity. When you have completed your own assessment of each statement, compare notes with those in your assigned group or in your class.

AC = Anglo Conformity   MP = Melting Pot
P = Pluralism   S = Separatism

_____ 1. My parents decided not to teach us Laotian. They hoped that this would enable us to move more quickly through the process of becoming an American.

_____ 2. More and more I think in family terms, less ambitiously, on a less than national scale. The differences involved in my being from an Italian family, and Catholic, and even growing up in a lower middle-class home seem more and more important to me.

_____ 3. The reliance of our race upon the progress and achievements of others for a consideration in sympathy, justice, and rights is like a dependence upon a broken stick: Resting upon it will eventually consign you to the ground. The Negro needs a nation and a country of his own, where he can best show evidence of his own ability in the art of human progress.

_____ 4. Now listen to me, Nikki, you are beginning to understand our American ways, so the sooner you drop your Puerto Rican notions, the more successful you will be.

_____ 5. Our blood is as the flood of the Amazon, made up of a thousand noble currents all pouring into one. We are not a nation, so much as a world.

_____ 6. The Japanese race is an enemy race, and while many second- and third-generation Japanese born on United States soil possess U.S. citizenship and have become "Americanized," the racial strains are unchanged.

_____ 7. Outwardly I lived the life of the white man, yet all the while I kept in direct contact with tribal life. While I learned all that I could of the white man's culture, I never forgot that of my people. I kept the language, tribal manners and usages, sang the songs, and danced the dances.

_____ 8. A few years ago, these Greek immigrants had nothing, and now most of them have made it. They're all well off. Of course, the richest ones have left the Greek neighborhoods and live in the suburbs.

_____ 9. Teachers must teach our children what they need to know, but the teachers must also have a profound knowledge of our culture when they work with our children. This is of paramount importance to the preservation of the Cherokee nation.

_____ 10. The Amish keep to themselves. They are tied together by religion, by kinship, and by custom, and they want to keep it that way.

_____ 11. That's right, I was ashamed of my name. Not only that, I was ashamed of being a Jew. There you have it. Exit Abraham Isaac Arshawsky, Enter Art Shaw! You see, of course, how simple this little transformation was. Presto, Change-o! A new name, a new personality. As simple as that!

_____ 12. Indian children are taught to "be like a white man, and think like a white man." They completely lose their self-identity as Navajos.

_____ 13. What I should like to do is come to a better and more profound knowledge of who I am, whence my community came, and where my son and daughter, and their children's children, might wish to head in the future: I want to have a history.

_____ 14. I only ask of the government to be treated as all other men are treated. If I cannot go to my own home, let me have a home in some country where my people will not die so fast.

_____ 15. It makes no difference to me whether my students are black, white, brown, green, red, yellow, or purple. They are *students* and I treat them all the same. After all, we are all human beings. Why can't we forget about color entirely and just treat each other like human beings?

ADAPTED FROM *EDUCATION IN A MULTICULTURAL SOCIETY* BY FRED RODRIGUEZ UNIVERSITY PRESS OF AMERICA (1983)

Clarification Exercise #2 Oppression: A Personal Insight Building Activity

Directions: In this exercise, consider the meaning of *power*. Steps for this activity appear in parts explained below.

Part One: Some people are members of groups with social, political, or monetary power and some have little power in the social, political, or monetary sense. Sometimes when we possess considerable power, we may react by joining our peers in blaming the victim rather than become more sensitive to those with less power. For example, a white male worker who is feeling oppressed may, as a white person, blame people of color for some of the anxiety he feels, or, as a

man, blame women, or, as a citizen, blame immigrants. Brainstorm with your class to complete columns one and two in the chart on page 168 of related persons or groups that have greater and less power.

Part Two: In your groups, identify some ways in which abuse occurs against people with less power. Record your suggestions in the third column in the chart on page 168.

Part Three: First discuss the Note of Explanation (Part One). Then respond in your discussion group, or as your instructor directs, to the four personal insight builder items:

Personal Insight Builders:

1. Explain how abusers justify their abuse and/or how we blame victims for their own harm.
2. From the perspective of one in power: List at least four ways that power can affect your perception of and reaction to others.
3. From the perspective of one NOT in power: List at least four ways that powerlessness can affect your perception of and reaction to others.
4. Be able to explain to the class—or to write about—how power and powerlessness reinforce our abilities to affect decisions of others.

Intergroup Exercises

In Chapter 8, two exercises promote discussion about our sensitivity to issues of oppression.

Intergroup Exercise #1 Majority vs. Minority: Limits of Pluralist Perspective Activity

Directions: Discuss each question on page 168 with your assigned team. Develop *separate* explanations for each situation *after* your team has reasoned out acceptable solutions. Be prepared to explain the extent to which your team would recommend that parents and school administrators go in advocating a pluralistic reply.

MORE POWER:	LESS POWER:	HOW ABUSE IS USED AGAINST POWERLESS PEOPLE:
Adults	Youth	_____
Men	Women	_____
_____	_____	_____
_____	_____	_____
Wealthy	Poor	_____
Whites	People of Color	_____
_____	_____	_____
_____	_____	_____
Bosses	Workers	_____
Heterosexuals	Gays and Lesbians	_____
_____	_____	_____
_____	_____	_____
Able-Bodied	People with Disabilities	_____
Christians	Jews	_____
_____	_____	_____
_____	_____	_____
Citizens	Immigrants	_____
_____	_____	_____
_____	_____	_____

1. Should schools in neighborhoods that serve predominantly Mexican American students serve primarily Mexican food in the cafeteria?
2. Should schools in neighborhoods that serve predominantly Jewish children serve primarily kosher food in the cafeteria? Substitute Jewish holidays for Christian holidays?
3. Should schools in predominantly black neighborhoods be allowed to enforce African American hair and dress codes? Serve primarily "soul" food? Require everyone to complete black history courses?

4. Now you or your group create a similar situational question here and pose it to other groups in your class.

_____
_____
_____
_____
_____

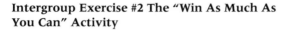

Intergroup Exercise #2 The "Win As Much As You Can" Activity

Directions: For ten successive rounds, four teams of two must individually choose either "X" or "Y"; after each round, compare choices with those of other teams within the group. Keep score on the grid provided. Be certain to follow rules, including explanations at the bottom of the score chart. The amount each team can win in each round is dependent upon the pattern of choices made in the group of four teams. (See below.)

Strategy: Partners should confer before each round to make a *joint decision*. For rounds 5, 8, and 10, teams may confer with others in the group before making and comparing choices.

If teams in the group choose . . .

4 Xs: Lose $100 each	2 Xs: Win $200 each	4 Ys: Win $200 each
	2 Ys: Lose $200 each	
3 Xs: Win $100 each		
1 Y: Lose $300	1 X: Win $300	
	3 Ys: Lose $100 each	

WIN AS MUCH AS YOU CAN!

Turn	Time	Conf. with	Choice	$ Won	$ Lost	Balance
1	2 min.	Partner				
2	1 min.	Partner				
3	1 min.	Partner				
4	1 min.	Partner				
5	3 min.	Group*				
	1 min.	Partner				
6	1 min.	Partner				
7	1 min.	Partner				
8	3 min.	Group**				
	1 min.	Partner				
9	1 min.	Partner				
10	3 min.	Group***				
	1 min.	Partner				

Bonus rounds: Payoff multiplied by — *: 3, **: 5, ***: 10

Contemporary Dilemmas for Intergroup Relations

Section 3 examines oppression currently experienced by members of diverse groups based on differences of race, gender, sexual orientation, social class, and disability. Although institutional discrimination is emphasized, cultural biases and individual prejudices and negative behaviors also will be addressed.

Although white supremacist attitudes described in Chapter 6 are no longer the cultural norm, Chapter 9 describes how white privilege is reflected in American culture. Ongoing individual racial prejudices have resulted in increased racial segregation in neighborhoods and schools. Overt and covert institutional discrimination is described

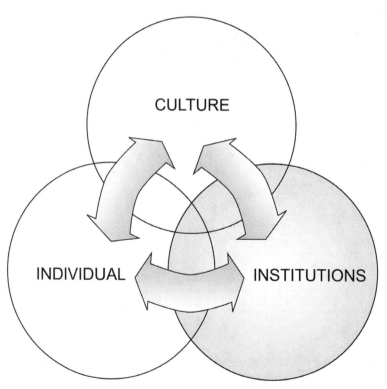

in such diverse practices as word-of-mouth hiring, tracking plans in schools, realtors steering clients to specific neighborhoods, and communities employing at-large elections to diminish or deny representation of racial minority groups.

Chapter 10 examines the sexist messages inherent in everyday words and phrases and provides nonsexist alternatives to language that has historically promoted sexist cultural attitudes. Not only does language present attitudinal disparity, but the nature of violence against women in the United States ranges from domestic abuse to rape: Institutional sexist inequity is reflected in salary disparity between men and women, exploitation of women as part-time workers, and sexual harassment in the workplace.

Chapter 11 provides an overview of historical influences shaping the European and American cultural bias against homosexuality and the myths that have emerged from that bias. Although many of these myths are contradicted by scientific studies of sexuality, many individual Americans maintain derogatory beliefs about gays and lesbians that justify their homophobia. Institutional discrimination is apparent in such areas as the workplace, the legal system, the military, and in schools; the campaign for "gay rights" represents the efforts of activists to demand equal legal status for all Americans regardless of sexual orientation.

Chapter 12 describes how American cultural values historically promulgate negative influences upon individual perceptions of poor people in terms of their deficiencies and personal responsibility for their own poverty. American cultural influence was interrupted in the 1930s when the Great Depression forced many Americans to demand that the federal government become involved in addressing the widespread problems of poverty. Even though many of those 1930s poverty programs are still in place, the previous negative attitudes have reappeared and are reinforced by derogatory beliefs concerning the poor, including myths about the capability of welfare recipients. Institutions contribute to the exploitation of the poor through government economic policies that favor the wealthiest Americans, resulting in a growing disparity between rich and poor. Vulnerable low-income families are also subjected to economic manipulation by banks and merchants, as illustrated by redlining practices, high interest rates, rent-to-own stores, and pawnshops.

Chapter 13 presents an overview of historical perceptions of people with disabilities and how these contributed to a cultural bias in America that resulted in the institutionalization of disabled people. Being kept apart from society reinforces negative perceptions of people with disabilities, especially the attitude that people with disabilities are unable to care for themselves, and results in discrimination against them even when they are living in one's community. Although many states have passed laws to reduce or eliminate these institutions today, people with disabilities encounter various forms of discrimination even when they may simply require minimal accommodations for personal needs.

CHAPTER 9

Racism: Confronting a Legacy of White Domination in America

"The problem of race remains America's greatest moral dilemma. When one considers the impact it has upon the nation, its resolution might well determine our destiny."

MARTIN LUTHER KING, JR. (1929–1968)

We have always divided people into categories based on physical differences: However, the concept of **racism,** which involves the creation of racial categories of human beings with one group superior to others, was not widely accepted until the nineteenth century. Even today, young children learn the lessons of difference.

When a city in the northwestern United States became home to a large Gypsy community, the elementary school teachers noted animosity between Gypsy children and other children. The teachers determined to implement curricula concerning Gypsy history and culture. The school district hired a consultant, Carlos Cortes, to assist them.

Cortes (2000) asked the teachers to find out what the children already knew about Gypsies, especially negative information or stereotypes. The teachers were confident that the children were too young to have learned stereotypes and believed that since the Gypsies had only recently arrived, it was highly unlikely that the children had heard much about them. Nevertheless, Cortes insisted that teachers talk to the children to find out what they knew about Gypsies. If they expressed prejudices or stereotypes, their misinformation would need to be addressed and corrected before new information could be accepted. When the teachers implemented Cortes' suggestion, they were shocked by what their children said about Gypsies: They

were dirty, they were thieves, and they kidnapped babies. It is sad to realize how easy it is for young children in America to learn to be racist; they have learned some of these lessons from their culture.

CULTURAL RACISM

Cultural racism is the practice of recognizing activities and contributions of one racial group in preference to others within a multiracial society. From its earliest days, America had a mix of races; however, the dominant culture that emerged did not tend to include all racial groups. Andrzejewski (1996) described one aspect of oppression as an **ethnocentric** group imposing its culture on others. Since schools are regarded as institutions that instill cultural knowledge and values in the next generation, our schools are an appropriate place to begin an analysis of cultural racism.

How is racism taught to children and youth in our schools?

One misinterpretation that could be taken from the Cortes experience is that schools work to confront and reduce racial prejudice. Although this is true to some degree, too many schools do not discuss issues of race, and all too often, they misrepresent the role

> At the start of the twentieth century, over 98 percent of blacks in the United States were native-born—a much higher percentage than for whites. Blacks are as American as you can get.
>
> MARGUERITE WRIGHT (CONTEMPORARY)

of race in the history of the United States and in contemporary American life. Students may be taught that the slave trade began because Europeans viewed Africans as a primitive and inferior people. Although some Europeans had this view, it was not shared by everyone. Evidence from English merchants engaged in trade with Africans reveals that they knew they were "dealing with people from well-organized sociopolitical systems, people who were sophisticated and intelligent" (Smedley, 1999, p. 92). Furthermore, Africans brought to Jamestown in 1619 and to New Haven in 1644 were laborers and indentured servants as were some Europeans; later, legislation separated Africans from other servants, reduced them to a status of permanent slaves, and created the stigma that has existed ever since.

Cultural racism is also evidenced when teachers and textbooks largely overlook indigenous people. If students are asked who settled the country now called the United States, the answer we have been taught to give is most likely "Pilgrims" or possibly "English colonists." We don't think of—or don't know about—Africans brought to South Carolina by the Spanish and left to establish a settlement in 1526. We tend to overlook Spanish settlements (in what are now Florida and New Mexico) that existed prior to English settlements at Jamestown and Plymouth. And ironically, American elementary and secondary students are unlikely to consider American Indians as "settlers." Loewen (1995) comments:

Part of the problem is the word *settle*. "Settlers" were white, a student once pointed out to me. "Indians" didn't settle. Students are not the only

people misled by *settle*. The film that introduces visitors to Plimoth Plantation tells how "they went about the work of civilizing a hostile wilderness." (p. 67)

Apparently "civilizing the wilderness" included stealing and desecrating graves. Loewen cited a colonist's journal reporting that on only their second day after arriving, two men from the Mayflower came upon an Indian dwelling where no one was at home and stole several items, noting in their journal that they intended to pay the Indians back later.

Pilgrims also took from caches where Indians stored food. During that first harsh winter when the Pilgrims were desperate for food, they dug up several Indian graves, knowing that food was buried with the bodies; then they thanked God for assisting their survival. Loewen (1995) explains the irony that Thanksgiving was never intended to be a holiday celebrating harmony between Indians and Pilgrims; it was declared a holiday by President Lincoln in the midst of the Civil War to foster patriotism. In spite of stereotypical textbook images showing Pilgrims and Indians sharing food at Thanksgiving, many Native Americans consider this holiday a form of cultural racism and do not participate in Thanksgiving celebrations.

How does our society reinforce the cultural racism taught in school?

Sometimes racist messages are communicated in subtle ways. Citron (1969) identified what he called a **rightness of whiteness** concept, meaning that children learn to regard being white as normal, and to make negative judgments of those who deviate from white norms. Children grow up seeing primarily white faces on television, in movies, in advertisements. They read fairy tales and stories about Snow White and Peter Pan, request Christmas presents from a white Santa Claus, and revere white heroes in history or literature. White children

FIGURE 9.1

Often found in public school textbooks, illustrations such as this one suggest that Native Americans and colonists had a peaceful, harmonious relationship, but the reality was one of consistent conflict as Indians were pushed off their lands and forced to move westward.

Source: First Thanksgiving at Plymouth, by Jeanne A. Brownscombe. Courtesy of Pilgrim Hall Museum, Plymouth, Massachusetts.

and youth usually attend schools with predominantly white students, learning a curriculum that emphasizes white people's perspectives and achievements. Consequently, white children are likely to unconsciously regard non-white people as less important.

In recent years, scholars have expanded Citron's insight into the concept of **white privilege,** referring to choices and behaviors white people take for granted that people of color cannot. McIntosh (2001) described white privilege as "an invisible package of unearned assets" and she identified many specific examples (p. 164). See Table 9.1 for some examples. Akbar (2003) defined white privilege as a set of options, opportunities, and opinions that are gained and maintained at the expense of people of color. To Akbar, white privilege can be as arrogant as people believing in a God who looks exactly like them or as poignant as a child reading Superman or Spiderman comic books and not needing to color the faces to identify with the heroes. Unless confronted, white privilege may create an unintended sense of white supremacy in white youth and adults, and white supremacy includes racist attitudes ranging from paternalism to antagonism.

White privilege not only fosters self-esteem and an attitude of superiority toward others, but also

has tangible benefits. White privilege creates a greater likelihood of being paid a higher salary, receiving promotions, and having loans approved. It also means being able to shape American conceptions of reality: allowing white people to dictate when and where philosophy begins, or mathematics or classical art. American history is said to begin when white people arrived; anything that happened prior to that time is relegated to a largely irrelevant category termed *prehistory.* In classrooms reflecting white privilege, textbooks, bulletin boards, classroom discussions, and assignments typically focus on white people; the contributions and concerns of other racial or ethnic groups may be minimally represented or omitted. Because understanding racial and ethnic groups has not been emphasized, white students entering college may be surprised and possibly annoyed to find requirements for courses in racial and ethnic studies.

As a consequence of receiving an ethnocentric education, white Americans may regard certain people of color as foreign. Howard (1999) and others have described white people who meet Asian Americans or Latinos and ask, "Where are you from?" When a hometown such as Chicago or Miami is identified, the next question often will be, "Okay, but where are you *from*?" If the person of color responds by saying he or she has always lived

T a b l e 9.1

White Privilege

Because of white privilege, the following activities illustrate assumptions white people can make that people of color cannot make:

1. If I should need to move, I can be pretty sure of renting or purchasing housing in an area which I can afford and in which I would want to live.
2. I can be pretty sure that my neighbors in such a location will be neutral or pleasant to me.
3. I can go shopping alone most of the time, pretty well assured that I will not be followed or harassed.
4. When I am told about our national heritage or about "civilization," I am shown that people of my color made it what it is.
5. I can be sure that my children will be given curricular materials that testify to the existence of their race.
6. Whether I use checks, credit cards, or cash, I can count on my skin color not to work against the appearance of financial reliability.
7. I can arrange to protect my children most of the time from people who might not like them.
8. I can swear, or dress in secondhand clothes, or not answer letters, without having people attribute these choices to the bad morals, the poverty, or the illiteracy of my race.
9. I can be pretty sure that if I ask to talk to "the person in charge," I will be facing a person of my own race.
10. If a traffic cop pulls me over or if the IRS audits my tax return, I can be sure I haven't been singled out because of my race.
11. I can easily buy posters, postcards, picture books, greeting cards, dolls, toys, and children's magazines featuring people of my race.
12. I can choose blemish cover or bandages in "flesh" color and have them more or less match my skin.

Source: McIntosh, P. *White Privilege: Unpacking the Invisible Knapsack.* In P. Rothenberg (Ed.), *Race, Class, and Gender in the United States: An Integrated Study.*

in Chicago or Miami, the white person may respond: "Okay, but I mean, where did you come from?" In an attempt to ascertain the person's ethnicity, the questioner implies a perception that the other person is from outside the United States, especially since the response about their American hometown was ignored. The questioner is suggesting, "You don't look like an American." And the message that "You don't belong here" is clear to the Latino or Asian American being questioned.

Consequences of racist attitudes promoted by our culture can range from mildly annoying to tragic. A few days after the terrorists' destruction of

F i g u r e 9.2

The Japanese American relocation camps of World War II illustrate the perception of these American citizens as "foreign." Rumors that there were spies from Japan circulating among them were enough to justify confiscating their property and keeping them behind barbed wire for the duration of the war.

Source: The Japanese American Citizens League

the World Trade towers in New York City, a white man walked into a convenience store in Mesa, Arizona, and shot and killed the store clerk because he wore a turban and looked Muslim and Middle Eastern. The murder victim was not foreign, but American; he was not Muslim, but a Sikh who had emigrated from India. The killer justified his act by rationalizing that he was not racist, that his behavior was an expression of patriotism.

INDIVIDUAL RACISM

Individual racism includes both racial prejudice and racist behavior. Racial prejudice refers to negative attitudes a person holds based on racial categories, and it is learned in many ways: from stereotypes in films to myths passed on from one generation to the next. Racist behavior occurs when someone responds to his or her racial prejudices by saying or doing something degrading or harmful toward a person or group. The murder of the Sikh man was an extreme example of individual racism; it is also illustrated by name-calling or by refusing to hire a person of color. In discussing individual racism, it is important to include an analysis of attitudes and rationalizations used to justify racist behavior.

> Come from where it may, racism divides.
>
> **JOSE MARTI (1853–1895)**

What denial rationalizations justify individual racism?

Although some people deny that racism is a cause of problems in the United States today, referring to studies finding that prejudice has diminished significantly among Americans, racial prejudice is still a strong influence, causing many acts of individual racism. Most Americans send their children to racially segregated public or private schools, but some white people deny that schools are segregated, arguing that the 1954 *Brown* v. *Board of Education* decision addressed the issue by ruling racial segregation of schools unconstitutional. Since the 1960s, desegregation plans have created turmoil,

and many white people believe that the outcome was the desegregation of most American school districts serving multiracial populations.

Denial rationalizations often reject a reality that has been documented, as in the denial of continuing segregation in American schools. In 1968, almost 55% of Latino students attended segregated schools. By 1986, that percentage had risen to over 71%, and by 1998, it was at 76% (Orfield, 2001; Wells, 1989). Latino students attend predominantly minority schools because the 1960s desegregation effort only succeeded in integrating students of color in urban schools. Few white students attended urban schools because their families had moved out of urban areas in a massive migration to segregated suburbs, a phenomenon called **white flight** (Thompson, 1999). Massey (2003) analyzed multiracial societies around the world and found that the only nation as segregated as the United States is today was South Africa under apartheid.

A study of African American students sponsored by the National School Boards Association revealed a similar pattern of school segregation in every state, although some states were greater offenders than others (Orfield, 2001). In Illinois, 19% of students are African American and 83% of them attended segregated schools. In the state of New York, a little over 16% of students were African American and over 80% attended segregated schools. Over 50% of Mississippi students were African American and 80% attended segregated schools. Obviously, segregation is not just an issue for southern states. In fact, 29% of North Carolina's students were African American, yet only 37% attended segregated schools. Although the North Carolina percentage is high, many states outside of the South are even higher. These comparisons clearly suggest the impact of white flight on public schools in America.

Many white people have argued, lobbied, and voted against affirmative action programs based on a denial rationalization related to the assumption that schools are no longer segregated. These white people believe and have expressed the myth that the "playing field" is now level, meaning that after high school graduation, white and non-white students can compete on equal terms for college scholarships, admission to vocational programs, and employment opportunities. The American reality is that in addition to attending segregated schools, students of color are more likely to live in areas of poverty, and be educated in deteriorating school buildings under debilitating conditions, as described by Kozol (1991) and others.

By contrast, middle- and upper-middle class white students in America today will likely attend schools with excellent facilities and programs because of generous funding resources. Mainly white suburban school students can enjoy state-of-the-art equipment in well-financed districts, sometimes including swimming pools, tennis courts, and other luxuries that urban schools cannot afford. Meanwhile, teachers in metropolitan schools often struggle to have minimally equipped chemistry or biology laboratories and reasonably current textbooks and instructional materials. In spite of these disparities, all students take the same standardized tests to qualify for admission to colleges, technical schools, and training programs.

Another denial rationalization white people use to justify their opposition to affirmative action is to deny that racism exists. Because a disproportionate number of Americans of color live in poverty, some white people argue that poverty is the real issue, and that it affects white people as well as people of color. In reality, race plays a role in *creating* poverty conditions. When white families moved to the suburbs, businesses abandoned inner cities, taking resources and jobs with them. As a result, urban schools are challenged to educate a diverse population of primarily students of color and to address problems based on disproportionate numbers of students living in poverty. Of 50,000 students attending Boston public schools, over 30,000 qualified for free or reduced-price lunches. In Baltimore, 65% of public school students qualified for free or reduced-price lunches (Koppelman, 1994).

To address the needs of students adequately, urban schools must be provided with funding equal to or greater than that for suburban schools. Instead, urban schools historically have operated with far less funding, creating a self-fulfilling prophecy for failure. When low-income students—especially students of color—are not successful in school, white people all too often insist that "those students" just aren't willing to work hard in school, a rationalization that moves beyond denial to become victim-blaming.

What victim-blaming rationalizations justify individual racism?

Surveys conducted by scholars at the University of Chicago have reported a high percentage of comments from white people that appear to blame black people and regard them as deficient. Researchers randomly selected hundreds of households in 300 different communities and conducted surveys concerning racial attitudes, especially white people's perceptions of African Americans (National Opinion Research Center, 1998).

A 1991 survey reported that 62% of white respondents believed that black people were more likely to be lazy than white people, 53% believed that black people were less intelligent than white people, and 56% believed that black people were more likely than white people to commit acts of violence. A 1998 survey found that 56% of white people still thought blacks were lazy. Believing blacks are lazier or less intelligent than whites can be used to justify the individual racism of an employer refusing to hire a black applicant.

Although fewer white people in 1998 thought black people were less intelligent than whites (down from 50% to 35%), white people perceiving blacks as more likely to be more violent than whites increased from 56% in 1991 to 79% in 1998. Regarding black people as violent has contributed to whites demanding more prisons and tougher sentences for violent crimes; perceiving blacks as violent affects how police officers respond to black suspects and contributes to racial profiling.

Perhaps the most curious 1991 survey response was to a question eliminated from later surveys: 51% of white respondents said black people were less patriotic than white people, which is surprising since a conventional measure of patriotism in

Most of the people I meet in America are compassionate. Why is it that individually we can be so compassionate and collectively we can be so harsh? . . . I don't have an answer to that.

JONATHAN KOZOL (1936–)

America is the willingness to risk one's life in service to the country. Buckley (2001) described African Americans who volunteered, fought, and died in every war in which the United States was involved: the Revolutionary War, Civil War, Spanish American War, and all conflicts, large and small, in the twentieth century.

Although African Americans constitute about 12% of the U.S. population, Buckley (2001) reported that 20% of combat troops in the Vietnam War were African American, as were 14% of U.S. casualties. Buckley also found that 20% of the military forces in the 1991 Gulf War were African American, and 55 of the 266 casualties (15%) were black. Despite the historical record, a majority of whites in 1991 thought black people were not patri-otic. Perhaps these white people based their belief on perceptions of black people complaining of racism and criticizing the United States for not doing more to address it. If so, their belief not only blamed the victim but also avoided the fact that blacks have legitimate reasons to complain about racism.

What avoidance rationalizations justify individual racism?

Avoidance rationalizations propose partial or false solutions or are intended to distract attention from racism as a cause of some problem. A common avoidance rationalization stems from white people's belief that the passage of the 1964 Civil Rights Act,

FIGURE 9.3

This photograph shows the black members of the Rough Riders who fought in the Spanish-American War; African American soldiers have rarely been acknowledged in films or in history books.

Source: North Wind Picture Archives.

ON THE BATTLE-GROUND OF LAS GUASIMAS—TROOPS GOING TO THE FRONT.

> As long as you keep a person down, some part of you has to be down there to hold him down, so it means you cannot soar as you otherwise might.
>
> **MARIAN ANDERSON (1897–1993)**

affirmative action plans, and a variety of other policies and programs since then have resulted in significant progress toward achieving the goal of eliminating racial prejudice and discrimination. Based on this belief, many white people have opposed a variety of programs intended to assist people of color—from recreational basketball activities to bilingual education.

Because of the highly visible role of African Americans in the civil rights movement, one would assume that they were the major beneficiaries of policies and programs developed in response to that movement, but an examination of African Americans' economic circumstances contradicts this rationalization. The good news according to Wellner (2000) is that more than 40% of all black families today are middle class. The bad news is that almost 49% of black families earn approximately $15,000 a year or less, and still face significant barriers stemming from race and class prejudice.

Black children are three and one-half times more likely to be part of a family living in poverty than are white children. Further, blacks are twice as likely as whites not to have health care insurance. Studies show that blacks are less likely than whites to graduate from high school or college, and about twice as likely to be employed in low-paying, low-status jobs. Other data from Morin (2001) and Mann (1996) report that blacks are twice as likely as whites to have difficulty paying their rent or mortgage and about half as likely to have money invested in stocks, bonds, or mutual funds. Despite such statistics, Morin (2001) cited a national survey conducted by the *Washington Post,* the Henry J. Kaiser Family Foundation, and Harvard University reporting that 40% to 60% of white Americans believe great progress has been made to reduce racial discrimination and that black people are almost economically equal to white people in the United States today.

When white Americans acknowledge problems of Americans of color, we often express no sense of responsibility. History provides numerous examples of the white majority in the United States discussing "the Negro problem" as if it had nothing to do with the white population. Novelist Richard Wright contradicted that assertion: "There isn't any Negro problem; there is only a white problem" (Lipsitz, 2002). Wright meant that the racial attitudes and behaviors of white people were the problem—that racism in America meant white racism. It is neither ethical nor practical for Americans of any color to avoid issues stemming from racism.

INSTITUTIONAL RACISM

Jones (1997) defined **institutional racism** as "established laws, customs, and practices that systematically reflect and produce racial inequities in American society" (p. 438). We rely on institutions in America. When immigrants arrive from third world countries, one of the most formidable aspects of American culture they must comprehend is the function of various institutions in our daily lives to get food, health care, social services, loans, job training, jobs, and education. Although individual racism is damaging, institutional racism is far more devastating because of the broader impact institutions have on people.

Institutional racism can be intentional when it is a result of a prejudiced person making a conscious decision about a person or group based on their race. Williams (2003) described a study in which pairs of black and white males, and pairs of Hispanic and white males applied for the same jobs. Identical qualifications were created on their résumés. The men were trained to present themselves in similar ways to minimize differences during interviews; still, white males received three times as many job offers as did black or Hispanic males. Williams

> The sad truth is that most evil is done by people who never make up their minds to be either good or evil.
>
> **HANNAH ARENDT (1898–1989)**

reported on another, similar study involving 149 companies where only 10% more whites than blacks were granted job interviews, but 50% of the whites interviewed received job offers compared to 11% of the blacks (p. 450).

We also know that institutional racism can be unintentional. Since most Americans seem to agree that it is wrong to discriminate based on race, ethnicity, gender, or other factors, it is important to understand how institutional racism occurs even when racial discrimination is *not* intended. Whether covert or overt, institutional racism results in negative consequences for people of color. Unemployment statistics document how race makes a difference when decisions are made about hiring people.

How is institutional racism reflected in statistics on employment?

There are disproportionate numbers of people of color in low-paying, low-status jobs, and people of color tend to have significantly higher unemployment rates compared to whites. The data for black teenagers alone is staggering. Tyson (1997) reported a 34% unemployment rate for black teenagers compared to 14.2% for white teenagers, and as high as 60% for black teenagers in some cities.

Despite affirmative action programs, studies by the Bureau of Labor Statistics (2001) document that disparity between unemployment rates for people of color compared to whites was slightly worse in 1990 (11% versus 4%) than it was in 1960 (10%

versus 5%). By 2000, the situation had improved slightly (7.6% versus 3.5%) principally because of a strong and sustained economy during the 1990s. Yet even with a strong economy, urban areas showed larger disparities in unemployment rates for white and black workers (see Table 9.2). In a study by the Center for Economic Development at the University of Wisconsin-Milwaukee, Levine and Callaghan (1998) compared black and white unemployment in selected urban areas. They found blacks four times more likely than whites to be unemployed in Milwaukee, three and one-half times more likely to be unemployed in Chicago, and three and one-third times more likely to be unemployed in Detroit. Such data clearly suggests that race, whether intentional or unintentional, was a factor in hiring employees.

How does institutional racism influence hiring decisions?

To understand why disparities in black and white unemployment exist, examine how hiring decisions are made. Studies repeatedly show that one of the most important methods used to recruit and hire employees is **word-of-mouth hiring.** If job seekers have relatives or friends already working for the company to recommend them, those job seekers have a better chance of being hired. Research suggests that 60% to 90% of blue-collar workers were hired because of recommendations from family or friends—and the same pattern has been observed in hiring decisions for white-collar jobs (Feagin and Feagin, 1986).

TABLE 9.2

Black/White Unemployment in Selected Metropolitan Areas

		UNEMPLOYMENT RATES		
		BLACKS	**WHITES**	**MULTIPLE**
1.	Milwaukee	12.4	3.1	4
2.	Pittsburgh	18.1	4.8	3.8
3.	Chicago	13.3	3.8	3.5
4.	Cincinnati	12.4	3.6	3.4
5.	Detroit	10.9	3.5	3.3

Source: Center for Economic Development, University of Wisconsin-Milwaukee

Employers feel they benefit from the word-of-mouth approach. If a trusted employee recommends someone, employers believe that the risk in determining the quality of the person being hired is greatly reduced. Another benefit is that hiring costs are minimal; jobs are filled without paying to advertise them. Because of word-of-mouth hiring, Lipsitz (2002) found that 86% of available jobs never appeared in the classified ads of local newspapers.

Word-of-mouth hiring disadvantages people of color because of the history of segregation and discrimination in the United States. In the past, white male employees were blatantly favored over applicants who were women or people of color. At one time the preference was so obvious that state and federal governments passed anti-discrimination laws to address the problem; still, white males constituted a disproportionate share of the workforce. Schaefer (2004) reviewed social distance studies indicating that people consistently indicate a preference for people most like themselves; therefore, white people may recommend other white people simply to make sure they will be with people with whom they are comfortable.

Furthermore, because of ongoing housing segregation, white Americans have not tended to become friends with people of color. When white workers recommend a friend or relative for a job, they may insist that they are not trying to prevent a person of color from being hired, but instead are helping someone they know. Intentional or not, word-of-mouth job recruitment offers a distinct advantage to white job applicants and contributes to discrimination documented by statistics on unemployment disparities between black and white workers.

Another way to secure employment is to join a labor union. However, admission policies of many unions still discriminate against people of color, particularly in unions for skilled trades that are historically dominated by white workers with records of past discrimination against people of color. Unions typically accept new members based primarily on recommendations of current members. As with word-of-mouth hiring, white union members may or may not recommend people of color, but they are more likely to know and recommend someone who is white (Lipsitz, 2002; Feagin and Feagin, 1986).

Discrimination also occurs in decisions regarding company location. Since neighborhoods in the United States still reveal a pattern of racial segregation, a company's decision to locate in a white suburb means that the employees hired will be primarily or exclusively white. Studies show that when a new company selects a location or an established company expands to a new location, employees who live within a 30- to 40-mile radius of the worksite tend to be hired.

In recent years, there has been a growing trend toward the *suburbanization of industry,* especially among retail trade companies (Wilson, 1996). White suburbs are advantaged because they tend to be more affluent than urban areas and usually offer more incentives to influence a company's decision to relocate. Wilson reported that when a number of low-income blacks were placed in suburban apartments, they were significantly more likely to find work than the low-income blacks placed in apartments in the city; the reason was the higher availability of jobs in the suburbs. A company's reasons for selecting a location may have more to do with economic incentives than with race, but the consequences of that decision have a racial impact.

How has institutional racism influenced the development of segregated neighborhoods?

Studies report that neighborhoods in the United States continue to reveal a pattern of racial segregation (Bonilla-Silva, 2001; Massey, 2001; Farley, 2000; Orser, 1990). Although there has been some improvement since the 1980s, Massey (2003) describes the level of black and white segregation in urban areas:

> The most common measure of residential segregation is an index that ranges from 0 to 100, where 0 indicates that blacks and whites are evenly distributed among neighborhoods and 100 means that blacks and whites share no neighborhood in common. Scores greater than 50 are considered to be "high"; those above 70 are "extreme." . . . The most segregated U.S. metropolitan area is Detroit, with an index of 85, followed by Milwaukee (82), New York (81), Newark, N.J. (80), and Chicago (80). Other areas with "extreme" segregation scores include Buffalo, Cincinnati, Cleveland, Kansas City, Philadelphia, and St. Louis. (p. 22)

Past practices of discrimination were overt, including the use of covenants by which homeowners guaranteed other homeowners in their neighborhood that if they sold their home it would not be sold to a family of color. Today such tactics are illegal, but other discriminatory practices still occur.

A tactic that promoted white flight of the 1960s and 1970s has been termed **blockbusting.** When a family of color purchased a home in an all-white neighborhood, realtors could exploit fears of neighboring white homeowners by persuading them to sell their homes because the realtor had clients—families of color—willing to purchase a home in the neighborhood for a purchase price at or above what the white homeowner could expect. Since home equity constitutes a significant portion of middle-class wealth, homeowners were persuaded to sell their homes rather than take a chance on getting their price at a later date. Homes sold to families of color could bring inflated prices since racial minorities typically had to pay higher prices to purchase homes because of the restricted market.

The consequence of blockbusting was that neighborhoods becoming integrated experienced a racial turnover, which resulted in the creation of a reverse segregated neighborhood. And realtors made significant commissions. Although blockbusting has diminished since it was first identified, it occasionally occurs in more subtle forms, and white homeowners continue to move out of neighborhoods that start to become integrated. Although a formerly all-white neighborhood will accept a few black families, Bonilla-Silva (2001) reported that when black families constitute as much as 7% of a neighborhood, whites begin moving out.

> An illustration of the craving people have to attach favorable symbols to themselves is seen in the community where white people banded together to force out a Negro family that had moved in. They called themselves 'Neighborly Endeavor' and chose as their motto the Golden Rule.
>
> **GORDON ALLPORT (1897–1967)**

Another example of racial discrimination is that realtors may keep files of homes for sale in white neighborhoods separate from those for sale in areas consisting predominantly or exclusively of families of color. Realtors may also separate files to engage in the practice of **steering,** where they show homes in neighborhoods that consist exclusively or primarily of people from the same racial group as the client. Clients may be shown homes in integrated neighborhoods, if there are any, in response to a specific request. If accused of racism, realtors may claim that white homeowners who don't want people of color moving into their neighborhoods will not list their home with a realtor whom they believe will show their home to people of color. Realtors could insist that they are not being racist, but are simply respecting the wishes of their clients.

Zoning ordinances might also contribute to racial segregation of neighborhoods. City councils often approve ordinances excluding multifamily dwellings in certain residential areas. The cost of homes in such areas is usually well beyond the means of many families of color. The rental price of units in a multifamily dwelling might be affordable to many clients of color. So the passage of a zoning ordinance expressly prohibiting multifamily housing virtually eliminates the possibility of families of color moving into the neighborhood.

Segregation aside, it is often more difficult for people of color to finance the purchase of homes. A study of the Federal Reserve Bank of Boston reported almost three times as many mortgage loans in low-income neighborhoods consisting of white homeowners than in those consisting of African American homeowners. Home loan officers seem more willing to dismiss the credit record problems of white applicants. Lipsitz (2002) also cites a Los Angeles study that found different standards of eligibility for white and black loan applicants. A study of a Houston bank reported that 13% of middle-income white applicants were denied loans compared to 36% of middle-income black applicants; a study of home loan institutions in Atlanta found that they approved five times as many loans to whites as to blacks. Given the typical preference of American families for their children to attend neighborhood schools, segregated neighborhoods have contributed to the establishment of similarly segregated schools.

How does institutional racism occur in schools?

Sometimes decisions about where to locate new schools can result in institutional racism. Studies report that sites for new schools tend to be selected *within* segregated neighborhoods rather than *between* neighborhoods where they could include both children from families of color and white families in adjoining neighborhoods. Because new elementary and secondary public schools in the United States have largely been built within segregated neighborhoods, school districts have been forced to transport students to create integrated schools (Farley, 2000). People of color have not always supported the use of busing to desegregate schools because busing plans tended to make their children bear the burden of being transported. Further, white families continue to move to suburbs, resulting in schools becoming segregated despite implementation of busing plans. Urban schools brought children from other racial groups together, but in most cities, few white children remain in metropolitan schools.

Some school districts, especially in urban areas, have attempted to overcome the impact of racial segregation by implementing multicultural curricula to make subject matter more inclusive, yet most elementary and secondary schools do not address adequately issues concerning people of color. In part, this problem stems from textbooks that continue to demonstrate a Eurocentric bias in history, literature, art, and music (Loewen, 1995, Sleeter and Grant, 1991; Kirp, 1991). Indeed, textbook bias can be a problem at all levels of education. In a review of college economics textbooks, Clawson (2002) found African Americans were disproportionately described as low-income families and were not usually featured in contexts such as the 1930s depression where readers might be more sympathetic to the poor. Textbook bias requires that conscientious teachers develop supplementary materials to provide students with information about multicultural perspectives. This is a difficult task since the major function of teaching is delivering curriculum, and teachers have limited time and resources to develop new material.

Another example of racism in schools is **tracking**—grouping students into categories by ability and assigning them to specific, ability-related

> If we were to select the most intelligent, imaginative, energetic, and stable third of mankind, all races would be represented.
>
> **FRANZ BOAS (1858–1942)**

classes. Most public elementary, middle, and high schools in America engage in some form of tracking. Based on supposedly objective tests of intellectual ability, children whose first language is not English have been inappropriately placed in remedial classes or even classes for mentally retarded students (Fattah, 2001). Students of color tend to be overrepresented in classes for slow learners, underrepresented in accelerated classes, and they are often placed in vocational or remedial classes in disproportionate numbers (Oakes, Quartz, Ryan, and Lipton, 2004; Oakes and Wells, 1996; Kershaw, 1992; Oakes, 1985). Nieto (1996) explained how tracking children who are still going through puberty influences economic and occupational outcomes when they become adults.

Research has found that tracking provides minimal value for accelerated learners, and it harms students tracked at lower levels, especially those at the lowest level. Since a large percentage of low-income students are racial minorities, tracking usually results in both race and class segregation because low-income students are typically placed in different tracks than middle- or upper-class students. Tracking has been justified by the argument that it improves education for all students, allowing teachers to teach to the students' level so they learn more efficiently. Research does not support this assumption. Academic outcomes for high-achieving students do not appear to be compromised in heterogeneous classes. Middle- and low-achieving students appear to benefit by interacting with high-achieving students; scholastic development is curtailed significantly when they are stratified with other equally low-achieving students (Oakes, Quartz, Ryan, and Lipton, 2000; Oakes and Wells, 1996; Oakes, 1985).

It is difficult for people of color to confront institutional racism in jobs, housing, and schools because that requires political power at local, state, and federal levels. Institutional racism curtails opportunities to be elected to local governing bodies—school boards, city councils, county commissions—and makes it even more difficult to win party primaries or elections at the state and national levels.

How does institutional racism affect politics?

Although the situation is improving in some state legislatures, people of color still tend to be underrepresented in the House of Representatives and Senate at both state and federal levels (Bonilla-Silva, 1999). And there are many problems for candidates of color to overcome. One major obstacle is the enormous cost of getting elected. For almost all political candidates today, fundraising is a critical factor in running for office and being elected. Only a small percentage of candidates of color have the personal resources to mount an effective campaign even at the local and state level.

One problem in fundraising for candidates of color is overcoming the perception that they cannot win elections. To raise funds for campaigns, candidates seldom rely on small donations from individual voters; they must attract support from corporations and wealthy individuals who often contribute funds to more than one candidate and who are especially generous to candidates perceived as most likely to win. Unfortunately, a candidate's likelihood of winning an election may have little to do with the donor's estimation of a candidate's ability, but possibly more with concern about racial prejudice among voters. Since there are people who will vote against candidates because of their race, candidates of color confront a significant obstacle in their efforts to raise funds sufficient to wage an effective campaign.

When Jesse Jackson campaigned for president in the Democratic primaries in 1984 and 1988, he was

> In a democracy the majority of citizens is capable of exercising the most cruel oppressions upon the minority.
>
> **EDMUND BURKE (1729–1797)**

able to use his celebrity status to overcome funding problems. National media gave extensive coverage to his campaign, calling it the first serious effort by a black man to run for president; however, despite media attention, Jackson encountered obstacles. Overton (2002) described media pundits criticizing Jackson because he had less political experience than his white opponents and questioning his qualifications for the office, a common criticism used against candidates of color.

Institutional racism in politics may involve the use of at-large candidates in which city council representatives or school board officials are elected by the entire city, instead of by their respective districts or wards. If the majority of voters in a city are white, electing at-large candidates will assure all-white representation on councils or boards, despite having areas within the city consisting primarily or exclusively of people of color. Imagine a city that is composed of twelve wards, where three wards are predominantly Mexican American. If each ward elects its own council member, it is likely that three of the twelve city council members would be Mexican American. To reduce or even eliminate that possible outcome, a city can require at-large elections to fill any available position. Each year, when city council elections are conducted, voters in all twelve districts vote to fill all vacancies, with candidates receiving the most votes being elected. Since nine of the twelve wards consist predominantly of white voters, they can cast enough votes to elect white candidates at each election, making it very difficult for a Mexican American candidate to be elected to the city council.

How can institutional racism be reduced in the United States?

Institutional racism involves complex problems that are not easily solved. In the 1970s, scholars began to emphasize that *intent* was not necessarily relevant to the issue of whether or not institutional policies and practices created advantages for white people and disadvantages for people of color. In the 1980s, however, the U.S. Supreme Court ruled that to prove a claim of discrimination, plaintiffs had to demonstrate that the intended purpose of institutional policies or practices was to discriminate against a particular group. Producing statistics documenting racial inequities was not enough; plaintiffs had to prove that those who developed policies or engaged in practices alleged as discriminatory were guilty of an *evil intent*. As Bonilla-Silva (1999) noted:

> The standards that the Supreme Court enacted . . . on discrimination (plaintiffs carrying the burden of proof in discrimination cases and the denial of statistical evidence as valid proof of discrimination) help to preserve intact contemporary forms for reproducing racial inequality in America. (p. 85)

The Supreme Court's ruling illustrates the difficulties involved in making much progress on institutional racism unless the people of the United States and the legal system acknowledge that evil intent is not always the cause of discrimination. When courts are willing to examine the issue of who is advantaged or disadvantaged by institutional policies or practices—regardless of the original goals that these policies or practices were intended to address—then we may see progress in the United States against subtle but widespread institutional practices of racism. In the meantime, people of color must rely on affirmative action programs and legal recourse to respond to blatant discrimination within American institution. Affirmative action has been effective to a degree, but it also has produced vigorous criticisms.

How do advocates and critics assess the effectiveness of affirmative action programs?

Advocates of affirmative action cite studies beginning in the 1960s showing that the number of workers of color decreased in their traditional occupations and increased significantly in other occupations. For example, the percentage of African Americans employed as domestic servants or other service occupations decreased while their numbers have increased in the ranks of bank tellers, fire fighters, electricians, and police officers. Professionals of color have moved into high status positions in larger numbers than ever before. Critics of affirmative action argue that gains have primarily benefited people of color who were already middle class. They propose changing affirmative action policies to focus on socioeconomic status rather than race, but Feagin and Sikes (1994) found extensive racism

encountered by middle-class people of color despite their economic success.

Critics of affirmative action charge that these programs engender **reverse discrimination** by giving applicants of color preferential treatment over whites, especially white males. Policies and practices involving preferential treatment are not new; what is new is people of color benefiting from preferential treatment. Affirmative action advocates note that white males have been beneficiaries of preferential treatment as established in the Constitution and perpetuated in policies and practices of United States government, and that affirmative action programs have been mandated to combat a history of discrimination.

Other examples of preferential treatment include primarily white veterans returning from World War II and Korea who received preferential treatment from the GI bill and FHA loans (Brodkin, 2002). In the *Bakke* decision, justices of the Supreme Court ruled that reserving places for a certain number of minority applicants created a disadvantage for white applicants, but the Court's decision permitted race to be used as one of the factors in admitting applicants as long as racial quotas were not employed. The Court said nothing about the policy at that same university of reserving five places each year for children of wealthy, usually white, donors to the university (Lipsitz, 2002).

Despite a history of affirmative action in favor of the white majority, there has been a demand that affirmative action be eliminated because reverse discrimination is alleged to be the more serious problem today. To support this allegation, studies have been cited showing that African Americans represented approximately 40% of new hires for police officers in U.S. cities from 1970 to 2000 (Reaves and Hickman, 2002). Since African Americans constitute only 12% of the population in the United States, this appears to justify the accusation that urban police departments are hiring an excessive number of African Americans.

On the other hand, African Americans constitute much more than 12% of the population in most urban areas, yet Jones (1997) reported that 95% of urban police officers in 1970 were white. To determine if hiring decisions by police departments have been fair, a useful measure would be to compare the percentage of officers of color with the percentage of people of color in an urban community. In police departments of many cities in the United States, the percentage of police officers of color still does not equal the percentage of the city's residents of color.

According to a Justice Department report, 63% of the police force in Detroit was African American, but African Americans comprise 82% of Detroit's population. Almost 39% of Baltimore's police officers were African American, while 65% of Baltimore's citizens are black. New York City's finest included 13.3% African American police officers, half of what it should be to equal the percentage of black people in New York City (Reaves and Hickman, 2002).

Such discrepancies do not just affect African Americans. Latinos represented 26% of New York City's population, but only 18% of NYPD. San Diego's police force was 16% Hispanic, but Latinos constituted 26% of the population; 18% of Houston's police officers were Hispanic, less than half of the percentage of Latinos living in Houston; and 12% of Phoenix police officers are Hispanic, but one-third of its citizens are Latino (Reaves and Hickman, 2002). Although people of color have constituted a significant percentage of the police officers hired over the past thirty years, claims of reverse discrimination can be countered by the argument that the hiring decisions were a justifiable effort to correct a history of discrimination.

What remedies have been proposed to address institutional racism?

To speak of remedies for problems as complex and widespread as those stemming from institutional racism is to speak of partial solutions and of good faith efforts. Solutions will require a cooperation and commitment that have never existed. Whatever progress can be made represents a step forward; with each, step America comes closer to resolving race problems.

> Washing one's hands of the conflict between the powerful and the powerless means to side with the powerful, not to be neutral.
>
> **PAOLO FREIRE (1921–1997)**

Remedies proposed to address problems stemming from racism have come from scholars such as Massey (2001), Wilson (1996), Kozol (1991), and Feagin and Feagin (1986). Among their proposed solutions for institutional racism are the following:

1. Ongoing research must be conducted on institutional racism in America. Racist outcomes of policies and practices often are not easily identified and vary from one region and one institution to the next.

2. A national agency should be created that has regional offices to coordinate anti-discrimination activities across the nation. Such an agency would improve enforcement of anti-discrimination legislation and provide better documentation and dissemination of information. Most experts agree there are adequate laws against discrimination, but enforcement of those laws is not adequate because the responsibility for enforcement is currently assigned to the Justice Department, which has so many other areas of responsibility.

3. There must be a national and statewide commitment to stop the deterioration of inner cities in America. By providing resources, we could better address conditions that create misery and despair. Examples of resources include tax incentives to attract businesses to inner cities, federally funded jobs similar to the 1930s Works Progress Administration, training programs to give people skills related to available jobs, and day care subsidies to provide quality and affordable child care so that more people could work.

4. There must be active monitoring of real estate practices pertaining to advertising and marketing. Such oversight would ensure that practices are consistent with guidelines established in federal fair-housing legislation.

5. A commitment must be made to improve public elementary, middle, and high schools serving low-income students. Schools in low-income areas include many students of color who could be provided opportunity to develop the abilities and skills needed to function effectively in our highly technical, global economy. Resources will be required to remodel or build new schools, replacing the deteriorating buildings that low-income students often have to attend. Resources will also be required to develop and implement

multicultural curriculum and to redesign teacher preparation programs.

6. Teachers must be taught how to work effectively with diverse student populations. They need to learn about the diversity of their students, not just students of color, but students with disabilities, low-income students, and students marginalized by the society or by other students. Teachers must learn how to support positive intergroup relationships between students in their classrooms. They also must be able to identify bias in instructional materials and to teach students how to recognize bias. Until textbooks reflect multicultural content, schools must have resources to purchase multicultural instructional materials to supplement textbooks.

AFTERWORD

In *The Souls of Black Folk* published originally in 1903, W.E.B. DuBois (1994) wrote that the problem of America was the problem of the "color line," that skin color divided America as if it were a line drawn in the sand, never to be crossed. The color line continues to prevent Americans from being united by a common vision, strengthened by an appreciation of diversity. DuBois challenged Americans to solve the problem of the color line in the twentieth century. That challenge still has not been met at the beginning of the twenty-first century.

What must Americans do to confront the problem of the color line? For people of color, the challenge continues to be the same as it was for DuBois, to overcome barriers created by racism. The challenge for white Americans is first to acknowledge the existence of racism, then to understand blatant and subtle ways it operates in society, and, finally, to join with Americans of good will to reduce racism in America's schools, neighborhoods, and institutions. If those of us who will commit to this goal are successful, we will bring this society closer to the ideals for which it stands: freedom, equality, and the opportunity for all people to pursue their vision of happiness. When we come closer to that goal, it will not just be a victory for Americans of color, it will be a victory for America.

> [America is] a vast and quarrelsome family, a family rent by racial, social, political and class division, but a family nonetheless.
>
> **LEONARD PITTS (1957–)**

TERMS AND DEFINITIONS

Blockbusting The practice by real estate agents of scaring whites into selling their houses because families of color are moving into the neighborhood, and then selling these houses to families of color at inflated prices, creating a racial turnover and continued segregation of neighborhoods

Cultural racism The societal recognition and promotion of activities and contributions of one racial group in preference to others within a multiracial society; the superimposition of history and traditions of one racial group over other racial groups

Ethnocentrism The belief that one's race, nation, or culture is superior to all others; also individual actions or institutional practices based on that belief

Individual racism Prejudiced attitudes and behavior against others based on skin color demonstrated whenever someone responds by saying or doing something degrading or harmful about people of another race

Institutional racism Established laws, customs, and practices in a society that allow systematic discrimination between people or groups based on skin color

Racism The creation of categories of human beings according to color, with one group establishing an artificial superiority to others; an attitude, action, or institutional structure that subordinates or limits a person on the basis of his or her race

Reverse discrimination The allegation that people of color are receiving preferential treatment with regard to decisions about hiring, promotion, participation, and admission to schools

Rightness of whiteness The belief that white people are the human norm against which all persons of color must be judged

Steering The practice of realtors of showing homes to prospective buyers in neighborhoods where residents are predominantly or exclusively of the same race

Tracking The process in which students are divided into categories so that they can be assigned in groups to various kinds of classes

White flight The migration of white families from an urban to a suburban location because of court rulings to desegregate urban schools

White privilege A set of options, opportunities, and opinions that are gained and maintained at the expense of people of color

Word-of-mouth hiring Employment of a job applicant based on the recommendation of current employees

REFERENCES

Akbar, N. (2003, April). *Black collaboration with white privilege*. Paper presented at the Fourth Annual White Privilege Conference, Pella, IA.

Discusses white privilege and ways that blacks collaborate with white privilege.

Andrzejewski, J. (1996). Definitions for understanding oppression and social justice. In J. Andrzejewski (Ed.)., *Impression and social justice: Critical frameworks* (5th ed., pp 52–58). Needham, MA: Simon and Schuster.

Provides definitions for a variety of terms essential for discussing intergroup relations.

Bonilla-Silva, E. (2001). *White supremacy and racism in the post-civil rights era*. Boulder, CO: Lynne Rienner.

Examines why blacks and other racial minorities remain behind whites financially, in educational attainment and other social indicators (see residential segregation on pp. 95–96).

Bonilla-Silva, E. (1999). The new racism: Racial structure in the United States, 1960s–1990s. In P. Wong (Ed.), *Race, ethnicity, and nationality in the United States: Toward the twenty-first century* (pp. 55–101). Boulder, CO: Westview.

Examines research on housing, education, politics, and social interactions to describe how the new racism perpetuates social and economic control of African Americans.

Brodkin, K. (2002). How Jews became white folks. In P. Rothenberg (Ed.), *White privilege: Essential readings on the other side of racism* (pp. 35–48). New York: Worth.

Discusses racism and anti-Semitism that has characterized anti-immigrant sentiment and factors resulting in the ultimate acceptance of white ethnic immigrants.

Buckley, G. (2001). *American patriots: The story of blacks in the military from the revolution to desert storm*. New York: Random House.

Includes statistics and stories about African Americans who fought in America's wars.

Citron, A. (1969). *The rightness of whiteness*. Detroit: Michigan-Ohio Regional Educational Laboratory.

Describes how cultural images create racial ethnocentrism in the United States.

Clawson, R. (2002, January). Poor people, black faces: The portrayal of poverty in economics textbooks. *Journal of Black Studies 32*(3), 352–361.

Examines images of African Americans in college economics textbooks and relates findings to previous studies of how women and minorities are portrayed in college textbooks.

Cortes, C. (2000). *The children are watching: How the media teach about diversity*. New York: Teachers College Press.

Analyzes media images, including news and entertainment, to identify themes and values related to diversity and describes media influence on public perceptions of diversity issues.

DuBois, W.E.B. (1994). *The souls of black folk*. New York: Dover.

Includes the famous "color line" phrase in "The Forethought" which precedes essays affirming African Americans and rejecting accommodations to white supremacy. For those interested in learning more about DuBois, read David Lewis Levering: *W.E.B. DuBois: Biography of a race (1868–1919)*, (1993) and *W.E.B. DuBois: The fight for equality and the American century, 1919–1963* (2000) both published by Henry Holt.

Farley, J. (2000). *Majority-minority relations* (4th ed.). Upper Saddle River, NJ: Prentice-Hall.

Provides an overview of racial segregation in the United States in Chapter 10, pp. 296–306, and examines the basis and consequences of busing in Chapter 12, pp. 413–424.

Fattah, C. (2001, October). *Racial bias in special education*. FDCH Congressional Testimony, Washington DC: eMediaMillWorks.

Testimony on special education issues, including a description of the boy placed in a low functioning category who graduated from school and obtained a PhD.

Feagin, J., & Feagin, C. (1986). *Discrimination American style* (2nd ed.). Malabar, FL: Krieger.

Describes theories of discrimination and examples of discrimination in employment, housing, politics, education, and more.

Feagin, J., & Sikes, M.P. (1994). *Living with Racism: The black middle class experience*. Boston: Beacon.

Examines overt and subtle discrimination experienced by middle-class African Americans.

Hacker, A. (1992). *Two nations: Black and white, separate, hostile, unequal*. New York: Charles Scribner.

Provides data in support of the allegation that the United States has developed separate societies based on race.

Howard, G.R. (1999). *We can't teach what we don't know: White teachers, multiracial schools*. New York: Teachers College Press.

Integrates theory, research, and personal experiences to describe problems created by racism and white privilege and discusses actions to bring about positive changes.

Jones, J. (1997). *Prejudice and racism* (2nd ed.). New York: McGraw Hill.

Integrates data from psychology, sociology, and history to explain the relationship between prejudice and racism in their appropriate sociocultural historical context.

Kershaw T. (1992). The effects of educational tracking on the social mobility of African Americans. *Journal of Black Studies 23*(1), 152–170.

Analyzes criteria used to determine student placement in tracking systems; explains how black students are discriminated against and the negative consequences of such decisions.

Kirp, D.L. (1991, Summer). Textbooks and tribalism in California. *Public Interest 104*, 20–37.

Discusses the dissatisfaction expressed by various minority groups with textbooks being considered for adoption by California's curriculum commission.

Koppelman, K. (1994, October). *Race and gender equity in urban America: The efforts of six cities to define the issues and provide solutions*. Paper presented to the Renaissance Group. San Antonio, TX.

Describes information gathered in six cities (Boston, Baltimore, Minneapolis, Kansas City, Seattle, and San Diego) on how problems based on race and gender were being addressed.

Kozol, J. (1991). *Savage inequalities: Children in America's schools*. New York: Crown.

Examines inequities in public school funding; the basis for a PBS documentary by Bill Moyers entitled "Children in America's Schools," available on videotape.

Levine, M., & Callaghan, S.J. (1998). *The economic state of Milwaukee: The city and the region*. Retrieved August 19, 2003, from *http://www.uwm.edu/Dept/CED/publications/milwecon/Cover.htm*.

Compares fourteen metropolitan areas on economic issues including unemployment based on race (see tables 5.16, 5.17, and 5.18).

Lipsitz, G. (2002). The possessive investment in whiteness. In P. Rothenberg (Ed.), *White privilege: Essential readings on the other side of racism* (pp. 61–84). New York: Worth.

Discusses the economic benefits of racism for white people in the United States.

Loewen, J. (1995). *Lies my teacher told me: Everything your American history textbook got wrong*. New York: The New Press.

Describes distortions and omissions concerning the role of people of color in U.S. history.

Mann, T. (1996). Profile of African Americans 1970–1995. *Black Collegian 26*(3), 64–69.

Analyzes data on incomes, education, and employment to identify trends and suggest future directions for African Americans.

Massey, D.S. (2003). The race case. *The American Prospect 14*(3), 22.

Describes the current status of housing segregation in the United States, especially in urban areas.

Massey, D.S. (2001). Residential segregation and neighborhood conditions in U.S. metropolitan areas. In N. Smelser, W. Wilson, & F. Mitchell (Eds.), *America becoming: Racial trends and their consequences*. East Lansing, MI: National Center for Research on Teacher Learning. (ERIC Document Reproduction Service No. ED449286.)

Describes how segregation has increased in recent years, especially for blacks, as well as the nature of segregation for Hispanics and Asian Americans.

McIntosh, P. (2001). White privilege: Unpacking the invisible knapsack. In P. Rothenberg (Ed.), *Race, class, and gender in the United States: An integrated study* (5th ed., pp. 163–168). New York: Worth.

Describes how her understanding of white privilege emerged from a feminist analysis of male privilege and provides a list of twenty-six examples of white privilege.

Morin, R. (2002). Misperceptions cloud whites' view of blacks. *Washington Post*. Retrieved May 22, 2002, from ⟨*http://www.washingtonpost.com*⟩.

Presents the results of a poll of 779 randomly selected white Americans in terms of their perceptions of the economic status of and opportunities available to black Americans.

National Opinion Research Center. (1998). *Race surveys*. University of Chicago. Retrieved August 10, 2003, from *www.norc.uchicago.edu/projects/gensoc4.asp*.

Access survey information dealing with racial attitudes on this Web site by going to "General Survey Data and Information Retrieval System."

Oakes, J. (1985). *Keeping track: How schools structure inequality.* New Haven, CT: Yale University Press.

Documents how tracking practices have perpetuated racial and social class inequalities.

Oakes, J., Selvin, M., Karoly, L., & Guiton, G. (1992). *Educational matchmaking: Academic and vocational tracking in comprehensive high schools.* Santa Monica, CA: RAND.

Examines tracking practices in five high schools in terms of curriculum, consequences, and participation by race and gender.

Oakes, J, Quartz, K.H., Ryan, S., & Lipton, M. (2000). *Becoming good American schools: The struggle for civic virtue in school reform.* San Francisco: Jossey-Bass.

Describes the effort of sixteen schools in five states to move away from tracked classes and implement other reforms to improve the education of all students.

Orfield, G. (2001). Schools more separate: Consequences of a decade of re-segregation. *Rethinking Schools 16*(1), 14–18.

Reviews the history and current status of school segregation, with an emphasis on blacks and Latinos. The complete 54-page report by the Civil Rights Project of Harvard University is available at (*www.law.havard.edu/groups/civilrights*).

Orser, W.E. (1990). Secondhand suburbs. *Journal of Urban History 16*(3), 227–263.

Describes blockbusting tactics and white flight occurring in Baltimore in the 1950s and 1960s and the economic consequences for black homeowners.

Overton, S. (2002). *Money and race: Campaign finance as a civil rights issue.* The Fannie Lou Hamer Project. Retrieved, August 12, 2003 from http://www.flhp.org.

Provides information on the difficulties of raising money for candidates of color; the Web site will continue to update this information.

Reaves, B.A., & Hickman, M.J. (2002). *Police departments in large cities, 1990–2000.* United States Department of Justice. Retrieved, May 12, 2003 from *http://www.ojp.usdoj.gov/bjs*.

A special report from the Bureau of Justice Statistics agency that includes statistics in the text and in tables concerning police departments in major U.S. cities.

Schaefer, R.T. (2004). Prejudice. In *Racial and ethnic groups* (9th ed., pp. 36–71). Upper Saddle River, NJ: Pearson Education.

Discusses causes and consequences of prejudice including the findings from research using the Social Distance Scale.

Sleeter, C.E., & Grant, C.A. (1991). Race, class, gender and disability in current textbooks. In M. Apple & L.K. Christian-Smith (Eds.), *The politics of the textbook* (pp. 78–110). New York: Routledge.

A textbook analysis instrument was employed to examine forty-seven elementary and middle-school textbooks in social studies, reading, language arts, science, and mathematics.

Smedley, A. (1999). The arrival of Africans and descent into slavery. *Race in North America: Origin and evolution of a world view.* Boulder, CO: Westview.

Describes the arrival of Africans to America and how they lost their equal status with other immigrants.

Thompson, H.A. (1999). Rethinking the politics of white flight in the postwar city. *Journal of Urban History 25*(2), 163–199.

Discusses the pattern of white flight in Detroit up to 1980 and explains how white flight has contributed to the economic devastation of Detroit's inner city.

Tyson, J.L. (1997). Jobless rate for blacks falls to 23-year low. *Christian Science Monitor 89*(214), 8.

Describes the decline in unemployment for black Americans in the 1990s while noting problems that remain, such as high unemployment for black youth.

United States Bureau of Labor Statistics. (2001). Counting minorities: A brief history and a look at the future. In *Report on the American Workforce.* Washington, DC: U.S. Department of Labor (*www.bls.gov/opub*).

Analyzes statistics pertaining to the American workforce and the role and nature of the participation of women and minorities in that workforce.

Wellner, A.S. (2000). The money in the middle. *American Demographics 22*(4), 56–64.

Examines the impact of the economic prosperity of the 1990s on incomes of racial and ethnic minorities and immigrant populations in the United States.

Wells, A.S. (1989). *Hispanic education in America: Separate and unequal.* ERIC Document Reproduction Service No ED316616.

Presents data from the 2000 Census on the growth of the Hispanic population in the United States, the percentage of Hispanic students in segregated schools, and the need for desegregation.

Wilson, W.J. (1996). *When work disappears: The world of the new urban poor.* New York: Knopf.

Discusses the causes of unemployment in inner cities and provides recommendations to address the problem. The study of blacks placed in suburbs is on pp. 38–39.

Summary Exercises

See page 19 for exercises to help you summarize the main points and define key terms in this chapter.

Personal Clarification Exercises

In Chapter 9, two exercises promote discussion about racist bias, stereotyping, prejudice, bigotry. and discrimination.

Clarification Exercise #1 Feelings About Race—A Personal Questionnaire

Directions: Team partners take turns reading aloud to each other the twelve statements below, each of which could be a reaction that you might hear concerning another person's feelings about race. Each person should give his or her partner a response that you think would be appropriate and explain why you think that way; base each reply on your personal values as they are developing in this course.

1. People should not be forced to integrate if they don't want to.
2. I don't believe I'm racist, but when it comes right down to it, I wouldn't marry a person of another race.
3. On the whole, the educated, the upper classes, the more sophisticated, or the more deeply religious people are much less racist.
4. I don't want to hear any more about the past and broken treaties; I should not be held responsible for what white people did to Indians a hundred years ago.
5. When I am around angry blacks, it makes me feel defensive because it's as if they want me to feel guilty or something.
6. Other ethnic groups had to struggle, so why should it be any different for Mexican Americans? Why should they get bilingual education and other special accommodations?
7. These days, whenever a black man sneezes, thirty-seven white people rush up to wipe his nose.
8. How can I be pro-Indian without being anti-white?
9. Don't tell me that blacks aren't more violent than whites. If you look at the statistics, you

have to admit that there is a higher crime rate in the ghetto.
10. In many situations, minorities—especially Jews and blacks—are paranoid and oversensitive; they read more into a situation than is really there.
11. Because of the civil rights legislation passed in the mid-1960s, great opportunities are now available to racial minorities, and it is up to them to take more responsibility for exploiting those increased opportunities.
12. No, I'm not going to take the *Understanding Diversity* course because I'm not interested in learning about minorities; further, I've been told that it's a white-bashing course; male-bashing, too.

Clarification Exercise #2 Understanding Recollections of Larry Kobori Activity

Directions: Read aloud to another person the Larry Kobori's School Story (below); take turns reading with the goal of learning the story and especially the feelings that Larry describes having had about the incident. When you are finished, first clarify between yourself and your partner any details of Larry's story. Then, take personal notes of your discussion of the three analysis questions that appear at the end. Take twenty minutes to read and create responses to the questions for analysis. Your group convener will direct you to larger discussion groups to share responses.

Larry Kobori's School Story

When I was young I noticed I was a little different from my friends. My father told me I was Japanese and that I should never be ashamed of being Japanese. He has emphasized this for as long as I remember.

When I started school everything was perfect until the fourth grade. Some kids called me a "Chink." I told them I'm Japanese, not Chinese. If I was going to be called a dirty name, at least use the proper dirty name. My friends always told me to forget those kids, that those kids were stupid. I was glad to hear my friends say that.

After a while the fourth grade things straightened out. But in the seventh grade we started to read about World War I and World War II. I knew that in World War II Japan attacked Pearl Harbor. So I worked real hard on World War I. I answered every question I could.

But when it came to World War II, I never answered any questions. I would just slouch in my chair.

I guess I was feeling ashamed and embarrassed at the atrocities of Japan during World War II. But what I didn't understand was why the textbooks and the teacher glorified America's bombing of Hiroshima and Nagasaki. My teacher said thousands of civilians, including women and children, were killed by the atom bombs, thus making Japan surrender. She then added that the bombings had saved many American lives.

I then asked my teacher, "Wouldn't that be considered an atrocity since so many civilians died? That's the way you describe Japanese atrocities." I'll never forget the way she stared at me and said, "There's a difference." Today that episode is still clear as a bell. It's something that I've never forgotten.

My three years in high school were the best years. I felt that now I was really being accepted. I was the varsity scorekeeper for three years in football, basketball, and baseball. I couldn't compete on the high school level so I did what I could to help. I learned the plays and found myself getting to know the other guys much better. I was then encouraged to write sport stories in the local newspaper. When these stories came out the sophomores and juniors wanted me to help them. As a result I got to know quite a few of them.

Outside of class sometimes it was a different story. Traveling with the basketball team, some blacks called me a "Jap." Remembering my promise I turned around and was about to call the blacks "Niggers." I restrained myself because I was sure it would lead to a fight. The same thing happened when some Mexicans called me a "Jap." Once again I refrained from retaliating.

I'll never understand why those people called me a "Jap."

Individual Insight Builder Questions:

1. What are your impressions of Larry Kobori?
2. Do you think Larry Kobori's responses to the racial incidents were appropriate ways to deal with the discrimination that he experiences?
3. Whether you agree it is appropriate or not, what alternatives did Larry have? Which of them would you recommend as the best strategy?
4. In your opinion, how should teachers present the Japanese role in World War II? The use of atomic bombs on Hiroshima and Nagasaki?

5. What conditions were favorable in his school experiences? What conditions were not favorable?
6. Suggest a generalization concerning America and race today.

Intergroup or Individual Exercises

In Chapter 9, two exercises promote discussion about attitudes toward race in modern American society.

Intergroup Exercise #1 White Benefits Checklist

Directions: In teams of three, explain what you can about your grandparents and parents, where they grew up and where they lived as adults. What work did they do? If you have been privileged and white, what are some of the benefits that have accrued to your family? If you are a student of color, what "white benefits" have you enjoyed due to other factors such as socioeconomic status? Discuss with your group the definition of "Privilege."

Part One: In the same teams of three, (a) Read aloud each item on the following benefits checklist. (b) Check all items that apply to you and note why in the space provided. (c) Write your own personal notes about why the other items do *not* apply to you. (d) Explain to your teammates what effect not having that benefit has had on your life.

My White Benefits Checklist

1. My ancestors were legal immigrants to this country during a period when immigrants from Asia, South and Central America, or Africa were restricted.
2. My ancestors came to this country of their own free will and have never had to unwillingly relocate once here.
3. I live on land that formerly belonged to Native Americans.
4. I live in or went to a school district where the textbooks and other classroom materials reflected my race as normal and as heroes and builders of the United States, and where there was little mention of the contributions of people of color to our society.

5. I was encouraged to go on to college by teachers, parents, or other advisors.

6. I attended a publicly funded university or a heavily endowed private university or college, and/or I received student loans.

7. My ancestors were immigrants who took jobs in railroads, streetcars, construction, shipbuilding, wagon and coach driving, house painting, tailoring, long shore work, bricklaying, table waiting, working in the mills, farriering, dressmaking, or any other trade or occupation where people of color were driven out or excluded.

8. I received job training in a program where there were few or no people of color.

9. I have received a job, job interview, job training, or internship through personal connections of family or friends.

10. My parents were able to vote in any election they wanted without worrying about poll taxes, literacy requirements, or other forms of discrimination.

11. I can always vote for candidates who reflect my race.

12. In the region in which I live, the hospital and medical services that I use or to which have access may be better than those of most people of color.

13. I have never had to worry that clearly labeled public facilities, such as swimming pools, restrooms, restaurants, and nightspots were in fact not open to me because of my skin color.

14. I see people who look like me in a wide variety of roles on television and in movies.

15. My skin color needn't be a factor in where I choose to live or where I send my children to school.

16. Poorly paid women and children of color in this country and abroad make a substantial percentage of the clothes I wear.

17. The house, office building, school, hotels and motels, or other buildings and grounds I use are cleaned or maintained by people of color.

18. People of color in this country and abroad make many of the electronic goods I use, such as TVs, microwave ovens, VCRs, telephones, CD players, and computers.

19. I don't need to think about race and racism every day. I can choose when and where I want to respond to racism.

Part Two: In teams of six, share what feelings you have when you think about the benefits that white people gain from racism. Do you feel angry or resentful? Guilty or uncomfortable?

Do you want to say "Yes, but . . ."?

Part Three: Volunteer members of each group of six take turns reading aloud portions of the summary statement below. Listeners: follow your copy and highlight or underline 2–5 passages that you feel are important. Share the passages you underline or highlight and explain how at least one of the passages is of value to you.

Recall that the purpose of this checklist is not to discount what we, our families, and relatives have achieved. But we do need to question any assumptions we retain that everyone started out with equal opportunity.

You may be thinking at this point, "If I'm doing so well how come I'm barely making it?" Benefits from racism are amplified or diminished by our relative privilege. People with disabilities, people with less formal education, and people who are lesbian, gay, or bisexual are generally discriminated against in major ways. All Caucasians benefit in some ways from whiteness, but some of us have cornered the market on significant benefits from being white to the exclusion of others.

ADAPTED FROM: PAUL KIVEL, *UPROOTING RACISM*,
NEW SOCIETY PUBLISHERS, 2002

Individual Exercise #2 African American Military Achievements Matching Game

Directions: Match the name in column A with the person's military achievement in column B. Consult with no more than two classmates in completing your selections.

Star (*) those items that you are certain to be correct. Place a question mark (?) next to those with whom you are completely unfamiliar.

Suggest other names to add to column A and clues to column B.

Personal Insight Builders:

1. What might your results suggest about your previous study of American history?

2. If you were not able to identify any black American military accomplishments, in what way might it be a deficiency in your educational program?

3. From any period in American history, what do you know of Hispanic Americans having fought in U.S. army units? Native Americans? Black Americans? Asian Americans?

African American Military Achievements Matching Game

COLUMN A	COLUMN B
_____ 1. Eugene Jacques Bullard	a. (American Revolution) One of five killed at the Boston massacre.
_____ 2. William H. Thompson	b. (American Revolution) Fought at Concord and Bunker Hill and Saratoga.
_____ 3. Emmanuel Stance	c. (War of 1812) Recognized for heroism at the Battle of New Orleans.
_____ 4. Isaiah Dorman	d. (Civil War) First black recipient of the Congressional Medal of Honor.
_____ 5. Milton Olive III	e. (Indian Wars) First Black Medal of Honor winner for the Indian Wars.
_____ 6. Crispus Attucks	f. (Indian Wars) First black military officer (graduated from West Point).
_____ 7. Charity Adams	g. (Indian Wars) Scout and interpreter for Custer, died at Little Big Horn.
_____ 8. Charles "Buster" Hall	h. (World War I) Enlisted in France to become first black military pilot.
_____ 9. Calvin Waller	i. (World War II) First hero shot down two Japanese planes at Pearl Harbor.
_____ 10. Colin Powell	j. (World War II) First black pilot to shoot down an enemy plane.
_____ 11. Henry Ossian Flipper	k. (World War II) Achieved the rank of Lieutenant Colonel with WACS.
_____ 12. Daniel "Chappie" James, Jr.	l. (Korea) First GI to be awarded the Medal of Honor in Korean conflict.
_____ 13. Dorie Miller	m. (Korea) First black officer to command an integrated fighter squadron.
_____ 14. Joseph Savary	n. (Vietnam) First black soldier to win the Medal of Honor in Vietnam.
_____ 15. Peter Salem	o. (Vietnam) First black officer in American history to win a Medal of Honor.
_____ 16. William H. Carney	p. (Gulf War) First black chairman of the joint chiefs-of-staff and Secretary of State.
_____ 17. Riley Leroy Pitts	q. (Gulf War) Only woman to launch a Patriot missile bringing down the target.
_____ 18. Phoebe Jeter	r. (Gulf War) Helped to plan and implement the "Desert Storm" strategy.

CHAPTER 10

Sexism: Where the Personal Becomes Political

"Male supremacy has kept woman down.
It has not knocked her out."

CLAIRE BOOTHE LUCE (1903–1987)

Segregation is the normal pattern for the relationship between dominant and oppressed groups. Most Americans have been segregated according to such differences as race, social class, and disabilities. Sexism, however, is a unique form of oppression because people who belong to the dominant and subordinate groups live together. Andrzejewski (1996) defines **sexism** as "an attitude, action, or institutional structure that subordinates or limits a person on the basis of sex" (p. 56). Although sexism is customarily regarded as the oppression and exploitation of women, the concept of sexism includes both men and women, and is an oppression stemming from cultural norms for femininity and masculinity that prevent us from achieving our full potential as human beings. Racism and most other forms of oppression are influenced by the isolation and alienation of dominant and subordinate groups; yet because daily personal relationships exist between most women and men, we believe we have intrinsic, intimate knowledge about sexism.

How does daily interaction between men and women influence sexist attitudes?

Most people grow up in families where they are likely to have close relationships with someone of the opposite sex—brother/sister, parent/child, grandparent/grandchild—and they often enjoy some degree of affection between males and females. Because they believe they genuinely like women, men are more likely to take gender issues lightly, to joke about them and discuss them without the fear and discomfort that usually affects discussions of racism or other forms of oppression. Unfortunately, men in our society are also more likely to make insensitive comments about women that they would never make about people of color.

To illustrate male insensitivity, consider the use of the *natural* argument. White Americans used to say people of color were naturally—meaning genetically—inferior to whites; this belief persisted through the first half of the twentieth century but is now mostly relegated to the ranks of white supremacy groups. Yet many white males in the United States have employed the natural argument in discussing male and female differences, usually to defend their beliefs about male superiority. To justify their argument, men may claim that "the male animal" is always larger than the female, illustrating nature's intent to make males the aggressive protector of females. Gould (1983) corrected this assumption by explaining that larger males are only true for mammals, and not all of them, whereas in the entire animal world—think of insects and fish—the more typical pattern is that females are larger than males.

In conversation, Americans are often more comfortable talking about gender issues than racial issues; men and women joke about the "war between the sexes" where any strategy is acceptable because "all's fair in love and war." When Virginia Congressman Howard Smith amended the Civil Rights Act of 1964 by adding gender, he was not expressing concern about gender discrimination in this country; as a southerner, he wanted the bill defeated. Smith gambled that the "absurd" addition of women as a group whose civil rights needed protecting would appear so ridiculous that it would prevent or at least delay the bill's passage. Needless to say, the tactic backfired. The majority of members of the House of Representatives and the Senate were committed to voting for civil rights and the bill was passed (Branch, 1998).

CULTURAL SEXISM

Cultural sexism in the United States originated in the gender roles brought by the English and other European colonists. Historically, men were expected to be in a superior role as head of the household, while women were assigned the subordinate role as the person responsible for domestic chores, including child care. English law stipulated that any property owned by a woman became her husband's property after marriage, and any money a wife earned had to be given to her husband. These gender roles shaped our culture's ideals for masculine and feminine behavior in ways that have been modified but not radically changed since those early years. Men are still expected to be in control, the leaders and decision makers, while women are expected to play a supportive role both at home and in the workplace.

What gender biases did women confront in the earliest years of the United States?

Although men were expected to provide for the family's needs, from the beginning women went beyond the limits of their gender role. To support the family some women took in laundry, sewing, taught neighbor children, or made things to sell or barter. During the American Revolution—and all subsequent American wars—women assumed additional responsibilities while their husbands were away. Women joined together during the

American Revolution to protest against certain merchants who were suspected of inflating prices. Angered by one exceptionally greedy merchant, a group of women attacked the man, took his keys, and helped themselves to the coffee stored at his warehouse (Riley, 1986a).

Because of women's active involvement during the war, it is not surprising that Abigail Adams urged her husband John to make sure women's rights were protected in the Constitution then being written. Evans (1989) quotes from an article appearing in a U.S. women's magazine in 1792,

> And in the new code of laws . . . remember the ladies, and be more generous and favorable to them than your ancestors. Do not put such unlimited power into the hands of the husbands. Remember, all men would be tyrants if they could . . . [women] are determined to foment a rebellion and will not hold ourselves bound by any laws in which we have no voice or representation.
>
> ABIGAIL ADAMS (1744–1818)

where a woman asserted "I object to the word 'obey' in the wedding service because it is a general word, without limitations or definition" (p. 63). In the early 1800s, American women continued to earn extra money at home, producing four times the textiles as were produced in textile factories. Women also began to protest against the common law stipulation that their property and earnings must be given to their husbands.

How and when did forms of discrimination change?

Women activists such as Elizabeth Cady Stanton and Susan B. Anthony lobbied successfully in many states for women's property rights, but they were not as successful in their demand for women's right to vote. By the 1830s, individual states began to consider legislation to grant women the right to own property and keep their earnings. In 1848, in Seneca Falls, New York, women—and men supporting women's rights—met and signed a declaration of women's rights claiming full citizenship rights for all women, including the right to vote.

As more textile factories were built and more young women employed, factory owners exploited them, forcing workers into unions to strike for better pay and working conditions. In addition to demanding gender equality, women became active in the anti-slavery movement. The Grimke sisters shocked those who felt it wasn't women's place to speak in public, especially not passionately about political issues. Women who defied society's norms provoked harsh criticism, as illustrated by this explanation of their "unladylike" behavior: "Some of them are old maids, whose personal charms were never very attractive and who have been sadly slighted by the masculine gender" (Evans, 1989, p. 102). These unladylike women continued to lobby for gender equality and against slavery as the Civil War approached.

What effect did the Civil War have on women's demands for gender equality?

During the Civil War, the wives of soldiers once again had to provide for themselves and their children. Women were hired to be office workers, government workers, factory workers, teachers, and nurses, yet they encountered a gauntlet of critics. Their morals were questioned and they were said to be a distraction to male workers. After the war, women continued to work and to be active politically, lobbying for such diverse causes as women's suffrage, immigrant issues, and temperance. The Women's Christian Temperance Union, formed in 1874, denounced the evils of alcohol and lobbied for adding the nineteenth amendment (Prohibition) to the Constitution.

In the late 1800s, Congress passed a bill outlawing contraception, perhaps hoping that women with children would be too busy to be politically active. American men usually did not appreciate women's political activities, especially those of college-educated women who provided much of the leadership. Studies warned women that only 28% of college-educated women would marry. A book by a

Harvard professor alleged that the rigors of a college education created a conflict between the brain and uterus, resulting in infertility (Faludi, 1991). Scientists like Paul Broca engaged in a study of brain size based on the theory that larger brains equaled greater intelligence. Not surprisingly, white male researchers reported that white males had the largest brains, with white women—and people of color—far behind. Based on his studies, Le Bon published his conclusions in 1879 about women's inferior intelligence:

> This inferiority is so obvious that no one can contest it for a moment; only its degree is worth discussion. All psychologists who have studied the intelligence of women . . . recognize today that they represent the most inferior forms of human evolution and that they are closer to children and savages than to an adult, civilized man. (Gould, 1981, pp. 104–105)

Still, new employment opportunities for women arose as the establishment of department stores required personnel who could assist predominantly female customers. By 1900, more than one-third of all clerical workers were women; twenty years later, women would be the majority. Women already constituted the majority of teachers, and their numbers steadily increased among librarians, social workers, and nurses (Evans, 1989). But as women tried to redefine their "place" in the early twentieth century, they encountered strong resistance.

What progress and what resistance to women's rights occurred in the early twentieth century?

In the early 1900s, more women were admitted to college, worked outside the home, and engaged in political activities such as women's suffrage. Some called themselves *feminists*. Using recently created psychological language, critics called them *lesbians*, accusing them of hating men. Yet women's efforts on behalf of suffrage succeeded after almost a century of struggle. Women cast their first votes for president in 1920; ironically, one year later, the first Miss America Beauty Pageant was held in Atlantic City, New Jersey. While the Pageant reminded women of their place and purpose, the National Woman's Party went to every state to lobby for an

> I'm just a person trapped inside a woman's body.
>
> **ELAYNE BOOSLER (CONTEMPORARY)**

Equal Rights Amendment (ERA). In 1923, the Party was able to get congressional hearings on the ERA statement: "Men and women shall have equal rights throughout the United States and every place subject to its jurisdiction" (Riley, 1986b, p. 81).

Soldiers returning from World War I had been shocked by the brutality of a new kind of warfare with tanks, planes, trenches, and chemical weapons. With a booming economy to enjoy, Americans wanted to forget the war and serious issues. The momentum of the women's rights movement seemed to dissipate; the ERA campaign encountered an unsympathetic audience and made no progress. When the Great Depression of the 1930s arrived, men and women struggled simply to survive. With high unemployment and few jobs, employers preferred to hire men until World War II began. As men left the workforce to join the military, women continued the pattern from earlier wars by doing the work that men were not available to do.

Did women workers during World War II prove their competence?

During the war, women became the majority (57%) of the workforce for the first time (Faludi, 1991). Several scientific studies from the 1930s and 1940s proved how research could be manipulated to support the prevailing needs in American society: When jobs were scarce during the Great Depression, studies concluded that menstruation reduced women's ability to be effective at work. One researcher even described the effects as debilitating; later, that same researcher conducted a study of working women during World War II and reported

FIGURE 10.1

Advertisements like the one on the left glorified efforts of working women during World War II. Although the pictures such as the one above often depicted white women, a significant number of wartime workers were women of color.

Source: (left) N. S. National Archives; (right) Brown Brothers.

that menstruation caused no adverse effects on their ability to perform their jobs (Tavris, 1992).

Wartime women workers were praised for the quality of their work, including advertising campaigns like the one celebrating "Rosie the Riveter," but no one expected them to stay in those jobs permanently—no one except the women. Seventy-five percent of women surveyed wanted to keep their jobs after the war. But industry had other ideas: Businesses that had praised the women's work during the war suddenly found them to have "bad attitudes" or to be incompetent. The aircraft industry was one of the first to act, firing over 800,000 women two months after the war ended (Faludi, 1991). The aggressive actions of the business community and the blatant bias of the media forced women out of the jobs they had proved they could do.

What role did the media play in women being forced out of their jobs?

In 1945, a *Fortune* magazine poll reported that a majority of Americans believed that if a husband earned enough money to provide for his family, his wife should not work—even if she wanted to (Evans, 1989). The media was telling women to stop taking the jobs that men should have and go home where they belonged. By 1946, more than three million women were eliminated from well-paying industrial jobs. More than 80% of them did not quit working, but took jobs with lower salaries instead. Three years after the war, the United States was the only nation in the western hemisphere that refused to sign a statement issued by the newly created United Nations that supported equal rights for women (Faludi, 1991).

From 1946 to 1952, there were huge increases in births, creating what is called the "Baby Boomer" generation. Women were reinforced in their role as wives and mothers. Evans (1989) described a 1950s *Look* magazine celebrating the "wondrous creature" who married young, had babies, and was still more feminine "than the emancipated girl of the 1920s" (p. 249). An additional factor that discouraged women from working was the growth of suburbs, which isolated them from cities, the site of most jobs. Still, women resisted these efforts to keep them in their place.

How did women respond to the pressure to stay home and not have a career?

In the 1950s, more women enrolled in college. Echoing research a half century earlier, a Cornell University study warned that 65% of college women were much more likely not to get married (Faludi, 1991). But women continued to enroll and continued to work, especially middle-class married women. Evans (1989) reported that middle-class married women "entered the labor force faster than any other group in the population through the 1950s and 1960s" (p. 254). By 1980, women represented 43% of the workforce and they were attending college in record numbers; studies were conducted again to warn them of the risks.

A 1986 Harvard–Yale study predicted that if Baby Boomer women postponed marriage to get their college diplomas, they would find few marriage partners available. According to the study, women had a 20% chance of marrying if they were thirty years old, a 5% chance at thirty-five, and a 1.3% chance at forty. But the prediction was based on an erroneous assumption: Earlier studies of marriage patterns had found that women tended to marry men two to three years older, and that assumption was used to produce the results of the Harvard–Yale study. By the 1980s, this pattern had changed as more women were marrying men closer to their age and even younger. Two other studies reported findings contradicting the conclusions of the Harvard–Yale study, but the popular press was not interested enough to report on them (Faludi, 1991).

In 1985, psychologist Srully Blotnick published the results of his longitudinal study of over 3,000 women in which he found that high-achieving career women were more likely not to marry and to have such unhappy personal lives that the quality of their work was affected. After the press reported the story, it attracted considerable attention. A background check by a newsmagazine reporter assigned to do a story on Blotnick revealed that he was not a licensed psychologist and that much information on his résumé was false. In fact, Blotnick would have been seventeen years old when he said he began his longitudinal study. Despite the presumably newsworthy scandal, the newsmagazine had no interest in the story, and it was not until the reporter took a position at a New York newspaper two years later that the exposé was finally published (Faludi, 1991).

In what ways is American culture sending sexist messages?

In America as in other countries, gender roles are both consciously and unconsciously transmitted to children; also conveyed are the inequalities inherent in those roles. Feminists have been confronting gender roles in our culture—and others around the world—to demand equality. An evolving global economy is demanding change as well. As the number of women in the workforce has increased and the dual-career couple has become the dominant family form in the United States, one would assume that men and women share domestic duties. Domestic sharing, however, has not occurred.

> Culture is the medium through which children fashion their individual and collective identities.
>
> **HENRY A. GIROUX (1943–)**

Too often, Badgett (2001) reports, men tend to do minimal housework if they are living with someone, and even less if they are married. It is not easy to change traditional gender roles.

Sexism is learned through images, especially everyday images in advertising where women have historically been presented in stereotypical roles or as sex objects to sell products. Citing surveys in which most women say their most important goal is to lose ten to fifteen pounds, Wolf (1991) argued that women's concern for weight loss is a consequence of cultural messages about beauty reinforced by the beauty industry to make profits. Sexist images illustrating cultural traditions are important influences in the development of sexist attitudes, yet perhaps the single most significant influence in the development of sexist attitudes is language.

How does learning sexist language influence attitudes and behavior?

Feminists have long recognized gender prejudice in language; they have been committed to changing the language by replacing sexist terms with nonsexist alternatives (Arliss, 1991; Nilsen, 1977a). Traditional labels such as mailman, fireman, and policeman imply that these jobs are exclusively for men and they do not describe the nature of the job. Current language—letter carrier, fire fighter, and police officer—is more inclusive and more descriptive (see Table 10.1). Language has changed, but has this resulted in changes in the attitudes and behaviors of our young people?

Studies suggest some evidence of changing attitudes. In the past, American high school senior boys listed more than twice as many possible career options as did their female peers; few careers appeared on both lists. Today, females are more likely to express interest in a career also identified by males. In a longitudinal study, Wulff and Steitz (1997) reported that junior high school students indicated interest in 45 careers, and 12 of them (26.7%) were identified by both girls and boys. Just before their high school graduation, the students expressed interest in 68 careers, with 16 (23.5%) identified by both genders. Female high school graduates are more likely to choose a nontraditional career than in the past, but it is still more common for female and male high school graduates to choose traditional careers based on gender (Trusty, Robinson, Plata, and Ng, 2000).

> The limits of my language are the limits of my world.
>
> **LUDWIG WITTGENSTEIN (1889-1951)**

Increased use of nonsexist language is not solely responsible for gender differences reported in career choice studies, but language conveying sexist attitudes has contributed to a *perception* of certain jobs being for men only, and that men are more significant in our culture. Feminists continue to lobby professional organizations, businesses, and institu-

TABLE 10.1

Examples of Sexist Words and Phrases and Nonsexist Alternatives

SEXIST WORD OR PHRASE	ALTERNATIVE	SEXIST WORD OR PHRASE	ALTERNATIVE
businessman	business executive	mailman	letter carrier
career girl	professional	man-sized job	big job
chairman	chair or chairperson	newsman	journalist
coed	student	policeman	police officer
congressman	representative	salesman	sales representative
craneman	crane operator	sauce girl	sauce canner
fireman	fire fighter	spokesman	spokesperson
layman	layperson	statesman	diplomat

tions about using nonsexist language, but opponents question the impact of language, insisting that changing our choice of words is a trivial and ineffective way to confront sexist attitudes. Yet there are examples of language being changed to accommodate men. After men won the right to work in the formerly all-female occupation of stewardess, airlines uniformly and rapidly revised the name to *flight attendant*. If it was so easy to change the language to be inclusive of men, why can't women be similarly accommodated?

Another gender-specific pattern in the English language involves condescending references to women as illustrated by diminutive endings such as *poetess*. To refer to an *aviatrix* implies that "She's the little woman who flies a plane." In fact, she is a pilot, as is any man who flies a plane. Although the Academy Awards still has a "Best Actress" category, most women who receive the award refer to themselves as actors.

American feminists have explained that the term *coed* is a condescending reference to an era when men believed that women lacked the intelligence required for college studies, it is comparable to the condescending phrase *colored people* for African Americans. Colleges that permitted women to attend were called *coeducational;* therefore, the term *coed* is regarded as reflecting the historic perception of women as intellectually inferior to men. Oberlin College became the first coeducational campus in 1833. Although Oberlin offered them opportunity, women admitted to Oberlin College were required to meet one condition in addition to those for men who were admitted: They had to agree to do the laundry for Oberlin's male students (Sadker and Sadker, 1994). Change is usually resisted, and never happens without sacrifice.

Another sexist pattern in American English is the consistent denigration of aging women, reinforcing the importance of female appearance: Women are valued only if they are beautiful. English novelist George Meredith argued that women die twice: Their first death occurs when they lose their beauty. Attractive young women are referred to as "kittenish," but with age they become "catty." The sexy young "chick" becomes the "old biddy" that "henpecks" her husband. And speaking of marriage, a man is considered a "good catch" but a woman is a "ball and chain." The old maid or spinster is to be pitied, whereas the bachelor is envied. Before marriage, women have a bridal shower to celebrate the coming event, but American men traditionally have had a stag party to mourn the groom's last night of freedom (Nilsen, 1977b). All too often, our language suggests that marriage is a state much to be desired for women, but to be avoided for as long as possible by men. Is there any evidence that marriage is really such a terrible burden for men?

What do studies say about who benefits from marriage in our culture?

Previously, studies found that married men tended to have fewer mental and physical health problems than single men; however, married women have more mental and physical health problems than single women (National Center for Health Statistics, 1999; Tavris and Wade, 1984). More women than men seek therapy for emotional problems, and the majority are married. Results from recent studies have challenged the previous studies, arguing that men and women both benefit from marriage. Simon (2002) reported that unmarried men and women were more likely to suffer from depression than men and women in stable marriages and that unmarried men were more likely to report alcohol abuse than married men. These studies would still seem to contradict the traditional belief that only women benefit from marriage.

INDIVIDUAL SEXISM

As a result of learning sexist attitudes from our culture and from the sexist attitudes of others, people of both genders may engage in **individual sexism** involving prejudiced attitudes and actions against women or men because of rigid beliefs about gender and gender roles. Although both men and women can become "male chauvinists," they can also choose to be "feminists" in support of gender equality.

What does it mean to be a "male chauvinist" or a "feminist"?

The term "chauvinist" is reported to have originated with a Frenchman named Chauvin, a zealous soldier intensely loyal to Napoleon Bonaparte. To be a *chauvinist* has evolved to designate someone who believes in the superiority of someone or something (Partridge, 1983). In Chapter 2, Kimmel (2000) referred to people being chauvinistic about their culture. French scholars have been accused of being chauvinistic about their language as demonstrated by their attempts to prevent foreign words, especially American phrases—"le hamburger" or "le weekend"—from polluting their native tongue. To call someone a *male chauvinist* is to accuse that person, who could be male or female, of believing men to be superior to women. A **male chauvinist** is a person who believes that men ought to be the leaders and decision makers and women should be subordinate. It is interesting that there are American men who publicly declare themselves male chauvinists yet would bristle at being called racists or bigots.

Confusion exists also with the word *feminist* and with those labeled as feminists. Too many people perceive a feminist as an angry woman; our media has reinforced that view by focusing on feminists who represent radical perspectives. In reality, a **feminist** is a woman—or a man—who advocates for the personal, social, and economic equality of women. The goal of feminist activists is to increase the opportunities available for both men and women as part of the larger goal of eliminating traditional, stereotypical gender roles. To eliminate gender stereotypes, feminists have advocated *androgyny,* a concept that promotes interchangeability of female and male roles or responsibilities in all areas beyond fundamental biological ones.

> People call me feminist whenever I express sentiments that differentiate me from a doormat or a prostitute.
>
> DAME REBECCA WEST (1892–1983)

What does it mean to be androgynous?

Androgyny has been confused with the unisex concept illustrated by unisex clothing, hair styling, and toilets, but the unisex concept denies differences between men and women and advocates treating members of both genders as if they were exactly the same. **Androgyny** is the belief that men and women share a variety of human traits that should be encouraged in both as opposed to fostering certain traits in each gender based on traditional cultural stereotypes about masculinity and femininity (Tavris and Wade, 1984).

Androgynous people respond to situations as needed, without being limited by their gender. If a situation calls for aggressive behavior, an androgynous person responds aggressively; if the situation requires a nurturing response, the androgynous person is nurturing. The person's gender does not matter since aggression and nurturance are traits every human being possesses. Does each androgynous person respond the same way in a given situation? No, because each *individual* is different, but if everyone in a society were androgynous, the differences between people would derive from their individual abilities and preferences, not from artificial differences created by teaching children to shape their identities and behavior to conform to rigid stereotypes about being male or female. Many feminists believe that promoting androgyny from childhood could have a positive impact on the traditional ideas about gender roles that contribute to a serious problem for women in this society: aggressive and abusive behaviors of men that are often harmful to women physically, socially, and psychologically.

What kind of abuse do women encounter in the United States?

According to a study by Tjaden and Thoennes (1998), one million women in the United States are stalked each year (half of them by an intimate partner); two million American women are physically assaulted annually, meaning three to four women are assaulted every minute. One-third of all women (and 20% of female high school students) are victims of physical or sexual abuse, usually from an intimate partner. Almost 900,000 women are raped every year (three women are raped every two minutes) and more than half are raped before they turned eighteen. One out of every four women attending college will be sexually assaulted before they graduate, and one out of eight will be victims of rape or attempted rape (RAINN, 2000).

Rape is an emotional issue that historically has often been misrepresented (McEvoy and Brookings, 1984). Simply put, **rape** is physical and psychological violence defined as forcing someone to submit to sexual intercourse or engaging in sexual intercourse without another's consent, and rape is a major factor in the problem of violence against women in the United States (RAINN, 2000). Unfortunately, rape continues to be misunderstood by unaffected men and women who have inaccurate information.

How has rape been misunderstood in the United States?

As the twentieth century was ending, *Newsweek* released a cover story on rape. The first 75% of the article was about "stranger rape"; the last section addressed the issue of "acquaintance rape," including date rape. The emphasis was the reverse of what really happens: Stranger rape accounts for 25%–30%

of all reported rapes (Tjaden and Thoennes, 1998; Russell, 1984). It is important to recognize misperceptions about rape in order to understand the reality of that experience. Some generally conceded myths and realities about rape include:

MYTH: Rape is an act of sexual arousal caused by an attractive, sexy woman who stimulated such sexual tension and passion that the man could not control himself.

REALITY: Rape is an act of power and humiliation, and any woman of any age is a potential victim regardless of her physical appearance.

MYTH: Rapes usually occur in dark alleys or poorly lit parking lots where the woman is isolated and therefore vulnerable.

REALITY: More than 60% of rapes occur in the victim's home or in a place where the woman would normally feel safe—the home of a friend, relative, or neighbor.

MYTH: Rapes are usually committed by violent strangers concealed somewhere usually at night waiting for an unwitting and unknown victim.

REALITY: Almost 66% of rapes are committed by someone the victim knows such as a lover, a friend, relative, or an acquaintance, while other potential rapists may be trusted authority figures such as a teacher, a minister, a counselor, or therapist.

MYTH: Since many women read and enjoy romance novels that typically include rape scenes, these women must fantasize about rape and secretly want to be raped.

REALITY: Romance novels are exciting fantasy adventures that tend to portray sex in terms of seduction. Although women may fantasize about being seduced by some handsome man, such fantasies bear no relationship to the brutality, violence, and violation associated with rape. It is well documented that boys and men enjoy reading novels and watching movies and television shows filled with murder and violence. Does that mean they secretly want to be murdered or assaulted?

One in six American women have been victims of rape or attempted rape in their lifetimes. As high as that statistic is, as well as the other statistics given above, law enforcement officials say this data would be even higher if all of the rapes and attempted rapes were reported.

Why do women choose not to report a rape or attempted rape?

Since rape is an underreported crime, feminists have argued that the one out of six rate that is reported for rape is conservative. Because of changes in police departments' processing of rape cases and new guidelines for rape trials, this crime is now more likely to be reported. Still, fear affects a

> There is no difference between being raped and being run over by a truck, except afterwards men ask if you liked it.
>
> MARGE PIERCY (1936–)

woman's decision to report a rape. According to MacKinnon (1987, p. 82), victims have given four reasons for not reporting a rape:

Threats: Rapists often threaten to return and to inflict even more violence if victims go to the police. Some rapists even threaten to kill their victims, and just by reading newspapers, women know this has happened to others.

Reactions: Some victims fear the reactions of their significant others. Women have been verbally abused, beaten, and even abandoned by partners who would not believe that the woman did nothing to cause the rape.

Disbelief: Some women fear that if they report the rape, the police might not believe her. Even if the police are convinced, some women fear they may not be able to persuade a jury. There is no guarantee of justice from the legal system.

Publicity: Some women fear the loss of privacy, and the feeling of being exposed and vulnerable, as well as being subjected to embarrassing allegations about their personal lives in court. They are also reluctant to recall and relive (in front of an

audience) a painful, humiliating incident they would rather forget.

The concerns of rape victims are the reason law enforcement officials and other experts have generally agreed with feminists that the number of reported rapes is probably much less than the number of incidents. Rape and domestic violence are painful consequences of sexism played, principally by men, as a power game in our culture.

INSTITUTIONAL SEXISM

Institutional sexism is the consequence of established laws, customs, and practices that systematically discriminate against people or groups based on gender. Institutional sexism takes many forms, but a persistent problem is the ongoing gender discrimination in hiring. Jones and George (2003) describe a study in Philadelphia where men and women applied for restaurant jobs offering good salaries. Although their résumés were carefully constructed to make them equally qualified, men were called in for interviews twice as often as women, and five times as many men as women received job offers. Jones and George also report that women constitute 46% of the workforce in 2000, yet:

> Only about 12 percent of corporate officers and boards of directors were women, less than 6 percent of employees with the highest status job titles are women, and only about 4 percent of women occupy positions with the highest earning levels. (p. 127)

Even if women are successful at finding jobs, another persistent problem is the salary inequity between men and women. Historically, there is ample evidence of inequities in the salaries of men and women, but attempts have been made to address this gender gap. There is disagreement about the extent to which gender salary inequities are being resolved, but most people concur that men earn more than women, even when they work in the same jobs (see Table 10.2).

Why are men earning more than women in the workforce?

Four arguments address the issue of salary inequity between men and women. The first argument is

RANK EARNINGS GAP		MEDIAN 1999 EARNINGS		FEMALE EARNINGS PER DOLLAR OF MALE EARNINGS
		MEN	WOMEN	
1	Wyoming	$34,442	$21,735	0.63
2	Louisiana	33,399	22,069	0.66
3	Utah	36,935	24,872	0.67
3	Michigan	41,897	28,159	0.67
5	Indiana	37,055	25,252	0.68
5	West Virginia	31,299	21,154	0.68
7	New Hampshire	39,689	27,488	0.69
7	North Dakota	30,488	20,893	0.69
7	Montana	30,503	20,914	0.69
10	Wisconsin	37,062	25,865	0.7
10	Idaho	32,603	22,939	0.7
10	Ohio	37,692	26,400	0.7
10	Alabama	32,383	22,518	0.7
14	Illinois	40,999	29,106	0.71
14	New Jersey	46,368	33,081	0.71
14	Arkansas	29,784	21,270	0.71
14	Mississippi	30,549	21,554	0.71
18	Kansas	35,104	25,249	0.72
18	Missouri	34,357	24,705	0.72
18	Oklahoma	31,123	22,473	0.72
18	Pennsylvania	37,051	26,687	0.72
18	Kentucky	32,357	23,285	0.72
23	Minnesota	39,364	28,208	0.73
23	South Dakota	29,677	21,520	0.73
23	Iowa	32,697	24,023	0.73
23	Connecticut	45,787	33,318	0.73
23	Rhode Island	37,587	27,358	0.73
23	South Carolina	32,027	23,329	0.73
29	Nebraska	31,965	23,598	0.74
29	Virginia	37,764	28,035	0.74
29	Massachusetts	43,048	32,059	0.74
29	Washington	40,687	30,021	0.74
29	Oregon	36,588	26,980	0.74
29	Tennessee	32,313	23,978	0.74
35	Maine	32,372	24,251	0.75
35	Georgia	35,791	26,679	0.75
35	Texas	34,925	26,168	0.75
38	Alaska	41,257	31,151	0.76
38	Colorado	38,446	29,324	0.76
38	Delaware	38,961	29,544	0.76
38	Nevada	35,794	27,089	0.76
38	New Mexico	31,310	23,658	0.76
38	Arizona	35,184	26,777	0.76

TABLE 10.2

Statewide Comparison of Gender Salaries

Minnesota is tied with Alaska for the highest percentage of working women, but women's earnings continue to lag behind men.

(Continues)

TABLE 10.2

(*Continued*)

RANK EARNINGS GAP		MEDIAN 1999 EARNINGS		FEMALE EARNINGS PER DOLLAR OF MALE EARNINGS
		MEN	WOMEN	
44	Maryland	41,640	32,155	0.77
44	New York	40,236	31,099	0.77
46	Vermont	32,457	25,322	0.78
46	North Carolina	32,132	24,978	0.78
46	California	40,627	31,722	0.78
49	Florida	32,212	25,480	0.79
50	Hawaii	35,535	28,546	0.8
51	District of Columbia	40,513	36,361	0.9
52	Puerto Rico	17,097	15,698	0.92

Source: Jane Roberts, St. Paul Pioneer Press, 2000 Census.

the claim that significant progress has been made in closing this income gap. According to the U.S. Bureau of Labor Statistics (2001), women earned approximately 60 cents for every dollar a man made from 1960–1980. In the next two decades the gap narrowed, so that by 2000, American women were earning an average of 75 cents for every dollar a man earned. The answer to the salary inequity question would seem to be that men are still earning more, but that women must be getting more raises and promotions and are apparently catching up.

Careful analysis of salary data tells a different story: The primary reason for the decreasing gap is that the salaries of male workers *have not been increasing;* they have even been decreasing in some areas. The claim that women's salaries are becoming closer to men's salaries is based on the reality of salary stagnation for men. In addition, 80% of working women still earn less than $20,000 a year. It seems debatable to say that "progress" is being made concerning men's and women's salaries if closing the gender gap is based on women making small wage gains while men are receiving no wage increases.

A second argument regarding gender salary inequity is based on data showing that young women entering the workforce are earning slightly more than 80 cents for every dollar a man makes. This statistic has been used to argue that the gender inequity problem is being solved and to predict that the salary gap will eventually disappear as more highly paid young women pursue their careers. Although entry-level salaries are becoming more equal, feminists argue that women who stay in the workforce lose ground to their male peers because they are not promoted as readily as men. The term

> The Glass Ceiling hinders not only individuals but society as a whole. It effectively cuts our pool of potential corporate leaders by half. It deprives our economy of new leaders, new sources of creativity.
>
> LYNN M. MARTIN (1939–)

glass ceiling was coined to refer to an upper limit, usually middle management, beyond which women are not promoted. Studies have confirmed that women are not being promoted at the same rate as men; few are promoted to top leadership roles (Redwood, 2002; U.S. Department of Labor, 2000).

In addition, our dominant cultural expectation for women to perform housekeeping duties and raise children results in less opportunity for developing abilities, experience, contacts, and reputation. For the last forty years it has been true that for entry-level jobs, the gap between men's and women's salaries was smaller; during that time it has also been true that the disparity between salaries increased as women and men continued in their careers.

A third argument about gender salary disparity is based on the fact that more American women earn college diplomas than ever before. Since more education is assumed to mean access to careers with higher salaries, gender disparity is predicted to decrease further, and eventually to disappear. Yet statistics show that college-educated women are still paid less than men. Reports indicate that women with college diplomas earn an average salary similar to that of white males with high school diplomas, and that women workers with high school diplomas make an average salary less than that of the average male high school dropout (U.S. Department of Labor, 2000; Benokraitis and Feagin, 1995).

A fourth argument for the gender salary inequity is that women tend to choose careers that pay lower salaries than the more highly paid professions men tend to choose. Although women account for 59% of low-paying jobs, including 70% of minimum-wage jobs, comparing the salaries of women and men within the same profession reveals that men are paid more—even in those professions where women constitute the majority of workers (Kim, 2000; U.S. Department of Labor, 2000; Benokraitis and Feagin, 1995).

What are economic consequences of institutional sexism for women?

While people debate gender disparity in wages, Day and Newburger (2002) report that during their lifetimes women with high school diplomas can expect to be paid $450,000 less than men with high school diplomas. They also predict that women with bachelors' degrees will earn almost $900,000 less than men with similar degrees; women with professional degrees will earn $2 million less than men with pro-

fessional degrees. Unfortunately, this isn't the only economic loss that women suffer. For a variety of reasons, women constitute the majority of people working less than forty-hour weeks or working forty or more hours a week on a temporary basis. In either case, part-time workers are typically denied most or all fringe benefits provided to full-time employees, including day care, health insurance, life insurance, and employer contributions to retirement accounts.

Another economic consequence of institutional sexism concerns child support payments. When the family unit is broken, mothers are most often awarded custody of children and, as part of legal divorce settlements, fathers are almost always required to provide child support for children under the age of majority. Despite their fiscal obligation, only 40% of American fathers are observed to pay full child support during the first year following a divorce. Another 26 percent of divorced fathers make partial payments for only the first year (Grall, 2000). After one year, almost half of paying fathers stop making payments altogether; of those who continue, few pay the full amount, even though most can afford to make the payments (Sorenson, 1997; Benokraitis and Feagin, 1995).

For low-income mothers, lack of child support often forces them to apply for public assistance, whereas middle-class mothers often return to college to upgrade their skills so they can compete for jobs in the labor market. If divorced custodial mothers applied for loans, they would likely be rejected since child support payments are not considered a reliable source of income! Lenders are familiar with the data on child support. Despite lower salaries, lack of child support, and other economic consequences, women often work for all the same reasons as men. And they do so regardless of discrimination in salaries and promotions, and despite another frustration encountered on the job: sexual harassment.

> Whatever women do they must do twice as well as men to be thought half as good.
>
> **CHARLOTTE WHITTON (1896–1975)**

How is sexual harassment a significant problem for women in the workforce?

The behavior called *sexual harassment* is not new, but it wasn't until 1979 that Catherine MacKinnon created the term in her writings on workplace behaviors and gender discrimination (Wetzel and Brown, 2000). According to Daft (2003), there were 17,000 sexual harassment complaints filed in 1998—twice as many as were filed in 1988. Sexual harassment in the workplace is not only a problem for women; men filed 10% of those complaints. Typically, **sexual harassment** is defined as unwelcome deliberate and repeated behavior of a sexual nature that is neither requested nor returned. Men tend to be responsible for sexual harassment, even when men are the victims. Sexual harassment is an issue of power, not sex. Most men do not engage in sexual harassment at work; rates are estimated as ranging from only 5%–10% of the American male workforce. Men who do harass are being pressured to change their behavior.

What are the most common behaviors that women regard as sexual harassment?

There are two common reasons that women complain about sexual harassment. The behaviors described can be regarded as illustrating a "cultural" conflict between men and women. One complaint: Men make a nuisance of themselves by persistently asking women for dates. In response, the explanation is that during childhood and adolescence, every American male is taught some version of the cliché "if at first you don't succeed, try, try again." Men taught to view persistence as a positive attribute are encouraged to be persistent in anything they do. Accused of harassment, some men have yet to understand that persistently approaching women for dates may initially be regarded as obnoxious, but eventually becomes threatening. American women tend to regard such harassment as a verbal form of stalking, and it is not surprising that many victims tend to describe harassers as disgusting, even ugly, regardless of the physical attractiveness of the harasser (Strauss and Espeland, 1992).

A second complaint has to do with men making unwelcome, sexually suggestive remarks to women,

often in the form of sexual jokes sometimes told by men to each other. Now constituting almost half of the workforce, most women find this kind of humor unequivocally offensive. As our workforce continues to change, it is inevitable that some previously established norms and behaviors will also change. Men must recognize the need for reform and respond appropriately. Men must also recognize that respecting rather than resisting or criticizing reasons for reform demonstrates their respect for women.

Throughout the global economy, corporations are confronted with sexual harassment and must establish clear policies on what they consider acceptable and unacceptable behavior. The European Equal Opportunities Commission has ruled that flirting becomes harassment if it continues after the recipient has made it clear that it is offensive (Webb, 2000). How are employers at all levels supposed to monitor employee behavior in a way that is fair? The U.S. Equal Opportunities Commission has established some reasonable guidelines.

What are the workplace guidelines for sexual harassment in the United States?

If sexual harassment is not severe—persistent requests for a date or telling sexual jokes—victims must tell the harasser that they regard this behavior as offensive. If the harasser continues the offensive behavior despite the victim's repeated objections, the victim can contact a supervisor to ask that he or she intervene or file a sexual harassment complaint. In cases where the behavior is not considered severe, it usually must be repeated a number of times before a sexual harassment complaint should be filed.

How many times must the victim be subjected to the behavior before filing a complaint? The courts use a "reasonable person" standard, meaning how long should a reasonable person have to tolerate such behavior before it is considered intolerable? On the other hand, if the behavior is considered severe, such as demanding sexual favors from an employee in return for a raise or promotion, it only has to occur once for the victim, or an advocate aware of the behavior, to file a sexual harassment complaint (Webb, 2000).

Are American employers following sexual harassment guidelines?

Most American employers have demonstrated a willingness to take aggressive action against sexual harassment, perhaps because of the history of large settlements awarded to women having filed complaints. As employers become aware of research findings, they have even more reason to follow workplace guidelines. Studies report that one effect of sexual harassment in the workplace is a reduction of profits, which is reason enough for any employer to aggressively enforce policies against sexual harassment. According to research, when sexual harassment is not stopped at worksites, the consequences include increased worker absenteeism, lower worker productivity, and higher training costs from employee turnover (Knappand Kustis, 1996). As American employers take aggressive actions to eliminate sexual harassment in the workplace, educators must take similar steps to eliminate sexual harassment from our schools.

How much of a problem is sexual harassment in the schools?

In 1993, the American Association of University Women (AAUW) commissioned a Harris poll to examine sexual harassment in schools. Over 1,600 students in grades 8–11 from seventy-nine school districts across the United States responded. The AAUW survey reported that 81% of girls and 76% of boys had experienced sexual harassment, and that for 30% of girls and 18% of boys, it was a frequent occurrence. The students described sexual harassment beginning in elementary school and continuing through middle school and high school. Although the most common form of sexual harassment involved only nonverbal and verbal behaviors such as sexual comments, jokes, and gestures, the second most common complaint involved being touched, grabbed, or pinched in a sexual way. The survey also reported that 13% of the girls had been forced to do something sexual other than kissing. The perpetrators of this sexual harassment were overwhelmingly peers (79%) rather than adults.

According to Wetzel and Brown (2000), studies conducted since 1993 have continued to find evidence of ongoing sexual harassment in schools. In 1999, the U.S. Supreme Court decision on Davis v. Monroe County Board of Education ruled that schools had a responsibility to take appropriate action to eliminate student sexual harassment and were legally liable. To reduce sexually harassing behavior, educators must make efforts to change sexist attitudes that encourage such behavior. Based on studies of attitude and behavioral change related to racial issues, Brandenburg (1997) recommended that educators confront sex role stereotypes as well as the issue of sexual harassment to increase student awareness of gender issues.

Is sexual harassment the main gender issue in schools?

Nonsexist educators have long advocated teaching strategies to confront sexist attitudes because gender problems in schools are not limited to sexual harassment. After collecting years of observational data on teacher–student interactions in K–12 classrooms, Sadker and Sadker (1994) reported consistent sexist patterns for both teacher and student behaviors. Boys were more likely to call out answers without raising their hands and they interrupted when others gave answers. Because boys were more aggressive, teachers tended to call on them, praise them, and discipline them more often than girls. Teachers were more likely to challenge boys to finish their homework, while they would help girls finish theirs. Although girls starting school have tended to test higher than boys in almost all areas, by middle school, boys overtake girls in math and science and by high school graduation, boys are outperforming girls in almost all areas. Despite excelling in these tests, boys continue to earn lower grades than girls.

In addition to declining test scores, girls encounter a curriculum that typically does not include much information on the achievements of women. Although recent textbooks have tried to be more inclusive, educators still have to supplement textbooks with other instructional materials on women's achievements and women's issues to provide more equitable coverage. Many teachers have experimented with a variety of classroom activities to ensure equal opportunities for both genders to give answers, share opinions, and receive praise for the quality of their work.

Achieving gender equity in schools is difficult because all of us have learned gender stereotypes and sexist attitudes, and it is easy to be unaware of how they affect our behavior, whether we are teachers or students, and in elementary, secondary, or college classrooms. But women are now almost half of the American workforce, and they are increasingly choosing nontraditional careers. It is in the best interest of everyone that teachers understand their own sexist attitudes and stereotypes so they can assist both male and female students in learning new and more positive ways to perceive and interact with each other.

AFTERWORD

This description of cultural, individual, and institutional sexism is the tip of an iceberg. Gender discrimination occurs in our laws and in our court system, in the arts and in athletics, and in the images encountered in media and in school textbooks. Sexism permeates our institutions. Some men believe that sexism works to their advantage and resist efforts to promote gender equality, but sexism hurts men and women, boys and girls. Anything that prevents people from using their talents and abilities results in a loss for us all. Anyone who is denied a chance to contribute to our society results in a nation that is less than it could have been. If Americans create a society that offers opportunities to all and receives the gifts each person has to offer, the male–female power game can cease—a victory for everyone.

> What is enough? Enough is when somebody says, 'Get me the best people you can find,' and nobody notices when half of them turn out to be women.
>
> **LOUISE RENNE (1937–)**

TERMS AND DEFINITIONS

Androgyny The interchangeability of male and female roles and responsibilities in all areas beyond fundamental biological ones

Cultural sexism The societal promotion of negative beliefs and practices that reinforce rigid gender roles in which men are traditionally accorded a superior role in society while women are assigned to subordinate roles; the artificial superimposition of authority of one gender over another

Feminist A woman or man committed to the struggle for the social, economic, and personal rights of women and men; an advocate for equality between women and men

Glass ceiling An informal upper limit that keeps women and minorities from being promoted to positions of greatest responsibility in work organizations

Individual sexism Prejudiced attitudes and behavior demeaning to women, or to men, because of beliefs about gender and gender roles, demonstrated whenever someone responds by saying or doing something degrading or harmful about persons of the other gender

Institutional sexism Established laws, customs, and practices in a society that allow systematic discrimination against people or groups based on gender

Male chauvinist A man or woman who believes that men ought to be the leaders and decision makers and women should be subordinate to them

Rape Forcing someone to submit to sexual intercourse or engaging in sexual intercourse without their consent

Sexism An attitude, action, or institutional structure that subordinates or limits a person on the basis of sex

Sexual harassment Deliberate and repeated behavior that has a sexual basis and is not welcomed, requested, or returned

REFERENCES

American Association of University Women. (1993). *Hostile hallways: The AAUW survey on sexual harassment in America's schools*. Washington, DC: Author.

Describes pervasive patterns of sexual harassment against both girls and boys in public schools in the United States.

Andrzejewski, J. (1996). Definitions for understanding oppression and social justice. In J. Andrzejewski (Ed.),

Oppression and social justice: Critical frameworks (5th ed., pp. 52–58). Needham, MA: Simon & Schuster.

Provides definitions for a variety of terms essential for discussing intergroup relations.

Arliss, L.P. (1991). *Gender communication.* Englewood Cliffs, NJ: Prentice Hall.

Provides examples of sexist language in Chapter 3, "Debates about Language and Sexism."

Badgett, M.V.L. (2001). *Money, myths, and change: The economic lives of lesbians and gay men.* Chicago: The University of Chicago Press.

Discusses the study of domestic duties in Chapter 6, "A Family Resemblance," page 147.

Benokraitis, N., & Feagin, J. (1995). *Modern sexism: Blatant, subtle and covert discrimination* (2nd ed.). Englewood Cliffs, NJ: Prentice Hall.

Analyzes gender discrimination in society, including issues specifically related to women of color, and provides recommendations to eliminate gender discrimination.

Branch, T. (1998). *Pillar of fire: America in the King years 1963–65.* New York: Simon & Schuster.

Describes the civil rights movement in the United States and the leadership role played by Martin Luther King, Jr. (the second volume of a trilogy).

Brandenburg, J.B. (1997). *Confronting sexual harassment: What schools and colleges can do.* New York: Teachers College Press.

Provides information and case studies to explore the psychology behind sexual harassment, examines the legal issues involved, and provides educators with a variety of educational strategies.

Daft, R.L. (2003). Managing diverse employees. In *Management.* (6th ed., pp. 436–468). Versailles, KY: Thompson Southwestern.

Discusses the current status of affirmative action, explores various dimensions of diversity in the workforce, and examines how corporate culture is changing to accommodate diversity.

Day, J.C., & Newburger, E.C. (2002, July). The big payoff: Educational attainment and synthetic estimates of work-life earnings. *Current Populations Reports.* Washington, DC: U.S. Department of Commerce. Retrieved July 12, 2003, from *http://www.census.gov/educational_attainment*

Compares earnings of men and women and projects work-life earnings in today's dollars.

Evans, S. (1989). *Born for liberty: A history of women in America.* New York: The Free Press.

Describes the experiences of women in America beginning with indigenous women and including women of color as well as European women immigrants.

Faludi, S. (1991). *Backlash: The undeclared war against American women.* New York: Crown.

Describes the backlash against the women's movement that has undermined and manipulated women in the media, the legal system, the fashion industry, politics, and business.

Gould, S.J. (1983). Big fish, little fish. In *Hen's teeth and horses toes* (pp. 21–31). New York: W. W. Norton.

Examines assumptions about "natural" differences between genders in the animal world.

Gould, S.J. (1981). *The mismeasure of man.* New York: W.W. Norton.

Discusses the belief in human intelligence as an entity that can be measured and quantified in each individual, producing a number to judge individuals as superior or inferior.

Grall, T. (2000, October). Child support for custodial mothers and fathers. *Current Population Reports.* Washington, DC: U.S. Department of Commerce.

Provides demographic and economic data on custodial parents from census reports.

Jones, G.R., & George, J.M. (2003). Managing diverse employees in a diverse environment. In *Contemporary management* (3rd ed., pp. 112–149). Boston: McGraw Hill.

Describes increasing diversity among consumers and in the workforce and provides strategies for managers to work effectively with diverse employees.

Kim, M. (2000, September). Women paid low wages: Who they are and where they work. Monthly Labor Review, 26–31.

Uses a national data set from the 1998 Current Population Survey (March) of 60,000 households in the United States to analyze salaries for women in the workforce.

Kimmel, P.R. (2000). Culture and conflict. In M. Deutsch & P. Coleman (Eds.), *The handbook of conflict resolution* (pp. 453–474). San Francisco, CA: Jossey-Bass Publishers.

Describes the influence of culture on individual communication and the need to practice cultural relativism to avoid conflict in intercultural communication.

Knapp, D.E., & Kustis, G.A. (1996). The real "Disclosure": Sexual harassment and the bottom line. In M. Stockdale (Ed.), *Sexual harassment in the workplace: Perspectives, frontiers, and response strategies* (pp. 199–213). Thousand Oaks, CA: Sage.

Examines the cost of sexual harassment including a "comprehensive behavior costing model" to determine economic consequences of tolerating sexual harassment.

MacKinnon, C.A. (1987). A rally against rape. In *Feminism unmodified: Discourses on life and law* (pp. 81–84). Cambridge, MA: Harvard University Press.

Discusses why women do not report rapes and calls on men to be supportive.

McEvoy, A.W., & Brookings, J.B. (1984). *If she is raped: A book for husbands, fathers, and male friends.* Holmes Beach, FL: Learning Publications.

Provides advice for men to help a loved one deal with the trauma of rape; reasons for not reporting a rape are stated in Chapter 8, "Reporting a Rape."

National Center for Health Statistics. (1999). *National Vital Statistics* 47(21). Retrieved July 12, 2003, from *http://www.cdc.gov/nchs*

Provides statistics on a variety of health issues including those related to marriage; studies are periodically updated and made available at this Web site.

Nilsen, A.P. (1977a). Sexism as shown through the English vocabulary. In A.P. Nilsen, H. Bosmajian, H.L. Gershuny, & J.P. Stanley (Eds.), *Sexism and language* (pp. 27–41). Urbana, IL: National Council of Teachers of English.

Examines how sexism is implicit in many words and phrases in American English.

Nilsen, A.P. (1977b). Sexism in the language of marriage. In A.P. Nilsen, H. Bosmajian, H.L. Gershuny, & J.P. Stanley (Eds.), *Sexism and language* (pp. 131–140). Urbana, IL: National Council of Teachers of English.

Examines the nature of sexism in words and phrases pertaining to marital relations.

Partridge, E. (1983). *Origins: A short etymological dictionary of modern English* (p. 92). New York: Greenwich House.

Citation notes that Nicolas Chauvin was often ridiculed for his loyalty to Napoleon.

RAINN (2000). Rape, Abuse, and Incest National Network. Retrieved June 12, 2003, from *http://www.rainn.org*

Provides statistics from the 2000 National Crime Victimization Survey conducted by the U.S. Department of Justice (at the Web site, look for "statistics"). Also go to National Domestic Violence Hotline (*www.ndvh.org*) for additional statistics.

Redwood, R. (2002). The glass ceiling. *Motion Magazine.* Retrieved June 12, 2003, from *http://www.inmotion magazine.com*

Discusses findings of the Federal Glass Ceiling Commission about the nature of the glass ceiling and ways to dismantle it; the complete report, *Good for Business: Making Full Use of the Nation's Human Capital* is available from the U.S. Government Printing Office.

Riley, G. (1986a). *Inventing the American woman: A perspective on women's history, 1607–1877: Vol. 1.* Arlington Heights, IL: Harlan Davidson.

Describes women's experiences from the colonial era to post–Civil War Reconstruction.

Riley, G. (1986b). *Inventing the American woman: A perspective on women's history, 1865–present: Vol. 2.* Arlington Heights, IL: Harlan Davidson.

Describes the experiences of women in the United States from the Civil War to the 1980s.

Russell, D.E.H. (1984). *Sexual exploitation: Rape, child sexual abuse, and workplace harassment.* Beverly Hills, CA: Sage.

Challenges several assumptions about rape based on results from a survey of 930 women.

Sadker, D., & Sadker, M. (1994). *Failing at fairness: How America's schools cheat girls.* New York: Charles Scribner.

Discusses sexist practices and their consequences in American schools; describes conditions women had to meet in order to attend Oberlin College in Chapter 2, pp. 21–22.

Simon, R.W. (2002, January). Revisiting the relationships among gender, marital status, and mental health. *American Journal of Sociology* 107(4), 1065–1097.

Describes survey data on differences in mental health for those married and unmarried.

Sorenson, E. (1997, November). A national profile of nonresident fathers and their ability to pay child support. *Journal of Marriage and the Family* 59(4), 785–798.

Describes demographic characteristics and child support paid by nonresident fathers.

Strauss, S., & Espeland, P. (1992). *Sexual harassment and teens: A program for positive change.* Minneapolis, MN: Free Spirit.

Addresses sexual harassment at the worksite, but focuses on sexual harassment in schools, including a program for implementing sexual harassment policy and procedures.

Tavris, C. (1992). *The mismeasure of woman.* New York: Simon & Schuster.

Analyzes scientific studies of women to expose the biases in them that have been used to justify the status quo by perpetuating sexist stereotypes and the devaluation of women.

Tavris, C., & Wade, C. (1984). *The longest war: Sex differences in perspective* (2nd ed.). New York: Harcourt Brace Jovanovich.

Examines an array of gender issues by reviewing research in anthropology, biology, human sexuality, education, psychology, and sociology.

Tjaden, P., & Thoennes, N. (1998). *Prevalence, incidence, and consequences of violence against women: Findings from the National Violence Against Women Survey.* Washington, DC: United States Department of Justice. Retrieved June 20, 2003, from *http://www.ojp.usdoj.gov*

Provides data on domestic violence that is regularly updated.

Trusty, J., Robinson, C.R., Plata, M., & Ng, K. (2000, Fall). Effects of gender, socioeconomic status, and early academic performance on postsecondary educational choice. *Journal of Counseling and Development* 78(4), 463–473.

Analyzes national data on academic performance and educational choices of eighth grade students and recent high school graduates to determine the influence of gender and class.

United States Bureau of Labor Statistics (2001). Chapter 1: Counting minorities. A brief history and a look at the future. *Report on the American workforce.* Washington DC: U.S. Department of Labor. Retrieved July 12, 2003, from *http://www.bls.gov/opub*

Analyzes statistics concerning women and minorities in the American workforce.

United States Department of Labor. (2000). Earnings differences between women and men. *Facts on working women.* Washington, DC: Author. Retrieved July 12, 2003, from the Women's Bureau, *http://www.dol.gov/dol/wb*

Provides information on the history of the wage gap between men and women.

Webb, S. (2000). *Step forward: Sexual harassment in the workplace* (2nd ed.). New York: Mastermedia.

Reviews the history of sexual harassment, offers solutions to prevent sexual harassment, and examines sexual harassment in the global workplace. For more information, read *Women's International Network News 28*(1).

Wetzel, R., & Brown, N.W. (2000). *Student-generated sexual harassment in secondary schools.* Westport, CT: Bergin & Garvey.

Describes legal rulings on sexual harassment, theories explaining why sexual harassment occurs, and guidelines for secondary schools to develop effective sexual harassment policies.

Wolf, N. (1991). *The beauty myth: How images of beauty are used against women.* New York: William Morrow.

Analyzes the ways in which the "consumer culture" manipulates women's images for profit but to the detriment of both women and the relationships between women and men.

Wulff, M.B., & Steitz, J.A. (1997). Curricular track, career choice, and androgyny among adolescent females. *Adolescent 32*(125), 43–50.

Describes their study of androgyny among twenty high school girls from a college-track upper-level math class and twenty girls from a vocational-track cosmetology class.

REVIEW AND DISCUSSION ACTIVITIES

Summary Exercises

See page 19 for exercises to help you summarize the main points and define key terms in this chapter.

Personal Clarification Exercises

In Chapter 10, two exercises promote discussion about sexism and sexual harassment.

Clarification Exercise #1 What Is Sexual Harassment?

Directions:
- Circle "T" for TRUE if you think the statement is generally or usually *true*.
- Circle "F" for FALSE if you think the statement is generally or usually *false*.

A Sexual Harassment Quiz

T F 1. If a woman or a girl dresses or behaves in a sexy way, she is suggesting that she is interested in being sexually active.

T F 2. Men and boys can be victims of sexual harassment.

T F 3. Sexual harassment can occur between people of the same sex.

T F 4. Women in professional jobs—teachers, lawyers, engineers, doctors, for example—are not as likely to be sexually harassed as women in blue-collar jobs like factory workers, secretaries, or truck drivers.

T F 5. Women who work in jobs that are usually held by men—construction workers, accountants, or surgeons—are more likely to be sexually harassed.

T F 6. Women and girls rarely file false charges of sexual harassment.

T F 7. Saying "NO" is usually enough to stop sexual harassment.

T F 8. If sexual harassment occurs in the school between students, it is illegal and the school is responsible.

T F 9. Most people—male or female—enjoy getting sexual attention at work and at school.

T F 10. One of the best ways to deal with sexual harassment is to ignore it.

T F 11. Women of color are sexually harassed more often than white women.

T F 12. If he didn't like the sexual attention, but she meant it only as flirting or joking, then it was not sexual harassment.

ADAPTED AND UPDATED FROM S. STRAUSS AND P. ESPELAUD (1992), *SEXUAL HARASSMENT AND TEENS* P. 61.

Clarification Exercise #2 Find the Problem: Analyzing Sexist Language

Directions: Read the following statements that have been termed "sexist." Determine why the language in each is biased; discuss with a team member how to revise the sentence or phrase; write in the space provided an appropriate nonsexist message to replace the sexist one. *Note:* There is probably more than one nonsexist alternative for each item, and each unit below will likely convey multiple discriminatory levels. [*Example:* The average American drinks his coffee black. Nonsexist revision: The average American drinks black coffee.]

1. Dear Sir:

   _____

2. Any student who is not satisfied with his performance on the pretest may take the posttest.

   _____

3. Mr. McAllister runs the garage in partnership with his wife, a striking blonde who mans the pumps.

   _____

4. The English teacher developed a wonderful thematic unit on "Man and his World."

   _____

5. Housewives are feeling the pinch of higher food prices.

   _____

6. A writer can become so involved in his work that he neglects his family.

   _____

7. NCTE convention-goers and their wives are invited to attend the gala event.

   _____

8. One of our prehistoric ancestors was the Neanderthal man.

_____

9. We are asking all the mothers to send cookies for our field trip tomorrow.

_____

10. Blacks finally received the vote in 1870.

_____

11. While lunch was delayed, the women gossiped about last night's meeting.

_____

12. A slave could not claim his wife or children as his own because the laws did not recognize slave marriages.

_____

13. The average student is worried about his grades.

_____

14. The ancient Egyptians allowed women considerable control over property.

_____

15. One of the political debates in the racial struggle taking place in South Africa is over the concept of "one man, one vote."

_____

Intergroup and Individual Exercises

In Chapter 10, two exercises promote discussion about attitudes toward race in modern American society.

Individual Exercise #1 What Would You Say? A Case Study: Susan Consults the Feminist

Directions: In male-female teams of two, read aloud to each other the case study below. As a team, compose a paragraph for Ms. Walker in response to Susan's essay: What would you write in response if you were Ms. Walker?

Susan Consults the Feminist

Susan was pouring herself some orange juice when her father walked into the kitchen. "I've been thinking about your college decision," he said, as he got out the cereal. "With your talents and interest in international relations, you should really consider the foreign service. I took the exam myself, you know."

Her mother frowned, "Michael, you shouldn't encourage that type of career. It's unrealistic." She turned to Susan, "I wanted to be a teacher partially because teachers are needed everywhere; I could follow my husband wherever he needed to go. If you were in the Foreign Service, it would be very difficult to have a family and take care of your children. You're going to have to put two careers together when you get married, and a Foreign Service career will be hard to work out."

Susan looked up, surprised. Her mother was the epitome of the "superwoman" with a wonderful career, happy kids, and a good marriage. She had always struck Susan as believing in the equality of women. And here she was, telling her daughter to give up her dreams for some man! "Why should women always have to have 'mobile' careers?" Susan thought. "Why couldn't it be the man who moved?"

Susan got up angrily and left for school. Men are different now, she thought. In class, Susan felt better. She was a high school junior, and everyone knew her. Her teachers were always telling her, "With your ability, you can do whatever you want." Her classmates respected her—even the boys listened to her advice on everything from relationships to schoolwork. At school Susan never had to fight to be equal. She knew that she was one of the brightest.

That afternoon Susan called Rob, her boyfriend. She related the conversation that she had had with her parents that morning. Rob immediately told her that he agreed with her mother.

"What do you mean?" Susan yelled. "I thought we were past all that. Why is it that at school I can do whatever I want, but then, when I'm married, some man who probably isn't as intelligent as I am can make me give up my dream? Why shouldn't *he* have the mobile job?"

Rob was sympathetic. "You've got a point, but society's just not that way. Men still expect to be the primary breadwinners, and women are still not equal. No man is going to sacrifice his job for a woman. You're never going to be happy if you expect to always get your way, especially when your way goes directly against the real world."

The next day Susan could hardly wait for English class, where she would have time to write in her journal. Ms. Walker, her English teacher, responded to each student's writing once a week and had built up rapport with each student. Susan knew that her teacher was a committed feminist—far more radical than Susan herself. She hoped that Ms. Walker would validate her views about women's careers. Here is her journal entry:

I'm so furious I could scream! Everybody tells me I'm so talented—blah, blah, blah—and I keep getting these college catalogs with women doing all sorts of amazing things; and then my own mother tells me to pick a job on the basis of some man's being able to live with my choice! Then my own boyfriend tells me it's intimidating for a girl to hold a better job than her husband!

Why don't teachers just tell us straight out, "You can be ten times smarter than any boy in the class, work harder, and go to a better college; but if you want a family, you might as well be content with Cs and a high school diploma. You're going to have to adapt your whole life around your husband's anyway, and the more intelligent you are, the harder that will be." Basically, women who have less initiative and fewer brains are going to be happier, because they won't have to give up as much! So why do teachers praise me for leadership and intelligence? They're so hypocritical!

Susan threw her journal onto the pile on her teacher's desk. She slumped into her chair and wondered how Ms. Walker would respond.

ADAPTED FROM RACHEL KLEINFELD

Intergroup Exercise #1 Difficult Dialogues Experience: Sexism

Directions: In groups of three, develop a dialogue based upon the scenario below. Use the situation as the basis for your 5-minute role play of the situation. Remain in character at the conclusion of your skit and respond to class questions about motivation, purpose, or intent behind your comments during the scene. Each team of three is asked to complete a 5-minute role play, regardless of similarity to others performed.

Difficult Dialogues: All Work and No Play Makes Xiong Less Fun

Characters:

- An experienced university professor and advisor to a college student group
- A university junior student in the group who has just led students in a successful state Supreme Court challenge to have their Native American school logo banned
- A high-achieving senior student [See below]

A student in your class complains that the H'mong woman in their class project can never make outside of class meetings because she has too many responsibilities. Further, upon rare occasions when she is free, she will not join the others in a bar to discuss the project because she thinks a bar is not respectable.

CHAPTER 11

Heterosexism: Transforming Homosexuality from Deviant to Different

"The only abnormality is the incapacity to love."

ANAIS NIN (1903–1977)

The word homosexual and the concept of homosexuality appear to have originated in the 1860s in the German medical writing of Dr. Karl Ulrichs. Homosexuality does not seem to enter into public discourse in a formal and explicit way until 1892, when scholars such as Havelock Ellis and Magnus Hirschfield published essays and books describing theories and research concerning human sexuality. In a highly regarded book published in 1886, Richard von Krafft-Ebing chose not to use "sexual inversion," the common term in America, but Ulrich's word, translated to English as *homosexuality*. Krafft-Ebing described a **homosexual** as someone sexually attracted to members of the same sex. Although same-sex liaisons had been documented throughout human history, the new term challenged the western world's traditional heterosexual assumption.

What is the heterosexual assumption?

Non-western cultures have a history of acknowledging and accepting sexual variation in human beings (Herdt, 1997; Williams, 1992). Western cultural attitudes about sexuality have been based on a **heterosexual assumption:** that all people were born **heterosexual** and that being attracted to opposite-sex partners was the natural condition of human beings. People who engaged in any sexual activity not conforming to heterosexual norms were assumed to be making deviant and unnatural choices, especially when sexual activity took place with a same-sex partner. The Bible was often used to justify beliefs about normal or deviant sexual behavior, and even twentieth century psychologists reinforced the assumption by regarding homosexuality as a mental illness. Homosexuals were widely perceived as aberrations in need of correction (a cure) to bring them back to their true heterosexual nature (Duberman, Vicinus, and Chauncey, 1989).

When was the heterosexual assumption challenged?

Krafft-Ebing provided the term that challenged the heterosexual assumption. Although he still believed that homosexuality was immoral and unacceptable, he defined it as one of many forms of sexual desire. Like fetishism or masochism, Krafft-Ebing argued that homosexuality was a condition, a mental defect that could be cured (Halperin, 1989).

Although the general public would not become familiar with the idea of homosexuality for another sixty years, Krafft-Ebing established the idea that there were various forms of sexual desire, and that one of these involved a desire for same-sex part-ners. His assertion was addressed by the evolving field of psychology as its practitioners searched for a way to remedy deviant behavior. The suggested "cures" included castration, sterilization, electric shock, and occasional lobotomies; however, none proved practically successful (Katz, 1976).

Although conventional wisdom among psycholo-gists continued to regard homosexuality as deviant and unnatural—a mental defect—the failure of rec-ommended remedies in the clinical setting caused a number of respected people in the field, including A. A. Brill, Magnus Hirschfield, and even Sigmund Freud, to conclude that homosexuality could not be cured and was probably a permanent condition. As psychologists became convinced that deviant sexual desires could not be redirected, they adopted approaches such as adjustment therapy to control homosexual behavior. These practices were the norm when the Kinsey Report was published in 1948.

How did the Kinsey Report challenge the heterosexual assumption?

With funding from the Rockefeller Foundation and Indiana University, a zoologist named Alfred Kinsey and his research staff engaged in a study of human sexual behavior from 1938 to 1956. The Kinsey Report issued in 1948 was controversial for many reasons, not the least of which was its proposition that **sexual orientation** was not a singular phe-nomenon, but a continuum of multiple possibilities ranging from exclusive heterosexuality to exclusive homosexuality, with a variety of bisexual orienta-tions in between (see Figure 11.1). Based on self-reports of dreams and fantasies as well as behavior, Kinsey and his staff concluded that only a small per-centage of their research subjects were exclusively heterosexual or exclusively homosexual (later a fig-ure of 10% became widely used). Most appeared to have some potential for **bisexual** behavior—being sexually attracted to members of either gender— although sexual attraction might be biased more toward one gender than another.

The Kinsey Report challenged the general assump-tion that all human beings possessed a heterosexual orientation. Americans were confronted with the radical concept of sexual orientation: that every human being is not heterosexual, but that human sexuality encompasses categories of different sex-ual attractions and behaviors, including an attrac-tion to and a desire for same-sex partners.

What was the impact of the Kinsey Report?

The term *homosexuality* provided a label for what Oscar Wilde's lover had called "the love that dare not speak its name," but most Americans were uncomfortable with the subject and refused to dis-cuss it. Most psychologists still regarded homosexu-ality as a defect, a form of mental illness, but homosexuals themselves began to reconsider their situation. There were, and always had been, same-sex–oriented people who were comfortable with their sexuality while being discreet in their behav-ior. These men and women were now convinced that attitudes in America needed to change, but they weren't sure how that could happen.

Homosexual friends of psychologist Evelyn Hooker argued that psychologists persisted in regard-ing homosexuality as a mental illness because the homosexual patients who sought treatment were not comfortable with their own sexuality. These individuals were often filled with guilt and anxiety because of society's condemnation or their religious upbringing. One gay man urged Dr. Hooker to engage in research involving well-adjusted gay men, and he volunteered a number of such men for the research (Marcus, 1992).

Hooker subsequently conducted a study involv-ing thirty homosexual men and thirty heterosexual men. She administered three different personality tests to each subject—Rorschach, Thematic Apper-ception, and Make a Picture Story—and submitted the results to a panel of internationally respected psychologists. None of the panelists could discern heterosexual from homosexual subjects, and they gave two-thirds of the subjects from each group a score of average or higher, clearly refuting the belief that homosexuality was associated with inherent mental problems. Hooker presented the findings of the panel evaluations in her research at the national conference of the American Psychological Associa-tion (APA) in 1956. It would take another seven-teen years for APA members to admit they had been wrong and take appropriate action.

In 1973, the American Psychological Association voted to remove homosexuality from its list of men-

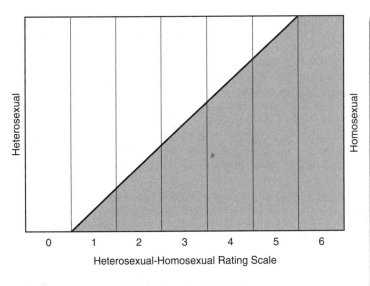

FIGURE 11.1

The Kinsey Continuum of Sexual Orientation

Based on dreams and fantasies as well as behavior, the continuum of sexual orientation ranges from exclusively heterosexual to exclusively homosexual, with the majority of people between the two exclusive positions.

Source: Sexual Behavior in the Human Male, by A. Kinsey, W. Pomeroy, and C. Martin, 1948, The Kinsey Institute, W.B. Saunders. Reprinted by permission of the Kinsey Institute for Research in Sex, Gender and Reproduction, Inc.

Heterosexual-Homosexual Rating Scale

0-Exclusively heterosexual with no homosexual
1-Predominantly heterosexual, only incidentally homosexual
2-Predominantly heterosexual, but more than incidentally homosexual
3-Equally heterosexual and homosexual
4-Predominantly homosexual, but more than incidentally heterosexual
5-Predominantly homosexual, only incidentally heterosexual
6-Exclusively homosexual

tal illnesses. The American Medical Association (AMA) would later join the APA in declaring that homosexuality was not a mental illness, affirming that gay men and lesbians could be just as healthy, competent, and capable of functioning effectively in society as heterosexuals. The decisions of the APA

> In my relationship with others, I have found that it does not help, in the long run, to act as if I am something I am not.
>
> **CARL ROGERS (1902–1987)**

and AMA sent a clear message to people who believed they were justified in discriminating against people who were not heterosexual. This resulted in the concept of **heterosexism**—the oppression or exploitation of human beings not biologically heterosexual.

What has current research reported with regard to homosexuality?

Research on human sexuality has continued and, based on the studies, researchers seem to agree that sexual orientation has a significant biological basis. Using anthropological evidence and studies in child development, Pillard (1997) proposed that sexual orientation is an innate characteristic, a deeply embedded personality trait that can be observed in young children:

> There seems to be a fundamental bias toward either a heterosexual or a homosexual developmental path, prefigured early in life, neither taught nor learned, and profoundly resistant to modification. (p. 233)

Le Vay (1996) argued that the influence of sex hormones on brain functioning at the primary drive center, the hypothalamus, appears to be a significant biological factor. Although not denying the importance of biological factors, anthropologists have described cultural influences on behavior and attitudes concerning human sexuality (Herdt, 1997). Researchers widely agree that there is no single cause for the sexual orientation of each individual, but that multiple factors are responsible (Stein, 1999; Le Vay, 1996).

Reinforcing the idea of sexual variation among humans, studies of animal behavior have reported sexual activities between same-sex animals (Stein, 1999). Money (1988) described research that experimentally manipulated prenatal hormones affecting the sexual pathways of the brain to successfully influence animals (other than primates) to engage in exclusively homosexual or heterosexual behavior during mating. Money did not claim that scientists could have the same success with humans, explaining that prenatal hormones are thought to have a less absolute influence on primates, but he did conclude that manipulation of sex hormones can create a predisposition for sexual activity with same-sex or opposite-sex partners.

Research regarding human sexual variation would seem to parallel the role that variation plays throughout nature. Gould (1981) provides an illustration in his explanation of the variety in striping patterns for zebras. One striping pattern has numerous, narrow, parallel stripes configured relatively straight up and down the body. Another pattern has fewer, thicker stripes on the body and three broad slightly curved stripes on the haunch. A third pattern has even fewer and thicker stripes on the front of the body, and even broader stripes starting from the middle of the belly and curving back to the haunch (see Figure 11.2).

The three striping variations result from the striping mechanism being initiated at different times during fetal development. Since variation occurs in something as simple as the striping pattern for zebras, it is difficult to maintain that all human beings possess the same heterosexual orientation, given the complexity of factors involved with the sexual development of the human fetus. It is far more logical to expect the kind of sexual variation described in the Kinsey Report, in the research conducted since 1948, and as recorded in human history.

CULTURAL HETEROSEXISM

Cultural heterosexism refers to a dominant culture defining heterosexuality as the norm and anything else as deviant. The heterosexual assumption is an example of cultural sexism. Although science has attempted to explain the complexity and variations in human sexual response, some people insist that the only acceptable way to love and make love is to be a heterosexual couple. History tells us, however, that homosexual feelings are not a contemporary aberration but have been reflected in human behavior in all cultures, in every era.

FIGURE 11.2

A simple genetic striping mechanism occurring at different times during fetal development produces these three striping patterns.

Source: From *Hen's Teeth and Horse's Toes: Further Reflections in Natural History* by Stephen Jay Gould. Copyright © 1983 by Stephen Jay Gould. Used by permission of W. W. Norton & Company, Inc.

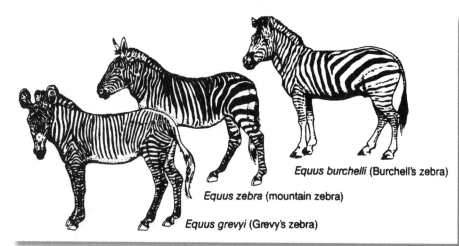

Equus burchelli (Burchell's zebra)

Equus zebra (mountain zebra)

Equus grevyi (Grevy's zebra)

> I can't understand any discussion of gays and lesbians as if they were something immoral or unsatisfactory. They're just doing what nature wants them to do.
>
> R. BUCKMINSTER FULLER (1895-1983)

What historical evidence has described the existence of homosexuality?

Love and sexual desire between men was accepted and widely practiced in ancient Greece. Greeks openly wrote about the love of one man for another. Although Sappho's poetry described women's love for other women, men were the primary authors of Greek literature that has been preserved. Approving of same-sex attraction wasn't an Athenian idiosyncrasy; it was also widely accepted in Sparta and other city-states. One of the most famous military units in Greek history was the Band of Thebes—150 pairs of lovers, a fighting force of 300 men; each pledged to stand by his lover in battle until death took one or both. The unit played a heroic part in Sparta's siege of Thebes: Fewer than 6,000 Theban defenders defeated more than 10,000 Spartan soldiers, a defeat from which Sparta never recovered, paving the way for the conquest of Greece by Philip of Macedonia. Philip's son, Alexander the Great, would become famous for conquering the known world during his lifetime and, according to contemporary accounts, was known to engage in sexual activity with male partners (Rowse, 1977).

One of the ironies of the history of homosexuality was recorded in nineteenth century England. At a time when English society was extremely homophobic, wealthy families sent their sons to male-only boarding schools, where they learned to read Latin and Greek texts, some with homosexual themes. Many memoirs recall upper-class boarding school experiences where English boys are described as engaging in homosexual behavior that they called "**Greek love,**" a euphemism for homosexual activity (Crompton, 1985).

Anthropologists have observed that culture often determines societal attitudes toward homosexuality.

Some Native American cultures believed that a homosexual is a special human being, considered to have great power by possessing traits of both males and females. Katz (1976) provided historical and anthropological documentation as evidence of the acceptance of homosexuality in various Native American cultures.

Some Polynesian and Caribbean cultures also view same-sex attraction and homosexual behavior as acceptable. The Mediterranean region, including southern Italy and countries such as Greece, Morocco, and Turkey, has historically been a haven for European homosexuals because same-sex relationships were tolerated. Aristocratic homosexuals traveled there primarily to act on their sexual attraction to same-sex partners (Williams, 1992; Crompton, 1985). According to Zeldin (1994), homosexuality has been accepted at one time or another by about two-thirds of human societies.

Early on, the Catholic Church played a major role in the denunciation of homosexuality in Europe. The Church regarded homosexuality as a sin, yet in 1102, the Archbishop of Canterbury called for lenient punishments for people engaging in same-sex activity because, "this sin has been so public that hardly anyone has blushed for it" (Zeldin, 1994, p. 123). As part of investigations by the Inquisition, Church persecution of homosexuals began in the thirteenth century as the Vatican sought to eliminate various heresies. The Inquisition lasted about four hundred years, but homosexuals continued to be persecuted in Europe for the next six hundred years (Boswell, 1994; Duberman, Vicinus, and Chauncey Jr., 1989).

Medieval churchmen executed both male and female homosexuals, although women were equally likely to be executed as witches, also justified in the Bible. The persecution and execution of men has suggested the origin of the term *faggot* as derived from *fagot*, referring to sticks tied in a bundle for kindling. When medieval judges condemned men to death for engaging in sexual activity with another man, the executioner sometimes tied up and piled the men on top of one another like bundles of kindling and burned them (Kantor, 1998).

Even royalty were not immune from persecution. Kings and queens were permitted a variety of sins as long as they were discreet, but English monarch Edward II was not discreet. His coronation festivities were almost disrupted by public reaction to the King's obvious preference for his friend Piers Gaveston rather than his Queen. Offended by the King's outrageous behavior, English nobles sent Gaveston back to France. Edward could not bear to be separated from his lover and pleaded that Gaveston be allowed to come back. Shortly after Gaveston returned to England, he was murdered, which led to a civil war that ended with Edward's death at the hands of Queen Isabella and her lover, Mortimer (Rowse, 1977). Still, Edward II was the exception. For royalty or aristocrats, or perhaps an artist under their protection, it was possible to escape persecution for having homosexual feelings or behaviors.

Despite some degree of tolerance for occasional royal family and aristocratic dalliances, England continued to reflect homophobic attitudes that forced those with fame and fortune, like the poet Lord Byron, to seek sexual pleasure outside the boundaries of Britain for fear of punishment in the country. Indeed, popular playwright Oscar Wilde was tried and sent to prison from 1895–1897 for his homosexual activity.

By the twentieth century, cultural attitudes about homosexuality in England had mellowed; this was true for most of Europe, but not for the United

> Whenever I behold someone who possesses any talent or displays any dexterity of mind, who can do or say something more appropriately than the rest of the world, I am compelled to fall in love with him, and give myself away to him so entirely that I am no longer my own property but wholly his.
>
> MICHELANGELO [BUONARROTI] (1475–1564)

States. The contrast between European and American attitudes was illustrated by the appointment of James Hormel as U.S. ambassador to Luxembourg during the Clinton administration. Officials in Luxembourg raised no objection to Hormel, who was openly gay, but his appointment was stalled in the Senate for two years because of objections from influential senators such as Jesse Helms.

How have attitudes of the American people changed concerning homosexuality?

As it did with racial minorities, World War II had an impact on American homosexuals returning from the war. The 1948 Kinsey Report had refuted the heterosexual assumption, and many gay and lesbian veterans thought their military experience earned them the right to be accepted regardless of sexual orientation. Because California courts had upheld the right of openly gay men and lesbians to patronize certain bars and businesses, it seemed the safest place to live. San Francisco had been a major port of departure for men and women sent to the Pacific, and many returning gays and lesbians chose to remain there. As their numbers grew, so did their political activism; by the 1970s, mayoral candidates such as George Moscone were openly courting gay voters.

San Francisco was one of many cities across the United States to witness gay and lesbian political activism, yet when Harvey Milk, an openly gay candidate, was elected San Francisco city supervisor in 1977, national media reported the story. One year later, a city supervisor who objected to serving with a gay man murdered both Milk and Mayor Moscone. As an indication that anti-gay prejudice had not disappeared, the jury convicted Dan White of the minimal penalty possible in such a case, manslaughter. The White verdict sparked a riot that lasted more than two hours in gay areas of San Francisco; police responded by shouting homophobic slurs and brutally beating any gay man or lesbian they encountered (D'Emilio, 1989).

The San Francisco riot on the West Coast, like the Stonewall riot a decade earlier in New York City, were two of many events in the late twentieth century that would force Americans everywhere to acknowledge the presence of homosexuals (see Table 11.1). The word **gay** became accepted as the self-chosen label of the homosexual community, although usage eventually was limited to men. The identification of homosexuals in popular culture and the acceptance of gays and lesbians by prominent people were important factors in changing historical anti-gay attitudes. By the 1970s, columnist Abigail van Buren ("Dear Abby") responded to questions about homosexuality based on her understanding of scientific research, emphasizing the need to accept it. In

TABLE 11.1

A Timetable of Important Events in the Twentieth Century for the Recognition of Gay Rights in the United States

1924	Formation of the first recognized activist group for gays and lesbians (Chicago).
1962	Illinois is the first state to repeal its sodomy laws.
1969	Police raid of the Stonewall Inn (a gay bar in New York City) results in riots that spark the beginning of the gay rights movement.
1970	First "Gay Pride" march (New York City) commemorates the Stonewall Riot.
1975	Retired NFL running back, Dave Kopay, is the first professional athlete to admit that he is gay.
1978	Harvey Milk, San Francisco's first openly gay City Supervisor, is assassinated.
1981	The Centers for Disease Control reports on the first case of what later becomes known as AIDS (initially called the "gay plague").
1982	Wisconsin is the first state to prohibit discrimination based on sexual orientation.
1982	Harvey Fierstein's play about a drag queen called "Torch Song Trilogy" opens on Broadway and wins the Tony Award for Best Play.
1984	Hollywood's legendary leading man Rock Hudson admits to being gay.
1987	Formation of ACT UP, which advocates for more funding for AIDS research.
1993	U.S. military adopts "don't ask, don't tell" policy as a compromise to address the problem of harassment of gay and lesbian soldiers.
1993	Hundreds of thousands participate in a march for equal rights for gays and lesbians (Washington, D.C.).
1996	U.S. Supreme Court declares equal rights for gays and lesbians.
1997	The popular television show "Ellen" is the first program to have a main character who admits to being gay (as does the actress, Ellen DeGeneres).
1998	The murder of Matthew Shepard gains national attention and is the catalyst in many states to include gays and lesbians in hate-crime legislation.
1999	Vermont's Supreme Court rules that same-sex couples have the same legal right to get married as heterosexual couples.
2003	U.S. Supreme Court rules that sodomy laws are unconstitutional, reversing its 1986 decision in *Hardwick* v. *Bowers*.

1975, David Kopay, a retired National Football League running back, published an autobiography in which he not only admitted his own homosexuality but also alleged that many professional athletes were gay. With the sexual identity of popular stars from the 1950s and 1960s such as Rock Hudson and Liberace being revealed to the public, gays and lesbians increasingly encountered more tolerant attitudes, especially in urban areas.

Most Americans tended to ignore the AIDS epidemic that arose in the early 1980s, although some radio and television ministers blamed homosexual behavior for causing this "gay disease." As Sontag (1989) explained "The unsafe behavior that produces AIDS (was) judged to be more than just weakness. It is indulgence, delinquency—addiction to chemicals that are illegal and to sex regarded as deviant" (p. 25). As the epidemic continued, Americans were forced to confront the American historic cultural bias against gays; people increasingly recognized HIV as a virus, not a punishment from God. The fact that a young boy, Ryan White, could

FIGURE 11.3

In this picture, Ryan White returns to school, after being sent home by school authorities who feared that having AIDS would make him a danger to the lives of the other students. Based on medical testimony, the courts disagreed.

Source: © Bettman/CORBIS

contract this fatal disease from a blood transfusion illustrated the point dramatically. For seven of his eight years as president, Ronald Reagan never publicly acknowledged the spread of AIDS (Shilts, 1987). It took another presidential election before Congress passed the Ryan White Comprehensive AIDS Resources Emergency Act in 1990. But anti-gay attitudes in the United States have persisted.

> God loves homosexuals as much as he loves everybody else.
>
> **RYAN WHITE (1971–1990)**

Why do so many Americans continue to have anti-gay attitudes?

Many Americans still cling to the cultural belief that homosexuality is unnatural, an accusation that calls for reasonable people to consider what it would mean for something to be natural. Some sexual activity, such as incest, is forbidden in every known culture, yet homosexual behavior is—or has been—accepted in most world cultures. Scientists have argued that anything observed and documented in nature should be considered natural. Stein (1999) found that scientific studies of animals in their nat-

ural habitat report occurrences of sexual activity between animals of the same sex in every group studied, suggesting that sexual activity between same-sex partners normally occurs in nature.

Although the Catholic Church accepts that homosexuality is a natural predisposition (that is, one is born with it), it continues to denounce homosexual activity as a sin—the only instance of the Church forbidding something it admits to be natural. The struggle within the Catholic Church over this issue is reflected in a letter from American bishops urging Catholic parents to accept and love their gay and lesbian children regardless of whether or not they refrain from acting on their homosexuality (Christian Century Foundation, 1997).

Protestant churches are divided on the issue of accepting homosexuality. Some Protestant theologians continue to condemn homosexuality. Others argue that certain Biblical passages have been mistranslated to justify regarding homosexual behavior as a sin—these passages actually denounce male and female prostitution, not homosexuality. Some feel Biblical criticism of men engaging in homosexual acts was based on the Biblical authors assuming everyone was heterosexual, and that anyone engaging in a homosexual act betrayed human nature (Doupe, 1992). Another argument has been that since Biblical injunctions against eating pork or making clothes out of two types of material are now regarded as historic but no longer relevant, any Biblical passage interpreted as an injunction against homosexual acts should also be regarded today as an example of historic prejudice. Protestant debates about accepting homosexuality certainly will continue as we have seen in the recent controversy in the Episcopal Church over the ordination of the first openly gay bishop. Time will tell if various Christian denominations will respond to research on sexual orientation and accept people who are not heterosexual.

INDIVIDUAL HETEROSEXISM

Despite increasing acceptance of homosexuality in western cultures outside the United States, as well as research findings, many Americans still regard homosexuality as unnatural and sinful. Sociological study confirms that **individual heterosexism,** negative attitudes and behaviors based on the belief that sexual orientations other than heterosexual are unnatural, is a major factor promoting one of the most common hate crimes in the United States, the physical assault of a person perceived to be gay known as **gay bashing.** Herek and Berill (1992) report that more than 75% of gay men and lesbians have experienced verbal abuse, almost half have been subjected to violent threats, and for 20% or more, the threats were carried out. Young males are the primary perpetrators of anti-gay violence, and most of them do so as part of a group. Although personal prejudice is ascribed as a major factor, studies of motivations for anti-gay violence have revealed that young men often believe cultural myths about homosexuality that justify their verbal abuse and physical attacks (Franklin, 1998). Each of us must confront myths that promote anti-gay behavior, and since gay bashers tend to be young men in high school, vocational school, or college, educators must play a role in giving our youth accurate information to refute these myths.

What are some myths about homosexuality?

Myths regarding homosexuality contribute to individual prejudice and homophobia in the United States (Blumenfeld, 1992). **Homophobia** is a stronger feeling than prejudice, usually defined as fear or hatred of homosexuals. Here are some examples of myths still perpetuated in American society about gays and lesbians:

MYTH: Anyone who has ever engaged in a homosexual act at any time is a homosexual.

REALITY: To be identified as a homosexual means that a person demonstrates a persistent erotic attraction for people of the same sex. Gays and lesbians are not attracted to every same-sex person they see, but when they feel physically and emotionally attracted to someone, that person is consistently someone of the same sex.

Some people engage in sexual activity with a person of the same sex one time and never again. Some people have only engaged in homosexual acts during unusual and temporary circumstances, such as being in situations where there is no easy access to members of the opposite sex (such as in prison or in the military). Men or women who engage in sexual acts with a partner of the same sex in an unusual situation typically do not persist in this behavior when circumstances return to the more typical situation and thus should not be identified as homosexual.

MYTH: Homosexuals tend to engage in criminal activity, and are especially likely to prey on children and molest them.

REALITY: Studies of criminal activity report that homosexuals are no more likely to engage in criminal activity than heterosexuals, and studies of child molesters reveal that over 99% are male and nearly 80% are white, heterosexual men who are married or were formerly married (Abel and Harlow, 2001).

Child molesters are **pedophiles**—adults who desire sexual contact with children. There are heterosexual pedophiles who desire children of the opposite sex and homosexual pedophiles who desire children of the same sex. As the data show, children are at greater risk from heterosexuals than from gays and lesbians. Pedophilia has nothing to do with being homosexual.

> **MYTH:** Homosexuals attempt to seduce vulnerable adolescents and recruit them into their lifestyle.
>
> **REALITY:** Individuals who engage in homosexual behavior during adolescence tend to do so with other adolescents, not adults (Sears, 1992).

> If . . . marriage can keep you in touch with your past, your emotional self, and your humanity, the notion that this should be any less true for gay or lesbian couples than it is for heterosexuals is absurd.
>
> **DERRICK BELL (1930–)**

This accusation is an ancient one, as we know from the life of Socrates, who was accused of corrupting the youth, found guilty, and ordered to drink a poisonous cup of hemlock for his punishment. Since the primary group responsible for gay bashing in the United States is adolescent males, gays are risking violence if they approach adolescents for sexual purposes.

> **MYTH:** Homosexuals do not have loving relationships, but are only interested in sex and engage in sexually promiscuous behavior.
>
> **REALITY:** Americans have historically denied gay men and lesbians the right to marry and refused to recognize domestic partnerships, tolerating sexual activities of gays and lesbians who are discreet but not sanctioning their activity.

This myth is especially egregious since American society has created conditions that promote the behavior being condemned. Gays and lesbians have been allowed to engage in sexual activity in gay bars and bathhouses, but they are not allowed to declare their affection publicly or to have their relationships acknowledged. Americans have vigorously resisted gays and lesbians who have sought public sanction for their relationships by demanding the right to marry or to be recognized in domestic partnerships. Although heterosexuals may engage in public displays of affection, gay men or lesbians are often verbally or physically assaulted for the same behavior.

Heterosexuals are encouraged to marry and be monogamous, yet the percentage engaging in premarital sex with many partners has increased, and it has been estimated that two-thirds of all marriages in the United States will end in separation or divorce (Cushner, McClelland, and Safford, 1996). Given such projections, it is hypocritical for the heterosexual community to accuse gays and lesbians of promiscuity and to insist that marriage is sacred and should be reserved exclusively for heterosexual couples. According to psychologists, gays and lesbians have the same need as heterosexuals for long-term, stable relationships. Because of the 2003 decision by the Massachusetts Supreme Court that gay and lesbian couples ought to have the same legal right to marry as heterosexuals, gay men and lesbians may have an opportunity to demonstrate their ability to have successful monogamous marital relationships.

> **MYTH:** People become homosexual because they had a bad experience while involved in heterosexual activity; therefore gay men or lesbians could change their sexual behavior if they had a positive heterosexual experience.
>
> **REALITY:** Many gay men and lesbians have been involved in heterosexual relationships, including marriage, because of the hostility directed against homosexuality.

Many gays and lesbians have engaged in heterosexual activities in an effort to convince themselves of their normality, but sexual orientation is not a choice. Some people still refer to *sexual preference* as if lesbians and gays prefer to love same-sex partners. But human sexuality is not a matter of preference, and past efforts to reorient an individual's sexuality have not been successful. Studies of human sexuality have concluded that sexual orientation is determined early in human development. Once we become aware of our sexual feelings, our only choice is to accept these feelings and act upon them or to reject and repress them. Some gays and lesbians have accepted their sexual orientation but—as with some heterosexuals—have chosen to be chaste. Sexual abstinence is a choice any individual can make, but it is no more likely to lead to happiness for homosexuals than for heterosexuals.

MYTH: Close personal relationships between adolescents or adults of the same sex could stimulate homosexual feelings and behavior; so intimate friendships should be avoided, especially between men.

REALITY: It is perfectly normal for a man or a woman to feel and express love and affection for a person of the same sex as can be observed in other cultures.

Displays of affection between men and between women are common in many cultures. In American culture, women are allowed some degree of public intimacy with each other such as holding hands, dancing together, or even kissing (as long as they don't kiss on the lips). Men are not allowed to engage in similar public behaviors with other men without being perceived as homosexual; this creates a burden for American men who have the same human need for affection and intimacy as do women.

Because of myths such as these, it should be easy to understand why most people would be reluctant to identify with such a reviled and persecuted group. Civil rights activists often claim that gays and lesbians encounter more blatant discrimination than any other group. In response to this discrimination, gays and lesbians have intensified their efforts to promote the concept of gay rights across America.

INSTITUTIONAL HETEROSEXISM

Although Kinsey suggested that the sexual orientation of approximately 10% of Americans is exclusively homosexual, recent surveys report

FIGURE 11.4

Parents, Families and Friends of Lesbians and Gays (PFLAG) is an advocacy organization that started when the mother of a gay man participated in a 1972 gay pride march in New York City after her son had been assaulted because of his sexual orientation. Today PFLAG has a national office in Washington, D.C., with 500 affiliates that promote respect for human differences and the acceptance of all people regardless of sexual orientation or gender identity.

Source: Photo Courtesy of PFLAG.

approximately 3% of men identify themselves as gay and about 1.5% of women identify themselves as lesbian (Jones and George, 2002). It is impossible to have a census of gay men and lesbians because of the number who conceal their sexual identity—or deny it—to protect themselves from other people's negative attitudes and behaviors. **Institutional heterosexism**—established laws, customs, and practices that systematically discriminate against people who are not heterosexual—has been so prevalent and so blatant that activists have increased their efforts to combat discrimination across America. They are promoting **gay rights,** insisting that gays and lesbians should have the same rights and privileges as heterosexual Americans.

Is the demand for gay rights really a demand for special privileges?

The goal of gay rights is to make it possible for gays and lesbians to be honest about their sexual orientation without being deprived of civil rights. These rights do not entail special privileges, but rather the rights of citizens in our democracy. It is a question of tolerance: One can support civil rights for gays and lesbians without necessarily condoning homosexual behavior. It does require us to agree that if gays and lesbians identify their sexual orientation publicly, they should not be discriminated against in being hired for jobs, renting or purchasing a home, running for political office, enlisting in the military, attending their church of choice, or any other rights that heterosexuals take for granted. Gay rights means having the same—not special—rights and responsibilities as other citizens of the United States. In most of the United States, gays and lesbians are often not extended the civil rights that heterosexuals enjoy unless they are **in the closet,** meaning they deny or disguise their sexual orientation.

Numerous examples exist of gays and lesbians who have been dismissed from jobs, not because they were inefficient or incompetent but because employers discovered their sexual orientation. A Baltimore civil rights advocate told the story of a lesbian manager of a diner who hired a gay dishwasher. When the owner of the diner realized the sexual orientation of the dishwasher, he insisted that the manager fire the man because he did not

> Tolerance is the positive and cordial effort to understand another's beliefs, practices, and habits without necessarily sharing or accepting them.
>
> **JOSHUA LIEBMAN (1907–1948)**

want gay employees on his payroll. The woman enjoyed a good relationship with her boss and had certainly proven her competence as a manager over the past ten years. She took a chance. She told the boss he already had a gay employee and he was looking at her. She also was fired. The civil rights advocate who related the incident insisted the story was not unusual. Twelve states—California, Connecticut, Hawaii, Maryland, Massachusetts, Minnesota, Nevada, New Hampshire, New Jersey, Rhode Island, Vermont, and Wisconsin—and the District of Columbia have laws against discrimination based on sexual orientation. In all other states, the only way gays and lesbians can be certain of keeping their job is to stay in the closet. And so they do.

How can homosexuals be discriminated against if they don't reveal their identity?

If gay men and lesbians are in the closet—not perceived by their employers, supervisors, and co-workers as homosexual—it seems logical to assume that they should not experience discrimination, but that assumption is only accurate for blatant kinds of discrimination. Subtle forms of discrimination can affect such concerns as job advancement. According to a Harvard Business School study, gays and lesbians who did not identify themselves at work were not promoted as readily as their heterosexual peers. Because of the need to keep their personal lives secret, gay men and lesbians often maintained their personal privacy at work, not engaging frequently in casual conversations and not socializing with others after work or on weekends. The study concluded that social isolation in protection of one's identity is a major factor for gays and lesbians not being promoted (Badgett, 2001).

Another form of discrimination based on sexual orientation involves health care coverage. Married employees typically include their spouses under their employer's health care plan: Partners of gays and lesbians are not allowed to participate, which is another consequence of keeping one's sexual identity private. Even if an employee were willing to risk being openly gay, almost 90 percent of businesses do not include domestic partnerships in their health care plans (Badgett, 2001). Today, American health care coverage is a benefit equaling approximately 6% of an individual's salary, and as health care costs increase, that amount is likely to increase. Although the cost of providing health care for domestic partners is affordable for most corporations and businesses, many continue to deny health coverage for partners of gay or lesbian employees, which essentially denies them the opportunity to receive equal compensation for equal work (McNaught, 1997).

Why do homosexuals want legal recognition for domestic partnerships?

Many gays and lesbians are willing to let marriage remain an exclusively heterosexual arrangement as long as the law recognizes **domestic partnerships,** which are defined as:

> An intimate, committed relationship between two individuals of legal age who are financially and emotionally interdependent, share the same residence, and intend to remain together indefinitely. (Badgett, 2001, p. 82)

The purpose of legal recognition for domestic partnerships is to provide gay couples with the same legal rights married couples enjoy: being covered by a partner's health insurance, being able to inherit a partner's property, being eligible for a partner's survival benefits, or having the right to make decisions for an incapacitated partner. Advocates for recognizing domestic partnerships support their cause by referring to the existence of such laws in Denmark, France, Hungary, Iceland, Norway, the Netherlands, and Sweden.

A dramatic example of the importance of recognizing domestic partnerships was illustrated in Minnesota. A head-on collision with a drunk driver left Sharon Kowalski paralyzed and unable to speak. Her long-term partner visited her at the hospital for as many as eight hours a day to read aloud to her,

massage her, and make sure Sharon received rehabilitative therapy. At first appreciative, Sharon's parents began to question the behavior of Sharon's friend until they were finally told that their daughter was a lesbian and that the friend was actually her domestic partner. Sharon's father immediately took steps to prevent Sharon's partner from seeing his daughter, even though hospital personnel confirmed that Sharon was improving largely because of the therapy her partner had been providing (Griscom, 2001).

Even though it offered minimal rehabilitation services, Sharon's father committed her to a nursing home. Sharon's partner pursued every possible course of action, and after eight years, the courts recognized that Sharon Kowalski was competent to make her own decisions and that it was her desire to be cared for by her partner. Since that incident, Minnesota legislators have added homosexuals to the list of protected groups in its Civil Rights law. With the U.S. Supreme Court's 2003 decision in

> If what we think is right and wrong divides still further the human family, there must be something wrong with what we think is right.
>
> **WILLIAM SLOAN COFFIN (1924–)**

Lawrence v. *Texas* that it is unconstitutional to criminalize gay sexual activity, opponents feared that the decision represents the first step toward sanctioning gay marriages.

If domestic partnerships were recognized, why would homosexuals wish to marry?

Gays and lesbians who desire state-recognized marriage give reasons similar to those of heterosexuals: to make public statements about their commitment to each other, including the pledge to maintain a monogamous relationship. Rather than a special privilege, marriage is a decision to participate in a legally and socially sanctioned activity. Church leaders may insist that marriage is a sacred rite reserved exclusively for people in heterosexual relationships; however, many gays and lesbians want to participate in a secular marriage ceremony performed in accordance with state law, not necessarily a religious marriage. To assert that marriage is a legal contract available exclusively for heterosexual couples is to engage in discrimination based on sexual orientation.

In recent years, gays and lesbians have taken legal action to force the courts to rule on the legality of same-sex marriage. In 1996, a Hawai'i Circuit Court found no legitimate legal basis for denying homosexuals the right to obtain marriage licenses, but the state court reversed that ruling three years later. In 1999, Vermont's Supreme Court ruled that denying gay and lesbian couples the opportunity to participate in legal, secular marriage violated the state constitution. In many states, the reaction to such rulings has been to pass legislation defining marriage as a legal contract between "a man and a woman," refusing to recognize same-sex marriages performed in other states. The 2003 Massachusetts Supreme Court decision in support of gay marriage has now made it even more likely that the United States Supreme Court will soon have to address the issue of whether gay men and lesbians have the legal right to get married. In the meantime, many gays and lesbians continue to enjoy stable, monogamous relationships, some choosing to have children, while they wait for state and federal law to acknowledge the reality of their relationships.

What harm is done to a child raised by gay parents?

It is harmful and immoral for a child to be abandoned, untouched, unloved, ridiculed, and physically or sexually abused. It is usually not harmful for a child to be cared for by his or her biological mother or father or to be adopted by loving parents, regardless of their sexual orientation. Many gays and lesbians are parents, bringing children to same-sex relationships from past failed heterosexual relationships. According to Badgett (2001), approximately 30% of lesbians have children in their homes and 27% of gay men are fathers, with 15% of them caring for children in their homes. Although gays and lesbians may have become parents as a result of denying their sexual orientation

in a heterosexual marriage, some choose to become parents because they want to raise a child. No matter how or why they have children, studies suggest that gays and lesbians appear to be conscientious about parenting.

According to Johnson and O'Connor (2002), research concludes that gay and lesbian couples are effective parents, providing for their children's physical and emotional needs to ensure a healthy and positive childhood. In evaluating children raised by gays or lesbians, studies have explored such factors as social interaction, intelligence, self-esteem, and ability to express feelings. Children of gays and lesbians not only appear to develop self-confidence and social skills, but also are more tolerant of differences than are other children (McLeod and Crawford, 1998). Research does not support the exclusion of gays and lesbians from any occupation or activity in which other U.S. citizens participate.

Why have homosexuals always been excluded from military service?

There is historic evidence that gays and lesbians have served in the military in the United States and in other countries. In addition to the Greek Band of Thebes, historic warriors such as Alexander the Great and Richard the Lion-Hearted had male lovers. As attitudes in the Western world have become more negative toward homosexuality, same-sex behavior in the military became more carefully concealed. Activities occasionally would be exposed, as in Germany's Eulenberg Affair where from 1907 to 1909, accusations of homosexual behavior were directed against officers in the German army, the diplomatic corps, and the cabinet of Kaiser Wilhelm (Steakly, 1989). Allegations were well-documented, which led to several resignations by cabinet members and military officers.

In America, a Navy investigation at Newport Naval Training Station following World War I similarly revealed widespread homosexual activity (Chauncey, 1989). During World War II, the Army conducted an investigation of alleged lesbian activity in the Women's Army Corps (WAC) in which a WAC officer testified about a letter she received from the Surgeon General's Office that said "homosexual relationships should be tolerated" as long as they were discreet and did not lead to disruptions in the unit (Bérubé, 1989, p. 384).

Homosexual participation in the armed forces is not new. What is new is periodic blatant discrimination against gays and lesbians by the U.S. military. In 1981, the Pentagon instituted a policy banning all gays and lesbians from the armed forces because the leaders believed that homosexuality was incompatible with military service. Patriotic gay and lesbian soldiers serving their country could be discharged, not for incompetence or misbehavior, but because they were homosexual. The first Clinton administration modified the policy, forbidding the military to inquire about a person's sexual orientation; neither recruits nor gays and lesbians already in the armed forces could be asked about their sexual orientation.

The "Don't Ask, Don't Tell" policy was intended to discourage attempts to identify and remove homosexuals from the military. According to the policy, gays and lesbians were required to keep quiet or lie about their identity, and could be discharged if their sexual identity were discovered or they admitted to being homosexual. Perhaps because of the increased militancy in the gay community or because of a growing reluctance to conceal their identity, the number of gays and lesbians discharged from the military actually has increased under the new policy (see Figure 11.5).

As the United States has hardened its resistance to gays in the military, attitudes in other countries have become more tolerant. Armies in Australia, France, Ireland, and the Netherlands actively recruit and train openly homosexual soldiers, many of whom worked with U.S. armed forces as part of the United Nations' peacekeeping forces in Bosnia (Palmer, 1997). Gay activists are demanding that gays and lesbians be accepted not only in the military but in other professions, such as education, where they have been excluded because of past prejudice.

Why should homosexuals be allowed to become teachers?

Accepting gays and lesbians as teachers illustrates another contrast between European and American attitudes. In the summer of 1988, some American students were in Austria, taking courses offered by American professors. One professor

FIGURE 11.5

Annual Gay Discharges Under "Don't Ask, Don't Tell, Don't Pursue, Don't Harass"

Source: Courtesy of Servicemembers Legal Defense Network (www.sldn.org), based on Department of Defense Figures.

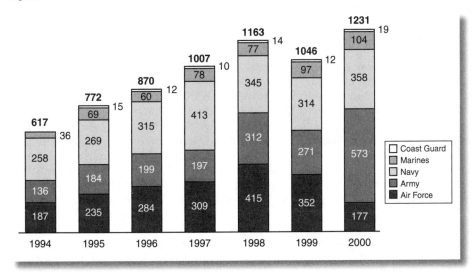

> You don't have to be straight to shoot straight.
>
> BARRY GOLDWATER (1909–1998)

required each student to interview Austrians using a series of questions based on issues of prejudice and discrimination discussed in his course. One of the questions puzzled the Austrians: "Should a homosexual be allowed to teach children?" People being interviewed consistently asked for a clarification of the question and often responded, "I don't understand. Is this person not a good teacher?" Knowing that the person was a good teacher was important; knowing the teacher's sexual orientation was not relevant. In years to come, perhaps Americans will also view such a question as irrelevant.

Having openly gay and lesbian teachers would be especially important for gay and lesbian youth. Children encounter many dilemmas growing up, especially learning to deal with peers and responding to the physiological and psychological changes of puberty. Adolescence is even more difficult for gay and lesbian youth because their emerging sexual feelings are not accepted by our culture and are often vehemently denounced. Name-calling in elementary schools includes epithets such as "faggot" and "queer." "That's so gay" has become a negative judgment. Gay and lesbian youth hear animosity expressed toward homosexuals at school, in their communities, and perhaps even in their homes. They may witness or hear accounts of gay bashing, and they are rarely able to resolve the conflict between their sexuality and the anti-gay hostility they observe in society. D'Augelli (1998) and Gibson (1994) each report that over half of gay youth consider committing suicide, and that 30 percent attempt suicide at least once.

During the early 1990s, the Republican governor of Massachusetts was concerned enough about the safety of gay youth to initiate an investigation. In its final report, the Governor's Commission described a disturbing pattern of abuse: Testimony from gay and lesbian youth and their parents described a constant barrage of taunts and slurs, being spit upon, and physical attacks. One boy left all his classes late and arrived late to every class so he could walk through empty hallways to avoid constant harassment. Another student *who was not gay* was assaulted every day at school simply because other students thought he was homosexual. Having heard such painful testimony of widespread anti-gay violence, the Commission's recommendations included implementing school policies to protect gay and lesbian youth from harassment and violence, establishing support groups for gay and lesbian students, and providing information in school curriculum and in school libraries on gay and lesbian issues (Massachusetts Governor's Commission on Gay and Lesbian Youth, 1994).

Gay and lesbian students have the right to attend public middle and high schools that are safe places to learn, but schools need to do more than announce policies and provide information. According to the Governor's Commission, over half of the gay and lesbian youth who testified had heard homophobic slurs from their teachers. When people in positions of authority such as teachers express their prejudice to children and youth, it legitimizes prejudiced attitudes. For that reason, the Commission recommended additional training for teachers and counselors. If schools become accepting of openly homosexual teachers, gay and lesbian youth will have needed role models, and school districts will send a message to homophobic teachers that discourages them from expressing anti-gay prejudices (Kissen, 1996; Harbeck, 1992).

AFTERWORD

The most important change that needs to be made at this time in the United States may be to establish policies and practices that promote tolerance for homosexuality to the extent that all gays and lesbians feel safe being open at school, at work, and in their neighborhoods. Young gays and lesbians are trying to change the language of hate by choosing the term **queer** to describe not only gays and lesbians but people who are bisexual, transgender, and transsexual (GLBT). Queer studies programs are appearing on some college campuses as scholars try to examine and disseminate information about issues in the lives of GLBT people.

Changing cultural attitudes will take a long time, but if it becomes more acceptable to be open about sexual identity, it is more likely that heterosexuals will find that they know someone who is homosexual. Simon (1998) has reported that when people know someone who is a gay man or lesbian, they tend to be less homophobic and to have a more positive attitude about the issue of sexual orientation and homosexuality. Change is possible if conditions are created to allow it. Accepting homosexuality is an ethical challenge confronting nations around the world, and every American institution and individual must decide how to meet it.

> I believe all Americans who believe in freedom, tolerance and human rights have a responsibility to oppose bigotry and prejudice based on sexual orientation.
>
> CORETTA SCOTT KING (1927–)

TERMS AND DEFINITIONS

Bisexual A normative category of sexual identity referring to lifelong sexual desires and/or erotic relations with members of both genders

Cultural heterosexism The societal promotion of negative beliefs and practices that reinforce dominant culture traits that define heterosexuality as the norm and anything else as deviant and unacceptable; the assumption of superiority of heterosexuals over those who are not heterosexual

Domestic partnership An intimate, committed relationship between two individuals, of legal age, who are financially and emotionally interdependent, share the same residence, and intend to indefinitely remain together

Gay, Gays A term in reference to homosexuality in general, but specifically to male homosexuals.

Gay bashing Physical assault on an individual who is perceived as being gay, which is motivated by the individual's sexual orientation

Gay rights The demand that gay men and lesbians be able to openly identify their sexual orientation and not be discriminated against with regard to the civil rights available to all other citizens

Greek love The nineteenth century code phrase invented by boys at British boarding schools to describe their sexual activities with other boys

Heterosexism The systematic oppression and exploitation of bisexuals, lesbians, gay men, and transgender individuals, especially policies and practices reinforcing heterosexuality as the only option for relationships and families

Heterosexual A normative category of sexual identity referring to exclusive lifelong sexual desire and erotic relations with the opposite gender

Heterosexual assumption The assumption that every human being is born a heterosexual

Homophobia The culturally influenced fear and hatred of homosexual persons, acts, and events

Homosexual A normative moral category of sexual identity referring to exclusive lifelong sexual desire and erotic relations with the same gender

Individual heterosexism Prejudiced attitudes and behavior against others based on the assumption that sexual orientations other than heterosexual are unnatural; this is demonstrated whenever someone responds by saying or doing something degrading or harmful about persons who are not heterosexual

Institutional heterosexism Established laws, customs, and practices in a society that allow systematic discrimination against people or groups who are not heterosexual

In the closet The concealment of sexual orientation from colleagues, heterosexual friends, and/or family

Pedophiles Adults who desire sexual contact with children

Queer Generic term used to refer to people who are gay, lesbian, bisexual, transgender, and transsexual (GLBT)

Sexual orientation The sexual identity of an individual based on lifelong sexual fantasies, desires, and practices

REFERENCES

Abel, G., & Harlow, N. (2001). *The stop child molestation book.* Philadelphia: Xlibris.

Analyzes responses from over 4,000 adults who had sexually molested children to determine characteristics of child molesters and to develop recommendations to curb child molestation.

Badgett, M.V.L. (2001). *Money, myths, and change: The economic lives of lesbians and gay men.* Chicago: The University of Chicago Press.

Describes economic myths and workplace discrimination against lesbians and gay men by examining various studies and analyzing statistical data.

Bérbubé, A. (1989). Marching to a different drummer: Lesbian and gay GIs in World War II. In M. Duberman, M. Vicinus, & G. Chauncey, Jr. (Eds.), *Hidden from History: Reclaiming the gay and lesbian past* (pp. 456–476). New York: Meridian.

Discusses the emergence of the gay political movement in the United States as a consequence of military policies attempting to manage the homosexual behavior of soldiers during World War II.

Blumenfeld, W.J. (Ed.). (1992). *Homophobia: How we all pay the price.* Boston: Beacon.

Addresses myths about homosexuality in many of the essays, and identifies and refutes twelve of these myths in the Appendix (pp. 293–294).

Boswell, J. (1994). *Same-sex unions in pre-modern Europe.* New York: Villard.

Reviews historical evidence for acceptance of same-sex relationships in Greek and Roman cultures and translates documents from Vatican archives suggesting that the Catholic Church sanctioned same-sex marriages during its early years.

Chauncey, G., Jr. (1989). Christian brotherhood or sexual perversion? Homosexual identities and the construction of sexual boundaries in the World War I era. In M. Duberman, M. Vicinus, & G. Chauncey, Jr. (Eds.), *Hidden from History: Reclaiming the gay and lesbian past* (pp. 456–476). New York: Meridian.

Discusses the Navy's investigation of the Newport naval training station (1919–1920) in terms of the social context and the self-awareness of sailors accused of homosexual behavior.

Christian Century Foundation. (1997). Accept Gay Orientation, Say Catholic Bishops. *Christian Century* 114(29), 936–937.

Highlights the pastoral statement "Always Our Children: A Pastoral Message to Parents of Homosexual Children and Suggestions for Pastoral Ministers" by the Catholic Bishops.

Crompton, L. (1985). *Byron and Greek love: Homophobia in 19th century England.* Berkeley: University of California Press.

Examines the influence of homoeroticism on Lord Byron and the homophobia of his time as revealed in sources such as the popular press, court documents, and parliamentary debates.

Cushner, K., McClelland, A., & Safford, P. (1996). Education in a changing society. In *Human diversity in education: An integrative approach.* New York: McGraw Hill.

Describes changes in American society and the implications of these changes for schools.

D'Augelli, A.R. (1998). Developmental implications of victimization of lesbian, gay, and bisexual youth. In G. Herek (Ed.), *Stigma and sexual orientation: Understanding prejudice against lesbians, gay men and bisexuals.* Thousand Oaks, CA: Sage.

Reviews research which explores the psychological impact of verbal and physical abuse directed against adolescents who are lesbian, gay, or bisexual.

D'Emilio, J. (1989). Gay politics and community in San Francisco since World War II. In M. Duberman, M. Vicinus, & G. Chauncey, Jr. (Eds.), *Hidden from history: Reclaiming the gay and lesbian past* (pp. 456–476). New York: Meridian.

Describes factors that attracted gay men and lesbians to San Francisco following World War II and how the development of the gay community promoted political activism.

Doupe, G.E. (1992). True to our tradition. In W. Blumenfeld (Ed.), *Homophobia: How we all pay the price* (pp. 187–204). Boston: Beacon.

Analyzes and rejects the Biblical justification used to denounce gay men and lesbians and provides an alternative Christian response grounded in Biblical principles.

Duberman, M., Vicinus, M., & Chauncey, G. Jr. (Eds.). (1989). *Hidden from history: Reclaiming the gay and lesbian past.* New York: Meridian.

Consists of essays from more than twenty scholars describing the historical experiences of gay men and lesbians in China, Japan, Russia, and South Africa as well as the United States and Europe.

Franklin, K. (1998). Unassuming motivations: Contextualizing the narratives of antigay assailants. In G. Herek (Ed.), *Stigma and sexual orientation: Understanding prejudice against lesbians, gay men and bisexuals* (pp. 339–363). Thousand Oaks, CA: Sage.

Analyzes the motivations provided in interviews with three young men who engaged in gay bashing, taken from the author's research on anti-gay attitudes and behaviors.

Gibson, P. (1994). Gay male and lesbian youth suicide. In G. Remafedi (Ed.), *Death by denial: Studies of suicide in gay and lesbian teenagers* (pp. 15–68). Boston: Alyson.

Describes factors contributing to the high percentage of gays and lesbians in the data on youth suicide and provides recommendations to reduce their suicide attempts.

Gould, S.J. (1981). How the Zebra gets its stripes. In *Hen's teeth and horse's toes* (pp. 366–375). New York: W. W. Norton.

Addresses genetic issues related to striping patterns on zebras.

Griscom, J.L. (2001). The case of Sharon Kowalski and Karen Thompson: Ableism, heterosexism, and sexism. In P. Rothenberg (Ed.), *Race, class, and gender in the United States: An integrated study* (5th ed., pp. 410–420). New York: Worth.

Describes an eight-year ordeal as a father opposed efforts of his daughter's lesbian partner to provide needed physical therapy following a traffic accident.

Halperin, D.M. (1989). Sex before sexuality: Pederasty, politics, and power in classical Athens. In M. Duberman, M. Vicinus, and G. Chauncey, Jr. (Eds.), *Hidden from history: Reclaiming the gay and lesbian past* (pp. 37–53). New York: Meridian.

Explains how homosexuality and heterosexuality are modern cultural categories that are alien to the cultural perspective of the ancient Greeks.

Harbeck, K.M. (Ed.). (1992). *Coming out of the classroom closet: Gay and lesbian students, teachers and curricula*. New York: Harrington Park Press.

Examines such topics as images of lesbians and gay men in the curricula, HIV education, and experiences of gay and lesbian students and teachers, both in the closet and out.

Herdt, G. (1997). *Same sex, different cultures. Exploring gay and lesbian lives*. Boulder, CO: Westview.

Reviews anthropological, and cross-cultural evidence on attitudes toward lesbians and gay men.

Herek, G.M., & Berrill, K.T. (Eds.). (1992). *Hate crimes: Confronting violence against lesbians and gay men*. Newbury Park, CA: Sage.

Includes essays examining statistical data, exploring the cultural context, analyzing motivations of perpetrators, and featuring first-person accounts of anti-gay violence.

Johnson, S.M., & O'Connor, E. (2002). *The gay baby boom: The psychology of gay parenthood*. New York: The New York University Press.

Reviews previous psychological studies of gay and lesbian families and discusses results from the author's "National Study of Gay and Lesbian Families."

Jones, G.R., & George, J.M. (2002). Managing diverse employees in a diverse environment. In *Contemporary Management* (3rd ed., pp. 112–149). Hightstown, NJ: McGraw Hill.

Describes increasing diversity among consumers and in the workforce and provides strategies for managers to work effectively with diverse employees.

Kantor, M. (1998). *Homophobia: Description, development, and dynamics of gay bashing*. Westport, CT: Praeger.

Analyzes homophobia as an emotional disorder and describes possible causes of homophobia a well as common traits and suggested therapy for homophobes.

Katz, J. (1976). *Gay American history: Lesbians and gay men in the U.S.A.* New York: Harper Colophon.

Provides documentary evidence of lesbians and gay men in America from the colonial period to the present with specific chapters devoted to Native Americans and women.

Kinsey, A.C., Pomeroy, W.B., & Martin, C.E. (1948). *Sexual behavior in the human male*. Philadelphia: W.B. Saunders.

Analyzed information collected from 18,000 male subjects concerning their sexual behavior and developed a continuum to describe the variety of sexual behavior reported.

Kissen, R.M. (1996). *The last closet: The real lives of lesbian and gay teachers*. Portsmouth, NH: Heinemann.

Describes the personal lives and professional struggles of lesbian and gay educators based on interviews with more than one hundred individuals.

LeVay, S. (1996). *Queer Science: The use and abuse of research into homosexuality*. Cambridge, MA: Massachusetts University Press.

Reviews research on sexual orientation with attention to the influence of the social context. Discusses findings of hormonal and brain mechanisms in Chapters 5 and 6.

Marcus, E. (1992). *Making history: The struggle for gay and lesbian equal rights, 1945–1990*. New York: HarperCollins.

Presents biographical descriptions of over forty individuals who played a significant role in assisting efforts of American lesbians and gays to combat heterosexism.

Massachusetts Governor's Commission on Gay and Lesbian Youth. (1994). Making Schools Safe for Gay and Lesbian Youth: Breaking the silence in schools and in families. In G. Remafedi (Ed.), *Death by denial: Studies of suicide in gay and lesbian teenagers* (pp. 151–205). Boston: Alyson.

Presents the results of the Commission's investigation into harassment and violence against gay and lesbian youth in Massachusetts' schools, with specific recommendations.

McLeod, A., & Crawford, I. (1998). The postmodern family: An examination of the psychosocial and legal perspectives of gay and lesbian parenting. In G. Herek (Ed.), *Stigma and sexual orientation: Understanding prejudice against lesbians, gay men and bisexuals* (pp. 211–222). Thousand Oaks, CA: Sage.
Examines issues related to lesbian and gay couples such as the desire to have and raise children, including the results of public polls and relevant court decisions.

McNaught, B. (1997). Gay and lesbian partners should receive employment benefits. In T. Roleff (Ed.), *Gay rights* (pp. 18–28). San Diego: Greenhaven.
Provides arguments justifying the right of lesbian and gay employees involved in domestic partnerships to have the same employment benefits as heterosexual employees.

Money, J. (1988). *Gay, straight, and in-between: The sexology of erotic orientation.* New York: Oxford.
Reviews research to describe the current state of knowledge about what determines human sexual orientation, including studies of the influence of prenatal hormones on animals.

Palmer, A. (1997). The military ban on gays and lesbians is based on prejudice. In T. Roleff (Ed.), *Gay rights* (pp. 126–131). San Diego: Greenhaven.
Describes the experience of countries recruiting lesbian and gay soldiers in an attempt to refute arguments that having gays in the military will cause problems for morale and discipline.

Pillard, R.C. (1977). The search for a genetic influence on sexual orientation. In V. Rosairo (Ed.), *Science and homosexualities* (pp. 226–241). New York: Routledge.
Reviews genetic research and anthropological studies to discuss the role of heredity and environment in determining sexual orientation.

Rowse, A.L. (1977). *Homosexuals in history: A study of ambivalence in society, literature and the arts.* New York: Dorset.
Describes the lives of many famous lesbian and gay individuals in the history of Europe, and the homophobic context in which they had to live their lives.

Sears, J.T. (1992). Educators, homosexuality, and homosexual students: Are personal feelings related to professional beliefs? In K. Narbeck, *Coming out of the classroom closet: Gay and lesbian students, teachers and curricula.* Binghamton, NY: Harrington Park Press.
Discusses survey data from school counselors, prospective teachers and lesbian and gay young adults from the southern United States.

Shilts, R. (1987). *And the band played on: Politics, people and the AIDS epidemic.* New York: St. Martin's Press.
Provides an account of the development of AIDS in the United States and the reactions of people, especially politicians, to the disease.

Simon, A. (1998). The relationship between stereotypes of and attitudes toward lesbians and gays. In G. Herek (Ed.), *Stigma and sexual orientation: Understanding prejudice against lesbians, gay men and bisexuals* (pp. 62–81). Thousand Oaks, CA: Sage.
Reviews research on the influence of stereotypes on attitudes of heterosexuals toward lesbians and gays, concluding with a discussion of strategies for prejudice reduction.

Sontag, S. (1989). *AIDS and its metaphors.* New York: Farrar, Straus, Giroux.
Analyzes the myths and prejudices associated with HIV and people with AIDS.

Steakley, J.D. (1989). Iconography of a scandal: Political cartoons and the Eulenberg affair in Wilhelmine Germany. In M. Duberman, M. Vicinus, & G. Chauncey, Jr. (Eds.), *Hidden from history: Reclaiming the gay and lesbian past* (pp. 233–263). New York: Meridian.
Describes the Eulenberg Affair and provides political cartoons from the period that not only illustrate public anxiety but also the connection of homophobia with other prejudices.

Stein, E. (1999). *The mismeasure of desire: The science, theory, and ethics of sexual orientation.* Oxford: Oxford University Press.
Reviews and critiques scientific studies on sexual orientation, and also examines questions stemming from theoretical and ethical considerations related to sexual orientation.

Williams, W.L. (1992). Benefits for non-homophobic societies: An anthropological perspective. In W. Blumenfeld (Ed.), *Homophobia: How we all pay the price* (pp. 258–274). Boston: Beacon.
Describes benefits gained for children, families, friendships, religion, and for the society as a whole based on studies of cultures that are not homophobic.

Zeldin, T. (1994). *An intimate history of humanity.* New York: HarperCollins.
Examines private lives and relationships, but expands to explore a universal human history through a variety of perspectives, employing a wide range of knowledge.

Summary Exercises

See page 19 for exercises to help you summarize the main points and define key terms in this chapter.

Personal Clarification Exercises

In Chapter 11, two exercises promote discussion about bias, stereotyping, prejudice, bigotry and discrimination regarding sexual orientation.

Clarification Exercise #1 Testing Our Knowledge about Homosexuality

Directions: Work with one other person; discuss each statement below, then agree whether the statement is true or false and record your response. Discuss your responses with the class.

Are the following statements True or False?

	True	False
1. Most homosexuals want to be members of the opposite sex.	___	___
2. A person becomes a homosexual—develops homosexual orientation—because he or she chooses to do so.	___	___
3. Sexual orientation is established at an early age.	___	___
4. 60% of pre-adolescent males report at least one homosexual experience.	___	___
5. A majority of homosexuals were seduced in adolescence by a person of the same sex, usually several years older.	___	___
6. There is a good chance of changing homosexual persons into heterosexual men and women.	___	___
7. Homosexual activity occurs in many animal species.	___	___
8. According to the American Psychological Association, homosexuality is a mental illness.	___	___
9. In most states, sexual relations between two people of the same sex is a criminal act.	___	___
10. Homosexual males are more likely to molest young boys than heterosexual males are to molest young girls.	___	___
11. Gay men are at least four times more likely to be victims of criminal violence as members of the general public.	___	___
12. Some church denominations have condemned the legal and social discrimination against gay men and lesbians.	___	___

ADAPTED FROM JAMES T. SEARS,
COMING OUT OF THE CLASSROOM CLOSET

Clarification Exercise #2 If I Were the Teacher . . . Sexual Orientation in the Classroom

Directions: Evaluate personally each statement below; make an individual tentative decision about what you might do as a teacher of children or youth. After completing your personal responses, meet with three others who have completed their personal assessments; discover why you agree or disagree about how you would approach issues of sexual orientation if you were teachers. Please: (a) Limit your "Undecided" to fewer than four items, (b) Keep notes of any reservations, qualifying conditions, or comments you would add in making your selection.

	Agree	Disagree	Undecided
1. *Classroom Interaction*			
A. I would discuss homosexuality in the classroom.	___	___	___
B. It would be difficult for me to deal fairly with an avowed homosexual student.	___	___	___
2. *Counseling*			
A. Providing homosexual high school students			

with supportive materials is appropriate for a teacher. ____ ____ ____
B. I would feel comfortable if a student talked with me about his or her sexual orientation. ____ ____ ____

3. *Student Harassment*
   A. I would ignore student jokes about homosexuals. ____ ____ ____
   B. I would discipline a student for making a derogatory remark about homosexuals or for harassing another student *suspected* of being gay or lesbian. ____ ____ ____
   C. I would openly disagree with a faculty member who made a disparaging comment about a suspected homosexual student. ____ ____ ____

4. *Homosexual Teachers*
   A. I believe homosexuals should not be allowed to teach in public schools and I would feel uncomfortable if my school hired an openly gay or lesbian teacher. ____ ____ ____
   B. Adolescents who know several homosexual teachers will be strongly influenced to be homosexual. ____ ____ ____

5. *Human Rights*
   A. A teacher must work in school to lessen all forms of prejudice, including homophobia. ____ ____ ____
   B. I would work in my community to fight against discrimination against gay men and lesbians. ____ ____ ____

ADAPTED FROM JAMES T. SEARS,
COMING OUT OF THE CLASSROOM CLOSET

Intergroup Exercises

In Chapter 11, two exercises promote discussion about attitudes about sexual orientation in modern American society.

Intergroup Exercise #1 Integration in the Military Exercise

Directions: Today, arguments often are made that oppose the presence of gay men and lesbians in the military. These are similar to those made by people opposed to racial integration of the American armed forces in the late 1940s.

In this exercise, teams of three are asked to read each statement where issues of homosexuality have been substituted for those of race. Replace the underlined words or phrases with those that refer to other groups. Attempt to rewrite one statement to refer instead to each of the following groups listed immediately below. At the conclusion of your reading, prepare a reply to the two questions at the end of the activity to share with the class.

Women   Disabled   Senior citizens   Blacks
Buddhists   Homeless   Arab Americans

Racial or Homosexual Integration?

1. **The opinion of soldiers**: Army studies show that 80% of the underline{heterosexual} soldiers oppose underline{homosexual} integration in the armed forces.
2. **The opinion of generals**: Respected generals such as Dwight David Eisenhower and current military leaders have been and remain staunchly opposed to underline{homosexual} integration in the armed forces.
3. **Objections based on unit cohesion**: According to the Secretary of the Army, underline{homosexual} integration would undermine unit cohesion—"Effective comradeship in battle calls for a warm and close personal relationship within a unit;" an Army Report opposing underline{homosexual} integration argued—"The soldier on the battlefield deserves to have, and must have, utmost confidence in his fellow soldiers."
4. **Objections based on opposition to using the military for social reforms:** As one general has said, "the Army is not out to make any social reforms. It will change that policy when the Nation as a whole changes it . . . experiments

within the Army in the solution of social problems are fraught with danger to efficiency, discipline and morale."

5. **Objections based on privacy**: Georgia's senior Senator says <u>homosexual</u> integration in the armed forces would compromise the privacy rights of all <u>heterosexual</u> soldiers—"There is no more intimate relationship known to men than that of enlisted men serving together at the squad level. They eat and sleep together. They use the same facilities day after day. They are compelled to stay together in the closest association."

6. **Objections based on health concerns**: The Senator from Georgia went on to say he had statistics "which will show that the incidence of (all venereal diseases) is appallingly higher among <u>homosexuals</u> than among <u>heterosexuals</u>."

7. **Objections based on religious beliefs**: A Congressman from Alabama has argued that <u>homosexual</u> integration in the armed forces would lower not just the morale but the "morals" of soldiers and quoted from the Bible to assert that being around <u>homosexuals</u> could taint the moral "purity" of the <u>heterosexual</u> soldiers which he said was a "gift from God."

8. **Objections based on the will of the majority**: The Department of Defense has taken the position that <u>homosexual</u> integration in the armed forces would erode public confidence in the military— "The Army can under no circumstances adopt a policy which is contrary to the dictates of a majority of people (because) to do so would alienate the people from the Army and lower their morale."

ACTIVITY DERIVED FROM INFORMATION AND DATA PROVIDED BY SERVICE MEMBERS LEGAL DEFENSE NETWORK, WWW.SLDN.ORG

Questions for discussion:

1. In what way is exclusion of homosexuals from the military similar to exclusion of any other minority group?

2. Develop your own rationale that might be used to justify excluding homosexuals from the American military. Have you heard—or used—those rationalizations? Where is the logic illogical?

Intergroup Exercise #2 Difficult Dialogues Experience: Homophobia

Directions: In groups of three, develop a dialogue based upon the scenario below. Use *The Situation* as the basis for your 4–5-minute role play. Remain in character at the conclusion of your skit and respond to class questions about motivation, purpose, or intent behind your comments during the scene. Each team of three is asked to complete a 5-minute role play, regardless of similarity to others performed.

At the conclusion of this exercise, pass to your convener a 3 × 5 index card with one general comment that you feel summarizes what you suggest should be the outcome of this situation.

The Situation: You are a teacher, and students are coming into your classroom and taking their seats. The students are high school juniors. Two students, both females, are talking about AIDS because one of them had gone to a see an AIDS quilt over the weekend. She was moved by the experience and is trying to describe it to her friend as they sit down at their desks in the front of the room near your [teacher's] desk. As Mary talks, however, Paul, who is sitting in the desk behind her, interrupts.

Mary: "I think it's so awful that all of these people have gotten so sick and are going to die. I just think . . ."

Paul: "Those fags get what they deserve. What makes me mad is that we're spending money trying to find a cure. If we just let God and Nature take its course, I won't have to worry about any queer ever bothering me again."

Mary: "Well . . . (Mary seems uncertain how to respond.) I don't know, I mean, I never thought about it that way before. (She turns to the teacher.) Mrs. (or Mr.) [Your name], what do you think about what Paul said?"

Ms./Mr. [Your name]: Do not respond directly to Mary's question. Instead, engage Mary and Paul in conversation so that they can each further explain their feelings about Paul's perspective on homosexuality.

CHAPTER 12

Classism: Myths and Misperceptions about Poverty

"The greatest of evils and the worst of crimes is poverty."

GEORGE BERNARD SHAW (1856–1950)

Classism refers to attitudes and discriminatory actions toward others based upon their low socioeconomic status. It is nearly impossible to grow up in the United States without being affected by pervasive cultural messages that engender antagonism and sometimes contempt for poor people. In our American capitalist economic system, which emphasizes competition for opportunity and reward, there are winners and there are losers. Americans are encouraged to admire winners. Stories of winners are told daily in newspapers and magazines, and we applaud their success. Americans do not tend to identify with losers. Poor people are usually perceived as losers. Historically, our culture has produced many negative messages about people living in poverty being deficient and inferior; these negative cultural messages represent **cultural classism** and they constitute one factor influencing the process by which Americans have learned to devalue poor people.

CULTURAL CLASSISM

When colonists came to the New World, they had a well-established tradition that caring for the poor was both a local responsibility and a religious obligation. Historically, the European Catholic Church provided food to the hungry, shelter for the homeless, and care for the sick; the legacy can still be found in Catholic and Protestant hospitals and social service agencies today. Problems of poverty remained local, affecting a small percentage of people, and church resources were adequate to the task. But in fourteenth and fifteenth century Europe, the number of poor people increased dramatically. Plagues, wars, and various economic changes dispossessed rural families of their livelihoods and land, forcing them to search for employment elsewhere, usually in major cities.

What was the response in England to people in poverty?

In England, the local response to poverty was termed *outdoor relief,* where food, funds, and other assistance were distributed to people as needed. However, because of the increasing numbers of people whose poverty did not seem temporary, vagrancy laws were created that proscribed punishment for beggars and vagrants: public whippings, then exile, forced labor, and, for people who persisted in being poor and making a nuisance of themselves, execution. Another strategy involved auctioning groups of poor people to the lowest bidder—the person who offered to care for the group for the fewest tax dollars. The purpose of punishment, banishment, auctions, and executions was not to address problems of poverty, but to be rid of the poor, and English colonists in particular brought these attitudes and strategies with them.

What was the response to poverty in America during the colonial period?

In the colonies, outdoor relief included sharing food, providing common grazing land (and "town cows"), building shelters for homeless families, and caring for sick persons in their homes when they had no family to give care. To reduce burdens of poverty in a community, potential settlers often were required to prove they could care for themselves. If they weren't convincing or if they failed to take care of their own needs as promised, they could be *warned out*—notified that they must leave the community. Komisar (1977) reported that in 1790, one Massachusetts community warned out almost one-third of its population.

Meanwhile, English poorhouses providing food and shelter became an alternative to outdoor relief. People living in poorhouses were required to work to pay for their care, thereby reducing the need for local revenue. According to Katz (1986), Boston established the first colonial poorhouse in 1664; later, others were established in Philadelphia (1732), New York (1736), and Baltimore (1773). Although poorhouses were never intended to offer compassionate care, they were "the best means of frightening the able bodied into going to work and discouraging people from applying for aid" (Komisar, 1977, p. 21). The physical conditions in many poorhouses were atrocious: too many people crowded together, many with contagious diseases and often too little food or medical care. Poorhouses also included people with additional problems such as mental illness and alcoholism. Even when poorhouses had decent conditions, people were reluctant to live there because of the stigma associated with them. Since anyone applying for outdoor relief could be referred to a poorhouse, it was hoped that the threat of referral would reduce relief applications. For many years in both America and England, sending people to the poorhouse was a major strategy for dealing with poverty.

County Poor House, Burlington, Iowa.

FIGURE 12.1

If you were in a poorhouse, you might be able to let family and friends know where you were by sending a postcard like this one from the County Poorhouse in Burlington, Iowa, early 1900s.

241

What happened to the "religious obligation" to help the poor?

Ironically, Christian faith in America was a major contributor to increasingly harsh attitudes toward the poor. Many colonial Protestants believed that poverty was a consequence of sin and slothfulness. They assumed the rich were rewarded for their thrift and virtue, while the poor were sinners needing reform. Americans often expressed their belief that anyone who wanted to work could find a job, as Matthew Carey noted in 1828:

> Many citizens entertain an idea that in the present state of society . . . every person able and willing to work may procure employment . . . [and that] the chief part of the distresses of the poor arises from idleness, dissipation, and worthlessness. (Katz, 1986, p. 7)

Carey believed that poverty was not a consequence of personal failure as much as it was low wages, poor working conditions resulting in accidents or illness, and the impact of economic downturns. Those who actually worked with poor people understood that many were industrious and virtuous, but still lived in poverty because of circumstances beyond their control. Despite the efforts of Carey and other advocates for poor people, negative attitudes prevailed, not only toward paupers but also toward the working poor who lived perilously on the brink of poverty.

Why were people who had a job so close to poverty?

Komisar (1977) described an 1833 economic analysis of a construction worker's salary that concluded it was hardly sufficient to support a wife and two children. A continuing flow of immigrants exacerbated the problems of the poor by increasing competition for jobs; this allowed employers to keep wages low or even reduce them. Schwarz (2000) quotes social reformer Joseph Tuckerman explaining that wages in 1830 were so low "because the number of laborers [was] essentially greater than the demand for them" (p. 17). Because unemployment remained high, poorhouses never lacked occupants even though conditions were usually unsanitary and unhealthy, filled as they were with people who were undernourished and often ill. Even so, Komisar provided an excerpt from a Mass-

achusetts report in 1833 that complained of poor people who regarded poorhouses as their "inns":

> Here they find rest, when too much worn with fatigue to travel, and medical aid when they are sick. And as they choose not to labor, they leave these stopping places when they have regained strength to enable them to travel; and pass from town to town *demanding* their portion of the State's allowances for them as *their right.* (pp. 21–22)

In reality, poorhouses included so many children, elderly, and people with disabilities or illness that there were in fact few able-bodied residents. Komisar referred to an 1848 report of a Philadelphia poorhouse where only 12% of the residents were capable of working. In some communities, poorhouses were built on farmland in the hope that residents could pay for their care by operating the farm, yet "poor farms" often hired people to do the work because there were not enough healthy, able-bodied people in residence. Men who could work stayed out of poorhouses and tried to find work; it wasn't easy.

Why was it so difficult to find work?

The rapid development and use of machines throughout the second half of the nineteenth century contributed to unemployment, even in rural areas where hand threshing was eliminated by threshing machines. In urban areas, unskilled factory workers replaced skilled artisans, diminishing the satisfaction derived from work. Schwarz (2000) quoted a social reformer commenting on the dehumanizing aspect of factory jobs:

> [Factory work] tends to dwarf the intellectual powers, by confining the activity of the individual to a narrow range, to a few details, perhaps to the heading of pins, the pointing of nails, or the tying together of broken strings. (p. 15)

Although working wages were low for men, they were lower for women. Even children worked to help cover family expenses. If everyone in the family worked and everyone stayed healthy, it was possible to save money to be self-sufficient in old age. Retirement was rare: Workers didn't usually retire, but worked as long as they could. When they could no longer work, they typically lived with their adult children, who often could not afford to keep that parent without outdoor relief. Elderly who could not stay with children usually lived in poorhouses.

Why did people think poorhouses were the solution to poverty?

In the early 1800s, institutions were promoted as a solution to social problems: prisons for criminals, mental hospitals for the insane, orphanages for children, reform schools for juvenile delinquents, and poorhouses for the poor. In addition to rehabilitating inmates, these institutions were supposed to require minimal tax dollars from state and local governments. By 1850, many people had been placed in institutions; however, expenses proved

> Of all the preposterous assumptions of humanity over humanity, nothing exceeds most of the criticisms made on the habits of the poor by the well-housed, well-warmed, well-fed.
>
> HERMAN MELVILLE (1819–1891)

more costly than anticipated. To make matters worse, Katz (1986) noted the realization that "Mental hospitals did not cure; prisons and reform schools did not rehabilitate; . . . and poorhouses did not check the growth of outdoor relief or promote industry" (p. 25). In fact, from the beginning, institutions tended to provide primarily custodial care to protect society from deviant individuals within.

Because of public opposition to providing relief to able-bodied men, the few men still in poorhouses in the late 1800s were expelled. They moved to cities to find work and often sought lodging with other poor families who were eager for the extra money lodgers would pay. Social activists were appalled because lodging indigent men gave them sexual access to women in the home. Katz (1986) explains that the word *lodger* became a derisive term; still the housing need could not be ignored

and Lodging Houses, later nicknamed *Flophouses*, evolved to provide inexpensive rooms for single, itinerant men. Shortly after men were barred from poorhouses, children were removed as well, and poorhouses evolved into nursing homes for elderly people without families to care for them.

Why were children removed from poorhouses?

Social activists believed that poverty was caused in part by *hereditary pauperism*, as if being poor was a genetic defect. They argued that adult paupers were beyond help, but that children in poverty could be saved. In state after state, legislation was passed mandating that children be removed from a parent or parents admitted to a poorhouse and placed in orphanages. By 1875, the majority of children in orphanages were not orphans; they had living parents who were poor.

Consequently, adoption patterns began to change. Low-income families had adopted children old enough to work outside the home or to assist with domestic chores, but middle- and upper-class families were increasingly adopting children based on the assumption that these infants would remember nothing of their impoverished origins and could be "saved" by being raised in good homes. Katz (1986) explains how social reformers defended the practice of taking children away from poor parents: "Only by snapping the bonds between pauper parents and their children could they prevent the transmission of dependence from one generation to another" (p. 106). Such negative attitudes were characteristic of this era, resulting in a minimal response to the needs of poor people.

What was the response to the needs of poor people?

In the late 1800s, charitable organizations including the *Association for Improving the Condition of the Poor* sent "friendly visitors" to homes of poor people to offer spiritual advice and to promote a Protestant work ethic, the notion that hard work is essential and that rewards come from one's willingness to work. Komisar (1977) reports that charitable organizations viewed a poor person asking for money to pay rent or purchase food as a "failure of character" (p. 33). Organizations provided minimal financial or material aid, believing people would work only if they were choosing between work and starvation. American society of the 1880s and 1890s tended to regard poverty as proof of moral misconduct; organizations denied aid to drunkards and would only help their families if the wife and children left the drunkard.

By the late 1890s, studies began to suggest that misconduct, especially alcohol abuse, was *not* a major cause of poverty. Data from one study suggested that alcohol abuse and other forms of misconduct affected only 10% to 30% of families living in poverty, but that circumstances beyond anyone's control accounted for 65% or more of families who were poor. Schwarz (2000) described social reformers such as Josephine Lowell defending poor people "who are not drunken and shiftless, but who lead lives of . . . heroic self-sacrifice and devotion" (p. 101). Social reformers began to challenge Christians to demonstrate a more altruistic attitude by helping people in poverty, and reformers often identified capitalists as the true cause of suffering among the poor.

By the early 1900s, attitudes had evolved to the point that social reformers no longer supported the practice of taking children from poor parents. Buttressed by new child development theories, they denounced orphanages as harmful to children and advocated foster parent placement and care as an alternative. They lobbied for outdoor relief to keep poor families together, reasoning that the presence of children was an incentive for parents to work. In response to studies, speeches, and arguments of social reformers, states began to initiate programs of financial assistance to single-parent mothers regardless of whether they had been abandoned by their husbands or had given birth to children without being married.

Financial support was necessary since it was hard for single women to make enough money to cover their own expenses, and even more difficult if they had children, because women were paid considerably less than male workers. Perhaps women's low pay was the reason they were the first to form unions and to initiate strikes demanding wage increases and better working conditions. Most early labor strikes were unsuccessful because impoverished women workers desperately needed money and could not afford to be out of work for long. Nevertheless, women workers—and men as well—

continued to organize into unions throughout the 1800s as their best option to stop exploitation by employers.

What did workers do to protest employer exploitation?

In the early 1870s, 20,000 unemployed workers in Chicago marched to City Hall demanding food, clothing, and shelter; textile workers went on strike in Massachusetts; and coal miners struck in Pennsylvania. Despite union activism, railroad owners drastically cut worker wages in 1877, causing strikes in several states; the owners hired newly arrived immigrants to break many of the strikes, fueling anti-immigrant sentiments among workers. Local citizens often supported strikers, but railroad owners had the law on their side. As strikers barricaded buildings and blocked tracks, police and state militias were called in to drive striking workers away, with many injuries resulting from the violent confrontations.

Zinn (1999) described solidarity between local people and striking workers during the Pittsburgh strike against the Pennsylvania Railroad in 1877. Owners believed local militias would not fire at the strikers for fear of killing them and demanded that local officials call federal troops from Philadelphia. When troops arrived, the workers refused to be intimidated. In the first confrontation with strikers, the federal troops killed ten people; Pittsburgh residents responded angrily, surrounding the troops as they retreated to the nearest building which was a railway roundhouse. Although the citizens surrounded the roundhouse and set fire to the building, the troops managed to escape and left the city.

How did unions ultimately help workers to gain higher salaries?

Despite union organizing and strikes, wages remained low. Komisar (1977) identified a 1904 economist who calculated that an annual salary of $460 was required to support a wife and three children. Most railroad workers made less than $375 a year. Out of all the jobs studied, the economist reported that one-third of them paid less than $300 a year. If more than one person in the family worked and if they were frugal, they might manage to save money, but instead of receiving praise for being thrifty, their savings were often used against them. Schwarz (2000) explained how: "When employers discovered that their workers earned enough to put something by, they concluded that they had been overpaying them" (p. 43).

In addition to low wages, laborers often toiled in dangerous workplaces. In 1908, the federal government reported that every year, over 35,000 workers were killed and 536,000 injured on the job. The U.S. rates for worker injuries and deaths were much higher than those in most European countries. Although workers did not often convince employers to raise wages, they did persuade state legislators to address the issue of workplace risks. Katz (1986) reported that 43 of 45 states passed workman's compensation laws between 1909 and 1920 over the

> The test of our progress is not whether we add more to the abundance of those who have much; it is whether we provide enough for those who have too little.
>
> **FRANKLIN ROOSEVELT (1882-1945)**

objections of employers who complained of the financial burden of compensating workers for injuries sustained at work. Americans continued to debate what was fair for employees and employers until the Great Depression of the 1930s, when widespread unemployment demanded an aggressive response from the federal government.

How did the federal government address unemployment in the 1930s?

By the spring of 1931, Komisar estimated five million unemployed U.S. workers; for the following year, he estimated a total of eight million. By 1933, when Franklin Roosevelt began his first presidential term, between twelve and fifteen million workers were unemployed, one-third of the U.S. labor force. Federal programs were installed as "New Deal" activities from Roosevelt's campaign pledge to offer a "new deal" for workers in America. When Roo-

sevelt signed a Federal Emergency Relief Act (FERA) to provide assistance for people suffering from poverty, he ended a tradition of local and state governments having exclusive responsibility for the poor. FERA distributed $250 million to the states based on a formula of $1 of federal money for every $3 the state spent for relief or economic assistance to individuals; another $250 million was given to states with the most severe poverty problems. In some states, 40% of the people were on relief. To add insult to injury, laws in 14 states prevented people who received relief from voting.

In addition to providing money for relief, the federal government became an employer. The Civilian Conservation Corps recruited 250,000 young men (but no women) to work on projects to prevent floods, fires, and soil erosion, and to develop recreational areas. The Works Progress Administration (WPA) employed about two million men, one-fourth of the workforce, to build roads or to construct bridges, public buildings, and parks. Some Americans did not support these actions; Komisar (1977) quoted a bank president who said: "I profoundly believe that society does not owe every man a living" (p. 56).

Although federal employment programs provided jobs, the numbers of unemployed continued to be significant, and employers took advantage of the oversupply of labor to keep wages low and (again) even reduce them, resulting in more worker protests and strikes. In response to this turmoil, the Wagner Act passed in 1935 created a National Labor Relations Board (NLRB) and granted unions legal status as collective bargaining agents for workers. The intent was that the NLRB would encourage peaceful resolutions of labor disputes by negotiation rather than through strikes and disruptive activities that often ended in violence.

What was the outcome of the New Deal?

Because of employment demands during World War II, the "make-work" New Deal programs were dismantled. Although European countries had been enacting social insurance programs since 1833, conservative critics had accused Roosevelt of aspiring to become a dictator and attacked his poverty programs, saying they would "threaten the integrity of our [capitalist] institutions" (Komisar, 1977, p. 62). Despite opposition, programs such as unemploy-

FIGURE 12.2

The Civilian Conservation Corps (top photo) gave young men jobs in the 1930s when jobs were scarce. The federal government (bottom photo) continues to engage young adults to work on conservation projects, but unlike the Civilian Conservation Corps, the Student Conservation Association's diverse membership includes women and people of color.

Source: Courtesy of Brown Brothers (top) and Student Conservation Association (bottom).

ment insurance and the social security and welfare programs that were created by the Economic Security Act of 1935 have been maintained to provide basic protection and support for people in need. A 1939 Gallup poll reported that 70% of Americans believed that the federal government should address the needs of unemployed people, and the same 70% approved the amount of relief available to the poor. Programs continue to function today because they have been successful, are still considered necessary, and enjoy widespread public support.

The legacy of Roosevelt's New Deal was not only social programs, but also the principle of federal government involvement in poverty issues. The Civilian Conservation Corps, which is no longer in existence, was the forerunner of Peace Corps and AmeriCorps that recruit young people to work on community projects locally and globally. Politicians may wish to reform the welfare program or propose privatizing social security, yet few would question the need for such programs or the appropriateness of the federal government providing them. Because of federal remedies to economic challenges of the 1930s, American culture developed new perceptions of poverty and the role of government in response to it. Unfortunately, some Americans cling to old attitudes and persist in accusing poor people of deficiencies as a cause of their poverty.

INDIVIDUAL CLASSISM

Individual classism refers to attitudes and discriminatory actions stemming from prejudice against poor people. According to a Harris poll, Taylor (2000) reports that 77% of Americans believe most unemployed people could find a job without much difficulty if they would make an effort, an interesting assertion in a capitalist society. Unlike most Americans, economists understand that capitalism requires a certain percentage of unemployed workers to keep wages low and to control inflation. Europeans seem to understand this economic principle better than Americans. In a 1990 survey of citizens from twelve European countries, 17% believed poverty was due to laziness or lack of will power, but 66% said poverty resulted from social injustice, from personal misfortune, or from changes in the modern world (Wilson, 1996).

In contrast to European attitudes, Wilson also reported surveys finding Americans more likely to blame poor people for being poor stemming from factors such as lack of effort, lack of ability, or loose morals. Ironically, our American penchant for blaming the victim overlooks the fact that children represent the largest percentage of poor people in the United States and that their numbers continue to increase. Even when Americans acknowledge poor children, all too often we blame them for not working harder in school to lift themselves out of poverty.

How are children from low-income families disadvantaged in schools?

Although Americans may argue that poor children should use free education provided in public schools to escape from poverty, Kozol (1991) and others have described the appalling conditions in the schools attended by those living in poverty. Among the world's industrialized nations, the United States is the only one without universal preschool and child support programs. Wilson (1996) described an alternative approach: French child-care programs of infant care, nursery schools, paid leave for parents of newborns, and medical care that includes a preventive care system for children and public health nurses to monitor children's health. The French support system sends a clear

> For every talent that poverty has stimulated it has blighted a hundred.
>
> JOHN GARDNER (1912–2002)

message that France values all children, not just middle- or upper-class children.

By 2010, Owen (1999) predicted that 40% of American children will experience poverty at some time in their lives, and poor children tend to have greater needs than middle- or upper-class children. Anyon (2001) reports that 25% of U.S. urban school budgets are typically expended to respond to psychological and social needs of students from low-income families, yet Americans often seem oblivious to the impact of poverty. Pipher (2002) provides this comment about American attitudes: "We were born on third base and we think we hit triples" (p. 21).

The consequences of educational advantages for children of the middle and upper classes can be ascertained by analyzing student SAT scores in relation to family income. According to multiple studies, higher family income in all races—socioeconomic standing—translates into higher scores on SAT tests. Owen (1999) argued that the power of socioeconomic standing should not be surprising, since studies also report that low-income families seldom have computers in their homes and that students from low-income homes rarely can afford fees paid by other students for coaching sessions to improve SAT scores. Despite the obvious explanation for their children's higher scores on SAT tests, Owen described how SAT scores provided middle- and upper-class families with:

> A scientific-sounding justification for the advantages they enjoyed. The wealthy lived in nice houses because they were smart; the poor were hungry because they were stupid. American society was just after all. (p. 175)

How can schools make a difference in the lives of poor children?

Herrnstein and Murray (1994) reported the same pattern concerning socioeconomic standing and IQ test scores as reported for SAT tests and concluded that genetic differences exist and therefore IQ disparity could not be reduced by improving education for poor children. Yet in a study comparing IQ scores of black and white children, IQ differences were almost completely eliminated when adjustments were made for poverty-related factors such as economic conditions and learning experiences available in home environments (Brooks-Gunn, Klebanov, and Duncan, 1996). There is ample evidence that all children can learn. Macedo and Bartolome (2001) cite several studies reporting on successful programs for disadvantaged children even when cultural and linguistic differences were present (p. 120). Other studies report that children from low-income families initially learn at a rate similar to middle- and upper-class children, but fall behind when they start school, and then lose further ground during summers when middle- and upper-class children take advantage of opportunities to travel, visit museums, and attend camps—activities that promote children's social and intellectual development (Entwhistle and Olson, 2001).

Anyon (2001) calculated that American suburban school districts spend up to ten times more funds per student than do urban districts; yet some American politicians oppose increased spending for schools of primarily low-income students, claiming that "throwing money at the problem" will do no good. Owen (1999) cited research on students from all races in which those in higher income brackets who attended excellent schools with state-of-the-art technology achieved higher test scores than did their low-income peers who often attended deteriorating schools with inadequate instructional resources. An obvious conclusion is that differences in socioeconomic privilege are significant factors in enhancing the cognitive development of children and youth. And research findings were available on this issue decades ago; in 1970, after reviewing considerable data including cross-cultural studies, Stein and Susser reported:

> Improvement in the social environment of groups at a marked social disadvantage can bring about a substantial improvement in IQ levels and a decline in the frequency of mild mental retardation. . . . It seems likely that the greatest advantage will come from a serious attack on poverty and its concomi-

tants in unemployment, deteriorated housing, physical environment, and poor and inappropriate schooling. (p. 64)

How has the federal government addressed the disadvantages for low-income students?

Since 1988, most presidential candidates have campaigned to be "the Education President." For the 2003 renewal of the Elementary and Secondary Education Act, President George W. Bush promoted and signed the "No Child Left Behind" (NCLB) Act, which requires rigorous testing of students, labels schools whose pupils earn scores below the established benchmarks as "failing" (now softened to "in need of improvement"), and identifies those students who do not achieve the designated test scores. Failing schools are in jeopardy of losing federal funds. NCLB makes no distinction between students attending underfunded deteriorating schools with inadequate facilities in poverty areas and students attending well-maintained schools with state-of-the-art facilities in wealthy suburbs. They all have to pass the same tests (Mathis, 2003).

Many educators have criticized NCLB for its reliance on standardized tests to determine student learning. Even makers of standardized tests admit that these tests measure only a portion of what a child learns, and that multiple measures are necessary for authentic assessment of learning. Yet the NCLB plan forces teachers to reduce their curriculum content in order to prepare students for the tests, including students learning English as a second language, at-risk students, and special education students. A fourth grade teacher who administered NCLB tests complained that NCLB testing "results in educational practices that are developmentally inappropriate and discriminatory for English language learners" (Dawson, 2003, p. 3). And while the NCLB is adding to the fiscal burden of local schools, President Bush has announced plans to eliminate funds for federal educational programs such as the National Writing Project, Rural Education, and Comprehensive School Reform, a program supporting school improvement initiatives in low-income school districts (Coles, 2003).

The financial toll of NCLB to school districts from increased administrative costs, remedial instruction, and other factors has been determined by several state studies. A Nebraska study concluded that per pupil expenditures would have to increase by 45% to implement NCLB. Combining costs for all fifty states, the minimum estimate of increased funding required to implement NCLB is approximately $80 billion. President Bush allocated $1 billion for NCLB in his 2004 budget (Mathis, 2003). States have a desperate need for more federal funding to increase the quality of education for children in low-income areas, but in its present configuration, NCLB does not seem likely to improve the ability of schools to prepare students either for further education or for the work force.

How will spending more for education solve unemployment problems of the poor?

If schools are provided resources to improve educational opportunity for low-income students, children and youth will be more likely to develop knowledge and skills needed for employment. Unfortunately, if students from low-income families maintain good grades and graduate from high school, they may still be unable to find a job. Historically, the United States has had inadequate school-to-work programs, usually the worst among industrialized nations. In Germany and Japan, employers with jobs commanding good wages, benefits, and potential for career advancement offer apprenticeships for high school graduates. Similar employers in the United States usually do not.

Nearly 50% of all U.S. high school graduates will seek immediate employment rather than pursue post-secondary education. Wilson (1996) quotes Ray Marshall, former Secretary of Labor, discussing that students not aspiring to further their educations "are left to sink or swim—without advice or career counseling and without any job placement assistance" (p. 216). High school graduates bound for the work force often receive inadequate education and little if any career counseling, and must seek employment in an economic system that requires millions of people to be unemployed or underemployed. Then they are often blamed when they cannot find work and seek help from social assistance agencies. Many Americans still believe the myth that welfare is paid to unemployed men.

FIGURE 12.3

The Southern Poverty Law Center (SPLC) is dedicated to protecting the legal and human rights of impoverished people and providing them with legal assistance as needed. SPLC offices are located in Montgomery, Alabama, across the street from the Civil Rights Memorial designed by Maya Lin, visited by thousands each year.

Source: Photo courtesy of Timothy Hursley, Southern Poverty Law Center.

Who is eligible for welfare payments?

There is confusion in the United States about who qualifies for welfare assistance. Weaver (2000) explains that aside from programs for widows, orphans, and people with disabilities, over 90% of social support comes through Transitional Assistance for Needy Families (TANF), a program that replaced Aid to Families with Dependent Children (AFDC) in 1996. As with AFDC, TANF assists single-parent families, rarely including men but typically consisting of women with dependent children; children represent two-thirds of recipients.

Americans have historically believed that all able-bodied men can and should be gainfully employed, and they have regarded those who are not employed as lazy. The mistaken belief that able-bodied men receive welfare has caused people to engage in individual classism, criticizing welfare recipients and demanding reductions in welfare benefits. A colleague once asked his college students to imagine that they could be invisible and go back to middle schools in their home town. He asked them to speculate on what prejudices would be most openly expressed by middle school students. Aware of expressions such as "That's so gay" and the frequent derisive use of "faggot," he assumed his students would say prejudice against gays and lesbians, but they all agreed that it would be prejudice against poor people, especially welfare recipients. The college students described myths about poverty and welfare they had learned, and they believed these same myths were still shaping negative attitudes, words, and actions toward welfare recipients today.

> Men in search of a myth will usually find one.
>
> **PUEBLO INDIAN PROVERB**

What are some myths about welfare recipients?

Johnson (1998) and others identify a variety of myths about welfare; many have been around for a number of years. The following list includes examples of myths that have fostered negative or even hostile attitudes and actions toward recipients; further information is included to provide a more accurate picture about people receiving social assistance:

MYTH #1: WELFARE ROLLS ARE INCREASING. This is a half-truth, and as the Yiddish proverb says, "A half truth is a whole lie." True, numbers of people on welfare are increasing, but so is the population. Since 1970, people receiving some form of social assistance as a percentage of overall population has been relatively stable, with increases or decreases reflecting economic conditions. Schorr (2001) explains that in good economic times, women find available jobs and leave welfare; during economic downturns, unemployment increases, as do applications for social assistance.

MYTH #2: WELFARE FAMILIES ARE LARGE. As the twentieth century ended, the average size of families receiving social assistance was 2.9 children, down from 4.0 children thirty years earlier. Over 40% of all TANF families have one child; 30% have two children. Weaver (2000) reports that the average size of families receiving assistance across the nation is about the same as the typical American family.

MYTH #3: PEOPLE ON WELFARE HAVE A COMFORTABLE LIFE BY ABUSING THE WELFARE SYSTEM. In seven states offering the most generous social assistance, family income—including food stamps received—is raised to meet the poverty level. In more than half the states, combined forms of social assistance only raise a recipient's gross income to 75% of the poverty level, and to 60% of the poverty level in twelve southern states. Despite such inadequate support, less than 2% of recipients have been documented as being engaged in welfare fraud. The myth of widespread fraud in the U.S. welfare system persists among middle-class Americans. Yet Allison and Lewis (2001) report Internal Revenue Service estimates revealing a considerably higher percentage of fraud in the tax returns of middle- and upper-class Americans.

MYTH #4: THE GOVERNMENT ONLY HELPS PEOPLE ON WELFARE. The U.S. Congress has helped corporations in fiscal trouble such as Chrysler and Boeing, and has offered assistance to corporations not in financial trouble. In one recent year, the federal government spent over $167 billion for corporate support, costing approximately $1,400 per taxpayer compared to $400 per taxpayer spent on welfare and food stamps for poor people. Critics of corporate welfare argue that U.S. government spending reduces competition by subsidizing a select few corporations, creating an uneven playing field by providing what they regard as unnecessary assistance. Moore and Stansel (1995) reason that corporate support is a "huge drain on the federal treasury for little economic benefit" (p. 4). Despite criticisms, corporations continue receiving taxpayer dollars.

MYTH #5: WELFARE RECIPIENTS ARE TOO LAZY TO GET A JOB. Two-thirds of Americans receiving social assistance are children, half of whom are five years old or less. Before TANF, most state assistance programs penalized enrolled mothers who were employed, deducting one dollar from their welfare check for every dollar they earned, and yet almost half of welfare mothers held at least part-time jobs. Mead (2000) found that one of the most generous states paid benefits of $673 per month to a welfare mother—regardless of the number of children—and required that she work a minimum of thirty hours per week with child care paid for by the state. However, if that mother were employed at minimum wages for forty hours a week she would earn $824 each month, but because she is not on welfare she would not qualify for child care benefits. The additional $150 a month earned at her minimum wage job would not cover the cost of quality child care and work-related expenses such as clothing and transportation. Further, minimum wage jobs frequently lack health insurance, and if insurance is provided, it is likely restricted to employees only, not their families. Welfare

assistance includes health care for families. It is not surprising that many mothers, forced to choose between such options, decide to swallow their pride and apply for assistance for the sake of their children.

MYTH #6: WELFARE RECIPIENTS STAY ON WELFARE FOREVER. Because so many people believed this myth, the 1996 U.S. welfare reform placed time limits on assistance to recipients. Historically, the AFDC program provided few incentives to leave, yet recipients tended to require only temporary assistance. Studies showed that more than 30% of recipients left welfare each year, and 75% left within five years. Less than half returned to welfare. Of those who returned, 65% to 75% left the program again within a year, and most of those left permanently (Isaacs and Lyon, 2000; Sandefur and Cook, 1998).

Myths about social assistance have shaped American attitudes and caused negative actions against welfare recipients. Although the negative actions illustrate individual classism, the inadequacies of American social assistance programs illustrate institutional classism.

INSTITUTIONAL CLASSISM

Individual prejudice based on socioeconomic status and negative behaviors rooted in that prejudice are especially problematic in a society with a disparity in wealth and income as wide as exists in the United States. Yet **institutional classism**—institutional policies and practices that exploit low-income people and benefit middle- or upper-class individuals—have contributed even more to the wealth and income disparity in America. The history of these policies and practices was discussed previously in examining cultural classism, but recent institutional policies and practices have contributed to a rise in the wealth and income disparity that dramatically increased in the early 1980s and has continued to the present.

Why is the disparity between the richest and poorest Americans increasing?

Federal policies have played a major role in diverting resources to the richest Americans. Some Americans regard income redistribution as a socialist scheme, yet each year the U.S. Internal Revenue Service collects income taxes—scaled according to income—to fund programs and projects approved by our elected representatives. Phillips (1990) estimates that during the 1980s, $160 billion collected from middle- and low-income taxpayers replaced funds lost from capital gains tax cuts benefiting wealthy Americans and funded programs such as providing subsidies for overseas corporate advertising. Social economists term such effects a *redistribution of income*. According to Hout and Lucas (2001), the United States surpassed France and Great Britain in the 1980s to become the leading nation in the world for disparity between incomes and wealth of families in the highest 20% and lowest 20% of our economy.

Income redistribution also occurs when federal and state governments offer tax breaks to wealthy individuals and corporations resulting in their taxes becoming a lower percentage of income than that of most Americans. Ogden Corporation, a diversified supplier of aviation, building, and waste management services, reported earning $217 million from 1991–1992, yet paid less than $200,000 in taxes, amounting to $1 for every $1,085 earned. If a working-class family of four earning $25,000 a year paid taxes at a level equal to the Ogden Corporation, they would pay approximately $25 annually (Macedo and Bartolome, 2001). In the 1950s, corporate taxes constituted 27% of federal revenue; in 2001 they were less than 10%.

Another indication of wealth and income disparity in the United States is the dramatic increase in billionaires. From the Reagan economic policies of the 1980s through the Internet expansion and economic boom of the 1990s, data document dramatic increases in wealth for the richest Americans and a contrasting decrease in resources for low-income Americans. Phillips (1990) reported two billionaires in the United States in 1980, but more than 50 by 1989, and Forbes (2002) identified 308 billionaires in 2002, representing 60% of all the world's billionaires. In the list of the wealthiest American families in 1982, the Du Pont family was on top with $8.6

billion. By 1999, the thirtieth family on the list had $7 billion, and Bill Gates of Microsoft had the top spot with $154 billion (Phillips, 2003). According to a Congressional Budget Office study, from 1979 to 1997, average incomes of the top 1% in the

> Wealth is a power usurped by the few to compel the many to labor for their benefit.
>
> **PERCY BYSSHE SHELLEY (1792–1822)**

United States increased from $263,700 to $697,900, while annual salaries of Americans in the lower 20% decreased $100 from 1979 to 1997 (Shapiro, Greenstein, and Primus, 2001).

How have salaries in the United States been affected by recent economic changes?

Starting in 1950, hourly wages for workers increased each decade until the 1980s, then declined by almost $1 per hour in that decade. Wages dropped another 50 cents in the first five years of the 1990s, but the economy prospered in the late 1990s and the 50 cents was regained. According to data from the Department of Labor Statistics, full-time male workers in the year 2000 earned a median weekly wage of $646, less than the $678 per week earned in 1979, a finding consistent across income levels (Children's Defense Fund, 2001). As Wilson (1996) stated, "The wage gap between low-skilled men and women shrank not because of gains made by female workers but mainly because of the decline in real wages for men" (p. 27). Historically, white males have enjoyed an economic advantage resulting in their salaries being the highest in all worker categories, yet even wages for white males declined, a major factor in the decreasing disparity between men and women's salaries (U.S. Department of Labor, 2000).

While wages for workers have declined, management has prospered. Sklar (1998) found that U.S. chief executive officer (CEO) salaries have climbed astronomically since 1980 when the average CEO earned 42 times the average worker's salary, which is more than generous when compared to German CEOs making an average of 14 times the average worker salary. By 1995, U.S. CEOs were paid a corporate average of 224 times what the average worker earned, making their salaries the highest in the world; nevertheless, U.S. CEO salaries doubled by 1999, making their compensation 475 times the average worker's salary (Edelman, 2001). While German, Japanese, and British CEOs earned average annual salaries of approximately a half million dollars, the average CEO salary in the United States was $3.5 million (Hout and Lucas, 2001; DeVries, 1999). (See Table 12.1.) In 1988, the ten highest paid CEOs averaged $19 million; in 2000, their average compensation was $154 million (Phillips, 2003). Large executive salaries are another factor in the increased disparity of wealth and income in the United States. Despite recent stockholder revolt over excessive executive pay, management salaries at even small industries exceed those of all other industrial countries.

How large is the disparity of wealth in the United States?

Income is generated by toil or investment; *wealth* refers to assets one already controls. Since wealth is an obvious means of designating upper class, that

group controls much of our wealth, but what level of concentrated wealth results in excessive influence? Wealth controlled by the top 1% of U.S. families declined slightly in each of the four decades after 1940 until 1980. The slight decrease in assets, due in part to higher tax rates, helped fund valuable social programs such as the GI Bill, FHA loans, and college loans that provided economic assistance to middle- and low-income families, creating a larger and more robust middle class.

In 1959, the top 4% of Americans had as much wealth as the lowest 35%; through the 1980s, wealthy Americans acquired even more wealth. In 1989, the top 4% held as much wealth as the lowest 51%, and by 1999, the top 1% had more wealth than 95% of Americans. At about the same time, between 1983 and 1995, middle-class Americans lost 11% of their net worth and the lowest 40% lost 80%. Comparing incomes from 1998 and 1999, the top 5% of American families—3.5 million people—enjoyed an average increase of $101,000 in earnings compared with the lowest 20%—14.5 million people—who lost an average of $184 a year from their average income of $13,500 (Edelman, 2001; DeVries, 1999; Barlett and Steele, 1992). Such figures document the fact that middle- and low-income families are increasingly losing their

HOME BASE OF CORPORATIONS	COMPARISON TO AVERAGE WORKER'S SALARY
Brazil	57 times
Mexico	45 times
Hong Kong	38 times
Britain	25 times
Australia	22 times
China	21 times
Italy	19 times
Spain	18 times
France	16 times
Taiwan	16 times
Germany	11 times
South Korea	11 times
Japan	10 times

TABLE 12.1

CEO Salaries in the Global Economy.

In comparison to the salaries on this chart, American CEOs earn 475 times the average worker's salary (Edelman, 2001).

The data from *Business Week* was reported in the June, 2003 edition of *The Hightower Lowdown*, edited by Jim Hightower and Philip Frazer.

share of our nation's wealth and income, and some analysts report even larger losses (see Table 12.2).

Why has there been so little protest from Americans about the tax cuts for the wealthiest people in our society that has contributed to this upward redistribution of wealth and loss of wealth for the middle class? Perhaps Americans feel they lack the power needed to succeed in a confrontation with such a powerful group as the wealthy, or perhaps too many Americans see these tax cuts as benefiting them now or in the future. According to one poll, 19% of Americans identify themselves as being in the top 1% of incomes, and another 20% believe they will be in the top 1% in the near future (Collins, 2003). There is obviously considerable confusion in our society about how much wealth exists in America and who controls it.

How do income levels determine social class in the United States?

The nature of wealth in America makes it difficult to define who comprises the middle-income class. Historically, some American politicians lobbying for economic relief for their "middle class" constituents have argued for extending tax cuts to those with annual earnings of up to $200,000 or higher. Bonilla-Silva (2001) reported that a 1992 Congressional Budget Office study defined "middle class" as a family of four with an annual income of $19,000–$78,000. More than 70% of Americans were middle class according to this definition. Wolfe (1998) reported the results of a 1993 survey where Americans were asked how much annual income would

make someone too rich to be considered middle class:

> 19% said $50,000–$75,000, 17% said $75,000–$100,000, and 15% said over $200,000. The general feeling in America is that you are middle class if you say so . . . **middle class** status (is) . . . a cluster of attitudes, beliefs, practices, and lifestyles that defines what it means to live in a way not too poor to be considered dependent on others and not too rich to be so luxuriously ostentatious that one loses touch with common sense. (pp. 2–3)

It is not difficult to define "low income." The federal government established criteria for determining poverty, including earnings and number of people in a family (see Table 12.3). As of June 2003, the federal definitions of **poverty levels** designate an income of $8,959 for a person living alone; $11,483 for a single person with one child; $13,423 for a single person with two children (U.S. Census Bureau, 2000). Keeping these poverty levels in mind, a full-time worker paid the minimum wage will earn $10,712 a year. Recognizing the inadequacy of the minimum wage, many U.S. communities are implementing a "living wage" to meet the needs of low-income families.

Who suffers most from poverty?

Social activists and organizations such as the Children's Defense Fund emphasize that poverty in America has become an issue of families and children. One out of six children in the United States lives in poverty; two out of three social assistance recipients are children; and one out of five new-

TABLE 12.2

Distribution of Wealth in the United States

WEALTH LEVEL	PERCENTAGE OF WEALTH CONTROLLED			
	1962	1983	1992	1998
Top 1%	33.4	33.8	37.2	38.1
Top 5%	54.6	56.1	60.0	59.4
Top 10%	67.0	68.2	71.8	70.9
Top 20%	81.0	81.3	83.8	83.4
Bottom 80%	19.1	18.7	16.2	16.6

Source: Robert Kuttner. (May 2003). "Sharing America's Wealth." *American Prospect*, Vol. 14, No. 5, pp. A3–A5. He cites the source of this data: *Analysis of Survey of Consumer Finance* by Edward Wolff.

MEMBERS IN FAMILY	ANNUAL INCOME
Single Person	$8,959
Single with One Child	$11,483
Single with Two Children	$13,423
Single with Three Children	$16,954
Two Adults with One Child	$13,410
Two Adults with Two Children	$16,895
Two Adults with Three Children	$19,882
Annual Income for Minimum Wage Earner = $10,712	

Source: United States Census Bureau, 2000. Available at www.census.gov.

TABLE 12.3

Official Poverty Levels in the United States

borns is born into poverty—the highest rate in the industrialized world.

Despite the enormous wealth in the United States, America ranks seventeenth among industrialized nations in low birth weights and twenty-third in infant mortality rates. Low birth weight means 5 pounds, 8 ounces or less; very low birth weight is 3 pounds, 4 ounces or less. In America a low birth-weight baby is born every two minutes and a very low birth-weight baby every nine minutes; a newborn baby dies every 19 minutes (Edelman, 2001). Middle- and upper-income families do not contribute as much to these statistics as do low-income Americans whose insufficient diets, lack of nutritional information, insufficient health care, and stressful existence force them to bear the brunt of infant mortality.

The U.S. federal government response to help children in poverty began with the Economic Security Act of 1935 that included Aid to Dependent Children (ADC), a program intended for mothers widowed or abandoned by their husband. In 1950, ADC was expanded to include any single parent with children and was termed Aid to Families with Dependent Children (AFDC). In 1964, food stamps were made available to low-income families. In 1996, Transitional Assistance to Needy Families (TANF) replaced AFDC. Rodgers (2000) notes, however, that the average value of TANF benefits in combination with food stamps was about the same as what low-income families received from AFDC alone in 1970.

In the late 1970s, studies assessed the impact of war-on-poverty programs initiated in the 1960s by President Lyndon Johnson, especially programs concerned with meeting nutritional needs of the poor. One study reported that hunger had been virtually eliminated (Edelman, 2001). However, the Children's Defense Fund (2001) estimated that in 2000, 12 million children were living in "food-insecure" households, and 2.4 million children were living in "extreme poverty," meaning those children faced frequent and regular occasions where they were not receiving proper nutrition. When children go to bed hungry in the richest nation in the world, it illustrates a failure of our institutions to fulfill their social obligations.

Despite social assistance programs such as TANF, Women, Infants and Children (WIC), food stamps, and Meals on Wheels, malnutrition exists primarily among the old and the young in the United States. Children who do not die from malnutrition may suffer brain damage due to protein-deficient diets and sometimes calorie-deficient diets. Brain damage

> I hold it for indisputable, that the first duty of a state is to see that every child born therein shall be well housed, clothed, fed and educated, till it attain years of discretion.
>
> **JOHN RUSKIN (1819–1900)**

resulting from malnutrition is just as devastating as physical violence because it is permanent; it cannot be reversed by free breakfasts or free lunches once a child starts school.

American healthcare systems also fail to provide adequate services to poor people because they are based on ability to pay. Poor people may visit free or low-cost clinics, yet these clinics are likely to be inadequately staffed and underfunded. Although the United States leads the world in medical technology, it is one of the worst among industrialized nations in health care delivery; the high infant mortality rate in the United States is primarily a consequence of inadequate prenatal care for pregnant women living in poverty (Children's Defense Fund, 2001). In addition to the failure of institutions to meet their needs, poor people must also contend with institutional exploitation from a variety of sources in the United States.

How do institutions exploit poor people?

Financial institutions exploit poor families simply by enforcing policies meant to protect them from losses. **Redlining** refers to banks and other lenders identifying a deteriorating portion of a city, and then refusing to lend money for mortgages in that area. For low-income workers, such areas are most likely to offer the best opportunity to purchase affordable homes, yet when they apply for mortgage loans, their applications may be denied. In such cases, denial is not based on bad credit ratings or lack of skills to maintain and improve property; it results from the age and/or current condition of properties in the redlined area and the average income levels of its residents. Although lenders claim it is just good business not to invest in declining areas, refusing to lend money for purchase and improvement of property makes it inevitable that an area will continue to deteriorate. The prediction becomes a self-fulfilling prophecy (Wilson, 1996; Feagin and Feagin, 1986).

Another way financial agencies may discriminate against the poor is by insisting on a minimum balance of $150 or $200 for checking accounts, making it impossible for workers living from paycheck to paycheck to maintain checking accounts. Families are then forced to live on a cash-only basis—and most banks charge a fee for cashing pay-

> Of course I believe in free enterprise, but in my system of free enterprise the democratic principle is that there never was, never has been, never will be, room for the ruthless exploitation of the many for the benefit of the few.
>
> **HARRY S. TRUMAN (1884–1972)**

roll checks unless an individual has an account at the bank. Many workers find it more convenient to take their paychecks to a neighborhood check-cashing store, even though the convenience may cost them as much as 10% of the amount of the check.

Check-cashing stores have proliferated as banks have abandoned central cities, and fewer banks mean less money available for businesses and homeowners. Based on an analysis of twelve cities, Kane (1996) reported that there were approximately equal numbers of banks per 1,000 residents in white and minority (primarily inner city) areas in 1970, but by the 1990s, there were three times as many banks in white areas as in minority areas. A decline in numbers of banks has led to an increase in private financial companies legally permitted to charge interest rates higher than banks; these companies are also allowed to combine several high-interest loans and sell them to a bank for the interest owed. The bank owning the high-interest loans can then collect interest at a rate well above what it would normally be permitted to charge (Kane, 1996). And banks are not the only business involved in the exploitation of low-income families and individuals.

How do businesses discriminate against poor people?

According to Feagin and Feagin (1986), retail businesses serving low-income people may charge higher prices for products than stores in suburban areas with similar merchandise. As described on the next page, merchants engage in a variety of practices to exploit the poor:

Blank price tags   Blank price tags on merchandise force the customer to ask for the price of an item and allows merchants to quote higher prices to customers they feel may be particularly naïve.

Bait and Switch   Although the practice is illegal, stores serving low-income customers may advertise a product at a low price to attract customers, who are then told that the product is of poor quality. Customers are encouraged to buy a similar product of better quality at a higher price.

Rent-To-Own   Customers rent a product that they can own by making weekly payments over a specified time. Rent-to-own customers may pay up to four times more for merchandise; only 25% eventually own the rented product. Store-owners are exempt from laws limiting interest rates; they insist that they are not charging interest but renting a product. One Virginia store rented a 20-inch Zenith television for $14.99 a week; the renter could own it after 74 payments totaling $1,109.26. Sears sold the same television for $329.99 (Hudson, 1996).

Pawnshops   An expensive option for low-income families is to surrender a possession as collateral for a loan. Pawnshops have proliferated in recent years, with interest rates up to 20% a month—240% a year. Even when customers pay the interest and reclaim the property, the loan repayment does not go on their credit record, so the transaction does not improve their credit rating (Minutaglio, 1996).

Poor people are exploited in other ways in America, but the preceding examples illustrate that exploitation occurs. One must overcome numerous economic obstacles to escape poverty, and no simple solutions exist. As was demonstrated in the 1930s, federal and state governments must address issues of poverty if any progress is to be made concerning the exploitation of and discrimination against poor people.

What can federal and state governments do to assist families living in poverty?

Scholars Abelda, Drago, and Shulman (1997), Entwhistle, Alexander, and Olson (2001), Haycock (2001) and social activist organizations such as the Children's Defense Fund (2001) have made suggestions regarding the role government must play in assisting people in poverty or in supporting those struggling to stay out of poverty:

1. Provide services to address critical needs; subsidies for battered women's shelters would provide options for women in abusive situations.

2. Subsidize child-care services for low-income women who are enrolled in education or training programs. Because of child-care expenses, the best financial option for a single mother working at minimum wage is to quit her job and receive support from social assistance programs.

3. Raise the minimum wage and strive for a living wage. It is difficult to take care of individual needs with the current minimum wage, yet in many families both parents have minimum wage jobs. When the parents' combined salary is barely over $10 an hour, a family will still live in poverty. Jones and George (2003) concluded that for a family earning $10–$15 an hour, "it is often difficult, if not impossible, for them to meet their families' needs" (p. 123).

4. Restructure public school funding so that taxes to support schools are collected by the state and disbursed to schools according to a variable per pupil funding formula that takes into account

> Governments exist to protect the rights of the poor and minorities; the loved and the rich need no protection.
>
> **WENDELL PHILLIPS (1811-1884)**

factors such as: (a) number of low-income students in a given school; (b) amount of budget devoted to special learners; (c) mobility rate of students. In 1990, the New Jersey Supreme Court ruled that such plans are economically feasible and morally justified (*Abbott* v. *Burke*). Only by making a commitment to all children can we hope to nourish their talents and reap the benefits of these children becoming adults who know and use their abilities to the fullest.

5. Provide tax relief for low-income families. Tax relief for wealthy Americans exists as capital gains tax cuts and corporate exemptions from

local property taxes for a specified number of years as incentive to locate. If tax relief is good for the wealthy, why not offer it to the poor? Some tax relief exists in the Earned Income Tax Credit (EITC) and child-care allowances, although some politicians persist in proposing to eliminate these programs. Another form of tax relief for low-income workers might be to exempt home purchases to allow time to make improvements and save money in preparation for paying the resulting higher taxes assessed because of improvements.

6. Offer tax incentives for corporations to locate in inner cities, and tax incentives for corporations creating day care centers at the worksite if they allow low-income families in the area to place children in the centers. Wilson (1996) suggests that reduction of businesses in inner cities has been a major factor in the increase of drug use and crime, and the general deterioration of those communities.

7. Strengthen educational opportunity by increasing support for Head Start programs, and funding quality preschools and summer school programs for low-income children, especially during summers just before and after first grade, so children can experience similar educational gains as middle- and upper-income children during the summer. For middle school and secondary school low-income students, high expectations reflected in clearly articulated standards must be accompanied by a challenging curriculum. Teacher salaries could be subsidized to ensure higher salaries for experienced, quality teachers willing to be assigned to schools in low-income areas.

8. Increase the opportunity for affordable housing. Almost five million families use over half their income to pay rent, often for substandard housing. The federal government could add 300,000 more housing vouchers each year for the next ten years. In addition, the Low-Income Home Energy Assistance Program could be expanded so low-income families can meet rising energy costs.

9. Maintain reasonable regulation of the private sector concerning job discrimination, possibly with affirmative action policies focused on socioeconomic status. State and federal governments could review policies pertaining to multi-national corporations that relocate outside the United States. Although inevitable in a global economy, there could be incentives to keep those corporate jobs in the United States, and disincentives for locating elsewhere. At the present time, American corporations have more incentives to locate overseas than to remain in this country.

AFTERWORD

Oppression is an inevitable consequence when power and resources are concentrated in one group. During the 1930s, U.S. Supreme Court Justice Louis Brandeis expressed his concern for the future of democracy in America by proposing that the United States could continue to be a democracy or it could continue to allow great wealth to be accumulated by a few people, but that it was not possible to accomplish both. Equity and justice depend on transferring resources and power to oppressed groups. People suffer the misery of poverty not because they deserve it, but most likely as a consequence of birth.

If needs of adults living in poverty are neglected, we will perpetuate a despair that often produces drug abuse, crime, and violence. In America today, one of every five babies is born into poverty. If the needs of children living in poverty are neglected, we will be guilty of abandoning American ideals and betraying the decency and compassion Americans have long associated with those ideals. If Americans reject our social conscience, we make achievement of social justice impossible. When we look at faces of poor children, we are not only confronted with a moral dilemma in the present, but with a question about what kind of society America will have in the years to come.

> Until the great mass of the people shall be filled with the sense of responsibility for each other's welfare, social justice can never be attained.
>
> HELEN KELLER (1880–1968)

TERMS AND DEFINITIONS

Bait and switch An illegal strategy whereby a merchant advertises a cheap product and when the customer comes in to purchase it, he or she is persuaded to buy a more expensive product

Classism An attitude, action, or institutional structure that subordinates or limits a person on the basis of his or her low socioeconomic status

Cultural classism The societal promotion of negative beliefs and practices that tend to portray poor, less educated, or socially unacceptable persons as deficient, inferior, and responsible for their own situation; the assumption of superiority by people or groups based upon wealth, employment, education, or social standing

Individual classism Prejudiced attitudes and behavior against others based on the perception of level of income, education, or status as inferior, demonstrated whenever someone responds by saying or doing something degrading or harmful about persons whose income, education, or social standing is looked upon as unacceptable

Institutional classism Established laws, customs, and practices in a society that allow systematic discrimination against low-income individuals or groups to the benefit of middle- or upper-class individuals or groups

Middle class A socioeconomic status determined partly by income and primarily by a cluster of attitudes, beliefs, practices, and lifestyles, which results in living in a way not too poor to be considered dependent on others but not in an ostentatious manner associated with being wealthy

Pawnshops Businesses that receive individual possessions as collateral for loans

Poverty level Income levels established by the federal government based on earnings and the number of individuals in a family

Redlining The practice of banks and other lenders of designating certain areas, especially inner-city neighborhoods (ghettoes or barrios), as "deteriorating," which means they are viewed as bad risks for mortgage loans

Rent-to-own Businesses that offer merchandise on a rental basis to customers who cannot afford the purchase price of that merchandise, stipulating that at the end of the rental period the merchandise will become the property of the renter

REFERENCES

Abelda, R., Drago, R., & Shulman, S. (1997). *Unlevel playing fields.* New York: McGraw Hill.

Describes the disadvantages faced by the poor in the game of economic survival in our society, and what could be done for the poor to make the competition more equal.

Allison, L., & Lewis, C. (2001). *The cheating of America: How tax avoidance and evasion by the super rich are costing the country billions and what you can do about it.* New York: W. Morrow.

Describes how wealthy Americans avoid paying taxes by employing simple solutions such as utilizing cash transactions to complicated financial transactions that permit accounting experts to use legal tax loopholes.

Anyon, J. (2001). Inner cities, affluent suburbs, and unequal educational opportunity. In J.A. Banks & C.M. Banks (Eds.), *Multicultural education: Issues & perspectives* (4th ed., pp. 85–102). New York: John Wiley.

Compares the education offered by inner city schools and suburban schools and describes the academic advantages of students in suburban schools.

Barlett, D., & Steele, J. (1992). *America: What went wrong?* Kansas City: Andrews & McMeel.

Analyzes economic changes that occurred in the 1980s and the impact of these changes, especially on the wealthiest Americans and the middle class.

Bonilla-Silva, E. (2001). *White supremacy and racism in the post-civil rights era.* Boulder, CO: Lynne Rienner.

Examines why blacks and other racial minorities remain behind whites financially, and in terms of occupation, health, educational attainment and other social indicators; the definition of *middle class* is given in the second footnote on page 14.

Brooks-Gunn, J., Klebanov, P., & Duncan, G. (1996). Ethnic differences in children's intelligence test scores: Role of economic deprivation, home environment and maternal characteristics. *Child Development 67,* 396–408.

Reports on the influence of poverty and home environment on the difference in IQ scores between black and white children and how that difference could be dramatically reduced.

Children's Defense Fund. (2001). *A Children's Defense Fund report: The state of America's children.* Boston: Beacon.

Examines statistics from federal and state sources to identify issues affecting children and families living in poverty and makes recommendations to address these problems.

Coles, G. (2003). Learning to read and the "W Principle." *Rethinking Schools 17*(4), 7–8.

Discusses the educational promises of George W. Bush as governor of Texas and as President of the United States and how in reality those promises have been contradicted.

Collins, C. (2003). Tax wealth to broaden wealth. *American Prospect 14*(5), A6–A7.

Explains how taxing the wealthy creates a more just tax system and a more stable society.

Dawson, K. (2003). E.S.E.A. watch. *Rethinking Schools 17*(4), 3–4.

Describes the inappropriateness of tests mandated by the No Child Left Behind Act for fourth grade students, especially bilingual children.

DeVries, J.T. (1999, April). The rich get richer . . . The poor get poorer! *USA political research.* Retrieved March 18, 2003 from *http://balderdashe.com/usapol*

Describes changes in income for CEOs in the United States and in other countries; for updates on CEO salaries, see *www.aflcio.org* "Executive Pay Watch."

Edelman, M.W. (2001). Introduction. *A Children's Defense Fund report: The state of America's children.* Boston: Beacon Press.

Focuses on data with regard to children in poverty today and explains why it is urgent for the United States to take immediate action to address their problems.

Entwhistle, D., Alexander, K., & Olson, L.S. (2001, Fall). Keep the faucet flowing: Summer learning and home environment. *American Educator 47,* 10–15, 47.

Describes why low-income children have a greater learning loss during summer than middle- or upper-class children, and what steps could be taken to minimize that loss.

Feagin, J., & Feagin, C.B. (1986). *Discrimination American style.* (2nd ed.). Malabar, FL: Robert E. Krieger.

Describes discrimination theories and practices with specific examples from research.

Forbes. (2002, March). *The global billionaires.* Retrieved April 12, 2003, from *http://www.forbes.com*

Identifies the top moneymakers of the 497 global billionaires and explains how they make their money. The list is updated each year and is available from this Web site.

Haycock, K. (2001). Closing the achievement gap. *Educational Leadership 58*(6), 6–11.

Compares data on the achievement of low-income students with middle- and upper-class students, and minority students with white students.

Herrnstein, R.J., & Murray, C. (1994). *The bell curve: Intelligence and class structure in American life.* New York: The Free Press.

Analyzes research to argue that differences in intelligence stem from race/ethnicity and are genetically determined, and economic success or failure is determined by intelligence.

Hout, M., & Lucas, S.R. (2001). Narrowing the income gap between rich and poor. In P. Rothenberg (Ed.), *Race, class and gender in the United States: An integrated study* (pp. 649–653). New York: Worth.

Reviews the gap between rich and poor and describes how *The Bell Curve* misled the public by claiming the gap is a result of inequality of ability.

Hudson, M. (1996). Rent to own: The slick cousin of paying on time. In M. Hudson (Ed.), *Merchants of misery: How corporate America profits from poverty* (pp. 146–152). Monroe, ME: Common Courage Press.

Explains how rent-to-own stores exploit low-income consumers.

Isaacs, J.B., & Lyon, M.R. (2000). *A cross-state examination of families leaving welfare: Finding from the ASPE-funded leavers studies.* Presented at the National Association for Welfare Research and Statistics Workshop, August, Scottsdale, AZ. Available: *http://www.dhhs.gov*

Describes preliminary outcomes for families in eleven states leaving welfare based on reports from studies funded by the Department of Health and Human Services.

Johnson, H.W. (1998). Public welfare and income maintenance. In *The social services: An introduction.* (5th ed.). Itasca, IL: F. E. Peacock.

Discusses the nature and causes of poverty in the United States and examines several federal programs implemented to reduce poverty.

Jones, G.R., & George, J.M. (2003). Managing diverse employees in a diverse environment. *Contemporary management* (3rd ed.). Boston: McGraw Hill.

Describes increasing diversity among consumers and in the work force and provides strategies for managers to work effectively with diverse employees.

Kane, M. (1996). Fringe banks. In M. Hudson (Ed.), *Merchants of misery: How corporate America profits from poverty* (pp. 52–57). Monroe, ME: Common Courage Press.

Describes the decline of banks and the increase in check-cashing stores in poverty areas.

Katz, M. B. (1986). *In the shadow of the poorhouse: A social history of welfare in America.* New York: Basic Books.

Describes poverty programs in colonial America, why the Poorhouse failed, and how social policies responded to the historic shifts in America's social and economic structure.

Komisar, L. (1977). *Down and out in the USA: A history of public welfare.* (Rev. ed.). New York: New Viewpoints.

Presents the history of American welfare including European antecedents, forms of relief established in the colonial period, and issues and actions taken up to the present.

Kozol, J. (1991). *Savage inequalities: Children in America's schools.* New York: Crown.

Describes the inadequate funding of schools consisting largely of low-income children compared to schools for middle- or upper-class children.

Macedo, D., & Bartolome, L.I. (2001). *Dancing with bigotry: Beyond the politics of tolerance.* New York: Palgrave.

Examines issues concerning language, race, ethnicity, and social class and the limitations of merely teaching tolerance in multicultural education.

Mathis, W.J. (2003). No Child Left Behind: Costs and benefits. *Kappan.* Retrieved August 15, 2003, from *http://www.pdkintl.org/kappan/k0305mat.htm, Phi Delta Kappa International.*

Analyzes costs to explain how much federal financial support is required for schools to have a realistic chance of achieving the goals identified in the No Child Left Behind Act.

Mead, L. (2000). The twilight of liberal welfare reform. *Public Interest 139,* 22–35.

Describes an experimental welfare program in Milwaukee called the New Hope Project and compares its effectiveness with the Wisconsin Works (W-2) welfare reform.

Minutaglio, B. (1996). Prince of pawns. In M. Hudson (Ed.), *Merchants of misery: How corporate America profits from poverty* (pp. 58–70). Monroe, ME: Common Courage.

Describes one highly successful pawnshop owner to discuss the growth of pawnshops and how they operate as an underground economy exploiting the financial needs of the poor.

Moore, S., & Stansel, D. (1995, May 12). Ending corporate welfare as we know it. *Policy Analysis No 225.* Retrieved June 12, 2003, from *http://www.cato.org/pa225.html*

Provides examples of corporate welfare and eight reasons explaining why corporate welfare is misguided and even harmful to the society.

Owen, D., & Doerr, M. (1999, Revised). *None of the above: The truth behind the SATs.* Lanham, MD: Rowman Littlefield.

Describes the origin of standardized tests in America and biases in the current SAT tests.

Phillips, K. (2003). How wealth defines power. *American Prospect 14*(5), A8–A9.

Compares the concentration of wealth since 1980 with that of the late 1800s and 1920s.

Phillips, K. (1990). Wealth and favoritism. In *The politics of rich and poor: Wealth and the American electorate in the Reagan aftermath.* New York: Random House.

Describes how wealthy Americans exploited federal policies during the Reagan era.

Pipher, M. (2002). *The middle of everywhere: The world's refugees come to our town.* New York: Harcourt.

Describes the nature of recent immigration to America using some statistical data, but primarily based on interviews with immigrants.

Rodgers Jr., H. (2000). *American poverty in a new era of reform.* Armonk, NY: M.E. Sharpe.

Describes poverty in America, provides a history of the welfare system, and gives an analysis of the recent welfare reforms.

Sandefur, G.D., & Cook, S. (1998). Permanent exits from public assistance: The impact of duration, family and work. *Social Forces 77*(2), 763–789.

Analysis of data to ascertain the length of time a woman receives welfare and the effect of marital status and work qualifications on the time an individual stays on welfare.

Schorr, A. L. (2001). *Welfare reform: Failure and remedies.* Westport, CT: Praeger.

Examines the successes and failures of previous efforts to reform welfare and the social forces that resulted in the 1996 welfare reform legislation.

Schwarz, J. (2000). *Fighting poverty with virtue: Moral reform and America's urban poor, 1825–2000.* Bloomington: Indiana University Press.

Examines the work of moral reformers with regard to poverty issues in the late 1800s and early 1900s and the implications for dealing with current poverty issues.

Shapiro, I., Greenstein, R., & Primus, W. (2001). *Path-breaking CBO study shows dramatic increases in income disparities in the 1980s and 1990s: An analysis of the CBO Data Center on Budget and Policy Priorities.* Retrieved May 31 from *http://www.cbpp.org*

Analyzes data from a Congressional Budget Office (CBO) study of changes in the economic status of those in the top 1%, middle fifth and bottom fifth of the U.S. population.

Sklar, H. (1998). CEO greed is out of control. *Z Magazine.* Retrieved May 12, 2003, from *http://www.third worldtraveler.com*

Describes the growing gap between average salaries of CEOs and workers, with specific examples of CEOs whose salaries increased while they released workers.

Stein, Z., & Susser, M. (1970). Mutability of intelligence and epidemiology of mild mental retardation. *Review of Educational Research 40,* 29–68.

Reviews research, including cross-cultural studies, and concludes that environmental conditions have a significant impact on student achievement. [*Note:* For a current perspective, refer to: Desimone, L. (1999). Linking parent involvement with student achievement: Do race and income matter? *Journal of Educational Research 93*(1), 1–31.]

Taylor, H. (2000, May 3). The public tends to blame the poor, the unemployed, and those on welfare for their problems. *Harris Poll #24.* Retrieved August 14, 2003, from *http://www.harrisinteractive.com*

Presents results of a Harris Poll on American attitudes concerning people living in poverty who are unemployed or on welfare.

United States Census Bureau. (2000). *Poverty thresholds/ 2002.* Retrieved June 10, 2003, from *http//www .census.gov*

Provides income levels defining poverty for families of various sizes.

U.S. Department of Labor. (2000). Earnings differences between women and men. Available from the Women's Bureau under *Facts on working women.* Retrieved April 12, 2003, from *http://www.dol.gov/ dol/wb*

Provides statistics on the history of the wage gap between men and women, including comparisons based on age, occupation, and education.

Weaver, R.K. (2000). *Ending welfare as we know it.* Washington, DC: Brookings Institution Press.

Describes the former welfare system and the arguments for the need to change it and analyzes the most recent welfare reform.

Wolfe, A. (1998). *One nation, after all: What middle-class Americans really think about God, country, family, racism, welfare, immigration, homosexuality, work, the right, the left, and each other.* New York: Viking Penguin.

A team of researchers interviewed and gathered information from middle-class families living in suburban areas across the United States.

Wilson, W.J. (1996). *When work disappears: The world of the new urban poor.* New York: Knopf.

Examines causes of inner city unemployment and makes recommendations to address the problem.

Zinn, H. (1999). *A people's history of the United States.* New York: HarperCollins.

Provides a detailed account of the history of union organization and employer resistance beginning with Chapter 10, "The Other Civil War."

REVIEW AND DISCUSSION ACTIVITIES

Summary Exercises

See page 19 for exercises to help you summarize the main points and define key terms in this chapter.

Personal Clarification Exercises

In Chapter 12, two exercises promote discussion about wealth, poverty, and income inequality.

Clarification Exercise #1 What Do You Believe? Contrasting Beliefs about Poverty

Directions: In groups of six, read the two selections below. After reading the opposing points of view, discuss the two contrasting beliefs, addressing at least three of the following questions.

1. How do you feel about each of these beliefs?
2. Why do you feel about them the way you do?
3. Do you think you feel the same way your parents do? Grandparents? Other relatives?
4. What do you think the majority of your friends believe?
5. Do you know people who are poor?
6. Are they on welfare?
7. Does what you know about them reinforce or contradict your beliefs about poverty?
8. In what ways might you have you experienced poverty yourself?

Contrasting Beliefs about Poverty

In the United States, many people seem to endorse one or the other of the following beliefs:

A. "Where there's a will there's a way" (or some variation of that expression); therefore, if anyone is poor, it's their fault. They haven't tried hard enough (or they might even be lazy and irresponsible). There are jobs out there for anyone who really wants to work. Furthermore, if a poor person needs and asks for help, it is NOT my obligation to help them. Let them help themselves by pulling themselves up by their own bootstraps just like I did. No one helped me or gave me any handouts and I wouldn't take them even if they were offered to me because I've got too much pride to take charity; so, I do NOT want my tax dollars used to help poor people, and I deeply resent it when the government takes my hard-earned money and spends it on these people.

B. "Nobody talks more [about] the best man winning than the man who inherited his father's store or farm." If anyone is poor it's probably because they were born into a low-income family, did not have the same advantages as those with more money, did not develop high expectations (and may even have dropped out of school). Since they will end up in the least desirable jobs, they will be most likely to be unemployed during tough economic times. If a poor person needs and asks for help, we should give them a helping hand until they get back on their feet again, especially if it involves training or retraining for a new job or making sure children are getting food and shelter. I'm willing to have my tax dollars used to help poor people because I'd want to be helped if I ever found myself in such a situation.

Clarification Exercise #2 Distribution of Wealth: The Ten Chairs of Equality

Introduction: Inequality of wealth is becoming more extreme in the United States. While billionaires double their wealth every three-to-five years, we have by far the highest poverty rate in the industrialized world. No industrialized country has a more skewed distribution of wealth. We need information about this concentration of wealth—and the power that accompanies it—in order to become critical thinkers and aware citizens. A Boston-based group, United for a Fair Economy, has developed the simulation activity below to dramatize the increasingly unequal distribution of wealth.

Ten Chairs of Equality

Directions: Ten chairs are placed in each of two facing rows. Ten persons may be seated on each of the ten chairs to the *left* of the head of the room.

Part One: Each chair on the *left* represents 10% of the wealth in the United States and each person seated represents 10% of the population. (Wealth is what one owns, such as sound systems, jewelry, clothing, automobiles, homes, companies, yachts, villas, and private jets.)

With the ten chairs of *equality* occupied, respond to the following questions:

Question 1: What is the approximate wealth each family would have in the United States if wealth were distributed equally?

(A) ___ 1 or 10% or less   (F) ___ 6 or 60%
(B) ___ 2 or 20%   (G) ___ 7 or 70%
(C) ___ 3 or 30%   (H) ___ 8 or 80%
(D) ___ 4 or 40%   (I) ___ 9 or 90%
(E) ___ 5 or 50%   or more

Question 2: What would the atmosphere here feel like if we knew that each person in this room could have 40% of their wealth paid toward a home, 2.5% invested in an automobile, and still have $140,000 in the bank?

[*Note:* Actually, we have nowhere near an equal distribution of wealth in the United States. The poorest 20% of the population are in debt and the next 30% average $5,000 in wealth, primarily in home equity.]

Part Two: Now agree upon another ten persons to sit on each of the ten chairs to the *right* of the head of the room. These chairs more accurately will represent the actual wealth of Americans today. With the ten chairs of *inequality* occupied, respond to the next questions:

Question 3: Recall that each chair represents 10% of the wealth in America. Speculate how many chairs you think in 1976 belonged to the wealthiest 10% of the population:

(A) ___ 1 or 10% or less   (F) ___ 6 or 60%
(B) ___ 2 or 20%   (G) ___ 7 or 70%
(C) ___ 3 or 30%   (H) ___ 8 or 80%
(D) ___ 4 or 40%   (I) ___ 9 or 90%
(E) ___ 5 or 50%   or more

Now: realign yourselves accordingly. One person will occupy ___ [number] chairs; the remainder of the 10 persons will jointly seat on ___ chairs. Can this be correct?

Wealthiest person: How do you feel now? Remaining 9 persons: How do you feel about needing to share the wealth that is left?

Question 4: Still keeping in mind that each chair represents 10% of the wealth in America, speculate how

many chairs you think in 1996 belonged to the wealthiest 10% of the population:

(A) ___ 1 or 10% or less   (F) ___ 6 or 60%
(B) ___ 2 or 20%   (G) ___ 7 or 70%
(C) ___ 3 or 30%   (H) ___ 8 or 80%
(D) ___ 4 or 40%   (I) ___ 9 or 90%
(E) ___ 5 or 50%   or more

Next: Realign yourselves once again. How many chairs will the wealthiest person occupy? How many chairs will the remaining nine persons share between them?

Question 5: Recognizing that 10% of America's wealthiest persons occupy most of the chairs—the percentage of wealth in the United States—what is your speculation regarding the percentage of America's wealth [at 10% of the wealth per chair] that the top 1% of persons controlled in 1979? In 1992?

(A) ___ 1 or 10% or less   (F) ___ 6 or 60%
(B) ___ 2 or 20%   (G) ___ 7 or 70%
(C) ___ 3 or 30%   (H) ___ 8 or 80%
(D) ___ 4 or 40%   (I) ___ 9 or 90%
(E) ___ 5 or 50%   or more

Now: Realign yourselves one last time according to the final number. Is the configuration a surprise in any way? *Wealthy person:* What can you suggest you can do for your fellow citizens? *Other citizens:* What feelings might your fellow citizens have when confronted with this ratio?

Part Three: Interviews with citizens

Wealthy citizens:
    What is your future?
    How are you managing your wealth?
    What do you recommend the common and poor citizens do to improve their lives?

Common citizens:
    What is your future? How are you managing your wealth?
    Why have you not organized for a redistribution of wealth?
    What would you like to do to improve your lives?

Poor citizens:
    Would there not be more money to go around if you and your friends weren't ripping off the welfare system?

Do you find that the super-wealthy are really helping you daily with living expenses and tax credits? What would you like to do to improve your lives?

Part Four: Class Interaction: What comes next?

Is there an inevitability to domination of our economy and society by the wealthy?

What do you foresee as the future for Americans as those with most widely disparate economy?

What questions should we be asking regarding distribution of wealth in the United States?

Is inequality of wealth a problem for Americans today? Why? And Why not?

[Answers: Q 1: *I;* Q 3: *E, 5, 5;* Q 4: *G, 7, 3;* Q 5: 1979: *B (22%),* 1992: *D (43%)*]

ADAPTED FROM EDWARD N. WOLFF, *RECENT TRENDS IN WEALTH OWNERSHIP, 1983–1998,* LEVY INSTITUTE WORKING PAPER NO. 300, TABLE 2. LEVY ECONOMICS INSTITUTE, APRIL 2000.

Intergroup Exercises

In Chapter 12, three exercises promote discussion about interviews, academic ethics, and wealth.

Intergroup Exercise #1 Information Gathering: Interviews

Directions: Sometimes, polling a particular population reveals attitudes that are not anticipated. The interview is one means of assessing attitudes of specifically identified groups, such as college faculty, undergraduate college students, neighborhoods, types of businesses, or service providers. This activity is to be prepared within the classroom or workshop and then immediately administered outside of class, either on the campus of the course or in the area where the class is being held. Alternatively, the questionnaire may also be taken to other parts of an agreed-upon city, suburb, or village with an extended time allowance.

Information Gathering: Interviews

1. With the assistance of your instructor, with prior approval for such activity, and based upon your summary exercise discussions of the chapter, develop an agreed-upon list of ten questions about the economics of wages, wealth, and employment that your class thinks should be asked of students, staff, instructors, and faculty on your campus or around your classroom meeting place.

2. Write those questions out and discuss what responses might be given if the questions were asked.

3. Discuss how to conduct interviews in which you actually ask those questions to others and record their responses, and agree upon how to administer interviews.

4. In teams of only two, select a portion of the area for each team to ask the same questions of six different persons; clarify all components of the interview and time process.

5. In the space of 55 minutes:
   • Leave for that assigned area.
   • Select and administer your interview questions to persons who are willing to respond.
   • Keep a record of their age ranges, gender, and status (faculty, student, administration, staff).

6. Return to the classroom for tallying and a report of the results of the interviews.

7. Include in your post–interview classroom discussion:
   • What is your conclusion about the sample of six persons you interviewed?
   • Were the responses honest?
   • How did your subjects respond when you asked your questions?
   • Do you conclude that your interview sample were aware of problems and concerns of lower economically placed persons in America today?
   • In your area?

Individual Exercise #2 An Economic Ethical Dilemma: The Power of the Course Grade

Directions: Read "College or Bust" case study aloud in groups of five; take turns in order that each person in the group has opportunity to participate. Then determine (a) What is the main issue or issues in this situation? (b) What can be said in favor of the student? In favor of the instructor? (c) What could be done to satisfy both needs and make a Win-Win situation? (d) What does your group recommend be done?

An Economic Ethical Dilemma: The Power of the Course Grade

It is the end of the school year and you have just finished calculating your grades for the semester.

A young woman from a low-income family who is a senior in high school comes to see you, her chemistry teacher, after school. She explains that a nearby college has offered her financial aid if she receives at least a B in Chemistry.

She shows you a letter from the college's admissions officer, which indicates that she has discussed her plans for a career in medical technology and the college believes that a grade of at least a B in Chemistry will be a strong predictor of success in their program. They will accept her into the program if she receives a passing grade (less than a B), but if she earns a B or better they have assured her that she will receive financial aid. If she does not receive financial aid, she cannot afford to go to college.

You have already determined that her grade for the semester is a C. You not only considered scores on objective tests but participation in class discussions, lab work, homework, and your own subjective judgment in arriving at that grade, but if you give her a C she will obviously not be eligible for financial aid, which will seriously jeopardize her goal of going on to college.

In your conversation with her, she says that she has applied to several other colleges, but this college is the only one that has offered her the financial aid she needs.

Will you change her grade from a C to a B and provide this student with an opportunity to continue her education, or do you stick to your decision to award a C despite the loss of financial aid that the student would otherwise receive?

If she can get a job and live at home, she might be able to attend the nearby college without financial aid, especially if she only takes classes on a part-time basis, but she will clearly be at a much greater risk of not completing her college degree without the financial assistance she could receive with the higher grade.

What will you do?

Individual Exercise #3 Broadening the Wealth in America: Can We Avoid Economic Domination by the Wealthy?

The Plan: Ideas for a more equitable distribution of economic resources in the United States have been discussed and implemented throughout the 20th century and include such strategies as pension plans, profit sharing, the GI bill, FHA loans, and Social Security. The following two ideas summarize some recent approaches to this issue. Proponents argue that the money for these plans could be raised by increasing income tax on the wealthiest 40% of Americans (those making $80,000 or more) by 2%.

Directions: In groups of five, review each plan below; make certain everyone is clear on the details of each proposal. Next, prepare cogent answers to each of the questions posed, then develop a five-to-ten minute panel presentation to the group using your discussion, expertise, experience, and background knowledge. Questions: Does either plan [below] seem to be a reasonable way to obtain funding to fulfill its objective? Which of the two plans seems more possible? What special considerations might need to be made in its implementation?

Broadening the Wealth in America

1. Individual Development Accounts (IDAs) would be established for all Americans at birth. The IRS would deposit part of an individual's income taxes (or that of the individual's parents as long as he or she is a dependent) in this account for each significant milestone or achievement that occurred during that year: passing a grade in school, graduating from high school, graduating from college, getting married, getting a job. The amount would vary from $500 for passing a grade in school to $1,500 for graduating from high school. If an individual did not pay enough in taxes to cover the cost of the amount to be deposited in a given year, the government would

subsidize the payment. Each individual would manage the assets in this account, and could receive the interest generated from these accounts, but he or she could not touch the principal. The interest generated by the accounts would not be taxed when withdrawn, but such withdrawals could only be made for a purpose related to the eventual enhancement of an individual's assets (such as paying for postsecondary education or the down payment on a house). The accounts could also be used as collateral for college loans, home loans, or for credit to open a business. (Adapted from: Sherraden, M. (1992). *Assets and the poor.* Armonk, NY: M.E. Sharpe.)

2. Every American would have a "wealth account" of $80,000 established for him or her at birth. A person could have access to this account when he or she turned twenty-one, but ONLY upon graduation from high school. For the rest of his or her life, a person could use this account to achieve desired goals, but anything taken from the account must be paid back. As an example of how the account could be used: eighteen-year-olds attending college would be permitted to access the account early to pay for college expenses (including the high school graduate trying to escape a violent and drug-ridden neighborhood); workers who are laid off their job could live off the interest until they found a new job or they could pay for further training for a related or different occupation; a young couple who just had their first child and wanted to buy a house could use the money for a down payment; a truck driver could use the money to begin his or her own trucking company. Any of the interest or principal used from this "wealth account" would eventually be repaid so that when an individual died, the money plus interest from the wealth account would be reclaimed by the government and used to finance an account for another person. If an account did not have the full amount it should have, the government would get to make the first claims on whatever assets the dead person left behind in order to get the full amount repaid. (Adapted from: Ackerman, B.A., & Alstott, A. (n.d.). $80,000 and a dream. *The American Prospect Online.* Retrieved December 22, 2003 from *http://www.prospect.org/print/V11/16/ackerman-b.html*)

CHAPTER 13

Ableism: Disability Does Not Mean Inability

"All governments treat disabled people badly. They all see us as a burden. All governments, whether capitalist or socialist, have separated us from the rest of society . . . Until we are businessmen, politicians, community leaders, people at all levels of society, we will be marginalized and segregated."

JOSHUA MALINGA (CONTEMPORARY)

In 1993, members of the United Nations declared people with disabilities an oppressed minority group. Writers of the U.N. Human Rights and Disabled Persons Report documented that around the world, people with disabilities were being treated as outcasts and that the situation was getting worse as their numbers increased. The 1995 representatives at the World Summit on Social Development in Copenhagen described disabled people as "one of the world's largest minority groups facing poverty and unemployment as well as social and cultural isolation" (Ervelles, 2001, p. 93). Despite the statements of these global organizations, the concept of *ableism* (sometimes erroneously called *handicapism*) has yet to be accepted by many people in the United States and around the world.

Ableism has been defined by Linton (1998) as the negative determination of an individual's abilities based upon his or her disabilities. Ableism promotes the belief that people with disabilities are inferior to able-bodied persons to justify discrimination against them. Linton's definition asserts that the dominant group oppresses people with disabilities, as do other minority groups. Many people, including some people with disabilities, reject that assumption. Hahn (1988) observed that:

Unlike other minorities . . . disabled men and women have not yet been able to refute the implicit and direct accusations of biological inferiority that have often been invoked to rationalize the oppression of groups whose appearance differs from the standards of the dominant majority. (p. 26)

Why should people with disabilities be considered a minority group?

The Fall 2001 issue of the *Journal of Disability Policy Studies* addressed the question of whether people with disabilities could be regarded as an oppressed minority. Although the contributors agreed that disabled people were oppressed, guest editor Andrew Batavia strongly disagreed. While acknowledging past problems, Batavia argued that people with disabilities in the United States live in conditions "dramatically better" than in other countries. Reacting to the high rate of unemployment for disabled people in the United States, Batavia said employers had the right to hire the most qualified person for a job regardless of disability, implying that disabled applicants were often not the most qualified.

Because of the efforts of disability rights advocates and with the passage of the Americans with

Disabilities Act (ADA) in 1990, Batavia argued that people with disabilities no longer experience the regrettable discrimination that occurred in the past and therefore do not qualify as an "oppressed minority." Apparently Batavia had not reviewed recent statistics: A survey of people with disabilities reported that the percent of unemployed adults had

FIGURE 13.1

Like other minority groups, people with disabilities and their advocates have had to protest and demonstrate to draw attention to the discrimination against them.

Source: Courtesy of Richard B. Levine

increased since the ADA became law, as had the percentage of people living in poverty (Wilson and Lewicki-Wilson, 2001). Batavia's denial rationalization that discrimination no longer affects people with disabilities today is unusual because such arguments are more likely to be expressed by a nondisabled person than someone like Batavia who has a disability.

Another argument denies that people with disabilities are oppressed because having a disability makes one part of the majority. According to the rationale of this argument, having a disability places a person on a continuum where mild physical disabilities, such as poor eyesight, can be corrected by wearing glasses, whereas a more severe physical disability may require someone to use a wheelchair. The logic continues that whether minimal or severe, almost all of us are disabled in one way or another and must learn to live with the condition. In response, Gill (1994) argues that to be a *person with a disability* means the disability has a significant impact on daily life: For example, the disability influences an individual's sense of identity, or others' perceptions of the disability have a significant influence on their reactions to the person, including the likelihood of negative attitudes of rejection or even discrimination. Our reactions reflect a similar rejection of or discrimination toward people from other minority groups.

Disability rights advocates argue that the concept of people with disabilities being an oppressed group would be more readily accepted if disability studies were included in secondary and higher education courses that examine women's issues, racial and ethnic problems, and negative social, cultural, and institutional experiences of other minority groups. Understanding experiences of people with disabilities requires recognition of dominant group privileges and power not shared. Linton (1998) suggests that such recognition could parallel that afforded other minority groups in viewing the dominant nondisabled group as "not the neutral, universal position from which disabled people deviate, rather, it is a category of people whose power and cultural capital keep them at the center" (p. 32).

The disability rights approach views disability as a natural phenomenon which occurs in every generation, and always will. It recognizes people with disabilities as a distinct minority group, subject at times to discrimination and segregation . . . but also capable of taking our rightful place in society.

LAURA HERSHEY (1962–)

CULTURAL ABLEISM

Negative attitudes toward people with disabilities are not recent phenomena. Whether perceived as wicked, violent, or merely foolish, people with physical, emotional, or mental disabilities have been identified consistently as **deviant** because they were not *normal,* leading to negative and sometimes hostile behaviors. In the early 1900s, the U.S. Public Health Service categorized people with retardation as "Defectives" along with criminals and delinquents, later labeling them "Mental Defectives" to distinguish them from the prostitutes, pimps, pickpockets, and paupers. But all such human beings were frequently placed together in institutions since they were nevertheless deviants, different from the norm, requiring their removal from communities. The historical record reveals a pattern of **cultural ableism,** images and beliefs perpetuated in society that promote the perception of people with disabilities as deviant or incompetent.

What are the historical perceptions of people with disabilities?

Understanding how societies have regarded people with various kinds of disabilities can explain not only negative individual attitudes, but also why different societies institutionalized people with disabilities. Wolfensberger (1970) explained some of the major historical perceptions of people with disabilities in the following categories:

A Subhuman Organism Although other groups (such as African Americans, Native Americans, and Jews) historically have been regarded as subhuman, the perception is still associated with people with disabilities, especially those labeled "mentally retarded" who have been occasionally referred to as "vegetables," alluding to medical terminology for performance of vital functions (heart rate, blood pressure) as vegetative functions. Logical thinking and other higher brain activity were assumed impossible for retarded persons. As late as the nineteenth century, "mental defectives" were housed in rooms not heated in winter nor cooled in summer because it was assumed that they were not sensitive to heat or cold like "normal" people. Even in the last half of the twentieth century, caregivers for institutionalized people with mental disabilities have been known to use cattle prods for control. Once we dehumanize a group to subhuman status, there are few limitations to what can be done. Another example of the subhuman perception was articulated in a 1960s *Atlantic Monthly* article suggesting that organs should be harvested from severely and profoundly retarded people, referred to by the author as "human vegetables," and donated to those on organ waiting lists in order to "increase the intellectual betterment of mankind" (Wolfensberger, 1970, p. 17).

Menace to Society This perception regards people with disabilities as evil. It is fostered in children's literature with villains such as Captain Hook, Long John Silver, and in fairy tales by an array of wicked goblins and trolls, evil giants, and other weird, frightening characters who are ultimately subjugated or eliminated (Fiedler, 1978). Although Franks (2001) reported a surprising number of positive characters with disabilities in Grimm's fairy tales, college students in her study tended to remember the negative images of disabled people in the fairy tales they read and discussed. Winzer (1997) described how adult literature continues the pattern, portraying disabled people as criminal, homicidal, or maladjusted monsters who are often sexual deviants as well. Charles Dickens created a dwarf called Quilp to be the evil villain in pursuit of the innocent Nell in *The Old Curiosity Shop* (see Figure 13.2). Shakespeare contributed to this cast of villainous characters in his depiction of Richard III, who is sometimes described as the model for the deformed villain whose visible disability is a manifestation of the invisible wickedness inside.

Object of Dread The origin of this perception is the medieval myth of the *changeling* where people believed that upon the birth of a normal child, evil spirits came in the night and stole the child, replacing it with a defective child such as one who was mentally retarded or with cerebral palsy. In Grimm's fairy tale "The Elves," a changeling with "fixed staring eyes" is substituted for the original baby (Franks, 2001). The belief that evil spirits were the source of changelings may have influenced Martin Luther's perception of defective children as spawn of Satan, denouncing them as a "mass of flesh" without a soul (Winzer, 1997). Today, some Christians regard deformity or disability as a sign of "moral failure" or as a visible stigma of sinfulness (Pelka, 1994). Some parents of children with disabilities regard the child as punishment from God; some mothers experience enough depression to seek therapy following the birth of such a child.

Object of Pity This perception may not seem negative because it appears to include compassion for disabled people, but it is a compassion seldom accompanied by respect. Fundraising campaigns by well-meaning organizations work to arouse pity with poster children or by having telethons that parade children with disabilities to stimulate viewers to make contributions. According to Charlton (1998), surveys conducted in the United States have concluded that more people form their attitudes about people with disabilities from telethons than from any other source. Because telethons tend to reinforce images of people with disabilities as helpless or dependent, the disability community in America has voiced objections to them, with some organizations responding by agreeing not to participate in telethons for fundraising purposes.

Diseased Organism This perception views a person's physical or mental disability as a temporary condition that can be cured by chemical or psychological treatments. Ancient Egyptians often regarded disability as a condition for which medical "cures" were prescribed. Egyptian doctors hoped to restore eyesight to blind people by applying a solution to their eyes made of copper, myrrh, Cyprus seeds, and other ingredients. Although many Greeks believed that supernatural forces caused disabilities, physicians including Hippocrates rejected superstition and attempted to identify physiological causes of disabilities (Winzer, 1997). In the United States

FIGURE 13.2

One of the original illustrations by Phiz (Halbot K. Browne) depicting Quilp the dwarf, the villain in *The Old Curiosity Shop* by Charles Dickens

Source: Michael Steig, *Dickens and Phiz.* Bloomington: Indiana University Press. Used with permission.

today, national fund drives solicit money for research to find cures for disabilities, presenting people with that disability not only as an object of pity, but also as a diseased organism: The disability is perceived as "unhealthy" and the person is portrayed as needing to be cured. This medical view of people with disabilities is pessimistic because until a cure can be found, people with disabilities are regarded as having "incurable diseases." Because of such perceptions, people with disabilities have been placed in institutions, which penalize them for the crime of being disabled.

Holy Innocent/Eternal Child This perception is normally identified with one group: people labeled "mentally retarded." Viewed as incapable of sin, the Holy Innocent image can be found in most countries, religions, and cultures, and is often regarded as a benign view. The perception suggests that people with mental retardation need to be protected and sheltered, isolated from the outside world to perpetuate their innocent, child-like qualities. But encouraging people with mental retardation to maintain childish behaviors rather than learn adult behaviors is a barrier to their ability to live independently. Linton (1998) observed that when people with disabilities are viewed as "living in the body, not in the mind, [they] are configured as childlike, even infant like, acting on primary drives rather than engaging in purposeful behavior" (pp. 95–96). This perception can become a self-fulfilling prophecy, illustrated in reports of people with mental retardation who have been constantly treated as children even during adolescence who persist in child-like behaviors as adults, requiring constant care (Wehmeyer, 2000).

Object of Ridicule In literature, folk stories, and jokes, people with disabilities are subject to humiliation for the sake of humor. People with mental retardation have been portrayed as village idiots and ridiculed in moron jokes. According to Fiedler (1978), pagan practices of displaying freaks for public entertainment were revived in the Middle Ages by the Catholic Church, which displayed disabled or deformed "monsters" on feast days. In the nineteenth century, carnival side shows with magicians and sword swallowers also featured freaks: giants, dwarves, human skeletons, and other physically

malformed or disabled people. Legendary showman P.T. Barnum popularized the freak show in the United States, exhibiting Chang and Eng (the original Siamese twins) and General Tom Thumb (a midget), along with anonymous pinheads and armless or legless wonders, now immortalized in wax at the Circus World Museum in Baraboo, Wisconsin. Living or dead, people with deformities or disabilities are still perceived as odd, ridiculous, or bizarre—anything but human.

According to Russell (1998), 20% of Americans have some form of disability, so it is surprising that these historical perceptions continue to influence individual concepts of people with physical or mental disabilities. In America, families were expected to keep disabled family members at home, hidden from the community, until the nineteenth century,

> The point is, we are all one great big family, and any one of us can get hurt at any moment. . . . We should never walk by somebody who's in a wheelchair and be afraid of them or think of them as a stranger.
>
> **CHRISTOPHER REEVE (1952–)**

when institutions were established for "defectives" (Pelka, 1994). Once they were institutionalized, people with disabilities could be completely isolated from their communities. Before examining these institutions, we need to examine and understand the individual attitudes that made such institutions possible.

INDIVIDUAL ABLEISM

Negative attitudes are reflected in the language we employ to identify disabled people. The word *disabled* implies inability; the prefix *dis* is generally regarded as signifying *not* or *no*. Derived from Latin, the prefix actually means *apart* or *asunder*, which is consistent with the historic practice of keeping disabled people apart from society.

How are negative attitudes reflected in the way people with disabilities are described?

We display our negative attitudes when nondisabled people describe people with disabilities as being "afflicted with" or a "victim of" a disability. Affliction is associated with disease, as is being a victim, so this language relates to the cultural image of the person with a disability as a diseased organism. Using words or phrases like *crippled, handicapped, impaired,* or *confined to a wheelchair* foster the belief that people with disabilities are incompetent or damaged, not capable of being independent. The term *confined to a wheelchair* is especially absurd. People in wheelchairs are not confined, but liberated by them. The wheelchair provides mobility to people who might be "confined" to their apartment or home if they did not have a wheelchair. And although physical barriers can be identified easily, it is much more difficult in America today to identify and overcome barriers created by **individual ableism**—prejudiced attitudes and actions toward people with a disability based on assumptions about their lack of ability. These assumptions are reinforced by our continued use of negative language.

How can negative attitudes constitute a barrier for people with disabilities?

At a large Midwestern university, a young woman born without arms enrolled in the nursing program. Although she had an excellent academic record, the nursing faculty was opposed to accepting her based on concerns that the young woman would not be able to perform physical tasks required of nurses. When a campus disability advocate became involved,

> Before I was paralyzed, there were 10,000 things I could do. Now there are 9,000. I could dwell on the 1,000 I lost or focus on the 9,000 I have left.
>
> **WALTER MITCHELL (CONTEMPORARY)**

a compromise was reached. The young woman was admitted to the nursing program, but would not be allowed to take licensure exams. This resolution was acceptable to the young woman; she had hoped to earn a nursing degree because of her interest in the subject matter. After graduation, the young woman wrote articles based on her research and observations for nursing journals, eventually becoming an editor. Nursing faculty had not focused on what the young woman could do, nor had they anticipated this outcome; their focus had been on tasks the disability would prevent the young woman from doing.

What labels represent legitimate ways of identifying people?

Adelman (1992) observes that most people believe the "mentally retarded" label is a well-defined, scientifically determined, unambiguous way to categorize human beings: It is not. In the early 1900s, people with Down Syndrome were considered profoundly retarded; today, it is estimated that 20% to 50% of people with Down Syndrome are mildly retarded. In 1952, the American Psychological Association (APA) recommended institutionalization of people with IQs less than 50 who were considered severely retarded. The current conclusion of the APA is that half of those with IQs of less than 50 can be considered moderately retarded and that neither moderate nor severely retarded individuals require continuous custodial care. In 1973, the American Association on Mental Deficiency eliminated the "borderline" category in its classification system when people of color protested the disproportionate number of racial and ethnic minority children so categorized (Kliewer and Biklin, 1996).

Another disability that professionals have been forced to re-evaluate is cerebral palsy. In 1960, experts assumed that 75% of people with cerebral palsy were retarded. After some alternative methods of communication and assessment were developed, from adaptations for typewriters to special computers, assumptions of mental retardation diminished significantly (Kliewer and Biklin, 1996).

The well-documented case of Sharisa Kochmeister illustrates how communication devices can make a significant difference. As a child, Sharisa was diagnosed as mentally retarded with a measured IQ of

15; then she learned to use a computer. Initially, someone held her hand while she hunted for letters on the keyboard; eventually, she could operate a computer independently. When she turned fifteen, her IQ was retested and her score was measured at 142. In a similar case, a seventeen-year-old girl with a previously measured IQ of 42 was asked what it felt like before she learned to communicate through her computer. She replied, "(As if) I was a clown in a world that was not a circus" (Kliewer and Biklin, 1996, p. 90). These examples of change reported in IQ evaluations, like the changes in defining labeled groups, do not reflect a transformation in the ability of the people being labeled; they do reflect a change in opportunities for those who were labeled as well as in the perceptions and assumptions of those responsible for the labeling.

How can negative attitudes be changed?

To create labels promoting a more positive image, the term *differently abled* has been proposed because it seems to emphasize the compensatory skills disabled people often develop to function effectively in society; the term has not garnered much support within the disability community. The use of *people with disabilities* began to be widely accepted in the 1970s as a substitute for *the disabled* and *the handicapped* (Linton, 1998). The term places people first to emphasize the humanity of the group and retains the word "disability" to acknowledge an existing mental or physical problem. Linton (1998) defined **people with disabilities** as referring to "people with behavioral or anatomical characteristics marked as deviant . . . that makes them targets of discrimination" (p. 12).

In an attempt to replace negative labels with positive terms, some have suggested using "challenged" instead of "impaired" when referring to visual or physical disabilities. Before comedians turned the idea into a joke, people in the disability community criticized the concept, saying challenges are confronted by individuals: Being "visually challenged" could be regarded as placing the burden on disabled people to overcome the challenge, thus exempting society from its responsibility to remove barriers that challenge people with disabilities (Russell, 1998).

Although there is no agreement in the United States regarding the acceptability of alternatives

> It is not the fact that [a person] cannot walk that is disabling but that society is organized for walking and not wheelchair-using individuals. [A person's] disability is not paraplegia but steps, pavement kerbs, buses and prejudiced shopkeepers.
>
> **Victor Finkelstein (Contemporary)**

such as *challenged* or *differently abled*, there is agreement on the offensiveness of negative terms such as *impaired, crippled,* and *handicapped*. These are words that contribute to the perception of people with disabilities being not just "disabled" but "unable," implying an inability to manage for themselves or to contribute to society. According to the World Health Organization, a disability is not a handicap. **Disability** refers to "a restriction of functional ability and activity caused by an impairment (e.g., hearing loss, reduced mobility)" whereas **handicap** generally is employed as a reference to "an environmental or attitudinal barrier that limits the opportunity for a person to participate fully in a role that is normal (depending on age, sex, and social and cultural factors) for that individual" (Bernell, 2003, p. 41).

Imagine a woman in a wheelchair approaching a building. Her legs do not function well enough for her to walk; the wheelchair provides mobility. As she nears the steps of the building, she discovers it has no access ramp. Now she is handicapped. She has found a way to be mobile, but due to the insensitivity or prejudice of the architect or building owners, the lack of a ramp is a barrier that denies her and any wheelchair user access to the building.

INSTITUTIONAL ABLEISM

Institutional ableism is a consequence of established laws, customs, and practices that systematically discriminate against people with disabilities. A unique consequence for this minority group has been their placement in institutions in the United States, comparable only to nineteenth century poorhouses for paupers. Poorhouses and poor farms have come and gone; yet institutions for people who have mental or physical disabilities remain, despite efforts in recent years to close them and to place people with disabilities into communities.

Why were people with disabilities placed in institutions?

The first institutions charged with caring for people with disabilities were hospices built within monasteries. An early reported example comes in the fourth century: a hospice for the blind at a monastery in Caesarea, now Turkey. According to the legend of St. Nicholas, as bishop of Mya in southwestern Turkey, he provided care for "idiots and imbeciles." For his efforts he was named the patron saint of the mentally retarded, although that part of his history was lost in his transformation into the American Santa Claus (Winzer, 1997). As monasteries were built in Europe, many included hospices to care for poor, homeless, or disabled people. Using hospices to satisfy Christian mandates to care for "the least of these" continued into the sixteenth century, when turmoil over church reforms created a schism termed the Reformation, resulting in Protestant churches as alternatives to the Catholic Church.

Even before the Reformation, the Catholic Church contributed to an increasingly negative attitude toward people with disabilities. St. Augustine sowed seeds for religious rejection when he refused to allow deaf people to become church members because of his literal interpretation of St. Paul (Romans 10:17): "Faith comes by hearing." During the Middle Ages, as Europe was devastated by plague and pestilence, especially the Black Death, fear fostered a growing hostility toward people exhibiting strange appearances or odd behavior (Barzun, 2000).

With the Reformation, monasteries were abandoned or forcibly closed and inhabitants evacuated. Communities were confronted with the problem of disabled people and beggars wandering the streets. Not surprisingly, attitudes toward the newly released people became increasingly negative. Laws were passed that vagrants be whipped (Ribton-Turner, 1972). By the fifteenth century, the Catholic Church declared a virtual war on witches, which resulted in the arrests, torture, and deaths of a great

many people who in some way were considered unusual or deviant. Evidence suggests that people who were mentally ill and people with disabilities were among the unfortunates serving as scapegoats.

The association with witchcraft often stemmed from people with mental retardation making odd comments or from mutterings of the mentally ill. Some citizens believed the strange talk was dialogue with the Devil; others regarded the conversations as divinely inspired. Whether they talked with God or the Devil, deviants were not tolerated on the streets. Some communities placed mentally retarded vagrants in the old city wall guard towers, which came to be called a "Fool's Tower" or "Idiot's Cage" (Winzer, 1997). In other communities, homeless people were charged with vagrancy, tortured, and expelled, or if they could work, they were forced into slavery (Ribton-Turner, 1972).

Reformation leaders John Calvin and Martin Luther did not question the prejudices behind this behavior; in fact, they contributed to them. According to Calvin, Satan possessed mentally retarded people; Luther believed Satan was responsible for fathering all mentally retarded children, and urged the parents of one mentally retarded child to drown it in a nearby river (Winzer, 1997).

When the centuries-old scourge of leprosy ended as the seventeenth century began, buildings used to quarantine lepers (leprosaria) became vacant. Communities found a solution to their dilemma of what to do with deviants: Europe initiated *the great confinement* to these newly christened "lunatic hospitals" (Foucault, 1965). Although the hospitals were initially used to house mentally ill people, they accepted "mental defectives," including people with various physical and mental disabilities, and eventually amassed a wide assortment of "defectives." Before long, only about 10% of inmates were considered insane in the average lunatic hospital. In addition to people with disabilities, other inmates included prostitutes, beggars, alcoholics, social dissidents, and people with syphilis (Winzer, 1997). Whereas hospices had protected disabled people from the wickedness of the world, lunatic hospitals protected the world from the wickedness of such morally, mentally, and physically deviant human beings.

It was apparent early on that hospitals could not provide treatment to rehabilitate inmates. The purpose of institutions was to remove defective people from society. Not surprisingly, the quality of "care" in such places was not good; rumors often circulated of inhumane treatment. In England, the Hospital of St. Mary of Bethlehem was referred to as "Bethlehem," which reduced to "Bedlam," coining a word to describe chaotic conditions there. By the nineteenth century, reformers visiting lunatic hospitals were appalled by the horrible conditions: some inmates wandering around naked and shivering, others chained to beds, some sitting in their own excrement, many bitten by rats or other vermin roaming the grounds. Reformers advocated for "moral treatment" of people in the institutions: eliminating chains, giving patients work, and treating patients with respect to develop self-esteem (Foucault, 1965).

Moral treatment involved not defining patients as deviant so much as regarding their defects as conditions requiring accommodations for them to function more effectively. Foucault (1965) tells the story of a mentally ill man who refused to eat because he thought he was dead and he was certain that dead people did not eat. One night, institutional staff came to the patient's bed looking pale, ashen, and dressed in clothing to simulate the look of a corpse. They brought in a table and some food, then sat down and began eating. When the patient asked why they were eating when they appeared to be dead, they replied that dead people had to eat like anyone else. They finished their meal and left. The next day the patient resumed eating. This approach was taken with patients who had mental or physical disabilities as well.

Instead of being defined as insurmountable deviance, *disability* gradually came to be regarded as a human condition; institutional staff began to provide accommodations to help individuals take better care of themselves and to function effectively with others. Although reforms were not universally applied, they constituted a practical alternative to the punitive treatment that had characterized previous institutional practices.

How were institutions for people with disabilities established in the United States?

When the United States entered the global community as a new nation, people with disabilities simply

> *Progress, far from consisting in change, depends on retentiveness. . . . Those who cannot remember the past are condemned to fulfill it.*
>
> **GEORGE SANTAYANA (1863–1952)**

lived in communities, primarily cared for by their families, although some religious facilities also provided care. Their situations varied widely—from being employed to being the town fool or even a pariah whom the family hid from the community. In nineteenth century America, attitudes toward people with disabilities were challenged. Americans were not to view people's disabilities as an act of God but instead in a biological context: rehabilitation was emphasized as the appropriate response.

Following the Civil War, a transformation of public attitudes seemed to be demonstrated by the construction of numerous institutions and residential schools that were often dedicated to a particular kind of disability. Institutionalizing people with disabilities was especially popular in urban areas, indicating a shift in responsibility for care from families and communities to the state as the nation moved into the twentieth century. Based on a biological view of human disability, the institutions were usually administered by people with medical training who claimed to use rehabilitative strategies. In reality, the function of institutions was usually custodial care—monitoring and restraining patients—reflecting ongoing negative American attitudes toward disabled people.

What evidence exists that negative attitudes prevailed in institutions and in society?

The negative attitude toward institutionalized patients is documented legal history. A 1913 Wisconsin law mandated the institutionalization of disabled people who constituted a "menace to society." A similar law passed the following year in Texas stated that people with disabilities mingling freely in the community was "a most baneful evil," describing people with disabilities as "defect(s) . . .

[that] wound our citizenry a thousand times more than any plague ... [they are] a blight on mankind" (Garrett History Brief, 2001, p. 72). Encouraged by the **eugenics** movement following World War I, every state in the United States passed laws singling out people with mental or physical disabilities for institutionalization. Some states went so far as to authorize the removal of children with disabilities from their homes, even against the wishes of parents.

With most disabled people confined to institutions, continuing prejudice was demonstrated in the 1930s when over thirty states enacted laws permitting involuntary sterilization of people in state funded institutions. Among the targets of this law were those identified as *feeble minded, idiots, morons,* and *mental defectives.* States justified their actions by claiming the need to eradicate the possibility of procreation for people who were such burdens on society (Russell, 1998; Garrett History Brief, 2001).

In Europe, German Nazis implemented a program of involuntary sterilization that was continued until the end of World War II. Subsequently, allies identified forced sterilization of people with disabilities for inclusion on the list of Nazi war crimes. Russell (1998) explained why it was deleted: "Allied authorities were unable to classify the sterilizations as war crimes, because similar laws had ... recently been upheld in the United States" (p. 22).

People with disabilities who were institutionalized in the United States were largely ignored until 1972, when Geraldo Rivera exposed the appalling conditions at New York's Willowbrook State School where "one hundred percent of all residents contracted hepatitis within six months of entering the institution.... Many lay on dayroom floors (naked) in their own feces" (Linton, 1998, p. 40). The description parallels conditions denounced by "moral treatment" reformers a century earlier, yet ten years after the Willowbrook scandal, problems persisted in American institutions. Linton (1988) cites a 1984 *New York Times* article about a community facility for physically and mentally disabled people in California that described staff serving spoiled food, not repairing malfunctioning toilets, and physically and sexually abusing patients.

FIGURE 13.3

The scandalous conditions at Willowbrook Institution finally got the attention of American society.

Source: Courtesy of the College of Staten Island Archives, Archives & Special Collections Department, College of Staten Island Libraries, CUNY.

Are institutions for people with disabilities providing good care today?

Although reduced in number, institutions for physically and mentally disabled people still exist despite the fact that national and state political leaders know they are harmful to the people in them. In 1996, a federal General Accounting Office (GAO) investigation of public institutions for mentally retarded people warned Congress of serious deficiencies in quality of care: "insufficient staffing, lack of active treatment and deficient medical and psychiatric care" (Garrett History Brief, 2001, p. 72). The GAO report described harm to residents including injuries, unnecessary illnesses, and physical degeneration—in a few instances the institutional "care" contributed to a resident's death.

Some states attempted to eliminate institutions by passing "deinstitutionalization" laws, but this has not solved the problem. When institutions have closed, residents are often relocated not to communities but to another form of institutional care—nursing homes. Care provided in nursing homes reportedly is no better, and is sometimes worse, than the care residents experienced in institutions (Russell, 1998).

What is the alternative to placing disabled people in institutions?

Instead of being placed in institutions, people with disabilities prefer to live in family homes or group homes in their communities. A 1996 federal court ruling found that some city zoning ordinances had limited or prevented the establishment of group homes in neighborhoods by including "density laws" restricting the number of "unrelated persons" in a house or the number of group homes within a certain area. Some cities have even passed so-called

> If our brothers are oppressed, then we are oppressed. If they hunger, we hunger. If their freedom is taken away, our freedom is not secure.
>
> **STEPHEN VINCENT BENÉT (1898–1943)**

"ugly laws" that forbid people with an unsightly appearance from appearing in public (Garrett History Brief, 2001, p. 72). The irony of such ordinances is that placing disabled people in communities to receive care not only increases their quality of life, it is also more cost-effective for taxpayers than providing care in nursing homes or institutions.

What is the cost of care for people with disabilities?

Taxpayers fund over 60% of the expenses for people with disabilities in nursing homes and institutions. Although people with disabilities overwhelmingly prefer to be cared for at home and require only minimal assistance, almost two million Americans with disabilities live in nursing homes at a cost of over $40,000 per person per year. According to Russell (1998), costs could total less than $10,000 per year to provide an individual with personal assistance services at home. State institutions are even more expensive: More than 75,000 people with developmental disabilities still live in state institutions at an average annual cost of more than $80,000 per person. Charlton (1998) estimated that the most expensive support system that could be created to provide adequate care for someone living in their own home within their community would cost no more than $30,000 per year.

Charlton (1998) reviewed numerous studies that consistently reported benefits for people with disabilities living in communities: "living at home, in a house or an apartment, is better psychologically, more fulfilling, and cheaper than living in nursing homes" (p. 47). By contrast, critics point out that nursing homes and institutions make substantial profits for private corporations while providing primarily low-wage jobs. As quoted in *Business First,* one private corporation providing "health care" said their three primary objectives were: "1. increase net profit, 2. increase net profit, and 3. increase net profit" (Russell, 1998, p. 103).

Advocates for **normalization** oppose confining disabled people in institutions. The concept refers to implementation of policies and practices to help create life conditions and opportunities for disabled people that are at least as good as those of average citizens. Normalization promotes strategies for disabled people to live and work in communities, and it challenges nondisabled people to eliminate barriers that prevent disabled people from being involved in community life. Based on the concept of normalization, disability advocates help people with disabilities move out of institutions and into communities, and they have lobbied for legislation to protect the civil rights of disabled people living in communities.

How do other countries respond to the needs of people with disabilities?

In 1995, the House of Representatives Ways and Means Committee reported that the United States spent less on long-term disability benefits than several European countries (Russell, 1998). Germany and Austria both provide cash benefits to disabled people regardless of their financial resources. Those receiving benefits can spend the money however they wish, including hiring family members to provide care. In Germany, cash benefits are half what can be obtained in service benefits, but it is at the discretion of the recipient to determine which kind of benefits to accept. Human services personnel pay random visits to recipients to assess the adequacy of their care. In 2000, Austria provided benefits for 310,000 people funded by general tax revenues, and Germany provided benefits for 1,280,000 people funded by a 1.7% tax on salaries and pensions, a cost shared by employers, employees, and retired workers (Batavia, 2002).

Austrian legislation has promoted hiring disabled workers, stipulating that for every twenty-five workers employed, one worker must be a disabled person. If the company fails to meet this standard, it is assessed a fine of approximately $155 a month that it must continue to pay until it hires the required number of disabled workers. Money collected from fines is retained in an account from which employers can receive funds to make physical modifications necessary to employ disabled workers (Koppelman, 2001).

In France, benefits to disabled people are not as generous as in Austria and Germany, but they exceed those of the United States. Benefits are based on financial resources of recipients, with a maximum national benefit. Local French governments responsible for providing benefits are funded from general tax revenues that supported approximately 86,000 people in 2000. Local agency representatives make annual home visits to recipients to assure that adequate services are being provided (Batavia, 2002).

How does the U.S. government provide support for people with disabilities?

European countries began providing social insurance and welfare assistance in the eighteenth and nineteenth centuries. In the United States, the federal Social Security program was established in 1935, although it did not include disabled people until the 1950s (Stone, 1984). Whereas European countries seem to have accepted their responsibility to provide care for disabled people, the United States has continually questioned its obligation. In 1996, Congress voted to add $320 million to the Social Security Administration, doubling the budget, but not to assist more disabled people. The budget increase was designated to fund reviews of recipients to determine if they could be removed from the list of those eligible for disability benefits. Ironically, that same year, Congress provided approximately $32 million for programs to protect disabled people from being discriminated against in hiring decisions (Russell, 1998).

The 1990 Americans with Disabilities Act (ADA) was enacted to prevent discrimination against people with disabilities. In the first four years after the law was passed, 3,600 complaints were filed charging employer hiring practices with discrimination against disabled workers: The Equal Employment Opportunities Commission (EEOC) approved 28 to be pursued in court. By 1995, the EEOC reported a backlog of over 20,000 complaints filed by people with disabilities concerning allegations of discrimination (Russell, 1998).

How does the United States support people with disabilities who want to live independently?

In 1973, the Supplemental Security Income (SSI) program was created to assist people with disabilities. The means-tested program offers a range of $400–$700 per month, but recipients must remain without other means of support to receive SSI funds. If recipients make extra money to be more financially secure, they are likely to lose the benefit.

In one case that exemplifies SSI policy, Lynn Thompson, a quadriplegic, was attempting to live on SSI payments of about $600 a month when she began earning extra income at home stuffing envelopes. After she reported her earnings, Social Security officials declared her income in excess of allowable limits and ordered her to return $10,000 of the benefits received or, if she couldn't pay the money, her benefits would be terminated until that amount was withheld. Termination of her benefits meant Thompson could no longer afford to hire a personal care attendant and she would need to leave her home and enter a nursing home. Thompson fought to overturn this decision, but the legal battle dragged on. Ms. Thompson committed suicide rather than be forced into a nursing home (Russell, 1998).

Is there discrimination against disabled people living in communities?

People with disabilities who are fortunate enough not to be institutionalized also encounter discrimination in the community. Hahn (1988) described the problems:

> Disabled persons have not only exhibited one of the highest rates of unemployment, welfare dependency, and poverty in the United States; but they also have experienced a more pervasive form of segregation in education, housing, transportation, and public accommodations than the most rigid policies of apartheid enacted by racist governments. (p. 26)

In addition to housing, already discussed, disabled people experience discrimination in four critical areas: jobs, mobility/accessibility, health care, and education.

Jobs Because of the shortage of men, women were hired for traditional male jobs during World War II; employment of people with disabilities also increased during the war. As was true for women workers, unemployment rates for disabled people increased after the war, as jobs were assigned to returning soldiers. The work performance of people with disabilities during the war proved that they not only wanted jobs, but they could perform their tasks competently. This lesson has apparently been lost on employers: Ongoing documentation reveals that people with disabilities continue to be discriminated against in hiring decisions.

As reported in the U.S. Current Population Survey database in 1998, 26.6% of disabled people were employed, yet a survey by the National Organization on Disability reported that 66% of working-age disabled adults want to work rather than rely on SSI benefits. Of disabled people who work, 80% are employed in sheltered workshops that hire only disabled workers for as little as 20% to 30% of the minimum wage, often earning as little as $11 a week. Although the unemployment rate was less than 4% in the late 1990s, unemployment for working-age disabled adults maintained the same range—from 65% to 71%—reaching a high of 80% in 2000 according to Harris poll data analyzed by Sowers, McLean, and Owens (2002).

In a case illustrating the difficulties of finding work, a disabled man in Maine with a PhD in chemistry asked the state agency for assistance in finding a job. The agency sent him to the Goodwill store to be trained to sort socks. Another case occurred in Rhode Island where the vocational rehabilitation agency refused to provide further education to a quadriplegic man, arguing that he was adequately taken care of by SSI benefits (Garrett History Brief, 2001). A 1987 Congressional survey of twenty-three state and local government agencies found that none was willing to hire blind applicants; many discriminated against applicants who had a history of cancer or who were amputees. Not surprisingly, the study concluded: "Public and private employers tend to be unaware of the capability of persons with developmental disabilities to be engaged competitive work in integrated settings" (Garrett History Brief, 2001, p. 70). Given this kind of discrimination, it should come as no surprise that

> I am not broken! I am not broken! I am a representative of the diversity of the human race.
>
> **NORMAN KUNC (CONTEMPORARY)**

in the United States, almost one-third of working-age adults with disabilities are living in poverty.

Mobility/Accessibility The ability of people in wheelchairs to function effectively in the community is affected by the existence of ramps, elevators, curb cuts, and wheelchair lifts on public buses. According to a Harris survey, 60% of people with disabilities report that their social, recreational, and employment opportunities are substantially limited due to lack of accessible public transportation. Accessibility problems have been cited as the reason why 40% of disabled people say they cannot participate in community activities such as attending church. Because of lack of access to buildings or restrooms, nondisabled people are twice as likely as disabled people to eat in a restaurant or socialize with friends, family, or neighbors at least once a week (Taylor, 1998). Accessibility problems can also impede a disabled citizen's right to vote. A 1996 study reported that almost 60% of New Hampshire's polling places were not accessible to disabled people, and a national study found that almost half of people with disabilities in their survey had experienced problems of accessibility at their polling places (Garrett History Brief, 2001).

Health Care Many disabled people encounter difficulty obtaining health insurance. The insurance industry openly uses personal health and genetic data in its review of potential clients: Health insurance organizations carry data on millions of Americans. Russell (1998) cited one study reporting that 47% of applicants identified to be screened for "defects" were ultimately denied health insurance—even though no defects were found. In addition, disabled people are twice as likely as nondisabled people to report that they did not receive needed medical services in the previous year (Taylor, 1998). People with disabilities receiving medical benefits from the U.S. government can jeopardize their health care just by taking a job. Once they are covered by an employer's health care plan, they can lose their federally funded medical benefits. Often, it takes up to two years to reclaim and receive federally funded health care if individuals with disabilities lose their jobs.

Education With the advent of mainstreaming and inclusion, schools have been challenged to integrate disabled students into regular classrooms with nondisabled students. The term **mainstreaming** means that students with disabilities are taught in the "least restrictive" and most acceptable available environment. Integrating disabled and nondisabled students is supported by studies reporting that exceptional children with physical or mental disabilities learned more when they were integrated

FIGURE 13.4

In the 1980s, Berke Breathed's "Bloom County" was one of the first comic strips to feature a character using a wheelchair.

Source: © 1982, The Washington Post Writer's Group. Reprinted with permission.

into regular classes than when they were taught in separate classes (Hines, 2001; Kochhar, West, and Taymans, 2000). Despite the research, administrators and teachers often object to mainstreaming. At a U.S. congressional hearing, legislators were informed of a girl in a wheelchair being denied admission to a public school because the principal decided she was a "fire hazard" (Garrett History Brief, 2001).

Because of such resistance, mainstreaming efforts vary widely in U.S. schools, causing disability advocates to favor **inclusion,** a more aggressive approach requiring total integration of students with disabilities into regular education classrooms. Opponents argue that disabled students take too much of teachers' time, that it is unfair to nondisabled students. Advocates for inclusion argue that teachers can utilize aides, peers, and classroom strategies to ensure that all students receive an appropriate educational experience. Linton (1998) insisted that inclusion "is not an educational plan to benefit disabled children. It is a model for educating all children equitably" (p. 61).

Inclusion advocates argue that the presence of disabled students can benefit nondisabled students by providing opportunities to develop attitudes and skills that enable them to work with people who may be different from themselves (Sapon-Shevin, 1999). Despite the efforts of inclusion advocates, school districts still may designate schools where all students with disabilities are assigned. One study found that 10% to 55% of students with severe disabilities were not allowed to attend their neighborhood schools (Garrett History Brief, 2001).

Disability advocates contend that most problems for people with disabilities stem from the attitudes of the nondisabled. Although many individuals and organizations advocate for people with disabilities and the Americans with Disabilities (ADA) provides legal recourse against discrimination, actions cannot be effective if nondisabled people perpetuate negative attitudes. Children are curious and interested in human differences; they do not demonstrate a fear of differences unless taught to do so (Coleman, 1997). Inclusion may be the most important long-term strategy to improve attitudes and increase opportunities for people with disabilities since it provides opportunities for interaction with nondisabled students and for teachers to model positive attitudes.

How difficult is it to change people's attitudes?

As Fiedler (2000) wrote, "Perhaps the greatest obstacle to school change efforts is the attitudes of the individuals who must implement the change" (p. 119). The effectiveness of school change efforts has varied according to the attitudes of the teachers and administrators involved; this is true for community change efforts as well. Posner (1979) described an incident from Israel illustrating the difficulties involved in changing attitudes. Two villages did not have enough orange pickers at harvest time, so they arranged for young men at a nearby institution for the mentally retarded to help with the harvest. Before the young men arrived, researchers came to the villages and conducted an attitude survey. The researchers reported that 66% of villagers said there should be no contact between retarded people and children; 68% thought retarded people should be permitted to work only in sheltered workshops; 95% said institutions were the best place for retarded people; 58% believed that retarded people should be forbidden to marry.

When the retarded workers came, they picked oranges with great care and an enthusiasm not often displayed by other workers. Workers were told that if fallen oranges had not been bruised they could be used; only the retarded men inspected oranges that had fallen or been dropped. The retarded men climbed to the tops of ladders to pick oranges from high branches; no other workers were willing to climb so high. As the days passed, townspeople invited the workers to join them for lunch and the retarded men played with the children from the village. When the harvest was over, the young men returned to their institution.

The researchers returned to conduct a second attitude survey to see if changes had occurred in the attitudes of village residents. They found that the same 66% still believed there should be no contact between retarded people and children; the same 68% still thought retarded people should not work alongside others; the same 95% said retarded people should be in institutions, and the same 58% believed they should not marry. But please, all the villagers asked, will you make sure they send those nice young men back again next year?

AFTERWORD

Our attitudes are resistant to change: Change occurs only when we first examine our attitudes for myths, misperceptions, or stereotypes. It is especially important for aspiring teachers to reflect on their attitudes since every teacher will teach children or youth with disabilities. But assessing personal attitudes is not only appropriate for teachers but for others as well: It is equally important for employers who have the choice of hiring a person with a disability and for employees who may work with that disabled person. According to Williams (2003), one out of five Americans—about 52 million people—has a disability. We can make a difference in the lives of people with disabilities who live in our communities. It is a choice each of us must make. If made wisely and compassionately, that choice will be a force for change.

> But in the ideal world, my differences, though noted, would not be devalued. Nor would I. Society would accept my experience as "disability culture," which would in turn be accepted as part of "human diversity." . . . In such a world, no one would mind being called Disabled.
>
> CAROL GILL (CONTEMPORARY)

TERMS AND DEFINITIONS

Ableism The determination of an individual's abilities based on his or her disabilities; any policy or practice promoting the belief that disabled people are inferior to able-bodied persons to justify discrimination against people with disabilities

Cultural ableism The societal promotion of negative beliefs and images concerning people with disabilities that tend to portray the less able as deviant or incompetent; an assumption of superiority by people or groups based upon physical, mental, and emotional attributes

Deviant/Deviancy Someone whose appearance or behavior differs from the norm, from acceptable standards, in society

Disability A restriction of functional ability and activity caused by an impairment (such as hearing loss or reduced mobility)

Eugenics The study of agencies under social control that may improve or repair the racial qualities of future generations, either physically or mentally

Handicap An environmental or attitudinal barrier that limits the opportunity for a person to participate fully in a role that is normal (depending on age, sex, and social and cultural factors) for that individual

Inclusion Integration of all students with a disability into regular education classrooms

Individual ableism Prejudiced attitudes and behavior against others based on the assumption that one's level of ability is deviant from the norm, demonstrated whenever someone responds by saying or doing something degrading or harmful about persons whose ability is looked upon as unacceptable

Institutional ableism Established laws, customs, and practices in a society that allow systematic discrimination against people with disabilities

Mainstreaming The responsibility of schools to educate all students, regardless of disability, in the least restrictive and most normally acceptable environment

Normalization Policies and practices that help create life conditions and opportunities for disabled people that are at least as good as those of average citizens

People with disabilities People with behavioral or anatomical characteristics marked as deviant, which identify them as targets for discrimination

REFERENCES

Adelman, H.S. (1992). The classification problem. In W. Stainback and S. Stainback (Eds.), *Controversial issues confronting special education: Divergent perspectives* (pp. 29–44). Boston: Allyn & Bacon.
Describes concerns, criticisms, and responses to labeling people in special education.

Barzun, J. (2000). *From dawn to decadence: 500 years of Western cultural life (1500 to the present)*. New York: HarperCollins.

Discusses significant historical events as well as the intellectual contributions of those individuals who have had a lasting impact on the culture of the Western world.

Batavia, A. (2002). Consumer direction, consumer choice, and the future of long-term care. In L. Powers (Ed.), *Journal of Disability Policy Studies 13*(2), 67–73.

Describes home care as an alternative to institutional care in the United States and other nations.

Batavia, A. (2001). The new paternalism: Portraying people with disabilities as an oppressed minority. *Journal of Disability Policy Studies 12*(2), 107–113.

Critiques the other articles in this issue that provide evidence or analysis supporting the idea that people with a disability represent an oppressed minority group.

Bernell, S. (2003). Theoretical and applied issues in defining disability in labor market research. *Journal of Disability Policy Studies 14*(1), 36–45.

Reviews various definitions of disability and examines problems related to definitions and research methods in labor market research.

Charlton, J.I. (1998). *Nothing about us without us*. Berkeley: University of California Press.

Describes the status of people with disabilities in various cultures and compares it with the treatment that people with disabilities in the United States receive.

Coleman, L.M. (1997). Stigma. In L. Davis (Ed.), *The disability studies reader* (pp. 216–233). New York: Routledge.

Discusses the origin of the concept of stigma and analyzes the reasons why some differences in human beings are valued and others are stigmatized.

Ervelles, N. (2001). In search of the disabled subject. In J.C. Wilson & C. Lewicki-Wilson (Eds.), *Embodied rhetorics: Disability in language and culture* (pp. 92–111). Carbondale: Southern Illinois University Press.

Explains how social differences such as disability, gender, race, and social class have been produced by and still operate within the context of global economic exploitation.

Fiedler, C. (2000). *Making a difference: Advocacy competencies for special education professionals*. Boston: Allyn & Bacon.

Discusses the need for teachers and parents to be advocates for people with disabilities and provides strategies, examples, and resources for being an effective advocate.

Fiedler, C., & Rylance, B. (Eds.). (2001, Fall). *Journal of Disability Policy Studies 12*(2).

Addresses the question of whether or not disabled people constitute a minority group.

Fiedler, L. (1978). *Freaks: Myths and images of the secret self*. New York: Simon & Schuster.

Provides a history of people with disabilities and deformities, describing how they were viewed in the past and how these perceptions have shaped contemporary attitudes.

Foucault, M. (1965). *Madness and civilization: A history of insanity in the age of reason*. New York: Mentor Books.

Describes perceptions of madness, the institutionalization of mentally ill people, and their treatment in such institutions from the Middle Ages to the eighteenth century.

Franks, B. (2001). Gutting the golden goose: Disability in Grimms' fairy tales. In J.C. Wilson & C. Lewicki-Wilson (Eds.), *Embodied rhetorics: Disability in language and culture* (pp. 244–258). Carbondale: Southern Illinois University Press.

Examines the first 100 fairy tales in the Brothers Grimm collection to identify and describe how characters with a disability are portrayed.

Garrett History Brief. (2001). *Journal of Disability Policy Studies 12*(2), 70–78.

Presents historical and contemporary evidence of discrimination against disabled people.

Gill, C.J. (1994). Questioning continuum. In B. Shaw (Ed.), *The ragged edge: The disability experience from the pages of the first fifteen years of "The Disability Rag"* (pp. 42–49). Louisville, KY: The Advocado Press.

Argues that placing all people at some point along a continuum of disability reflects a discomfort with differences and is an attempt to minimize them.

Hahn, H. (1988, Winter). Can disability be beautiful? *Social Policy 18*, 26–32.

Examines cross-cultural perceptions of people with a disability and provides historic examples of disabled people being valued for their differences.

Hines, R.A. (2001). *Inclusion in Middle Schools*. (Report No. EDO-PS-01-13). Champaign, IL: ERIC Clearinghouse on Elementary and Early Childhood Education, Children's Research Center, University of Illinois. (ERIC Document Reproduction Service No. 459000).

Discusses research on inclusion and benefits for nondisabled and disabled students.

Kliewer, C., & Biklin, D. (1996). Labeling: Who wants to be called retarded? In J. Stainbeck & S. Stainbeck (Eds.), *Controversial issues confronting special education: Divergent perspectives* (pp. 83–95). Baltimore: Brookes.

Describes changes in labeling people mentally retarded in the past and currently, and the changing perspectives on independent living for those individuals who have been labeled.

Kochhar, C.A., West, L.L., & Taymans, J.M. (2000). *Successful inclusion: Practical strategies for a shared responsibility.* Upper Saddle River, NJ: Prentice-Hall.

Describes the history and philosophy of inclusion and successful classroom practices; the benefits of inclusion are described in Chapter 9, pp. 37–40.

Koppelman, K. (2001). The only thing we have to fear. *Values in the key of life: Making harmony in the human community* (pp. 24–28). Amityville, NY: Baywood.

Uses a personal example to discuss the inadequate social services available in the United States, and compares U.S. social services with social services in Austria.

Linton, S. (1998). *Claiming disability: Knowledge and identity.* New York: New York University Press.

Discusses the need for disability studies to understand the experience of disabled people as a minority group; defines ableism and other relevant terms in Chapter 2, pp. 8–33.

Pelka, F. (1994, July/August). Hating the sick: Health chauvinism and its cure. *Humanist 54*(4), 17–21.

Examines current evidence that attitudes in the United States reflect a "health chauvinist society" that is prejudiced against disabled people and blames them for having a disability.

Posner, B. (1979). Israel: A tale of two people. *Disabled USA 2*(8), 16–17.

Describes negative attitudes in the United States toward people who are mentally retarded and uses an incident from Israel to illustrate the difficulty of changing such attitudes.

Ribton-Turner, C.J. (1972). *A history of vagrants and vagrancy.* Montclair, NJ: Patterson Smith.

Describes the history of societal responses to vagrancy primarily in England, but with chapters on Russia, Turkey, and countries in Western Europe (first published in 1887).

Russell, M. (1998). *Beyond ramps: Disability at the end of the social contract.* Monroe, ME: Common Courage Press.

Examines historical examples of the oppression of disabled people and contemporary issues concerning poverty, institutionalization, and denial of civil rights.

Sapon-Shevin, M. (1999). *Because we can change the world: A practical guide to building cooperative, inclusive classroom communities.* Boston: Allyn & Bacon.

Provides strategies and activities that reflect principles of multicultural education although primarily intended for creating cohesive classrooms in elementary schools.

Sowers, J., McLean, D., & Owens, C. (2002). Self-directed employment for people with developmental disabilities: Issues, characteristics, and illustrations. *Journal of Disability Policy Studies 13*(2), 96–103.

Describes a customer-directed employment service system and provides an example of how such an approach can more effectively find employment for people with disabilities.

Stone, D.A. (1984). *The disabled state.* Philadelphia: Temple University Press.

Discusses the complex issues affecting the medical basis for determining who is disabled and eligible for disability benefits and who is not.

Taylor, H. (1998). Americans with disabilities still pervasively disadvantaged on a broad range of key indicators. *Harris Poll #56.* Retrieved July 30, 2003, from *http://www. harrisinteractive.com*

Presents results of the Harris Poll on issues for people with disabilities.

Wehmeyer, M. (2000, Summer). Riding the third wave. *Focus on Autism & Other Developmental Disabilities 15*(2), 106–116.

Describes three waves of the disability movement with professionalism superseded by the parent movement that is now being challenged by those promoting self-advocacy.

Williams, C. (2003). Managing individuals in a diverse work force. In *Management* (2nd ed., pp. 434–471). Versailles, KY: Thompson Southwestern.

Explains why diversity is being promoted in the corporate world, the benefits of diversity, and principles for being an effective manager of diverse employees.

Wilson, J.C., & Lewicki-Wilson, C. (2001). Disability, rhetoric, and the body. In J.C. Wilson & C. Lewicki-Wilson (Eds.), *Embodied rhetorics: Disability in language and culture* (pp. 1–24). Carbondale: Southern Illinois University Press.

Examines the relationship between language and behavior and describes how rhetorical analysis can be an aid for people with disabilities as they define themselves.

Winzer, M.A. (1997). Disability and society before the Eighteenth Century: Dread and despair. In L. Davis (Ed.), *The disability studies reader* (pp. 75–109). London: Routledge.

Describes the experiences of disabled people from ancient times including how they were portrayed in literature and the evolution of institutions to care for them.

Wolfensberger, W. (1970). *The principle of normalization in human services.* Toronto: National Institute on Mental Retardation.

Analyzes the role of ideology and concepts of deviancy in shaping attitudes toward disabled people; describes how the principle of normalization could change human services.

Summary Exercises

See page 19 for exercises to help you summarize the main points and define key terms in this chapter.

Personal Clarification Exercises

In Chapter 13, two exercises promote discussion about physical, emotional, and mental disabilities.

Clarification Exercise #1 Tolerance vs. Control: Group Home Discussion Activity

Directions: Realizing the limitations and abilities of a developmentally disabled individual, which of these activities—listed below under four general areas of human behavior—should a mentally retarded (MR), cerebral palsied (CP), epileptic (E), or physically disabled (PD) person be allowed to do? Write "all" under the "should" or "should not" column if you feel that all people having the aforementioned disabilities should or should not be allowed to do the particular activity. If you want to make a distinction, write the abbreviation for the particular disability. For example, if you feel that all disabled persons except for the mentally retarded should be allowed to engage in a particular activity, then place an MR in the "should not" column and the initials of the other three in the "should" column.

Category/Action	Should	Should Not	Comment
I. Interpersonal Relationships			
1. Date	____	____	_____
2. Engage in sexual activities	____	____	_____
3. Use birth control devices	____	____	_____
4. Marry	____	____	_____
5. Have and raise children	____	____	_____
II. Lifestyle Concerns			
1. Choose their own clothing	____	____	_____
2. Dress and look the way they want	____	____	_____
3. Participate actively in the church of their choice	____	____	_____
4. Plan their own leisure time	____	____	_____
5. Engage in recreational activities of their choice	____	____	_____
III. Economic Issues			
1. Choose the job they want	____	____	_____
2. Support themselves	____	____	_____
3. Be financially independent	____	____	_____
4. Enter into contracts	____	____	_____
5. Live where they choose	____	____	_____
IV. Rights and Responsibilities			
1. Vote in political elections	____	____	_____
2. Drive a car	____	____	_____
3. Drink beer and/or liquor	____	____	_____
4. Have medical insurance	____	____	_____
5. Be educated to their fullest potential	____	____	_____
6. Be held responsible for their actions	____	____	_____

Clarification Exercise #2 "I Only Wanted to Help" Attitude Analysis

Directions: Participating with others in the class, read aloud the position paper below that was written by a college professor regarding his disposition toward college students with disabilities. Then, after reading the document, as a person with a disability, propose your reply to two questions: What accommodations and dispositions does the author demonstrate regarding students with disabilities? and How else might college professors provide disabled students with equitable opportunity for learning, make appropriate "reasonable accommodations," and yet not treat them in a way that encourages and reinforces dependency or that belittles and insults?

"I Only Wanted to Help" Attitude Analysis

As I reflect on my years of teaching, I see many situations where I used different standards of grading and evaluations for disabled and able-bodied students. At first my double standards were fairly blatant, but I had all sorts of "good" rationalizations to support them. For example: "They haven't been adequately prepared by the system, so I shouldn't expect them to perform at the same level." Or, "It takes them more time and effort to accomplish the same as other students, so I should adjust my evaluation accordingly." Or, "They've worked so hard to get this far, I can't blow it for them now."

I have come to realize that by using these rationalizations as justification for differential grading, I was continuing to foster dependency in disabled students. I was giving them a false picture of their abilities and successes and I was not giving them opportunities to grow by confrontation with critical feedback and honest challenges; however, I was not yet ready to take the risk of allowing my disabled students their right to learn from honest criticism and even failure. After all, by not grading so hard it was easier to see myself as a helping person; therefore, my rationalizations became even more subtle, "I'll evaluate them on the basis of how much improvement they exhibit from the beginning to the end of the course."

But this was just avoiding the issue and in the end was just as unequal, because I was not applying the same criteria to other students. Another thing I found myself doing was over-praising disabled students. If they did anything, I would tell them how well they did. This hap-

pened most frequently with good students. I was so pleased to see a disabled student perform well that I reinforced them as if they had done even better. What such behavior revealed was my own prejudice reflected in the lower expectations that I had for my disabled students. And once again, I was giving them a false sense of their abilities.

Although all of these excuses and rationalizations still tempt me, I think I've finally come to the realization that I cannot justify unequal standards for my able-bodied and disabled students. Whenever I do, I am facilitating the continued dependence of disabled students and making it even harder for them to deal with the real world.

Now, I don't mean to suggest that I have no responsibilities to disabled students beyond those I have to able-bodied students. I do indeed have many additional responsibilities, and these vary extensively with the type and severity of the disability. For example, it may mean that for students with certain visual and coordination problems I may have to make my texts available several months in advance for taping and, working with the student, I will probably have to make arrangements for test taking, writing papers, and so on.

These kinds of "reasonable accommodations" do mean more work for the instructor. In fact, that may be one distinction between fair accommodation and differential grading. It doesn't take any effort on my part to simply give someone a better grade than they deserve. But it may take a lot of effort to make sure that every student has an equal opportunity to learn in my classes. At the same time, the disabled student must also take significant responsibility for his or her own education and behavior and not expect me to do it all. The dividing line between reasonable accommodation and differential treatment is not always clear, but I must accept the necessity of continually living in the tension of attempting to distinguish between the two.

It should also be said that as I begin to expect disabled students to take responsibility for their own education, I may encounter some who have never been expected to be responsible and who may get angry at me for what they perceive to be excessive demands. I need to be prepared for this reaction and to deal with it creatively, helping the student learn from his or her own responses to this situation.

Finally, there are times when my responsibility moves beyond the classroom to intervention within the institution itself. If I have disabled students who simply should not be in college, I owe it to them to be honest with them.

I must give them an honest grade and help them explore alternatives rather than just pass them through, but I must also confront the admissions office (or whoever makes those decisions) for admitting students who lack the appropriate minimal skills and abilities to be in college. And I must press for action in the public schools so that disabled students get the skills they need much earlier. In short, I must become an advocate for change so that disabled students are treated honestly and fairly from the start.

JOEL MUGGE—AUGSBURG COLLEGE
ADAPTED FROM: *ACCESS AWARENESS NEWSLETTER*
VOL. 2, NO. 2, NOVEMBER 1980

Intergroup or Individual Exercises

In Chapter 13, two exercises promote discussion about physical, emotional, and mental disabilities.

Intergroup Exercise #1 Disability Awareness Activity

Directions: What is a disability? How much do we know about disabilities? How prevalent are our disabilities? For this activity, take turns listing disabilities in your group or create team lists to share.

Part One: Utilize your instructor, group leader, or designated recording secretary to list *all* the disabilities that you can think of; you will be reminded of additional disabilities as you listen to the suggestions of others. Rotate the turn taking for at least five rounds; if you have no disability to suggest, indicate that you "Pass" to allow others opportunity to contribute. Attempt to identify at least 150 different disabilities. "Paraplegic" may be combined with "quadriplegic" for example, in order that there be room for a wide representation of true human disabilities. Take time for discussion and clarification as needed to be certain that all members of the group understand each disability.

Part Two: As a group, sort your disabilities list into three principal groups: physical, emotional or chemical. (For example, Multiple Sclerosis is a physical degeneration of one's muscular system; schizophrenia is commonly identified as a brain chemistry imbalance.) If you are uncertain of the category of a disability, discuss it with others and investigate to be

sure. Recall from the chapter that disabilities may be permanent or temporary, evident and observable, or invisible.

Part Three: Based upon the activity in which you participated, make three generalizations regarding how humans are different according to disability. (For example: Do you suggest any policy modification that would more readily accommodate persons with disabilities? Can you venture estimates of instances of unjustifiable discrimination against persons with disabilities? What attitudinal adjustments might be made within the general United States population regarding our attitudes toward persons with disabilities?)

Intergroup Exercise #2 Difficult Dialogues Experience

Directions: In groups of three, develop a dialogue based upon the scenario below. Use the situation as the basis for your 5-minute role play of the situation. Remain in character at the conclusion of your skit and respond to class questions about the motivation, purpose, or intent behind your comments during the scene. Each team of three is asked to complete a 5-minute role play, regardless of similarity to others performed.

Difficult Dialogues: Physical Facility Handicaps and the Common Student

Characters:

- Wheelchair user who is a graduate teaching assistant
- Undergraduate third-year business management major
- University classroom building custodian [See below]

As a custodian is working in a hallway between classes, a teaching assistant asks her for help to circumvent an open door very near the top of a staircase in order to safely reach the elevator that is behind the door. The business major makes a rather unkind remark about the limited nature of students with disabilities on the campus and makes her way down the steps.

The Challenge of Diversity to American Institutions

This section will describe the changes in the United States that take advantage of American population diversity.

Elementary, middle, and secondary schools have historically been considered the vehicle by which we transmit our cultural values and knowledge to future generations, and Chapter 14 describes the philosophy and practices of school multicultural education curriculums. Following a brief review of America's traditional educational philosophy known as "essentialism," this chapter describes the changes necessary to create schools and classrooms where policies, practices, curricu-

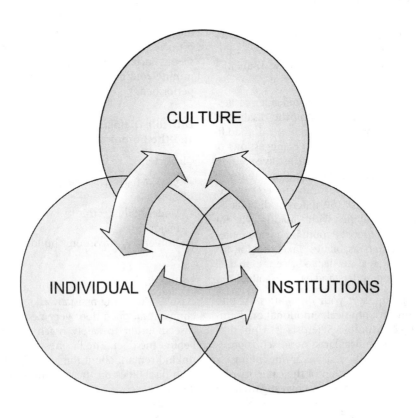

lum, and instruction reflect the purposes and goals of multicultural education. The chapter concludes with an explanation of why multicultural education represents an educational reform that needs to be pursued for the benefit
of all our students and for the future of our diverse society.

Currently, considerable effort is being made to instill in the American workforce a more inclusive attitude toward diversity. Chapter 15 describes changes occurring in major institutions of our society that reflect the growing influence of pluralism as the preferred perspective in response to the ongoing and growing diversity of the American people. Our government continues to require affirmative action plans to ensure that opportunities are provided to members of groups that were discriminated against in the past and continue to be discriminated against. Higher education administrators have embraced the value of affirmative plans to broaden the diversity of faculty as well as student populations and to argue that such diversity enhances the education of all students.

In the corporate world, business leaders have recognized the growing diversity of the workforce and consumers and are increasingly implementing diversity training to take advantage of both. Mass media organizations have promoted diversity by placing more women and people of color in positions that have a high public visibility, and the diversity in this profession is likely to increase given the significantly increasing numbers of women and people of color currently majoring in journalism or mass communication on college campuses. The military has taken aggressive action to promote gender and racial equality in its recruitment, in promotion policies and practices, and in its diversity training programs.

Change occurring in institutions across the United States reinforces the need to prepare new generations to appreciate and participate effectively in the unique and increasing diversity that defines our American society in the twenty-first century.

CHAPTER 14

Pluralism in Schools: The Promise of Multicultural Education

"Learning to read was, for slaves, not an immediate passport to freedom but rather a way of gaining access to one of the powerful instruments of their oppressors: the book."

ALBERTO MANGUEL (1948–)

Learning and schooling are critical for every person in any society. The future of our diverse society will depend upon how schools educate the coming generations, and pluralism must be a significant factor in that education. During an interview for a college administrative position, an African American candidate asked about his views on diversity responded, "First, let me say that I'm a pluralist. After all, we had a diverse society when we had slaves." This is an important distinction. Many people refer to *diversity* and *pluralism* as if the two terms were synonymous, but diversity simply describes the existence of many different groups of people within a society, while pluralism describes a society in which diversity is accepted and supported. A pluralistic society is one in which diverse groups function together effectively with mutual respect. In a society that is diverse but not pluralistic, schools tend to teach principally about the dominant group—its influence on the evolution of society, and its literature, art, and music. In a diverse society committed to pluralism, schools would teach about all groups within the society, from most ancient to most recent.

Misunderstanding of terms occurs when we fail to clarify meanings and intentions. No study of human differences is complete without special terms, and precise communication exists only when everyone involved is clear about their meaning. So we must begin by clarifying our definition of multicultural education and explaining our vision of its importance for the future of our diverse society.

DEFINING MULTICULTURAL EDUCATION

Multicultural education is based on a commitment to pluralism; its guiding purpose is to prepare students to be active participants in a diverse, democratic society. There is confusion and considerable debate about multicultural education, even among educators who advocate for it. Some people regard multicultural education simply as the process of integrating issues and information about race and ethnicity into school curricula, but that describes what Banks (1994) defines as **multiethnic education.** Some regard multicultural education as a curriculum for teaching about cultures around the world, but that is usually called **global (or inter-**

national) education. Others say multicultural education includes recognition of women, gays and lesbians, people with disabilities, and other minority groups; opponents to this idea argue that such groups do not constitute distinct cultures and therefore should not be included. This confusion raises many questions that must be answered before we can understand what multicultural education is and recognize schools that are engaged in an authentic form of this educational approach.

In addition to conflicting opinions about the definition of the term *multicultural education* and about who should be included, there are numerous perceptions about who benefits from it. Americans seem to agree that students of color benefit from multicultural education, especially in urban multiracial and multiethnic classrooms; yet many educators and parents in suburban or rural school districts consisting predominantly or exclusively of white students appear to believe that multicultural education provides no benefits. Although some educators in the predominantly white elementary and secondary schools have added to their curriculums some names of people of color and their contributions to society and called the curriculum "multicultural," this is not what we mean by that term.

What does it mean for education to be called *multicultural*?

As early as 1974, Hilliard wrote that **multicultural** refers to a society "made up of a number of cultural groups based upon race, ethnicity, religion, language, nationality, income, etc." (p. 41). Since income level is not usually regarded as representing a different culture—rich or poor, we're all Americans—Hilliard's comment is assumed to mean that the term *multicultural* includes other subordinate groups that he did not specifically identify, such as women, gays and lesbians, and people with disabilities.

As for the term *education*, we must distinguish between *education* and *training*. Some dictionaries suggest that education and training are synonyms,

but people take classes to train them in a particular skill. A person can be trained to drive or cook, or even be trained to train a dog. Education is a broader concept. Partridge (1983) explained that *educate* derives from the Latin word *ducere* which means to lead; "educere" means to lead out or bring forth (p. 169). By extrapolation, *education* means to bring forth the potential of an individual. In addition to developing cognitive skill and affective sensitivity, education entails developing an understanding of previous achievements in subjects such as history, literature, and science as a basis for making individual and societal choices in the future. Carse (1986) distinguished education from training:

> Education discovers an increasing richness in the past because it sees what is unfinished there. Training regards the past as finished and the future to be finished. Education leads toward a continuing self-discovery; training leads toward a final self-definition. (p. 23)

Multicultural education integrates information about past issues with achievements of diverse groups to describe how they have influenced our society. Children and youth from all groups are thereby provided with a sense of belonging to our society by understanding how their group has helped to shape what it is and by appreciating the potential they have for influencing what it will become.

What is an appropriate definition for multicultural education?

Multicultural education is a journey that leads students to self-discovery and to a sense of personal efficacy. Nieto (2004) provides a comprehensive definition and description of multicultural education that includes the components to be addressed in this chapter:

> **Multicultural education** is a process of comprehensive school reform and basic education for all students. It challenges and rejects racism and other

FIGURE 14.1

Frank and Ernest

© 1998 Thaves / Reprinted with permission. Newspaper dist. by NEA, Inc.

forms of discrimination in schools and society and accepts and affirms the pluralism (ethnic, racial, linguistic, religious, economic, and gender, among others) that students, their communities, and teachers reflect. Multicultural education permeates the schools' curriculum and instructional strategies, as well as the interactions among teachers, students, and families, and the very way that schools conceptualize the nature of teaching and learning. Because it uses critical pedagogy as its underlying philosophy . . . multicultural education promotes democratic principles of social justice. (p. 346)

Nieto's definition and description of multicultural education emphasizes that it is not a "business-as-usual" approach to schooling. It requires changes in teaching methods and perspectives on learning because of critical philosophical differences between traditional education and multicultural education.

TRADITIONAL ASSUMPTIONS IN AMERICAN EDUCATION

The development of American schools has been based upon a conservative philosophy that was eventually labeled *essentialism*, and essentialist assumptions are still in place. The term stems from the belief that an essential body of knowledge and essential human values that have stood the test of time can be identified and transmitted to students. Essentialists describe the purpose of schools as the transmission of the most significant accumulated knowledge and values from previous generations to the coming generation.

What body of knowledge have essentialists identified?

Essentialist scholars maintain that knowledge from four disciplines is essential: social studies, science, mathematics, and English language and literature; therefore these four subjects are emphasized in elementary, middle, and high school. Graduation requirements for high school students usually include a minimum of two years of course work, often three or even four, in social studies, science, mathematics, and English. To essentialists, subjects such as art, music, and physical education are accepted principally to make school more enjoyable, but they are regarded as additional rather than essential. When administrators consider budget reductions, programs in art, music, and physical education are scrutinized and are most likely to be reduced or eliminated. Similar assumptions continue into college, where general education programs often require students to choose among a selection of courses in social studies, science, math, and English literature and composition.

What essential human values do schools teach?

As indicated in Chapter 1, Myrdal (1944) identified core American values embraced by most citizens and taught in most schools. In addition, Americans presume that certain values represent the American middle class: promptness, honesty, hard work, competitiveness, and efficiency. Teachers implement traditional approaches to teaching values (see Chapter 1) to convince children and youth that the core values are worthwhile and should be adopted. Students may say they believe in these values because it's expected of them, even though their behavior often does not suggest that they yet have genuine commitment.

How do essentialists define or describe learning?

Essentialists define learning as the acquisition of essential knowledge and values. Metaphors used by essentialists to describe learning portray knowledge as water and students as empty vessels to be filled or as sponges ready to absorb. To assess learning, essentialists favor objective tests with questions about factual information to ascertain if students absorbed the information. (If not, teachers may review the information and test students again.) In extreme cases, students may repeat a grade to have a second chance to learn material in the hope that the teacher, perhaps a different teacher, will be more successful helping them acquire the information. Maturity and readiness are considered secondary in this process.

> Teachers open the door, but you must enter by yourself.
>
> **CHINESE PROVERB**

What is the role of the essentialist teacher in helping students learn?

An essentialist teacher is supposed to be a skillful transmitter of information and an advocate for American values. Teachers are expected to be role models for our society's values—both inside and outside the classroom. As transmitters of information, teachers are expected to use technology to make information interesting and thereby promote acquisition of knowledge. Although teachers may select from a variety of pedagogical techniques, the goal is to motivate students to remember information provided in textbooks, lectures, and films. The problem is that few students can demonstrate that they are learning what teachers are teaching.

Why are students not learning in essentialist schools?

The first problem has to do with what has been considered essential. During the past several decades, research in various fields, especially the sciences, has generated what scholars have called a *knowledge explosion*. Given so much new knowledge, how is one to determine which facts are most important? Feminists and scholars of color have developed alternative interpretations of historical events that challenge conventional views; they believe their perspectives should be included in school curricula. Whereas women and writers of color were minimally represented in previous literature anthologies, advocates are increasingly demanding that their voices and ideas be acknowledged. Curriculum reformers suggest that most students regard traditional essentialist curriculum as inaccurate, irrelevant, and not at all motivational.

Another problem is that we know students learn at different rates. If teachers transmit information at the same rate, some students learn all of it, some learn most of it, and some very little of it; yet teachers often must proceed as if all students learned equally. The solution essentialists have developed to address incomplete learning is to group students according to ability, which known as *tracking*. Studies of tracking have found that excellent students learn just as well in heterogeneous groups as in homogeneous groups where they are grouped by ability, but that the achievement of moderate and slow learners improves significantly when they are in mixed groups rather than when they are grouped according to academic ability (Oakes, Quartz, Ryan, and Lipton, 2000; Oakes and Wells, 1996; Kershaw, 1992; Oakes, 1985). Despite these consistent research conclusions, essentialist schools tend to continue to group students according to ability.

Perhaps the most significant obstacle to learning in essentialist schools is the problem of retention and transfer. **Retention** refers to student recall of knowledge; **transfer** is the ability of students to apply that knowledge both inside and outside the classroom. Students have long complained about "cramming" before taking exams that require them to memorize material. Studies have consistently found that when tested for retention of information, students tend to recall no more than 20% of what they had "learned" the first time they took the exam.

ASSUMPTIONS OF MULTICULTURAL EDUCATION

In order to resolve problems related to student learning, as parents or educators, we must change our assumptions about curriculum content, learning, teaching, and the purpose of schools. As described by Nieto (2004), Banks (1999), Sleeter (1996) and others, multicultural education challenges us to change those assumptions.

What assumptions do multicultural educators make about curriculum?

Nieto's widely accepted 1996 definition of multicultural education includes an affirmation of diversity that must permeate the curriculum in order to provide honest representations of diversity in American society. At present, textbooks continue to be dominated by the art, music, history, literature, perspectives, and images of white Americans. Sleeter and Grant (1999) reviewed 47 textbooks in social studies, reading, language arts, science, and mathematics for elementary and middle level students. They reported that whites were featured predominantly in all of them. Although some improvements have been found in more recent textbooks, when people of color are included, the textbooks typically have provided:

A sketchy account of Black history and little sense of contemporary Black life. Asian Americans appear mainly as figures on the landscape with virtually no history or contemporary ethnic experience. . . . Native Americans appear mainly as historical figures. (p. 22)

American elementary, middle, and secondary textbooks also tend to omit or provide only minimal representation of other groups: women, gays and lesbians, people with disabilities, and low-income families. School textbooks not only represent a problem for minority children, but also are apt to teach white children a dishonest perspective of their society. As Baker (1983) explained, "Non-minority children are led to believe that their behavior, the

> It is probably never really wise, or even necessary, or anything better than harmful, to educate a human being toward a good end by telling him lies.
>
> **JAMES AGEE (1910–1955)**

ways they are taught to respond, are the only accepted ways of behaving" (p. 8). To present a realistic understanding of our multicultural society and the influence of diverse groups on our society, advocates support a multicultural curriculum for all students, not just for students of color.

A multicultural curriculum examines the influences of diverse groups on historical events, literary developments, musical styles, artistic expression, athletic achievements, and other facets of American society—but the goal is not simply to memorize facts. Appleton (1983) described multicultural curriculum as "a conceptual approach that provides a framework for understanding the experience and perspectives of all the groups" (p. 211). The need for a conceptual approach is another assumption about curriculum by multicultural educators.

Why is it necessary to take a conceptual approach to curriculum?

Because of the knowledge explosion, it is impractical to emphasize memorization. It is not possible for us to remember all available information in every subject; we also know that much information soon will be obsolete, supplanted by new knowledge. In a multicultural curriculum, understanding broad concepts is preferable to memorizing facts. Gay (1977) described a multicultural curriculum design based on a thematic approach and a conceptual framework. In the thematic approach, students employ information from different disciplines to explore universal themes such as the search for identity, communication and conflict resolution, human interdependence, economics and exploitation, or the struggle for a just society.

Curriculum based on a conceptual framework also requires an interdisciplinary approach. Beginning with a concept such as power, alienation, or socialization, students could collect data from various sources addressing the concept, leading them to the identification and exploration of related concepts. Gay (1977) argued that both curriculum designs must be interdisciplinary because they require "the use of knowledge, concepts, and principles from many different disciplines" (p. 101). In either a thematic or a conceptual framework approach, students examine past and present experiences to develop an integrated understanding of principles and relationships between concepts.

Because multicultural curriculum is based on concepts rather than on specific content, students are involved in an ongoing and dynamic search for knowledge that is never finished, whereas the monocultural curriculum traditionally presented in schools is a finished product. As Nieto (2004) wrote:

> When reality is presented in schools as static, finished, and flat, the underlying tensions, controversies, passions and problems faced by people throughout history and today disappear. (p. 358)

Identifying concepts for students to analyze and discuss in order to clarify their understanding is the foundation of multicultural curriculum; to be effective, it is critical that the curriculum not be sabotaged by the hidden curriculum in school.

What is the hidden curriculum?

Pai and Adler (1997) define **hidden curriculum** as the indirect means by which schools teach students "the norms and values of their society" (p. 148). They describe the hidden curriculum as subtle messages learned from pictures displayed on bulletin boards or from school policies such as tardy slips and tracking. Messages may be intentional or unintentional; still, they have an impact on learners. Through the hidden curriculum, schools can promote such values as punctuality, assertiveness, or competitiveness. Pai and Adler suggest that the hidden curriculum may vary according to socioeconomic status, with upper-class children being taught leadership skills and having opportunities for creativity and problem solving in contrast to low-income students being taught to respect authority and receiving rewards for compliance and conformity.

Everyday situations reveal a hidden curriculum in school policies and practices, and subtle messages can even be found in formal curriculum. An education professor entered a Los Angeles high school English classroom, where 80% of the students were Hispanic; she noticed that only white authors were featured on wall posters. An unmarried high school student was expelled from the local chapter of the National Honor Society because she was pregnant. A student teacher in a fourth-grade classroom of predominantly white students wanted to make a "Black History Month" bulletin board for February, but her supervising teacher rejected the idea because she believed that the students were "too young" for that.

Teaching that Columbus discovered America tells children that Native Americans were irrelevant and can be ignored; perhaps it is no coincidence that the white majority ignores Native Americans who protest Indian mascots for school sports teams. Brigham Young took his followers to Mexican territory because of the oppression and violence Mormons had encountered in the United States. Teaching that Mormons settled in Utah instead of Mexican territory implies that religious groups have always been able to practice their beliefs freely in the United States and ignores the difficulty America has experienced living up to the principle of religious freedom. Teaching that "old world art" refers only to ancient Greek and Roman cultures denies

> Until lions have their historians, tales of the hunt will always glorify the hunter.
>
> **AFRICAN PROVERB**

the artistic heritage of many—especially non-Western—countries. Nieto (2004) argued that presenting history only from the perspective of the dominant group teaches a skewed version of the truth. Educators implementing multicultural curricula must be especially sensitive to subtle messages provided by the hidden curriculum.

Why have schools implemented multicultural curriculum?

Many schools across the United States, especially in urban areas, have developed their own multicultural materials to supplement inadequate textbooks. Banks (1999) categorized the efforts into four approaches, two of which also satisfy Nieto's definition of multicultural education: the transformation approach and the social action approach (see Figure 14.2).

A *transformation* approach to multicultural curriculum design emphasizes concepts and themes. Students are presented with multiple perspectives on issues, and the goal is not to identify a "right perspective," but to understand how each perspective contributes to a richer understanding of issues. Critical thinking skills are emphasized as students develop their own insights and conclusions and logically justify them.

A *social action* approach to multicultural curriculum design encourages students to take action based upon their ideas and conclusions. Students—individually or collectively—pursue projects at school and in their community to address problems they identify and study. The goal of a social action approach is to empower students and to demonstrate that learning is not a game of *Trivial Pursuit:* Knowledge can lead to social action and create positive change. By encouraging critical thinking and

FIGURE 14.2

Approaches to Multicultural Curriculum Reform

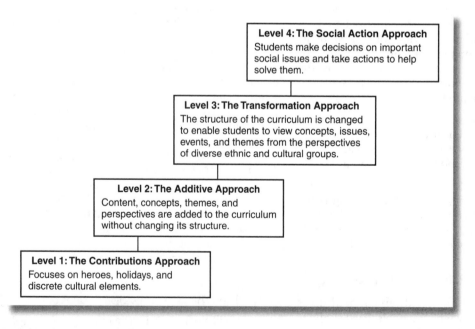

Level 4: The Social Action Approach
Students make decisions on important social issues and take actions to help solve them.

Level 3: The Transformation Approach
The structure of the curriculum is changed to enable students to view concepts, issues, events, and themes from the perspectives of diverse ethnic and cultural groups.

Level 2: The Additive Approach
Content, concepts, themes, and perspectives are added to the curriculum without changing its structure.

Level 1: The Contributions Approach
Focuses on heroes, holidays, and discrete cultural elements.

Source: From *Multicultural Education: Issues and Perspectives,* 9/e by James A. Banks and Cherry A. McGee Banks. Copyright © 2004. This material is used by permission of John Wiley & Sons, Inc.

active learning, multicultural educators combine theory and practice about conditions necessary to promote effective learning.

How do multicultural educators describe learning?

Advocates for multicultural education rely on cognitive development theory to describe how people learn. In essence, learning is a process of meaning making. Learners organize ideas, information, and experiences they encounter to make sense of them. They may categorize, seek relationships, and simplify complex issues to achieve understanding. According to Sleeter and Grant (1999), "Learning is a process of constructing knowledge through the interaction of mind and experience" (p. 196). Piaget (1974) observed that children learn by interacting physically and intellectually with their environment. If students are provided information through lecture, they may attempt to extract relevant meaning from it, but if they perceive no relevance in the information, they are not likely to make the effort.

Learning results from the interaction learners encounter when they are required to be active. Learning also requires meaningfulness. Information regarded as meaningless will not be learned. Being an active learner promotes the development of competence and confidence, the basis for Dewey's insistence that children "learn by doing." Feeling competent and gaining self-confidence leads to a sense of power. As Hilliard (1974) wrote, "Learning is related to a sense of power over some of the forces which impinge upon our lives" (p. 47). If students feel powerless, they have little motivation to learn; when students are active, they develop skills and demonstrate abilities that reinforce self-confidence and give a sense of personal competence, and they acquire an enthusiasm for learning.

With regard to skill development, learning must not be limited to basic academic skills—reading, writing, computing—but must include a multitude of skills related to critical thinking, creativity, decision making, problem solving, information accessing, interpersonal and cross-cultural communication, conflict resolution, visual literacy, and self-analysis. Gay (1977) argued that an education that "does not include the development of skills that will increase and enhance student's capabili-

> In every child who is born, under no matter what circumstances, and of no matter what parents, the potentiality of the human race is born again; and in (that child) . . . and in each of us, our terrific responsibility towards human life; toward the utmost idea of goodness.
>
> JAMES AGEE (1910–1955)

ties to live and function in a culturally pluralistic setting is incomplete" (p. 98). Although students may develop skills, an obstacle to facilitating skill development is that students have multiple ways of learning; therefore a single teaching strategy may be inadequate. Teachers committed to multicultural education must believe that all children can learn—if learning activities are designed to accommodate each child.

In what different ways do individuals learn?

Considerable research has been conducted to identify and explain styles of learning, but the result has been to categorize learning so specifically that, as Nieto (2004) said, "As many as 14 learning styles and 13 different learning style theories have been suggested" (p. 150). In recent years, multicultural educators have been attracted to the work of Gardner (1993), whose theory of multiple intelligences is regarded by many as one of the best explanations of the diversity in learning. Gardner defines intelligence as the ability to process information and to generate solutions or products of value within in a particular context.

Gardner identified eight distinct ways that people demonstrate intelligence (see Table 14.1). According to Gardner, each person has the potential to engage in all nine means of processing information, although an individual is likely to be more competent in certain dimensions based on personal idiosyncrasies or as influenced by his or her culture. The theory rejects the educational practice of

TABLE 14.1

Descriptions of
Multiple
Intelligences

1. *Logical-Mathematical:* Ability to understand and solve logical problems, especially involving the use and manipulation of numbers.
2. *Linguistic:* Ability to understand nuances of meanings and multiple meanings of words, including a special appreciation for the sounds and rhythms of language.
3. *Bodily-Kinesthetic:* Ability to learn and master physical tasks involving motion and balance, and including manual manipulation of objects.
4. *Musical:* Ability to understand, reproduce, and appreciate musical sounds and rhythms in a range of musical expressions.
5. *Spatial:* Ability to understand spatial relationships in the environment and to cognitively modify those relationships for particular purposes.
6. *Interpersonal:* Sensitivity to nonverbal expressions of feelings and desires of other people and the ability to respond appropriately to them.
7. *Intrapersonal:* Ability for self-analysis, to understand clearly one's own feelings and desires and to apply that knowledge in one's choices and behaviors.
8. *Naturalist:* Ability to discern similarities and differences in plants and animals that leads to an enhanced understanding of established classifications.

Source: Gardner (1993).

recognizing and rewarding primarily two intelligences: logical-mathematical and linguistic. Gardner's theory describes a more complete means of understanding intelligence and identifying intellectual abilities. The challenge for teachers is to create instructional strategies and assessment procedures that accommodate more than one kind of intelligence. If teachers can meet this challenge, more students will have successful learning experiences, which will promote self-confidence.

Why is self-confidence necessary for learning?

Attitudes affect learning. It is generally understood that if students think they cannot learn something, they aren't likely to learn it. Combs (1979) claimed, "People behave in terms of what they believe about themselves. Whether we feel adequate or inadequate greatly affects how we approach a task" (p. 108). Research studies have confirmed that attitudes of teachers (and others)

can positively or negatively affect student self-confidence. Research cited by Baker (1983) concluded "There appears to be a high correlation between achievement in school and students' self-concept of academic ability as determined by the expectations and evaluations of significant others" (p. 9). By "significant others" Baker meant teachers and other school personnel. Although expectations should not be unrealistic, teachers must express high expectations for students in order to facilitate learning.

What must teachers do to implement a multicultural education approach?

Educators must determine which multicultural education approach they will implement. Sleeter and Grant (1999) identified five distinct approaches, two of which also satisfy the criteria included in Nieto's description: multicultural education and education that is multicultural *and* social reconstructionist (see Table 14.2). For purposes of clarity, the latter will be referred to as the *social reconstructionist approach.*

Principles underlying a multicultural education approach are reflected in a statement entitled "No One Model American" issued by the Commission on Multicultural Education (Hunter, 1974):

> Multicultural education values cultural pluralism. Multicultural education rejects the view that schools should seek to melt away cultural differ-ences or the view that schools should merely tolerate cultural pluralism. Instead, multicultural education affirms that schools should be oriented toward the cultural enrichment of all children and youth through programs rooted to the preservation and extension of cultural diversity as a fact of life in American society. (p. 21)

A *multicultural education approach* insists that a diverse society can achieve unity through diversity; it need not eliminate cultural differences. Although

TABLE 14.2

Approaches to Multicultural Education

Teaching the Exceptional and the Culturally Different

GOALS: To help low-achieving students succeed within traditional education by building bridges between them and the curriculum, and providing special assistance.

CURRICULUM: Based on the traditional curriculum but incorporates students' experiences (especially those who are culturally different). Uses classroom materials that include meaningful contexts for the students.

INSTRUCTION: Implements English as a Second Language or transitional bilingual education for language minority students and culturally relevant teaching for culturally different students; provides remedial classes including special education placement for temporary but intensive remediation; displays images relevant to students on wall posters and bulletin boards.

Human Relations

GOALS: To maintain traditional educational assumptions but with an emphasis on reducing prejudice, developing positive student self-concepts, and promoting acceptance of individual diversity.

CURRICULUM: Based on the traditional curriculum but including content on prejudice and stereotypes, similarities and differences among groups and individuals, and societal contributions from members of diverse groups in society, especially those groups represented by the students in the school.

INSTRUCTION: Uses strategies that build student–student relationships such as conflict mediation, role playing, simulations that address interpersonal relationships, and cooperative learning; displays student work on walls and bulletin boards.

Single Group Studies

GOALS: To provide knowledge about a particular group (Women's Studies, Chicano Studies, etc.) including an examination of structural inequalities affecting members of this group and encouraging students to work for social change.

CURRICULUM: Provides information (for a unit or course) about cultural characteristics and historical experiences of a group with emphasis on perspectives of group members and how this group has been and still is oppressed.

INSTRUCTION: Responds to learning style differences of the group with accommodations for individual learning styles; incorporates media, music, performances, and guest speakers to address aspects of the culture or issues related to the group; wall displays and bulletin boards emphasize societal contributions from individual members of the group.

Multicultural Education

GOALS: To promote cultural pluralism by emphasizing respect for human differences, including individual lifestyles, equal opportunity for all in school and society, and the need for power equity among diverse groups in society.

CURRICULUM: Provides content on diverse groups and their contributions to society with emphasis on perspectives from members of each group; incorporates student experiences to enhance curriculum relevance, and emphasizes the need to be aware of and understand alternative perspectives on issues; addresses "hidden curriculum" by including diversity in special events, holidays, school menus, etc.

INSTRUCTION: Responds to student learning styles and skill levels with emphasis on an analysis of curriculum content and critical thinking activities; promotes respect for and use of other languages and dialects while learning standard English; displays wall posters and bulletin boards that reflect human diversity represented by race, ethnicity, gender, disability, religion, and other diverse groups, as well as issues reflecting individual student interests.

Education That Is Multicultural and Social Reconstructionist

GOALS: To promote cultural pluralism and structural equality for diverse groups in our society, to prepare students to be active participants in our democratic society by understanding structural inequalities and promoting equal opportunity.

CURRICULUM: Provides content on current social issues of oppression and structural inequalities for diverse groups using perspectives of members of those groups including the perspectives of students and community members; emphasizes historic and contemporary life experiences for self-reflection, for analyzing oppression, and for understanding alternative perspectives; addresses "hidden curriculum" by including diversity in special events, holidays, school menus, etc.

INSTRUCTION: Responds to student learning styles and skill levels with emphasis on active student involvement in democratic decision making in the school; engages students in critical thinking and in problem solving to promote the development of social action skills that empower students; employs cooperative learning and group projects, especially those involving the community; avoids testing and tracking procedures that represent narrow views of student learning that label some students as failures; displays wall posters and bulletin boards that reflect cultural diversity, social action themes, and student interests.

Source: Grant and Sleeter (1999).

some advocates of this approach focus on racial and ethnic groups, most promote an inclusive view of diversity by incorporating information on women, gays and lesbians, low-income families, and people with disabilities.

Multicultural education advocates support integration, inclusion, and "de-tracking" to create heterogeneous classrooms emphasizing skill development to gain knowledge and a better understanding of diverse groups in American society. Further, a multicultural education approach calls for curricular reform to correct omissions and distortions in textbooks concerning diverse groups, and provides multiple perspectives on important historical or contemporary events. Advocates have criticized visual images in textbooks for not representing diversity in American society adequately and for continuing to depict certain groups in stereotypical ways. They urge teachers to use bulletin boards and media to provide accurate representations of diverse groups.

Advocates for the multicultural education approach challenge teachers to be sensitive to language that is derogatory toward any group and to model use of inclusive language. Teachers must study and understand diverse ways of learning and design or modify lessons to accommodate differences. In addition to having high expectations for students, multicultural teachers encourage cooperation between students in the classroom through group activities. Teachers need not strive to treat students equally—treating all students the same—but to address students equitably with responses based on the diverse needs of individual students.

A *social reconstructionist approach* shares many principles and practices of a multicultural education approach. Four major differences include: (1) attention to structural inequalities in America; (2) emphasis on democratic decision making in the classroom; (3) development of social action skills to empower students; and (4) use of an activist curriculum with student projects addressing problems in schools and communities.

Social reconstructionism has roots in the Progressive Education movement and in Dewey's 1920 book, *Reconstruction in Philosophy* that inspired the term. In the early 1930s, Counts and Rugg, leaders of a group called "Frontier Thinkers," were concerned about inequities in American society and urged that schools play a more active role to create a more equitable society (Kneller, 1971). In his 1956 book, *Toward a Reconstructed Philosophy of Education,* Brameld became an influential advocate for reconstructionism, suggesting that schools create a new social order by fostering democratic principles and demanding more citizen control over major institutions and resources.

A social reconstructionist approach to multicultural education focuses less on awareness of cultural diversity and more on the ongoing struggles of diverse groups against oppression. The curriculum includes examples of successful resistance to oppression by subordinate groups and actions against injustice by individuals from the dominant group. This approach emphasizes democratic classroom practices to develop student decision-making skills and to encourage social action projects.

What does it mean to implement democratic practices in schools?

In describing schools employing democratic practices, Apple and Beane (1995) noted that all people in these schools must participate in governance issues and policymaking. In classrooms, students and teachers must work together to create learning environments responsive to student questions, interests, issues, and aspirations; however, as stated in Sleeter and Grant (1999), "Democratizing power relationships in the classroom does not mean turning all power over to the students" (p. 197). Teachers still represent adult authority and, like the state or federal government, they must take action if a majority of students makes decisions creating inequity or injustice in the classroom. In the history of the United States there have been numerous occasions when the majority was wrong, and as Griffin said, "Rule by majority is a great idea, but the majority has no right to rule wrong based on prejudice" (Terkel, 1980, p. 311).

In addition to emphasizing democratic practices, a social reconstructionist approach encourages students to analyze their own lives, reflecting Dewey's insistence that education take account of students' life experiences. Analyzing their own lives can lead students to a better understanding of their experiences with injustice, and provide a basis for developing constructive responses for future encounters. Self-analysis leading to action not only strengthens a student's self-concept, but also develops social action and interaction skills when coalitions are necessary to address issues. Social action projects can be as simple as examining the nutritional value of various fast foods or as complex as examining factors influencing a pattern of lower scores on standardized tests for females or students of color. By making curriculum personal, it becomes relevant; by emphasizing social action, it becomes empowering. Students are encouraged to regard citizenship in a democracy as active participation by individuals and groups to resolve personal and social dilemmas.

Engaging in democratic practices has enormous implications for a teacher's choice of instructional approaches. Before describing teaching strategies, it is important to recall an important point from Hilliard (1974), that teachers implementing multicultural education must believe "a multicultural orientation is beneficial to them personally" (p. 49). Howard (1999) argued that teachers have no choice about dealing with diversity; their only choice is how they will respond to diversity. If teachers implement strategies for multicultural education merely to *help* students, especially students of color, they are not likely to be effective.

What specific instructional strategies are recommended for teachers?

Sleeter (1996) insisted that implementing multicultural education effectively requires that teaching not be regarded as experimenting with a variety of classroom strategies; instead she described the importance of "listening to oppressed people, including scholars, with the aim of learning to hear and understand what is being said" (p. 134). By listening to students and their parents, teachers will develop appreciation for and understanding of their students, and will genuinely project high regard and

> The wise person can see a question from all sides without bias. The foolish person is biased and can see a question only from one side.
>
> CONFUCIUS (551–479 BCE)

high expectations for all students. As Nieto (2004) described it: "Becoming a multicultural teacher . . . means first becoming a multicultural person" (p. 383). Becoming a multicultural person means knowing about human differences and desiring to learn more; examining attitudes for biases, stereotypes, and prejudices; and understanding the need to look at issues from more than one perspective.

Advocates for either of the two multicultural education approaches described above agree that for a multicultural curriculum, teachers must employ **critical pedagogy.** Nieto (2004) described learning experiences where "students critically analyze perspectives and use them to understand and act on the inconsistencies they discover" (p. 359). Critical pedagogy is also illustrated by Sleeter's (1996) description of *Why? Papers:* In this activity students are assigned the task of asking a question about some issue involving race, social class, or gender. In doing research and writing their responses to the questions, students are asked to take the perspective of the oppressed group identified in the question. Examples of "Why?" questions include:

- Why are Mexican American children frequently absent from school?
- Why do Native American students drop out of school?
- Why are many African American males in prison? (p. 120)

According to Sleeter, taking the minority perspective has been effective because students talk with members of oppressed groups as they search for answers; this provides them with unique insights on the group's past experiences and their perspectives on problems addressed. Multiple insights and perspectives influence the analysis and conclusions students present in their papers:

> They framed concrete observations of inequality in terms of institutional discrimination and uncovered strategies oppressed groups use to cope with or attempt to advance from a minority position. (p. 123)

Appleton (1983) recommended process-oriented teaching strategies such as role playing, simulation games, using students as discussion leaders, and assigning individual or group projects based on student interests. Using the community to create learning experiences is essential for social action activities, but communities also have human resources—such as students' parents—who can be invited to the classroom to discuss the impact of past or current issues on the community. For students who struggle with nonstructured tasks, teachers might provide a mastery learning activity in which learning is partitioned into a series of sequential tasks and students can periodically evaluate themselves to determine when they achieve mastery. Effective multicultural teaching must allow for the flexibility to modify learning activities in order to provide students with opportunity to be successful learners.

Multicultural educators deplore tracking and encourage the use of learning centers or cooperative groups as effective strategies in heterogeneous classrooms. Tiedt and Tiedt (2002) describe a learning center as a part of the classroom set aside for the study of a specific topic or for the purpose of developing a specific set of skills; it may be devoted to studying the issue of prejudice or filled with exercises requiring critical thinking. Before using a learning center, students are given directions concerning the center's activities and instructions for using equipment or materials. Students involved in learning center activities can proceed as individuals learning at their own pace or they can be organized into teams.

Cooperative learning strategies are especially attractive to advocates of multicultural education because they involve students of mixed abilities in learning tasks that have clearly defined responsibilities for each group member. Each person must complete his or her task in order for the group to complete the project. According to Sleeter and Grant (1999), research findings suggest that this strategy works well with children from diverse racial and ethnic groups, not only in terms of academic achievement but also in terms of developing positive interpersonal relationships. In reviewing research on cooperative learning, Stephan (1999) reported its effectiveness in reducing student prejudice and improving intergroup relations for diverse groups of students.

How can multicultural education help to reduce student prejudice?

Reducing prejudice and developing conflict resolution skills are important objectives in multicultural education. Referring to a review of prejudice reduc-

tion programs, Nieto (2004) reported that activities designed to reduce prejudice were more effective if students viewed cognitive learning as the primary objective. When prejudice reduction was the primary objective of an activity, students tended to feel as if they were being manipulated to "say the right thing" and they became defensive or resentful. The success of indirect approaches emphasizing cognitive tasks for reducing student prejudice may explain why studies have found cooperative learning strategies to be effective in this area.

OUTCOMES OF MULTICULTURAL EDUCATION

Teaching conflict resolution skills can reduce the influence of prejudice on intergroup relations in schools (Stephan, 1999). One study reported that helping students develop conflict resolution skills "improved students' abilities to manage conflicts, increased their social support from other students, and decreased victimization by others" (p. 70). Stephan added that teaching conflict resolution skills to students had a positive effect on decreasing student anxiety, increasing self-esteem, and improving intergroup relations. Strategies for prejudice reduction or developing conflict resolution skills clearly are related to issues of student values. A dilemma for teachers is to determine how to discuss values in a classroom without being perceived as attempting to indoctrinate students.

How do multicultural educators address individual values?

Stephan (1999) described studies finding inconsistencies "between the inequalities in our society and our democratic values of equality and freedom" (p. 93), the same inconsistency Myrdal described in *An American Dilemma* in 1944. However, Stephan recommended that students examine how people in power have used myths and half-truths to legitimize their position in the social hierarchy—and that students investigate their own inconsistencies.

If students engage in self-analysis, they may come to understand their own values and how these values are consistent with their own reactions and behaviors. Multicultural teachers must ask students to agree on one central value: to respect differences in others. Only in the context of mutual respect can students debate and defend their values as they decide what is really meaningful to them. Using role-playing exercises and moral dilemmas, multicultural educators can stimulate discussions of inconsistent behavior reflecting conflicting values. Studies have found that as long as students do not feel they are being coerced into accepting certain values, discussions of values tend to increase the sophistication of the moral reasoning expressed (Stephan, 1999).

How do we know when people are becoming more sophisticated in their moral reasoning?

Different theories of moral reasoning have been described, but some have not been carefully researched; others do not seem widely applicable to different cultures or genders. Perry (1970) developed a theory of moral reasoning that suggests an accurate description of moral reasoning engaged in by people of different ages, from different cultures or subcultures, and from both genders (King and Kitchener, 1994; Belenky, Clinchy, Goldberger, and Tarulle, 1986). Using this theory, multicultural teachers can analyze student moral reasoning and engage students in values discussions to improve the quality of their moral reasoning.

PERRY'S CONTINUUM OF MORAL DEVELOPMENT

Perry's theory is based on the assumption that changes in moral reasoning are related to cognitive development: Increased cognitive ability allows individuals the possibility of increasing the complexity of their moral reasoning. Although there are nine developmental positions in Perry's continuum, as an introduction to the theory, it is sufficient to understand two major areas Perry has identified—**Dualism** and **Relativism**—and the mental shift that occurs within each: A Dualistic thinker transitions into Multiplicity, a Relativistic thinker transitions into Making Commitments (see Figure 14.3).

Dualism

All human beings begin as dualistic thinkers when confronted with moral decisions; children tend to operate simplistically with absolute categories of right and wrong. In dualistic thinking every moral issue is a question of either/or: either it's right or it's wrong, it's true or it's false, it's good or it's bad. This is also called "black and white" thinking because there are no "shades of gray" for dualistic thinkers. To be dualistic is to believe that what is true must be regarded as an Absolute Truth: It has always been and will always be true.

Believing in absolutes is challenged when a person is confronted with problems that don't lend themselves to the either/or style of thinking. A popular moral dilemma exercise is to ask people what they would have done if they were hiding Jews in the early 1940s and Gestapo officers came to their home to ask if they knew where there were any Jews. For the person who believes "honesty is the best policy," this is a difficult question to answer. Complex issues that challenge dualistic thinking may not occur until a student enters high school or college, but when students confront such issues, they often feel compelled to move away from rigid dualistic thinking and engage in the kind of moral reasoning called **multiplicity.**

FIGURE 14.3

A Continuum of Moral Reasoning

Source: Perry, W. (1970). Intellectual and Ethical Development in the College Years: A Scheme.

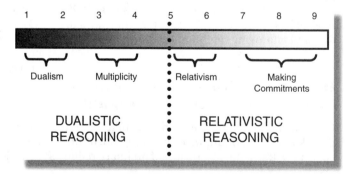

Multiplicity

This perspective recognizes the difficulty of knowing "the right answer" in every situation. When the right answer is not obvious, the only recourse is for the individual to examine various opinions or multiple perspectives without being certain which one is right. Each person must consider the different perspectives and decide which one seems best. This is not satisfying for people at the multiplicity position, because they are still influenced by dualistic thinking. They would prefer to know the answer or the truth in a given situation, and often complain that all we have are opinions. Because of the influence of dualistic thinking, people at a multiplicity position still believe the truth can be known and will be known some day, but for the moment, they reluctantly accept that they do not know the answer for a number of issues.

Relativism

When people move beyond multiplicity to **relativism,** they tend to exhibit a change in attitude from reluctantly accepting the existence of multiple perspectives to becoming intrigued by the idea that each person must decide what is right. Relativism is based on the assumption that there are no absolute truths, and that truth is relative, a concept reflected in the familiar phrases: "One man's meat is another man's poison" and "One person's treasure is another person's junk." The relativist is stimulated by differences of opinions, is interested in debates, and may enjoy playing the "devil's advocate" in a discussion by articulating arguments and ideas to defend a particular perspective without really believing in it.

Some people may become relativistic thinkers briefly, but return to dualistic thinking as an expression of their need for more certainty in a complex, uncertain world. Others may never progress beyond basic relativistic thinking, often resulting in a cynical attitude, since at this stage, a person has not become personally invested in any issue or cause. Many become dissatisfied with the moral ambiguity of relativism and begin to search for their own answers.

Commitment

Relativistic thinkers who continue to develop their moral reasoning are attracted to the idea of making commitments to certain personal truths, ideals, or causes that seem to give meaning to their lives. Most people need to believe in something and to feel a sense of satisfaction that their belief enhances the quality of their lives. **Commitments** may include being active in a political party or joining a church, an advocacy group, or some other organization. A commitment may result in volunteer work or influence a person's career decision. Whatever the choice, it is made from among many alternatives and represents a decision to which relativists are committed because it reflects their values.

Once people make commitments, they often become advocates for that particular cause or perspective. Because commitment is made in the context of relativistic thinking, people who reflect this perspective do not advocate like dualistic thinkers whose arguments are based on a sense of certainty. Relativistic thinkers may emphasize the sense of satisfaction they feel that their commitment provides a stronger sense of meaning and purpose in their lives, and they invite others to join them. In contrast, when dualistic thinkers advocate for truths they believe are absolute, they tend to view those who agree with them as right and those who disagree as wrong. There is no other option. When committed relativists argue on behalf of their commitments, they do not tend to judge those who agree or disagree. Relativists acknowledge that it is an individual's obligation to make his or her own choices, and they respect the person's right to choose.

> The question should never be who is right, but what is right.
>
> **GLENN GARDINER (CONTEMPORARY)**

How have Perry's ideas about moral reasoning influenced teachers?

Educators have employed Perry's continuum to determine growth in the complexity of student moral reasoning. If teachers begin by listening to student responses concerning moral issues, they may be able to determine where a student's moral reasoning places him or her on Perry's continuum. Students can be organized in small groups for discussions of moral dilemmas based on their continuum position. For example, students who are dualistic can be placed with multiplicity thinkers, and multiplicity thinkers can be placed with relativistic thinkers based on Perry's belief that someone slightly further along the continuum can intellectually challenge a person at an earlier position on the continuum. However, placing dualistic and relativistic thinkers in the same group is likely to lead to frustration since the gap between them will make it more difficult for students to find common ground for discussion. Most teachers may not use Perry's ideas in such a structured way; still, they may find his continuum helpful as they work to understand and develop student moral reasoning.

Is multicultural education too idealistic?

The purpose of multicultural education is to prepare children and youth to be active, positive participants in a diverse, democratic society. Although this chapter can only provide an overview of multicultural education, the intent is to provide a framework that describes schools committed to multicultural education and teachers who have implemented multicultural education in their classrooms. Educators may not achieve the ideals of multicultural education, but they can have a significant impact on students by engaging in efforts consistent with the purpose of multicultural education. If teachers address that purpose with students now and in the future, this diverse nation we live in will make progress toward achieving two related goals: more effective schools for all students and a more accepting society.

Elementary, middle level, and secondary educators committed to principles of multicultural education have implemented strategies and activities described in this chapter. The National Education Association (NEA) has promoted multicultural education since the 1960s and the National Council for Accreditation of Teacher Education (NCATE) requires teacher education programs to address diversity issues and to include principles and practices of multicultural education to receive accreditation for the preparation of teachers. Professional organizations advocate pluralism not just as a response to diversity but to meet our needs as a

> Ideals are like stars: you will not succeed in touching them with your hands, but like the seafarer . . . you choose them as your guides and following them you reach your destiny.
>
> CARL SCHURZ (1829–1906)

democratic society. Pai and Adler (1997) succinctly state the relationship between democracy, diversity, and multicultural education:

> In a truly democratic society, no single group rules over others because of the implicit faith in the human capacity for intelligent behavior. Democracy requires a method of resolving conflicts by inquiry, discussion, and persuasion rather than by violence. Hence, the kind of education that cultivates reflective thinking and conflict resolution through discussion and persuasion is essential. (p. 110)

AFTERWORD

Diversity is not just an issue for K–12 schools; most universities and colleges mandate diversity courses in their general education programs, and corporations implement policies promoting diversity and provide diversity training for managers and employees. Churches, community organizations, and civic groups already articulate pluralistic mission statements about the value of diversity in our society. Idealistic or not, multicultural education is likely to become increasingly influential in American schools in the twenty-first century. Fortunately, we have many excellent resources that describe teaching strategies based on principles of multicultural education (Tiedt and Tiedt, 2002; Ladsdon-Billings, 2001; Sapon-Shevin, 1999; Sleeter and Grant, 1998; Shade, Kelly, and Oberg, 1997; Derman-Sparks, 1989; Pasternak, 1979).

The challenge confronting us today is how to become multicultural individuals. In the teaching profession, that question will be answered primarily by white, middle-class people—primarily women. As our schools increasingly consist of students from subordinate groups—students of color, students from low-income families, children and youth who are not Christian, gay and lesbian youth, learners with disabilities—teachers continue to enter the profession from our dominant societal group. Cochran-Smith (2003) cites demographers analyzing 2000 Census data and reporting that 86% of all teachers are white, while students of color constitute almost 40% of the school population (p. 4); although the percentage of white teachers is predicted to remain stable, the percentage of students of color is predicted to be 57% by 2035 (see Table 14.3).

Pang (2001) has urged white teachers to engage in self-analysis in order to understand how being white has shaped their identity, and how oppression has affected and shaped the identities of members of subordinate groups in our society. Self-analysis is part of the journey toward becoming a multicultural teacher; it may often feel uncomfortable, but if pursued, it can also be liberating. In the end, white teachers can develop a profound appreciation for both diversity and democracy—and the need to be pluralistic to promote and sustain both in our schools and in our society.

TABLE 14.3

U.S. Public School Teachers

CATEGORY	PERCENT
Gender	
Female	74.4
Male	25.6
Race	
White	90.7
Black	7.3
Other	2.0
Highest Degree	
Bachelor's	43.6
Master's	54.5
Beyond Master's	1.7
Average Age	44 years

Source: U.S. Department of Education. (1997). National Center for Education Statistics.

> The role of the teacher remains the highest calling of a free people. To the teacher, America entrusts her most precious resource, her children; and asks that they be prepared, in all their glorious diversity, to face the rigors of individual participation in a democratic society."
>
> **SHIRLEY HUFSTEDLER (1925–)**

TERMS AND DEFINITIONS

Commitment Moral reasoning in a relativist context that recognizes the importance of becoming actively committed to certain personal truths to strengthen and deepen the meaningfulness of one's life experiences

Critical pedagogy Providing opportunities for students to analyze perspectives and use their analysis to understand and act on perceived inconsistencies

Diversity The presence of human beings with perceived or actual differences based on a variety of human characteristics

Dualism Moral reasoning involving a belief in absolute truths and unambiguous categories of right and wrong behavior; also called "either/or reasoning"

Global (International) education Teaching about the cultures of nations around the world

Hidden curriculum Indirect means by which schools teach the norms and values of a society

Multicultural Any society composed of a number of subordinate groups based upon race, ethnicity, religion, language, nationality, income, gender, sexual orientation, and degree of physical, mental or emotional ability

Multicultural education A process of comprehensive school reform that rejects discrimination in schools and society and accepts and affirms pluralism

Multiethnic education Integrating issues and information about race and ethnicity into school curricula

Multiplicity Moral reasoning in a dualistic context, recognizing that it isn't possible to know what is the right behavior in certain situations, in which case opinions from multiple perspectives must be examined; a person can't be confident of the final decision since he or she can't be certain of having made the right choice

Pluralism The equal coexistence of diverse cultures, institutions, and/or individuals within a mutually supportive relationship within the boundaries of one nation

Relativism Moral reasoning that rejects absolute truth and is based on the assumption that all truth is relative and determining the right behavior depends on the individual and the situation

Retention The ability of students to recall knowledge they have been taught

Transfer The ability of students to apply retained knowledge to situations occurring inside and outside the classroom

REFERENCES

Apple, M.W., & Beane, J.A. (Eds.). (1995). *Democratic schools*. Alexandria, VA: Association for Supervision and Curriculum Development.

Includes narratives written by those involved in reform efforts in four schools and describes how educators and students established democratic policies and practices.

Appleton, N. (1983). *Cultural pluralism in education: Theoretical foundations*. New York: Longman.

Examines how the United States has become pluralistic, how American education has responded to pluralism, and what our pluralistic society might look like in the future.

Baker, G.C. (1983). *Planning and organizing for multicultural instruction*. Reading, MA: Addison Wesley.

Presents a conceptual approach to multicultural education and practical suggestions for implementing multicultural education in curriculum and instruction.

Banks, J.A. (1999). *An introduction to multicultural education* (2nd ed.). Boston: Allyn & Bacon.

Explains major concepts, principles, theories, and practices in multicultural education.

Banks, J.A. (1994). *Multiethnic education: Theory and practice* (3rd ed.). Boston: Allyn & Bacon.

Discusses the evolution of multiethnic, pluralistic education and analyzes curricular issues and teaching strategies for implementing multiethnic content.

Belenky, M.F., Clinchy, B.M., Goldberger, N.R., & Tarulle, J.M. (1986). *Women's ways of knowing: The development of self, voice, and mind*. New York: Basic Books.

Describes the ways of gaining knowledge that women have developed and the obstacles women must overcome in developing their intellectual abilities.

Carse, J. (1986). *Finite and infinite games: A vision of life as play and possibility*. New York: Free Press.

Describes two philosophical orientations toward life, one collaborative and the other competitive, and explains their divergent responses to life experiences.

Cochran-Smith, M. (2003). Standing at the crossroads: Multicultural teacher education at the beginning of the 21st century. *Multicultural Perspectives 5*(3), 3–11.

Describes three issues of critical interest to U.S. educators: teacher/student demographic data and trends, competing school reform agendas, and criticisms of educational research.

Combs, A.W. (1979). *Myths in education: Beliefs that hinder progress and their alternatives*. Boston: Allyn & Bacon.

Analyzes many myths about values, human nature, and education that influence educators and students and interfere with students learning and being successful in school.

Derman-Sparks, L. (1989). *Anti-bias curriculum: Tools for empowering young children*. Washington, DC: National Association for the Education of Young Children.

Provides activities and strategies for preschool and early elementary teachers to engage young children in an anti-racist approach to learning.

Gardner, H. (1993). *Multiple intelligences: The theory in practice*. New York: Basic Books.

Reviews earlier theories of intelligence and discusses the evidence in support of the existence of a number of intelligences and the implications of this theory for educators.

Gay, G. (1977). Curriculum design for multicultural education. In C.A. Grant (Ed.), *Multicultural education: Commitments, issues, and applications* (pp. 94–104). Washington, DC: Association for Supervision and Curriculum Development.

Describes a philosophy of multicultural education as a basis for developing specific objectives and organizational principles for designing a multicultural curriculum.

Hilliard, A. (1974). Restructuring teacher education for multicultural imperatives. In W.A. Hunter (Ed.), *Multicultural education through competency-based teacher education* (pp. 40–55). Washington, DC: American Association of Colleges for Teacher Education.

Provides definitions, rationale, general aims, methods, and content for a multicultural preparation of teacher education students.

Howard, G.R. (1999). *We can't teach what we don't know: White teachers, multiracial schools.* New York: Teachers College Press.

Discusses issues such as social dominance and racial identity development in relation to helping teachers, especially white teachers, become effective multicultural educators.

Hunter, W.A. (1974). Antecedents to development of and emphasis on multicultural education. In W.A. Hunter (Ed.), *Multicultural education through competency-based teacher education* (pp. 11–31). Washington, DC: American Association of Colleges for Teacher Education.

Provides a historical overview of intergroup relations in the United States, the rise of cultural pluralism, and the need and support for multicultural education.

Kershaw, T. (1992). The effects of educational tracking on the social mobility of African Americans. *Journal of Black Studies 23*(1), 152–170.

Analyzes criteria used to determine student placement in tracking systems; explains how black students are discriminated against and the negative consequences of such decisions.

King, P.M., & Kitchener, K.S. (1994). *Developing reflective judgment: Understanding and promoting intellectual growth and critical thinking in adolescents and adults.* San Francisco: Jossey-Bass.

Reviews research on the development of reflective judgment from childhood through adult years and includes cross-cultural and gender comparisons.

Kneller, G.F. (1971). *Introduction to the philosophy of education* (2nd ed.). New York: Macmillan.

Examines the intellectual foundations for five contemporary educational philosophies.

Ladsdon-Billings, G. (2001). *Crossing over to Canaan: The journey of new teachers in diverse classrooms.* San Francisco: Jossey-Bass.

Describes the experiences of eight teachers starting their careers in urban elementary schools and their use of student cultures to enhance academic achievement.

Laosa, L. (1974). Toward a research model of multicultural competency-based education. In W. Hunter (Ed.), *Multicultural education through competency-based education.* Washington, DC: American Association of Colleges for Teacher Education.

Discusses the value of cultural diversity and the need for competency-based programs to prepare teachers for working with culturally diverse students.

Myrdal, G. (1944). *An American dilemma: The Negro problem and modern democracy.* New York: Harper & Row.

Describes values and contradictions in American culture and how they relate to the pervasive prejudice in American society.

Nieto, S. (2004). *Affirming diversity: The sociopolitical context of multicultural education* (4th ed.). Boston: Pearson.

Provides a comprehensive analysis of how schools are failing to meet the needs of students of color and suggests strategies for more effective teaching based on research and practice.

Oakes, J. (1985). *Keeping track: How schools structure inequality.* New Haven, CT: Yale University Press.

Documents how tracking practices have perpetuated racial and social class inequalities.

Oakes, J., Selvin, M., Karoly, L., & Guiton, G. (1992). *Educational matchmaking: Academic and vocational tracking in comprehensive high schools.* Santa Monica, CA: RAND.

Examines tracking practices in five high schools in terms of curriculum, consequences, and participation by race and gender.

Oakes, J., Quartz, K.H., Ryan, S., & Lipton, M. (2000). *Becoming good American schools: The struggle for civic virtue in school reform.* San Francisco: Jossey-Bass.

Describes the effort of sixteen schools in five states to move away from tracked classes and implement other reforms to improve the education of all students.

Pai, Y., & Adler, S. (1997). *Cultural foundations of education* (2nd ed.). Upper Saddle River, NJ: Merrill Prentice Hall.

Examines education as a cultural phenomenon, the implications for schooling, and provides information about curriculum and pedagogy as a foundation for multicultural education.

Pang, V.O. (2001). *Multicultural education: A caring-centered, reflective approach.* Boston: McGraw Hill.

Presents stories and classroom examples to illustrate concepts of culture, discrimination, and social justice, explaining how teachers can effectively address these concepts. Uses actual experiences to illustrate major concepts in multicultural education and explains how these concepts can be incorporated into school classrooms.

Partridge, E. (1983). *Origins: A short etymological dictionary of modern English* (p. 92). New York: Greenwich.

Citation notes that the Latin "ducere" means to lead and is the basis for Duke, p. 169.

Pasternak, M.G. (1979). *Helping kids learn multi-cultural concepts: A handbook of strategies.* Champaign, IL: Research Press.

Describes activities developed for an urban school system to create a multicultural environment for a multiethnic student population.

Perry Jr., W.G. (1970). *Forms of intellectual and ethical development in the college years: A scheme.* New York: Holt, Rinehart, Winston.

Describes nine positions in the development of moral reasoning based on interviews with Harvard students and including interview excerpts illustrating developmental positions.

Piaget, J. (1974). *The language and thought of the child* (Rev. ed.). New York: New American Library.

Includes a collection of preliminary studies on the exchange of thought between children, their verbal understanding, and how social conditions affect the development of thought.

Sapon-Shevin, M. (1999). *Because we can change the world: A practical guide to building cooperative, inclusive classroom communities.* Boston: Allyn & Bacon.

Provides strategies and activities that reflect principles of multicultural education, although it is primarily intended for creating cohesive classrooms in elementary schools.

Shade, B.J., Kelly, C., & Oberg, M. (1997). *Creating culturally responsive classrooms.* Washington, DC: American Psychological Association.

Examines the impact of culture on learning and suggests strategies to motivate students from diverse cultural groups in the United States.

Sleeter, C.E. (1996). *Multicultural education as social activism.* Albany: State University of New York Press.

Explores the value of multicultural education for white people and the impact of the connections between race, gender, and class in the struggle for social justice.

Sleeter, C.E., & Grant, C.A. (1999). *Making choices for multicultural education: Five approaches to race, class, and gender* (3rd ed.). Upper Saddle River, NJ: Merrill.

Examines how concepts of race, class, and gender are presented to students and how students are asked to respond in five different approaches to multicultural education.

Sleeter, C.E., & Grant, C.A. (1998). *Turning on learning: Five approaches for multicultural teaching plans for race, class, gender, and disability* (2nd ed.). Upper Saddle River, NJ: Merrill Prentice Hall.

Provides lesson plans consistent with each of the five approaches to multicultural education the authors identified in previous research.

Stephan, W. (1999). *Reducing prejudice and stereotyping in schools.* New York: Teachers College Press.

Reviews theories of prejudice and stereotyping, examines conditions to promote changes in negative attitudes and describes techniques for improving race relations in schools.

Terkel, S. (1980). *American dreams: Lost and found.* New York: Ballantine.

Includes interviews with diverse people about their perceptions of America, including the author of *Black Like Me*, John Howard Griffin.

Tiedt, P.L., & Tiedt, I.M. (2002). *Multicultural teaching: A handbook of activities, information, and resources* (6th ed.). Boston: Allyn & Bacon.

Provides strategies for thematic studies and learning modules with specific multicultural lessons in various disciplines for teachers in elementary and middle level classrooms.

Summary Exercises

See page 19 for exercises to help you summarize the main points and define key terms in this chapter.

Personal Clarification Exercises

In Chapter 14, two exercises promote discussion about essential and multicultural curriculum and about Perry's moral development continuum.

Clarification Exercise #1 Keeping Secrets: A Morality Tale

Directions: Read the scenario below; the situation illustrates persons operating at several of Perry's value levels. Also, it gives us an opportunity to learn values through discussion.

(a) Review the events with one person of your choice from the group to be certain you are clear about what occurred. (b) Next, share your personal value judgments with your discussion partner and jointly determine the morality of each of the four characters. Rank them Most Moral = 1 to Least Moral = 4. Space is provided at the end of the vignette. Take time in your deliberations to mutually agree to the rankings assigned. Keep notes about why each character was given their rank to explain to the class when rankings are aggregated to determine overall scores. (c) Use the questions for discussion that follow as discussion departure points regarding our cultural and personal value systems.

Keeping Secrets: A Morality Tale

Teri met Clint during her junior year at college. After several dates they went to a party one Friday night and both had too much to drink. They ended up having sex. Teri thought she loved Clint and that he loved her. Their relationship continued to be a sexual one until it became obvious that Clint did not intend to marry her. Teri broke off the relationship.

During her senior year, Teri met Alex and it was love at first sight for both. Alex was going to state college 25 miles away, and he saw Teri every weekend. They developed a loving relationship and Alex asked her to marry him. Because Alex was a born-again Christian,

Teri was reluctant to tell him about Clint. She asked her best friend Clair what to do, but Clair said that Teri had to make the decision herself. Clair emphasized that Teri was a good person and no matter what decision she made, Clair would always support her and be her friend.

Teri agonized for months. She loved Alex and didn't want to ruin their relationship, but she knew she should tell him. Ten days before the wedding, she mailed Alex a letter telling him what had happened with Clint. She saw Alex every day and he said nothing about her letter. Teri was convinced this meant that Alex had forgiven her. The day before the wedding, Teri found a letter marked "Return to Sender" in her mail. She had inadvertently turned around two numbers on Alex's street address so the letter had never been delivered. Teri panicked, but she didn't want to cancel the wedding at this point.

On the first night of their honeymoon, Alex confessed he had had an affair with a graduate student when he was a sophomore. He had met her at a party and he had been flattered that this sexually experienced woman was attracted to him. He knew that having sex with her violated his religious beliefs and after a few weeks he stopped seeing her. He asked Teri to forgive him. She forgave him and immediately told him about Clint and asked him to forgive her as well. Alex was upset to hear about Clint. He said he could have forgiven her the mistake of getting drunk and Clint taking advantage of her, but he couldn't forgive her continuing to have sex with him. He packed up his suitcase and left. Teri called Clair, who tried to console her.

A few days later, Teri got a call from Clint. He had talked to Clair and heard what Alex had done. He wanted to get back together with Teri and accused Alex of being a hypocrite. In fact, he admitted that he was so angry he found out where Alex lived and had gone to see him. The two had gotten into an argument and Clint beat Alex up.

Teri cried and said he shouldn't have done that, but Clint said Teri was too good for Alex and that he deserved what he got. Clint told Teri that he loved her. He asked her to go out with him the following night. Teri was confused and did not know what to say. Clint said to think about it and he'd call her back tomorrow. Teri called Clair to ask her advice. Clair said that she should do what her heart told her to do.

Rank the four characters from the most moral (#1) to the least moral (#4):

_____ Alex _____ Clint _____ Clair _____ Teri

Questions for discussion:

1. In your judgment, is the scenario a realistic one? If yes, why? If not, how do you suggest it could better reflect reality in your culture?
2. How is it possible for your team of two to mutually agree on a ranking order?
3. Under what circumstances would it be possible for the entire group to reach consensus on a most, next, less, and least moral ranking?
4. What individual action could any one of the characters take that would alter your most–least moral rankings?
5. At what levels in Perry's continuum would you suggest each character is operating?
6. Propose a new vignette based upon your team assigning specific heritages or other human difference traits to Alex, Clint, Clair, and Teri. How would your proposed vignette be different with characters representing other racial or ethnic heritages?

ADAPTED FROM *TESS OF THE D'URBERVILLES*
BY THOMAS HARDY

Clarification Exercise #2 Statements Illustrating Perry's Continuum

Directions: Read the following statements and identify each according to the four broad areas in Perry's Continuum of Moral Development. You will find three examples from each area. Mark your answers as follows:

(a) Dualism   (b) Multiplicity
(c) Relativism   (d) Commitment

Statements Illustrating Perry's Continuum

_____ 1. In areas where even the experts disagree, everyone has a right to his own opinion. I mean, if answers aren't given, like in lots of things, then it has to be just anyone's opinion.

_____ 2. Understanding another point of view, especially a contrary one, helps me understand my own point of view. So trying to see through the other person's eyes helps my own understanding of the issue.

_____ 3. I came here from a small town in the Midwest where everyone believed the same things and everyone is, like, Methodist and Republican. But here, there is a variety of Protestants and Catholics and a Chinese boy who follows the teaching of Confucius . . . Some people are quite disturbing; they say they're atheists, but I don't think they are.

_____ 4. I'm not sure how to make any decision at all. When you are here and having the issues thrust at you and reading about the people who pushed their thought to the absolute limit and seeing how that did not result in an all-encompassing answer . . . , you begin to have respect for how great their thought could be even though it did fall short.

_____ 5. The science lectures are all right. They sort of say the facts, but when you get to a humanities course, they are awful!! The lecturer is just reading things into the book that were never meant to be there.

_____ 6. This place is full of bull. If you turn in a speech or a paper that is well written, whether it has one single fact in it or not is beside the point . . . So you sit down and write a paper in an hour, just because you know that whatever it is isn't going to make any difference to anyone.

_____ 7. I get frustrated in class when the teacher only looks at things from her point of view. There are other ideas to consider. What is important to me is trying to understand and evaluate ideas and to come up with my own. I dislike discussions in which everyone just voices an opinion without backing it up. What good are opinions unless you put them to the test?

_____ 8. When I have an idea about something and it differs from the way another person is thinking about it, I will usually try to look at it from that person's point of view, see how they could say that, why they think they are right, why it makes sense.

_____ 9. In science you don't really want to say that something is true. We're dealing with a model and models are always simpler than the real world, which is more complex than anything we can create. We simplify so we can work with it. When we try to describe things, we leave out the truth because we are oversimplifying.

_____ 10. About the only thing I guess I would say to a prospective student is that if you come to this college, you had better do everything you are supposed to do and then you will be all right. That's just about all.

_____ 11. As soon as someone tells me his point of view, I immediately start arguing in my head the opposite point of view. When someone is saying something, I can't help turning it upside down.

_____ 12. I can't really say that one opinion is better than another. It depends on your beliefs. I am the type of person who would never tell someone that their opinion is wrong. If they have searched, well, even if they haven't searched, if they just believe it, that's cool for them.

Intergroup Exercises

In Chapter 14, three exercises promote discussion about multicultural education and moral development.

Intergroup Exercise #1 Examining Multicultural Education

Directions: Create a team of four members who have not worked together. For each of the questions below, record at least 4–5 responses that could be legitimate possible answers. If you do not represent the minority group about whom each item is directed, respond nevertheless as if you were a member of that group. Present your selections and rationale to another team of four so that they are convinced of at least half of your lists.

Examining Multicultural Education

1. Why do many *people of color* insist that multicultural education is good for all students?

2. How might elementary, middle school, or secondary *educators* who promote multicultural education reply to criticism that multicultural education is unpatriotic? [Note: Some Americans argue that the concept of multiculturalism is destructive in that it forces children and youth to study racial, ethnic, and cultural issues at a time when there is no longer a need to rekindle the conflicts of past American history.]

3. What could be outcomes of a multicultural education for each of the groups listed below:
   a. Native Americans
   b. Foreign-born naturalized Americans
   c. Women in science
   d. White sales representatives
   e. Bank presidents
   f. Amputees
   g. Men aspiring to be music teachers
   h. Americans of Hungarian descent
   i. Mormons
   j. Ford automobile dealership employees

4. What basic skills or subjects would each of the groups above advocate as being "essential" in a traditional elementary, middle, or secondary school curriculum?

Intergroup Exercise #2 *Sally's Dilemma*

Sally's Dilemma

The situation: Sally's dilemma is about a low-income family just barely making ends meet where the woman (Sally) discovers that she is pregnant for the fourth time. Furthermore, the doctor has indicated that there is a high probability that the child may have Down Syndrome. Sally's husband doesn't want Sally to have an abortion, yet he has also said he will refuse to accept any kind of social services to help with the child if it does have Down syndrome because he considers the services equivalent to welfare and he refuses to accept welfare assistance. All of these issues appear in the arguments below.

Directions: In the following two conversations, identify the following arguments according to Perry's Continuum of Moral Reasoning as:

[D] Dualism   [M] Multiplicity
[R] Relativism   [C] Commitment

First Conversation (Dualistic and Multiplicity thinkers):

____ *Della:* Sally should not have an abortion because abortion is murder and if she has an abortion God will punish her. She will go to Hell.

____ *Mary:* I'm not so sure. What I do know is that abortions are legal and I know there are some good reasons why some people choose to have an abortion. In America we are supposed to make our own decisions based on our own beliefs and opinions. It is Sally's decision and she might decide to have an abortion for reasons as good any reasons you or I could come up with.

____ *Mike:* I don't think any of us can say what's the right thing for Sally to do, but I do believe that Sally's happiness will depend on this decision. Having an abortion would probably cause her to feel so much guilt that she would be better off having the child. Some people probably feel that the child will be an added burden on this family, but I know I would never encourage my wife to have an abortion, no matter what. If Sally feels like I do, then she should not have the abortion.

____ *Doug:* There's no law against abortion, so the most important issue here is that no one should have more children than they can take care of. Sally's family is barely making ends meet, and if the child is retarded they will have to get help from social services no matter what her husband says. Taxpayers will have to bear the burden of taking care of this child and that's not right. I think Sally should have an abortion; that's the fairest solution for everyone.

____ *Della:* Everyone but the baby! Listen, I know there's no law against abortion, but I think the Supreme Court was wrong! I support the

people trying to get a constitutional amendment outlawing abortions because I believe in the Ten Commandments, and I believe that "Thou shalt not kill" applies to a fetus just as much as it applies to anyone else.

Second Conversation (Relativistic and Commitment thinkers):

____ *Rick:* Sally's got to consider a lot of factors. Another pregnancy and delivery might weaken her physically, and the mental stress alone could be damaging. There also could be complications with the delivery. There are risks involved in having an abortion, but I think in this case the benefits from having an abortion outweigh the risks.

____ *Chuck:* Although abortions are legal, I believe there is a higher law, God-given to everyone regardless of race, color, creed, disabilities, or anything else, and that law is the right of every human being to live. Human beings represent the pinnacle of God's creation, so who are we to interfere with the unfolding of that creation?

____ *Christine:* Life is about more than mere existence; it is about the quality of that existence. This family already suffers from insufficient resources and they are living a marginal existence. To have even less because of the needs of raising another child, especially a retarded child, would be to force them to struggle with demands beyond what they are capable of meeting. The emotional and financial strain could destroy the family and end in divorce. If Sally values her family above all else, then she should have an abortion.

____ *Rita:* I understand why you believe Sally should have an abortion, but what if Sally believes that life starts at conception? Then she has to regard that fetus as a human being, and every human being in America deserves the rights we guarantee to Americans, especially the right to life. If the child is retarded, well, we provide services in this country to help couples that have retarded children, and I would hope her husband would understand that taking such help isn't like going on welfare but is a way of getting something back for all the taxes he has paid over the years.

_____ *Rick:* Our society tends to support the right of individuals to make their own decisions, and that was the point of the Supreme Court when it ruled that abortions could be performed legally. Sally has to look at her options and make the best decision for herself and her family. If this were my situation, I would tell my wife that I would support whatever decision she made, but I would encourage her to have an abortion. Their resources are spread thin as it is, and to have another child, especially a retarded child, is going to add more burdens, heartache, and expense to an already vulnerable family.

Intergroup Exercise #3 Difficult Dialogues Experience

Directions: In groups of three, develop a dialogue based upon the scenario below. Use the situation as the basis for your 5-minute role play of the situation. Remain in character at the conclusion of your skit and respond to class questions about motivation, purpose, or intent behind your comments during the scene. Each team of three is asked to complete a 5-minute role play, regardless of similarity to others performed.

Difficult Dialogues: Universal Truths

Characters:

- Russian graduate teaching assistant who is convening a required general sciences physics lab class
- Naturalized African American from Somalia hoping to complete her undergraduate degree and teach in Africa
- Serious physics major who has contributed significantly to fundamental laser research knowledge while still an undergraduate [See below]

A student in a physics class is heard to remark: "I'm glad we're in this course. It is good to be away from all those diversity, multicultural, and pluralism issues we have to talk about in our *Understanding Human Differences* course. At least we can deal with some facts and not have to worry about such issues as race, gender, ethnic origin, or homosexuality."

CHAPTER 15

Pluralism in Society: Creating Unity in a Diverse America

"How many goodly creatures are there here!
How beauteous mankind is! O brave new world
That has such people in't."

WILLIAM SHAKESPEARE (1564–1616)

All around us, a brave new world is indeed taking shape in America. Despite a wealth of diversity, America has not yet become a pluralistic society. Being **pluralistic** entails perceiving human differences as enriching, and valuing that diversity in our society. Yet Americans are still wary of one another, and fearful when conflicts occur between groups. Nevertheless, changes are taking place that encourage us to become more accepting of others and more pluralistic. It is obvious that students in K–12 schools and colleges today will shape our society in the future; yet many Americans don't realize that almost 40% of all K–12 children and youth are students of color. According to 2000 Census data, students of color in California and Texas comprise 50% of the K–12 population. Immigrants constitute 12% of the American workforce, and 20% of all K–12 students are foreign-born or have foreign-born parents (Cochran-Smith, 2003; Pipher, 2002). U.S. trade agreements guarantee that these figures will increase.

The diversity and location of racial and ethnic groups have changed dramatically: for example, more than 600 Somali refugees live in Owatonna, Minnesota. And although our media still tend to present U.S. diversity as principally African American, Hispanic Americans have become the largest ethnic minority group. As these societal changes occur, they are reflected in organizations such as the American military: More than 1,400 Muslims and 1,240 Buddhists serve in the U.S. Armed Forces. One out of every five soldiers recruited by the Army is a woman, and half are African American (Katzenstein and Reppy, 1999; Matthews, 1999).

To capitalize on these unprecedented demographic changes, Americans must realize the need for new approaches to living and working together and must create new partnerships with people in their communities. In Billings, Montana, a Jewish family decorated their home for Hanukkah and placed a menorah by their front window. After a vandal threw a cinder block through their window, thousands of Christian families put pictures of menorahs in their windows so vandals could not identify for certain which homes in their community had Jewish families (Eck, 2000).

America is the most diverse society in our diverse world: The global presence of major U.S. corporations requires sensitivity to diverse global issues and cultures. Americans come from almost every country on the planet; our diversity is represented by differences not only in geographical origins (ethnicity) but also in religion, social class, disabilities, gender, sexual orientation, age, region, and dialect, as well as individuals in multiple categories.

> For each age is a dream that is dying.
> Or one that is coming to birth.
>
> ARTHUR O'SHAUGHNESSY (1844–1881)

Forces at work in all areas of society increasingly recognize pluralism as a preferred alternative to the Anglo conformity demanded in the past. Although the transformation from America's preference for conformity to an unequivocal acceptance of human differences will not be resolved for decades to come, we must be aware of recent changes and prepare for future challenges. This chapter reports on five major societal areas—the federal government, higher education, business, mass media, and the military—and how each is making conscious and deliberate efforts to respond positively to diversity in the United States. The information provided is based on these three questions:

How do advocates promote pluralism?
How do detractors oppose pluralism?
What changes illustrate progress toward pluralism?

Regardless of the profession chosen, most individuals starting their careers are likely to encounter some form of the challenges and changes described in this chapter.

FEDERAL GOVERNMENT

With the passage of the 1964 Civil Rights Act, the U.S. federal government mandated **affirmative action** programs as a major initiative to promote pluralism by reducing acts of discrimination and providing opportunity for women and people of color. Title VII of the Civil Rights Act stated that if a court rules that a finding of discrimination is justified, the court might order an employer "to take such affirmative action as may be appropriate." A 1972 Title VII amendment added "or any other equitable relief as the courts deem appropriate"

(Greene, 1989, p. 15). Title VII has been controversial from the moment the Civil Rights Act became law, consistently keeping the issue of equal opportunity for all Americans in the public eye.

According to the Civil Rights Act, affirmative action plans represent voluntary programs unless a court orders that an affirmative action plan be designed and implemented. Determining the need for an affirmative action plan begins by analyzing the diversity of employees at a business or agency, or the student population at a university. If population variation is similar to that of available applicants, there is said to be no equity problem. If disparities exist, however, each phase of the application and selection process is evaluated for bias that may advantage some applicants and disadvantage others.

The Affirmative Action Debate

Debate concerning affirmative action has resonated from the public square to the U.S. Supreme Court. The crux of the debate concerns whether affirmative action was intended only to redress victims of intentional discrimination or if it mandates that programs create a more just distribution of women and minorities in the work force and in higher education. In the business community, the principal emphasis has been on compensating victims of discrimination; institutions of higher education have implemented admissions policies designed to increase the numbers of women and minorities admitted.

Affirmative action advocates argue that aggressive action is required to address inequities in hiring and college admissions. Proponents insist our society must guarantee equal opportunity to every citizen, and argue that ample evidence demonstrates our failure to achieve this goal. Since a college education is required to become qualified for certain jobs, policies and practices of college admission are scrutinized, just as businesses and corporations are monitored to ensure that women and minorities have the same opportunity as white males to work and to receive promotions. Affirmative action advocates explain that monitoring is not intended as punitive, but rather that it meets a broader goal of strengthening our society by creating racial, gender, and ethnic unity. Greene (1989) argued that if white males "continue to hold positions of power and prestige to the exclusion of other groups . . . divisions will continue to exist" (p. 10).

Affirmative action opponents counter that equal opportunity programs have created greater American disunity. They denounce affirmative action plans as racist when race is emphasized to create quotas, establishing what they term "preferential treatment." Opponents also claim that businesses and schools have often been forced to accept women and minorities who are less qualified than the rejected white males. They say it is ironic that affirmative action with a goal of reducing discrimination is engaging in "reverse discrimination"—decreasing opportunity for qualified white males. Eastland (2000) expressed gratitude for reverse discrimination lawsuits because they remind us of the principle "that no one in America should be discriminated against on account of race" (p. 175). Opponents also suggest that affirmative action plans have an adverse effect on society because quality and competence are being compromised, making the "solution" worse than the problem.

Judicial Limitations on Affirmative Action

Quality and competence was the focus of the *Griggs* v. *Duke Power* case heard by the U.S. Supreme Court in 1971. Job applicants at the Duke Power Company were required to have a high school diploma or passing scores on a specific standardized test. Lawyers argued that the requirement excluded a higher percentage of blacks than whites because unequal educational opportunities and other inequities prevented more black than white youth from earning high school diplomas. The U.S. Supreme Court ruled that any hiring practice that was intended to select the most qualified candidates was legitimate. Companies could not be held accountable for past discrimination that adversely affected individuals in the present. As long as job requirements were related to work performance,

they could not be labeled discriminatory, even if they did advantage some job applicants.

Based on the same concept, the U.S. Supreme Court also upheld the *seniority system* to determine layoffs during economic downturns. Because of past discrimination against women and minorities, adhering to **seniority system** priorities required employers to lay off people with least seniority: "last hired is the first fired." Although the procedure seemed race-neutral, lawyers provided evidence that the majority of women and minority employees had low seniority and were most likely to be dismissed. Supreme Court justices acknowledged the problem, but consistently have found the seniority system constitutional because it does not represent intentional discrimination. The Court has ruled with the same consistency on cases where the affirmative action plan appears to include a racial quota; that is a specific number of people hired or accepted based on race.

Affirmative Action and Quotas

Whenever **racial quotas** have been employed, the U.S. Supreme Court has always ruled against them, declaring that Title VII of the Civil Rights Act never mandated racial (or other) quotas. Indeed, the justices are correct. There is no mention of quotas in Title VII, nor anything to suggest that employers must hire unqualified applicants; as Greene (1989) noted, section 703 (j) of Title VII states:

> Nothing contained in this title shall be interpreted to require any employer, employment agency, labor organization, or joint labor-management committee subject to this title to grant preferential treatment to any individual or group. (p. 60)

One of the clearest judgments against racial quotas was the Supreme Court's ruling in the case of *Regents of California* v. *Bakke.* In 1970, 80% of the 800 students of color attending medical school in the United States were enrolled in programs at two historically black universities. Because minorities were never more than 3% of students at the University of California–Davis Medical School, the university decided to reserve eight of their admissions places (16%) for minority applicants. For two consecutive years, Alan Bakke was rejected by UC–Davis despite having a grade point average and Medical College

> One who gains strength by overcoming obstacles possesses the only strength which can overcome adversity.
>
> **ALBERT SCHWEITZER (1875–1965)**

Admissions Test scores higher than those of several minority applicants admitted. Ball (2000) explained the strategy of Bakke's lawyers in arguing relentlessly against the concept of racial quotas while UC–Davis lawyers argued that the university only accepted academically qualified applicants to their medical school and that preferential treatment of minorities was necessary to increase the numbers of minorities in professions "from which minorities were long excluded because of generations of pervasive racial discrimination" (p. 92).

The final decision on Bakke in 1978 fragmented the Court. Four justices approved UC–Davis affirmative action procedures, and four justices rejected them, arguing that race should play no role whatsoever on admission decisions. Justice Powell cast the deciding vote. In his written opinion, Powell declared that racial quotas were an unconstitutional strategy for achieving affirmative action goals, but that race could be used as one factor among others in considerations of college applicants.

Affirmative Action for Minority-Owned Businesses

Another affirmative action strategy rejected by the courts was the practice of setting aside a certain percentage of tax-funded projects for minority-owned business. In 1983, the city of Richmond, Virginia, was 50% African American, but in the previous five years, less than 1% of funds spent on city projects had been paid to minority-owned businesses. The Richmond city council approved an affirmative action plan to require recipients of city construction projects to subcontract at least 30% of the dollar value of these projects to minority-owned businesses. When J.A. Croson Company insisted it could not find any suitable minority-owned businesses and asked for a waiver of the subcontracting requirement, the city refused and informed the

company that it would resubmit their part of the project for new bids. The company brought the case to federal court, and the Supreme Court ruled on the case in 1989.

Writing for the majority in the *City of Richmond* v. *J.A. Croson Co.,* Sandra Day O'Connor criticized Richmond's **set-aside** program for its apparently arbitrary determination of the 30% figure and for not providing evidence demonstrating that previous major contractors had intentionally discriminated against minority-owned businesses. O'Connor said the Richmond City Council could have implemented effective, race-neutral strategies rather than establishing set-aside quotas. The court affirmed the right to remedy past discrimination, but again rejected racial quotas as a legitimate constitutional strategy (Crosby and VanDeVeer, 2000).

The Future of Affirmative Action

Because of continuing criticism of affirmative action, President Clinton appointed a task force in 1995 to review all federal affirmative action programs. Although some changes were recommended, the task force concluded that programs reviewed did not include quotas, did not mandate preferences for unqualified individuals, and did not engage in reverse discrimination. Instead, the programs were designed to remedy past discrimination and "lead the nation toward the goal of equal opportunity" (Ball, 2000, p. 163).

California voters did not agree. In 1996, they voted to approve **Proposition 209,** prohibiting preferential treatment to individuals or groups in hiring, awarding public contracts, and college admissions. According to Ball (2000), African American admissions to California law schools dropped 72% the year after the proposition was approved, and admission of all students of color to UC–Berkeley dropped 50%. The following year, UCLA and Berkeley reported continuing decreases in numbers of students of color. In response to complaints of increased segregation on state university campuses, California legislators voted to guarantee admission to any California university campus for all high school students graduating in the top 4% of their class. Critics said the vote represented a cynical recognition of racial segregation in California high schools. Although other states such as Oregon have passed propositions similar to Proposition 209, advocates argued that eliminating affirmative action was premature, and most would agree with the perspective expressed by Clayton and Crosby (2000):

> When the goals of true equality have been reached . . . affirmative action will be unnecessary. We have not yet reached such a happy state of being. Sexism and racism are still strong forces in American society, and both hostility toward and stereotypes about women and people of color influence decisions. (p. 88)

HIGHER EDUCATION

Since the 1960s, colleges and universities have implemented affirmative action plans to increase the numbers of students of color on their campuses. Although many administrators initially viewed affirmative action as unnecessary interference, in recent years administrators have displayed a pluralistic attitude, arguing that diversity of all kinds benefits the entire student population. Administrators, faculty, and student leaders on college campuses have consistently supported setting diversity goals. Musil (1996) summarized their perspective:

> To invite that diversity onto campus is not simply an act of charity. It is an act of raw self-interest. . . . it will make higher education better than it is. It expands our notion of learning. It widens what we study and how we study it. It improves our pedagogy. It adds to our resources in human capital. (p. 225)

Criticism of Diversity Goals in Higher Education

Affirmative action plans in higher education and the increased diversity they have helped produce have been the subject of much criticism. Even some people of color say affirmative action has stigmatized students of color, as white students question their academic ability and believe students of color are admitted through lower standards. Some faculty blame affirmative action for a perceived decline

FIGURE 15.1

Source: Courtesy of *The Daily Cardinal*, University of Wisconsin.

in academic standards and for promoting a multicultural curriculum that has caused a decline in the rigor of traditional college education.

Critics persist in denouncing changes in traditional curriculum, accusing faculty who are creating a more inclusive curriculum of having a "political agenda" rather than purely academic objectives. However, it would seem equally appropriate to accuse advocates for the preservation of a curriculum emphasizing white people as having a political agenda as well. One persistent criticism is that there has been widespread elimination of traditional Western Civilization courses by universities responding to pressure from "multiculturalists." According to a 1999 survey, almost 60% of college faculty believed that Western Civilization courses are the foundation of undergraduate education, and more than half of all U.S. colleges still require Western Civilization courses (Yamane, 2001).

The critics are correct in insisting that feminists and people of color are challenging the lack of relevance and inclusiveness in college curricula. Duncan (2002) noted that women and students of color in college courses encounter minimal information written by or about their groups, and often the information provided misrepresents or distorts the group being described. Even worse, Duncan claimed that students of color find "both explicit and subtle racist themes in what they . . . study" (p. 45). What is included in college curricula is a critical issue, as Groff and Cain explained: "Curriculum is a microcosm of the culture: its inclusions and exclusions are an index of what the culture deems important" (Yamane, 2001, p. 6).

Diversity in College Faculty and Course Content

In addition to the omission of people of color in curriculum, few faculty of color are represented at most universities. Tusmith and Reddy (2002) reported that people of color constitute less than 15% of higher education faculty, and that the majority were nontenured lecturers or instructors. Browne-Miller (1996) quoted an Asian American student observing that the teaching styles of her white professors were "geared to white middle-class males, overlooking the fact that this may not be the most effective . . . with non-white students and women" (p. 90). Courses taught by faculty of color

would benefit all students, including white students, by presenting perspectives they are not likely to have encountered. Reddy (2002) noted:

> Students—especially but not exclusively white students—arrive in our college classrooms with predictable baggage. Prepared by virtually every element of the society in which we live, they come ready to accept white authority, intelligence and rightness while discounting the views and experiences of people of color. (p. 54)

Because of Reddy's "predictable baggage," it is not inevitable that positive outcomes will occur if white students and students of color are brought together on a college campus; they may or may not enjoy each other or learn from each other. Almost a century ago, journalist John Reed observed that participating in a diverse community may bring "pain, isolation of separateness, [or] intellectual exhilaration, greater self-knowledge and . . . human reconciliation (Lowe, 1999, p. 22). To ensure productive interactions between members of diverse groups, colleges sponsor frequent diversity workshops and seminars, require all students to take at least one course on diversity, encourage relevant academic departments to include at least one course with significant content on diversity issues in their majors and minors, and encourage all faculty to integrate content about diversity issues into the courses they teach.

Since the 1960s, professors in numerous institutions of higher education have created scholarly courses focusing on one or more diverse groups. As they have grappled with diversity issues, their efforts have been learning experiences for themselves as well as their students. To struggle with diversity issues is to engage in an evolutionary process of change. According to Musil (1996), colleges cannot assume that they can "simply add diversity and stir and think the recipe will not be fundamentally altered" (p. 224). To illustrate, Musil went on to describe the limitations of initial courses developed to examine diversity issues, and what professors and students involved in those courses learned:

> Black studies were typically about only men. Women's studies were typically only about white women. Gay and lesbian studies had no practicing Christians or Jews. And none of the three paid much attention to those in the group who were old,

working class or disabled. Today it is largely commonplace in the most influential texts . . . in these kinds of courses to recognize the reality of our multiple identities. (p. 228)

Unfortunately, enrollment figures indicate that only a few white students take ethnic studies courses, and there have been few men enrolled in women's studies courses. Duncan (2002) believes that most white students, especially white males, are so accustomed to white experience being the focus of curriculum that they feel strange, defensive, and uncomfortable as they struggle to understand information that focuses on experiences of women or people of color. Despite these difficulties, colleges and universities continue to promote the goal of students gaining knowledge about diverse groups. Although designed to heighten student acceptance of diverse populations, courses on diversity have tended to be an addition to rather than a replacement for traditional curriculum. Kolodny (1998) addressed the importance of adding diversity content to the traditional curriculum:

We are expanding our students' repertoire of reading and interpretive strategies, teaching them to comprehend and appreciate the aesthetic rules and cultural practices governing the Zuni story of emergence as well as those governing the composition of a Shakespeare play. (p. 49)

In 1989, the University of Wisconsin System—consisting of 13 four-year and 12 two-year institutions of higher education—implemented a **Design for Diversity** plan mandating changes in policies and practices on all campuses to make them more welcoming places for students of color. Across America, universities have instituted changes to create positive environments for the increasingly diverse college student population. Humphreys (2000) presented results of a survey finding that 63% of colleges and universities either have at least one diversity course as a graduation requirement or are developing such a course; 42% require more than one course; 25% have had such a requirement for more than ten years.

Results and Possibilities

Diversity courses not only provide greater understanding of diverse groups, but they also help students appreciate the benefits of diversity. In Browne-Miller (1996), one student learned "More diversity allows for more possibilities, be it knowledge, friends, understanding between people" (p. 83). In a society as diverse and democratic as the United States, colleges and universities must actively facilitate understanding between diverse groups. Ball (2000) commented "For democracy to flourish, college students have to be able to interact with other students who are different from them" (p. 13). In a series of diversity reports, the American Association of Colleges and Universities (AACU) argued that diversity challenges democratic commitments: "instead of creating fragmentation and alienation . . . [AACU] asserts that only through diversity can we achieve a deeper and lasting national unity" (Musil, 1996, p. 226).

Diversity does not only refer to obvious differences of race, ethnicity, gender, or disabilities. Diversity includes other changes taking place in students attending college today: Almost 50% of all college students are over 24 years old, more than 50% are the first in their family to attend college, and students with learning disabilities are the fastest growing category of disabled students on our campuses. Individuals accepted today may require modifications of and accommodations within traditional policies and practices governing campuses. Yet as demographic developments and affirmative action plans change the face of our campuses, opponents struggle to maintain the status quo. White students filed suit against both graduate and undergraduate admissions programs at the University of Michigan for including race in their admissions procedures. In 2003, the Supreme Court's ruling on this case maintained its consistent position of allowing race to be used as a factor in admissions procedures while rejecting approaches that appear to establish racial quotas. Although there are likely to be further

> Democracy is a way of life . . . a vibrant, living sweep of hope and progress which constantly strives for the fulfillment of its objective in life—the search for truth, justice, and human dignity.
>
> **SAUL ALINSKY (1909–1972)**

cases, this ruling affirmed the university's argument that having a diverse student body benefited all students at the University of Michigan; in addition, the justices provided further clarification concerning how universities can include race as a factor in admissions procedures.

CORPORATE AND SMALL BUSINESS

It surprised some opponents of affirmative action to discover that several Fortune 500 corporations filed *amicus* briefs in support of Michigan's program; for the past two decades, the private sector has been in support of affirmative action. In the early 1980s, many corporations opposed Reagan administration efforts to reduce the demand for contractor compliance on federal projects. According to responses from Corporate Executive Officers (CEOs) reported by Reskin (2000), 122 of 128 major corporations would "retain their affirmative action plans [even] if the Federal government ended [required] affirmative action" (p. 111). Reskin also cites a 1996 survey where CEOs agreed that affirmative action had improved hiring procedures, marketing, and productivity. American corporations have embraced and promoted diversity because they understand how diversity benefits them.

In recent years, American business has become more attentive to diversity. It has no choice. The American work force has become much more diverse, and this trend is destined to continue. White males already represent less than half of the work force. According to Daft (2003), racial and ethnic minorities will constitute 40% of those entering the work force by 2010, and women will represent half the work force by 2020. Business leaders understand that responding positively to diversity by implementing pluralistic policies and practices is necessary because not only is the work force becoming more diverse, so are the customers.

The numbers of women and people of color in the work force mirror the percentage they represent as consumers, one certain to increase. In 2000, Secretary of Commerce Norman Mineta predicted: "America's population will increase 50% over the next 50 years, with almost 90% of that increase in the minority community" (Williams, 2003, p. 442). When people have money to spend, they command attention from American business. Williams claimed that people of color represent almost $800 billion of purchasing power, and 134 million American women have $1.1 trillion of purchasing power (see Table 15.1). One corporate president has insisted that more women must be appointed to corporate boards of directors primarily because "Women either control or influence nearly all consumer purchases" (Jones and George, 2003, p. 118).

Corporate Litigation

American demographic changes represent compelling reasons for corporate America to value diversity. Discrimination litigation has also provided motivation. In the 1980s and early 1990s, Denny's

GROUP	POPULATION NUMBERS	PURCHASING POWER
Gays and Lesbians	20 million	$514 million
People with Disabilities	49 million	$100 billion
African Americans	34 million	$400 billion
Asian Americans	10 million	$150 billion
Hispanic Americans	28 million	$235 billion
Women	134 million	$1.1 trillion

TABLE 15.1

Diversity and Purchasing Power Among U.S. Consumers

Source: Ellison and Bond, Diversity: The Bottom Line for Small Business, *Inc.,* 19 May, 1998, cited in Williams (2003).

RACIST INCIDENTS AT DENNY'S RESTAURANTS

At about 1:00 a.m., 32 African American high school students attending a conference for high school students at San Jose State (CA) University enter a Denny's restaurant but are told by the manager that Denny's policy regarding late night customers requires that they must pay for their meals after ordering and that there is a $2 cover charge per person. Although there are white customers in Denny's at this time, none has been asked to prepay or to pay a cover charge.

En route to Annapolis, MD, to make security preparations for a Presidential visit, 21 Secret Service agents stop at Denny's for supper. The restaurant is not crowded and all 21 agents are seated together; however, the white agents receive their food promptly while six African American agents receive no food. Half an hour after food was served to the white agents, the African American agents ask about their order. The waitress shakes her head and walks away. Other white customers arrive and are served, yet no food is brought to the African American agents who ask for the regional manager's phone number and leave.

Because Denny's advertised that its customers could eat for free on their birthday, an African American girl celebrates her 13th birthday at Denny's. The waitress is not pleasant, and when the girl's baptismal certificate is produced to prove that it is her birthday, the waitress becomes angry. She calls the manager, who refuses to accept the baptismal certificate as proof and demands to see the girl's school I.D. card. After the girl produces the card, the manager rejects it as well and begins yelling angrily at the family, who leave the restaurant.

Restaurants were the sites for several alleged racist incidents (see the box). Despite being one of the largest restaurant chains in the United States, Denny's hired few minority employees, and none of its major suppliers was a minority-owned firm. At the time of its purchase by Advantica Corporation, Denny's had just paid $54 million out of court to settle discrimination claims. According to Williams (2003), Advantica's CEO said the lawsuits had turned Denny's into "a poster child for racism" (p. 467).

Advantica took aggressive action to change the Denny image. As the twenty-first century began, 42% of Denny's employees were minorities, as were 33% of its managers. Nearly 20% of its suppliers were minority-owned firms, and 35% of its franchises were minority-owned. Denny's commitment to diversity was recognized by *Fortune* magazine identifying it as one of the top ten companies in its support of minorities.

Denny's experience provides a dramatic example of business responding to diversity issues; however, it is not the only example. Shoney's Restaurants paid $132.8 million to settle a claim of racial discrimination in hiring; Edison International paid $11 million for the same offense. Bell Atlantic Telephone paid $500 million for discrimination against blacks in employee promotions. After making significant changes in policies and practices, all three companies are now listed among *Fortune* magazine's top 50 companies for their support of minorities (Williams, 2003).

Workplace Diversity

Most businesses do not address diversity issues in response to legal action, but because they recognize the advantages of promoting workplace diversity. Employing diverse managers and employees increases the likelihood of more appropriate responses to customer needs. In areas with significant Hispanic populations, Sears and Target Stores have profited by accommodating Hispanic consumers, as have Darden's Restaurants by providing Spanish menus (Jones and George, 2003). Griffin

> Wrongdoing can only be avoided if those who are not wronged feel the same indignation at it as those who are.
>
> SOLON (640–558 BCE)

(2002) described the hypothetical example of Avon Cosmetics pursuing African American consumers. To be successful, they would want to have "African American managers . . . available to provide input into product development, design, packaging, advertising" (p. 176). Williams (2003) described the current American corporate attitude:

> We are living in an increasingly multicultural country, and new ethnic groups are quickly gaining consumer power. Our company needs a demographically more diverse work force to help us gain access to (them). (p. 462)

In addition to improving external marketing strategies, having a positive work environment to accommodate diversity improves productivity and reduces turnover costs. The Employment Management Association estimates the average costs for hiring new employees is $10,000 (Jones and George, 2003). According to Griffin (2002), one pharmaceutical corporation saved $50,000 by lowering its turnover rate among women and minorities. The creation of positive work environments for diverse employees may be one reason why 62% of job seekers said they would prefer to work for organizations demonstrating a commitment to diversity (Daft, 2003). (See Table 15.2.)

Creating a positive work environment is not a simple task, but it must be done. In discussing current issues, Griffin (2002) stated that a fundamental trend in business "is that virtually all organizations . . . are becoming more diverse" (p. 169). Businesses define diversity as not only the obvious differences of race and gender, but also less obvious differences including status as single parents or dual-career couples. To accommodate diversity, some U.S. companies have created day care centers at their work sites or have instituted flexible working hours. Benefits packages have been structured to address the diverse needs of employees. Being flexible does not have to be expensive, even when providing accommodations for people with disabilities. According to Williams (2003), the average cost of accommodating workers with disabilities was $250; 20% of accommodations involved no direct cost.

Diversity Programs and Workplace Training

Other components useful in creating a positive work environment may include disseminating sexual harassment policies, holding diversity seminars, and enforcing zero-tolerance policies toward prejudicial comments and behaviors. Because 50% of its

TABLE 15.2

America's Best Companies for Minorities

Company	Board of Directors	Officials and Managers	Total Workforce	Minorities as a % of New Hires
Advantica Spartanburg, S.C	4 of 11	33.4%	49.9%	69%
Avis Rent A Car Garden City, N.Y.	2 of 11	25%	48%	63%
Dole Food Westlake Village, CA	1 of 7	36.6%	55.6%	71%
Fannie Mae Washington, D.C.	N.A.	27.6%	40.2%	46%
Levi Strauss & Co. San Francisco	2 of 12	35.3%	58%	51%
SBC Communications San Antonio, TX	4 of 24	26.1%	34.4%	52%
Xerox Stamford, CT	2 of 16	23.4%	28.7%	40%

Source: Fortune, July 10, 2000, pp. 190–193.

employees were Hispanic, a San Antonio company provided copies of the employee handbook in Spanish and translated staff meetings into Spanish (Griffin, 2002). Some companies reward managers for working effectively with diverse groups of employees. A quarterly survey of Allstate Insurance employees included a "diversity index" for evaluating managers on diversity issues: 25% of a manager's bonus pay was determined by that score (Daft, 2003).

To promote a positive environment for diversity at the worksite, some U.S. companies have instituted **diversity training** programs for managers and employees. Training programs may include **diversity pairing,** where people from diverse backgrounds are paired to provide them with opportunities to interact and become better acquainted. Such pairs may be combined with mentoring as when a white male manager is paired with an employee of color or a woman. Many businesses create multicultural teams for more effective problem solving that also provide an opportunity for workers to learn more about their colleagues.

Jones and George (2003) described the diversity training program at United Parcel Service (UPS) that requires upper-level managers to participate in community programs for a full month. Approximately 40 managers per year work in organizations such as homeless shelters, Head Start centers, migrant farm worker assistance groups, and detention centers. Since 1968, over 800 managers have been involved in the program, and UPS believes it has had a positive impact on the abilities of its managers to respond more effectively to diversity issues.

Lingering Problems

Diversity problems still arise in the business community. Jones and George report that women and minorities continue to be disadvantaged because of how they are regarded by white colleagues, especially at worksites where they are a numerical minority. Daft (2003) cited two studies; one reported that 59% of minority managers believed there was a "racially motivated double standard in the delegation of assignments" (p. 443). Another study found that employees of color believed they had to work longer hours and make extra efforts to be given the same respect as white co-workers. Salary data documents that women and minorities

still earn substantially less money than white males and that minorities are still underrepresented in management. Although African Americans and Hispanics constitute 26% of the U.S. population, they represent only 13% of managers—8% and 5% respectively (Daft, 2003).

Women hold 49.5% of managerial positions and appear to be fairly represented, but the **glass ceiling** prevents them from rising as high as their abilities should permit. Jones and George (2003) reported on evidence of women's managerial ability, with one study concluding that female executives outperformed males on listening, motivating others, communicating effectively, and producing high-quality work. Another study of 425 top executives assessed 52 skills and found that women received higher ratings than men on 42 of them; yet women remain underrepresented in top executive positions. Williams (2003) reported that 90% of women executives said the glass ceiling had restricted their career growth; 80% indicated that they left their last job because the glass ceiling hurt their chances for promotion. Studies show that women are increasingly leaving organizations to start their own businesses because of their perception of a glass ceiling at work.

Corporate leaders know that problems arising from human differences must be resolved if U.S. businesses are to remain competitive in the global economy. These leaders will continue to publicly promote diversity, hire job seekers who appreciate corporate commitments to diversity, and provide diversity training to create a positive work environment for diverse employees. As Williams (2003) stated:

> The general purpose of diversity programs is to create a positive work environment where no one is advantaged or disadvantaged, where "we" is everyone, where everyone can do their best work, where differences are respected and not ignored, where everyone feels comfortable. (pp. 438–439)

MASS MEDIA

Ellmore (1991) defines **mass media:** "The various vehicles used for sending information to a mass audience: radio, television, CATV, newspapers, magazines, books, discs" (p. 351). The best evidence of mass media promoting pluralism is the increasing involvement of women and minorities. Because it is a visible medium, increased presence of people of color on television has been noticeable. In the 1950s and 1960s, few television programs cast minority characters; of those who were featured, most appeared in stereotypical roles. Stereotypes in television remain, but Americans also see people of color as news reporters, as anchors on local and network news programs, and as actors on television and in films. In 2002, Oscars for Best Performances by an Actor and Actress were both awarded to African Americans. Media spokespersons explain that diversity is promoted and appreciated in media because the industry understands the economic advantages of rewarding talent, regardless of gender, race, or ethnicity.

Actually, a weakness of the media industry argument is suggested in the representation of human diversity in media: People of color constitute 28% of the population, yet Popper (2000) found that people of color occupied 11.6% of the positions on newspaper staffs. And although diversity is represented on television and theater screens, the vast majority of jobs in television are behind the camera—writers, producers, camera operators, and technicians. According to Larson (1999), a study of U.S. news stations reported that in the top 25 markets, 81% of the news staff was white. Of the 19% minority staff, 9% was African American, 7% was Latino, 3% was Asian American, and 1% was Native American. In the 26–50 top markets, 91% of the news staff was white; in the 51–100 top markets—which included cities like Las Vegas, Nevada, and Jackson, Mississippi—94% of the staff was white. Popper (2000) responded to the question of future changes: "Most industry people expect on-air staff to remain diverse, since that's what the audience sees. What happens behind the scenes is less clear" (p. 67).

In entertainment programming, Johnson (2000) identified 55 African Americans among 839 writers for prime time shows—6.6% of the total—with 45 of the 55 writing for black-themed shows. Only one black writer was employed by a white-themed show, a seemingly blatant form of segregation suggesting that black writers can't write scripts for white actors even though white writers have written for black actors for years. In reference to segregation, the majority of black-themed shows are on the UPN and WB networks.

Increasing Media Representation of Human Diversity

Jones and George (2003) explained that the NAACP and Children Now, an advocacy group, are lobbying the entertainment industry to increase diversity in televised programs. The need for increased diversity has been documented. According to the Center for Media and Public Affairs, Hispanic reporters provided less than 2% of the stories for network television news, even though Hispanics make up 13% of the American population—representing 35 million potential television viewers. A study conducted by Children Now identified about 2% of the characters in prime time shows as Hispanic: 47 of 2,251 characters examined (p. 119).

Because of underrepresentation of people of color among television employees, the Federal Communications Commission (FCC) disseminated ambitious requirements for affirmative action plans to be submitted by communications corporations, but in 1998, a federal appeals court overturned the FCC requirements. Affirmative action advocates were encouraged, however, when the 15 largest broadcast networks agreed to follow FCC requirements as guidelines in developing their affirmative action plans (Childs, 1998).

Media Presentation and Language

Another area of concern is how American media report diversity issues such as affirmative action. Gabriel (1998) analyzed news media presentation of affirmative action controversies, including the 1995 headline in *U.S. News:* "NO WHITE MEN NEED APPLY?" The article ignored the history of discrimination against women and minorities to focus on the question of whether white men were being discriminated against. From his review of media coverage of affirmative action controversies, Gabriel found a tendency to reinforce misperceptions such as "affirmative action = quotas = lowering standards = discrimination against white males = racism" (p. 87). Gabriel also reported that media coverage typically stated or implied that affirmative action benefited people of color at the expense of white males, yet only peripherally recognized that white women have been major beneficiaries of affirmative action programs.

In terms of how people of color are presented on newscasts, Ferguson (1998) cited a study of 29 North American cities where newscasts included a pattern of stereotyping African Americans. Positive stereotypes were involved in the coverage of successful black athletes and musicians, but negative stereotypes were frequently reinforced in images of criminals, welfare mothers, and others representing a range of anti-social behaviors. External factors influencing the conditions for low-income blacks were never presented, leaving the viewer to assume that "these people" weren't willing to work hard enough to escape their poverty.

Bacon (2003) found a double standard in news coverage of black public figures. Although social activist Jesse Jackson ran two credible campaigns for the president of the United States, reporters and columnists frequently describe him as a "publicity hound" and "a race hustler." Betraying a total lack of understanding and respect for African American oral traditions, one Boston columnist chided Jackson because he "regularly substitutes rhyme for reason" (p. 27). Although professor Cornel West has consistently engaged in social justice issues, newspaper articles have referred to him as "a con man" and a "clownish minstrel." Some reporters have excerpted difficult passages from West's scholarly writing to illustrate their contention that West is impossible to understand. By creating such distractions, reporters have avoided addressing substantive issues being raised by Jackson and West. In Bacon's conclusion, she asks:

> Why do mainstream media approach progressive African American leaders with such evident contempt? . . . Why are they so reluctant to engage in arguments, preferring instead to ridicule and misrepresent them? (p. 29)

Perhaps part of the answer stems from white dominance of mainstream media. To grow up white in America is to believe in a world defined by white perspectives that are reinforced in schools and in media. As Ferguson (1998) stated: "Whiteness, and the power that goes with it, have been represented as so utterly normal that any other possibility seems like an aberration" (pp. 180–181). Gabriel (1998) cites June Jordan's reflection on media use of language to frame issues and images in stereotypes familiar to their white audience:

> I came to recognize media constructions such as "The Heartland" or "Politically Correct" or "The Welfare Queen" or "Illegal Alien" or "Terrorist" . . . for what they were: Multiplying scattershots intended . . . to establish and preserve white supremacy. (p. 11)

Critics have described media manipulation of language in the 1991 Gulf War to shape our perceptions of "us" versus "them," and some media critics have claimed that similar language patterns were prevalent in media coverage of the 2003 Iraqi conflict as well. Ferguson (1998) provided specific examples of how the 1991 news reports consistently used different language to describe American and Iraqi military actions:

The American Military	*The Iraqi Military*
had reporting guidelines	had censorship
was cautious	was cowardly
was confident	was desperate
was loyal	was blindly obedient
was resolute	was ruthless
was brave	was fanatical (p. 139)

Ferguson also noted that while American missiles caused "collateral damage," Iraqi missiles created "civilian casualties."

Representation of Diversity in Media: Present and Future

The creation of positive or negative images is not restricted to news reporting or television. Films have portrayed women and people of color in both positive and negative ways. Although American films have featured female characters overcoming obstacles, filmmakers have long been criticized for consistently producing films that link sex and violence. Similarly, people of color have been portrayed as admirable and heroic individuals; still we are offered more negative images of people of color as drug dealers, thieves, and violent criminals.

When filmmakers depict oppression, the result often seems self-serving. Gabriel (1998) observed that films like "To Kill a Mockingbird" (1962) and "A Time to Kill" (1996) are part of a pattern of films that denounce racism but present blacks as powerless, requiring white people to save them. "Mississippi Burning" (1988) incensed people who knew that many black men, women, and children in Mississippi had courageously defied racist authorities and were jailed—some were killed—while the FBI did little to help them, instead tapping Martin Luther King Jr.'s telephone to gather evidence that might prove a communist connection. For the film to portray white FBI agents as heroes saving frightened blacks was an outrageously racist revision of historical truth.

Media critics suggest that increasing the diversity of people writing and producing mass media in the United States will be the best way to reduce bias and stereotypes. Data show that women and people of color are entering media professions in increasing numbers. McQueen (2002) reported that 61% of journalism and mass communication students were female and that 27% were students of color. McQueen also noted that only 35% of journalism and mass communication faculty was female and 15% were faculty of color. By 2035, experts predict that 40% of students in journalism and mass com-

> You see things; and you say, 'Why?'
> But I dream things that never were;
> And I say, 'Why not?'
>
> **GEORGE BERNARD SHAW (1856–1950)**

munication will be students of color. In mission statements, media organizations often claim to reflect the diversity of their community. That does not describe the reality, but it should be the goal.

MILITARY SERVICES

Diversity in the armed forces of the United States is not a new issue; it is only the nature of the diversity that has changed. Although the military kept no records in its earliest years, there is anecdotal evidence that ethnic diversity in society was reflected in its military, and we know of at least one woman—Deborah Sampson—who disguised herself as a man and engaged in combat during the Revolutionary War (Craft-Fairchild, 1997).

Starting in 1856, records exist showing a significant percentage of ethnic immigrants serving in the Army—a short cut to being granted citizenship—but they also reveal problems. During the Mexican American War, many Irish Catholic soldiers were reluctant to kill Mexican Catholics, and a number of them deserted to avoid doing so (Johnson, 1999). Nevertheless, diversity continued to exist in the U.S. Army. According to Buckley (2001), at the end of the Civil War there were 140 black regiments with over 100,000 soldiers, and the army continued to recruit blacks and immigrants. Johnson (1999) cited an 1896 Army report documenting that 7% of that year's recruits were black and 33% were ethnic immigrants.

Significant differences concerning diversity in the military today include racial desegregation, inclusion of women, and exclusive reliance on volunteers. Each difference has created unique problems for military leadership to address, parallel to similar problems stemming from race and gender in the larger society. Dansby, Stewart, and Webb (2001) wrote, "In many ways the military has always been a mirror of American society, reflecting back the scars and blemishes as well as the face of the nation" (p. xvii). Although diversity problems have not yet been resolved, the U.S. military has made substantial progress, even more than society in general has made, according to sociologists Moskos and Butler (1996).

Military Desegregation

Desegregation in the military began with a research project during World War II. Black army platoons were integrated into white infantry companies and the social experiment was carefully monitored. The research team found that no unusual problems occurred and that all soldiers functioned effectively. Despite positive results, military leaders continued to oppose racial desegregation, even after President Truman issued an executive order mandating military racial desegregation. Because of racist attitudes among military leaders, the executive order was not fulfilled until the Korean War when desegregation became necessary for the sake of efficiency.

Dansby, Stewart, and Webb (2001) described problems with desegregation that came to the forefront during the Vietnam War. African Americans protesting against unequal treatment rioted at Fort

Dix, Fort Bragg, on two aircraft carriers, and at Travis Air Force base. As the Vietnam War was ending in the early 1970s, General Creighton Abrams testified that poor race relations had had a negative impact on combat effectiveness. Complicating matters further, in 1973, Congress ended the draft and established an all-volunteer Army. Recruiting and retaining quality soldiers would be affected by how the Army addressed issues of race relations.

The Army's response was to create a Defense Race Relations Institute charged with the responsibility of creating a race relations training program. The initial program lasted for six weeks; it was later expanded to include sexual harassment and discrimination, and now has become one of the Army's most ambitious programs. Dansby and Landis (2001) report that the current training program lasts 16 weeks and, according to the American Council on Education, is equivalent to 23 undergraduate semester college credits. A major objective is "To create an environment that values diversity and fosters mutual respect and cooperation" (p. 9).

Integration Problems

Johnson (2001) evaluated the Defense Race Relations program and concluded that the training had an immediate positive effect on participant attitudes and improved subsequent work performance. Even so, problems with race relations in the United States military persist. Katzenstein and Reppy (1999) referred to a 1996 task force that found evidence of racism at 4 of 19 military facilities evaluated. Individual soldiers have been involved in incidents of racial violence; some continue to be members of extremist groups promoting racism or white supremacy, even though military policy prohibits active participation in such groups. Waldman (1996) explained the reason for that policy: "The nature of the military means that anything that gets in the way of mission accomplishment is unacceptable. Racism gets in the way" (p. 27).

Sexism gets in the way as well. Prior to the establishment of the all-volunteer Army, fewer than 2% of recruits were female, with 90% of them receiving medical or administrative assignments (Katzenstein and Reppy, 1999); in order to maintain recruitment standards, however, the pool of candidates was expanded. According to Peterson (1999),

female recruits have tended to be better educated, to have higher scores on aptitude tests, and to be less likely to cause disciplinary problems. According to Katzenstein and Reppy (1999), women represent approximately 14% of enlisted personnel, 14% of officers, and 20% of those in basic training. Peterson (1999) concluded, "The Army fields the highest quality force in its history owing to the gains brought about by the all-volunteer force" (p. 100).

Increasing the role of minorities and women in the military has challenged male recruits because of cultural messages some men have internalized about masculinity. Katzenstein and Reppy (1999) explain: "Cultural ideas of masculinity encourage recruits to prove their fitness for military life by flaunting their masculine prowess in bigoted and sexist behavior" (p. 2). Military leaders did not understand this cultural influence at first. Defense directives about **sexual harassment** had been in place for many years before the 1991 Tailhook incident, in which drunken Navy pilots forced female officers to walk through a gauntlet while they were groped and verbally humiliated. The chief of naval operations said later, "Until Tailhook we dealt too often with sexual harassment . . . one case at a time, rather than understanding it as a cultural issue" (Katzenstein and Reppy, 1999, p. 2). The problem was intensified five years later when rape charges were brought against drill sergeants at the Aberdeen Army base. In 2002, cadet women of the Air Force Academy reported allegations of sexual

> Injustice anywhere is a threat to justice everywhere. We are caught in an inescapable network of mutuality, tied in a single garment of destiny. Whatever affects one directly affects all indirectly.
>
> **MARTIN LUTHER KING, JR. (1929–1968)**

assault, indicating the ongoing challenge for the U.S. military to address male concepts of power and gender superiority.

Diversity Policy and Gender

As military leaders study the gender problem, they realize that rules are not always being observed. Kier (1999) reported that no action was taken for 56% of all sexual harassment complaints. Women had reported sexual harassment for years, but had been ignored or encouraged to drop their complaint; some encountered hostile reactions from their male superiors. Katzenstein and Reppy (1999) conclude, "It was not a failure to have rules; [these] are problems emerging out of a culture at odds with [military] institutional policy" (p. 3). The 2002 and 2003 allegations of sexual harassment and even sexual assault at the Air Force Academy demonstrated that more must be done to resolve these problems.

Some people opposed to women in the military argue that sexual harassment is a reaction to double standards that allow women to perform at lower levels of competence. The Army's response is that levels are adjusted to take account of physiological differences for men as well as for women. Roush (1999) pointed out that for soldiers of the same height, men are allowed to weigh 30 pounds more than women before being required to enter weight control programs. In areas where no weight adjustment is necessary, women and men compete on an equal basis. Women soldiers have demonstrated excellent marksmanship by winning the Army's highest awards, and have participated on marksmanship teams at the Olympics (Carter, 2002). Shooting skills are only part of women's impressive record of achievement that has opened doors to new responsibilities.

During the 1970s and 1980s, the U.S. Army employed a **risk rule** that measured how close certain roles would bring a participant to battle and did not assign women to roles that would bring them into combat. Carter (2002) observed that the 1989 Panama invasion altered the rules when women soldiers engaged in battle while working in support units that were fired upon. Women driving convoy trucks and flying helicopters to transport wounded men to safety were fired upon and women in military police units assisted with cordoning off neighborhoods in search of guerillas. Some women would have earned medals if their assignments officially had listed them as combatants.

In 1991, Desert Storm provided another opportunity for women to prove their combat readiness. Despite predictions of critics, mixed-gender units displayed as much cohesiveness as single-gender units. Because of their performance in the Gulf War, women are now assigned to command military police companies, pilot helicopters, and serve in artillery units. The 2003 Iraq war placed thousands of women in battle zones, and actual combat assignments no longer seem unthinkable. Guenther-Schlesinger (1999) reported that 70% of women soldiers want to be assigned combat roles because major promotions are the most available to those who prove themselves on the battlefield. Kier (1999) argued that women would never be treated as equals in the military culture as long as their names are "missing from the rostrum of heroes, stories, and myths" arising from combat (p. 49).

Having studied demographic predictions, military leaders expect the percentage of women and minorities in the armed forces to increase; they are prepared to do much more recruiting from the growing pool of Hispanic American and Asian American candidates. Although there will be twice as many African Americans in the candidate pool by 2050, half of the U.S. population growth from 2000 to 2050 will occur among Latinos, with a smaller yet significant growth of Southeast Asians. Recruiters are encouraged by 1997 data showing that more Hispanics joined the military than any other ethnic group, but a major concern is the high dropout rate: Army policy requires that 90% of all recruits must have high school diplomas. According to a 1996 study by the National Center for Educational Statistics, 30% to 35% of Hispanic students drop out of high school, the highest rate of all groups included in their study (Diaz, 1999).

Religion and Sexual Orientation

Racial, ethnic, and gender diversity is only the beginning. The American military now has procedures for accommodating religious differences. And although the issue of lesbians and gays in the military is still debated, there is a growing sentiment that openly gay men and lesbians should be allowed to serve their country: "To be denied the right to serve is to have one's citizenship denied, and to be restricted in one's form of military service is to have one's citizenship restricted" (Segal, Segal and Booth, 1999, p. 225).

Although military leaders express opposition to gay and lesbian soldiers, Matthews (1999) reported results of a survey of 270 male soldiers, finding only 36% strongly opposed to serving with gay soldiers; twice as many women soldiers said they would serve with lesbians as those who said they would not. Opponents to gays and lesbians serving in the military say the Army is not the place for social experiments, but Katzenstein and Reppy (1999) note that the Army and other units of America's armed forces have always been affected by societal changes: "The American military has at different times trailed, led or simply mirrored efforts to combat prejudice, but it has never been isolated from those prejudices" (p. 10).

Military Leadership

As military recruiters make contact with an increasingly diverse pool of candidates, they must offer evidence that advancement is possible. According to Stewart and Firestone (2001), minorities are underrepresented at the general officer level. Jones (1999) recommended that military services immediately identify and attract more minority officer candidates to function as a "source of inspiration" for minority soldiers. Sayles (1999) discussed the importance of women and minority role models at all levels in the military organizational structure to provide women and minorities proof of genuine opportunity for advancement in the military—rather than a glass ceiling. All branches of the service have been asked to address the need for minority officers in their affirmative action plans; as

an example, the Navy goal is to commission at least 7% black and 4% Hispanic officers each year. Jones (1999) stated: "Commitment to diversity and equal opportunity is the keystone to our entire value structure" (62).

AFTERWORD

In his discussion of diversity issues in the military, Jones (1999) commented: "Americans tend to be ignorant about other societies and even about subcultures within their own society" (p. 62). His comment echoes a concern multicultural education advocates have expressed for several years: that too many K–12 schools do not address diversity issues adequately. This book was written to address diversity issues with college students, but the issues need to be addressed in K–12 classrooms as well. Schools in rural or suburban areas with predominately white students tend to offer too little information about diversity. White teachers are often uncomfortable with controversies related to diverse groups, some insisting that they don't need to address diversity because there are no—or few—students of color in their schools!

If white students rarely encounter people of color, it is even more important for teachers to provide accurate cognitive information about history, contributions, and issues affecting diverse populations in this country both historically and today. Further, this is not just a need for white students: Jones's comment referred to American recruits from diverse groups. African American students may know little about cultures or experiences of Native Americans; Native American students may only know about the "model minority" and have little knowledge of the past oppression, achievements, and current barriers of Asian Americans. Latino students may not understand why Somali students are in their school, and Somali students may have learned negative stereotypes about Latinos. Middle-class students need to understand the realities for low-income families; nondisabled students must confront misperceptions about people with disabilities; heterosexual students can unlearn myths they have been taught about gays and lesbians. In a diverse society, everyone needs to learn more about the diverse groups of people calling themselves Americans.

> One of the most successful institutions in American society in dealing with racial integration has been the United States Army. At the other extreme . . . (public) schools are among the most segregated associations in the country.
>
>   **E**UGENE **Y. L**OWE, **J**R. **(C**ONTEMPORARY**)**

We are all Americans. We share a culture, yet we are different in many ways. We live in a nation that adopted the motto "E Pluribus Unum" in 1782, originally meaning: "from many states, one nation." The motto has also been a metaphor for the people in a nation built on foundations established by Native Americans, profiting from import of Africans, and exploiting the labor of immigrants and women: Each group has struggled to find its place in the kaleidoscope of changing images and altered realities. Their achievements were based on an American Dream of a good life for themselves and their families, of a nation where they had freedom to work, worship, and live as they pleased among diverse people who were also guaranteed equal rights and equal opportunities.

That American Dream has always been an ideal. Some groups were granted this ideal more readily than others, but all have sought it. America's history is a history of that struggle. We are farther along than ever today, yet we still have much to do to bring the dream closer to reality for all Americans. Pluralism represents a vehicle to move us forward. Committing ourselves to being pluralistic represents a commitment to the American Dream, a commitment to make our nation's motto—"out of the many, one"—a description of the nation we are becoming. That is a dream worth dreaming.

> When we dream alone, we are merely dreaming; But when we dream together, that's the beginning of reality.
>
> BRAZILIAN PROVERB

TERMS AND DEFINITIONS

Affirmative action A written plan required of businesses and institutions of higher education to reduce discrimination in hiring, public contracting, and college admissions

Design for Diversity A Wisconsin program that mandates changes in policies and practices on all thirteen UW System campuses to make them more welcoming places for diverse students

Diversity The presence of human beings with perceived or actual differences based on a variety of human characteristics

Diversity pairing A diversity training strategy where two people from diverse backgrounds are paired to provide them with opportunities to interact and become better acquainted

Diversity training Programs designed by businesses to promote a positive environment for diverse employees and managers at the worksite

Glass ceiling An informal upper limit that keeps women and minorities from being promoted to positions of greatest responsibility in work organizations

Mass media The various vehicles employed to provide information to a mass audience: radio, television, CATV, newspapers, magazines, books, discs, etc.

Pluralism The equal coexistence of diverse cultures in a mutually supportive relationship within the boundaries of one nation

Proposition 209 A California statute prohibiting preferential treatment to individuals or groups in hiring, awarding public contracts, and college admissions

Racial quota Designation of a specific number of applicants to be hired or admitted based on their race

Risk rule An army practice of measuring how close certain roles would bring a participant to combat and not assigning women to any role that would bring them too close

Seniority system Requires employees with least seniority to be laid off work if the employer needs to release a certain number of employees

Set-aside program Requiring contractors to hire a certain percentage of minority subcontractors if they are awarded a project funded by tax dollars

Sexual harassment Deliberate and repeated behavior that has a sexual basis and is not welcomed, requested, or returned

REFERENCES

Bacon, J. (2003) Disrespect, distortion and double binds: Media treatment of progressive black leaders. *Extra! 16*(2), 27–29.

Analyzes media treatment of three black social activists and describes a pattern of remarks reflecting personal attacks without responding to the issues they raise.

Ball, H. (2000). *The Bakke case: Race, education, and affirmative action.* Lawrence: University Press of Kansas.

Examines law and politics providing a context for the Bakke case, presents key arguments from both sides, and reviews more recent events stemming from the Bakke decision.

Browne-Miller, A. (1996). *Shameful admissions: The losing battle to serve everyone in our universities.* San Francisco: Jossey-Bass.

Discusses college admissions policies and practices and how they help or hinder fair access to equal opportunity for all applicants and what happens after a person is accepted to college.

Buckley, G. (2001). *American patriots: The story of blacks in the military from the Revolution to Desert Storm.* New York: Random House.

Includes statistics and stories about African Americans who fought in America's wars.

Carter, P. (2002). War dames. *The Washington Monthly 34*(12), 32–37.

Reviews recent history of women in the military and how their role has evolved from serving only in support units to having responsibilities that bring them into combat.

Childs, K. (1998). Media affirmative action pact. *Editor & Publisher 131*(32), 11.

Describes the reaction of broadcast networks to a federal court's ruling against affirmative action requirements established by the Federal Communications Commission.

Clayton, S.D., & Crosby, F.J. (2000). Justice, gender, and affirmative action. In F.J. Crosby & C. VanDeVeer (Eds.), *Sex, race, and merit: Debating affirmative action in education and employment* (pp. 81–88). Ann Arbor: The University of Michigan Press.

Explains the purpose of affirmative action, examines the denial of discrimination by victims of discrimination, and discusses the future of affirmative action.

Cochran-Smith, M. (2003). Standing at the crossroads: Multicultural teacher education at the beginning of the 21st century. *Multicultural Perspectives 5*(3), 3–11.

Describes three issues of critical interest to U.S. educators: teacher/student demographic data and trends, competing school reform agendas, and criticisms of educational research.

Craft-Fairchild, C. (1997, Fall). Women warriors in the 18th century. *St. Thomas,* 32–35.

Describes eighteenth century women who dressed as men in Great Britain or the United States, in some cases becoming soldiers, in order to have the advantages of men.

Crosby, F.J., & VanDeVeer, C. (Eds.). (2000). *City of Richmond* v. *J.A. Croson Co.* In *Sex, race, and merit: Debating affirmative action in education and employment* (pp. 280–293). Ann Arbor: The University of Michigan Press.

Contains a brief introduction by the editors and presents an abridged version of Sandra Day O'Connor's text explaining the court's decision with comments from other justices.

Daft, R.L. (2003). Managing diverse employees. In *Management* (4th ed., pp. 436–468). Versailles, KY: Thompson Southwestern.

Discusses the current status of affirmative action, various dimensions of diversity in the work force, and how corporate culture is changing to accommodate diversity.

Dansby, M.R., & Landis, D. (2001). Intercultural training in the Unites States military. In M.R. Dansby, J.B. Stewart, & S.C. Webb (Eds.), *Managing diversity in the military: Research perspectives from the defense equal opportunity management institute* (pp. 9–28). New Brunswick, NJ: Transaction.

Describes the background, philosophy, and status of intercultural training in the military.

Dansby, M.R., Stewart, J.B., & Webb, S.C. (Eds.). (2001). Overview. In *Managing diversity in the military: Research perspectives from the defense equal opportunity management institute* (pp. xvii–xxxii). New Brunswick, NJ: Transaction.

Summarizes the role of women and minorities in military history as a context for the essays in this book and explains the organization of the book.

Diaz, R.F. (1999). The Hispanic market: An overview. In L.J. Matthews & T. Pavri (Eds.), *Population diversity and the U.S. Army* (pp. 87–98). Carlisle, PA: Strategic Studies Institute.

Describes the current location and predicted growth of Hispanics and strategies for effectively recruiting Hispanics at the present time and in the future.

Duncan, P. (2002). Decentering whiteness: Resisting racism in the women's studies classroom. *Race in the college classroom: Pedagogy and politics.* In B. Tusmith &

M.T. Reddy (Eds.), *Race in the college classroom: Pedagogy and politics* (pp. 40–50). New Brunswick, NJ: Rutgers University Press.

Describes conflicting racial perspectives between white students and students of color in college and how professors often behave as if white students are of primary concern.

Eastland, T. (2000). Ending affirmative action: The case for colorblind justice. In F.J. Crosby & C. VanDeVeer (Eds.), *Sex, race, and merit: Debating affirmative action in education and employment* (pp. 174–175). Ann Arbor: The University of Michigan Press.

Argues that affirmative action has failed by harming those it was intended to help.

Eck, D.L. (2001). *A new religious America: How a "Christian Country" has become the world's most religiously diverse nation.* New York: HarperCollins.

Examines the growth of diverse religions in the United States, especially with regard to immigration patterns since 1965, and describes its impact and its potential.

Ellmore, R.T. (1991). *NTC's mass media dictionary.* Lincolnwood, IL: National Textbook.

Includes definitions of numerous terms related to mass media.

Ferguson, R. (1998). *Representing "race": Ideology, identity and the media.* London: Arnold.

Reviews research to discuss relationships between racism and media representations of reality, and analyzes the ideology employed in maintaining racial hierarchies.

Gabriel, J. (1998). *Whitewash: Racialized politics and the media.* London: Routledge.

Focuses on case studies to analyze media dissemination of language that normalizes white privilege and creates a racialized discourse influencing political and economic change.

Greene, K.W. (1989). *Affirmative action and principles of justice.* New York: Greenwood.

Analyzes the philosophical and legal issues related to affirmative action and responds to the emotional reactions created by the affirmative action debate.

Griffin, R. (2002). The cultural and multicultural environment. In *Management* (7th ed., pp. 162–191). Boston: Houghton Mifflin.

Discusses how trends in diversity affect the corporate environment, advantages of diversity, and suggests strategies for effective management of diversity.

Guenther-Schlesinger, S. (2001). Persistence of sexual harassment: The impact of military culture on policy implementation. In M.F. Katzenstein & J. Reppy (Eds.), *Beyond zero tolerance: Discrimination in military culture* (pp. 195–212). Lanham, MD: Rowman & Littlefield.

Reviews the history of sexual harassment in the military and identifies unique aspects of military culture that enable sexual harassment to persist.

Humphreys, D. (Ed.). (2000, Fall). National survey finds diversity requirements common around the country. *Diversity Digest,* 1–2.

Presents results from a survey of 543 colleges and universities from every region of the country and representing an array of types of institutions.

Johnson, D. (1999). The U.S. Army and ethnic diversity: A historical overview. In L.J. Matthews & T. Pavri (Eds.), *Population diversity and the U.S. Army* (pp. 45–56). Carlisle, PA: Strategic Studies Institute.

Describes the ethnic composition of the U.S. army in the past, reasons why ethnic groups joined the army, and issues related to the historic diversity of the American army.

Johnson, J.L. (2001). Local effects and global impact of Defense Equal Opportunity Management Institute Training. In M.R. Dansby, J.B. Stewart, & S.C. Webb (Eds.), *Managing diversity in the military: Research perspectives from the defense equal opportunity management institute* (pp. 178–188). New Brunswick, NJ: Transaction.

Evaluates effectiveness of DEOMI training in terms of local effects (mastery of content, development of skills and attitudes) and global impact (subsequent work performance).

Johnson, S.D. (2000, June). Keep the pressure on. *Essence 1*(2), 184.

Discusses the participation of African American writers in prime-time television shows.

Jones, G.R., & George, J.M. (2003). Managing diverse employees in a diverse environment. *Contemporary Management* (3rd ed., pp. 112–149). New York: McGraw-Hill.

Describes increasing diversity among consumers and in the work force and provides strategies for managers to work effectively with diverse employees.

Jones, J.C. (1999). Diversity in the 21st Century: Leadership issues. In L.J. Matthews & T. Pavri (Eds.),

Population diversity and the U.S. Army (pp. 57–68). Carlisle, PA: Strategic Studies Institute.

Analyzes predicted demographic trends for implications on future recruitment and the importance of having more women and minority officers to enhance recruitment.

Katzenstein, M.F., & Reppy, J. (Eds.). (1999). Introduction: Rethinking military culture. *Beyond zero tolerance: Discrimination in military culture* (pp. 1–21). Lanham, MD: Rowman & Littlefield.

Describes American military culture, how it has functioned as a social laboratory, and why it needs to change because of the increasing numbers of women and minorities.

Kier, E. (1999). Discrimination and military cohesion: An organizational perspective. In M.F. Katzenstein & J. Reppy (Eds.), *Beyond zero tolerance: Discrimination in military culture* (pp. 25–32). Lanham, MD: Rowman & Littlefield.

Uses knowledge from organizational theory to discuss the military's organizational culture and how that culture must change to end discrimination against women, gays, and lesbians.

Kolodny, A. (1998). *Failing the future: A dean looks at higher education in the Twenty-First Century.* Durham, NC: Duke University Press.

Describes issues in higher education, especially in a public research university, from perspectives of students, teachers, and administrators, and recommends changes.

Larson, M. (1999, November). News hues. *Brandweek 40*(43), 4043.

Discusses participation of racial minorities in news stations at various market levels.

Lowe Jr., E.Y. (Ed.). (1999). Promise and dilemma: Incorporating racial diversity in selective higher education. *Promise and dilemma: Perspectives on racial diversity and higher education* (pp. 3–43). Princeton: Princeton University Press.

Examines the history of societal efforts to accommodate racial diversity and identifies recurring phenomena that have helped or hindered these efforts.

Matthews, L. (1999). Introduction: Primer on future recruitment of diversity. In L.J. Matthews & T. Pavri (Eds.), *Population diversity and the U.S. Army* (pp. 116). Carlisle, PA: Strategic Studies Institute.

Discusses issues affecting future recruitment, such as accepting gay and lesbian soldiers, increasing religious diversity in the army, and women engaging in combat.

McQueen, M. (2002, July/August). What about diverse faculty? *Quill 90*(6), 19–22.

Discusses the presence of women and minorities as students and faculty in journalism/mass communication departments in higher education.

Moskos, C.C., & Butler, J.S. (1996). *All that we can be: Black leadership and racial integration in the Army.* New York: Basic Books.

Provides evidence and arguments in support of their thesis that racial integration has been successfully achieved in the U.S. Army.

Musil, C.M. (1996 November/December). The maturing diversity initiatives on American campuses. *American Behavioral Scientist 40*(2), 222–232.

Describes the increasing value for diversity expressed in corporate culture and in higher education and how the two mutually reinforce each other.

Peterson, M.J. (1999). Women in the U.S. military. In L.J. Matthews & T. Pavri (Eds.), *Population diversity and the U.S. Army* (pp. 99–106). Carlisle, PA: Strategic Studies Institute.

Describes characteristics of women in the military, issues affecting them, and how their presence has enhanced the quality of the army.

Pipher, M. (2002). *The middle of everywhere: The world's refugees come to our town.* New York: Harcourt.

Presents stories about a variety of recent immigrants, the conditions that forced them to immigrate, and the difficulties they encounter trying to adjust to American culture.

Popper, B. (2000). Minority hiring may be facing retrenchment. *USA Today Magazine 128*(2658), 66–67.

Discusses the participation of racial minorities in newspapers and television news.

Reddy, M.T. (2002). Smashing the rules of racial standing. In B. Tusmith & M.T. Reddy (Eds.), *Race in the college classroom: Pedagogy and politics* (pp. 51–61). New Brunswick, NJ: Rutgers University Press.

Examines strategies—and describes the mixed outcomes—for dealing with presumptions of authority based on whiteness and for decentering whiteness in the classroom.

Reskin, B.F. (2000). The realities of affirmative action in employment. In F.J. Crosby & C. VanDeVeer, (Eds.), *Sex, race, and merit: Debating affirmative action in education and employment* (pp. 103–113). Ann Arbor: The University of Michigan Press.

Compares employers with and without affirmative action plans, and examines how affirmative action affects the workplace and the people it was designed to help.

Roush, P.E. (1999). A tangled Webb the Navy can't afford. In M.F. Katzenstein & J. Reppy (Eds.), *Beyond zero tolerance: Discrimination in military culture* (pp. 81–100). Lanham, MD: Rowman & Littlefield.

Responds to James Webb's arguments against women being in the military.

Sayles, A.H. (1999). Person to person: The diversity challenge for the Army after next. In L.J. Matthews & T. Pavri (Eds.), *Population diversity and the U.S. Army* (pp. 107–124). Carlisle, PA: Strategic Studies Institute.

Discusses the benefits of diversity in the military and describes a program called Consideration of Others that is designed to enhance appreciation for diversity.

Segal, D.R., Segal, M.W., & Booth, B. (1999). Gender and sexual orientation diversity in modern military forces: Cross-national patterns. In M.F. Katzenstein & J. Reppy (Eds.), *Beyond zero tolerance: Discrimination in military culture* (pp. 225–250). Rowman & Littlefield.

Discusses issues affecting the acceptance of women, gay men, and lesbians in the military and the role of the "citizenship revolution" in promoting change in the military culture.

Stewart, J.B., & Firestone, J.M. (2001). Looking for a few good men: Predicting patterns of retention, promotion, and accession of minority and women officers. In M.R. Dansby, J.B. Stewart, & S.C. Webb (Eds.), *Managing diversity in the military: Research perspectives from the defense equal opportunity management institute* (pp. 231–256). New Brunswick, NJ: Transaction.

Reviews the literature on officer promotion, explains the issue of white male dominance, and makes recommendations to increase the numbers of women and minority officers.

Tusmith, B., & Reddy, M.T. (2002). Introduction: Race in the college classroom. In B. Tusmith & M.T. Reddy (Eds.), *Race in the college classroom: Pedagogy and politics* (pp. 1–3). New Brunswick, NJ: Rutgers University Press.

Defines affirmative action, summarizes the main arguments in the debate over affirmative action, and describes the organization of the book.

Waldman, A. (1996, November). GIs: Not your average Joes: What the military can teach us about race, class, and citizenship. *The Washington Monthly*, 26–33.

Discusses the military's historic role in assimilating immigrants for future success in society and how the military has now achieved the same result for people of color.

Williams, C. (2003). Managing individuals and a diverse work force. In *Management* (2nd ed., pp. 434–471). Versailles, KY: Thompson Southwestern.

Explains why diversity is being promoted in the corporate world, the benefits of diversity, and principles for being an effective manager of diverse employees.

Yamane, D. (2001). *Student movements for multiculturalism: Challenging the curricular color line in higher education.* Baltimore, MD: The Johns Hopkins University Press.

Addresses the problem of the color line in higher education curriculum and the process by which students have challenged this color line by demanding multicultural courses.

Summary Exercises

See page 19 for exercises to help you summarize the main points and define key terms in this chapter.

Personal Clarification Exercises

In Chapter 15, two exercises promote discussion about diversity and pluralism in major American institutions.

Clarification Exercise #1 Diversity in America: Comments That Deserve Responses

Directions: With a team member, take turns reading aloud the statements below. Each statement in some way represents a perspective of diversity in America today; consider that the topic of each remark is our federal judiciary, the business community, K–12 education, higher education, and/or American media sources. As you progress, mark whether you *Approve* or *Disapprove* of the statement. Then, in any order, explain to your teammate *Why* the statement is appropriate or ill-advised. Be certain that your partner clearly understands your explanation. Where needed, suggest a revised remark that might better reflect your judgment of the issue. The goal is not to persuade, but to be able to express your analysis clearly and concisely. Your instructor may ask you to share your responses with the entire class before concluding the exercise.

1. I don't have enough time to comprehend all these new ideas and content. Besides, people in their profession who are directly affected can handle diversity issues better by themselves. I prefer not to be involved.

   Approve _____   Don't approve _____
   Why? _____

2. I really don't plan on working in that sector. Besides, I won't be in an area with a large ethnic or racial population, so diversity won't be an issue to me or my employer.

   Approve _____   Don't approve _____
   Why? _____

3. I am concerned with American children and youth becoming pluralistic, but I am more concerned with whether they can qualify for college or do a good job in the work force.

Approve _____   Don't approve _____
Why? _____

4. Why make such a big deal out of human differences? We're all Americans here. We don't need to emphasize diversity and pluralism. We just need to learn to contribute to the U.S. economy and not be supported by it.

   Approve _____   Don't approve _____
   Why? _____

5. The more time we spend studying multiculturalism, the more we will really be promoting separatism rather than uniting all of our citizenry. I went though the system when there was no multicultural focus and I don't think I was limited by it.

   Approve _____   Don't approve _____
   Why? _____

6. America is a melting pot. Everyone has an equal chance. If you want to make it in this country, all you need is a little desire and initiative.

   Approve _____   Don't approve _____
   Why? _____

7. Why focus on diversity and how everyone in America is different? Besides, more than 90% of all human characteristics are alike, not different.

   Approve _____   Don't approve _____
   Why? _____

8. I recognize that America is a diverse country. Aren't we doing a good enough job getting along as it is? Why do we need to go the next step and expect to be a pluralistic society?

   Approve _____   Don't approve _____
   Why? _____

ADAPTED FROM AN ACTIVITY IN *EDUCATION IN A MULTICULTURAL SOCIETY*, PP. 33–37 BY FRED RODRIGUEZ UNIVERSITY PRESS OF AMERICA, 1983

Clarification Exercise #2 Assessing Diversity and Pluralism in America

Directions: Each member of the class joins one of four groups: Each group agrees to represent one of the following four categories below: Biology, Ideology, Geography, Economy. (a) Individual groups should identify within each subcategory ways in which the United States is *diverse* and create a table of results. (b) Groups continue with the category and subcategories by identifying ways in which the current U.S. population meets—or could meet—its diversity goals with what could be termed *pluralist* behavior or policy. For both (a) and (b), cite examples from Chapter 15 as well as from discussion within your group. Prepare to share your responses with the class and to hear the responses of those who studied other categories.

[*Example:* Races are well represented in the United States today, but we must rid ourselves of job discrimination based on race. Interracial marriage is breaking racial barricades, but we need to be more accepting of groups of people of other races.]

Intergroup Exercises

In Chapter 15, two exercises promote discussion about diversity and pluralism in major American institutes.

Intergroup Exercise #1 Whom Would You Hire? Selecting Elementary Teachers

Directions: Imagine that you are a school board member and committee member to an elementary school administrator with responsibility for hiring new teachers. You have four positions open in grades 1–3 and eight applicants from whom to choose. You have interviewed all eight, each of whom impressed you favorably.

Assessing Diversity and Pluralism in America

CATEGORY	HOW ARE WE DIVERSE?	HOW CAN WE BE PLURALISTIC?
Humans are different according to our . . .		
BIOLOGY		
Race	_____	_____
Gender	_____	_____
Age	_____	_____
Sexual orientation	_____	_____
Health	_____	_____
Physical attributes	_____	_____
IDEOLOGY		
Religion	_____	_____
Politics	_____	_____
Education	_____	_____
GEOGRAPHY		
Ethnicity	_____	_____
Nationality	_____	_____
Dialect and language	_____	_____
ECONOMY		
Wages	_____	_____
Occupations	_____	_____
Wealth	_____	_____

Part One: Read through the brief descriptions below and select the four you would hire. [*Note:* Although the sketches provide much less information than one would have in reality, no matter how much material one has, it would undoubtedly never be enough.]

Candidate 1: Forty-year-old female, single, lives alone with eighteen years outstanding experience; highly successful with typically unsuccessful children. Possibly in a lesbian relationship.

Candidate 2: Twenty-four-year-old male, single, two years experience in a ghetto school. A near-genius, he brings outstanding recommendations. Leader of local black power group; his students use African names and openly reject "slave" names.

Candidate 3: Thirty-five-year-old male, married, father of six. Community-minded, interested in Cub Scouts. Known for having very well-organized, planned lessons and classes. Ten years experience. Native American heritage.

Candidate 4: Forty-year-old male, single, living with aged parents. The candidate has extensive experience from being a local business entrepreneur before returning to college for credentials. Just completed requirements, and received a $20,000 grant to work with junior high school students in distributive education. Native of India; practicing Catholic.

Candidate 5: Twenty-six-year-old female, divorced, supports self and three small children. Highly creative; three years experience; outstanding recommendations on professional capability. Native of Puerto Rico.

Candidate 6: Fifty-eight-year-old male, highly respected former Episcopal minister who left pulpit to work full time with children. Has just completed teaching credentials.

Candidate 7: Forty-eight-year old female, widowed. Twenty-five years experience, including three years in the Infants School of England. Wants to incorporate Infant School concepts here. Independently wealthy through both her own and her spouse's families.

Candidate 8: Twenty-two-year-old female, single, one year experience, excellent recommendations. Voluntarily tutored all four years in college, including full time in summers. Living openly in the community with a man of another race.

Part Two: When you have selected four, collaborate with other members of your assigned group of five in order to function as a personnel committee for the school. Establish ground rules for the operation of your committee, including leadership, decision-making process (majority vote or consensus), and whatever other considerations you feel important.

Part Three: Discuss the selections of each committee member to agree on candidates. When your group has selected four teacher candidates for the jobs, post your selections and compare your choices with those of other groups. Summarize the reasoning behind your group's choices.

Intergroup Exercise #2 Difficult Dialogues Experience

Directions: In groups of three, develop a dialogue based upon the scenario below. Use the situation as the basis for your 5-minute role play of the situation. Remain in character at the conclusion of your skit and respond to class questions about motivation, purpose, or intent behind your comments during the scene. Each team of three is asked to complete a 5-minute role play, regardless of similarity to others performed.

Difficult Dialogues: Plan 2008

Characters:

- Asian American 21-year-old junior with strong ties to her parents
- Highly enthusiastic white 24-year-old woman active in multiple human rights events

- Campus student activities director; convener of campus students for input regarding The Plan [See below]

A group of 24 students is discussing "The Plan 2008 for Campus Diversity" and its impact on the university. The enthusiastic woman points out that the plan calls for ethnic and racial diversity, but that the institution is also dealing with a broader definition of diversity that includes people's disabilities, sexual orientation, gender, age, and ideologies. An Asian American student questions this, saying that she feels diversity means race and ethnicity alone. The student activities director is interested in the students discussing the definition in detail before drawing any conclusions.

How Can Understanding Human Differences Resolve Dilemmas in a Multicultural Society?

Reading about the past and discussing the present reality of human differences in America represent the beginning of a new and vital awareness of interactions between people. But it is only a beginning. Knowing how interpersonal communication occurs and how to avoid or resolve conflicts between people and groups is of little value to the bigot, since bigots are constrained from action only when the consequences appear to be more severe to themselves than to those they hate. Knowing the causes of prejudice is of little value to the worker who allows prejudice to corrode an appreciation for the worth of other individuals or groups. Recognizing historical precedents for our current actions does little for the neighbor who ignores this knowledge and denounces those who complain of continuing discrimination. And being able to recognize racism, sexism, homophobia, and other markers of majority oppression toward minority persons or groups is of no use to any person whose harassment, contempt, and oppression is allowed to continue.

Positive attitudes about diversity must be demonstrated, and when positive behaviors are demonstrated, positive attitudes are strengthened. Follow the rules for respect of others and respect will accrue in return. Apply the lessons in this study of how humans are different and discover the scientific truth reported in genome research that human beings are 96% alike, no matter where we live, no matter what we've done.

So why spend so much time studying differences that are no more than 4% of who we are? Because that 4% has been allowed to overpower us, to divide, separate, anger, segregate, offend, and hurt. Our emphasis on the 4% has permitted us to classify, rank, categorize, and demean others. It has allowed us to watch as others grow weary, become discouraged, starve, suffocate, and die.

Practice and repetition are important. Discussion and debate are vital. Proposition and negotiation are necessary. Nothing we have written in this text has any value for a reader unless that reader agrees to follow a positive and constructive philosophy based on optimism about diversity and then demonstrates that optimism in word and deed. We know that it is possible, and we believe that it is necessary. If enough Americans believe this is the right thing to do, then together we can sustain this noble experiment with a democracy that promises freedom and opportunity for all its citizens.

No experience is complete without reflecting upon one's learning and without opportunity to aggregate thoughts, values, opinions, and beliefs into a coherent personal statement. These exercises allow for summarizing and for drawing conclusions about how humans are different in America today.

Personal Clarification Exercises

Two exercises promote discussion of human differences in the United States today.

Clarification Exercise #1 A Personal Post-Test Self Check: What Will You Be?

Directions: Respond to each of the items below with brief remarks. Then, at an agreed upon time after writing out your remarks, exchange all ten resulting replies with those from each of three other group members. Take approximately 10 minutes with each person; be sure to explain your responses *and* to hear and comment on the responses from your three selected partners. Following your three partner discussions, prepare to explain to the group the similarities, differences, and most exciting replies of your own or those of your discussants.

A Personal Post-Test Self Check

1. List what you believe personally to be three of the most important human differences.
   - _____
   - _____
   - _____

2. Explain one instance where you have witnessed racism as the belief that some human population groups are inherently superior or inferior to others because of genetically transmitted characteristics. Tell your personal suggestion of how that situation could have been avoided.
   - _____
   - _____

3. Give an example of a situation that illustrates cultural blindness. Explain how it could be remedied.
   - _____
   - _____

4. Describe a real or imagined situation in which you might confront "ethnocentrism."
   - _____
   - _____

5. List three terms that you think are acceptable replacements for "handicapped" or "disabled."
   - _____
   - _____
   - _____

6. Describe your current ability at cultural communication.
   - _____

7. List four recommendations for how one might better recognize cultural and ethnic heritage when communicating.
   - _____
   - _____
   - _____
   - _____

8. Suggest two or more ways that you could be an active advocate for diversity.
   - _____
   - _____

9. Name several ways that current American culture—workplace and personal—affects women, disabled, or any other minority groups because of human differences.
   - _____
   - _____
   - _____
   - _____

10. Tell what one practice you have resolved to adopt to be an active pluralist within our diverse America.
    - _____
    - _____

ADOPTED FROM EVELYN HARDEN *RURAL HEALTH CARE: CULTURAL COMPETENCY TRAINING WORKBOOK* NATIONAL RURAL HEALTH ASSOCIATION, 2002

Clarification Exercise #2 Personal Assessment: How Tolerant Are You?

Directions: It is possible to sample a person's attitudes to assess tolerance levels. If you respond honestly to each item below, this exercise may suggest areas of which to be aware. For each of the following questions, circle the answer that best describes you. When you have completed the exercise, add up your converted scores using the conversion chart below, and then total the converted scores to obtain a final figure. Compare that figure with the scale at the end of this exercise. As time permits, analyze each item, comparing your score for each item with the answer having the lowest numerical weight.

How Tolerant Are You?

1. Most of your friends are:
   a. Similar to you
   b. Very different from you and from each other
   c. Like you in some respects, but different in others
2. When someone does something of which you disapprove, you:
   a. Break off the relationship
   b. Tell how you feel but keep in touch
   c. Tell yourself it matters little and behave as you always have
3. Which virtue is most important to you:
   a. Kindness
   b. Objectivity
   c. Obedience
4. When it comes to beliefs, you
   a. Do all you can to make others see things the same way you do
   b. Actively advance your point of view but stop short of argument
   c. Keep your feelings to yourself
5. Would you hire a person who has had emotional problems?
   a. No
   b. Yes, provided there is evidence of complete recovery
   c. Yes, if the person is suitable for the job
6. Do you voluntarily read material that supports views different from your own?
   a. Never
   b. Sometimes
   c. Often
7. You react to old people with
   a. Patience
   b. Annoyance
   c. Sometimes a, sometimes b
8. Do you agree with the statement "What is right and wrong depends upon the time, place, and circumstance"?
   a. Strongly agree
   b. Agree to a point
   c. Strongly disagree
9. Would (or did) you marry someone from a different race?
   a. Yes
   b. No
   c. Probably not
10. If someone in your family were homosexual, you would:
    a. View this as a problem and try to change the person to a heterosexual orientation
    b. Accept the person as a homosexual with no change in feelings or treatment
    c. Avoid and/or reject that person
11. You react to little children with:
    a. Patience
    b. Annoyance
    c. Sometimes a, sometimes b
12. Other people's personal habits annoy you
    a. Often
    b. Not at all
    c. Only if extreme
13. If you stay in a household run differently from yours—cleanliness, manners, meals, other customs—you:
    a. Adapt readily
    b. Quickly become uncomfortable and irritated
    c. Adjust for a while, but not for long
14. Which statement do you agree with most?
    a. We should avoid judging others because no one can fully understand the motives of another person.
    b. People are responsible for their actions and have to accept the consequences.
    c. Both motives and actions are important when considering questions of right and wrong.

Circle your score of each of the answers below and total your scores:

1. a = 4; b = 0; c = 2
2. a = 4; b = 2; c = 0
3. a = 0; b = 2; c = 4
4. a = 4; b = 2; c = 0
5. a = 4; b = 2; c = 0
6. a = 4; b = 2; c = 0
7. a = 0; b = 4; c = 2
8. a = 0; b = 2; c = 4
9. a = 0; b = 4; c = 2
10. a = 2; b = 2; c = 4
11. a = 0; b = 4; c = 2
12. a = 4; b = 0; c = 2
13. a = 0; b = 4; c = 2
14. a = 0; b = 4; c = 2

Total score:

- 0–14: If you score 14 or below, you are a very tolerant person, and dealing with diversity comes easily to you.
- 15–28: You are basically a tolerant person and others think of you as tolerant. In general, diversity presents few problems for you, but you may be broadminded in some areas and have less tolerant ideas in other areas of life, such as attitudes toward older people or male–female social roles.
- 29–42: You are less tolerant than most people and should work on developing greater tolerance of people different form you. Your low tolerance level could affect your business or personal relationships.
- 43–56: You have a very low tolerance for diversity. The only people you are likely to respect are those with beliefs similar to your own. You reflect a level of intolerance that could cause difficulties in today's multicultural environment.

ADAPTED FROM THE TOLERANCE SCALE
MARIA HEISELMAN, NAOMI MILLER, AND BOB SCHLORMAN
NORTHERN KENTUCKY UNIVERSITY, 1982,
BY GEORGE MANNING, KENT CURTIS, AND STEVE MCMILLEN,
IN *BUILDING COMMUNITY: THE HUMAN SIDE OF WORK,*
CINCINNATI: THOMSON EXECUTIVE PRESS, 1966, PP. 272–277

Intergroup or Individual Exercises

Intergroup Exercise #1 What You Can Do to Change the World: Idea Exchange

Directions: While standing, read aloud the comment [below] to the person on your right. Then listen to the same selection read by the person on your left. After reading, and again after listening, take 3–5 minutes to discuss the question: What do you feel is the most important purpose one can fulfill in life? Then move to What You Can Do part two, below.

When I was a young person, I wanted to change the world. I found it was difficult to change the world, so I tried to change my nation.

When I found I couldn't change my nation, I began to focus on my town.

I couldn't change the town and as an older person, I tried to change my family.

Now as an old person, I realize the only thing I can change is myself, and suddenly I realize that if long ago I had changed myself, I could have made an impact on my family.

My family and I could have made an impact on our town. Their impact could have changed the nation and I could indeed have changed the world.

UNKNOWN, 1100 A.D.

What Can You Do to Change the World?

Directions: With the entire group standing, (a) take turns reading aloud the items below, until everyone has read an item. (b) Continue rereading the list aloud until it has been read four times. (c) As you read and listen, place an *x* next to the number of those actions that you could perform. Then standing, (d) exchange an additional action you suggest with one from a neighbor. (e) List your suggestion on the board or on paper provided so that each class member has written an additional action that can be taken by those in the class. (f) Read aloud your item to the entire class. (g) Still standing, suggest other additions, if any. (h) Sit with two other class members. Tell them which items are marked with an *x*. Listen to them tell you their lists of actions they could take. (i) Select five items from the entire extended list that you intend to carry out. Tell your two partners what items you selected and when you will do each of them. Your instructor may distribute index cards for you to record your intentions as part of course requirements.

What Can You Do to Change the World? You Can . . .

1. Listen to other people's stories to understand their understanding.
2. Tell jokes only when they don't make fun of people because of their ethnicity, gender, sexual orientation, health condition, or religion.
3. Walk away rather than listen to others tell jokes that make fun of people. Laughing or remaining silent is a sign of acceptance.
4. Speak up when you see someone being discriminated against.

5. Spend time with people who are different from you.
6. Read books by authors who have a different perspective from yours.
7. Spend time talking with people about discrimination; in order to have best results, make your friends as diverse as possible.
8. Recognize how institutionalized oppression permeates our society and therefore influences your understanding when reading newspapers or magazines or when listening or watching news reports.
9. Understand the privilege that you have as a result of the group of which you are a member, such as your gender, ethnicity, sexual orientation, class, religion, or disability.
10. Write letters to the editor that point out discrimination in your community.
11. Support groups that fight discrimination.
12. Don't support businesses or other organizations that discriminate.
13. Be aware that prejudice and discrimination come in many forms and accepting one is in effect promoting all.
14. Become aware of your own prejudices.
15. Make sure that your children and other children within the community have an education that appreciates the contributions of all people in our society.
16. Write letters or e-mails to your congressional representatives advocating legislation that is nondiscriminatory.
17. Become aware of the language that you use and try to use language that is inclusive and nondiscriminatory.
18. Don't use racist, sexist, or other language that identifies your sentiments as prejudiced.
19. Ask questions, but don't make assumptions about people.
20. Take next steps even though there have been major strides in fighting discrimination. Not everyone is treated fairly and equitably.
21. Be forgiving.
22. Let people know when they do or say things that are offensive to you. If you do not, it becomes your problem rather than theirs.
23. Be respectful and be honest with yourself about what you do, say, and think.

Remember: Everything starts with our own behavior. We cannot decide how others must behave.

Intergroup Exercise #2 Difficult Dialogues: Resolving Cultural Conflicts

Directions: In teams of four, read the following four scenarios; select one to use as the basis for a scene that your group will act out for the class. Discuss the question at the end; then create four characters to present the predicament to the class. Each student in your group must have a part to play in this scene. The scenes should not take more than five minutes.

Friendship

1. Eric, an African American student, is new to State University. During the first week of classes he is put in a discussion group where he becomes friends with Bob, who is white. As the semester goes on, he meets many black students at the Multicultural Resource Center and becomes friends with several of them. One day two of his black friends see Eric eating lunch with Bob and they don't come over to their table. Eric begins to worry that his black friends might see him as a "sell out" for having a white friend, but he and Bob have had a lot of fun together and he doesn't want to end their friendship. What does Eric do?

Look Who's Talking

2. Maria, a Hispanic student, is upset by the behavior of three white girls in her art appreciation class. They seem to be friends because they are always together and they always sit in the back of the room and talk until class begins, but Maria notices that they stop talking whenever she comes near them. If she starts to walk by them, they will suddenly become quiet and stare at

her, and the expression on their faces is not friendly. What could Maria do?

Are We Our Brothers' Keepers?

3. Ben, a Native American student, hears one of his Native American friends talk about African Americans in a very demeaning way. Ben does not like to hear such prejudicial comments, but he notices that his other friends smile and seem to agree with these comments. What could Ben do?

Is She Too Unaware to Realize She's Stereotyping?

4. Kim, a white student, tells Amy, an Asian student, that she is very lucky. When Amy asks why Kim thinks she is lucky, Kim says Amy must be getting a lot of money to go to college since she is a minority. This comment upsets Amy even though she has heard it before. In the past she has tried to ignore such comments, but she doesn't feel like ignoring it today. What could Amy say or do?

Human Relations
Attitude Inventory

This attitude inventory allows a student to assess any change in his or her attitudes as a result of reading this book. The statements in the inventory pertain to issues addressed and information provided in this book. During the first week of the semester, students are encouraged to respond to the statements in the inventory as described in the directions and keep a copy of their responses, then respond again at the end of the semester. Look for any changes when comparing the responses from the beginning and the end of the semester. The course instructor may also want to use this inventory to compare changes in the group means of student responses at the beginning and end of the semester rather than analyzing changes for individual students.

A HUMAN RELATIONS ATTITUDE INVENTORY©

for

Understanding Human Differences: Multicultural Education for a Diverse America

BASED ON AN INVENTORY DEVELOPED BY DR. FLAVIO VEGA

Part 1—Demographic Information

Please provide the following information by blackening the corresponding numbered spaces for questions 1 through 6 on your computer answer sheet.

1. Based on your major, identify the general discipline area in which you are enrolled:

    1. Arts and Humanities   2. Science, Medicine or Nursing   3. Education
    4. Business Administration   5. Mathematics or Engineering   6. Other

2. Gender: 1. Female   2. Male

3. Student Status: 1. Graduate   2. Traditional undergraduate student (age 16–24)
                      3. Nontraditional undergraduate (age 25 or over)

4. Race: 1. White   2. Black   3. Hispanic/Latino 4. American Indian
            5. Asian/Pacific Islander   6. Bi-racial (Check all that apply)
            7. Other: Please specify _____

5. Class: 1. Freshman   2. Sophomore   3. Junior   4. Senior   5. Graduate

6. Overall GPA: 1. 3.5–4.0   2. 3.0–3.49   3. 2.5–2.99   4. 2.0–2.49   5. 1.99 or less

NOTE: Reference to "minority" or "minorities" in this inventory is to racial minorities in the U.S. (i.e., African Americans, Hispanic Americans, Asian/Pacific Island Americans and American Indians) and does not include white ethnic groups and/or religious minorities.

Part II—Attitude Inventory

Instructions: This instrument is composed of 64 statements representative of various attitudes on race, gender and social class in the United States. Each statement is followed by five possible responses: SA, A, U, D, and SD (Strongly Agree, Agree, Undecided, Disagree and Strongly Disagree). SELECT THE RESPONSE MOST REPRESENTATIVE OF YOUR OWN THINKING for each statement and blacken the numbered space on your computer answer sheet corresponding to that response.

EXAMPLE: Our schools teach sexism	SA	A	U	D	SD
(Computer answer sheet response)	1	2	3	4	5

MAKE EACH RESPONSE A SEPARATE AND INDEPENDENT ONE. Respond as honestly as possible and work through the inventory as quickly as possible.

PROCEED WITH NUMBER 7 OF THIS INVENTORY. PLEASE RESPOND TO ALL STATEMENTS.

7. One's gender has little to do with one's educational opportunity   SA   A   U   D   SD

8. Our welfare system doesn't give people enough money to get off welfare   SA   A   U   D   SD

9. Minorities do not achieve as much in our society because they do not aspire to achieve as much as white people do   SA   A   U   D   SD

10. Homosexuality is unnatural because it is contrary to human nature   SA   A   U   D   SD

11. The sex role stereotypes of employers and supervisors prevent women from being promoted to positions of authority in our society   SA   A   U   D   SD

12. People on welfare don't have the will power needed to get off welfare   SA   A   U   D   SD

13. Most white people in our society are not aware of their racist attitudes   SA   A   U   D   SD

14. Gay rights means gay men and lesbians demanding special privileges   SA   A   U   D   SD

15. Because they are so angry, feminists increase the problems of sexism   SA   A   U   D   SD

16. Schools are biased against low-income students   SA   A   U   D   SD

17. We should not notice differences in people's skin color   SA   A   U   D   SD

18. There are many cultures in the world which accept homosexuality   SA   A   U   D   SD

19. Both females and males are victims of sexism   SA   A   U   D   SD

20. Most people receiving welfare benefits don't really want to work   SA   A   U   D   SD

21. Institutional racism is always due to racial prejudice   SA   A   U   D   SD

22. Most psychologists no longer consider homosexuality a mental illness   SA   A   U   D   SD

23. The issue of discrimination against women is overly exaggerated   SA   A   U   D   SD

24. Very few people who are receiving welfare assistance are white   SA   A   U   D   SD

25. Racism isn't going to end overnight so minorities need to be patient   SA   A   U   D   SD

26. Homosexuals are mainly interested in having sex with many partners   SA   A   U   D   SD

27. Legislation requiring employers to recruit women into traditionally male occupations should be more strictly enforced   SA   A   U   D   SD

28. Women on welfare have illegitimate babies to get more money   SA   A   U   D   SD

29. Most school textbooks and instructional materials are racist because they emphasize white people and omit or stereotype minorities   SA   A   U   D   SD

30. People who fantasize about homosexual activities really want to be gay   SA   A   U   D   SD

31. Most feminists are just too sensitive about sexism   SA   A   U   D   SD

32. Poverty is a serious problem which our society must address   SA   A   U   D   SD

33. Affirmative action requires employers to hire unqualified minorities   SA   A   U   D   SD

34. Homosexuals have made many contributions to their societies   SA   A   U   D   SD

35. Courses on sexism should be required in our schools   SA   A   U   D   SD

36. The homeless are never going to be successful so people advocating for them should spend their time on more worthy causes   SA   A   U   D   SD

37. White people often get hired because their white friends recommend them   SA   A   U   D   SD

38. Homosexuals are more promiscuous than heterosexuals   SA   A   U   D   SD

39. Women shouldn't be given the rights feminists are demanding; women must first work hard and earn them   SA   A   U   D   SD

40. School textbooks and instructional materials are biased toward the middle class because they omit or stereotype working class people   SA   A   U   D   SD
41. Racism is not a serious problem in all-white communities   SA   A   U   D   SD
42. Employers should have the right to fire someone who is a homosexual   SA   A   U   D   SD
43. All occupations should be open to both men and women   SA   A   U   D   SD
44. Welfare makes people dependent, which is why most never get off welfare   SA   A   U   D   SD
45. Minorities would be successful if they worked hard and stopped complaining   SA   A   U   D   SD
46. Most gay men are child molesters who should be kept away from children   SA   A   U   D   SD
47. The problem with feminists is that they are women who hate men   SA   A   U   D   SD
48. Poverty today is a problem primarily affecting children   SA   A   U   D   SD
49. White people benefit from racism whether they want to or not   SA   A   U   D   SD
50. Much of one's sexual orientation is determined during fetal development   SA   A   U   D   SD
51. Much of our everyday language is sexist   SA   A   U   D   SD
52. Too many welfare recipients are living well off our tax dollars   SA   A   U   D   SD
53. Teachers need to understand how schools perpetuate cultural racism   SA   A   U   D   SD
54. Intimate same-sex relationships often evolve into homosexual relationships   SA   A   U   D   SD
55. Today men and women are paid about the same for doing the same job   SA   A   U   D   SD
56. Most of the adults on welfare want to work and get off welfare   SA   A   U   D   SD
57. Minorities have the same opportunity as whites to succeed in our society   SA   A   U   D   SD
58. Landlords should have the right to evict a tenant that is gay   SA   A   U   D   SD
59. Most men in our society are not aware of their sexist attitudes   SA   A   U   D   SD
60. Our government gives more help to the rich than to the poor   SA   A   U   D   SD
61. Racial segregation in our schools and neighborhoods remains a problem   SA   A   U   D   SD
62. If anyone engages in a homosexual act it proves that they're gay   SA   A   U   D   SD
63. Most rapes are perpetrated by strangers hiding in poorly lighted places   SA   A   U   D   SD
64. Achievement tests discriminate against children from low income homes   SA   A   U   D   SD
65. Whites are just as likely to be victims of racism as racial minorities   SA   A   U   D   SD
66. A significant percentage of gay men commit violent crimes   SA   A   U   D   SD
67. Violence against women is a serious problem in our society   SA   A   U   D   SD
68. Poverty is just a natural way of life for some people   SA   A   U   D   SD
69. Affirmative action has resulted in discrimination against white males   SA   A   U   D   SD
70. All men and women have a choice to be homosexual or not   SA   A   U   D   SD

Index